To Bob and Pushpa Schwartz

World Politics Debated

A Reader in Contemporary Issues

Herbert M. Levine

University of Southwestern Louisiana

McGraw-Hill Book Company

New York   St. Louis   San Francisco   Auckland   Bogotá   Hamburg
Johannesburg   London   Madrid   Mexico   Montreal   New Delhi
Panama   Paris   São Paulo   Singapore   Sydney   Tokyo   Toronto

This book was set in Times Roman by Black Dot, Inc. (ECU).
The editor was Eric M. Munson;
the production supervisor was Rosann E. Raspini.
Project supervision was done by The Total Book.
The cover was designed by Suzanne Haldane.
R. R. Donnelley & Sons Company was printer and binder.

WORLD POLITICS DEBATED
A Reader in Contemporary Issues

ISBN 0-07-037433-3

Library of Congress Cataloging in Publication Data
Main entry under title:

World politics debated.

    Includes bibliographies.
    1. World politics—1975–1985—Addresses, essays,
lectures. 2. International economic relations—
Addresses, essays, lectures. I. Levine, Herbert M.
D849.W69 1983   327'.0904   82-10001
ISBN 0-07-037433-3   AACR2

Contents

List of Contributors

DENNIS T. AVERY is Senior Agricultural Analyst, Office of Economics, Bureau of Intelligence and Research in the U.S. Department of State.

DESMOND BALL is a Fellow in the Strategic and Defence Studies Centre at the Australian National University, Canberra

PETER BAUER is Professor of Economics at the London School of Economics, Fellow of Gonville and Gaius College, Cambridge, and Fellow of the British Academy.

C. FRED BERGSTEN served as Assistant Secretary of the Treasury for International Affairs in the Carter administration. He is the author of several books on international economics.

HAROLD BROWN was Secretary of Defense in the administration of President Jimmy Carter.

HEDLEY BULL is Montague Burton Professor of International Relations at Oxford University.

DONALD L. CLARK is Assistant to the President and a lecturer at Montana State University, Bozeman.

STEPHEN F. COHEN is Professor of Politics at Princeton University.

EDWARD CRANKSHAW is a British writer, widely known for his books on Russia.

ALONA E. EVANS, who died in 1980, was Elizabeth Kimball Kendall Professor of Political Science, Wellesley College, and President of the American Society of International Law

NEAL B. FREEMAN is a writer for *National Review*.

RAYMOND D. GASTIL is Director of the Comparative Survey of Freedom at Freedom House.

CARL GERSHMAN was Executive Director of Social Democrats, USA, and is a member of the United States delegation to the United Nations.

L. C. GREEN is a professor at the University of Alberta, Canada, and a member of the ILA Terrorism Committee. He is the author of numerous journal publications and several books: *International Law through the Cases, Law and Society,* and *Superior Orders in National and International Law.*

MAHBUB UL HAQ was Director of Policy Planning at the International Bank for Reconstruction and Development and is now Deputy Chairman of the Planning Commission, Government of Pakistan.

ROBERT G. HAWKINS is Professor of Finance and Economics at New York University.

STANLEY HOFFMAN is Douglas Dillon Professor of the Civilization of France and Chairman of the Center for European Studies at Harvard University.

PAUL JOHNSON, former editor of *The New Statesman*, is a historian and journalist and is author of *History of Christianity* and *Enemies of Society.*

HERMAN KAHN is Director of the Hudson Institute and has written books on military affairs and economic development.

DONALD M. KENDALL is Chairman of the Board and Chief Executive Officer of Pepsico, Inc.

SIR JOHN KILLICK is a former Ambassador and United Kingdom Permanent Representative to NATO.

G. B. KISTIAKOWSKY was Special Assistant for Science and Technology to President Eisenhower from 1959 to 1961.

IRVING KRISTOL is a Professor of Social Thought at the Graduate School of Business Administration at New York University.

CHARLES M. KUPPERMAN is Defense Analyst and Research Associate for the Committee on the Present Danger.

WALTER LAQUEUR is chairman of the research council at the Center for Strategic and International Studies at Georgetown University.

ERNEST W. LEFEVER is a faculty associate of the Center for Strategic and International Studies and President of the Ethics and Public Policy Center at Georgetown University.

EDWARD N. LUTTWAK is an associate of the Georgetown Center for Strategic and International Studies.

RICHARD L. McCALL served as Assistant Secretary of State for International Organization Affairs in the administration of President Jimmy Carter.

ROBERT MOSS, who was editor of Foreign Report, the intelligence bulletin of *The Economist*, is a writer who specializes in terrorism and foreign policy. He is also a novelist.

JOHN O'SULLIVAN is editor of *Policy Review*, published by the Heritage Foundation.

JULIANA G. PILON is Policy Analyst with the Heritage Foundation. She was a Visiting Scholar and Earhart Fellow at the Hoover Institution at Stanford University and a Research Fellow at the Institute for Humane Studies in Menlo Park, California.

RICHARD PIPES is Frank B. Baird, Jr. Professor of History at Harvard. He is a member of the National Security Council staff in the Reagan administration.

SAMUEL PISAR, an international lawyer, is author of *Coexistence and Commerce: Guidelines for Transactions between East and West.*

YOSHIKAZU SAKAMOTO is a Professor of Law at the University of Tokyo.

ERNEST SCHNEIDER is a member of the professional staff at the Hudson Institute.

ELIAS M. SCHWARZBART is a writer who specializes in Far Eastern Affairs.

JOHN SPANIER is a Professor of Political Science at the University of Florida.

HAROLD SPROUT was the Chairman of the Politics Department at Princeton University and author of numerous books in international politics. After his retirement in 1969, he served as a research associate at Princeton's Center of International Studies.

MARGARET SPROUT is the co-author with Harold Sprout of several books in international relations, including *The Context of Environmental Politics* and *The Rise of American Naval Power, 1776-1918.* She is also a research associate in the Center of International Studies at Princeton University.

PAUL M. SWEEZY is a Marxian economist and is co-editor of *Monthly Review.*

CYRUS VANCE was Secretary of State in the administration of President Jimmy Carter.

INGO WALTER is Professor of Finance and Economics at New York University.

ALLEN S. WHITING is Professor of Political Science at the University of Arizona.

WILLIAM APPLEMAN WILLIAMS teaches in the Department of History at Oregon State University. He was President of the Organization of American Historians.

DANIEL YERGIN lectures at Harvard University and is the author of *Shattered Peace: The Origins of the Cold War and the National Security State* and co-editor of *Energy Future: Report of the Energy Project at the Harvard Business School.*

Introduction

Power is a central concept of politics. It is also an ambiguous concept. A standard definition of power, which is used in this book, is the ability to make someone do what he or she may not want to do.

This book deals with the changing nature of power in world politics since the end of World War II. It is organized into sections discussing actors, the international system, goals, instruments of power, constraints on war, modes of interaction, and the future world order.

Each chapter begins with headnotes describing the significant power relationships in the postwar period. Issues are selected, and there is a Yes and a No position for each issue. Questions and suggested readings follow the debates to allow for further thought and study.

The purpose of the debate format is to stimulate interest in the subject matter of world politics. The debates are taken from different sources, such as magazine articles, government documents, and books. The debates reflect a variety of ideological viewpoints and are selected because of their value in a debate framework.

The debate format is a pedagogical device to encourage critical thinking of issues. As such, it presents some problems. Of necessity, it restricts attention to focusing on a single issue from only two sides. When evaluating the affirmative and negative side of an issue, consequently, readers should keep in mind that there is often no "yes" or "no" answer to a debate question. Often, there is some merit in each of two views of an issue, and readers must decide for themselves what to accept and what to reject from both the affirmative and the negative positions.

Another problem of the debate format is that the necessity to choose one debate question on a topic may give the impression that there is only one issue worthy of consideration for that topic. The introductory essay in each chapter, however, often suggests other questions requiring examination although space limitations of the book prevent them from being examined.

The debate format, moreover, may also give the impression that the arguments presented for saying yes or no on an issue are always those given in the selections. In fact, on many of the issues, entirely different positions are sometimes taken that reject the arguments made on both of the sides presented in the selections. There may really be a much wider variety of views than implied by the format.

In spite of the problems, the debate format offers opportunities for critical investigation. A useful way to evaluate a debate is, first, to discover the specific differences between the two viewpoints, and, then, to analyze the differences by answering the following questions:

1 Do the contending authors disagree about the facts?

2 Is there a disagreement about the consequences of certain actions?

3 Does the disagreement arise because the background of the authors differs so that each author perceives events from a different perspective?

4 Are the disagreements related to differing ideological orientations of the authors?

5 Are there ways of looking at the issues involved other than those presented in the selections?

These five questions do not constitute the only ones which may be considered. They do, however, offer a framework for evaluating the selections.

ACKNOWLEDGMENTS

I am grateful to the editorial consultants for this book: B. David Meyers, University of North Carolina, Greensboro; Whitney Perkins, Brown University; David Rosen, Cook College, Rutgers University; Edward Thomas Rowe, University of Denver; and Herbert Tillema, University of Missouri at Columbia. They made many comments on the draft of the book, and their recommendations for changes were of enormous help. Marvin Maurer, chairman of the Department of Government at Monmouth College, also read the entire manuscript and made suggestions for improvement.

I wish to express my appreciation to Ron Labbé, my department head at the University of Southwestern Louisiana, for granting me a reduced teaching schedule during one semester so that I could work on this book. I acknowledge, too, the expert assistance of the staff of McGraw-Hill—particularly the political science editor Eric Munson and the production editor Annette Bodzin.

World Politics Debated

A Reader in Contemporary Issues

Chapter One

Actors

Even before World War II came to an end, some political observers looked with hope to the establishment of new institutions to cope with the problems facing the postwar world. The war had produced horrendous destruction of life and property in Europe, Asia, and Africa. The economies of many countries in the world—whether victors or vanquished— were shattered as a result of military devastation or the distorted priorities of the war. The old colonial political rule in Africa and Asia was already being challenged because of the war, the rise of nationalism among the peoples of Africa and Asia, the declining economic power of Western colonial countries, and ideologies committed to ending colonialism.

Political observers differed in predicting the character of world politics in the postwar world. Some believed that the system of independent states would survive the war, and that power considerations should be based on this reality. Others looked to the creation or strengthening of international organizations—both public and private—to transform world politics so that the problems of war and economic development could be solved. The more idealistic hoped for a world government to emerge as the principal actor in the global arena.

Any view of the future had to consider who the principal actors in world politics would be. In the nearly four decades since the end of the war, these have been diverse in character and have experienced change. That change reflects the political, military, economic, and social forces that have shaped the postwar world.

The principal actors in the postwar period have been states, private groups, and international governmental organizations. These actors are not new to world politics.

States have been in existence for the past four hundred years. Private groups have had an even older history, and international governmental organizations antedate the Congress of Vienna, which assembled in 1814.

States are defined as political institutions that are characterized by territory, population, government, and sovereignty. By the end of World War II, there were about fifty states in the world. By late 1945, two states stood out as superpowers—the United States and the Soviet Union. Because the United States possessed vast economic resources and because it had not been attacked on its mainland during the war, it emerged as the strongest country in the world. It had preeminence in military power in part because it possessed a rich economy that could sustain a strong defense establishment and in part because it was a master of military technology, most notably in its leadership in producing the atomic bomb. The Soviet Union had the strongest army in Europe. Although the U.S.S.R. experienced the most destruction of life and property of any allied power during the war, it came out of the war with its power strong, relative to other states. Germany was wrecked by the war and was divided into occupation zones. Britain and France were recovering from the economic problems of the war. The other states of the world varied in power and independence.

By the 1980s, the character of the state system had experienced many changes. Rather than wither away to be replaced by a world government, states grew in number and diversity. By 1982, the number of states rose to about 160. Most of the new states had been under colonial rule and had achieved their independence either through war or through voluntary agreement by the colonial powers. The emergence of these independent states (many in Africa and Asia) had a profound impact on world politics as power shifted to them. Because of their strategic location, vital resources, military strength, and diplomatic leverage, these new states made demands on the world community— particularly in areas such as economic development, redistribution of the world's income, arms transfers, and disarmament.

A prominent feature of post-World War II states was nationalism, the feeling of a strong attachment to a state. Not only did the nations under colonial rule seek independence, but national communities within the newly independent states sought self-rule from those states. The unsuccessful attempt by Biafra in Nigeria to achieve independence from 1967 to 1970 and the successful effort by Bangladesh to secede from Pakistan in 1971 are two cases in point. In general, the new states have sought to prevent their secessionist groups from forming additional states.

States have not been the only prominent actors in the international arena in the postwar period. Private groups have played an important role in shaping world politics. Some of these have exercised their primary influence within states rather than across state boundary lines. Economic groups have sought to promote their interests through influencing such matters as the level of tariffs, immigration, government subsidies to domestic producers, and export assistance. Ethnic, religious, and racial groups have attempted to get government help to achieve their objectives, including such matters as immigration laws and foreign-policy support for kindred groups around the world.

Private groups have also acted in the international arena. The most prominent new economic groups are the multinational corporations (MNCs). These corporations are organizations with personnel and offices located in more than one country and whose commercial interests are global in nature. Although the MNCs have received attention in the past decade, there have been such international economic groups for many centuries. The most prominent early economic groups were the great trading companies of the seventeenth and eighteenth centuries, such as the East India Company, the Hudson Bay Company, and La Compagnie des Indes. In the more recent past, the United Fruit

Company, a private United States firm, held enormous economic investments in Latin America. International Telephone and Telegraph (ITT) was operating internationally even before World War II. Nevertheless, the MNCs have grown in importance in the postwar period. Their influence in directing the flow of capital, building factories, and employing a labor force has become an important feature in the economic plans of developing nations.

Private groups continue to play a role in areas other than economics, such as in religious and ethnic matters. The Catholic church, for example, is one international religious institution with political interests in every continent. As was the case in 1945, the Catholic church is today involved in many matters not necessarily religious. The church played an important role in 1981 in mediating between government and the trade unions in the management of the Polish economy.

Ethnic groups in 1945 generally acted domestically to wield influence by getting their governments to support their policies. They have, however, been more likely to act across national lines in the past decades. A notable example is the Palestine Liberation Organization (PLO), which has sought an independent Arab Palestine.

In addition to states and private groups, international government organizations have been formed to play a role in the conduct of world politics. These associations include economic organizations, cartels, military alliances, regional associations, and general international organizations.

During World War II, allied powers prepared for the postwar period through the establishment of international organizations, such as the International Monetary Fund (IMF) and the International Bank for Reconstruction and Development (now known as the World Bank). The IMF was created to act as a clearing agency and monitor of monetary transactions among states. The World Bank was established to aid postwar recovery, and its work later encompassed aid for economic development in the third world. Since 1945, other international economic institutions such as the Common Market and the Organization for Economic Cooperation and Development (OECD) have been established. In 1949, the Soviet Union formed the Council for Mutual Economic Assistance (Comecon), which included East European economic cooperation in a manner separate from the West.

International government cartels in essential commodities were nonexistent in 1945. A cartel is an organization of suppliers who control the production and price of scarce items. The most successful cartel of the postwar period is the Organization of Petroleum Exporting Countries (OPEC), which was formed in 1960 by five states—Iran, Iraq, Kuwait, Saudi Arabia, and Venezuela. Other international organizations have been formed with a goal of strengthening the producers' position with respect to such products as bauxite, tin, iron ore, coffee, and bananas. None has met with the success of OPEC, however, since the latter has raised prices more than ten times the 1973 level in less than a decade.

Military alliances have existed as long as the state system itself. There were military alliances even in ancient Greece. In 1945, however, the grand alliance against Germany came to an end as the Soviet Union and the United States—allies in the war against Germany—became bitter foes. In the 1940s and 1950s, military alliances became widespread. The North Atlantic Treaty Organization (NATO) was born in 1949 and continues to the present day. In response to the joining of NATO by the Federal Republic of Germany in 1955, the Soviet Union established the Warsaw Pact of seven communist countries. Military alliances such as these formed permanent institutions that transcended state boundaries and continue to exercise an influence in the 1980s.

Some regional organizations were in existence in 1945 but became more institutionalized in the following decades. New regional organizations, such as the Organization of American States (OAS) and the Organization of African Unity (OAU), were formed. They played important political and economic roles in world politics.

The most notable of international institutions is the United Nations (UN). Formed during World War II, it was organized in response to the failure of its predecessor organization, the League of Nations, and in the hope of providing an institutional environment conducive to peace.

The UN was established with great popular hope for its survival and its active participation in world politics. The people who drafted the UN Charter had no vision that they were establishing a world government. Rather, they created an organization that would be effective provided the big powers who dominated that organization—principally the United States and the Soviet Union—maintained the same degree of unity that they had shown during World War II.

When the UN was formed, it was dominated by the United States because of U.S. preeminence over its allies in Latin America and Europe. The history of the UN is also a history of the decline of American power in that organization, as the new states of Africa and Asia joined the world organization on their independence. Today, the smaller powers of Latin America, Asia, and Africa dominate the UN.

This chapter deals with some of the actors in world politics: states, multinational corporations, cartels, and the UN.

STATES

The growth of states in the postwar period has produced questions about their role in world politics. Some people wonder whether the existence of the state system encourages wars. Still others ask whether states are the political institutions best organized for promoting security and prosperity, and whether economic groups rather than governments are the real manipulators of power in many states.

The debate that follows centers on the power of states as actors in contemporary world politics. Although states have grown in numbers since 1945, it is questionable if this development is a reflection of the increasing power of states. Harold Sprout and Margaret Sprout argue that state sovereignty is declining because the state cannot by itself provide for its own military security, economic well-being, psychological support, and health and ecological needs. Personal safety, public order, and survival of the human species, they contend, require new international institutions.

This view of the decline of the state is challenged by Hedley Bull, who feels that the state is not a decaying and endangered species. Bull argues that the state is here to stay and is growing. He contends that the absence of the state system will not produce a better world and that the states perform positive functions in relationship to world order. He sees no consensus on what will replace the state system and asserts that Western countries have a special interest in preserving the system.

MULTINATIONAL CORPORATIONS

The involvement of MNCs in the third world has evoked many questions about these groups. Some writers ask whether MNCs are a force for good in third world nations; others wonder whether new nations benefit more from foreign aid and technical assistance than they do from investment by foreign private companies.

MNCs have received much notoriety since the end of World War II. The MNCs have hailed the contributions that they make to economic development, employment, and technological know-how in the third world. The involvement of MNCs in the internal political affairs of developing nations, however, has also brought international attention to their activities. The participation of the United Fruit Company in internal Guatemalan politics in the 1950s and the efforts of ITT in toppling Salvador Allende from power as President of Chile in 1973 are two striking examples. In both cases, the MNCs were depicted as exercising extraordinary influence in world politics—an influence rivaling or surpassing that of states. But are such organizations dominant actors in the international arena?

Paul Sweezy, a Marxist economist, argues that the rise of MNCs reflects the most advanced form of capitalist development. According to him, it is capitalist organizations rather than states that are the principal actors in the international arena. American intervention in such places as Vietnam, the Dominican Republic, Iran, and Guatemala was instigated to support capitalist enterprises. American arms transfers to third world countries and American support for right-wing dictatorships, Sweezy says, are intended to aid the capitalists in exploiting the masses of people in Africa, Asia, and Latin America.

Robert G. Hawkins and Ingo Walter provide a different portrait of the MNCs. If MNCs are the dominant actors, then they can manipulate host countries at will. Hawkins and Walter describe the formidable restrictions that host countries impose on MNCs— restrictions that involve ownership and control. Host countries may require that the MNCs have a proportion of local ownership. Host-country controls are exercised at different pressure points: controls on entry before an MNC operation is underway, controls on existing and successful MNC operations, controls on MNC affiliates, and terminal controls leading to a phaseout of foreign participation in local ventures. Hawkins and Walter argue that controls of MNCs in third world countries are far more stringent than similar controls in advanced industrial societies.

CARTELS

The enormous success of OPEC in raising the price of oil in the 1970s won the approval of some supporters of third world countries. The view was expressed that at last the Western countries that had exploited the economies of third world peoples for so long would now get their comeuppance.

The OPEC cartel had a profound impact on world politics. Non-oil-producing developing nations found that their economies were severely damaged by OPEC's high oil prices and they had to restructure their development plans. Most advanced Western nations discovered that they were vulnerable to OPEC demands because without imported oil, their industrial societies could not function. The high price of oil contributed to worldwide inflation and recession.

Many questions were raised about OPEC. Would economic chaos be the permanent condition for oil-importing countries? Would the Middle East—particularly Saudi Arabia—become the stage for political instability brought on by the quest for economic prosperity and political opportunities? Would the Soviet Union or the United States resort to war in the Middle East because of the vast oil resources in the area?

One important question involved the future of cartels. Although many third world nations suffered from high energy prices, they also saw opportunities of their own, which the OPEC model suggested. As producers of basic raw materials, they could conceivably establish cartels for their commodities. If so, they would be able to get higher commodity prices that could help finance their development programs.

At the height of its influence, OPEC made decisions that affected policymakers in governments throughout the world. Will OPEC-type cartels become principal actors in world politics? Writing in 1973 when OPEC was beginning to exercise its power, C. Fred Bergsten notes the increased reliance by the United States on third world energy supplies and other natural resources. Bergsten points to the fact that a few countries account for the bulk of exportable raw materials, such as copper, tin, natural rubber, bauxite, and coffee. Some countries, moreover, possess abundant supplies of key raw materials and agricultural products. Many third world countries have potential for strategic market power in the manner of OPEC and could exercise that power for political and economic purposes, according to Bergsten.

Writing from the vantage point of 1981, agricultural analyst Dennis T. Avery evaluates the attempt by less-developed countries (LDCs) through the United Nations Conference on Trade and Development (UNCTAD) to organize international agreements for their important commodity exports. Avery concludes that LDCs did not succeed in altering the terms of trade for commodity producers. Rising commodity prices encourage a shift to the purchase of substitutes, which results in an inability to sustain high prices for commodities. There is little likelihood that the non-oil-producing LDCs will be able to achieve the same political and economic benefits as the oil-producing third world countries, according to Avery.

UNITED NATIONS

In part because of the great expectations surrounding the creation of the UN, much disenchantment, sometimes bordering on cynicism, marks the comments of observers—particularly American observers—of that organization. Does the UN play a meaningful role in world politics? Richard L. McCall, Assistant Secretary of State for International Organization Affairs in the Carter administration, argues that the UN has some impressive accomplishments in spite of its many shortcomings. Specifically, he notes: (1) the UN has become a universal organization; (2) it has been the source of innovative measures to reduce international tensions; and (3) it has helped to transform the colonial world into independent states. He points to the benefits of the UN in promoting international rules for improving health, communications, human rights, and economic activities. He highlights the UN as a forum for diplomatic initiatives from different countries. The UN, he concludes, will play an important role in East-West relations, the North-South dialogue, and global economic management.

Juliana Geran Pilon, a policy analyst who has studied the world organization for the Heritage Foundation, argues that the UN has not only failed to meet the hopes of its founders but has also been a major cause of global disharmony. Pilon points to institutional blocks to effective UN action, such as the provision in the UN Charter preventing UN intervention in matters that are essentially within the domestic jurisdiction of any state, and the practices of staffing the UN Secretariat. Both the Security Council and the General Assembly have been disappointing to those people favoring effective action. The UN has been the stage for inflammatory rhetoric and for anticapitalist third world claims to redistribute Western wealth to developing nations. It has sought to promote censorship in news coverage of the third world and has aided terrorists. Although some UN activities have been successful, Pilon concludes that the UN is more suspect than at any time in its history.

1 Is the State Declining in Significance as an Actor in World Politics?

YES

Harold Sprout and Margaret Sprout

Tribal Sovereignty vs. Interdependence

NO

Hedley Bull

The State's Positive Role in World Politics

Tribal Sovereignty vs. Interdependence
Harold Sprout
Margaret Sprout

. . . The present chapter focuses specifically on the phenomena that progressively erode in practice the sovereignty to which statesmen and their fellow citizens cling so tenaciously in principle. We shall be concerned especially with two facets of this sovereignty-limiting interdependence: (1) the vulnerability of all political communities—the more modernized the more vulnerable—to adverse intrusions from abroad; and (2) the rising, though often seemingly helpless, concern of their members to control or influence conditions and events outside their sovereign jurisdictions.

One of the elemental realities, stressed in this chapter . . . is the tendency of thinking and acting to lag far behind events in this era of unprecedentedly rapid change. The human population of the earth may be bound together in a common fate, but parochial tribalism continues to sustain a fragmented international order more relevant to the seventeenth than to the late-twentieth century. Notions of sovereignty, national self-determination and independence still rank high in the scale of political values in every country. Something vaguely thought of as *national* security is still envisaged as the prime objective of *national* statecraft. With rare exceptions, people look to their own rulers, not to some international organization, for protection against real or imagined dangers from abroad. Economic autonomy is a widely proclaimed goal, especially among the former colonial subjects of Western empires. Statesmen try to exclude from their countries foreign persons and ideas deemed to be subversive or otherwise dangerous to the *national* community. Many governments and private entrepreneurs strive for possession or exploitive control of the resources within and beneath the international oceans and seas.

However, it is becoming increasingly evident that interrelatedness, and interdependencies that interrelatedness entails in the modern world cannot be escaped. All political communities are exposed in some degree, most in very large degree, to adverse intrusions from abroad. None can prevent or evade undesired consequences of events originating outside their jurisdictional boundaries.

This vulnerability extends over many fields of activity. We shall concentrate in this chapter on five that are especially salient: (1) military penetrability, (2) economic constraints, (3) transnational communications, (4) pollution of the state's geographic space, and (5) the terms of access to resources outside the sovereign jurisdiction of any state.

TWILIGHT OF MILITARY SECURITY

Military technology has evolved from nonexplosive projectiles (stones, clubs, spears) thrown by hand, to rocket-propelled explosive charges capable of reaching any target upon the face of the earth. . . .

Since the introduction of chemical explosives in the fifteenth century, the upward trend of destructive force has been spectacular. There seems to be little ground for doubt that weapons now in existence are far more than sufficient to destroy any country, and perhaps sufficient to make all or most of the earth uninhabitable. Many reputable scientists and engineers doubt that antiballistic missiles or any other technical devices are likely to restore any significant fraction of the security which conventional military forces formerly provided. This is the context within which we consider several further aspects of the interdependence arising from the advance of military technology.

Formation of the modern state system coincided in history with the introduction of chemical explosives into the technology of war. This was the so-called "gunpowder revolution." On this issue all students of international politics are indebted to John Herz, Professor of International Relations in the City University of New York.[1] As he and a few others have emphasized, it was chiefly the introduction of explosive firepower, especially in the form of mobile artillery, that rendered medieval castles and walled towns indefensible in a military sense. Artillery fire could knock down the strongest walls, and did so on many

[1] See J. Herz, "The Rise and Demise of the Territorial State," *World Politics,* 9 (July 1957), pp. 473 ff.

From Harold Sprout and Margaret Sprout, *Toward a Politics of the Planet Earth.* New York: Van Nostrand Reinhold, 1971, pp. 401–425.

occasions, most notably in the historic siege of Constantinople in 1453.

Development of more destructive cannon and more mobile gun carriages, together with some improvement in roads, made it possible to defend a larger geographic perimeter against military intrusion, as well as to administer and police a larger area from a central capital. Thus the "gunpowder revolution," together with other innovations, expedited the emergence of larger political entities, larger both in population and in territory. In due course, these "sovereign states" superseded castles and walled towns as the basic units of public order and personal security in the Europe of the fifteenth century and thereafter.

A prime concern of the rulers of those larger communities was to make their domain as secure (that is, as impenetrable) as possible. Much attention was given to acquiring "naturally strong" boundaries. Seacoasts ranked highest. A state that was entirely insular, like Britain, enjoyed the strongest "natural defenses." Other types of more-or-less strong frontiers included mountain ranges, other rough terrain, and rivers.

Statesmen strove tirelessly to improve on nature. Labor and materials were lavishly expended on fortifications designed to make the country as nearly impenetrable to hostile force as possible. Roads and (later) railways were laid out to serve defensive purposes first and commerce second. As repeatedly demonstrated in our own time, when military planners and bureaucrats have their way, military installations are located with scant regard to the health, safety, convenience or comfort of the civil population.

Geographic space—the distance between a state's territorial perimeter and its centers of population and production—was long considered another prime defensive asset. Where space was deemed inadequate, a powerful government might succeed in establishing a "buffer zone" of protected, semi-independent states —satellites in today's idiom—for the purpose of absorbing the initial shock of military onslaught. This was precisely what Russian statesmen set out to accomplish after World War II. They successfully established a tier of Communist-ruled satellite states reaching from the Baltic to the Black Sea; but, as is well known, their efforts to extend the buffer zones through the Near East and inner Asia met with insuperable obstacles.

The First World War (1914-1918) convinced a few percipient military theorists that expanding firepower and mobility of weapons were fatally eroding the military security of all but the very largest countries. A long sequence of inventions had raised the destructive capability of a single soldier by several orders of magnitude. Railroads, more and better roads, and more reliable and capacious overland vehicles had given unprecedented mobility to this expanding firepower. Development of marine mines, automotive torpedoes, and submarines comparably undermined the previously strong "natural defenses" of insular countries. Aircraft, though still primitive and unreliable by today's standards, foreshadowed the possibility of overleaping even the most strongly defended land and sea frontiers.

Subsequent events transformed the hint into reality. In the Second World War for the first time in history, crowded cities and their industrial plants located hundreds of miles inside a country's interior were laid waste without blasting a way across fortified land frontiers or storming ashore upon strongly defended beaches. *The effect in the aggregate was reminiscent of the destructive impact of the gunpowder revolution on medieval castles and walled towns.*

However, to the end of World War II, geographic space still counted heavily as a defensive cushion— but only for a large country. No country in Western Europe proved large enough to absorb the shock of modern mobile armies. None possessed sufficient geographic depth for protracted retreat and protective dispersal of vital industries and population. In Russia, on the contrary, defending armies could retreat through hundreds of miles, and factories could be bodily transported to the comparative safety of inner Asia.

Introduction of nuclear explosives in 1945 and the vastly more destructive weapons that followed within a decade, accompanied by increase in the range and capacity of airborne and ballistic carriers, have further depreciated the military value of space, even for countries of continental size. Today, no country, however large, can reasonably expect to escape crippling devastation if attacked with the thermonuclear weapons now deployed. There is literally no place to hide. Historic two-dimensional security has evolved into today's three-dimensional vulnerability. In the historic seesaw between offensive and defensive military innovations, the technology of offense has decisively outstripped the defense, at least for the near future.

The implications are much in dispute. Some optimistic technocrats express confidence that defensive weapons will catch up, as has happened repeatedly in the past. There are well-known projects for antiballistic missiles and rumors of other innovations that might restore to some extent the defensibility of territory, at least for two or three polities of continental size, advanced technology, and huge material resources.

Other experts are pessimistic of ever achieving any effective *military* defense, almost certainly not with resources likely to be at the disposal of any contemporary government. This pessimism becomes more impressive when one considers the still unsolved problem of defense against biological-chemical weapons that might utterly shatter the ecology of any society— at a fraction of the cost of thermonuclear warheads and missiles.

Development of so-called "internal war" has still further eroded the territorial facade of military defense. The war in Indochina and comparable operations in other areas have demonstrated how difficult, if not utterly impossible, it is to block infiltration across any land frontier. And conventional defenses lose yet more of their waning credibility when a whole society is the battleground and the "enemy" is everywhere.

We are not suggesting that the sovereign territorial state is about to wither away from erosion of its military viability. As we have said before, institutions tend to live on long after they have ceased to perform the essential functions for which they were created. The thrust of the evidence is simply that the goal of national security as traditionally conceived—and as still very much alive—presents problems that are becoming increasingly resistant to military solutions. To the extent that this is perceived to be so, it imposes constraints on the actions of statesmen quite at variance with the historic myths of sovereignty and independence, myths that in many if not in most societies still inform the attitudes of rulers and citizens alike.

It was noted in Chapter 15 [*Editor's note*: omitted here.] that expanding domestic demands and social and environmental imperatives are putting military budgets under growing pressure in numerous countries, a trend that is likely to spread. The resulting crisis of priorities has already produced significant military retrenchment in several countries, notably in Britain, several other European countries, Canada, and the United States. These pressures encourage reexamination of military commitments and curtailment of weapons research and development. Indica-

tions point to steadily rising pressure on every government's disposable resources with no respite in sight. Such pressures may in time provide stronger incentives toward stabilizing military forces by international agreement, *thereby tightening still further the interdependence of nations in the sphere of military security*.

THE TIGHTENING SCREW OF ECONOMIC INTERDEPENDENCE

Legally sovereign political communities have become economically interdependent to an extent not generally appreciated. Such interdependence derives from various sources. These include economic specialization, growth of external commerce, transnational flows of capital, industrial enterprises that operate simultaneously in several or many countries more or less beyond effective control by host governments, the international monetary system, and the working of the balance of payments. In general, economic interdependence increases with progress along the road of modernization. All facets of such interdependence present opportunities for political leverage and conversely impose constraints on the effective exercise of the autonomy legally vested in the sovereign state.

Contemporary economic interdependence evolved largely as a by-product of the Industrial Revolution which encouraged specialization and the resultant growth of commerce among nations. Economic interdependence spread and tightened throughout the nineteenth century. Despite all efforts to counteract it, this trend has accelerated in the twentieth century. It is a salient feature of the milieu in which international politics is carried on, and seems likely to attain additional dimensions of constraint in the years ahead.

For reasons beyond the scope of this discussion, the Industrial Revolution began earlier in Britain than elsewhere. For several decades British industries held a strong lead over foreign competitors. British imports of food and raw materials, paid for by coal, manufactures, and essential services, came by the middle of the nineteenth century to constitute by far the largest national component of the total commerce among nations. Most of the profits were reinvested, increasingly overseas. To facilitate this worldwide complex of trade and investment, British bankers evolved an international monetary system. Its essence was unrestricted movement of gold and convertibility of British currency, sterling, into all foreign currencies. London became the world center of banking, insurance, and other financial services—in short, the financial capital of an economic empire that came to embrace not only the British dominions and colonies but also most of the sovereign political communities in every continent.

In consequence, without much evident planning, economies throughout the world became attuned to Britain's. Foreign societies acquired a vested interest in uninterrupted access to British manufactures, markets, capital, and financial services. It was a state of affairs in which British commercial and fiscal policies, as well as the flow of commerce, affected the structure of societies and imposed constraints on the behavior of statesmen throughout the world.

The spread of industrialism to the Continent, to North America, to Japan and elsewhere eventually destroyed the primacy of Britain, but did not diminish the interdependence of nations. On the contrary! The volume of international commerce continued to increase. And the pattern of commerce continued to reflect specialization, including the exchange of manufactures and services from the industrialized societies in return for foodstuffs and raw materials both from the unindustrialized colonies of the European empires and from the nominally sovereign but economically less modernized polities of Asia, Latin America, and elsewhere.

The dependence of the primary producers upon the industrialized economies is self-evident. Less evident perhaps, but scarcely less restrictive in the long run, has been the growth of interdependence among the industrialized economies themselves. This trend has persisted despite determined efforts in numerous countries to diversify and thereby to make the economy less dependent upon imports. Even more important has been the universal impact of industrialization upon population growth . . . [I]ndustrialization has generally produced sufficient improvement in living conditions to reduce mortality, with consequent rise of population. In many countries, such growth has outstripped the capacity of the land to support the inhabitants at anywhere near the prevailing level should they be cut off from imported food and other materials. The dependence of the more modernized economies on each other and upon the primary producers is as indisputable as the dependence of the latter upon the former.

Interdependence can be a source of either political strength or of political weakness. British experience exemplifies both conditions. Vulnerability was dramatically revealed in the British government's ill-fated attempt to repossess the Suez Canal in 1956. Most of the liquid fuels consumed in Britain came from the region around the Persian Gulf. This oil was paid for in British currency (sterling) or in local Middle Eastern currencies with which the British economy was adequately supplied. When (for reasons that need not concern us here) President Nasser of Egypt dispossessed the private corporation that owned and operated the Canal, the British and French governments reacted violently. By this act Nasser had gained presumptive ability to set the terms on which tankers could bring oil to Western Europe. This was an intolerable state of affairs from the French and British perspective. When their forces invaded Egypt to repossess the Canal, Nasser blocked it by sinking ships in the channel. In consequence the British community had to obtain oil elsewhere, chiefly in the Americas. But American oil had to be paid for in dollars, and the British economy was short of dollars. Thus the British government found itself at the mercy of those who controlled the dollars and who demanded that the invaders withdraw—which they did!

A century ago such an outcome would have been scarcely conceivable. The British economy in the 1850s was as interdependent with the outside world as in the 1950s. But as previously indicated, interdependence in that era contributed to towering strength—for Britain. Why? In large degree, it would seem, because of Britain's concomitant naval primacy. In those days the British navy wielded a largely undisputed command of the seas. *The combination of fleets and finance* enabled British statesmen to exert an influence abroad which neither ingredient alone could have accomplished. As long as British naval power was widely perceived to be presumptively supreme, no foreign adversary could exploit Britain's heavy dependence upon imported food and raw materials. With advances in technology, accompanied by changes in the geography of international politics, Britain's economic interdependence with the outside world was insidiously transformed into a position of extreme vulnerability.

Put more generally, if the ratio of exports and imports to the total national product is high, it indicates that the nation's economic life (in the words of a British report) "is linked with the outside world in many different ways," with the consequence, as a rule, that foreign economic events and trends "can have a profound effect upon it." Such an economy is inherently more sensitive, often extremely vulnerable, to foreign commercial regulations (tariffs, import quotas, and others), to exchange fluctuations and controls, to foreign dumping (sales of goods abroad at ruinous prices), to changes in world prices of commodities, especially *differential* changes in the prices of primary materials and manufactures, and to other external events.

For various reasons the trend nearly everywhere is toward greater interdependence among national economies. Even the United States, once more nearly self-contained than any other industrial society, has become increasingly sensitive to external conditions and events. The same trend seems certain to overtake the Soviet Union in the near future, and Communist China too in due course. No government today, not even the United States, can buttress interdependence with a global military primacy that was the essence of the mid-nineteenth-century Pax Britannica.

Three contemporary patterns of economic interdependence merit some further attention. One is the emergence of international organizations invested with authority over limited sectors of economic life previously within the exclusive jurisdiction of the member states. The second is the mushrooming growth and spread of gigantic industrial enterprises which spill over and increasingly ignore the jurisdictional boundaries of states. The third is the constraining effect that the international monetary system may impose on the national policies of sovereign states.

We shall consider the constraining economic role of international organizations in the next chapter. [*Editor's note*: omitted here.] Here we simply note that the extent to which organizations such as the European Community (Common Market) function as intended, they encroach in some degree on the freedom of choice hypothetically inherent in the governments of sovereign states.

With respect to the transnational operations of business corporations, George Modelski, of the University of Washington, describes the size, scope, and power of these industrial giants, some of which surpass all but the major sovereign states in resources and financial power.

In 1965, 87 corporations (of which 60 were domiciled in the United States, 25 in Western Europe and two in Japan) each had a sales volume in excess of one billion United States dollars. . . . In the same year no more than approximately 40 states had central government expenditures of a similar magnitude. . . . Only 69 countries (out of a total of 126) had a Gross National Product in excess of that figure. . . .

In 1965 (admittedly a good year) 40 corporations (33 in the United States and seven elsewhere) each showed net profits after taxes in excess of one hundred million dollars. As these in effect represent liquid resources at the disposal of the top management, and as we set these against the fact that no more than 52 states had a defense budget of these proportions, we become aware of how large are the resources commanded by the corporate structure.[2]

These industrial giants (typified by such corporations as General Motors, International Business Machines, Royal Dutch Shell, and Unilever) determine what goods shall be produced in what countries. They set prices that vary from one country to another. They influence the mobility of labor and the level of wages. They sponsor research and development of new technology, and influence the diffusion of new knowledge from country to country. Confronted with restrictive national regulations, they may threaten to move their operations to another country. With business policy measured primarily by profits, such corporations may approach maximum efficiency in utilization of capital, raw materials, and labor. But there is no assurance that their managers will be responsive to another increasingly important value—distribution of the wealth that they produce in accord with priorities prevailing within the societies where it is produced.

As we write this section, the rulers of oil-rich countries in North Africa and the Near East are challenging the omnipotence of several huge foreign oil producers operating in those countries. Similar challenges in numerous economic fields have occurred, or are impending, in other parts of the world, chiefly within the less modernized regions. Local sovereigns, weak by conventional military and economic criteria, are exhibiting a lot of "political mus-

[2] George Modelski, "The Corporation in World Society," *The Yearbook of World Affairs, 1968* (London: London Institute of World Affairs, 1969), p. 68.

cle" in their dealings with foreign industrial giants. In particular, they are increasingly setting the terms on which foreign corporations may develop and dispose of mineral and other resources in their territories— especially, as in the Near East, if the local sovereigns receive support and aid from one or other of the superpowers. No clear trend is yet discernible in the contests between local state authorities and foreign corporations. But one conclusion seems quite clear.

As one commentator puts it, "Unless the world corporations are somehow required to pass on to the workers the fruits of their production, and unless taxes can be levied on the international companies so that pressing (but unprofitable) needs of the world can be financed, one can imagine that the result of this corporate efficiency could simply be that the rich, white, northern part of the world will get richer while the rest of it will get relatively poorer."[3]

The managers of gigantic transnational business enterprises negotiate with each other, with host governments, and with a wide variety of organizations domestic and international. Increasingly their operations resemble those of legally sovereign governments. For this reason some students of international politics would elevate them to the status of primary actors of the international political system. Short of that, they can be treated as ubiquitous and increasingly important features of the world community in which organized political communities interact. They are environmental features that restrict both the effective choices of national statesmen and their ability to achieve desired goals. Viewed either way, the internationalization of business indubitably reduces to some extent, often to a large extent, the effective independence of even the largest and most powerful states.

The growth of commerce during the nineteenth century among legally sovereign communities, each with its own separate currency and its own priorities and mode of allocating goods and services, produced the phenomena now called the balance of payments. In essence a state's balance of payments is the record of all transfers of goods, services, claims, and/or monetary gold across its jurisdictional boundaries. If purchases of foreign goods, services, and claims (investments), plus gifts or subsidies to foreign nations (if any), exceed receipts in a given statistical period,

the state's economy as a whole shows net indebtedness by so much to the outside world.

Continuing failure to maintain a substantial equivalence of exports to imports will produce various consequences, including scarcity of foreign currencies with which to pay external claims and ultimately depreciation of the external value of the state's own currency and reduced purchasing power of its government and citizens abroad. To avoid or correct this state of affairs, a government may take various actions, the following among others: It may export gold, and thereby deplete its monetary reserve. It may seek foreign gifts or loans to cover urgent external commitments. It may take steps to expand exports or, conversely, to reduce imports.

All such actions affect in some degree the allocation of goods and services within the national community in question, always more or less adversely for particular categories of consumers. Adverse effects may take such forms as higher taxes, higher prices for imported goods, or restrictions on foreign travel. Actions required to correct an imbalance of payments may also affect the government's ability to sustain foreign commitments and policies. For example, chronic balance-of-payments difficulties were unquestionably one of the considerations that moved British statesmen to reduce progressively their overseas military expenditures during the 1950s and 1960s. It is also clear that the huge total of American military expenditures abroad, together with large grants to modernizing societies and subsidies to military allies and satellites, contributed to the severe depletion of U.S. gold reserves during the same period.

PSYCHOLOGICAL PENETRATION AND INTERDEPENDENCE

Interdependence is also manifest in the growing psychological penetration of national communities. One has to go back no further than the early nineteenth century to appreciate how recently psychological isolation was the normal, nearly universal state of affairs. Today the situation is reversed in many countries, and in process of reversal in the rest. News of the outside world penetrates "iron curtains," "bamboo curtains," and every other kind of man-made barrier to transnational communications. Ideologies —systems of ideas and beliefs—circulate without much regard for political geography and censorship. In many countries—and the number is increasing—

[3] Editorial, *War/Peace Report,* October 1968, p. 13.

television brings the outside world into uncounted millions of homes; and in less affluent societies radio broadcasts perform a similar if less dramatic function.

Transnational carriers of information, values, and beliefs are numerous and varied. The more obvious ones include tourists and other travelers, interpersonal letters, telegrams and telephone calls, books, newspapers and magazines, and above all radio and television mentioned above. By these and other means, information is transmitted, social movements are organized and directed, and ideologies are insinuated into the minds of men.

Governments everywhere are giving attention to the transnational flows of news, ideas, and ideologies. Directly and indirectly they influence the substance of what is communicated. News may be censored in ways both obvious and subtle. Reading matter may be intercepted and banned. Subversive movements and organizations may be outlawed. But even the strictest surveillance and suppression rarely cut off altogether the flow of influential communications into and out of a country. Nor can the most elaborate propaganda completely neutralize the effects of words and other symbols that cross national frontiers and infiltrate people's minds. Psychological penetration, in short, is a "given," a "fact of life," which statesmen can modify or manipulate in some degree, but (even in the most tightly organized dictatorships) cannot completely control or eradicate.

Ideologies have long been recognized as formidable instruments of psychological penetration. An ideology, as used here, is any system of received ideas. There are nonpolitical as well as political ideologies. Examples of the former are religious creeds, moral codes, and economic doctrines; prime examples of the latter, constitutional democracy, communism, nationalism, and internationalism.

The political effect of ideological intrusion may be trivial or revolutionary. In some instances it has been explosively disruptive. More often the effect is a subtle, gradual erosion of preexisting beliefs and loyalties. In either case, the intrusion may significantly affect the morale, sense of purpose, or other facets of a nation's behavior and capabilities. Frequently a state's rulers resort to harsh and oppressive measures to counteract these effects, and such measures may themselves be socially disruptive in the longer run.

Largely for these reasons, most political ideologies have come to be widely regarded as potent and dangerous instruments of statecraft. It is also widely

believed that ideologies which stand for change are more effective: for example, liberal democracy in the nineteenth century; militant communism in our time.

Use of ideology as an instrument for penetrating national communities on a significant scale dates from the later years of the eighteenth century. One of the early experiments in ideological penetration was the American Declaration of Independence. The Continental Congress asserted:

> We hold these truths to be self evident: that all men are created equal; that they are endowed by their Creator with certain inalienable rights; that to secure these rights, governments are instituted among men, deriving their just powers from the consent of the governed. . . .

This was dangerous, incendiary doctrine in the eyes of eighteenth century monarchs and aristocrats. Even more dangerous and subversive were the slogans of the French Revolution. The doctrine of "liberty, equality, fraternity" assailed the citadel of dynastic legitimacy and aristocratic privilege. It drew anguished protests from the frightened aristocrats of Europe, who ordered their soldiers into battle in a vain attempt to put out the fire.

However, until well into the nineteenth century, the opportunities for ideological penetration remained severely limited. Formidable obstacles confronted the purveyor of disruptive slogans before the era of modern rapid communications. Travel was slow and expensive—a barrier to spreading ideas by word of mouth. Books, pamphlets, and newspapers circulated mainly among the upper classes, and not too widely even there. The biggest obstacle of all was nearly universal illiteracy. Inability to read blocked off the mass of humanity from easy access to the universe of ideas that existed beyond the local farm or village.

The Industrial Revolution started a transformation that continues to this day. The transition from hand labor to power-driven machinery was accompanied everywhere by human dislocation, exploitation, and misery. Such conditions evoked radical prescriptions for reform and various utopian and revolutionary social philosophies. These latter ranged from democratic socialism to Marxian communism. More efficient means of disseminating ideas—improved printing machinery, cheaper paper, faster ships and overland transport, and eventually planes and the modern apparatus of electronic communication— progressively expanded the areas of circulation. The growth of literacy simultaneously enlarged the audience which could be reached.

The consequences of this transformation are well known. The circulation of people and ideas has doubled and redoubled many times. Contacts between national communities have become ever more varied and continuous. One has only to think of the millions of persons who cross national frontiers every year to travel or reside for short or longer periods; or the huge quantities of personal letters, newspapers, books and other reading matter that circulate among countries; or the radio broadcasts that overleap every frontier, increasingly supplemented by the far more evocative images upon the video screen.

This spread and circulation of news and ideas is widely regarded as a prime source of the discontents which afflict not merely the underdeveloped countries but also the most affluent urban societies as well. The more pervasive the discontents, the more receptive a community seems to become to new prescriptions for reform. Hence the widespread use and fear of ideological intrusion calculated to focus and channel frustration, demands, and expectations, and otherwise to influence the behavior of whole populations.

An aspect of psychological penetration that deserves more attention than it generally receives has been the disruptive impact of American affluence on the underdeveloped societies. The popular view in America and generally in the West has been that communism is the most disruptive psychological force in those societies. It is doubtless difficult for most Americans to conceive of their own culture as a force inspiring revolt and even fostering the spread of communism. Yet a by-product, perhaps in the long run the most important by-product, of the display of American affluence abroad during and since World War II appears to have been precisely that. American soldiers, civil servants, business men, and a flood of American tourists have carried willy-nilly the message that ordinary citizens can possess and enjoy the material amenities restricted in most Asian, African, and Latin American countries to a tiny privileged elite at the top of the social pyramid. From this perspective Americans appear as the "terrible instigators of social change and revolution."[4]

Some writers on international politics appear to believe that psychological penetration operates only in one direction—from the strong to the weak. In this view, Great Powers are masters of their own destiny. Only those political communities that are small, poorly organized, economically underdeveloped, or otherwise weak and vulnerable, are likely to be significantly "penetrated" by external influences. Such is plainly not the case. Even the Superpowers can be penetrated by the weak—and are! One has only to consider such examples as Israeli influence in Washington, the influence of Chiang Kai-shek on American attitudes through the 1950s and '60s, or the more recent influence exerted on successive administrations by client regimes in Vietnam and elsewhere. In the words of one percipient observer, "Informal penetration is a pervasive phenomenon in contemporary international politics which works in both directions: Small states can penetrate large ones as well as vice versa."[5]

INSIDIOUS INTRUDERS

Less attention has been given to another class of intruders into sovereign national communities, intruders that present far greater dangers in many instances than the most pervasive human subverters and ideologies. We refer to the pollutants that degrade the quality of human life, and may severely affect the health of entire populations. These insidious intruders are chiefly though not exclusively air- and waterborne. The latter include domestic and industrial wastes that are discharged into lakes and rivers and into the oceans and connecting narrow seas. The former include noxious gases and particulates, including radioactive materials, that are discharged into the atmosphere. A third category includes plant and animal pests and diseases; and a fourth, the parasites, bacteria, and viruses that attack human organisms.

Advances in technology—especially in the technology of economic production and transportation— have enormously increased the quantity of air- and waterborne pollution and the mobility of organisms that attack plants, animals, and humans. In general, air and water pollution is most severe where per

[4] I. C. Lundberg, "World Revolution—American Plan," *Harper's Magazine,* December 1948, p. 39.

[5] R. O. Keohane, "Lilliputians' Dilemmas: Small States in International Politics," *International Organization,* 23 (Spring 1969), p. 306.

capita productivity is highest and the consuming population large. It becomes a transnational menace, thus an international problem, where winds and currents carry the pollutants from their source in one country across political boundaries into others.

Pollution of transnational rivers and lakes has been a persistent if relatively minor focus of concern, chiefly in Europe, for half a century and more. Airborne pollution was recognized as a major international problem only after World War II. In recent years there have been recurrent charges that airborne pollutants, chiefly from industrial sources in Western Europe, are endangering health in neighboring countries. Largely because of prevailing winds and geographical location, the massive airborne pollutions from industrial plants, highway vehicles, and airplanes in the United States have not become as yet a major source of international concern, and the same holds for Japan.

Invention and testing of atomic and thermonuclear explosives raised the danger from airborne pollution. Following test explosions by the United States, Soviet Union, Britain, France and China, lethal fallout has invariably appeared quickly, at great distances from the testing site, and over vast areas, emphasizing the global continuity of the earth's atmosphere. Scientists and engineers engaged in weapons research and development have generally minimized the risk to plants, animals, and humans. But nagging uncertainty persists, buttressed by considerable evidence regarding the longer-range injurious effects of radioactive fallout. This concern is reflected in the "strenuous efforts" of the Russian and American governments "to universalize worldwide control of the proliferation of nuclear tests in the atmosphere."[6]

The migratory habits of pests, parasites and other invasive organisms have been well known for a century or more. Governments have fought against these insidious intruders with embargoes, border quarantines and other inhibitory regulations. Such measures have been only partially effective. Development of antibiotics and other drugs have provided additional defenses. Working in the opposite direction has been the rising speed and volume of intercountry and intercontinental commerce and travel. The 1918 pandemic of virulent influenza was a frightening reminder of the catastrophic worldwide effects of a swiftly

migrating deadly new disease. No one knows for certain when and where a virulent invasive new disease, or remedy-resistant variant of some known disease, will appear next. But the probability of its arising is greater where population is dense and people are weakened by chronic malnutrition and debilitating endemic diseases. The certainty of its rapid spread was dramatically exhibited in the pandemic of the fortunately mild "Hongkong flu" a few years ago. Sovereignty and border quarantines are no more effective against such epidemics than they are against air- and waterborne pollution. All these insidious intruders dramatize the elemental reality that in many respects vital to human health and survival, we are all parts of a single ecosystem coterminous with the earth.

There is a persistent tendency in affluent societies, especially in the United States, to spurn this elemental reality. Those who favor ending, or drastically reducing, economic and technical assistance to the modernizing countries habitually minimize any risk in doing so. Their prescription: quarantine the plague spots, and forget about them! Apart from the inhumanity of such an attitude, it reflects gross ignorance or reckless disregard of the mobility of migratory pollutants and other insidious intruders. As has been argued on many occasions by some of the most sophisticated and best informed experts: the United States cannot exist indefinitely as an island of health and affluence in an ocean of malnutrition, disease, and destitution.

THE INTERRELATING OCEAN

The oceans and connecting seas present a clutch of problems just the reverse of those examined in the preceding sections. The salient common feature of those latter problems is the fading ability of even the most powerful states (in a military and economic sense) to provide collective and personal security against unwanted intrusions from outside the territory over which they have indisputable legal sovereignty. With respect to the oceans and seas, the problems of confronting sovereign communities include: (1) how to get a fair share of the foodstuffs and industrial raw materials that lie outside every state's sovereign jurisdiction; (2) how to prevent contamination and needless destruction of these resources which every year become more important for the earth's growing population, especially for those communities

---

[6] Abel Wolman, "Pollution As an International Issue," *Foreign Affairs,* 47 (1968), p. 172.

that are struggling up the ladder of modernization; and (3) how to prevent man-made contamination of the oceans and seas from fatally disrupting the ecological chain-of-life upon which future human survival precariously depends. . . .

We are accustomed to thinking of the oceans as several distinct bodies of water—Atlantic, Pacific, Indian, Arctic and Antarctic—and the connecting seas —North Sea, Mediterranean, Caribbean, and all the others—as likewise separate and distinct. However, in a geographical sense, the oceans and connecting seas are not several but one—a single uninterrupted expanse of water, over 300 million cubic miles in volume and covering 70 percent of the face of the earth.

The water of the global ocean is perpetually in motion, not merely at the surface but far below the surface as well. Seawater flows according to established, well-known patterns. These flows can be likened to vast marine rivers of a magnitude many, many times the combined flow of all the great and little inland waterways. Ocean currents convey immense quantities of heat thousands of miles, moderating climates from the equator to the poles. They also carry many other things, including a huge and rapidly growing quantity of man-made pollutants, a somber reality to which we shall return later in this section.

In most places, the ocean floor, or seabed, slopes downward more or less gradually from the shore to a depth of about 600 feet—a zone called the continental shelf. From the edge of this shelf the floor drops away sharply to depths that range from a few thousand feet to over seven miles. The deep ocean floor includes vast plains and rugged mountain ranges, with some totally submerged "seamounts" higher than Mount Everest. Knowledge of this seabed topography is still far from complete. But underwater photography, television, echo-sounders, and other still more sophisticated instruments have produced more knowledge of the ocean floor "in the past fifteen years than in the preceding two thousand years."[7]

For thousands of years the oceans and larger seas separated and isolated human communities. Transoceanic migrations occurred in prehistoric eras, but infrequently and on a very small scale. Even as late as the 1400s, the oceans presented a formidable barrier to human movement and served more to separate

than to integrate the widely scattered aggregates of humanity.

. . . [A]ll this changed rather abruptly following the historic voyages of the later fifteenth century. Once it became reasonably safe to venture beyond sight of land and technically possible to make preselected landfalls across any body of water however wide, the oceans and larger seas provided highways that became progressively interrelating. Ships carried goods, colonists, and armed men to lands thousands of miles overseas. Until well into the twentieth century, the surface of these waters carried virtually all intercontinental commerce and much of the local traffic between coastal points on the same continent. Command of the sea became a prize of prime political value; and . . . the layout of the continents and narrow seas profoundly affected the geopolitical patterns of international politics for several centuries. The prodigious growth of overland transport and of intercontinental airborne traffic, supplemented in the military sphere by long-range ballistic missiles, has reduced the importance historically attributed to "command" of the ocean's surface. But the global ocean and its connecting seas have acquired other values that stimulate new rivalries, alter conceptions of national interest, and in various ways extend and tighten the interdependence of nations.

These contemporary values derive, in the main, from four sources: (1) from the rising importance of the ocean as a source of food and industrial raw materials; (2) from developments in military and economic technology; (3) from the disposition of governments and corporations that command the latest technologies to preempt the seabed for their own exclusive purposes; and (4) from accumulating evidence that human activities are polluting the ocean in ways that threaten disaster for the world community as a whole.

The ocean, as a source of food and raw materials and the locus of natural processes essential to life upon this planet, is receiving much more attention than formerly. Interest focuses chiefly on three points: (1) the ocean as the environment of marine organisms important for the human future both as a source of food and as the photosynthesizers that provide up to 70 percent or more of the free oxygen essential to the survival of all air breathing organisms including humans; (2) seawater as the carrier of huge quantities of dissolved chemicals of many kinds; and (3) the ocean floor, or seabed, as the locus of mineral

[7] Arvid Pardo, "Who Will Control the Seabed?" *Foreign Affairs,* 47 (October 1968), p. 125.

deposits possibly greater than all known sources upon or beneath dry land. . . .

According to traditional international law, the ocean and connecting seas (except for a narrow coastal zone) constitute the "high sea" that lies outside the sovereign jurisdiction of any state. The coastal zone of "territorial waters" historically extended about three miles from shore. During the past half century, various governments have asserted a "right" to exercise jurisdiction for various purposes farther from their shores. In 1958 a major breach in the traditional law was made by an international treaty which extended the jurisdiction of maritime states over the resources upon and beneath the seabed of the continental shelf to a depth of 600 feet, "or beyond that limit to where the depth of the superadjacent water admits to the exploration of the natural resources of the said areas."

In short, such sovereignty "may be exercised over a continuous stretch of seafloor starting with the beach and extending outwards and downwards to whatever depth the nation is able to work its benthic resources [that is, resources upon or beneath the seafloor]."[8]

There are plenty of indications that this is only the beginning of what may become another phase of ruthless international competition and conflict, or alternatively, the forerunner of a massive experiment in international order. As things stood in the early 1970s, the only effective constraints on exploitation of the seafloor to any depth were those imposed by the transient limitations of a rapidly advancing technology and the availability of huge amounts of capital. Since only a very few political communities commanded both the necessary technology and the capital, the outlook was that those few—U.S.A., U.S.S.R., Japan, and perhaps two or three others—would progressively preempt development and control of the resources in the more remote ocean depths. A review of the situation in 1969 concluded that "the great powers will not accept control by an international body," and that "the great industrial complexes that have been doing preliminary work will not look favorably on the idea of sharing profits" with other nations which lack the marine frontage, or the requisite technology, or the necessary capital to exploit the ocean depths.[9]

In the same year a leading authority on deep-sea technology noted a "worldwide trend by maritime nations to claim more offshore territory," a concomitant trend toward "head-on confrontation between rival claimants," and reluctance of governments and corporations in the forefront of deep-sea explorations to accept the principle of internationalization—reluctance, in short, to admit the principle that the resources upon and beneath the ocean floor are part of the *common wealth* of the world community as a whole.[10]

While nationalistic rivals mobilize to contest control of the resources of the seabed, two sets of forces are eroding the ecology of the ocean as a whole. These forces are excessive fishing and progressive pollution of the environment in which fish and other marine organisms subsist.

The fact and potentially disastrous consequences of large-scale industrialization of fishing—especially but not exclusively by Russians and Japanese—have evoked protests of alarm from ecologists in numerous countries. In the measured rhetoric of a recent United Nations report, it is stated with no qualification that

> destruction or depletion of marine resources has been a continuing process in the absence of effective control and management. The decline of certain species of whales and seals, of sea turtles, of the Pacific sardine and Atlantic salmon fisheries, as well as the continuing over-exploitation of the eastern Pacific anchoveta fishery are examples. The growing dependence of mankind upon the sea as a source of protein requires that its resources be properly managed.[11]

The U.N. report asserts further that "pollution of the sea is a continued threat to its future productivity." The report cites specifically the ecological damage caused by oil spills from tankers and from underwater oil drilling and pumping rigs. But these are by no means all, or necessarily the most serious, sources of marine pollution. Hundreds of millions of tons of sewage and industrial wastes from scores of countries are being dumped annually into coastal waters and

[8] E. W. Seabrook Hull, "The Political Ocean," *Foreign Affairs,* 45 (April 1967), p. 498. Copyright 1967 by the Council on Foreign Relations; reprinted by permission.

[9] "For Planners at the U.N., the Ocean Floor Is New Frontier," New York *Times,* November 24, 1969.

[10] The quoted phrases are from Paul Cohen, *The Realm of the Submarine* (New York: Macmillan, 1969), pp. 258, 259. Mr. Cohen is president of a private consulting firm in underwater technology.

[11] *Problems of the Human Environment, Report of the Secretary-General,* United Nations, May 26, 1969, Economic and Social Council, 47th Session, Agenda Item 10, par. 48.

thence out to sea—with the volume rising steadily year by year. Destruction of spawning sites by these pollutants and by the draining of tidal marshes, damming of rivers that discharge into the sea, and other projects and operations go on around the world without regard to their destructive effects on marine ecology.

Recurrent testing of nuclear weapons in marine areas, chiefly in the western Pacific, has released incalculable quantities of lethal radioactive debris, carried around the earth by the currents of the global ocean. Some radioactive contamination as well as a large amount of heat find their way into coastal waters via the spent coolant of atomic power plants, the number of which is steadily increasing. Ecologists view with concern the tendency of radioactivity to accumulate and concentrate in marine organisms through time, to become in the not distant future a menace to human consumers of the products of the sea.

It is further regarded as virtually certain that, in the absence of adequate and rigorously enforced regulations, mining of minerals upon and beneath the ocean floor will produce at least as much environmental damage as comparable operations on land have produced, and are still producing, in scores of countries.

Finally, one notes the grim warnings from ecologists that continued drainage of pesticide residues, industrial effluents, and other pollutants into the ocean will sooner or later slow down, possibly even utterly disrupt, the photosynthesis in marine organisms, starting chain reactions that could eventually so transform the ecology of the ocean as to endanger *all life upon the earth*.[12]

This is admittedly a controversial issue on which many expert opinions are still tentative and even agnostic. As usual, when experts disagree or seem uncertain, politicians and most of their constituents opt for quick gains at least cost and let the future take care of itself. In this instance, as Paul Ehrlich, the Stanford University biologist, reminds us, the risks may be more than minimal:

No one knows how long we can continue to pollute the seas with chlorinated hydrocarbon insecticides, polychlorinated biphenyls, and hundreds of thousands of other pollutants without bringing on a

worldwide ecological disaster. Subtle changes may already have started a chain reaction in that direction.[13]

Whether and when a marine catastrophe occurs as predicted from these and other causes depends upon the human response. Much remains to be learned about the short- and longer-range effects of the conditions and trends outlined above. But certain possibilities are no longer in doubt. Sooner or later, what happens within and beneath the water of the global ocean is likely to produce major consequences for the human condition everywhere, even for communities hundreds or thousands of miles from tidewater. Unregulated nationalistic competition for, and exploitation of, marine life and the minerals in seawater and upon and beneath the ocean floor are likely to hasten the worst ecological effects predicted. The ancient British maxim, "The sea is one," expresses an international reality that picks up new dimensions and salience with every passing year.

SUMMATION

In the preceding pages we have identified and examined several sectors of the interrelatedness and resulting interdependencies that characterize the milieu in which statecraft is conducted and increasingly determine its substance. Implicit throughout is the proposition that statesmen ignore these interdependencies at their peril. Also implicit is the further proposition that interrelatedness and interdependence limit the political capabilities of all states. Some national communities are manifestly more easily penetrated or otherwise adversely affected than others. It is likewise evident that states with large populations, vast territory, advanced economic development, and superior technology are prima facie less vulnerable than those less advantageously equipped. But interdependence, we repeat, is a pervasive worldwide phenomenon and, in different ways and in varying degrees, affects the external policies and potentials of all nations.

The thrust of this chapter . . . poses inescapable queries regarding the future of the sovereign state and its parochially tribal citizens. As previously emphasized, we do not predict that the nation-state is about

---

[12] See, for example, the somber scenario depicted by biologist Paul Ehrlich, "Eco-Catastrophe," *Ramparts*, September 1969, p. 24.

[13] P. R. and A. H. Ehrlich, *Population, Resources, Environment: Issues in Human Ecology* (San Francisco: Freeman, 1970), p. 180.

to wither away. Social structures often persist long after they have become potentially unviable, even a menace to the welfare of those who ostensibly derive benefit from them. Such may well be the future history of the state system. But historians of the twenty-first century might just possibly conclude that the combination of unattainable military security, diminishing economic autonomy, increasing psycho-logical penetrability, migratory pollutants and invasive pests and diseases, and looming ecological disaster within the global ocean had by the 1970s rendered sovereign territorial states unviable for the purposes of providing personal safety, public order, and survival of the human species—as unviable indeed as medieval castles and walled towns became after the "gunpowder revolution."

The State's Positive Role in World Affairs
Hedley Bull

We are constantly being told, at least in the Western world, that the state (and along with it, the system of states) is an obstacle to the achievement of a viable world order. First, the state is said to be an obstacle to peace and security: while the world continues to be organized politically as a system of states, war will remain endemic—a condition of affairs that could be tolerated before the advent of nuclear weapons but can be no longer. Second, the state is said to stand in the way of the promotion of economic and social justice in world society. It is the sovereign state that enables the rich peoples of the world to consume their greedy, mammoth portions of the world's resources, while refusing transfers to poor countries; and it is the sovereign state, again, that makes it possible for the squalid and corrupt governments of many poor (and some not so poor) countries to ignore the basic needs of their own citizens and to violate their human rights. Third, the state is held to be a barrier to man's grappling effectively with the problem of living in harmony with his environment. The connected issues of the control of the world's population, the production and distribution of food, the utilization of the world's resources, and the conservation of the natural environment, it is said, have to be tackled on a global basis, and this is prevented by the division of mankind into states.

Those who see the problem of world order as one of getting "beyond the state" (or the sovereign state or the nation-state) are not necessarily agreed as to what form of universal political organization should replace the system of states, or what combination of suprastate, substate, or transstate actors should deprive the state of its role. But they all feel that there is some basic contradiction between, on the one hand, the unity or interconnectedness of the global economy, the global society, the global polity, and, on the other, the system under which each state claims exclusive jurisdiction over a particular area of the earth's surface and of the human population. Thus political economists tell us that we must transcend the state in order to manage "the economics of interdependence," lawyers sound the clarion call of an advance "from international law to world law," and political scientists speak of the need to disavow the "states-centric paradigm."[1] The term "statist" is applied in a new pejorative sense to describe those unable to free themselves from the bad old ways.

No doubt the system of sovereign states, when compared with other forms of universal political organization that have existed in the past or might come to exist in the future (e.g., a world government, a neo-medieval order in which there is no central authority but in which states are not "sovereign," or an order composed of geographically isolated or autarchic communities) does have its own particular

[1] See, for example, Miriam Camps, *"First World Relationships": The Role of the OECD* (Paris: Atlantic Institute for International Affairs; New York: Council on Foreign Relations, 1975) and Joseph Nye and Robert Keohane, *Transnational Relations and World Politics* (Cambridge, Mass.: Harvard University Press, 1972). Also Richard A. Falk, *This Endangered Planet* (New York: Random House, 1971), and *A Study of Future Worlds* (New York: Free Press, 1975).

From Hedley Bull, "The State's Positive Role in World Politics," *Daedalus* **108** (Fall 1979): 111–123.

disadvantages. But the attack on the state is misconceived.

In the first place it seems likely that the state, whether we approve of it or not, is here to stay. If this is so, the argument that we can advance the cause of world order only by getting "beyond the state" is a counsel of despair, at all events if it means that we have to begin by abolishing or subverting the state, rather than that there is a need to build upon it. Of course, the state is not the only important actor on the stage of world politics: nonstate groups and movements of various kinds play a role, as do individual persons. There never was a time in the history of the modern international system when this was otherwise: in eighteenth and nineteenth century Europe, too, states shared the stage with chartered companies, revolutionary and counterrevolutionary political parties, and national liberation movements. Indeed, it is difficult to believe that anyone ever asserted the "states-centric" view of international politics that is today so knowingly rejected by those who seek to emphasize the role of "the new international actors."[2] What was widely asserted about European international relations from the time of Vattel in the mid-eighteenth century until the end of the First World War was the *legal fiction* of a political universe that consisted of states alone, the doctrine that only states had rights and duties in international law. But assertion of such a doctrine does not imply that the actual course of international political events can be understood in terms of this fiction rather than in terms of the actions of actual persons and groups of persons, such as are set out in any history of the period.

It is sometimes suggested that in recent decades "other actors" have increased their role in world politics at the expense of that of the state, but even this—although it may be so—is difficult to establish conclusively because of the impossibility of reducing the question to quantitative terms.[3] It is true that international governmental and nongovernmental organizations have multiplied visibly, that multinational corporations have had a dramatic impact on the world economy, and that vast new networks of contact and

intercourse have grown up at the transnational level. But the state's role in world politics has been growing dramatically also.

There has been a geographical spreading of the state, from Europe outward. Two centuries ago most of the non-European world lay beyond the boundaries of any sovereign state, in the sphere of the Islamic system or of Oriental empires or of tribal societies. Today the sovereign state is established throughout the world. No doubt the multiplication of states—the United Nations began with 51 member states and now has 151—has been accompanied by an increase in heterogeneity among them. There has been a certain debasing of the currency of statehood as a consequence of the growth of ministates and microstates, and many of the non-European ones—to which Michael Oakeshott contemptuously refers as "imitation states"—are imperfectly established and unlike the originals in important respects.[4] But for the first time the sovereign state is the common political form experienced by the whole of mankind.

At the same time the role of the state in world affairs has expanded functionally. Whereas a few decades ago states in their dealings with one another confined themselves to diplomatic and strategic issues and allowed economic, social, and ideological relations among peoples to be determined for the most part by the private sector, today the state has extended its tentacles in such a way as to deprive businessmen and bankers, labor organizations and sporting teams, churches and political parties of the standing as international actors independent of state control that they once enjoyed. It has been said that the growth of transnational relations has deprived traditional interstate politics of its previous autonomy.[5] But what is rather the case is that the growth of state involvement in trade, in exchange and payments, in the control of migration, and in science and culture and international sporting events has brought an end to the autonomy of transnational relations.

It is difficult to see evidence of the decline of the sovereign state in the various movements for the regional integration of states that have developed in the post-1945 world, such as the European Economic Community, the Organization of African Unity, the

[2] See especially Nye and Keohane, *Transnational Relations*.

[3] See, for example, Richard W. Mansbach, Yale H. Ferguson, and Donald E. Lamport, *The Web of World Politics. Non-state Actors in the Global System* (Englewood Cliffs, N. J.: Prentice-Hall Inc., 1976).

[4] Michael Oakeshott, *On Human Conduct* (New York: Oxford University Press, 1975).

[5] Nye and Keohane, *Transnational Relations*, Introduction.

Organization of American States, or the Association of South East Asian Nations. It is not merely that the EEC, which provides the most impressive example of progress toward a goal of regional integration, has not in fact undermined the sovereignty of its member states in the sense of their legal independence of external control. Nor is it merely that the very considerable achievements of the Community in promoting peace, reconciliation, prosperity, and cooperation in Western Europe have depended more upon intergovernmental cooperation than on Community institutions bypassing the constituent states. It is that the movement for European integration has been led from the beginning by the conception that the end goal of the process is the creation of a European superstate, a continental United States of Europe—a conception that only confirms the continuing vitality of "statist" premises.

Nor is there much evidence of any threat to the state as an institution in the attempts—sometimes successful, sometimes not—of nationalist separatist groups to bring about the disintegration of existing states, as in Nigeria, Pakistan, Yugoslavia, Canada, the United Kingdom, or Iraq, to name only a few. For if we ask what have been the goals of the separatist Biafrans, East Bengalis, Croats, Quebecois, Scots, or Kurds, the answer is that they have been trying to create new states. While the regional integrationists seek to reduce the number of states in the world, and the nationalist separatists seek to increase it, both are as committed as the defendants of existing states to the continuation of the state as an institution. It might be thought that a serious challenge to the position of the state lies in the tendency of Socialist and Third World states to accord rights and duties in international law to nations that are not states; and that, in particular, national liberation movements—most notably, the Palestine Liberation Organization—have achieved a degree of recognition in the United Nations and elsewhere that in some way sounds the death knell of the state, or at all events brings to an end its claims to a privileged position among political groups in the world today. But again, what we have to notice is that the thinking both of the national liberation groups and of the states that lend support to them is confined within statist logic. What national liberation movements seek to do is to capture control of existing states (as in the case of the PLO or the FLN in Algeria), to create new states (as in Eritrea or Nagaland), or to change the boundaries of states (as

in Ireland). In seeking recognition of their claims in international society, the starting point of their argument is the principle that nations ought to be states, and the strongest card they have to play is that they represent nations that seek to be states.

It is not a matter for celebration that regional integrationists and nationalist disintegrationists are as unable as they appear to be to think beyond the old confines of the states-system. There are other ways in which their aspirations might be satisfied than by seeking to control sovereign states.

One may imagine, for example, that a regional integration movement, like that in the countries of the European Community, might seek to undermine the sovereignty of its member states, yet at the same time stop short of transferring this sovereignty to any regional authority. If they were to bring about a situation in which authorities existed both at the national and at the European level, but no one such authority claimed supremacy over the others in terms of superior jurisdiction or its claims on the loyalties of individual persons, the sovereign state would have been transcended. Similarly, one may imagine that if nationalist separatist groups were content to reject the sovereignty of the states to which they are at present subject, but at the same time refrained from advancing any claims to sovereign statehood themselves, some genuine innovation in the structure of the world political system might take place.

We may envisage a situation in which, say, a Scottish authority in Edinburgh, a British authority in London, and a European authority in Brussels were all actors in world politics and all enjoyed representation in world political organizations, together with rights and duties of various kinds in world law, but in which no one of them claimed sovereignty or supremacy over the others, and a person living in Glasgow had no exclusive or overriding loyalty to any one of them. Such an outcome would take us truly "beyond the sovereign state" and is by no means implausible, but it is striking how little interest has been displayed in it by either the regional integrationists or the subnationalist "disintegrationists."

In the second place, those who say that what we have to do is get "beyond the states-system" forget that war, economic injustice, and ecological mismanagement have deeper causes than those embodied in any particular form of universal political organization. The states-system we have today is indeed associated with violent conflict and insecurity, with economic and social inequality and misery on a vast scale, and with failures of every kind to live in harmony with our environment. But this is no reason to assume that a world government, a neo-medieval order of overlapping sovereignties and jurisdictions, a system of isolated or semi-isolated communities, or any other alternative global order we might imagine would not be associated with these things also. Violence, economic injustice, and disharmony between man and nature have a longer history than the modern states-system. The causes that lead to them will be operative, and our need to work against them imperative, whatever the political structure of the world.

Let us take, for example, the central "world order goal" of peace. It is true that the states-system gives rise to its own peculiar dangers of war, such as those that have been stressed by exponents of "the international anarchy" (C. Lowes Dickinson), "the great illusion" (Norman Angell), "the arms race" (Philip Noel-Baker), or "the old game, now forever discredited, of the balance of power" (Woodrow Wilson). It is true that war is endemic in the present states-system, not in the sense that it is made "inevitable" (particular wars are avoidable, and even war in general is inevitable only in the sense of being statistically probable), but in the sense that it is institutionalized, that it is a built-in feature of our arrangements and expectations. We may agree also that nuclear weapons and other advanced military technology have made this state of affairs intolerable, if it was not so before.

But the idea that if states are abolished, war will be abolished, rests simply on the verbal confusion between war in the broad sense of armed conflict between political groups and war in the narrow sense of armed conflict between sovereign states. Armed conflicts, including nuclear ones, will not be less terrible because they are conducted among groups other than states, or called police actions or civil uprisings. The causes of war lie ultimately in the existence of weapons and armed forces and the will of political groups to use them rather than accept defeat. Some forms of universal political organization may offer better prospects than others that these causes can be controlled, but none is exempt from their operation.

Of course, it is possible to imagine a world government or other alternative form of universal political organization from which war, economic injustice, and ecological mismanagement have been banished. But so is it possible to imagine a states-system so reformed that it has these utopian features: a world of separate states disciplined by the arts of peace, cooperating in the implementation of an agreed universal standard of human welfare and respectful of a globally agreed environmental code. It is a perfectly legitimate exercise to compare these different utopias and to consider whether some are more feasible than others. What is not acceptable—but what critics of the states-system commonly do—is to compare a utopian vision of a world central authority, or of whatever other alternative universal political order they favor, with the states-system, not in a utopian form but as it exists now.

In the third place, the critics neglect to take account of the positive functions that the state and the states-system have fulfilled in relation to world order in the past. The modern state—as a government supreme over a particular territory and population—has provided order on a local scale. To the extent that Europe, and at a later stage other continents, were covered by states that actually maintained their authority and were not constantly breaking down as a result of internal or external conflicts, local areas of order have been sustained by states over vast areas of the world. Most of our experience of order in modern times derives from these local areas of order established by the authority of states; and the chief meaning that we have been able to give to the concept of world order before very recent times is that it has been simply the sum of the local areas of order provided collectively by states.

States, moreover, have cooperated with one another in maintaining a structure of interstate, or international, order in which they confirm one another's domestic authority and preserve a framework of coexistence. For all the conflict and violence that have arisen out of their contact and intercourse with one another, they have formed not only an international system, but also a rudimentary international society. They have sensed common interests in preserving the framework of coexistence that limits and restrains the rivalry among them; they have evolved rules of the road that translate these common interests into specific guides to conduct; and they have cooperated in working common institutions such as international law, the diplomatic system, and the conventions of war that facilitate observance of the rules. Experts on "the international anarchy" will tell us, and rightly so, how precarious and imperfect this inherited structure of international order is, and exponents of "spaceship earth" will show how inadequate it is to meet the needs of the present time. But it does represent the form of universal political order that has actually existed in modern history, and if we are to talk of extending the scope of order in world affairs, we need first to understand the conditions under which there is any order at all. The critics of the states-system contrast it with the more perfect world order they would like to see; but the historical alternative to it was more ubiquitous violence and disorder.

We associate states with war: they have claimed, and still claim, a legal right to resort to it and to require individual citizens to wage it in their name. They dispose of most of the arms and armed forces with which it is waged, and notwithstanding the large role played in modern war by civil factions of one kind or another and by so-called barbarian powers beyond the confines of European international society, states have been the principal political groups actually engaged in war. But if we compare war among modern states with other historical violence or with future violence that we can readily enough imagine, we have to note that, with all its horrors, it has embodied a certain normative regime, without which violence has been and might be more horrible still.

Thus states when they go to war have recognized a need to provide one another and international society at large with an explanation in terms of a common doctrine of just causes of war, at the heart of which there has always been the notion that a war is just if it is fought in self-defense. No doubt there is great ambiguity and much disagreement about the meaning of this rule; other causes have been thought to be just in addition to that of self-defense. It is only in this century that limitations on the right of a state to go to war have been clearly expressed in legal terms, and the limitations are in any case observed more in the breach than in observance. Yet the conception that resort to war requires an explanation in terms of rules acknowledged on both sides is a mark of the existence at least of a rudimentary society; it imparts some element of stability to the expectations independent political communities can have about one another's behavior. Where—as in the encounter between political communities that do not belong to a common states-system or international society—war can be begun without any feeling of a need for an explana-

tion, or the explanation felt to be necessary derives from rules accepted on one side only and not on the other—as in Europe's belief in its civilizing mission, or the Mongols' belief in the Mandate of Heaven, or in the conception of a crusade or holy war—no such element of stability can be achieved.

Modern states, moreover, wage war under the discipline of the belief that some means are legitimate in war and some are not, a belief expressed sometimes in a doctrine of morally just means in war, sometimes in a body of laws of war, sometimes simply in an unthinking acceptance of what Michael Walzer calls "the war convention."[6] At the heart of this is the notion that the soldiers or military agents of the enemy state are legitimate objects of the use of force and that others are not. On the one hand, this notion sanctifies a particular kind of killing and maiming, breaking down the ordinary civil prohibition of taking life and causing physical injury; on the other hand, it establishes boundaries between the kinds of killing and injury that are part of war and the kinds that are not. On the basis of these boundaries, states have built up rules to limit the force they employ against one another, to distinguish belligerents and neutrals and thus contain the spread of conflict, and to uphold standards of humanity and protect the innocent. Of course, it is not only in the special case of war in the strict sense, war between states, that war takes place in a normative framework: such a framework sometimes surrounded the armed conflicts of primitive, feudal, and oriental societies also. But in modern times there has been a sophisticated body of rules that are held to apply to war between states but not to armed conflicts in which one or both parties is a nonstate group, such as a civil faction or a "barbarian" power. These rules for the conduct of war are notoriously prone to be disregarded, and in the twentieth century they have been subject to special strain, but they are part of the heritage that has been bequeathed to us by the states-system.

More important even than the conceptions of legitimate ends and of legitimate means in war has been the notion that war to be legitimate must be begun, as Aquinas put it, on the proper authority. Cardinal to the distinction between war and mere brigandage or private killing is the idea that the former is waged by

[6] Michael Walzer, *Just and Unjust Wars. An Argument with Historical Illustrations* (New York: Basic Books, 1977).

the agents of a public authority, which is recognized to be entitled to resort to force against its adversaries, and signifies that it has done so by issuing a declaration of war or in some other way. In the modern states-system it has been held that states alone have this authority: deeply divided though they have been, states have usually been united in maintaining that they are entitled to a monopoly of the legitimate use of force, both domestically and across state frontiers. Of course, they have not always been successful in preserving their monopoly, which has been broken from time to time by civil factions, by "barbarian" powers, and by pirates. States also experience difficulty in maintaining a united front, on the issue: the Socialist and Third World countries at present, for example, uphold the right of national liberation groups to resort to force internationally, and in the Second World War both the Western powers and the Soviet Union supported partisan groups in their struggle against Germany. Nevertheless, the idea that the right to engage in war should be confined to certain public authorities and should not be generally available to self-appointed political groups of all kinds is one of the most vital barriers we have against anarchy, and the modern states-system has passed on to us a rule embodying this idea that has proved workable.

At present, of course, the state's monopoly of the legitimate use of force is under some challenge, especially from national liberation groups. This is not new or unusual, and the challenge is mitigated to the extent that these groups are themselves would-be states whose claims to legitimacy and recognition rest in large measure upon the belief of their supporters that they should be states. Neither national liberation groups themselves nor their supporters in the Socialist countries and the Third World (they enjoy in some cases considerable support in the West also) put forward any general attack upon the state's monopoly position or advocate a wide or indiscriminate license to resort to force. We do, however, find that some Western critics of the states-system put forward a general attack on the state's monopoly position, as if the attempt of states to confine to themselves the right to use force were some unwarranted attempt to cling to an unfair privilege, to be opposed in the same spirit in which men opposed the Big Trusts or the propertied franchise. We are told that the "elite claims" of states are inappropriate now that there is "a rich

diversity of authorized participants in the processes on international law."[7] The suggestion seems to be that "a rich diversity" of actors in world politics should be entitled to maintain "private armies" and go to war to support their demands, so long as these demands measure up to certain policy criteria ("world order with human dignity") drawn up in New Haven or elsewhere.

This kind of talk is not only dangerous in an era of frequent resort to force by small armed groups with no claims to representative status of any kind, and widespread availability of destructive weapons; it is also shallow in overlooking the difference between a modern state, endowed with authority as well as mere power and exercising rights to the use of force recognized by the domestic and the international legal order, and a mere political cabal or party that has chosen to turn itself into an armed band. No doubt there are illegitimate governments and insurgent or vigilante groups with just causes. But in the absence of authority to resort to force across international boundaries, possession of a just cause should be regarded as totally irrelevant. International society does not maintain that groups within a state have no right of revolution against an illegitimate government. It does, however, seek to protect itself against the use of force by civil factions across state boundaries. The convention we have restricting the use of force across international boundaries to states accomplishes this. The rule confining the right to the international use of force to states is readily recognizable and widely accepted, even if it is sometimes violated. A rule that confers this right upon any political group with a cause we regard as just is one that imposes no barrier at all.

We associate states not only with war but also with sovereignty—which in internal affairs connotes supremacy, the supreme jurisdiction of the state over citizens and territory, and in external affairs connotes independence, freedom from external control. The claims of the state to a right of external sovereignty or independence are sometimes taken to imply rejection of all moral or legal authority other than that of the state, and indeed such claims have sometimes been

[7] Michael Reisman, "Private Armies in a Global War System," in *Law and Civil War in the Modern World,* John Norton Moore (ed.), (Baltimore: Johns Hopkins University Press, 1974), p. 257.

put forward in its name. When they are (as by Hegel or Treitschke), they are a menace to international order. Λ state's rights to sovereignty, however, are not asserted against the international legal order but conferred by it (from which it follows that they can be qualified by it, and even taken away). A state's right to sovereignty or independence is not a "natural right," analogous to the rights of individuals in Locke's state of nature: it is a right enjoyed to the extent that is is recognized to exist by other states. So far from it being the case that the sovereignty of the state is something antithetical to international order, it is the foundation of the whole edifice.

The order provided by the states-system, founded upon the exchange of recognition of sovereignty, is rightly said to be inferior to that provided within a properly functioning modern state. Within the states-system there is still no authoritative legislature, empowered to make laws, amend and rescind them in accordance with the will of the community; no independent judicial authority to which the impartial interpretation and application of the laws is entrusted; no central authority commanding a monopoly of force to ensure that the law will prevail. It is this perception of the contrast between the more perfect order enjoyed by individual persons in domestic political systems and the less perfect order enjoyed by states in international society that provides the impulse behind the desire to create a central world authority that will reproduce the conditions of domestic society on a universal scale. The states-system does, however, provide an imperfect and rudimentary form of order that holds anarchy at bay. It provides external support to the internal order created by states in areas where their writs run. And it maintains among states a regime of mutual tolerance and forebearance that limits conflict, sustains intercourse, and provides the conditions in which cooperation can grow.

The case for the states-system as it has operated in the past is that it is the form of universal political organization most able to provide minimum order in a political society in which there is not a consensus broad enough to sustain acceptance of a common government, but in which there is a consensus that can sustain the coexistence of a plurality of separate governments. When independent political communities have little or no intercourse with one another—as between European communities and pre-Columbian American communities, or between the former and China before the nineteenth century—a states-system is not necessary. Where such intercourse exists but consists of almost unmitigated hostility, as between Europe and Islam during much of the history of their encounter, a states-system is not possible. But in relation to European political society from, say, the sixteenth to the early twentieth centuries, a strong argument was put forward to the effect that the attempt to create strong central authorities, or to restore and develop the central authorities that had existed in the past, would lead only to division and disorder; whereas there could be fashioned—out of the surviving rules and practices inherited from Christendom and the new body of precedent emerging from the experience of secular Europe—a decentralized form of interstate society. The question now is how far this argument is still valid in relation to the decentralized interstate society of today, now expanded to encompass the whole globe and inevitably diluted and modified in the process.

Today, order in world affairs still depends vitally upon the positive role of the state. It is true that the framework of mere coexistence, of what is sometimes called "minimum world order," inherited from the European states-system, is no longer by itself adequate. The involvement of states in economic, social, cultural, and communications matters has led us to judge the international political system by standards which it would not have occurred to a nineteenth century European to apply. We now expect the states-system not only to enable independent political communities to coexist, but also to facilitate the management of the world economy, the eradication of poverty, the promotion of racial equality and women's rights, the raising of literacy and labor standards, and so on. All of this points to a universal political system that can promote "optimum world order," a system that can sustain not only coexistence but cooperation in the pursuit of a vast array of shared goals.

If one believed that states were inherently incapable of cooperation with one another and were condemned—as on the Hobbesian theory—to exist permanently in a state of war, there would be no escape from the conclusion that the requirements of world order in our time and the continued existence of states are in contradiction of one another. In fact, states can and do cooperate with one another both on a regional and on a global basis. So far is it from being the case that states are antithetical to the need that we recognize to inculcate a greater sense of unity in human society, that it is upon the states-system that our hopes for the latter, at least in the short run, must principally depend. It is the system of states that is at present the only political expression of the unity of mankind, and it is to cooperation among states, in the United Nations and elsewhere, that we have chiefly to look if we are to preserve such sense of common human interests as there may be, to extend it, and to translate it into concrete actions. We do not live in a world in which states are prepared to act as agents of the international community, taking their instructions from the UN or some such body; but we do have to restore the element of consensus among states, without which appeals for a sense of "spaceship earth" are voices crying in the wilderness.

In the fourth place, there is no consensus in the world behind the program of Western solidarists or global centralists for "transcending the states-system." In the Socialist countries and among the countries of the Third World there is no echo of these views. From the perspective of the two weaker sections of the world political system, the globalist doctrine is the ideology of the dominant Western powers. The barriers of state sovereignty that are to be swept away, they suspect, are the barriers that they, the weaker countries, have set up against Western penetration: the barriers that protect Socialist countries from capitalism and Third World countries from imperialism. The outlook of the Western globalist does indeed express, among other things, an exuberant desire to reshape the world that is born of confidence that the economic and technological power to accomplish it lies at hand. One senses in it a feeling of impatience that the political and legal obstacles ("ethnocentric nationalism," "the absurd political architecture of the world," "the obsolete doctrine of state sovereignty") cannot be brushed aside. It is also notable that the prescriptions they put forward for restructuring the world, high-minded though they are, derive wholly from the liberal, social-democratic, and internationalist traditions of the West, and take no account of the values entertained in other parts of the world, with which compromises may have to be reached.

For the Soviet Union and other Socialist countries the state is not an obstacle to peace but the bulwark of security against the imperialist aggressors; not an obstacle to economic justice but the instrument of proletarian dictatorship that has brought such justice

about; not a barrier to the solution of environmental problems, for these exist only in capitalist countries. It is true that the Socialist countries are heirs to a profoundly antistatist ideology. Classical Marxism looks forward to the withering away of the state and hence of the states-system, while also (although the point is less clear) treating the nation as a transitory phenomenon; it is neither interstate nor international but class struggle that provides the main theme of world history. But the outlook of the Socialist countries is shaped less by ideology than by practical interest: finding themselves a minority bloc of states in a world dominated by the military power, the industrial, commercial, and managerial enterprise, and the scientific and technological excellence of the capitalist countries, they have had a greater need than the West to avail themselves of the rights to sovereignty, equality, and noninterference. In a period when the Western leaders have talked of expanding the role of the United Nations, of accepting the implications of increased international "interdependence," or of the need for a unified, global approach to the environment, the Soviet Union has seemed to stand for a dogged defense of the entrenched legal rights of sovereign states. Of course, where the entrenched legal rights in question have been those of colonialist or white supremacist states, the Soviet Union had been willing enough to attack them. So also the Soviet Union was willing enough to proclaim the subordination of the sovereignty of Socialist states to the higher law of "proletarian internationalism" in intervening against Czechoslovakia in 1968. But in responding to the aggressive challenge of American globalism—as in rejecting the Baruch Plan in the 1940s or the UN's Korean action in the 1950s or the Congo action in the 1960s, the Soviet Union and its Socialist allies have adopted a conservatively statist position.

Among the Third World countries the idea that we must all now bend our efforts to get "beyond the state" is so alien to recent experience as to be almost unintelligible. Because they did not have states that were strong enough to withstand European or Western aggression, the African, Asian, and Oceanic peoples, as they see it, were subject to domination, exploration, and humiliation. It is by gaining control of states that they have been able to take charge of their own destiny. It is by the use of state power, by claiming the rights due to them as states, that they have been able to resist foreign military interference, to protect their economic interests by excluding or controlling multinational corporations, expropriating foreign assets, planning the development of their economies, and bargaining to improve the terms of trade. It is by insisting upon their privileges of sovereignty that they are able to defend their newly won independence against the foreign tutelage implicit in such phrases as "basic human needs," "the international protection of human rights," or (more sinister still) "humanitarian intervention."

Of course Third World countries have not displayed the same solicitude about the sovereign rights of Western countries with which they have been in conflict that they have shown for their own. Like the Socialist countries, they have been strong champions of interference in the domestic affairs of colonialist and white supremacist states, which they have seen not as interference but as assistance to peoples who are victims of aggression. While they insist on the right of developing states to have wealth and resources transferred to them, it is the *duty* of the advanced countries to transfer their resources that they are insistent upon, rather than any corresponding rights—as emerges from the Charter of Economic Rights and Duties of States, which the UN General Assembly endorsed in 1974.

In the controversy over establishment of an International Seabed Authority controlled by the developing countries—where it is the advanced countries whose deepsea mining operations will be subject to the Authority's control, and the developing countries that will gain from distribution of the rewards—the Third World countries are the champions of subordinating sovereignty to a common effort to preserve "the common heritage of mankind."

Finally, those in the West who disparage the states-system underestimate the special interests the Western countries themselves have in its preservation and development. We have noted that distrust of the state and the states-system appears to flourish especially in Western societies. A number of factors account for this. The liberal or individualist political tradition, so much more deeply rooted in the West than elsewhere, has always insisted that the rights of states are subordinate to those of the human beings that compose them. Loyalties that compete with loyalty to the state—allegiances to class or ethnic group or race or religious sect—can be openly proclaimed and cultivated in Western societies and often cannot be elsewhere. Moreover, it is only in the West that it has

been possible to assume that if the barriers separating states were abolished, it would be our way of life and not some other that would be universally enthroned.

It is the last point that is the crucial one. We in the West have not had—to the same degree as the Socialist countries and the Third World—a sense of dependence on the structure of the states-system. We assume that if the division of the world into separate states were to come to an end, and a global economy, society, and polity were allowed to grow up, it would be our economies, our ways of doing things, our social customs and ideas and conceptions of human rights, the forces of modernization that we represent, that would prevail. On the one hand, we have not had the feeling of vulnerability to "nonstate actors" shaping us from outside that Socialist countries have about Western libertarian ideas, or that developing countries have about Western-based multinational corporations, or that Islamic countries have about atheistic materialism. On the other hand, we have believed that our impact on the rest of the world does not depend merely on the exercise of state power. Our ways of doing things attract the peoples of Socialist countries even without efforts by our governments to promote them, and the withdrawal of Western governors, garrisons, and gunboats from the Third World countries has not brought the processes of Westernization at work in these countries to an end. Socialist and Third World states have sought to combat our influence—by withdrawing from the international economy, by excluding or controlling foreign investment, by building walls around their frontiers, by suppressing the flow of ideas—and the designs of Western globalists or "one-worlders," as we have noted, are designs to remove these obstacles. But Socialist and Third World states are in part in league with us. For while Socialist states seek to remain untainted by capitalism, Third World states to be free of imperialism, and both to diminish the West's dominant power, both are also seeking to become more modern; and because they cannot fail to recognize in the societies of North America, Western Europe, and Japan specimens of modernity more perfect than themselves, are compelled to imitate and to borrow. In Western attitudes toward the rest of the world there is still the belief, more deep-seated perhaps than that of the heirs of Marx and Lenin who rule the Soviet Union today, that the triumph of our own ways is historically inevitable.

There is some question whether this belief is well-founded. In the 1970s there has occurred a shift of power against the West and toward the Soviet Union and certain of the Third World countries. It has become more apparent that the revolt against Western tutelage that has played so large a part in the history of this century is a revolt not only against Western power and privilege, but also in large measure against Western values and institutions. Although the evidence is contradictory (consider, for example, the contrary cases at the present time of China and Iran) and we cannot now foresee what the outcome of the process will be, there are many signs in the extra-Western world of a conscious rejection of Western ways, not merely of capitalism and liberal democracy but even of modernity itself. In many parts of the world there is under way an attempt to revert to indigenous traditions, to restore institutions to the condition in which they were before they became contaminated by contact with the West, or at least to create the illusion that they have been restored. Just as the Western powers for more than a decade have found themselves a beleaguered minority in the United Nations, so they are coming to see themselves as forming a redoubt in a hostile world. There is a new attitude of defensiveness, even of belligerence, in Western attitudes toward the Soviet Union; and the countries of the Third World, until recently regarded as weak and dependent states in need of our help, are increasingly viewed as alien, hostile, and in some cases powerful and competitive states against which we need to defend ourselves.

At all events, the preservation of world order is not a matter of removing state barriers to the triumph of our own preferred values and institutions, but rather a matter of finding some *modus vivendi* as between these and the very different values and institutions in other parts of the world with which they will have to coexist. In thinking about world order it is wrong to begin, as the critics of the states-system do, by elaborating "goals" or "relevant Utopias" and drawing up plans for reaching them. This is how the "policy-scientist's" mind works but it is not what happens in world politics. It is better to begin with the elements of world order that actually exist, and consider how they might be cultivated. This must lead us to the state and the states-system, without which there would not be any order at all.

QUESTIONS FOR DISCUSSION

1 What information must one have to determine whether states are declining in power as actors in the international arena?
2 Is the state system harmful to world order?
3 Does state sovereignty prevent effective treatment of international problems?
4 Are states any longer capable of dealing with problems of common defense, public order, and providing for the general welfare of their citizenry?
5 What is the impact of increased global economic interdependence on the power of states as actors in the international political arena?

SUGGESTED READINGS

Angell, Robert Cooley. *The Quest for World Order.* Ann Arbor, Mich.: University of Michigan Press, 1979.

Brown, Lester R. *World Without Borders: The Interdependence of Nations.* New York: Foreign Policy Association, Headline Series, 1972.

Brucan, Silviu. "The Nation-State: Will It Keep Order or Wither Away?" *International Social Science Journal* **30** (1978): 9–30.

Hanreider, W. F. "Dissolving International Politics: Reflections on the Nation-State." *American Political Science Review* **72** (December 1978): 1276–1287.

Howard, Michael. "War and the Nation-State." *Daedalus* **108** (Fall 1979): 101–110.

Keohane, Robert O., and Joseph S. Nye. *Power and Interdependence: World Politics in Transition.* Boston: Little, Brown, 1977.

Nye, Joseph S., and Robert O. Keohane (eds.). *Transnational Relations and World Politics.* Cambridge: Harvard University Press, 1975.

Ronen, Dov. *The Quest for Self-Determination.* New Haven: Yale University Press, 1979.

Smith, Anthony D. S. *Nationalism in the Twentieth Century.* New York: New York University Press, 1979.

Waltz, Kenneth. "The Myth of National Interdependence," in Charles P. Kindleberger (ed.). *The International Corporation.* Cambridge: MIT Press, 1970, pp. 205–223.

2 Are the Multinational Corporations Dominant Actors in the International Arena?

YES

Paul M. Sweezy

Corporations, the State, and Imperialism

NO

Robert G. Hawkins and Ingo Walter

Multinational Corporations: Current Trends and Future Prospects

Corporations, the State, and Imperialism[1]
Paul M. Sweezy

The fact that the title for this talk was given to me by the organizers of this lecture series reflects what is doubtless a widespread conviction that corporations, the state, and imperialism are intimately interrelated both in theory and in practice. My assignment, I take it, is to attempt to throw light on the nature of these interrelations. And the most logical way to proceed is first to define the three concepts individually and then to inquire as to how they are related to each other.

1 Corporations are the typical twentieth-century units of business enterprise—first and foremost in production but also in commerce and finance.

2 The state is the institution which makes the laws and enforces them through an apparatus of armed force (including police), courts, prisons, etc. The state has a definite territorial identity: the area in which it operates is a nation, and within the nation's borders it is said to be "sovereign." The two characteristic features of sovereignty are a monopoly of (a) the legal use of armed force, and (b) the legal creation of money.

3 Imperialism is the process by which the corporations and the state team up to expand their activities, their interests, and their power beyond their borders.

The essential components of the corporation are capital and labor. Capital is money and means of production *in relation to* living labor. Only in combination with living labor is capital "productive," i.e., only thus is a product turned out which is sufficient to sustain the laborers and leave a surplus for the owners of capital.

How does it happen that the laborers are willing to play this role? Why don't they use their own money and means of production, keep the whole product for themselves, and eliminate the capitalists altogether? The answer of course is that as the result of a long historical process reaching back into the fifteenth and sixteenth centuries, the laborers have been separated from their means of production and are obliged to sell

their labor power to capitalists as the only way to avoid destitution and starvation. In other words, the means of production have been concentrated in the hands of capitalists, which today means corporations, and the workers have been transformed into wage-earners. In the United States this process was compressed into the relatively short span of two centuries. When the United States became a nation, more than three quarters of the workers were self-employed (owned their own means of production); today perhaps as many as 90 percent work for others, mostly corporations. The question is, why do workers tolerate this state of affairs? There are of course several reasons, but the most important one which underlies all the others is the system of private property, deeply imbedded in the constitution and the laws and vigilantly enforced by the state.

Thus the corporations are completely dependent on the state for their very existence, and the state in turn lives off the surplus produced by the workers and accruing to the capitalists, which means in the first instance to the corporations. The state and the corporations thus exist in a condition of symbiosis, each deeply dependent on the other.

Coming now to the problem of imperialism, we have to ask why this symbiotic relationship between corporations and state should result in a process of expansion in which the two mutually support each other. In other words, why isn't the relationship a static one which simply reproduces itself without essential change from one period to the next? To answer this it is essential to understand the nature of a unit of capital, which is what a corporation is, in the overall capitalist economy.

Here we can call on an extremely useful pedagogical device, comparing capitalism to simple commodity production, a mode of production which never actually existed independently of other modes of production. It should be emphasized, however, that simple commodity production is in no sense an *imaginary* mode of production: its component elements have existed in many historical societies, and in some regions at certain times it has come close to realization as an integrated and coherent form (for example,

---

[1] This is a reconstruction from notes of a lecture given at Stanford University in April 1978.

From Paul M. Sweezy, "Corporations, the State, and Imperialism," *Monthly Review* (November 1978): 1–10.

in certain parts of North America in the century or so surrounding the American Revolution). The defining characteristic of simple commodity production is that producers own their own means of production and satisfy their needs through exchange with other similarly situated producers. Farmers owning their own land, implements, and animals produce more food than they need, weavers more cloth, tailors more suits, hatters more hats, shoemakers more shoes, etc. Each producer takes his surplus to market and exchanges it for money, and with the money so acquired he buys the products of the others which he requires to satisfy his family's needs. Symbolically, this process can be represented, following Marx, by the formula C-M-C where the first C stands for a specific commodity being marketed by its producer, the M for the money the producer gets in exchange, and the second C for the bundle of useful commodities which he buys with his money. Here, obviously, we are talking about a system of production for use. The link is indirect: producers do not use their own products (or at least by no means all of them), but nevertheless their purpose in producing is to satisfy their needs, not to add to their wealth. In such a society—and indeed this tends to be true of all precapitalist societies—anyone whose purpose is to amass wealth as such is looked upon as a deviant, a miser, not a rational person.[2]

Matters are radically different when we come to capitalism, a society in which the actual producers own no means of production, are unable to initiate a process of production, and hence must sell their labor power to capitalists who do own means of production and are therefore in control of the processes of production. Here the defining formula C-M-C loses its relevance and must be replaced by its "opposite," M-C-M. What this symbolizes is that the capitalist who is the initiator of the production process starts with money (M). With this he purchases commodities (C) consisting of means of production and labor power which he transforms through a process of production into finished commodities ready for sale. When the sale has been completed he finds himself once again with money (M): the circuit is closed.

In the C-M-C case the first and last terms can be, and indeed are normally expected to be, quantitatively equal, i.e., to have the same exchange value. The

rationale of the operation lies not in the realm of exchange value but in that of use value: for the simple commodity producer the C at the end has a greater use value than the C at the beginning, and it is this increase in use value which motivates his behavior. Nothing of the sort exists in the M-C-M case. The first and last terms are both money which is qualitatively homogeneous and possesses no use value of its own. It follows that if the two Ms are also quantitatively equal, the operation totally lacks any rationale: no capitalist is going to lay out money and organize a process of production in order to end up with the same amount of money as he had at the outset. From this we can deduce that for capitalism to exist at all the M at the end must be larger than the M at the beginning. We can therefore rewrite the formula as M-C-M′ where M′ = M + Δ M. Here Δ M represents more money or, as Marx called it, more value (*Mehrwert*), which is customarily translated into English as surplus value.[3]

So far we have been considering what happens in a given period, say a year: the capitalist lays out M at the beginning of the year and ends up with M′ at the end. But this is only the start of an analysis: the capitalist does not wind up his enterprise at the end of a single production cycle. The enterprise continues to operate from one cycle to the next into the indefinite future, often outliving generations of its capitalist owners. And the enterprise which had a capital of M at the beginning of the first year starts the second with M′, and this in turn becomes M″, M‴, M⁗, and so on and on in successive years. This is what Marx meant when he defined capital as self-expanding value. Of course, not every individual unit of capital succeeds in living up to its ideal: many fall by the wayside or are gobbled up by luckier or more efficient rivals. But this only increases the importance of "trying harder," and the harder they all try the more marked becomes capitalism's essential nature as an expanding universe. Considered as a whole, capital *must* expand: the alternative is not a relaxed and happy condition of zero growth, as some liberal reformists would like to believe, but convulsive contraction and deepening crisis.

Given the symbiotic relation between the corporate

---

[2] In Webster's unabridged dictionary the first meaning given for "miser" is "a wretched or severely afflicted person."

[3] We are not concerned in the present context with the *origin* of surplus value but rather with (1) its presence as a necessary condition for the existence of capitalism, and (2) with some of its crucially important implications for the way capitalism functions.

units of capital and the state, it is but a logical corollary that the state is as expansion-minded as the corporations. This docs not mean that the state is necessarily fixated on its own expansion; it means simply that the state's primary concern is the expansion of capital, for the very simple reason that any faltering in this respect means crisis for the whole society including, of course, the state. How this primary concern of the state is implemented, however, depends on the circumstances of time and place.

In an earlier period of capitalist history when the individual units of capital were small and capitalist relations were expanding rapidly into a precapitalist environment, the domestic tasks of the state were relatively simple: helping to create a suitable wage-labor force through direct or indirect expropriation of independent farmers and artisans; providing infrastructure in the forms of roads, canals, and railways; and maintaining a reasonably orderly monetary and financial system. In the international sphere, the main task of the state was to assure for its own producers access to external markets on the most favorable terms possible—a task which involved continuous conflict with foreign states and led to innumerable commercial and colonial wars.

But as capitalism in a given area approaches maturity—i.e., as the size of the units of capital grows, taking on the corporate form with an attendant development of monopolies and oligopolies; as the precapitalist segment of the population dwindles; and as the problems of cyclical recessions and secular stagnation become increasingly serious—as these and other factors operate to multiply and intensify the obstacles to the continued expansion of capital, the role of the state takes on new dimensions of magnitude and complexity. Many of its new or enlarged functions have to do primarily with internal matters (e.g., fiscal and monetary policies), while others are essentially international.[4] Here our point is mainly in the latter.

---

[4] An important point which cannot be developed in the present context is that internal policies of the state often involve significant conflicts of interest within the national ruling class which under certain conditions may become so serious as to impair or even paralyze effective state action—a problem which has received far less attention than it deserves in discussions of the Marxist theory of the state. Such conflicts are much less likely to be involved in the external policies of the state; the entire national capitalist class is normally interested in maximizing gains at the expense of foreign nations and peoples.

The starting point, as always, is the conditions and requirements of the expansion of capital (I keep insisting on this because it is the *sine qua non* of *any* understanding of how capitalist societies actually work). Starting in a single industry and contributing a small share of the industry's total output, the typical unit of capital grows by accumulation, acquisition, and merger to be large relative to the industry's total output—in other words, it grows faster than the industry as a whole and as a consequence conquers an increasing degree of monopoly power. But there comes a time when this process reaches a limit. Theoretically, it could continue until one firm controlled the whole industry, but this situation is rarely reached: the normal situation is oligopoly (a few sellers) rather than monopoly (one seller), with each of the oligopolists powerful enough to hold its own against its rivals. When this stage has been reached, the conditions of further expansion are basically altered. The achievement of oligopoly status usually brings greater profitability, hence ability to accumulate more rapidly, at the same time that possibility of expansion within the industry is restricted to the rate of growth of the industry as a whole. Under these circumstances accumulation increasingly takes the form of conglomeration (expansion into other industries which have not yet reached the same degree of maturity) and multinationalization (expansion beyond existing national boundaries). It is the latter which sets new tasks for the state.

There are two kinds of multinationalization which need to be distinguished. The first takes place within the developed core of the global capitalist system (interpenetration of each other's territory by national oligopolists), and the second takes place between the developed core countries and the underdeveloped periphery. The first kind, interpenetration, does not pose any particularly urgent problems for the state. It has taken place on a vast scale since the Second World War, with the main direction of movement being from the United States to Western Europe and, to a much smaller extent, Japan. In the last few years, however, there has been an increasing flow in the opposite directions, with European and Japanese firms setting up branches or affiliates in the United States. Since all these countries have well developed capitalist systems and stable state structures, and since they are all deterred from putting obstacles in the way of this kind of capital movement by the credible threat of retaliation, the states involved have not found it necessary or useful to adopt policies or apply measures with respect to foreign capital greatly different from those in force domestically. (This had been less true of Japan which, for historical reasons, developed its own capitalism behind an elaborate screen of protective devices. But here, too, the mutual pressures of multi-nationalization have been slowly prying Japan open to foreign capital: Japanese "exceptionalism" seems to be more a matter of the past than of the present or future.)

When it comes to the other kind of multinationali-zation, however, matters are very different. It can be said without fear of exaggeration that the expansion of capital into the underdeveloped periphery on the scale desired, and in a real sense needed, by the oligopolistic corporations of the advanced countries would be totally impossible without the massive and unremitting application of the power of their states, either individually or collectively (including through such agencies as the International Monetary Fund and the World Bank), to the shaping and maintenance of an institutional setting and what is known as an "investment climate" favorable to the functioning of profit-oriented capitalist enterprise. This application of power takes place directly (as in Greece in the 1940s, Vietnam, and the Dominican Republic; or the recent French intervention in Zaire; or a long string of CIA-organized coups in Iran, Guatemala, Greece in 1967, Bangladesh, etc.) or indirectly through arm-ing, financing, and politically supporting client re-gimes throughout the Third World to repress their own people, and in some cases to act in addition as subimperialist gendarmes in their respective geo-graphical regions. The enormous apparatus of power necessary to sustain this world-wide enterprise in geopolitical engineering is centered in the United States and benefits from important and sometimes vital support from the other advanced capitalist coun-tries acting as junior partners; it involves the deploy-ment of military bases with their complements of military personnel and weapons over three quarters or so of the surface of the globe; and its bitter fruit is a fearsome crop of increasingly numerous and brutal dictatorships seeking to make the world safe for capital, and in the process making it less and less habitable for human beings.

In the ideology of capitalism, of course, this very dark cloud has a silver lining. The repression, the suffering, the misery of the present are supposed to be temporary, unavoidable aspects of a transition from underdevelopment and backwardness to the promised land of full-fledged capitalism. And not surprisingly in

this ideological fairy tale it is precisely the expansion of the multinational corporations—which we too have placed at the center of our analysis—which is sup-posed to provide the motor force. Wasn't it the accumulation of capital which led from the poverty of the Middle Ages to the affluence of today's advanced capitalist countries? And aren't the multinational corporate giants of our time infinitely more effective accumulators than the relative pygmies that pio-neered the economic development of Western Eu-rope, North America, and Japan? And if this is so, aren't we justified in looking forward to rapid prog-ress and a happy ending?

The answer, unfortunately, is no—flatly and un-conditionally. Multinational capital in migrating to the Third World today has absolutely no intention or interest in transforming those societies. It plans to adapt to and exploit the conditions which exist there. Whatever transformation takes place is a by-product of this process and cannot but intensify rather than alleviate the tragic conditions which are already deep-ly rooted in a long history. The general case can be most effectively presented by means of a particular example, the expansion of foreign (predominantly U.S.) capital into Brazil, one of the biggest and potentially richest countries in the Third World. Mul-tinational corporations based in the advanced capital-ist countries go to Brazil to supply and profit from markets which already exist and can be expected to grow with the general expansion of global capitalism. Some of these are domestic Brazilian markets, fueled by the spending of perhaps 20 percent of the popula-tion in the highest income brackets. Others are inter-national markets for agricultural products, raw mate-rials, and certain kinds of manufactured goods the costs of which can be kept low through the employ-ment of cheap labor. But there is one market, poten-tially by far the largest, which does not exist and which the multinational corporations have no inten-tion whatever of creating, the market which would burgeon along with a rising real standard of living for the Brazilian masses. The reason for what may at first sight seem a paradox is simple: for capitalists, both Brazilian and foreign, the masses are looked upon as costs, not as customers: the lower their real wages, the higher the profits from selling to the local upper class and the international market. The vicious dy-namic at work here has resulted in a drastic decline in the level of real wages in Brazil since the military coup of 1964, amounting by some estimates to as much as 40 percent. A stunning illustration of what

Marx called the general law of capitalist accumulation —growing riches on the one hand, deepening poverty on the other. And Brazil, far from being an exception, is a perfect example of what is happening and will undoubtedly continue to happen throughout the underdeveloped periphery of the world capitalist system.

I think you will agree with me that the conclusion to be drawn from this analysis is obvious. For the great mass of people living in the Third World—and that means for well over half of the human race—who are the special victims of this stage of capitalist development, the only possible way forward is to break out of the straitjacket which has been imposed upon them by the raw power of the metropolitan centers and to enter upon their own self-reliant course of development. This means revolution, the most massive and profound revolution in human history. And that is the final term in the logic of "corporation, the state, and imperialism."

Multinational Corporations: Current Trends and Future Prospects

Robert G. Hawkins
Ingo Walter

HOST-COUNTRY POLICIES TOWARD FOREIGN INVESTMENT

. . . While the policies of MNC home governments will be an important determinant of the growth and shape of multinationals in the future, equally significant are the policies and strategies of the host countries. This is particularly important for developing countries as hosts to MNC's, where policies are highly varied from country to country, and have changed in major ways over time. These can be separated into policies toward ownership and policies toward control. Both represent rapidly evolving phenomena among host countries, but each tends to originate in a more or less distinct set of underlying pressures.

Ownership policies reflect principally political pressures in host countries. Apart from questions of public versus private ownership that almost always are subjects of debate in host countries, the issue of foreign ownership of productive facilities tends to raise fears of foreign "domination" of the economy and society through the MNC's parent-affiliate relationship. In this view, fundamental decisions that affect the host economy are made from afar—at corporate headquarters by people not directly concerned with local conditions. And there is the parallel fear that home-country governments will try to influence the behavior of "their" multinationals on domestic or foreign policy issues in the host country. Such considerations, in a climate of nationalism, can generate pressures for local ownership, especially in "sensitive" sectors like mining, telecommunications and banking.

Control policies primarily reflect economic considerations, aimed at improving the relationship of benefits to costs in the involvement of multinational companies in host-country economies. Often ownership and control issues are intertwined, especially when governments decide (often erroneously) that the latter cannot be achieved without the former. Politically, governments cannot and will not allow multinationals totally free reign in their local operations—laissez faire in an era of giant firms and giant governments is simply no longer feasible, even in an age of "deregulation."

From the point of view of a nation, the purpose of host-country controls and pressures for national ownership is to achieve a closer correspondence between the effects of MNC activities and national policy

From Robert G. Hawkins and Ingo Walter, "Multinational Corporations: Current Trends and Future Prospects," in U.S. Cong., *Special Study on Economic Change, Volume 9, The International Economy: U.S. Role in a World Market*, prepared for the use of the Special Study on Economic Change of the Joint Economic Committee, 96th Cong., 2d Sess., Dec. 17, 1980, pp. 705–723.

objectives than would exist in their absence. This often means that the host country tries to obtain for itself a greater share of the benefits to economic efficiency and growth which MNC's bring about. It may attempt to obtain greater tax revenue, more local production and employment, or less repatriation of profits, relative to what it would get in an uncontrolled situation. But a major problem for host-country policy and regulations toward MNC's is that the results often are not clear in prospect or even in retrospect.[1] It is not easy to predict how MNC management will react to a given government policy initiative, whether or not it will bring about the desired result or whether, indeed, the opposite might occur.[2] This illustrates the critical importance of policymakers' understanding of how MNC's behave in terms of their own goal structures, how they react to external pressures when achievement of those goals may be compromised, and what alternatives may be open to MNC's.

Host-country policies toward the MNC may be constrained by the relative bargaining leverage of the country itself and by the ability of the firm to "escape" or "avoid" the effects of restrictions imposed upon it. The greater the leverage of the individual MNC relative to the host country in which it is operating, the less likely it is that effective controls can be established covering aspects of the firm's operations where actual or potential conflict exists. The host-country's bargaining power will be higher: *(a)* the larger the internal market and the more rapid its rate of growth; *(b)* the more valuable to the firm the indigenous resources such as a stable, inexpensive and well-trained labor force or desirable natural resources; *(c)* the more favorable to foreign-owned firms the domestic political conditions—i.e., the lower the perceived level of "country risk"; *(d)* the lower the economic and managerial costs of doing business locally, encompassing economic and social infrastructure (especially communications and transport), bribery, corruption, political meddling, and bureaucratic red tape; *(e)* the healthier the country's balance of payments outlook, promising adequate

foreign exchange availablity for imports and profit remittances; *(f)* the more stable its external political relations, promising freedom from war, insurgency, or other externally imposed violence; and *(g)* the larger the number of options available to the country for obtaining the "package" of services that the MNC in question promises, whether from one or more competing multinationals or from alternative independent sources, such as foreign technical assistance.

From this we can infer that a country with a large, dynamic, resource-rich economy, a stable and capable government with a high-quality infrastructure and low transactions cost, will be highly attractive to multinationals and other types of foreign business ventures. It can thus avail itself of a wide variety of control devices and relatively restrictive policies. On the other hand, for a country that is uninteresting from a market or resources standpoint, that has a corrupt, inefficient, complex or hostile environment, or is threatened with internal or external political instability, policies to control foreign MNC's become largely hypothetical, since few MNC's will be interested in investing. Each host country will have a distinct "leverage profile" comprising the various characteristics just mentioned. It is perhaps an indication of the complexity of this profile that governments' ability to take stock of their own assets and liabilities in a bargaining context often seems limited, resulting either in excessive or inadequate control and failure to successfully come to grips with basic regulatory problems affecting MNC's.

On the company's side, its bargaining position for limiting controls or achieving favorable treatment from a host government will be greater: *(a)* the greater its "packaged" technology, marketing and management inputs, and the degree of monopoly or uniqueness in that package; *(b)* the greater its prospective contribution to national employment, income, balance of payments, human-resource development, and related economic variables, as well as the more extensive its linkages to the remainder of the host economy; *(c)* the greater the coincidence of the firm's prospective economic contributions and the direction of national political and economic planning; *(d)* the more impressive its activities in other host countries as "showcases" for its prospective activities in the country concerned; and *(e)* the larger the number of options available to the firm in terms of investment opportunities and alternative ventures. Again, each firm will have a particular profile in terms of its own sources of bargaining strength, and their

---

[1] For a general discussion, see R. G. Hawkins (ed.), The Economic Effects of Multinational Corporations (Greenwich, Conn.: JAI Press, 1979).

[2] This discussion is based on T. N. Gladwin and Ingo Walter, Multinationals Under Fire: Lessons in the Management of Conflict (New York: John Wiley, 1980), Chapter 8.

accurate perception on the part of management will determine its reactions to the imposition or prospects of host-country controls.

The sources of country and company leverage are arrayed opposite each other, both in a general and specific context. That is, they figure into a country's overall ability to set terms and conditions for MNC operations more or less closely aligned with its own objectives. They also figure into its negotiating stance on a given MNC project, and whether the general policy measures will be applied in that particular case strictly, or not at all. For example, the overall policy may be that no foreign ownership of telecommunications facilities is allowed, yet a satellite communications firm may be allowed in on an equity basis.[3] Or a commercial bank proposing a new branch may be told of an overall prohibition against foreign investment in that sector, but may be encouraged to enter into a consortium banking venture with local interests. Some host countries may also set explicit policy differentials among groups of projects. For example, a firm may under certain conditions apply for especially favorable or "pioneer industry" status, involving tax concessions, guaranteed profit repatriation, and the like. Or it may fall into a "normal" category, or even an "undesirable" category where adequate local firms already exist and foreign firms are perceived to offer minimal net benefits—so they are either kept out, admitted only on a joint-venture basis with local firms, or subjected to several restrictive operating criteria.

Policy Options for Host Countries

It is convenient to consider host-country policies toward foreign direct investment in terms of when in the "project life-cycle" of that investment such controls are applied. There are four more or less distinct (but not mutually exclusive) "pressure points" that suggest themselves for the application of host-country policies: *(a)* control on entry, before a proposed project has gotten underway or an MNC commitment has been made; *(b)* controls on the operations of the foreign affiliate once it has gotten off the ground and is operating successfully; *(c)* financial controls on MNC affiliates, especially on earnings remittances, affecting their profitability from the standpoint of the parent; and *(d)* terminal controls which ultimately

[3] Ibid.

bring about a phaseout of foreign participation in the local venture.

Entry Control   Under this option, the host country sets the specific terms and conditions whereby the MNC may operate within its national borders. It will normally establish some type of "gatekeeper" mechanism, such as registration and screening procedures. Foreign firms interested in entering a particular line of economic activity must first register with a "board of investments" or similar institution set up for that purpose. To obtain permission, the investing firm may be asked to disclose the nature of the investment, the source of financing, whether it is a new project or the takeover of an existing firm, whether it will be wholly owned or a joint venture, whether raw materials and intermediate inputs will be imported or procured locally, and similar details. If the country offers special incentives for certain types of investments, the firm will apply for them at this point.

The proposal is then examined by the screening agency for its fit into the national economic plan, its prospective effects on employment, competition, the balance of payments, and other important variables in order to determine the desirability of the project from a host-country point of view. It will then set the terms for entry, ranging from "permission denied," to nondiscriminatory "national treatment," to major incentives for highly desirable projects. The response may include restrictions on location, financing, ownership, technology, local sourcing of inputs, earnings repatriation, and the like. The critical point is, however, that the terms and conditions are set before the commitment to a project by the multinational firm, and there is at least the implicit assumption that these will remain relatively constant over the life of the project.

Entry control has the advantage of minimum uncertainty and maximum freedom to negotiate on both sides. The country can determine how a particular venture fits into its objectives, and may be able to select from among competing foreign firms. The company can weigh the host-country's offer in the light of its own alternatives and, once committed, be reasonably sure of the rules of the game for the foreseeable future—at least within the limits of sovereign risk. So it can afford to be content with a relatively lower rate of return on invested capital, which in turn benefits the host country. Within the entry bargaining context, the firm may benefit from maximum negotiating leverage, since it is not yet committed and still has its options open.

Operating Controls An alternative approach to host-country policies toward foreign investment is to pursue a relatively liberal entry policy, perhaps without careful screening at the outset but with controls on various facets of the affiliate's operations once it is a going concern. The MNC may be asked to reduce its equity holdings from a majority to a minority position, for example. Or it may be required to source a minimum percentage of a product's total value locally, or to export a certain percentage of its production. Sometimes various tie-in schemes are devised, as when firms are permitted $1 worth of imports every $2 worth of exports—the foreign exchange can be used for needed inputs or capital equipment, or the firm might go into the business of importing and distributing goods not otherwise obtainable in the host country. Other operating controls include maximum price limits (e.g., on products like drugs and gasoline), minimum price limits to protect locally owned competitors, wage and credit controls, quantitative limits on the number of foreign workers or managers who may be hired, tax policies, environmental and plant safety restrictions, product quality controls and market restrictions, fringe benefit requirements, and many more.

Presumably the firm should be able to assess the host-country environment in terms of operating controls *ex ante*, so it knows the rules of the game before it makes a commitment. But rules have a way of changing, and host countries that rely heavily on operating controls are particularly subject to conflict with multinational companies as a result of revisions of those controls over the life of investment projects. Operating controls thus may be more prone to conflict than entry controls, and more subject to change. The greater uncertainty may require a higher return on investment in order to justify a particular foreign investment. At the same time, the multinational firm itself is committed, and so it is more vulnerable to external pressure and has less bargaining power than in an entry-type situation. On the other hand, the host country has to make sure that the pressure of operating controls does not drive the firm out. If the marginal cost to the firm of compliance is perceived to be higher than the losses associated with pulling out, it is likely to do so.

Operating controls may well be inefficient from the host-country's own point of view. Price and wage controls, rationing and related measures tend to distort resource allocation, and can thus be costly—possibly serious enough to eat into the benefits the controls are supposed to achieve or nullify them altogether. The adverse effects of operating controls are often difficult to identify and measure, especially before the fact, and this can lead to the imposition of self-defeating measures that the host country could better do without. Extensive and especially unstable operating controls have a way of souring a country's reputation as a place to invest, thus eroding its bargaining leverage for future investment projects by foreign-owned firms. On the other hand, operating controls are not cast in concrete, and can be altered over time as circumstances change, thus avoiding the rigidities that are often inherent in entry controls.

Financial Controls A third option for host countries is to permit relatively liberal entry and impose minimal operating controls, thus giving foreign MNC's a fairly free hand in the activities they undertake and how they carry them out, and then to apply a single set of controls on the "bottom line"—remittances of earnings. The firm may be able to set prices and incur costs according to market conditions, and its proffers in local currency may likewise tend to be largely market-determined. But at the point payments are to be made abroad, controls are imposed. These might involve, for example, a maximum percentage of registered capital repatriated as profit per year (that) would be granted, but no more. The necessary foreign exchange to make the permitted earnings remittances would be set accordingly.

Financial controls of this type have both advantages and disadvantages. They are comparatively simple, and avoid the array of bureaucrats and economic inefficiencies and complexities associated with operating controls. They also avoid some of the conflicts that entry and operating controls are subject to. And they share with entry controls the relative certainty of the rules of the game, which can be assessed and acted upon by MNC's prior to making a commitment. On the negative side, financial controls lend themselves to avoidance and evasion. For example, the registered capital of the MNC affiliate may be inflated through excessive valuation of equipment in order to boost the base upon which the remittance limit will be calculated. Firms may also repatriate funds via charges for technology, management fees, and other services, or they may achieve *de facto* repatriation through transfer pricing on imports and exports. Since the allocation of costs and revenues within a large MNC must, to a certain extent, be arbitrary and respond to international differences in tax rates, exchange controls, and other policies, the policing of financial controls is difficult and may involve major monitoring costs. As one observer notes, ". . . the ability of MNC's to shift funds and profits internally represents a constraint on national policies, a constraint which must be observed if governments do not wish to encourage the growth of MNC's beyond levels justified by national conditions in goods and factor markets."[4]

The point is that financial controls set up powerful incentives to avoid them, which itself leads to pressures for more comprehensive controls, or erodes the effectiveness of the measures themselves. Most importantly, financial controls relate to only a single facet of MNC operations of concern to the host country. They have no effect on employment, ownership, technology, and other dimensions that the host country may wish to influence from a policy perspective.

Terminal Controls A fourth way of executing policies toward foreign direct investment on the part of host countries is at the very end of their involvement, whether such disengagement is voluntary or not. At the one is expropriation with compensation, where the foreign-owned enterprise is taken over by the host-country government. Compensation to foreign owners may be in full, by means of cash payments in hard currencies, in local currency with guaranteed convertibility, in government bonds, in products, or some combination of these. Compensation, like the act of expropriation itself, may be instantaneous or phased-in over a period of months or years. The "fullness" of the compensation is, of course, in the eye of the beholder, and so the terms and conditions are generally the product of extended negotiations and often the source of serious conflict.

At the other extreme is expropriation without compensation, or confiscation, undertaken unilateral-

ly by the host-country government. Often the case for no compensation is based on past "excess profits" remitted by the firm, which generally equal or exceed the book value of the firm's assets—so that, it is argued, adequate and full compensation has already occurred.

Expropriation without compensation clearly involves a situation where national sovereignty is the determining variable and where the MNC has very little power to avoid it. The defenses against uncompensated expropriation are both specific and general. There is the loss of the link between the multinational and its expropriated affiliate which, depending on the value of the "package" of services the MNC was providing at the time, will be served after the expropriation. If market access, management skills or technologies are important enough, then the cost to the host country can be high, and the incentive to expropriate small. This does not necessarily mean that expropriation will not occur, since host countries have sometimes overestimated their own capabilities to provide the needed resources and operate the enterprise.

More common than expropriation is nationalization or indigenization, where the host country may require the MNC to sell off its affiliates' assets, either to the government or to local investors. Nationalization may be phased in under gradual "fadeout" formulas, or it may be quite abrupt. It may require total divestiture of assets, or only partial divestiture ending, for example, in minority participation in a joint venture. While perhaps somewhat milder than expropriation, there remain several areas of potential conflict. Adequate compensation is one, especially when the buyer is a government entity; another involves the terms under which the parent company will collaborate with the divested successor firm. Responses to divestiture pressures by multinational firms will of course vary, and views may change over time. Firms that previously would not consider joint ventures may now be ready to do so, perhaps because it is a good way to spread risk and reduce conflict, or more likely because their perceived alternatives are less than before.

MNC's may attempt to protect themselves against terminal controls in a variety of ways. One is to subdivide the production process so that only a very small part is carried out in any single host country. Expropriation then gives the host country no capacity to produce a final product that is competitive in the

---

[4] Donald R. Lessard, "Transfer Prices, Taxes and Financial Markets: Implications of Internal Financial Transfers Within the Multinational Corporations," in R. G. Hawkins (ed.), op. cit., p. 103.

marketplace. Sources of supply or export markets may be controlled by the firm with much the same result. Or an MNC may enter a cooperative consortium with others, not only to spread the risk but also to increase the cost of precipitous host-country action in terms of its relations with various foreign nations. Or it may include, on a joint basis, host-country firms or governmental agencies in such cooperative arrangement, in order to reduce the likelihood of terminal-type actions. As indicated above, such cooperative arrangements are increasing. The best shield, though, still remains a unique competitive advantage that cannot be replaced by the host country after expropriation or indigenization.

Policy Trends in Host Countries

How have the four available host-country conduits for exerting control over foreign direct investment been used in the recent past, and what are the prospects for the future? The first point that arises is diversity. The four strategies are not, of course, mutually exclusive—they can be and are used both simultaneously and sequentially. Yet different host countries have tended to rely on individual control techniques to a greater or lesser extent than others.[5] The Philippines, for example, has appeared to prefer entry controls, and the country has a rather well-developed institutional framework for this purpose. India has traditionally used a complex of operating controls, with government interference in virtually all facets of day-to-day corporate activities. Brazil has in the past seemed to prefer greater freedom and reliance on market mechanisms in MNC entry and operations, yet has maintained strict limits on earnings repatriation. Sri Lanka, under its previous socialist government, opted for terminal controls in nationalizing and expropriating foreign-owned tea plantations, with very little new investment coming in. Selective terminal controls have been used from time to time in specific sectors by countries as diverse as Chile, Venezuela, France, and Peru—not to mention Cuba, Angola, Mozambique, and similar countries undergoing drastic change in economic and political systems.

There is little doubt that developing countries on average apply more controls over inward MNC activity than do advanced industrial countries. The advanced countries which are members of the OECD [Organization for Economic Cooperation and Devel-

opment] have accepted, in principle, "national treatment" of inward direct investment, as evidenced by the OECD "Guidelines for Multinational Corporations." This policy presumes that foreign-owned businesses should not be treated differently than domestically owned business in the same activity. Each country, however, reserves certain "strategic" activities for local ownership. The United States, for example, does not permit foreign ownership in defense contracting, nuclear, and communications industries. Other countries (e.g., France) define "Strategic" more broadly. Japan is perhaps the most restrictive industrial country with respect to inward direct investment. In the United States, several (over 20) state governments have limited or banned foreign purchase of agricultural land. Such departures from the "right of establishment" by foreign companies under nondiscriminatory "national treatment" are still relatively rare, but they are increasing.

All the same, since 70 percent of world MNC activities are in advanced industrial countries, they have been accorded relatively liberal treatment by host countries. The 30 percent in developing countries exists under a more significant complex of controls over entry, operation, and financial transfers. As this group of nations and the communist countries become more important in worldwide MNC activities, the share of foreign direct investment under significant government controls will increase. At the same time, the trend in several industrial countries is to introduce selectively additional controls over certain activities by foreign enterprises.

The Use of Entry Controls Argentina, Chile, Colombia, Cyprus, India, Indonesia, South Korea, and Yugoslavia, among many other developing countries, all require government approval before an investment can be made by a foreign firm. Restrictions on foreign ownership at the entry level vary widely. Most host countries restrict foreign investments in defense, public utilities, and the media. Argentina requires that, in the automobile industry, at least 51 percent of the capital of firms be owned by nationals, and a minimum of 80 percent of the directors and 90 percent of the professional and technical staff must be nationals living in Argentina. Spain generally requires prior approval for all projects where foreign ownership exceeds 50 percent except that no such approval is required in the high-priority iron and steel, cement, food processing, and textile sectors. Spain also will

[5] See T. N. Gladwin and Ingo Walter, op. cit.

not approve any project that proposes to restrict exports or that impedes access to technology. India's Foreign Exchange Regulation Act of 1974 (FERA) requires all foreign affiliates to be 60 percent Indian-owned unless they produce exclusively for export—although there is a very restricted but constantly changing group of industries at the top of the priority list where the general rule against majority participation by foreign firms can be waived—and industrial licenses granted to foreign firms are predicated upon raising at least part of the equity capital within India. The 1972 Mexican law on foreign investment reserves petroleum, petrochemicals, nuclear energy, electricity, railroads, telecommunications and part of the mining sector exclusively for the government, and ownership of the media, road and air transport, forestry and gas distribution is confined to Mexican citizens. In other sectors maximum percentages of foreign ownership are specified, all under the control of the National Commission on Foreign Investment and requiring all foreign participations in business to be recorded in a National Registry of Foreign Investments.

Entry controls to force more of the financing of MNC affiliate operations offshore—and increase the net balance of payments capital inflow—are used by various developing countries. One recent study claims that only 17 percent of the capital invested by U.S. firms in Latin America during the 1957–65 period actually represented inflows from abroad, the rest being raised locally.[6] Tariff policy is another instrument to control MNC's at the entry level on the part of developing countries, and the promise of tariff protection can be used as an inducement for investments to serve the host-country market. Similarly, foreign investment projects may be accorded duty-free treatment for capital equipment and inputs, provided that local raw materials are used in the production process. When production is for export, free-trade zone treatment or tariff drawbacks (the rebating of tariffs on inputs when the final product is exported) are sometimes provided. Even more narrowly, Singapore, which has rather liberal entry requirements, evaluates investment applications in part on the proportion of scientific and technical personnel to be included in the work force.

Entry controls of several kinds also exist in some industrial countries.[7] For example in Italy, the Libyan purchase of 10 percent of Fiat stock for $415 million at the end of 1976 triggered Communist and other demands for a parliamentary debate on the issue and prompted Fiat's chairman Giovanni Agnelli to inform Italy's President Giovanni Leone well in advance of announcing the transaction. Especially controversial was the Soviet Union's alleged role in bringing the two sides together with a view of strengthening Fiat's ability to expand its Russian automobile activities. . . .

Use of Operating and Financial Controls   Like entry controls, operating and financial controls are employed in many developing countries and a few developed countries. Although the advanced countries employ a wide variety of controls that bear on domestic and foreign firms alike, these are not to be confused with specific measures to control foreign direct investment. Because advanced host countries are likely to have their own multinationals operating abroad, they are much more sensitive to reciprocity and retaliation against discriminatory measures aimed at foreign investment.

Manning controls are one example of operating restrictions. Countries as diverse as Nigeria and Morocco have limits on foreign workers employed by MNC's, and in Indonesia three-fourths of all employees must be local nationals within 5–8 years of start-up. In Argentina 85 percent of the combined scientific, technical, administrative, and managerial personnel must be local nationals. India and Turkey require periodic reports from foreign-owned firms about the number of nationals employed and progress made in the replacement of foreign managerial and technical staff.[8]

Frequently, operating controls are used to encourage extension of linkages between the MNC and the local economy in order to improve the developmental benefits from foreign investment. Escalating local-content targets, which set the minimum percentage of total product cost that must be of local origin, have been used effectively by Mexico and other countries over the years. This is often backed up by measures to cut off imports of parts and components after the

---

[6] Ronald E. Muller, "Poverty is the Product," Foreign Policy, Winter 1973–74.

[7] See A. E. Safarian and J. Bell, "Issues Raised by National Control of the Multinational Corporation," Columbia Journal of World Business, December 1973.

[8] T. N. Gladwin and I. Walter, op. cit.

"adjustment period" has passed, although there is usually an escape valve in case local sourcing is impossible within the time available.

Banking is one industry that has increasingly come under tight national operating controls in many developing countries, presumably because the costs of such policies are relatively small and because close regulation of the financial sector by national authorities is considered essential. Mexico, for example, in 1972 considerably tightened regulations on foreign banks in part to limit foreign indebtedness by Mexican firms. Representative offices of foreign banks were placed on the same regulatory basis as domestic banks, and continued to be barred from commercial banking operations in Mexico. Foreign-owned financial institutions may not accept Mexican funds for placement abroad, must restrict domestic loans to those permitted by Mexican credit policies and must provide the government with detailed monthly reports of operations. In addition, they must operate strictly within the confines of Mexican law, rather than their home-country regulations, and the government reserves the right to revoke the registration of foreign credit institutions at any time, at its own discretion.[9] Similar restrictions on foreign company activities in the financial sector exist in many developing countries and several industrial countries.

With respect to outright financial controls, the specifics of remittance policies vary widely from one country to the next.[10] Colombia places an annual ceiling of 14 percent of invested capital. Greece limits repatriation in previous years. Greece also permits firms engaged in exports to make larger remittances than firms that are not, up to a limit of 70 percent of export sales. Pakistan permits repatriation of foreign exchange costs that can be shown to have been incurred in introducing a new investment project. Chile allows companies to revalue local assets in accordance with exchange-rate changes, and permitted remittances are based on the revised asset values. Brazil limits profit repatriation to 12 percent of registered capital, subject to a 25 percent withholding tax. Thereafter, profit remittances are subject to taxes of 40–60 percent. Argentina likewise has a 12 percent limit, with excess profit remissions subject to taxes of 15–25 percent. Chile's ceiling is 14 percent, with no

additional remissions allowed, and the investment itself must have been subject to prior government approval. Colombia and Peru likewise have a 14 percent limit. In some countries there are extensive delays in the approval of permitted profit remittances.

Use of Terminal Controls   Terminal measures involving expropriation and indigenization have been a significant part of policies toward foreign direct investment, particularly in developing host countries. Table 6 lists the various identifiable terminal controls aimed at U.S. companies during the 15-year period 1962–77. [*Editor's note:* omitted here.] These include a number of well-known expropriation cases involving U.S. affiliates in Latin America. For example, the revolutionary government of Peru in 1968 seized the oil properties of International Petroleum (Exxon), which began a process of takeovers of foreign firms including Cerro (mining), W.R. Grace (chemicals and paper), and Utah International (iron ore). The Allende government of Chile in 1971–73 completed the takeover of the copper mining properties of Anaconda, Kennecott and Cerro and then proceeded to expropriate ITT and Boise-Cascade assets (utilities), as well as manufacturing facilities operated by Ford, DuPont, Dow, and Ralston-Purina. The Venezuelan Government in 1974 nationalized both the iron ore and petroleum industries, including properties owned by U.S. Steel, Bethlehem Steel, Exxon, Mobil, and Texaco.

In Africa and the Middle East, the petroleum industry has been the principal target of expropriation actions. The governments of Nigeria, Algeria, Iran, Kuwait, Libya, Morocco, Saudi Arabia, and Syria have nationalized the production and distribution of facilities of such prominent petroleum MNC's as Exxon, Gulf, Mobil, Socal, and Texaco, as well as the holdings of French, Dutch, and British oil companies. . . .

In addition, foreign-owned assets in such diverse fields as banking, insurance, trade, and manufacturing have been brought under national control in Ethiopia, Sudan, Tanzania, Uganda, and Zambia.

Affiliates of U.S. multinationals in Asia, although less subjected to explicit expropriation actions, have encountered broad nationalization programs and a hardening of host-government attitudes toward foreign investment. The insurance industry in India, the jute industry in Bangladesh, and petroleum and plantation properties in Indonesia are examples of broad

---

[9] See "Mexico Issues Rules Tightening Controls on Foreign Financing," The Wall Street Journal, April 1972

[10] Cf. Don Lessard, op. cit.

nationalization programs instituted by Asian nations. Burma, Indonesia, Malaysia, and Singapore have enacted laws which prohibit or severely restrict foreign involvement in certain sectors of the economy, resulting in MNC withdrawal. Other governments, such as India, Pakistan, the Philippines, Sri Lanka, and Thailand have adopted strict policies limiting foreign investors to minority participation in business ventures involving such firms as Coca-Cola, IBM, Goodyear, NCR, Singer, and Union Carbide.

Over half of all takeover cases in table 6 involved formal expropriation. Others have centered on forced sales, extra-legal interventions and contract renegotiations. Formal expropriation was the dominant form of takeover during the entire period covered. In many of these cases, the U.S. Government was subsequently directly involved in compensation negotiations with the host government. In addition, some of the properties expropriated by the Allende (Chile) and Sukarno (Indonesia) governments have been restored to their private ownership since the overthrow of those regimes. Final settlement terms, compensation arrangements and legal actions in many of the cases cited, however, have not yet been resolved.

Examination of the exercise of terminal controls by host-country governments reveals that they are not random occurrences, but reflect distinct trends related to combinations of certain MNC and host-country characteristics. Takeover cases have often resulted in political conflict between host and home countries. The history of terminal controls in the 1960's and 1970's also holds a number of lessons: (1) The incidence of takeovers has risen markedly since the early 1960's; (2) a few high-incidence countries like Algeria, Chile, Indonesia, Libya, Peru, Tanzania, Uganda, and Zambia, undergoing radical transformations in economic and social policy, accounted for a disproportionate share of the takeovers; (3) the extractive sector is clearly the most vulnerable, followed by manufacturing, financial services and utilities; (4) affiliates of large MNC's seem to be more susceptible to takeovers than smaller firms; (5) wholly owned affiliates appear to be more vulnerable than joint ventures with host-country firms; (6) both very high and very low technology firms tend to be more susceptible to takeovers than firms which fall into the middle range; (7) multinationals with a higher degree of vertical integration on the supply and/or market side seem to be less vulnerable to takeovers than less

integrated operations; and (8) takeovers of all firms in an industry and those specifically targeted on a particular MNC remain important. Sectors like mining and banking are especially susceptible by industry-wide actions, while manufacturing is more subject to firm-specific actions.

Many host countries have provided guarantees against expropriation, either for foreign-owned assets specifically or as part of a more general assurance that private industry will not be nationalized. Cyprus, Greece, Israel, Malta, Singapore, and Spain are among the countries providing such guarantees, sometimes as part of a package of incentives that contains tax holidays, tariff exemptions, and occasionally "most favored enterprise" provisions which assure investors parity in the event that foreign firms are given more favorable treatment in the future. Nor can expropriation be undertaken lightly. It signals to other firms that the same thing might happen to them, particularly if there is systemic political change away from a market system or private ownership of productive facilities. Despite government assurances to the contrary, sovereign risk rises, and to compensate for it, firms require higher expected profits or forms of risk-offsets. This reduces the net benefits to the host country, and may in turn bring on pressures for additional MNC expropriations in the same or other sectors of the economy. The application of such measures as the U.S. Hickenlooper Amendment and other national measures in various MNC home countries can further increase the cost of uncompensated expropriations to the host country, and shift the focus of the conflict from the MNC alone to its home government. Certainly uncompensated or inadequately compensated expropriation is deserving of careful consideration by host countries.

Prospective Future Policy Directions

The foregoing suggests certain plausible future trends with respect to policies toward inward foreign investment. As an industrial nation which has been and continues to be the preeminent home country for MNC's, considerations of reciprocity and possible retaliation suggest that the United States will continue to follow relatively liberal policies toward inward foreign direct investment. The fact that such investment tends to create jobs, supports capital formation and productivity at a time when both are lagging domestically, and may make positive balance of payments contributions further reduces the likelihood of controls. At the same time, there is some sensitivity to foreign ownership by various groups in the United States, including organized labor. As we have noted, sensitivities exist with respect to foreign ownership of farmland, defense-related industries including transportation, and financial institutions. With the possible exception of additional restrictions on foreign ownership or control of the traditionally restricted sectors of banking and real estate (applied largely at the state [and] local level) there is unlikely to be any trend toward restrictive policies on inward foreign investment applied by the United States.

One possible exception may be worthy of note. The fact that affiliates of foreign firms operating in the United States are usually not subject to as many SEC [Securities and Exchange Commission] disclosure requirements as publicly owned U.S. companies may give rise to pressures for greater "transparency." This could involve some sort of "registration" procedure for existing and new foreign ventures, coupled to disclosure requirements for operating and financial information similar to those contained in the OECD Guidelines and comparable to U.S. SEC public company requirements. This would not involve "screening" as such, and may be viewed as being consistent with parity in the treatment of foreign-owned and domestically owned firms.

As noted earlier, policies toward inward foreign investment differ somewhat among other developed market-economy countries, and will continue to do so, broadly in accordance with national policies toward domestically owned firms. The fact [that] the countries of Western Europe, and to a lesser extent Japan, have been following the U.S. lead in liberal policies toward inward direct investment means that they are increasingly aware of the need for reciprocity in the treatment of MNC's. Moreover, greatly liberalized trade barriers, including free trade within the EEC, has circumscribed the ability of these countries to pursue restrictive policies toward inward foreign direct investment without running the risk of losing the affected projects altogether. Much more likely is an intensification of "competitive laxity" and "subsidy wars" [by] host countries competing for foreign investment along neo-mercantilist lines. Carried to extremes, such policies can be as wasteful of productive resources, and as distortive of allocative efficiency as restrictive policies toward foreign investment. As this

realization gains currency among policymakers, it is likely that some initiatives will emerge to set international or multi-country rules of the game that will inhibit future "investment wars" among the industrial nations.

As in the case of the United States, a few sectors in the other developed market economy countries will continue to be considered "sensitive" with respect to foreign ownership or control, including agriculture, minerals and fuels, financial institutions, defense-related industries and selected high-technology industries. Preoccupation with policies toward inward foreign investment will continue to be concentrated primarily in Canada, Australia, and Japan, although the last will increasingly be forced to liberalize inward investment policy as it rises in the hierarchy of home countries of MNC's. If Japanese MNC's are to continue to be afforded liberal treatment in other industrial countries, the quid pro quo for Japan will increasingly require liberal treatment of inward investment.

Among the developing countries the focus will continue to involve several types of ownership and control issues. Despite attempts to devise common policy frameworks at the regional level, as in the Andean Pact or ASEAN [Association of Southeast Asian Nations], or at the global level through the United Nations, the focus of such policies will continue to be primarily at the national level. This is because the needs and priorities of individual countries, subject to highly variegated political systems and economic endowments, are so different as to virtually preclude extensive harmonization in the foreseeable future. Hence common policy pronouncements are likely to be violated as often as they are observed and there will continue to be a wide gap between the rhetoric in international organizations and the reality as practiced by policymakers "on the ground" at the national level.

It follows that pressures for nationalization, expropriation, confiscation, indigenization, and the like will also reflect primarily national determinants, although there may be cross-national demonstration effects as well. Countries will go through "waves" of indigenization based on domestic political currents. Many have already done so, like India, Nigeria, Malaysia, Venezuela, and Libya. Indigenization may be either universal or sectoral, but most likely some version of the latter, with "sensitive" sectors such as banking, insurance, energy, telecommunications, transport, agriculture, and real estate being vulnerable, followed by wholesale and retail trade, import-export services, food and beverages, and consumer goods industries. Manufacture of capital goods, industrial intermediates and high-technology industries appear less vulnerable, but even here countries like Brazil have pushed hard to indigenize foreign company activities so as to force the internal diffusion of know-how. MNC's that fill a demonstrated need, generally by virtue of persistently superior technology and access to markets or imports, will continue to face fewer pressures as long as their contributions continue to be valued, and alternative sources on more favorable terms remain unavailable.

Because of the continued value of MNC involvement, and the fact that MNC's hold access to much of the world's commercial technology, companies will find profitable opportunities even among those developing countries that have gone farthest down the road toward restriction on foreign investment. This is clear from the receptivity to MNC initiatives shown by the socialist countries of Eastern Europe and Asia. Their desire to close technological gaps with the West, and their awareness of MNC capabilities, will present profitable opportunities for MNC involvement on a non-equity basis in both the capital-goods and consumer-goods sectors in Communist countries. Such opportunities for "industrial cooperation" projects will continue to expand, and no doubt be used as patterns for policymaking toward MNC's by some developing countries. . . .

QUESTIONS FOR DISCUSSION

1 What information should one have to evaluate the power of MNCs in developing nations?
2 Are the interests of Western states and the interests of Western capitalists similar?
3 What are the instruments of influence or the relative capabilities of the MNC and the host state?

4 Are the interests of the MNCs and governing elites and general populations in host countries likely to be the same?
5 When communist states permit multinational corporations to invest in their economies, are they promoting imperialism?

SUGGESTED READINGS

Ball, George W. (ed.). *Global Companies: The Political Economy of World Business*. Englewood Cliffs, N.J.: Prentice-Hall, 1975.

Barnet, Richard J., and Ronald E. Müller. *Global Reach: The Power of the Multinational Corporations*. New York: Simon & Schuster, 1975.

Drucker, Peter F. "Multinationals and Developing Countries: Myths and Realities." *Foreign Affairs* **53** (October 1974): 121–134.

Gilpin, Robert. "The Multinational Corporation and American Foreign Policy," in Richard Rosecrance (ed.). *America as an Ordinary Country*. Ithaca, N.Y.: Cornell University Press, 1976, pp. 174–198.

Krarr, Louis. "The Multinationals Get Smarter About Political Risks." *Fortune* (March 24, 1980): 86–88.

Leonard, H. Jeffrey. "Multinational Corporations and Politics in Developing Countries." *World Politics* **32** (April 1980): 454–483.

Sauvant, Karl P., and Farid G. Lavipous (eds.). *Controlling Multinational Enterprises: Problems, Strategies, Counterstrategies*. Boulder, Colo.: Westview Press, 1976.

Sweezy, Paul M. "Multinational Corporations and Banks." *Monthly Review* (January 1978): 1–9.

Vernon, Raymond. *Storm Over the Multinationals*. Cambridge: Harvard University Press, 1977.

Wattenberg, Ben J., and Richard J. Whalen. *The Wealth Weapon: U.S. Foreign Policy and Multinational Corporations*. New Brunswick, N.J.: Transaction Books, 1980.

3 Will OPEC-Type Cartels Become Principal Actors in World Politics?

YES

C. Fred Bergsten

The Threat from the Third World

NO

Dennis T. Avery

International Commodity Agreements

The Threat from the Third World
C. Fred Bergsten

THE THIRD WORLD AND U.S. ECONOMIC INTERESTS

. . . The Third World retains some importance for U.S. security. But its new and major impact on the United States is economic.

Much of the impact, however, relates to the position of the United States in its triangular economic relationship with Europe and Japan. The pervasive and growing economic interpenetration among these three industrialized areas is increasingly important to the welfare of key groups in each. At the same time, it threatens the welfare of other key groups. Severe political tensions thus arise. The foreign economic policies of each area are increasingly politicized and increasingly polarized, and have become potentially explosive. They could easily come to dominate the over-all relationships among the areas, if new ways are not soon found to resolve cooperatively the disputes which inevitably arise. They have already done so on particular occasions, as when the British Prime Minister refused to meet with the President of the United States to talk about high politics in late 1971 until the United States initiated steps to end the international economic crisis triggered by its New Economic Policy.

Such an outcome is now possible because the security blanket which had previously smothered such economic disputes is being steadily nudged aside. Serious intra-alliance disputes over economics could brake the progress toward East-West détente, by breaking the solidarity of the "West" on which détente in part depends. Economic conflict could thus leave us further from, rather than nearer to, a true generation of peace.

But the acceleration of international economic interpenetration, with its complex sets of costs and benefits, is not limited to the industrialized world. It is global. The U.S. stake in the Third World is growing, and the leverage of the Third World to affect the United States is growing.

NATURAL RESOURCES

First, the United States is rapidly joining the rest of the industrialized countries in depending on the Third World for a critical share of its energy supplies and other natural resources. For oil alone, annual U.S. imports are expected to rise by $20 billion by the end of the decade. But it is not only much-publicized oil; accelerating imports of other raw materials will raise these figures significantly.

Four countries control more than 80 percent of the exportable supply of world copper, have already organized, and have already begun to use their oligopoly power. Two countries account for more than 70 percent of world tin exports, and four countries raise the total close to 95 percent. Four countries combine for more than 50 percent of the world supply of natural rubber. Four countries possess over one-half the world supply of bauxite, and the inclusion of Australia (which might well join the "Third World" for such purposes) brings the total above 90 percent. In coffee, the four major suppliers have begun to collude (even within the framework of the International Coffee Agreement, which includes the main consuming countries) to boost prices. A few countries are coming to dominate each of the regional markets for timber, the closest present approximation to a truly vanishing resource. The percentages are less, but still quite impressive, for several other key raw materials and agricultural products. And the United States already meets an overwhelming share of its needs for most of these commodities from imports, or will soon be doing so.

A wide range of Third World countries thus have sizeable potential for strategic market power. They could use that power against all buyers, or in a discriminatory way through differential pricing or supply conditions—for example, to avoid higher costs to other LDC's or against the United States alone to favor Europe or Japan.

Supplying countries could exercise maximum lever-

From C. Fred Bergsten, "The Threat from the Third World," *Foreign Policy* No. **11** (Summer 1973): 107–111.

age through withholding supplies altogether, at least from a single customer such as the United States. Withholding is a feasible policy when there are no substitute products available on short notice, and when the foreign exchange reserves of the suppliers become sizeable enough that they have no need for current earnings.

The suppliers would be even more likely to use their monopoly power to charge higher prices for their raw materials, directly or through such techniques as insisting that they process the materials themselves. Either withholding or price-gouging could hurt U.S. security. The threat of either could pressure the United States to compromise its positions on international political and economic issues. Either would hurt U.S. efforts to combat domestic inflation and restore equilibrium in our international balance of payments.

The price and balance-of-payments effects on the United States of withholding or price-gouging by suppliers of raw materials could not be attacked through conventional policy instruments. Domestic demand for raw materials could be dampened only at the cost of additional unemployment. Foreign suppliers are outside the jurisdiction of U.S. price controls. Substitution of domestic resources would also raise costs significantly. Stockpile sales help only for a short time. Devaluations make resource imports more costly without much dampening their volume. Such actions could thus cause major new problems for the U.S. economy and international position.

Such Third World leverage could have a double bite on the United States if used discriminatorily against it, thereby benefiting the competitive positions of Europe and Japan. Such discriminatory action, triggered either by the suppliers or by our industrialized competitors, is by no means impossible. It was attempted in oil by some Arab countries in 1967 and has been actively sought at least by Italy and France in the recent past. The spectre of "cannibalistic competition" among the rich for natural resources is unfortunately a real possibility which suggests that the owners of those resources have tremendous clout.

The Third World suppliers could also cause major problems by the way in which they use their huge export earnings. Oil earnings alone could rise to at least $50 billion per year by the end of the decade. It is hard to see how more than $20 billion of the total

can be spent on imports. These countries could thus add $30 billion *per year* to their portfolios seeking profitable (or mischievous) outlets. They could use the money to disrupt international money markets overtly, and we have already seen that they generate great monetary instability, perhaps without consciously trying, by pushing the world toward a multiple reserve currency system. Aimed specifically at particular currencies, they could seek to force the United States (or anyone else) to adopt policies which clashed with its national objectives of the moment—as a few Arab countries, from a much weaker financial base, attacked the United Kingdom by converting sterling balances in June 1967 and again in 1971.[1] At a minimum, the uncertain destination of these huge resources will add to the already formidable problems faced by the international monetary system, which can affect the United States quite adversely.

The oil situation is, of course, the prototype. The concerted action of the OPEC countries in raising oil prices has raised energy costs throughout the world and dramatically increased their revenues. Such extortion by the oil producers—including such "normal" LDC'S as Nigeria, Indonesia, Iran, and Venezuela—is likely to continue. This economic pressure is unlikely to be reduced as a result of the takeover of the production facilities by the OPEC countries from the international companies,[2] because the countries themselves—including "opposition" politicians in each—have well learned from the companies that *each* benefits from getting the highest possible price for *all*, and that price-cutting by one would be counterproductive because it would quickly be emulated by the others to preserve existing market shares. Equally important is the fact that OPEC has

[1] Feeling no responsibility for the system, they hold their assets in whichever national currency appears most likely to appreciate in value and/or has the highest yield at the moment—switching rapidly among currencies (and even buying gold in the free market) as the situation changes. Some of those oil countries which are members of the IMF have even opted out of the SDR [Special Drawing Rights] scheme, which was a first step toward reducing such problems. For the problems involved, see C. Fred Bergsten, "Reforming the Dollar: An International Monetary Policy for the United States," *Council on Foreign Relations Paper on International Affairs No. 2* (New York: Council on Foreign Relations, September 1972), esp. pp. 9-13.

[2] As argued by Theodore H. Moran, "Coups and Costs," *Foreign Policy* 8 (Fall 1972).

shown other countries how to do it. Oil may be merely the start.

To be sure, each of the specific commodity situations presents different and complex problems. There are serious obstacles to concerted supplier action: the economic option of using substitutes for some of the commodities, the political problem of achieving adequate cooperation among the suppliers, and the risk of overt retaliation by the industrialized world (or just the United States).

But the two obstacles specific to commodity action can be largely overcome within the Third World itself. Subtle pricing and marketing strategies could boost consumer costs and producer gains significantly without pushing consuming countries to the development of substitutes, which requires heavy initial investments and start-up costs. Concerted action by copper, tin, and bauxite producers would sharply reduce the risk to each that cheaper aluminum or tin would substitute for higher priced copper, or vice versa. An alliance among the producers of coffee, cocoa, and tea could preempt substitution by drinkers around the world. Objective calculations of the benefits to all producers could provide a basis for "equitable" division of the spoils.

All that is needed to permit political cooperation is increased knowledge of the market and the potential gains from concerted action, self-confidence and leadership. Whether such action actually eventuates would seem to depend quite importantly on the policy milieu of the future. The countries involved will certainly be more likely to act if the industrialized world frustrates their efforts to achieve their goals more constructively, and if they are barred from participating effectively in global decisions which vitally affect their own destinies. They are more likely to act against the United States alone if the United States is the most obstinate or neglectful of all. Even a perception of such obstinancy or neglect, sufficiently plausible to be widely believed in both the Third World and the industrialized countries themselves, could trigger action. It would seem far better for the United States, and for all the industrialized countries, to try to preempt such risks by taking initiatives to help these countries fulfill their aspirations by more stable means. . . .

International Commodity Agreements
Dennis T. Avery

SUMMARY

In 1976, the less-developed countries (LDCs) undertook a major effort sponsored by the U.N. Conference on Trade and Development (UNCTAD IV) to organize international agreements for their important commodity exports. They hoped that such agreements would help stabilize and/or enhance their earnings.

The resulting UNCTAD integrated program for commodities has not succeeded significantly in altering the terms of trade for commodity producers, and little prospect remains that it will succeed in doing so. Theoretically, such agreements could produce modest benefits by facilitating the commitment of a more appropriate level of resources to production over time. It has proven extremely difficult to realize these benefits in practice, however, due to the continuing vagaries of supply and demand and continuing competition for market shares.

Raising commodity prices to artificially high levels attracts added production, both from agreement members and from nonmembers. It also discourages consumption and encourages substitution. These powerful reactions all work toward creating surpluses of targeted commodities and explain why commodity agreements have been unable to sustain higher price levels. In fact, price stabilization efforts can themselves stimulate output if producers believe that their risk of low prices has been decreased.

Recent commodity agreements have tried several means for dealing with market competition problems:

From Dennis T. Avery, "International Commodity Agreements," *Department of State Bulletin* (November 1981), pp. 34 and 39–43.

keeping price goals modest, signing up all major producers, and enrolling importer nations, which agree not to increase their purchases from nonmembers. It has been a practical impossibility to include all producers and potential producers of major commodities, however. It has also been difficult to get importers to agree with producers on appropriate stabilization mechanisms and price levels for the agreements.

Competition from synthetics and substitutes has been an even more intractable problem. Modern technology has produced major competitors for nearly every commodity, from synthetic rubber and plastics to high-fructose corn sweetener and glass-fiber telephone cable. Only the beverages—coffee, tea, and cocoa—have so far escaped serious inroads from synthetics and substitutes.

Commodity agreements have also exhibited some serious limitations as an aid mechanism. Their benefits are distributed on the basis of commodity production, rather than need, so they assist only indirectly in reaching economic, political, or social goals within the recipient country. They also encourage added production, which either boosts donor costs or dilutes benefits.

There is little prospect that international commodity agreements can overcome their inherent limitations and provide greater benefits for commodity exporters in the future. Prices can be expected to continue to fluctuate widely around the trends dictated by demand, competition, and long-term production costs. . . .

EVALUATION

Despite Third World countries' rapid growth in manufactured exports, commodity exports still account for more than half of the export earnings for the Third World countries which do not export oil. For some, returns from one to two commodities weigh heavily in the country's foreign-exchange receipts or budget. The prices for most of these commodities are historically volatile. In addition, commodity-exporting countries have perceived themselves at an increasing disadvantage in trading with manufacturing nations.

The LDCs at the UNCTAD IV session in 1976 put forward international commodity agreements as a means of stabilizing prices and LDC earnings from commodity exports. Implicit in the strategy, at least for some, was the idea that such agreements would also raise real returns for commodity exports, in effect transferring resources from rich commodity-importing nations to poor commodity-exporting nations. The UNCTAD resolution euphemistically expressed this as securing prices "remunerative and just to producers and equitable to consumers."

A weighted 30-year index of non-fuel commodity prices would indicate that, if there has been a discernible trend in volatile commodity prices, it has been downward. Moreover, the World Bank's projections indicate only a slight upward trend in real commodity prices over the next decade.

Price Volatility in Major Commodities

The prices of primary commodities typically are volatile, on occasion rising as much as 750% in a few months or falling precipitously. For a variety of reasons, commodity prices are far more variable than prices of most manufactures or other classes of goods or services.

Demand for most primary commodities is not very responsive to short-term price changes. People usually buy about the same amounts of food and beverages unless prices rise very high or fall very low. Some substitution naturally takes place, but such items as grain, potatoes, and sugar are regarded as basic necessities. Tea and coffee take only a small portion of consumer budgets and are objects of strong preference patterns. Purchasers of raw materials tend to be unresponsive to price changes, because the price of an individual material is likely to be a minor factor in the cost of the finished product. For example, the price of tin has little effect on the cost of a can of tomatoes, and the price of copper for electrical wiring has little influence on the cost of a new house. Unlike price changes, business cycles can have a strong effect on demand for raw materials.

The supply of most major commodities responds poorly in the short term to price changes. In most cases, primary commodity producers cannot readily change their production schedules. Increases in production require planning, investments, and time. Developing a new copper mine, for example, takes several years. Tree crops probably have the most lagged response to a price increase, because the trees take up to 12 years to reach bearing age. Conversely, production is slow to decline when prices fall. Many of the resources used in commodity production cannot be shifted quickly to alternative uses.

Production of some commodities varies with extraneous factors. The output of commodities produced as byproducts may be more responsive to changes in the prices of associated products than to changes in their own prices. Vegetable oil, for example, is produced as a byproduct of soybean meal; cobalt as a byproduct of copper. The supply of practically all primary commodities produced in agriculture is subject to unpredictable and sometimes sharp variations resulting from the vagaries of nature. Droughts, severe winters, and wet harvest seasons can slash yields. A freeze in a coffee-growing area may affect harvests for several seasons. Crop diseases and insect infestations can develop quickly.

Competition from new producing areas and competition from synthetics and substitutes tend to put a ceiling on commodity prices over the long term. Most agricultural commodities and some minerals can be produced fairly widely, although costs vary from place to place. Potential competitors could begin production if the long-run outlook strengthened. For example, Africa has long been the leading cocoa producer, but recently Brazil and Malaysia have been increasing their cocoa plantings. Most raw materials must compete with synthetic substitutes: synthetic rubber versus natural rubber, synthetic fibers versus cotton and jute, glass fibers and microwave relays versus copper cables, and plastic coatings versus tin plating.

Commodity Agreement Goals

One view of commodity agreements is that they should mute short-term fluctuations in the market, following instead the long-term trends in supply and demand. Such agreements:

• Would preserve the price mechanism for adjusting to changes in supply and demand fundamentals while narrowing the range of short-term fluctuations around the trend line;
• Would help forestall overreactions to short-term price variations;
• Would facilitate financial planning in developing countries dependent on the revenues from commodities;
• Could lead to a greater and more reliable supply because of an improved investment climate; and
• Might marginally improve the competitive position of the commodity by reducing the volatility of consumer prices.

A second view of commodity agreements concedes value to stabilization but adopts a long-term goal of raising producer prices. The industrialized countries tend to be importers, and the LDCs exporters, of the commodities identified by UNCTAD for special attention. Sustaining prices of these commodities above market-clearing levels thus would result in a transfer of resources from developed to developing nations.

A stabilizing-type agreement, which is theoretically self-financing, would have to deal alternately with surpluses and shortages. An agreement designed to raise prices above market levels would have to deal with the tendency of higher prices to increase production and depress consumption. Efforts to cope with or somehow avert persistent surpluses would have to be financed by industrialized-country consumers or governments or a combination of both.

Commodity Agreement Mechanisms

International commodity agreements have been used since the 1920s in a wide variety of situations. By using one of two mechanisms—buffer stocks and export quotas—most agreements have attempted to control the amount of a commodity reaching the market. The buffer stock mechanism requires a fund that can be used to buy up stocks of the commodity when prices slump; the stocks are sold when prices rise above agreement objectives. Export quotas defend a price floor, reducing total supply by limiting the amount of the commodity that each member nation is permitted to market. Export controls generally require producing nations to stockpile or limit production individually, but stockpiling can be costly and limiting production can be politically painful. Some producers may elect to remain outside an agreement. The cooperation of consuming-country members may strengthen a commodity agreement; consumers can be asked to agree not to import commodities marketed in violation of the agreement. Some commodity agreements contain consultative provisions intended to facilitate planning and minimize price fluctuation due to faulty assessment of demand. Market-development measures sometimes are included.

Not all commodities lend themselves equally well to the commodity agreement concept. The most fundamental success factor is relative inelasticity of demand: the less elastic the demand, the more producer revenues can be raised by withholding supply. Otherwise, falling sales volume can offset price gains. Other success factors include perishability, transportation costs, industry concentration, the range of production costs, and the existence of a homogeneous product and organized international market. Low storage and transportation costs generally enhance an agreement's chances for success (bananas and fresh meat would be poor candidates for a buffer stock agreement). Success also depends on the proportion of a product's production that reaches the market; so an industry with fewer and more concentrated producers likely would have a greater market share than one with widely dispersed production. It also helps if producers' costs are generally equal, so that no one group of producers feels it can afford to expand its market share through price competition.

The Integrated Program for Commodities

The integrated program for commodities had an immediate goal of establishing international agreements covering the 10 "core" commodities of special importance to the Third World. The integrated program for commodities also planned eventual development of measures for eight additional commodities: bananas, bauxite, iron ore, manganese, meat, phosphates, tropical timber, and vegetable oils. Integrated program for commodities operations were to be financed by a common fund, projected at $6 billion, to be contributed by both importer and exporter governments. About $4.5 billion of the fund was earmarked for buffer stock operations. The remainder was to be used for lending operations in support of other commodities for which buffer stocks were not considered suitable.

After 4 years, the integrated program for commodities has made little progress. Only one new agreement has been signed since the UNCTAD IV conference—the International Natural Rubber Agreement. It entered into force in 1980, and its buffer stock will probably become operational in 1981. The sugar and coffee agreements, already in effect at the time of the UNCTAD conference, have been renewed but face market conditions that make their long-term economic effectiveness questionable. The International Cocoa Agreement has been renewed but without the largest producer (Ivory Coast) and the largest consumer (the United States). Negotiations are underway to replace the fifth International Tin Agreement, which is due to expire in June 1982. The International Wheat Agreement remains in effect, but only as a consultative mechanism, without economic provisions. Prices for the 10 core commodities have continued to fluctuate widely.

Enthusiasm for the common fund has waned among the LDCs, because the fund's size is much smaller than originally envisioned ($750 million instead of $6 billion). The fund has been scaled down drastically because only a few commodity agreements now seem likely to associate with it and because attention has shifted from stabilization of commodity prices to stabilization of commodity export earnings. The latter goal requires less intervention, because lower prices often are associated with increased supply rather than reduced demand.

Has the integrated program for commodities failed? Or will it merely require more time to develop than UNCTAD IV envisioned? Does recent experience with commodity agreements indicate eventual success? Have flaws emerged in commodity agreement designs? Is intransigence on the part of consumers or producers to blame for the integrated program for commodities' slow progress? Should the Third World redouble its efforts on the integrated program for commodities or turn to other means of increasing its income?

These questions bear importantly on the development strategies and potential of many Third World nations and on the interest of developed ones as well. Ultimately, these questions will be assessed in the broadest possible economic, political, and sociological terms. However, the primary focus of this paper is economic constraints shaping the potential of commodity agreements to affect international markets and producer incomes.

Stabilization Success of Commodity Agreements

Even a quick reading of commodity agreements history suggests that international commodity agreements have produced little price stability. Economic studies strongly support this conclusion. Alton D. Law in *International Commodity Agreements* (Toronto, 1975) determined that the average coffee price fluctuation was at least 50% greater during the agreement years of 1965–72 than in the preceding nonagreement period of 1950–63. For sugar, he found the fluctuation at least 75% greater for 12 recent years of control than for 11 noncontrol years, even eliminating the years when the U.S.-Cuban confrontation disrupted the sugar market. Only in wheat and tea did Law find more stable prices during the tenure of international agreements—and the wheat stability resulted primarily from national stockpiling by the United States and Canada. Gordon W. Smith and George R. Schink, writing on "The International Tin Agreement: A Reassessment" in *The Economic Journal* of December 1976, concluded that the U.S. tin stockpile has lent far more stability to the tin market than has the International Tin Agreement, in large part because it is many times larger than the agreement's tin buffer stock.

Those commodities with the most volatile market fundamentals—least elastic demand, longest supply response lags, greatest vulnerability to business cycles, etc.—have had volatile price patterns even when commodity agreements have been in effect. Tea, on the other hand, has had a relatively stable and uneventful price history both with and without a commodity agreement.

Limitations of Stabilization Schemes

The potential gains to be had from stabilization are relatively modest and enormously difficult to achieve.

In the first place, stabilization gains depend importantly on committing a more appropriate level of resources to production over time. It is extremely difficult, however, to determine the correct level at any given moment. Demand for many commodities swings in pronounced and erratic cycles. With other commodities, supply is the more important variable. For most, the overall market is growing, slowly—and judgments of when to add new production are extremely important. Production of most commodities must be developed in sizable units to achieve economies of scale, and this, too, complicates stabilization. Once such resources as ore deposits, groves of trees, and specialized processing machinery have been committed, they have little alternative use in the short or even medium term. Even with an international agreement, it is difficult to improve resource efficiency.

Any benefits achieved from stabilization must also be balanced against the costs involved. To the extent that they rely on export controls, commodity agreements may raise production costs by locking in the production patterns that exist at the time of negotiation. In order to maintain peak efficiency, these patterns normally would tend to change with new technology, new opportunities for resources, new entrants into the industry, and other factors. The recent shift of cotton production from the developed to the developing countries is such a change, which might well have been hindered by a strong commodity agreement. If the agreements encourage less efficient use of a nation's resources, that loss of efficiency must be balanced against the gains in stability.

Finally, of course, producer proponents of com-

modity agreements need to bear in mind that the benefits of stability in a commodity are shared between producers and consumers. Ezriel Brook and Enzo Grilli indicate in an article, "Commodity Price Stabilization and the Developing World," in *Finance and Development*, March 1977, that the source of market instability is a key factor in the distribution of these benefits, with producers gaining the principal benefits only when instability results from production factors.

On a more pragmatic level, stabilization itself can affect resource commitment and lead to increased—and sometimes surplus—production. Effective stabilization in the short run reduces producers' risks—and thus encourages them to expand output to the point where their variable costs are covered by the minimum price. This phenomenon has been frequently documented in connection with agricultural price-support policies in the developed nations (notably the United States). It is also noted in a World Bank study of the international jute market. This tendency toward increased production undermines even the most limited goal that has been outlined for commodity agreements—protecting exporters with a floor price.

Because agreements require a political consensus, the economic foundation of some agreements is shaky from the start. Export quotas are often the first area of compromise, because producing nations threaten not to join unless they receive attractive quotas. The second area of compromise, of course, is price objectives. Producers argue for higher prices; consumers for lower. For example, the recently renewed cocoa agreement has not been signed by Ivory Coast, the largest producer, because the price range is too low, while the United States, as the largest consumer, refuses to join because it believes the price is too high and that consequently the agreement will be overwhelmed by surplus cocoa. Some may have believed the price range was unrealistic but signed the agreement anyway to avoid seeming obstructionist. They may have assumed the costs to them would be small, because such agreements have a history of breaking down.

Competition among producers has probably been the most important factor in the collapse of stabilization efforts. Producer incomes, of course, are determined not only by prices but also by sales volume. So even when the agreement sets a price range, producers continue to compete for market shares. Often producing nations are under balance-of-payments pressure. Sometimes they attempt to market some of their production by subterfuge outside the agreement. Market pressure almost always comes from producers who are not party to the agreement.

Have Commodity Agreements Enhanced Producer Prices?

Economic theory holds that raising commodity prices to artifically high levels will attract additional production, encourage substitution, and cut back quantities demanded. These reactions create surpluses, and they basically explain why the price increases achieved by international commodity agreements have been limited to the short run. In fact, many of the short-term gains have turned into long-term losses.

Historically, price enhancement was tried first by individual companies, which found they lacked the market power to maintain high prices. It has been tried by cartels of companies, which found their prices undercut by producers outside the cartels. It has been tried by governments, which found themselves undercut by producers in other nations. It has been tried by groups of producer nations, which found their markets invaded by nonmember nations. Finally, it has been tried by broad alliances of producer and consumer nations, which have not yet discovered mutual interests strong enough to survive long-term pressures.

Jere R. Behrman, writing "Stabilizing Prices Through International Buffer Stock Commodity Agreements" in *National Development*, May 1980, found that most of the organized international arrangements that have attempted to raise prices have been unsuccessful. He documented 51 attempts, which lasted a median 2½ years each. Even those which have been successful in the short run have not lasted long; 4 years has been their median duration. These relatively successful efforts have been associated with "higher concentrations of production and foreign trade"; more inelastic demand; fewer possibilities of short-term substitution; small cost differences among producers; and less government involvement.

The Problem of Increased Production

Increased production has plagued nearly every commodity agreement. No matter how high the proportion of existing production included in the agreement, output by producers both inside and outside the agreement tended to increase with the expectation of

price enhancement and/or stability. Behrman concluded that organizations that had succeeded for a time broke down most often due to competition among the members, with competition from nonmembers the second most frequent cause.

The international commodity agreements have tried to deal with the nonmember competition problem in two ways: by signing up nonmembers and by including importing nations in the agreements. Neither approach has worked very well. Frequently nonmembers can only be enticed into the agreement through attractive quotas or other inducements that dilute the benefits available for the existing members. When importers are included in the agreements, it is often difficult to agree on price objectives (the recent cocoa and coffee negotiations illustrate this).

Competition From Synthetics and Substitutes

The problem of synthetics and substitutes may be even more intractable in the long run. Modern technology has produced major competitors for nearly every primary commodity (see Table 1). Sugar is the most recent commodity to come under heavy attack from a synthetic product (the new high-fructose corn

Table 1

Primary commodity	Competitors
Rubber	Synthetic rubber, plastics.
Cotton	Other natural and synthetic textile fibers.
Tin	New technology that permits thinner tin plating; plastic can linings; aluminum, paper, and plastic containers.
Jute	Polypropylene and polyethylene fibers and sheets.
Sugar	Corn sweeteners (especially the recently developed high-fructose corn sweetener), and noncaloric sweeteners.
Copper	Microwave communications; steel-reinforced aluminum and glass-fiber cables; plastic plumbing pipe; electronic replacements for electric devices.
Bauxite	Other metals and plastics that offer some of aluminum's lightweight and weather-resistent properties; aluminum recycling efforts.
Cocoa	Cocoa flavorings; vegetable oils used as extenders.
Coffee	Other beverages.
Tea	Other beverages.

sweeteners), and copper is probably under the most varied attack, from a whole host of technological innovations.

For some commodities, the synthetics and substitutes have essentially set the long-term market prices for the primary commodities—as in rubber and jute. In most markets, the substitutes are an important price factor, as in tin, sugar, and copper. The beverages—coffee, cocoa, and tea—are the only major commodity group whose markets have not been seriously constrained by outside competitors, although cocoa has felt the impact of extenders.

International Commodity Agreements as Aid Mechanisms

One of the arguments made for international commodity agreements is that they can transfer income from wealthy nations to poor ones. However, commodity agreements have some serious limitations as aid mechanisms.

• Price benefits are distributed among recipient nations on the basis of their production rather than their need.
• A commodity agreement price policy fails to target any economic, political, or social goals within a recipient country. Coffee price supports, for example, may benefit the plantation owners more than the coffee workers. A U.S. Agency for International Development grant, on the other hand, can be targeted more selectively.
• Producing nations will be encouraged to increase production, increasing the costs of the aid and/or diluting the benefits.

The International Coffee Agreement of the late 1960s and early 1970s came closest to the idea of transferring resources from wealthy importing states to developing exporters. It probably transferred $500-600 million per year. Even in this agreement, however, the producer-consumer compromise broke down rather quickly. Coffee drinkers rebelled when they felt prices had risen too high.

Conclusions and Policy Implications

The prices of primary commodities probably will continue to fluctuate widely in response to demand, competition, and long-term production costs. Recent international commodity agreements have not succeeded beyond the limited goal of protecting modest price floors for relatively short time periods, and there is little prospect that future commodity agreements will be more effective. Even if an agreement got full government financing, competition among producers for increased market shares and external competition from substitutes might drive costs to politically untenable levels. Moreover, the benefits of true stabilization are seldom sufficient to overcome the diversity of interests among affected nations.

There is virtually no evidence to indicate that primary commodities can be utilized to generate much larger amounts of development capital for LDCs. The International Tin Agreement is often pointed to as the most successful of the agreements. It has effectively defended its floor price over a long period (aided by Malaysia's ability to shut down its gravel-pump tin production when prices are unattractive). The real price of tin has also trended upward, albeit erratically. However, tin producers have often been squeezed between rising labor costs and the prices of competing materials. If tin is, indeed, the outstanding success story among recent international commodity agreements, then such agreements hardly seem to offer LDCs a powerful force for economic growth.

Based on analysis of supply and demand projections for primary commodities and on the lack of success in UNCTAD's integrated program for commodities, expansion of manufacturing appears to be a far more promising development strategy than reliance on exports of primary products under the aegis of international commodity agreements. In "The Changing Composition of Developing Country Exports," staff working paper 314 of January 1979, the World Bank notes that LDC exports have shifted dramatically toward manufactured goods in the last 15 years. Manufactures now account for nearly half of LDCs' non-oil exports. If the expansion of manufacturing continues over the next few years, the World Bank projects it will lead to an export growth rate for LDCs roughly equal to that of the rest of the world. The Bank notes that the greatest success to date has been achieved by the most advanced LDCs, but that this situation is changing rapidly as increasing numbers of LDCs move toward manufacturing (see Table 2).

Table 2   Past and Projected Rates of Export Growth by Broad Product Groups (in constant 1975 prices)

	World 1960–75	LDCs 1960–75	World 1975–85	LDCs 1975–85	Percent of LDC exports			Percent share of increase	
					1960	1975	1985	1960–75	1975–85
Fuel and energy	6.3	6.2	3.6	3.4	39	40	30	42	18
Agricultural products	4.2	2.6	4.4	3.1	43	27	20	16	12
Non-fuel minerals	3.9	4.8	4.2	5.8	7	7	7	6	6
Manufactures	8.9	12.3	7.8	12.2	11	26	43	36	64
Total merchandise	7.1	5.9	6.4	6.4	100	100	100	100	100

Source: World Bank, *World Development Report, 1978*, Tables 13 and 25, and unpublished projections for future WDR issues.

QUESTIONS FOR DISCUSSION

1 Can other cartels of third world countries be successfully formed on the OPEC model?
2 What conditions make a successful cartel possible?
3 What impact would commodity cartels have on world politics?
4 What policies should third world countries pursue to avoid sharp fluctuations in the world market price of commodities?
5 What groups in the third world benefit from commodity cartels?

SUGGESTED READINGS

Barraclough, Geoffrey. "Wealth and Power: The Politics of Food and Oil." *The New York Review of Books*, Aug. 7, 1976, pp. 23–30.

Brown, William, and Herman Kahn. "Why OPEC Is Vulnerable?" *Fortune* (July 14, 1980): 67–68.

Cline, William R. (ed.). *Policy Alternatives for a New International Economic Order: An Economic Analysis*. New York: Praeger, 1979.

Collins, Frank. "The OPEC Revolution: The World Will Never Be the Same." *Progressive* (February 1980): 22–27.

Laqueur, Walter. "Third World Fantasies." *Commentary* (February 1977): 43–48.

Perlman, Robert, and Anthony Murray. "Resources and Conflict: Requirements and Vulnerabilities of the Industrialized World," in *Third World Conflict and International Security: Part II*. Adelphi Papers No. **167**. London: International Institute for Strategic Studies, Summer 1981, pp. 51–59.

Rothstein, Robert L. *Global Bargaining: UNCTAD and the Quest for a New International Economic Order*. Princeton, N.J.: Princeton University Press, 1979.

Sauvant, Karl P. "The Poor Countries and the Rich—A Few Steps Forward." *Dissent* **25** (Winter 1978): 43–53.

Smith, Tony. "The Underdevelopment of Development Literature: The Case of Dependency Theory." *World Politics* **31** (January 1979): 247–288.

Wriggins, W. Howard, and Gunnar Adler-Karlsson. *Reducing Global Inequities: 1980s Project/Council on Foreign Relations*. New York: McGraw-Hill, 1978.

4 Does the United Nations Play a Meaningful Role in World Politics?

YES

Richard L. McCall

The United Nations and U.S. Policy

NO

Juliana Geran Pilon

The United States and the United Nations: A Balance Sheet

The United Nations and U.S. Policy
Richard L. McCall

Pollsters have taken a pretty bad shellacking lately—they, therefore, may not be the most authoritative source to establish my basic premise for this discussion. The point is, however, that contrary to conventional wisdom, public perception does support the notion that there is room for the United Nations in American foreign policy. According to recent polls by Gallup and Roper, Americans by a two-to-one margin want to increase U.S. participation in the U.N. system.

Nonetheless, the consumers of conventional wisdom continue to purport that American public support for the United Nations is on the decline and, accordingly, we ought to be reducing our financial assistance to the U.N. family. In dollars and cents terms, these advocates of retrenchment have succeeded to a considerable extent. Thirty years ago, the United States contributed almost one-half (47.5%) of the United Nations' budget. Today, our share is only 25.6%, a little over $1 billion, about $4 for each American—less than what each of us spent to see the movie "Apocalypse Now."

Along with this less than adequate performance, outlays for programs, such as foreign aid, which are critical in creating a more harmonious international community, have also declined over time and in comparison with other countries. For example, in the past 15 years, the net U.S. official development assistance decreased from 0.49% of our GNP to 0.17%. In contrast, the total development assistance effort of other traditional aid-giving countries has increased five-fold during the same period.

Why the discrepancy between our professed beliefs and our willingness to provide adequate financial resources which would reinforce these beliefs?

There are probably lists of reasons for it, none of them fully explanatory but each of them sufficient to raise doubts. Perhaps in its genesis, we have ascribed greater hopes to the United Nations than it could possibly fulfill in our lifetimes. Idealistic measuring sticks are bad bases for judgment.

THE U.N.'s RECORD

Almost 30 years ago when the United Nations was created, it was seen as the great global instrument that would banish forever the scourge of war. Since then, there have been at least five major military conflicts on the average every year. As we celebrate the 35th anniversary of the United Nations' founding, a war is going on unabated between Iraq and Iran, violent conflicts continue in at least four areas in Africa, direct Soviet, or Soviet-backed, military interventions violate the sovereignty of three countries in Asia, and civil strife has taken 8,000 lives in El Salvador this year alone. Annually, the world spends over $400 billion on armaments and as many as 35 countries (and even terrorist groups) could have nuclear weapons by the end of this century.

Thirty years ago nations pledged to adhere to the Universal Declaration of Human Rights. Today there are some 16 million refugees, one-fourth of this Earth's population is malnourished, and millions face starvation. Torture and imprisonment have remained convenient tools of governance irrespective of race, religion, or sex.

The United Nations has had a checkered history in the peaceful resolution of conflicts. It was either impotent to act, as in the cases of repeated Soviet aggression in Hungary, Czechoslovakia, and Afghanistan, or fearing impotency did not even get involved, as in the case of recent African wars. It has become bogged down in negotiations on the global economy, and its impact on global arms control is more exhortatory than real.

For a country that has placed so much faith in the imperatives of world order, that has spent so much effort and sacrificed so much for it—these are indeed legitimate causes for disappointment. It is not surprising then that the majority of Americans are critical of the United Nations—53% according to the polls—for falling short of their hopes and expectations about resolving international problems.

Falling short, however, is not the same as fail-

From Richard L. McCall, "The United Nations and U.S. Policy," *Department of State Bulletin* (February 1981), pp. 60–62. (Address before the Harvard Model United Nations in Cambridge, Massachusetts, on Dec. 4, 1980.)

ure. As we acknowledge shortcomings—serious shortcomings—let us also be mindful of certain facts and salient achievements.

The United Nations has become a truly universal organization. Its membership, tripling since its founding, now numbers 154 nations. Its budget has increased 16 times; its agenda has grown by leaps and bounds to encompass practically all aspects of international behavior. The General Assembly, which was once an annual affair, has become for all practical purposes—counting all the special and emergency sessions and full membership conferences—a year-round meeting. The Security Council, which had fallen into such disuse in the 1950s, meeting 5 or 10 times a year, now meets on the average of 100 times a year.

The United Nations has become the source of innovative measures to reduce international tensions. Peace-keeping forces—not even envisioned in the original charter—are in place in Cyprus and the Middle East. These forces have prevented local conflicts from festering into major wars and have been some of the United Nations' least heralded success stories.

The United Nations has had a steady, calming, and steering presence in the greatest transformation of the political geography of this Earth—aiding formerly colonialized people to achieve independence without major conflicts and in a relatively orderly fashion.

The United Nations' purview over what constitutes threats to collective security has expanded to include global economic security. At the present, almost 90% of its resources are devoted to this task—to development, to environmental protection, to international trade, finance, investment, and to other measures of economic, social, cultural, and scientific cooperation. Through its specialized agencies and programs, the United Nations has increased concessional assistance to developing countries in the past decade from less than $500 million to over $1.6 billion. Together with the multilateral development banks (such as the World Bank and the regional banks) it has been the channel for the growth of net flow of resources to the Third World from less than $1 billion to $4 billion annually in that same period.

The United Nations has had a pioneering role in setting standards and rules that make the life of all of us more secure, healthier and better—in international aviation; in communications; in the protection of the environment; in the husbandry of our resources in the deep seas and in outer space; in the promotion of health standards; and in the entire range of protection of civil, political, social, cultural, and economic rights.

The list is almost endless, and with such selective illustrations I have probably failed to mention some very important ones. There is little question that the United Nations has become the central forum for diplomatic initiatives of many small countries; that through its direct and joint oversight development efforts it has transformed formerly "basket case" countries into food sufficient states. It has been a major facilitator for American investment and export, and its networks of solidarity among labor groups gave birth to concrete measures to make life better for the workers. And perhaps more than any other international institution it has successfully promoted women's rights.

Such is not a record of failure. I do not, however, want to dwell too long on what the United Nations has done or failed to do in making my point about the challenges we must confront today and in the future. The United Nations will certainly remain an arena of conflict between East and West as it has also come center stage in the continuing dialogue between North and South. Yet it must also become a springboard for our collective efforts to address the common problems which this entire planet faces in the decades ahead. Permit me then to focus on the critical role of the United Nations in the context of the East-West rivalry, the North-South relationships, and in light of the prospects we hold for the future.

EAST-WEST RELATIONS

The past year bore witness to portentous events in world affairs, events that have neither run their full course nor are they as yet fully predictable in their outcome. We see the flagrant violation of the most elementary norms of international diplomatic practice and decency in Tehran; the naked aggression against the people of Afghanistan, Kampuchea, and Laos; the unceasing armed conflicts in the Horn of Africa; war and renewed threats to peace in the Middle East; and the current crisis in Poland. Each of these events has posed and will continue to pose major obstacles in the path of reasoned relationships between the Soviet Union and the United States.

Each event in direct or in subtle ways affects or is affected by the state of relationships between the two giant nuclear powers. We need not be so Pollyannaish as to presume that global interests always coincide with ours, but we need not be so simple-minded, either, as to assert that every threat to our interest is automatically a net gain for the Soviets.

The recent Soviet globetrotting from Angola to Grenada does not exactly reveal great success for their brand of adventurism. Nor does the emergence of numerous and busy Russian advisers in the area, now called the arc of crisis, suggest the tip of the iceberg of some grand plan of world domination. It does, however, point to the Soviet propensity of opportunism: to take advantage of the opportunities created by the correlation of forces and to extend their sphere of influence.

In the coming years, I am sure, there will be a lot of rethinking and debate about the appropriate American foreign policy stance toward such Soviet behavior. One thing is, however, certain; we will either have to confront them at a point or place of their own choosing—once they are already on the move—or, alternately, work for a world order in which the correlation of forces does not favor them.

Which approach is more expensive, more risky, I leave to your imagination and common sense. Today we spend about 5% of our GNP on defense purposes and there are persuasive arguments to increase this to 7%. At the same time, we devote less than 0.05% of our GNP to the United Nations, and there are some who consider even this little amount to be too much. But the arguments about the appropriate level of defense spending is not my issue here. My point is that it is reasonable to assume that a stronger United Nations would be more capable of dealing with political upheavals and tensions.

In several recent instances, the United Nations has proven to be the preferred instrument with sufficient international support to lead the search for political solutions to international problems. In each case, this approach also closed the door on Soviet mischief.

• The United Nations provided the mechanism through which a peaceful resolution was found to the challenge of majority rule and independence for Zimbabwe.
• The Security Council resolutions laid the basis for the successful Camp David negotiations leading toward greater peace between Egypt and Israel.

• Continuing efforts for the peaceful settlement of disputes in southern Africa, specifically Namibia, could not go forward without the leading role of the United Nations.

I do not intend to suggest that the United Nations can always act as a great buffer against Soviet designs. Realism dictates that we accept the limits imposed on the United Nations' ability to act in every case. But I do suggest that the United Nations can have a tempering influence on Soviet behavior and can serve, as it has served in the past, as a forum of diplomatic initiative to avoid direct East-West confrontations.

NORTH-SOUTH DIALOGUE

In 1945, the United States emerged indisputably as the most powerful and influential nation on Earth. We shaped the United Nations in our own image and likeness and provided for it the necessary economic muscle. Over time, we were the principal architect of the International Monetary Fund to insure monetary order and stability; of the World Bank to promote the reconstruction of Europe and economic growth all over the world; and of the General Agreement on Tariffs and Trade to stimulate world trade.

For a while these worked ideally. We commanded the primary influence because the United States accounted for 60% of the world's industrial production and 50% of its monetary reserves. But this is no longer the case. Only 30% of the world's industrial production and less than 7% of its monetary reserves are ours today. Western Europe and Japan have emerged as major and competitive economic powers. Cartels, such as the Organization of Petroleum Exporting Countries (OPEC), drastically rewrote the rules of global economy. And a new bloc of nations, the Third World, emerged demanding a fairer share and a greater voice in the world economy.

It is this new bloc, comprised of the developing countries, that commands majorities in the United Nations and demands attention to its own priority–a new international economic order. It wants systemic changes in the world monetary system, greater resource transfers from the industrialized countries, better access to technology, and a greater voice in international economic decision making.

The developing countries' demands do not always make economic sense, but there is a ring of justice in their call. After all, they comprise a substantial majority of the world's population but receive only 15% of the global income. Yet they are vitally important to the industrialized countries. The dependence of the North on the oil supplies from the South only dramatizes but does not complete the picture of how mutually dependent—indeed interdependent—we have become. And the dynamics of this interdependence also imply a condition of mutual vulnerability which begs for intensive search and drastic resolution of the outstanding differences.

The welfare, progress, and economic stability of these developing countries have become critically important to the West and to the United States. Our trade with the Third World surpasses that with Western Europe, Japan, and the Soviet Union. The United States sells one-third of its exports to developing nations, and they supply 42% of our imports. Approximately 1 million American jobs depend on U.S. exports to these countries, as does one quarter of our agricultural productivity. We have more than $40 billion in investment riding on the fortunes of the developing world.

This is why we press continuously, in a spirit of compromise, for agreement in the current round of global negotiations. And this is again why the United Nations has become an indispensable forum for the rich as well as the poor countries to fashion international institutions that are capable of responding to the growing global economic crises.

GLOBAL 2000 REPORT

This year saw the publication of two important studies dealing with our future. These studies, the Brandt Commission's *Programme for Survival* and the *Global 2000 Report to the President of the United States*, are not for the faint-hearted. They both diagnose the current state of global economy and ecology as dismal. Their prognoses are identical—the worst is yet to come.

I could cite dozens of other studies. They all point to the same conclusion, and they all urge unprecedented global cooperation as the only way to avoid global catastrophe. Yet, I am struck by the fact of how the glaringly obvious has failed to penetrate our collective psyche, how oblivious we continue to remain in the face of the clear and present danger that world hunger and poverty present to our countries, to our economic prosperity, and to our freedoms.

We are hurtling toward a future world population of 2½ billion more people than inhabit the Earth today, most of them destined to live in the poorest countries, with per capita incomes hovering at a level of abject poverty, with arable land running out, with forests receding, fresh waters disappearing, and deserts expanding.

Today, one-third of humanity exists in the absence of adequate shelter or food, ill and idle, with no glimpse of a better future and enraged by the injustice of it all. This creates a dangerous global climate—a climate where oceans of suffering breed hurricanes of hate, lashing out with destructive force not only where they are spawned but wherever they reach as well.

In this shrinking world of ours, distance no longer guarantees safety. The crises we face do not respect national boundaries or ideological frontiers. Let me select a few pertinent projections of the future.

- In the next 20 years there will be 2½ billion more people.
- The food deficit for the Third World alone will hover around 75 million metric tons by the year 1990, drawing down global food reserves and leading to worldwide competition for food and to a rapid rise of price levels.
- The search for alternative sources of food will cause drastic depletion of fishery resources.
- Increased fossil fuel consumption and the greater use of fluorocarbons for this growing population will correspondingly raise atmospheric carbon dioxide and will cause ozone depletion, both of which entail serious climatic changes—in turn affecting our ability to produce food.
- The inability of the developing countries to meet the growing demands—for food and energy alone—of their growing populations will deplete their foreign exchange reserves, raise their debts, in turn lead to defaults and global monetary instability.
- Growing scarcities as well as the growing demands of more and more people will place unacceptable strains on the stability of many developing countries, leading to frequent political upheavals threatening every nation's security.

In a world where billions are subjected to the degradation of poverty—abject poverty—the struggle for survival will become the paramount human endeavor. Abject poverty dehumanizes because it subjects life to the exigencies of mere existence. It is a condition in which people exhaust their energies at the grueling task of just being, with never a chance of becoming. It is a condition in which people squander their energies in the fight for mere physical survival, with their talents unchallenged, their human potential unfulfilled.

Where the basic human needs of food, health, and shelter remain the sole object of unfulfilled wants, no desire can emerge for liberty and no strength is left to protect rights. Where the struggle for liberation from daily necessities overwhelms the necessity for freedom, neither basic human needs nor human rights will ever be satisfied. And in a world where tyranny becomes the order of things, no nation, however prosperous and free, can long remain an island of virtue.

To confront these growing threats to global security, each nation, each government must do its share. None of the problems can be tackled by one country alone, and no country alone can long endure to carry the principal burden.

It is clear that the followup to the *Global 2000 Report* will require an extended program of cooperative interaction within the worldwide system of international organizations. The United Nations is the ideal focal point for strategists in formulating an agenda which could deflect projected ecological, economic, and social catastrophes in the coming millennium. The very nature of the entity that is the United Nations lends it to the creative long-range effort which could bring to fruition the massive economic development that the current world environment demands. Yet we can no longer attack problems in a piecemeal fashion.

It will not be enough merely to ask for increased funding from the world's financial institutions. We must evolve a precise strategy that will coalesce hardware with human resources, that points toward a convergence of intellectual and technological tools which concentrate our collective efforts in problem solving for both developed and developing nations.

THE CHALLENGES OF CHANGE

East and West, North and South, our present and our future—they are symbols of our concerns. Pitted against each other in dynamic tension, they reveal the promise and possibilities of change.

Will we control this change or will we permit events to control our lives? Can we allow the prognoses of the *Global 2000 Report* to come true? Can we resign ourselves to an unbridled East-West conflict and prepare to live in a world where the structures of global cooperation will have been replaced by the worst kind of international struggle for the survival of the unfittest? I need not posit the answer.

We Americans have never feared change. To the contrary, I sincerely feel that most of the change for the better that is taking place today has been prompted by our very presence in the world, our ideals, our ways, and our responses. We created the United Nations not to put the brakes on change but to design our future.

In a month or so, I will be leaving my post as Assistant Secretary of State in charge of U.N. affairs. I am proud to have been associated with an American foreign policy that has steadfastly supported the United Nations. To be sure we saw changes coming, yet we did not fear them. We understood the changes taking place in the United Nations, and we tried to steer them in a direction consistent with our values and beliefs. So as I leave office, I am confident that the seeds of our ideals that we planted with the United Nations 35 years ago will grow into a bountiful harvest—as long as we have the will and foresight to cultivate with care and compassion this fragile structure of global cooperation.

The United States and the United Nations: A Balance Sheet
Juliana Geran Pilon

INTRODUCTION

Born from the ashes of a devastating world war, the United Nations was to many a new hope for a more peaceful world. The United States gave its blessings: on July 28, 1945, the U.S. Senate ratified the U.N. Charter by a vote of 89 to 2. Were the vote to be taken today, the tally probably would be reversed. Not only has the U.N. failed to fulfill the lofty hopes of its founders, but it has itself become—in the eyes of growing numbers of American observers—a major cause of global disharmony. To some, indeed, the U.N. has become—to cite the titles of two books about the organization—"a dangerous place."[1] And to many Americans, the U.N. has become an object of suspicion and, perhaps worse, of ridicule and derision.

What has happened to the U.N. since its founding? Or, at least, what has happened to American perception of that institution? Why does the U.S. find itself under almost constant siege at the U.N.? These are questions which American policymakers ought to be and are asking. How they are answered may well determine for the rest of this century the role of the U.S. in the U.N.—or even whether the U.S. chooses to stay in the U.N.

By almost any measure, the U.S. has been the world's most enthusiastic booster of the U.N. From the outset, American generosity exceeded that of any other nation. Until 1964, the U.S. paid almost 40 percent of the U.N. assessed budget, gradually reducing this to 25 percent in 1974 (still the current percentage). By contrast, the U.S.S.R. pays less than 13 percent. From 1946 to 1980, the U.N. cost U.S. taxpayers nearly $10 billion. In 1980 alone, the U.S. paid more than $500 million in voluntary contributions, in addition to its $350 million membership assessment. This does not include the billions of U.S. dollars for direct or indirect foreign aid, which often find their way to the U.N. and other international organizations since many developing nations are dependent on Washington for the money with which they pay their dues.

Nothing has changed the nature of the U.N. as much as its exploding membership. In his article "The United States in Opposition," former U.S. Ambassador to the U.N. Daniel Patrick Moynihan traces the problem to "the British revolution" of 1947, when Britain granted India independence.[2] The other great empires, except the Russian, soon broke up as well, resulting in a tripling of U.N. membership within less than four decades. From 51 members in 1945, the U.N. grew to 82 by 1958, 115 in 1964, and now stands at 157; three states were admitted in 1981. Few observers realized in the early years that the new nations, most of them plagued with internal economic and political problems, would be interested less in international stability and more in asserting "the international power to which [they] feel entitled by virtue of their numbers."[3]

U.N. membership did not inevitably have to expand so rapidly. The Charter had stipulated that membership be restricted to "peace-loving states" which are both "able and willing to carry out the [Charter] obligations." This provision, however, was modified substantially in practice: in 1955, ignoring an advisory opinion by the International Court that each application for membership be considered on its own merits,[4] the Soviet Union and the United States agreed to a "package deal" whereby sixteen new

---

[1] Abraham Yeselson & Anthony Gaglione, *A Dangerous Place: The United Nations as a Weapon in World Politics* (New York: Grossman Publishers, 1974); Daniel Patrick Moynihan, *A Dangerous Place* (New York: Berkley Books, 1980).

[2] Daniel Patrick Moynihan, "The United States in Opposition," *Commentary*, March 1975.

[3] Joseph E. Johnson, "Helping to Build New States," in Francis O. Wilcox and H. Field Haviland, Jr., *The United States and the United Nations* (Baltimore, Maryland: Johns Hopkins Press, 1961), p. 3.

[4] In 1947, the General Assembly (on Western initiative) requested the International Court to define membership criteria more clearly—in particular, to decide whether a member was juridically entitled to make its consent to admission dependent on an additional condition that other states be admitted simultaneously. In 1948, the court advised that it was *not* so entitled; the vote was 9-6. Cited in Ruth B. Russell, *The United Nations and United States Security Policy* (Washington, D.C.: The Brookings Institution, 1968), p. 360.

From Juliana Geran Pilon, "The United States and the United Nations: A Balance Sheet," *Backgrounder* No. 162, Jan. 21, 1982, Washington, D.C.: The Heritage Foundation.

states were admitted to membership. Such a package seemed necessary to avoid a paralyzing stalemate. By 1964 sixty-six additional members had joined the U.N., many of them freshly emerged from colonial dependency, not always able or willing to carry out their Charter obligations.[5]

Problems were quick to surface. Since each member is entitled to an equal voice in the General Assembly, a discrepancy between voting power and financial contribution is inevitable. As Ambassador Edward Hambro of Norway remarked in 1970: "It is ridiculous, of course, that we have a voting majority that pays only 3% of the budget."[6] During fiscal year 1980-1981, for example, rich Saudi Arabia paid only .58 percent of the U.N. budget and Kuwait paid a mere .2 percent, compared to 4.4 percent for the relatively poor United Kingdom, .5 percent for Norway and 1.7 percent for Spain.[7] In fact, the entire "Group of 77," whose more than 120 members—among them Saudi Arabia—aggressively urge economic redistribution to benefit developing countries, contributes only about 8.8 percent of the total U.N. budget. Yet the policies endorsed by many of the smallest U.N. contributors have serious negative implications—both political and economic—for its largest supporter, the U.S. It is no wonder, therefore, that the American public is becoming increasingly disenchanted with the U.N.

THE PUBLIC VIEW

The American public originally had welcomed the U.N.[8] Even in 1959, the Gallup Poll reported that 87 percent of Americans thought the U.N. was doing a good job. But within little over a decade, on October 24, 1970, Thomas Vail, a member of the President's

Commission for the Observance of the 25th Anniversary of the U.N., was to report that public faith in the U.N.'s peacekeeping ability had declined to 50 percent. The following year, the Gallup Poll reported a drop to 35 percent. On November 19, 1980, George Gallup revealed that the public's rating of the U.N. performance had dropped to a 35-year low: only three out of ten Americans felt the U.N. was doing a "good job" in trying to solve the problems it has had to face, while 53 percent felt it was doing a "poor job." In his report, Gallup noted that his poll "has measured the public attitudes toward the U.N. since its formation in 1945, using questionnaires appropriate to the internal situation at the time. At no point since then has satisfaction with the overall performance of the world organization been so low as it is today."[9] The trend-line continues to plunge. A March 1981 Roper poll indicates that only 10 percent of the American public believes the U.N. has been "highly effective" in keeping world peace or in carrying out other functions. Americans, it seems, are well aware that the U.N. is not fulfilling its dream and has become an increasingly dangerous place.

INSTITUTIONAL BARRIERS TO EFFECTIVE U.N. ACTION

Many in the United States had unrealistically high hopes for the U.N. Coming back from the Yalta conference, President Franklin Roosevelt said the U.N.:

> spells the end of the system of unilateral action and exclusive alliances and spheres of influence and the balances of power, and all the other expedients which have been tried for centuries—and have failed. We propose to substitute for all these a universal organization in which all peace-loving nations will finally have a chance to join.[10]

But the U.N. can do no more than what its Charter—and its members—allow. Professor Ruth Russell observes:

> The system provided for in that Charter could come fully into being only as the Members of the United Nations fulfilled their commitments to its

---

[5] The nations admitted in 1955 were: Albania, Austria, Bulgaria, Cambodia, Ceylon, Finland, Hungary, Iceland, Italy, Jordan, Laos, Libya, Nepal, Portugal, Romania, and Spain.

[6] Thomas A. Hoge, "The United Nations' Happy (?) 25th Birthday," *The American Legion Magazine*, July 1970, p. 4.

[7] See "Statement of Assessment of Member States' Contributions to the United Nations Regular Budget for 1981," ST/ADM/Ser. B/250, January 2, 1981, pp. 3–9.

[8] See *Public Attitudes Toward the U.N.*, Hearings before the Subcommittee on International Operations of the Committee on Foreign Relations, U.S. Senate, July 27, 1977. Also, William A. Scott and Stephen B. Withey, *The U.S. and The U.N.: The Public View 1945-1955* (New York: Manhattan Publishing Company, 1958).

[9] *The Gallup Poll*, released November 20, 1980, p. 3.

[10] Cited in Ruth B. Russell, *A History of the U.N. Charter* (Washington, D.C.: The Brookings Institution, 1958), p. 547.

peaceful purposes and principles. Such a state of affairs did not obtain after the end of the war. Instead, the United States found the Soviet Union seeking to achieve atomic standing and to force world politics into a mold very different from that hoped for by the United States and outlined in the Charter. Lesser powers also complicated the picture with their own conflicts.[11]

Even the lofty language of the Charter was to be used against the intentions of the idealistic American Founders. The provision "to employ international machinery for the promotion of the economic and social advancement of all peoples" has become the banner of the underdeveloped Third World governments' attempt to grab the wealth of the developed nations.[12] The provision that nothing contained in the Charter "shall authorize the U.N. to intervene in matters which are essentially within the domestic jurisdiction of any state" did not prevent Soviet tanks from rumbling into Czechoslovakia in 1968. As the Soviet delegate to the U.N. argued at the time, "events in Czechoslovakia were a matter for the Czechoslovakian people and the states of the Socialist community, linked together as they were by common responsibilities, and for them alone."[13] The Security Council, as a result, did nothing to help the Czechs.

Another institutional flaw was soon reflected in the staffing problems of the U.N. Secretariat. In addition to the pathetic inefficiency for which that office is now known,[14] there is growing evidence of "political pressure and interference exerted by member governments at all levels of the Secretariat in the areas of

recruitment and promotion."[15] Major offenders are the Soviet Union and its satellites, which regard as legitimate the use of political pressure to affect personnel decisions. According to Moynihan, moreover, Moscow has violated Article 100 of the U.N. Charter, by placing Soviet KGB agents in the Secretariat.[16] Two Soviet U.N. employees arrested by the FBI in 1979 were subsequently convicted of espionage. Former U.N. Secretary General Kurt Waldheim even appointed a KGB officer as head of Personnel in Geneva, where the U.N. now has more employees than at its New York headquarters. In fact, according to Arkady Shevchenko, the highest ranked Soviet official at the U.N. before his defection in 1978, a very high percentage of Soviet delegates assigned to the U.N. Secretariat and other internationally staffed U.N. organizations, as well as the Soviets' own U.N. mission, report in one way or another to the KGB. A highly respected Swiss daily, the *Tribune de Geneve*, noted in its March 12, 1980, article "The KGB in Geneva," that "in terms of numbers, the Genevan capital represents the No. 1 stronghold of the Soviet secret service"—anywhere from 25 to 60 percent according to Western counterespionage. And Arnaud de Borchgrave wrote in *Newsweek* on May 7, 1979:

Recently, the United Nations organization in Geneva and a dozen other international organizations in Geneva have been infiltrated by a rapidly increasing number of Soviet and East European spies. According to Western intelligence sources and Swiss security officials, 78 of the 300 Soviet employees serving the various organizations are agents of the KGB or GRU, Moscow's civilian and military intelligence services. They work closely with 50 intelligence operatives at the Soviet consulate and mission, with about 130 Swiss-based spies from East Europe and Cuba and with an additional 100 Third World or Swiss nationals recruited by Communist agents. Geneva, with a population of 325,000, has more Soviet-bloc spies per capita than

[11] Russell, *The United Nations and United States Security Policy*, p. 3.

[12] For an attempt at defining the "Third World," see Alfred Reifman, "Developing Countries—Definitions and Data; or Third World, Fourth World, OPEC, and Other Countries," Congressional Research Service, Library of Congress, March 22, 1976.

[13] "Situation in Czechoslovakia," *UN Monthly Chronicle*, August-September 1968, p. 40. For the broader legal and political context of this action see William O. Miller, "Collective Intervention and the Law of the Charter," *Naval War College Review*, April 1970, pp. 71-100.

[14] See Robert Rhodes James, *Staffing the U.N. Secretariat* (Sussex, England: Institute for the Study of International Organizations, 1970); *Report of the Joint Inspection Unit on Personnel Problems in the U.N.*, a/6454, October 5, 1971 (New York: UN, 1971); also Richard Gardner, ed., *The Future of the U.N. Secretariat* (New York: UNITAR, 1977).

[15] Seymour Maxwell Finger and Nina Hanan, "The United Nations Secretariat Revisited," *Orbis*, Spring 1981, p. 198. It is noteworthy that the Under Secretary for Political and Security Council Affairs has always been a Russian appointee.

[16] Testimony of Senator Daniel Patrick Moynihan of New York in Hearings before the Subcommittee on International Organizations of the Committee on Foreign Affairs, House of Representatives, *U.S. Participation in the U.N. and U.N. Reform*, March 22, 1979, p. 11.

any other city in the West—and many diplomats contend that their presence is undermining the work of the United Nations.

The exact number of KGB spies at the U.N. cannot, of course, be known in the West. Yet the FBI appears to have a fairly good idea; Senator Jesse Helms of North Carolina has repeatedly requested publication of those figures.[17] Finally, allegations that Secretariat officials have been taking payoffs from individuals seeking jobs are currently being investigated by a Secretariat committee.

In addition to the potential espionage activities of Secretariat staffers, there are many opportunities for spying for members of the various delegations to the U.N. This may have been one of the reasons why the U.S.S.R. insisted that the U.N. be located in the U.S.[18] Some U.N. diplomats have also expressed concern over the inexplicably large number of staff members of other Communist missions, notably the Cuban.[19]

Though the Charter and Secretariat bear considerable responsibility for today's disillusion with the U.N., the major culprits are the Security Council and the General Assembly and its affiliated agencies.

DISAPPOINTMENT WITH THE SECURITY COUNCIL

The Security Council might have been a powerful instrument for keeping peace. But given the ideologi-

cal gulf between the Soviet Union and the other permanent members of the Security Council (the United Kingdom, France, Nationalist China, and the U.S.), it could never have performed its principal function. In the first two decades alone, the Soviet Union cast over 100 vetoes. Half of them killed membership applications from countries with non-communist governments. This made it impossible to create an international organization as broad as possible (within the limits of the Charter) and certainly frustrated the desires of the U.S.

Other Soviet vetoes:

• five vetoes (on September 20, 1946, July 29, twice on August 19, September 15, 1947) to protect Greece's Communist neighbors during the Greek civil war of 1946–1947, by refusing to endorse Security Council resolutions to investigate the conflicts in Northern Greece;

• the veto on May 24, 1948 of a U.N. probe into the Communist take-over of Czechoslovakia;

• the veto on October 25, 1948 of U.N. efforts calling for action to resolve the Berlin blockade;

• vetoes of resolutions on Korea on September 6, 12, and November 30, 1950, where U.N. action against Communist aggression was originally undertaken only because the Soviet Union had been absent from the Security Council on June 25, 1950;

• the veto of a Security Council resolution on November 4, 1956, calling upon the U.S.S.R. to desist from the use of force in Hungary;

• vetoes of U.N. actions concerning the Congo (on September 16 and December 13, 1960, and then again in 1961—two vetoes on February 20 and two on November 24).

The Congo provides a good example of Soviet tactics and American response. Dissatisfied with U.N. activities in that area, Moscow decided not to pay its assessed $40 million share of the cost of African peace-keeping, despite a ruling by the International Court of Justice that it was obliged to pay. In the face of Soviet adamancy, the U.S. backed down and chose to ignore Article 19 of the Charter, which stipulates that a two-year payment delinquency by a member state is punishable by expulsion. Though Congress approved a $100 million bond issue in 1962 to bail out the U.N. only after obtaining a firm pledge that Washington would not let the Soviet Union get away with nonpayment, the U.S. nevertheless decided not to press the issue two years later. According to the latest State Department figures, the Soviet Union

---

[17] The discussion of KGB infiltration in the U.N. may be found in "Nomination of Jeane J. Kirkpatrick," Hearing before the Committee on Foreign Relations, U.S. Senate, 97th Congress, 1st Session, especially pp. 99–106.

[18] Trygve Lie in his book *In the Cause of Peace: Seven Years with the U.N.* (New York: The Macmillan Company, 1954) records that the British delegate Philip Noel-Baker had been against a U.S. site, while "Andrei Gromyko of the U.S.S.R. had come out flatly for the U.S. As to where in the U.S., let the American Government decide, he had blandly told his colleagues. Later the Soviet Union modified its stand to support the East Coast." (p. 60). See also Angie L. Magnusson, "Location of the United Nations," Library of Congress Study, July 27, 1967, unpublished.

[19] "Many Western diplomats believe that Cuba's U.N. mission is, indeed, a nest of spies. . . . Westerners point out that Cuba's U.N. mission numbers 43, while countries of comparable population such as Madagascar, Belgium, and Greece maintain staffs of a dozen or under. 'If the Cubans are not spying, what do they need all those people for?' asks one suspicious European diplomat. 'There just isn't that much paperwork for a nation that small.'" *U.S. News & World Report,* September 22, 1980, p. 21.

remains delinquent: it owes the U.N. a staggering $180,035,000—most of it for peace-keeping operations.

Equally troublesome has been U.S. readiness to endorse the Security Council double-standard. On November 20, 1965, and then again on May 29, 1968, the Council voted mandatory sanctions against Rhodesia's new government headed by Ian Smith. Some observers questioned the wisdom of having the U.S. delegation go along with this: *U.S. News & World Report*, for instance, saw the action as "cracking down on a country at peace" while the U.N. ignored "Red aggression in Asia."[20] But U.S. Ambassador Arthur Goldberg countered that in Rhodesia "we have witnessed an illegal seizure of power by a small minority bent on perpetuating the subjugation of the vast majority."[21] Could the same not be said of the Soviet Union? Indeed, the sanctions against Rhodesia forced the U.S. to buy chrome, a strategic mineral, from the Soviet Union, at a greatly increased price. Senator Harry F. Byrd, Jr., of Virginia was thus prompted to introduce an amendment—not approved by the Congress until 1977—to permit the U.S. to import strategic materials from Rhodesia if those items were also being bought from Communist nations.

In the seventies, the U.S. found itself increasingly on the losing side. The Security Council seat of Nationalist China was given to the People's Republic of China in 1971, while the U.S. compromise proposal that Taiwan be allowed to retain a seat in the General Assembly was soundly defeated.

Now finding itself, as Moynihan puts it, "in opposition," the U.S. turned reluctantly to the weapon it had abjured for a quarter century: the veto. Washington cast its first Security Council nay on March 17, 1970, joining the United Kingdom in blocking a resolution which would have condemned Britain's refusal to use force against the Ian Smith regime in Southern Rhodesia, and would have severed all diplomatic, consular, economic, military, and other relations with that country. Then-U.S. Ambassador to the U.N. Charles W. Yost said that it was a "most serious" decision for the U.S. to veto a resolution of the Security Council but that the U.S. could not support a move implicitly calling on Britain to use force to overthrow the Smith regime, nor could it

agree to measures that cut off the means by which Americans might leave Rhodesia.

Two years later, on September 10, 1972, the U.S. stood alone in its veto of a resolution that called for an immediate halt to military operations in the Middle East but failed to mention the terrorist acts—the Israeli Olympic team murders—that led to Israeli strikes against Syria and Lebanon. U.S. Secretary of State William P. Rogers said that the U.S. intended to use the veto again; too often in the past, he told reporters, other delegations had persuaded the U.S. to soften its position so that the Soviet Union or some other permanent member of the Security Council would not use the veto.[22] In 1973, the U.S. vetoed another Security Council resolution concerning the Middle East, only to witness, a year later, the spectacle of the General Assembly welcoming to its podium Yassir Arafat, the Chairman of the Palestine Liberation Organization, a Soviet-backed terrorist organization dedicated to the annihilation of Israel. This was the first time that a representative of any group lacking official U.N. status had appeared before the General Assembly.

Also in 1974, the U.S., along with Britain and France, blocked a resolution to expel South Africa from the U.N. Whatever one may think of South Africa's separatist policies, they argue, that country represents no great threat to international peace—no greater, certainly, than the U.S.S.R.—and is thus entitled to participate in the Assembly.

Some comfort might be gained from the belief that the Security Council, if often ineffective, at least did not harm the U.S. But according to another point of view, ably articulated by Senator Henry Jackson of Washington, the U.N. prevented the U.S. from acting more vigorously in pursuit of its own interests. And the very existence of the U.N. might have hampered a wiser definition of American national interest.

DISAPPOINTMENTS IN THE GENERAL ASSEMBLY

The principal action of the U.N. takes place in the General Assembly. This is due in part to the paralysis of the Security Council. Indeed, as soon as the U.S. recognized that the Security Council would be at the mercy of Soviet vetoes, it turned to the General Assembly in the hope that it could appeal to the moral sense of the majority of its members. The U.S. took

[20] "Double Standard for U.N.? Action on Rhodesia and Vietnam," *U.S. News & World Report*, April 25, 1966, p. 50.

[21] U.S. Department of State Press Release 304, December 29, 1966, p. 6.

[22] M. A. Farrar, "U.S. to Use U.N. Veto More, Rogers Says," *New York Times*, October 15, 1972.

advantage of Article 10, which empowers the Assembly to discuss any questions or matter "within the scope of the present Charter or relating to the powers and functions of any organs provided for in the present Charter." This made it possible for the U.S. to propose the "Uniting for Peace Resolution" on November 3, 1950, to deal with the Korean crisis. The General Assembly asserted its right to meet in emergency session whenever there was a threat to the peace and the Security Council was unable to agree upon a course of action. That resolution added to the prestige, if not the power, of the General Assembly.[23] In retrospect, however, it is questionable whether the prestige of the Assembly should have been enhanced. By the mid-1970s, the Assembly had become a center of anti-Western rhetoric and action. Some examples are:

• inflammatory rhetoric condemning the U.S. and its allies on almost every political, economic and social issue;
• measures designed to redistribute to the developing states the economic resources of the industrial nations, especially the U.S., and to control the activities of Western businessmen;
• measures designed to curtail the free flow of information;
• measures to aid terrorists.

INFLAMMATORY RHETORIC

The crescendo of inflammatory rhetoric under the auspices of the General Assembly is one of the most disturbing features of that organization. Initially, it was the Soviet Union that delivered the anti-American speeches. After 1961, when the size of U.N. membership had more than doubled, the attacks echoed in other quarters as well. Ideology was being formed, and terms redefined. In 1961, for example, India's Krishna Menon stated that "colonialism is permanent aggression." The phrase was soon to assume a life of its own. Professor Ali A. Mazrui explains:

This became an important theme in Afro-Asian

argumentation mainly following India's annexation of Goa. . . . The more militant attitude toward colonialism which now characterizes the General Assembly both reflects and helps to consolidate new attitudes toward that phenomenon. And even the criteria of what constitutes domestic jurisdiction and external intervention and interference may imperceptibly be undergoing a legal *re*-definition as the old principles are newly tossed around in the tussle of United Nations politics.[24]

A few years later, in 1965 and in 1966, the General Assembly declared the continuation of colonial rule and the practice of racial discrimination to be crimes against humanity and threats to international peace. These words later would be used by the Soviet Union and Third World delegates to attack the U.S. action in Vietnam, the policies of South Africa and the actions of Israel—among others.

Throughout the sixties, the U.S. was charged increasingly with enormous crimes against humanity. Among them was "racism." As early as 1964, when the U.S. joined Belgium to send a mercy mission to Stanleyville in the Congo to rescue not only whites but Asians and blacks as well who were suffering from the war in that area, eighteen black African governments protested that the mercy lift was an act of aggression, colonialism, and imperialism.

By 1971, the U.S. was routinely being condemned as an imperialist aggressor in the halls of the General Assembly. In November of that year, when the representative of the People's Republic of China replaced the Taiwanese delegate at the U.N., a decisive turn against the U.S. had taken place. The U.S. had previously been able to marshall enough support

---

[24] Ali A. Mazrui writes in his article "The U.N. and Some African Political Attitudes":

Krishna Menon started invoking the concept of "permanent aggression" to reporters (the BBC broadcasted the doctrine) even before he arrived at the U.N. . . . Professor W. H. Abraham of Ghana lent philosophical backing to Menon's approach by reaffirming that "colonialism is aggression." [See his *Mind of Africa* (London: Weidenfeld and Nicholson, 1962), p. 152.] This idiom may have started as merely figurative use of the word "aggression." But it would not be the first instance in which a figurative use of a given term later took on a literal meaning as well.

International Organization, vol. XVIII, No. 3, Summer 1964, p. 506.

---

[23] Besides being invoked during the Korean crisis, the "Uniting for Peace" Resolution has been used eight times. One recent case was in 1980 to respond to the Soviet invasion of Afghanistan, and another was in September of 1981 to condemn South Africa's occupation in Namibia.

to block Peking's admission to the U.N. The seating of Peking symbolized America's shrinking power in the U.N. In his acceptance speech, the Chinese ambassador accused the U.S. of aggression for sending U.S. naval forces into the Taiwan Strait, and for military intervention in Vietnam, Cambodia, and Laos. George Bush, then-U.S. Ambassador to the U.N., chastised the Chinese for "intemperate language" and for firing "empty cannons of rhetoric."

Volleys were fired constantly from other Third World nations. Consider the outrageous statement by M. S. Aulagi, representative of South Yemen, in the General Assembly on October 11, 1971:

> The insistence of the U.S. in continuing [its imperialist and colonialist] policies, which are in contradiction of the interests of humanity in progress and cooperation, will lead that country once again into isolation and eclipse, against its own will.

In fact, reading through speeches made by representatives from Cuba, Libya, Niger, Albania, and most of the other Third World nations over the next decade reveals a disturbing rhetorical battle. Yet is has taken years for the U.S. to realize its significance. It is this which prompted Moynihan in 1975 to accuse the U.S. of "complacency" which could only be due, he charged, to "the failure to perceive that a distinctive ideology was at work [in the Third World], and that skill and intelligence were required to deal with it successfully."[25]

A major victory for the proponents of that ideology was the condemnation, on November 10, 1975, of Zionism as a "form of racism." This move so outraged American lawmakers, who saw the resolution as an insult to language and to common sense, that many questioned whether the U.S. should continue contributing money to the U.N. The following day, the Senate unanimously called for prompt hearings to "reassess the U.S.' further participation in the U.N."[26] In the Senate debate, Robert Packwood of

Oregon said, "I can't think of anything in the last 30 years as odious. Wherever Hitler may be I am sure he drank a toast to the devil last night."[27]

A more recent case of the anti-American offensive took place at the end of September 1981, when ninety-three Third World nations endorsed a document accusing the U.S. of being the only threat to world peace and prosperity today. Then on October 1, Ethiopian Foreign Minister Feleke Gedle-Giorgis unleashed a tirade from the General Assembly podium.

> International imperialism, spearheaded by the United States, has intensified its futile effort to reverse national liberation and social emancipation in southern Africa. . . . We are being daily threatened by United States imperialism. There are some ten United States military bases in and around our region alone. These keep a constant watch on countries in the region which are not amenable to Washington's dictate. The now all too familiar bogey being employed is, of course, the Soviet threat. No one, except those who worship the demi-god in Washington, will be fooled by such a smoke-screen.

Gedle-Giorgis went on to claim that the U.S. was "bent on dominating the people of Africa, Asia, Latin America and the Caribbean."

The next afternoon, U.S. Ambassador to the U.N. Jeane Kirkpatrick stingingly countered with a hard-hitting speech condemning the Ethiopian minister's "strident and vituperative attack on the United States." She accused him of the "Big Lie":

> The pattern is a simple one: He accuses others of committing crimes which have, in fact, been perpetrated by his own regime and by those countries with which his regime is allied. . . . He speaks, for example, of "the determination of Africans". . . . In fact, it is his own regime that is guilty of the very savagery of which he speaks. . . . It is estimated that some 30,000 persons in Ethiopia were summarily executed for political reasons between 1974 and 1978—10,000 in 1977 alone.

Adding that Cambodia "is occupied by 200,000 troops

---

[25] "The United States in Opposition," p. 36.

[26] This was not a move to get the U.S. out of the U.N. Rather, it was a call for a reassessment of U.S. participation in the U.N. Calls to get the U.S. out of the U.N. have been made in Congress ever since 1950 (H.R. 5080 and H.R. 5081, both asking to rescind membership of the U.S. in the U.N.). Many other similar bills have been introduced (e.g., H.R. 164 on January 4, 1965; H.R. 11465 on July 13, 1967; H.R. 360 and H.R. 2632, both in January 1971) but none have met with much support.

[27] See Daniel Patrick Moynihan, *A Dangerous Place*, Chapters 9 and 10, for a detailed description of the circumstances surrounding the vote.

from Vietnam,'' the Ambassador said *these* are the 'imperialist meddlers.'" In her closing words, she expressed U.S. commitment to international cooperation, but warned that this country, "cannot sit by quietly when the Big Lie echoes in these chambers." The speech expressed well the frustration of the American people when faced with such rhetoric.

It is this Big Lie that has made a mockery of General Assembly human rights discussions. As Ambassador Kirkpatrick said on November 24, 1981, "no aspect of United Nations affairs has been more perverted by politicization in the last decade than have its human rights activities." Moreover, what the U.N. has not done is no less part of the record, with all the cries of outrage it has not uttered, all the moral indignation it did not express. The human rights agencies of the United Nations have been silent while 3 million Cambodians died in Pol Pot's murderous Utopia; the human rights agencies of the United Nations have been silent while a quarter of a million Ugandans died at the hands of Idi Amin. The human rights organizations of the United Nations have been silent about the thousands of Soviet citizens denied equal rights, equal protection of the law, denied the right to think, write, publish, work freely, or to emigrate to some place of their own choosing.

ECONOMIC MEASURES

More serious than the rhetorical offensive, however, are the actions by the General Assembly and its related agencies which attempt to redistribute U.S. resources and to regulate activities of American businessmen dealing in the Third World. Although not explicitly coordinated, the regulatory programs debated and sometimes adopted at the U.N. share common principles and common methods of implementation.

One of the earliest attempts to use the U.N. to transform rapidly the economics of the Third World was the U.N. Conference on Trade and Development (UNCTAD). Established in 1964 as a permanent body for formulating general rules on trade between rich and poor countries, UNCTAD soon began working on so-called codes of conduct designed specifically to help non-Western nations. UNCTAD also served as midwife at the birth of the U.N. Charter of Economic Rights and Duties of States, adopted on December 12, 1974, by a General Assembly vote of 120 to 6

(including the U.S.), with 10 abstentions.[28] A new breed of self-styled international regulators cites this charter, along with The New International Economic Order (NIEO), to justify schemes for recasting world economic relations.[29] In essence, these efforts aim at creating an elaborate system of redistribution which would compel the U.S. to share its technological resources and output with developing nations.[30]

Perhaps the most celebrated of the efforts for a new economic order is the draft treaty by the U.N. Conference on the Law of the Sea which has been meeting since 1973. It would create a major multilateral body called "the Seabed Authority," authorized to allocate mining sites, conduct its own seabed explorations, control private competitors and levy its own taxes.

In March 1981, before the opening of what was to be the Law of the Sea Conference's final session, the Reagan Administration announced that it would not, as the Carter Administration had agreed, conclude the treaty by May 1981. The reasons for the delay, explained by the Administration, are that the Law of the Sea treaty, as it stands,

- discriminates against private mining enterprise;
- inadequately protects development investments made before the treaty's effective date;
- fails to make any provisions for arbitration of disputes between the mining industry and governments; and
- fails to make any provisions for arbitration of

[28] The Economic Charter was adopted in GA Res. 3281 (XXIX), 29 UN GAOR, Supp. (No. 31) 50, UN Doc. A/9631 (1974). The countries that joined the U.S. in its vote against the Charter were Belgium, Denmark, the Federal Republic of Germany, Luxemburg, and the United Kingdom.

[29] "The Economic Charter, a consensual U.N. declaration, arguably has legal force that delineates the rights and duties of member states." Edward A. Laing, "International Economic Law and Public Order in the Age of Equality," *Law & Policy in International Business*, vol. 12: 727, 1980, p. 754. Laing's article provides useful background discussion and analysis of the history and implications of the Economic Charter.

[30] See Richard Berryman and Richard Schifter, "A Global Straightjacket," *Regulation*, September/October 1981, pp. 19–28. For a good discussion of the implications of U.N. regulatory action see Raymond J. Waldham, *Regulating International Business Through Code of Conduct* (Washington and London: American Enterprise Institute, 1980).

disputes between the mining industry and governments; and

- subjects U.S. interests to decisions made by a forum in which the U.S. would carry very little weight.

Other areas potentially rich in important natural resources are also targets of U.N.-inspired international regulation. An Agreement Governing the Activities of States on the Moon and Other Celestial Bodies took effect in 1980; it establishes an international regime to govern exploration and extraction activities in outer space with an eye to favoring the enterprises of developing nations. Lacing this agreement are theoretical implications hostile to the principles of free enterprise. Though Jimmy Carter eventually decided not to endorse the treaty, the issue is by no means dead.

Another scheme designed to benefit the developing nations at potentially great cost to the Western industrial societies is the Code of Restrictive Business Practices, adopted by the General Assembly in 1980. This Code forces multinational corporations to sell their technology and know-how more cheaply and less efficiently for the benefit of Third World nations.[31]

An equally alarming UNCTAD action is the Code of Conduct for Liner Conferences to take effect when the European Economic Community ratifies it, as it soon is expected to do. This Code aims at promoting the maritime industries of developing nations by allocating shipping tonnage.[32] If the Code goes into effect this year—and it may—it could bring some far-reaching changes to American shipping:

- freight rates would be subject to large jumps every fifteen months;

- the U.S. could lose liner cargoes because these would be shifted to more specialized carriers;
- American laws would have to be changed extensively, resulting in increased regulations; and
- disputes would be settled by a conciliation process; this reverses the longstanding U.S. practice of maintaining open liner conferences and ignores U.S. laws requiring that government and government-financed shipments be carried by U.S. flagships.

The disadvantages to signing the Code may be less onerous, however, than outright refusal to ratify, which would leave the U.S. out of important negotiations that might permit working out mutually acceptable arrangements.[33]

Another major target of U.N. regulatory activity is the pharmaceutical industry. During the past six years, four different U.N. entities—UNCTAD, the U.N. Center for Transnational Corporations, the U.N. Industrial Development Organization (UNIDO), and the World Health Organization (WHO)—have begun trying to control pharmaceuticals. WHO, for instance, has passed a code recommending regulation of breast-milk substitutes; this has serious implications for the regulation of food products in general, and drugs in particular. UNIDO is trying to redistribute the revenues of the pharmaceutical companies by limiting royalties and prices; it is also seeking ways to obtain licensing information and technology transfer for the benefit of underdeveloped countries. Moreover, WHO is planning to regulate drug quality by establishing a body that would, in effect, supersede the U.S. Food and Drug Administration. In his "Background Paper on the North/South Dialogue and the New International Economic Order," prepared for the Pharmaceutical Manufacturers Association in June 1980, Paul Belford complains: these efforts "have generally been politically motivated, poorly researched, and biased against private industry."

The regulatory efforts of the U.N. and its agencies are heading full-speed ahead into 1982. The General Assembly, for example, has instructed the Centre on

---

[31] A useful discussion of international regulation affecting the transnational corporation may be found in *Studies in Transnational Economic Law*, vol. I: *Legal Problems of Codes of Conduct for Multinational Enterprises*, edited by Norbert Horn (Deventer, the Netherlands: Kluwer Publishers, 1980).

[32] For a useful recent analysis of the Liner Code see Stefan Lopatin, "The UNCTAD Code of Conduct for Liner Conferences: Time for a U.S. Response," 22 *Harvard International Law Journal*, 1981, pp. 355 ff. For a brief discussion of the development of the liner conference system, see Department of Transportation, "Potential Economic Impact Non-Market Cargo Allocation in U.S. Foreign Trade," Report No. DOT-TSC OST-76-31, pp. 19–20.

[33] For a fine, thorough study of the Liner Code and various options available to the U.S., see the four-volume study by E. G. Frankel, Inc., entitled "Impact of Cargo Sharing on U.S. Liner Trade with Countries in the Far East and South East Asia," released by the Federal Maritime Commission in late December 1981.

Transnational Corporations on December 22, 1981, to prepare a "register" of profits as part of an effort to regulate the economic activities of foreign interests which ostensibly impede the achievement of independence by peoples under "colonial domination" as defined in the Declaration of Independence to Colonial Countries and Peoples. The United States and other Western countries strongly opposed the resolution calling for this "register" on the grounds that it was ideologically motivated and completely failed to recognize the benefits of foreign investments in developing areas.

The economic offensive against the industrial nations shows no sign of abating. Indeed, the new Secretary General of the U.N., Javier Perez de Cuellar of Peru, has called on the U.N. to continue and accelerate its efforts at redistribution. In his speech of December 15, 1981, Cuellar noted that he was assuming his new post at a time when "the longstanding initiative for the renewal of global negotiations between North and South is coming back within the purview of the U.N. . . . This coincides with one of the most serious world economic crises of the past few decades, the most sorely pressed victims of which are the populations of the developing countries." By way of relief, he proposes to champion the cause of those whose "right to a better distribution of wealth and social well-being [is] in fact being infringed."

THREATS TO THE FREE FLOW OF INFORMATION

Better covered by the press than efforts to regulate business activities are plans by the U.N. Educational, Scientific, and Cultural Organization (UNESCO) to censor the flow of information. Since a 1976 Conference in Nairobi, UNESCO has been at work outlining a New World Information Order (NWIO) whose principal purpose is to alter the role of the media.[34] The Third World governments want to use the press to further their national ideologies. To this end, UNESCO produced a study in 1980 entitled *Many Voices—One World* which recommends that journalists be "licensed" and "protected" and calls for a code of ethics for journalists. Congressman John J. Rhodes of Arizona commented:

Understandably, the U.S.—and, in fact, all nations that cherish a free press and the free flow of information—strongly oppose implementation of the NWIO. Questions of news content and news values do not belong on intergovernmental agendas.[35]

An amendment to a State Department Authorization bill, which goes to conference in February 1982, would provide that none of the funds that go toward the assessed U.S. contribution to UNESCO will be paid in the event that the NWIO is implemented.

This is not the first time the U.S. has threatened to cut off funds to a U.N. agency. In November 1975, for example, the U.S. withdrew from the International Labor Organization (ILO) largely because of objections by American labor organizations. The list of American grievances included the ILO's recognition in June 1974 of an observer from the PLO, as well as the double-standard implicit in the ILO attacks on the human rights record of such countries as Chile and Tanzania while remaining silent on the Soviet and Eastern European dictatorships. At congressional hearings on May 12, 1981, Ambassador Kirkpatrick recommended the U.S. cut off funds from the ILO and urged using that method again. "I think that we have in a way acquiesced in the perversion of a good many of the U.N. agencies and activities," she said, "by failing to object as vigorously as we should have, or to demonstrate our unhappiness, for example, by withholding funds." She was especially concerned that such agencies as UNESCO, the U.N. Environment Program (UNEP), and the Women's Decade Conference, have been transformed into platforms for anti-U.S. demagoguery.

U.N. AID TO TERRORISTS

Since November 13, 1974, when Yassir Arafat appeared before the General Assembly, the PLO has enjoyed observer status at the U.N. Food and Agricultural Organization, joined the U.N. Economic and Social Council's Commission for Western Asia (the first time a non-nation had been granted full membership in a U.N. agency), and was authorized to use U.N. funds for propaganda purposes by the U.N.-sponsored Mid-Decade Women's Conference held in Copenhagen in July 1980.

---

[34] An enormous amount of material has been written on the NWIO. A concise set of papers was included in The Media Institute's *Issues in International Information*, vol. I, distributed on November 13, 1981, and vol. II, forthcoming.

[35] *Human Events*, December 12, 1981, p. 17.

As Evelyn Sommer testified before Congress in May 1981, she was shocked by the fact that *Forum 80*, the daily newspaper of the Copenhagen conference funded by the U.S., carried interviews with PLO members. On January 30, 1981, the U.N. Postal Administration even went so far as to issue a set of three stamps commemorating the "Inalienable Rights of the Palestinian People." The main sponsor of the stamp project was the Committee on the Exercise of the Inalienable Rights of the Palestinian People which, according to Congressman Hamilton Fish, Jr., of New York, "is merely a front in the U.N. for the PLO."

Another terrorist group that receives U.N. assistance is the South West African People's Organization (SWAPO). According to a 1979 study by the London-based Foreign Affairs Research Institute:

> The United Nations Commissioner for Namibia, his three offices in New York, Luanda and Botswana, the UN Council for Namibia, the UN Fund for Namibia and the UN approved Institute for Namibia are all organizations which co-operate closely with SWAPO as the "sole authentic representative of the Namibian People." All are bodies in receipt of generous funds from the UN budget. The UN Commission for Refugees and the Economic and Social Council's United Nations Development Programme are other organizations providing "humanitarian aid" on a lavish scale for refugees and others from Namibia. The United Nations Development Programme (UNDP) provided $31,500 to SWAPO for "education and training in the field of public information" during the year 1976–1977. It has also provided $151,000 in general education assistance to SWAPO within Angola.[36]

Almost as an aside, the report adds: "During the course of raids by the South African Army on SWAPO bases in Angola during the summer of 1979, food cartons . . . originating from the UN's world food programme were found in the camps."

On October 2, 1978, SWAPO president Sam Nujo-

ma told a meeting of non-aligned nations in New York that his organization shares a common bond of militant comradery and solidarity with Rhodesia's terrorist Patriotic Front, the terrorist PLO, and "other gallant forces of liberation."

Moreover, there is evidence that UNICEF has been helping terrorists: for example, in 1979, UNICEF money turned up in Mozambique following a raid by troops from Zimbabwe-Rhodesia. Consequently, there are calls in Congress for both the State Department appropriations bill and the Foreign Assistance Act appropriations bill to contain a specific prohibition against the use of tax dollars by the U.N. to finance terrorism.[37] Neither of these bills, however, contains any provision to prohibit tax dollars from use in programs that finance SWAPO.

SELECTED ABUSES

In addition to measures which could seriously impair the activities of American businessmen and journalists, the U.N. is plagued by other abuses which call into question the organization's usefulness. Among them:

• Fraud. According to *Business Week* on July 20, 1981:

> The evidence is mounting that the U.N.'s $300 million plus economic research programmes are being manipulated to promote the "new international economic order". . . . Appointments to the organization's professional staff of 3,000 economists have become increasingly politicized and, more important, numerous studies of world trade and growth—many of them by outside experts—have been suppressed, altered, or so stripped of detail that they have become useless as a basis for setting policy.

> Professor Ingo Walter of New York University and other consultants charge that some of the most egregious instances of altered work have occurred at UNCTAD.

• Misallocation of Resources. On November 15, 1981, CBS-TV's "60 Minutes" spotlighted the inefficiencies of UNICEF and other U.N. organizations in helping refugees, particularly in Uganda in the Spring of 1980. At UNICEF, politicization is also a serious

---

[36] Cited in Robert E. Lee, *The United Nations Conspiracy*, pp. 208–209. Elsewhere, the F.A.R.I. report asserts: "Despite its [SWAPO's] lack of military success, incessant lobbying at the United Nations resulted in the astonishing decision [by the General Assembly] to grant it recognition as the sole legal representative of the Namibian people despite the known minority nature of its support."

[37] See *Congressional Record*, October 5, 1981, p. E4628.

problem. The UNICEF Executive Board, for example, in 1970 approved a $200,000 purchase of cloth for North Vietnamese children's clothing. It was purchased from the Soviet Union and supposedly was delivered to North Vietnam by the Soviet Union in 1972. UNICEF has no way of making sure, however, that the supplies were actually distributed to children.

• Indoctrination. Some U.N. activities are used to indoctrinate the participants. As Evelyn Sommer told Congress in May 1981, the Women's Decade Conference shocked her with "the brutal indoctrination espoused by many of the forum's participants"; she was also disturbed by the draft declaration submitted originally by East Germany and other Communist and so-called non-aligned countries, which is "an anti-West, hypocritical, controversial document that has no value whatsoever in achieving progress for women."

• Puerto Rico. In September of 1972, by a 12 to 0 vote, with 10 abstentions, the U.N. Special Committee on Colonialism ordered a study of Puerto Rico as a colonial territory of the U.S. Washington objected that consideration of the island's status was "totally improper" and interfered in the "purely domestic affairs of the U.S." On August 20, 1981, however, the Committee—composed largely of Soviet bloc and Third World nations—returned to the issue over the protest of the U.S. For the moment, the U.S. has prevented a General Assembly discussion of the issue; should the Assembly take it up in the future, however, it would undoubtedly become a real problem.

• Representation in the Statistical Commission. For the first time in U.N. history, the U.S. in May 1981 was denied a seat on the Statistical Commission. This shocked the U.S. and its allies. Said Ambassador Kirkpatrick, "we—by not sitting on that commission —are denied an opportunity to effectively or even ineffectively work hard to influence its policies." She suggested "that our contribution in the form, for example, of technical expertise, ought also to be reduced commensurate with our opportunity for input and policies."

CONCLUSION

Not all U.N. activities are flawed, of course. Ambassador Kirkpatrick has praised some of the programs of the World Health Organization, the refugee ef-forts, and meteorological organizations, as well as some of those agencies fighting hunger and advancing science.

The ultimate question, of course, is whether these relatively few praiseworthy programs are worth the cost. While the World Health Organization distributes vaccines, for instance, it is also drafting codes to control Western food and drug companies for the sake of Third World nations. The refugee programs, besides helping the homeless, also aid terrorists. Even the scientific organizations are not immune to politicization. The U.N. Civil Aviation Organization (CAO), for example, granted observer status to the PLO in 1977. It was undoubtedly highly instructive to the terrorists, for the CAO then was discussing ways to prevent air piracy. Other examples abound.

For good reason, therefore, the worth of the U.N. is more suspect than at any time in its history. It was not solely an exaggeration when James J. Kilpatrick wrote on September 22, 1981, in *The Baltimore Sun* that "the purpose [of the U.N.] as a forum has been reduced to a nullity," and suggested that the media "should carry news of the U.N. back on the comic pages to dwell with Doonesbury and his friends." There are questions, too, as to whether the U.S. is benefiting from its U.N. membership, given the paralysis of the Security Council and the anti-American, anti-Western, anti-industrial, anti-capitalist majority in the General Assembly. Is the U.S. getting much of value for all that it is spending in resources and energy on the U.N.? These are questions which the Reagan Administration and the U.S. public must—with urgency—begin addressing.

QUESTIONS FOR DISCUSSION

1 What information should one have to evaluate the effectiveness of the UN?
2 Whose interests does the UN serve?
3 What would be the effect of United States withdrawal from the UN (a) on the UN? and (b) on world politics?
4 Should the UN be most appropriately analyzed simply as an arena within which world politics is played out or as an instrument for multilateral cooperation and decision making by the world community?
5 How can the UN be made a more effective actor in the world political arena?

SUGGESTED READINGS

Buckley, William F., Jr. *United Nations Journal: A Delegate's Odyssey.* New York: Putnam, 1974.

Claude, Inis L., Jr. *Swords into Plowshares: The Problems and Progress of International Organization*, 4th ed. New York: Random House, 1971.

Crozier, B. "Who Needs the UN?" *National Review* (Nov. 28, 1980): 1442.

Finger, Seymour Maxwell, and Joseph R. Harbert (eds.). *U.S. Policy in International Institutions: Defining Reasonable Options in an Unreasonable World.* Foreword by Cyrus Vance. Boulder, Colo.: Westview Press, 1978.

Hazzard, Shirley, *Defeat of an Ideal: A Study of the Self-Destruction of the United Nations.* Boston: Little, Brown, 1973.

Kim, Samuel S. *China, the United Nations, and World Order.* Princeton, N.J.: Princeton University Press, 1979.

Maynes, Charles William. "What's Wrong with the UN and What's Right." *Department of State Bulletin* (January 1979): 46–50.

Moynihan, Daniel Patrick, with Suzanne Weaver. *A Dangerous Place.* Boston: Little, Brown, 1978.

Stoessinger, John G. *The United Nations and the Superpowers: China, Russia, and America.* New York: Random House, 1977.

Waldheim, Kurt. *The Challenge of Peace.* New York: Rawson Wade Publishers, 1980.

Chapter Two

The International System

World War II unleashed forces of political, military, and economic change that transformed power relationships in the global arena. Just as the defeat of Napoleon in 1815 and the defeat of the Central Powers in Europe in 1918 produced new regimes and a new map of the world, so, too, did the conquest of the Axis powers in 1945.

Before World War II, power was dispersed among several countries—principally, Germany, Russia, France, Britain, and Italy—with the United States and Japan playing increasingly prominent roles. The colonial powers of the world—primarily Great Britain and France—ruled over millions of square miles of Africa, Asia, and Latin America.

The Soviet Union and the United States emerged from the war as the two strongest powers of the world. The United States was clearly the stronger power—a superpower in economic and military terms. The United States came out of the war with a vigorous economy—a giant industrial nation. Not only had the United States proved triumphant against its foes, but its military establishment was the only one to possess the atomic bomb, a weapon that has transformed the character of power in the global arena.

The strongest land power in Europe was the Soviet Union, which, as a result of the war, had swept westward to dominate Eastern Europe. Although it had suffered 20 million deaths and enormous property destruction, it was clearly a big power.

Germany was decimated by the war and its territory split into occupation zones by the victorious allies. Japan was suffering economic problems from wartime destruction even before the atomic bombs burst on Hiroshima and Nagasaki. Italy lay in ruins from allied air bombardment and invasion. Britain and France paid a heavy price in lives and wealth for their victory in war.

As indicated in Chapter 1, political observers in 1945 considered the character of the international system in the postwar world. From 1945 to the present, much discussion has centered on the impact of the balance of power and on the interdependence of nations as factors that could possibly transform the international system, and these subjects are considered in this chapter.

The expression, "balance of power," has been used in many ways, and there is no agreement about its definition. It can mean a state of equality or preponderance in power, stability or instability in a political system, and peace or war. The concept has its modern origin in the period following the Treaty of Westphalia in 1648, which ended the devastating Thirty Years War.

We will define a *balance-of-power system* as one characterized by several powerful states in which no one is dominant. In such a system, states seek to maintain their security by preventing any one state from becoming too powerful. In the European balance-of-power system of the period between 1648 and the late eighteenth century, there were several powerful states, no one of which was dominant. The leaders of the European countries shared a common cultural heritage and many were linked through family ties. They also shared a concern for territorial security and took measures to strengthen security. These measures included acquiring territory, strengthening armed forces, and making alliances with other countries.

When in the late seventeenth and early eighteenth centuries, Louis XIV sought to expand the power of France to a degree that the other powers found dangerous, the other powers united to put down that French monarch. The system worked, moreover, to defeat Napoleon's armies, which had gone to war against most of Europe in the late eighteenth and early nineteenth centuries.

Although the balance-of-power system continued after the defeat of Napoleon, new forces undermined that system. These forces included ideologies, democracy, the industrial revolution, and military technology.

As indicated above, the classical balance-of-power system required that the political leaders make foreign-policy decisions based on security considerations. The appearance of new ideologies—most notably nationalism, but also liberalism and socialism—often restrained leaders from acting according to security considerations. With the appearance of nationalism, the discretion of political leaders to redraw boundary lines became constrained. Groups committed to aiding liberal or socialist causes in foreign countries influenced state behavior by urging governments to base foreign policy on considerations of human rights or class solidarity.

Democratic institutions further limited the actions of policymakers. Ethnic, economic, religious, and racial groups influenced foreign policy although their views were at times contrary to the state's security interests.

The industrial revolution created new classes—business and labor—that played important foreign-policy roles. Pressures on governments to promote trade, secure cheap sources of raw materials, and collect debts were powerful forces in the nineteenth and twentieth centuries. Military technology produced more destructive weapons. These weapons affected the civilian population whose popular support for foreign policy became increasingly important.

The classical balance of power was influenced by these new forces. It was not really until the post-World War II period, however, that these forces became global. Before the twentieth century, the balance of power was primarily a European system. This is not to say that non-European countries, such as the United States and Japan, played no role, but rather that the major players of the balancing game were European.

In the post-World War II period, the balance-of-power system took a different form from the classical European model. The new system was characterized by two superpowers whose military strength was so overwhelming that no other nation could become their rival. The system, moreover, was influenced by nuclear weapons.

Nuclear weapons in the arsenals of both superpowers increased enormously so that each side has developed the capacity to annihilate the other. Not only have the superpowers increased their nuclear arsenals (vertical proliferation), but so, too, are more countries becoming nuclear powers (horizontal proliferation). Britain, France, and the People's Republic of China are nuclear-weapons states. India detonated a nuclear device, which it labeled as a peaceful nuclear explosion, in 1974. Israel is reported to possess many of these weapons although it has not tested them. Many more countries could build these weapons in the decades ahead.

The rise of the superpowers, the increase in the number of states playing important global roles, and the appearance and proliferation of nuclear weapons have had an impact on the character of the balance of power.

In addition to the balance of power, the interdependence of nations suggests possible changes in the international system. The interdependence of nations in military, economic, political, social, and ecological matters has led some observers to use expressions like "global village," "spaceship earth," and "the politics of the planet earth" to describe central features of world politics since the end of World War II. Interdependence, like balance of power, lacks a precise meaning, but we shall use it here to signify a situation in which the entire world is tightly linked in an unprecedented way in such matters as military security, trade, monetary exchange, economic investment, ecology, and communications. Such ties may influence the willingness and ability of states to act.

In military matters, the invention, development, and production of nuclear weapons constitute one form of interdependence. Nuclear weapons are so powerful that nearly every nation is concerned with their possible use either by the superpowers or by other countries. The mere above-ground testing of these weapons produces stratospheric fallout containing Strontium 90 and Cesium 137, which can cause cancer and leukemia in distant nations. Countries that are nonnuclear weapons states, consequently, are as much concerned with regulating nuclear tests as are the nuclear-weapons states.

It is perhaps in economic matters that interdependence is most clearly seen. Since the end of World War II, there has been an increase in trade and capital transfers across state lines. Some countries, such as Japan and Great Britain, have been heavily dependent on foreign trade. In contrast, the United States has had only a small percentage of its gross national product directed to foreign trade. Even the United States, however, has been dependent on other countries for the importation of essential resources, such as oil, copper, and uranium—a dependency that has made it vulnerable to political events in distant countries.

The rise in the power of OPEC in the 1970s highlights the importance of oil and the economic interdependence of nations. When the Yom Kippur war took place in 1973 between Israel and some of its neighbors, the Arab members of OPEC announced an embargo of oil exports to the West. That action and subsequent steep rises in the price of OPEC oil promoted inflation and unemployment in the Western economies and severely impeded the economies of third world countries that lacked their own oil resources.

The post-World War II period also featured an increase in capital transfers across national boundary lines. These transfers, in the form of aid, business investments, and loans, made some countries dependent on others. The increase in the number and influence of the multinational corporations is a reflection of the transnational character of economic interdependence, moreover.

As mentioned in Chapter 1, new institutions particularly in the economic realm, were established to cope with the many problems that states could not deal with by themselves. The International Monetary Fund and the International Bank for Reconstruction and Development (World Bank) were two of the most important.

One of the most prominent of the international organizations formed primarily to deal with economic matters among European nations was the European Economic Community (EEC), established in 1958. Originally, the EEC (Common Market) was formed by six European nations—Belgium, France, Italy, Luxembourg, The Netherlands, and West Germany—but now also includes Great Britain, Denmark, Ireland, and Greece. Its goal is to lower tariffs among its members and to stimulate economic growth by reducing the barriers that impede economic development.

Politically, many alliances among nations and meetings among diplomats reflected the new state of interdependence. In the West, the North Atlantic Treaty Organization, and the Organization of American States are examples of the political interaction. The Soviet Union established the Warsaw Pact for its communist allies. The Organization of African Unity served as a vehicle for third world African states to discuss and resolve their common political problems.

Political leaders met in various international arenas. The UN provided a forum for continuous negotiation among diplomats. Summit conferences of heads of government became periodic events, made easier by jet airplanes. Communication networks linked to satellites provided immediate means for discussion among diplomats and political leaders.

In the period since the end of World War II, there has been an increasing flow of people from one country to another. Refugees seeking political freedom or economic opportunities flocked to countries that would receive them. After World War II, the flow originated primarily from Europe. Later, there were major refugee exoduses from countries such as India, Vietnam, Cuba, and Haiti. Tourists used jet aircraft to vacation outside their own countries. Even communist countries that had been closed to most Westerners were opened up largely because of a need for hard currency.

Ecological interdependence in a world becoming more economically developed took many forms. Pollution of the oceans endangered fishing interests and created an international need for control. Infectious diseases respected no territorial limits.

Few would argue with the fact of interdependence in many areas. What is in dispute, however, is the significance of this interdependence on the character of world politics.

BALANCE OF POWER

As a central concept of international politics, balance of power continues to engage the attention of social scientists. Does the balance of power work in the nuclear age? To answer that question, an assessment must be made as to whether the number of actors affects the balance of power, whether nuclear weapons make the balance of power irrelevant, and whether the traditional functions of the balance of power are performed in contemporary world politics either on a global or regional scale.

Hedley Bull argues that a balance-of-power system operates today and fulfills the same functions in relation to international order that it has performed in other historical periods. It is a complex or multilateral balance of power involving China, the United States, the Soviet Union, Japan, and potentially a united Western Europe. Power in such a system does not mean that each principal actor is equal in influence to the other. Rather, different actors have variable power to make international moves on different "chessboards," such as nuclear weapons, conventional military strength, international monetary affairs and international trade and investment, and ideological appeal. According to Bull, the contemporary balance of power, like earlier balancing systems, fulfills the same three functions: (1) it prevents the system of states from becoming a universal empire; (2) local balances of power, where they exist, serve to protect the independence of states in particular areas from absorption or domination by a locally predominant power; and (3) it allows the conditions for those institutions on which international order depends, such as international law, diplomacy, and the management of the system by the great powers.

To political scientist Stanley Hoffmann, the balance-of-power system is outmoded because the conditions for such a system to exist are no longer present. These conditions are: (1) five or six major actors; (2) a central balancing mechanism in which the main actors would coalesce to prevent the expansion of one or more powers; (3) the existence of a common language and code of behavior among the major actors; and (4) a hierarchy in the international system that is relatively simple. Hoffmann points to the contemporary forces that make the balance of power irrelevant: the emergence of two superpowers; the development of nuclear weapons; misperceptions, misunderstandings, and differing goals among the world's leaders as well as the heterogeneity of many nations along ethnic, class, and ideological lines; the increase in the number of nations; and the rise of global economic interdependence.

INTERDEPENDENCE

Some degree of interdependence has been prevalent in the world for centuries. The debate below deals with the impact of interdependence on changing the character of the international system. To evaluate the arguments, it is essential to consider whether the world is becoming more or less interdependent; whether countries that are interdependent are more or less likely to resort to war with each other; and whether security goals are made subordinate to welfare and economic objectives for those countries experiencing a high level of interdependence.

Yoshikazu Sakamoto, Professor of Law at the University of Tokyo, argues that the nation-state system is being modified by three main trends: depolarization, denationalization, and increasing interdependence. According to Sakamoto, the world is moving from a bipolar to a polypolar structure, and even to depolarization. Such a change leads to independence of nations within and outside superpower spheres of influence. The major global issue is shifting from military security to socioeconomic security. With such a development, transnational interactions are increasing, promoting forces undermining the nation-state as a primary cultural reference group. The world, moreover, is characterized by economic interdependence in which competition and cooperation will replace confrontation among the advanced industrial states. The developing nations, Sakamoto contends, could benefit from these forces.

John Spanier is critical of the view that interdependence is transforming the international political system by reducing the importance of power politics. He makes the following points: (1) the major global problems require national solutions; (2) security, and not welfare, remains the highest priority of states; (3) the degree of interdependence among states varies; (4) some states retain great choice of policies they can pursue; (5) political considerations dominate economic objectives in state behavior; (6) much of interdependence theory is prescriptive and not descriptive; (7) the beneficiaries of much of the thinking of interdependence advocates would be the socialist and third world countries, and not the West; and (8) even in an age of interdependence, states emphasize their national interests.

5 Does the Balance of Power Work in the Nuclear
Age?

YES

Hedley Bull

The Present Relevance of the Balance of Power

NO

Stanley Hoffmann

The Balance of Power

The Present Relevance of the Balance of Power
Hedley Bull

It is clear that in contemporary international politics there does exist a balance of power which fulfils the same functions in relation to international order which it has performed in other periods. If any important qualification needs to be made to this statement it is that since the late 1950s there has existed another phenomenon which in some respects is a special case of the balance of power but in other respects is different: mutual nuclear deterrence. In a final section of this chapter I shall consider the meaning of mutual nuclear deterrence and its relation to the balance of power. [*Editor's note:* omitted here.]

There clearly does now exist a general balance of power in the sense that no one state is preponderant in power in the international system as a whole. The chief characteristic of this general balance is that whereas in the 1950s it took the form of a simple balance (though not a perfectly simple one), and in the 1960s was in a state of transition, in the 1970s it takes the form of a complex balance. At least in the Asian and Pacific region China has to be counted as a great power alongside the United States and the Soviet Union; while Japan figures as a potential fourth great power and a united Western Europe may in time become a fifth. However, the statement that there is now a complex or multilateral balance of power has given rise to a number of misunderstandings, and it is necessary to clear these away.

To speak of a complex or multiple balance among these three or four powers is not to imply that they are equal in strength. Whereas in a system dominated by two powers a situation of balance or absence of preponderance can be achieved only if there is some rough parity of strength between the powers concerned, in a system of three or more powers balance can be achieved without a relationship of equality among the powers concerned because of the possibility of combination of the lesser against the greater.

Moreover, to speak of such a complex balance of power is not to imply that all four great states command the same kind of power or influence. Clearly, in international politics moves are made on "many chess-boards". On the chess-board of strategic nuclear deterrence the United States and the Soviet Union are supreme players, China is a novice and Japan does not figure at all. On the chess-board of conventional military strength the United States and the Soviet Union, again, are leading players because of their ability to deploy non-nuclear armed force in many parts of the world, China is a less important player because the armed force it has can be deployed only in its own immediate vicinity, and Japan is only a minor player. On the chess-boards of international monetary affairs and international trade and investment the United States and Japan are leading players, the Soviet Union much less important and China relatively unimportant. On the chess-board of influence derived from ideological appeal it is arguable that China is the pre-eminent player.

However, the play on each of these chess-boards is related to the play on each of the others. An advantageous position in the international politics of trade or investment may be used to procure advantages in the international politics of military security; a weak position on the politics of strategic nuclear deterrence may limit and circumscribe the options available in other fields. It is from this interrelatedness of the various chess-boards that we derive the conception of over-all power and influence in international politics, the common denominator in respect of which we say that there is balance rather than preponderance. Over-all power in this sense cannot be precisely quantified: the relative importance of strategic, economic and politico-psychological ingredients in national power (and of different kinds of each of these) is both uncertain and changing. But the relative position of states in terms of over-all power nevertheless makes itself apparent in bargaining among states, and the conception of over-all power is one we cannot do without.

Furthermore, to speak of the present relations of the great powers as a complex balance is not to imply that they are politically equidistant from one another, or that there is complete diplomatic mobility among them. At the time of writing a *détente* exists between the United States and the Soviet Union, and between the United States and China, but not between the Soviet Union and China. Japan, while it has asserted a

From Hedley Bull, *The Anarchical Society: A Study of Order in World Politics.* New York: Columbia University Press, 1977, pp. 112–117.

measure of independence of the United States and improved its relations with both the Soviet Union and China, is still more closely linked both strategically and economically to the United States than to any of the others. While, therefore, the four major powers have more diplomatic mobility than they had in the period of the simple balance of power, their mobility is still limited, especially by the persistence of tension between the two communist great powers so considerable as to preclude effective collaboration between them.

We have also to note that the complex balance of power that now exists does not rest on any system of general collaboration or concert among the great powers concerned. There is not any general agreement among the United States, the Soviet Union, China and Japan on the proposition that the maintenance of a general balance of power is a common objective, the proposition proclaimed by the European great powers in the Treaty of Utrecht. Nor is there any general agreement about a system of rules for avoiding or controlling crises, or for limiting wars. . . .

The present balance of power is not wholly fortuitous in the sense defined above, for there is an element of contrivance present in the 'rational' pursuit by the United States, the Soviet Union and China of policies aimed at preventing the preponderance of any of the others. It may be argued also that there is a further element of contrivance in the agreement between the United States and the Soviet Union on the common objective of maintaining a balance between themselves, at least in the limited sphere of strategic nuclear weapons. There is not, however, a contrived balance of power in the sense that all three or four great powers accept it as common objective— indeed, it is only the United States that explicitly avows the balance of power as a goal. Nor is there any evidence that such a balance of power is generally thought to imply self-restraint on the part of the great powers themselves, as distinct from the attempt to restrain or constrain one another.

The United States and the Soviet Union have developed some agreed rules in relation to the avoidance and control of crises and the limitation of war. There is not, however, any general system of rules among the great powers as a whole in these areas. Neither in the field of Sino-Soviet relations nor in that of Sino-American relations does there exist any equivalent of the nascent system of rules evolving

between the two global great powers. In the absence of any such general system of rules, we cannot speak of there being, in addition to a balance among the great powers, a concert of great powers concerned with the management of this balance.

Finally, the present complex balance of power does not rest on a common culture shared by the major states participating in it, comparable with that shared by the European great powers that made up the complex balances of the eighteenth and nineteenth centuries. . . . In the European international system of those centuries one factor that facilitated both the maintenance of the balance itself and co-operation among the powers that contributed to it was their sharing of a common culture, both in the sense of a common intellectual tradition and stock of ideas that facilitated communication, and in the sense of common values, in relation to which conflicts of interest could be moderated. Among the United States, the Soviet Union, China and Japan there does exist, as will be argued later, some common stock of ideas, but there is no equivalent of the bonds of common culture among European powers in earlier centuries.

All five of the misunderstandings that have been mentioned arise from the fact that in present-day thinking the idea of a balance of power tends to be confused with the European balance-of-power system, particularly that of the nineteenth century. The latter system is commonly said to have been characterised by rough equality among the five principal powers (Britain, France, Austria-Hungary, Russia and Prussia-Germany); by comparability in the kind of power available to each, which could be measured in terms of numbers of troops; by political equidistance among the powers and maximum diplomatic mobility; by general agreement as to the rules of the game; and by an underlying common culture.

Whether or not the European system of the last century in fact possessed all these qualities might be disputed. Thus there were substantial inequalities between the five powers at different times. It was never possible to reduce British sea power and financial power, and continental land power, to a common denominator. There were ideological inhibitions to diplomatic mobility arising from associations such as the Holy Alliance, the *Dreikaiserbund* and the 'Liberal Alliance' of Britain and France. We do have to recognise, however, that the European balance of the nineteenth century was only one historical manifestation of a phenomenon that has occurred in many periods and continents, and that in asserting that there exists a complex balance of power at the present time we are not contending that this embodies every feature of the European model of the last century.

This presently existing balance of power appears to fulfil the same three functions in relation to international order that it has performed in earlier periods, and that were mentioned in the last section. First, the general balance of power serves to prevent the system of states from being transformed by conquest into a universal empire. While the balance continues to be maintained, no one of the great powers has the option of establishing a world government by force. . . .

Second, local balances of power—where they exist —serve to protect the independence of states in particular areas from absorption or domination by a locally preponderant power. At the present time the independence of states in the Middle East, in the Indian subcontinent, in the Korean peninsula and in peninsular South-east Asia is assisted by the existence in these areas of local balances of power. By contrast, in Eastern Europe where there is a Soviet preponderance and in Central America and the Caribbean, where there is a U.S. preponderance, local states cannot be said to be independent in the normal sense. It would be going too far to assert that the existence of a local balance of power is a necessary condition of the independence of states in any area. To assert this would be to ignore the existence of the factor of a sense of political community in the relations between the two states, the consequence of which may be that

a locally preponderant state is able, up to a point, to respect the independence of a weaker neighbour, as the United States respects the independence of Canada, or Britain respects the independence of Eire. We have also to recognise that the independence of states in a particular area may owe less to the existence or non-existence of a balance among the local powers than to the part played in the local equilibrium by powers external to the region: if a balance exists at present between Israel and her Arab neighbours, for example, this balance owes its existence to the role played in the area by great powers external to it.

Third, both the general balance of power, and such local balances as exist at present, help to provide the conditions in which other institutions on which international order depends are able to operate. International law, the diplomatic system, war and the management of the international system by the great powers assume a situation in which no one power is preponderant in strength. All are institutions which depend heavily on the possibility that if one state violates the rules, others can take reciprocal action. But a state which is in a position of preponderant power, either in the system as a whole or in a particular area, may be in a position to ignore international law, to disregard the rules and procedures of diplomatic intercourse, to deprive its adversaries of the possibility of resort to war in defence of their interests and rights, or to ignore the conventions of the comity of great powers, all with impunity.

The Balance of Power
Stanley Hoffmann

. . . It [the theory of the balance of power] has two assets. It rests on the nature of world politics, rather than requiring a utopia. As long as there is a fragmented structure, with power unevenly divided among the states, whatever their own nature or their social or economic systems, the states will block each other's ambitions and attempts at domination, and, either through deliberate creation or not, balances of power will occur. Indeed, the second asset of the theory is historical confirmation. There have been

balance of power systems, i.e., systems in which the basic "law" of politics just mentioned operated in specific conditions (concerning the number of major players, the relative homogeneity of the structure and domestic regimes, and so on). These resulted in certain methods, peaceful or coercive, for the maintenance of the balance, and in the moderation of violence. These two advantages explain why the model has to be treated seriously. Nevertheless, its relevance to the present world is limited. For there is

From Stanley Hoffmann, *Primacy or World Order: American Foreign Policy Since the Cold War*, New York: McGraw-Hill, 1978, pp. 168–177.

a difference between the maintenance of the central nuclear balance, which provides, so to speak, the steel framework of the whole construction and which results from the two superpowers' policies, and the establishment, in order to moderate conflict, of a balance of power *system* inspired by such systems of the past.

The balance was essentially a technique for the management of the strategic-diplomatic arena, which constituted, if not the exclusive, at least the principal functional realm of interstate politics. (In the days of mercantilist economic policies, economic gains and losses were treated exactly like strategic gains or losses, since economics was regarded not as a net of transactions but as a mass of goods to be seized or held in a zero-sum game; the logic of the power struggle, what I have called above the logic of separateness, and the rules of conflictual interaction, applied across the board.) Now, the idea of a new balancing system has many of the same attractions as the Kissinger design, which it certainly inspired. But the traditional arena, in the present world, does not lend itself to the restoration of a balancing system for a variety of reasons, many of which we indicated when we discussed the fate of this design. The "game of nations," even though it is still played in a decentralized milieu, has changed and does not fit the model.

For such a game to be played according to the rules of the balance of power, various conditions had, in the past, to be met. First, there had to be a number of major actors—it usually was around five or six—of comparable if not equal power. Today's distribution of power among the top actors is quite different. Only two states are actual world powers, militarily present and influential over most of the globe, and indispensable for all important settlements. China is still mainly a regional power, more concerned with breaking out of encirclement than with active involvement outside. While Chinese leaders assert that China will never want to become a superpower, there is no way of predicting that this will be the case. Even if both dogma and growing power should push Peking toward a world role, given its enormous internal problems of authority and development, the transition will be long. China is bound to remain in the meantime a potential superpower, i.e., a major player presently limited in the geographical scope and in the means of his activity albeit exerting considerable attraction on the global scene. There are no other two "poles."

Both Japan and Western Europe are military dependents of the United States. Neither, despite huge but fragile economic power, behaves on the strategic-diplomatic chess-board as if it intended to play a world role under the American nuclear umbrella. Japan, so far, does not have even a clear regional policy. Western Europe is a perpetual promise—a tease—not a real political entity.

A second condition for the functioning of past balance of power systems was the presence of a central balancing mechanism: the ability of several of the main actors to coalesce, in order to deter or to blunt the expansion of one or more powers. This corresponded to two fundamental realities: the inability of any one power to annihilate another and the usefulness of force. Aggressively, force was a productive instrument of expansion; preventively or repressively, the call to arms against a trouble maker served as the moment of truth. The invention of nuclear weapons and their present distribution have thoroughly transformed the situation. The resort to nuclear weapons can obviously not be a balancing technique. Indeed, the central mechanism's purpose in a nuclear world is the *avoidance* of nuclear conflict. This central mechanism of deterrence is likely to remain bipolar for a long time. Only the United States and the U.S.S.R. have the capacity to annihilate each other—a capacity distinct from that, which France, Britain, and China possess, of severely wounding a superpower but suffering either total or unbearable destruction in return. Only the superpowers have an oversupply of nuclear weapons to deter each other not merely from nuclear but also from large-scale conventional wars and from the nuclear blackmail of third parties. Their quantitative and qualitative advance over other nuclear powers remains enormous. It is doubtful that Peking could find the indispensable short-cuts to catch up with Moscow and Washington. Nor is an eventual nuclear Japan likely to outstrip the Americans and the Russians; political and psychological inhibitions in the Japanese polity are likely to delay a decision to join the nuclear race and to limit the scope of any nuclear effort. Western Europe continues to have an internal problem not unlike that of squaring a vicious circle: the British and the French deterrents remain separate; they are threatened with obsolescence and unlikely to grow much. But a genuine "West European" deterrent would require a central political and military decision-making process of which there are no traces. Nor is there a willingness of Bonn to consecrate the Franco-British nuclear duopoly, or a willingness of London and Paris to include Bonn.

A pentagon or hexagon of nuclear powers is not necessary and could be dangerous. The deterrence of nuclear war is not a matter of coalitions. What deters Moscow, or Peking, from nuclear war is the certainty of destruction. To add the potential nuclear strength of a Japanese or West European strategic force to that of the United States may theoretically complicate an aggressor's calculations, but it does not change the picture. Furthermore, a world of several *major* nuclear powers would be of dubious stability by itself and would probably foster further proliferation. Maybe five or six strategic forces of comparable levels could be "stable": each would-be aggressor would be deterred, not by a coalition, or by a third party's guarantee of the victim, but by that potential victim's own force. But here we are talking about very uneven forces. The balance of uncertainty that up to now has leaned toward deterrence and restraint could begin oscillating furiously. Even if it should never settle on the side of nuclear war, it would promote an arms race among the five or six. The very argument that stresses that nuclear guarantees are not credible would incite more states to follow the examples of Western Europe or Japan. Some would have a second-strike capacity against each other, and a first-strike capacity against others. It would be difficult to devise a "moderate" international system under these circumstances.

What of a return to a *conventional* balancing mechanism comparable to that of the past? It has been asserted that the very unusability of nuclear weapons actually restores the conditions of traditional war. But the model does not apply any better. Against a nuclear power, conventional forces are simply not a sufficient credible deterrent. Deterrence of nuclear attack, or of nuclear escalation by the side that finds its conventional forces stopped or beaten, depends on either the possession of nuclear forces or on protection by a credible nuclear guarantor. In a nuclear world, even if conventional war provides moments of partial truth, ultimate truth is either nuclear war or its effective, i.e., nuclear, deterrence. Moreover, from the theoretical viewpoint of a conventional balance, a world of several major actors would not resemble the great powers system of the past. The balance of power was predominantly about Europe. All its members sought a world role. It is

difficult to imagine either a West European entity or a conventionally rearmed Japan seeking such a role. Each one could become an important part of a regional balance of power—not more. There is no central, worldwide, balancing mechanism: the logic of fragmentation operates.

In this arena, then, three phenomena are likely. First, only the two superpowers are likely to remain, for a long time, capable of sending forces and supplies to distant parts of the globe. The world conceived as a single theater of military calculations and operations is likely to stay bipolar. Second, as long as the fear of nuclear disaster obliges the superpowers to avoid deliberate military provocation and direct armed clashes, and as long as China, Western Europe, and Japan remain at least partly hemmed in, endowed only with modest conventional means, and largely neutralized militarily by their very connection to the central nuclear balance of deterrence, other states, independently (like India) or, more likely, equipped or protected by a superpower, and in pursuit of objectives that are of vital importance to them, will continue to be able to provoke their own "moment of truth" and to build themselves up as regional centers of military power, as Israel has done in the Middle East, or North Vietnam in Southeast Asia, and as Saudi Arabia, Iran, and Brazil are doing now. A coalition of states with great power but limited stakes is not enough to stop a local player with limited power but huge stakes. For the superpowers and for such local players, conventional force used outside their borders still has considerable productivity (although, paradoxically, the superpowers can use such force only in small doses, through proxies, or in limited spheres). For France, Britain, or China, however, the greatest utility of conventional force is likely to be negative: its contribution to deterrence. Third, the fragmentation that results both from the impact of nuclear weapons on world politics and from the regional nature of several of the present or emerging military powers suggests that a future conventional balance of power would have to be regionalized some more. A strong Japan or a strong Western Europe could not ensure a sufficient balance in the Middle East, or in South Asia, or in the Western Pacific.

Nuclear weapons have obviously not abolished war, they have displaced it. The central mechanism of the past was aimed at the problem of large military intervention by the main actors. Their restraint now depends less on a global mechanism than on a local one. No amount of military coalition building would have saved Czechoslovakia. No adversary coalition could have prevented the United States from moving into the Vietnam quagmire. Moreover, because of the fear of escalation, much of international politics on the diplomatic-strategic chessboard becomes a game of influence—less violent but more intense. There is an art of knowing how to deploy force rather than to use it, how to exploit internal circumstances to dislodge a rival. Whereas the traditional balancing mechanism may not work against war, it still functions where the stakes are influence, not conquest; for military strength in an area can deter or restrict the subtle access that influence requires. A strong Western Europe still associated with the United States would be guaranteed against "finlandization," for instance. Yet there are grave complications even here. Precisely insofar as violence is curtailed, a coalition aimed at stopping a great power may actually goad it into expanding its influence by "leaping" over the coalition and leaning on local parties determined to preserve their own freedom of maneuver (a United States-Chinese coalition in Asia or Africa is not sure to stop Soviet influence, for instance). Also, a superpower has other ways of strengthening an area against the influence of a rival than by military build-ups. Most importantly, much depends on the internal circumstances in the area. Neither military build-ups nor coalitions may compensate for domestic weakness. There are too many local balances for the great powers, singly or jointly, to be able to control them all, as was shown in Southeast Asia. Finally, moderation at a global or even at a regional levels is compatible with occasional setbacks.

The traditional mechanism, geared to different stakes, is too gross for the modern variety of the old game. Indeed, the logic of the traditional mechanism, as applied to the present international system, is a logic of arms races, nuclear or conventional. A game of influence partly played with weapons supplies in a world in which many statesmen continue to see in force the only effective way of reaching vital goals risks—as balance of power systems did before—leading to multiple wars. In past centuries, global moderation was compatible with such explosions; but in a nuclear world there is no assurance that they would be as limited as, and more localized than, before.

A third requirement for an effective balance of power used to be the existence of a common language

and code of behavior among the major actors. This did not mean identical regimes, or the complete insulation of foreign policy from domestic politics, or a code of cooperation, but a diplomatic Internationale capable of reducing misperceptions, if not miscalculations, and of coping with crises. But today, summits too are fragmentary—our presidents meet either with our allies, or with Brezhnev, or with Chinese leaders. Even if we look only at the major powers, we are still very far from a common language. Even a tacit code prescribing how to handle conflicts, how to avoid or resolve crises, how to climb down from high horses, and how to save one another's face remains a dream, for several reasons. There is still the Sino-Soviet conflict, deepened by mutual charges of heresy; it makes the triangular relationship something quite different from a moderate balance of power. Next, neither Moscow nor Peking subscribes to a code of general self-restraint. In the past, an effective balance of power required either agreements on spheres of influence and dividing lines, or hands-off arrangements that took the form of neutralizing or internationalizing certain areas. Of course, today, some spheres of influence are being respected: the Soviet's in Eastern Europe, ours in Latin America. But Moscow and Peking both apply to the world a conceptual framework that dictates the exploitation of capitalist weaknesses and contradictions whenever possible and safe. Regimes in which the state molds the society are better at granting priority to foreign affairs than regimes in which the impulses of the society actually control the state's freedom of action.

Further, the heterogeneity of many nations split along ethnic, class, or ideological lines, makes it impossible even for an angelic diplomacy dedicated to the principle of nonintervention to carry out its intentions. But it offers irresistible opportunities for diplomacies tied to a strategic (which does not necessarily mean warlike) vision of politics and to a dynamic reading of history. Prudence, yes; the simple preservation of the status quo, no. Indeed, the very delicacy of the status quo in the one area where Moscow most assuredly tries to perpetuate it—Eastern Europe—the Soviet Union's inability, for domestic and external reasons, to separate security from domination there, the fact that, however (in its own eyes) unideological, the West cannot easily accept an equation that enslaves half of Europe, all this is likely to oblige the Soviet Union to keep trying to weaken the West in Europe, or at least to prevent it from strengthening itself, because even after the Western nations' recognition of the territorial division of the continent, their power and prosperity could serve as magnets. In the Middle East, in South Asia, in Southern Africa, on the world's oceans, the Soviets, without encouraging violence where it would backfire, but supporting it where it works, behave as if any retreat, voluntary or not, of the United States and its allies, or any weak spot created by Western diplomacy, constitutes a vacuum to be filled or a position to be held. This is not the code of behavior we would like Moscow to observe. But multipolarity is not Moscow's game, or interest.

Such tactics, if skillfully used, do not destroy moderation. But they test self-restraint. Of course, Moscow could be constrained to adjust its behavior to *our* code, should we encourage, in balance of power logic, other actors to fill the vacuum and to strengthen the weak spots. But we are caught between our desire for a détente and the fear that it would be compromised if we built up the power of those allies whom our adversaries most suspect. Our rivals' game is to improve their relations with us insofar as we tend toward disengagement without substitution—in which case, our self-restraint could benefit them. In other words, two requirements for a new balance of power —relaxed relations with former enemies and greater power for former dependents—are in conflict. Such will be America's dilemma as long as our interest in "flexible alignments" is matched by our rivals' search for clients; as long as their revolutionary ideology (not to be ignored just because their vision is, literally, millenial, their means are prudent, and their tactics flexible), as well as their great-power fears or drives, result in an extensive demand for security tantamount to a claim for either permanent domination where it already exists or regional hegemony to exclude any rival. Indeed, regardless of whether Western Europe and Japan become major actors, Eastern Europe and East or Southeast Asia will remain potential sources of instability.

Multiple asymmetries are at work, therefore, insofar as moving toward a common code is concerned. There is the asymmetry between the dynamic ideologies of the communists and our more static conceptions, which envisage order as a set of procedures rather than as a social process, as a web of norms rather than as the ever-changing outcome of struggles. There is an asymmetry between the active policies of the superpowers and the still nebulous ones

of Western Europe and Japan. Far from being two poles of diplomatic-strategic power, they are stakes in the contest between the United States, the U.S.S.R., and China. There is an asymmetry between the exhausting global involvement of the United States and a Soviet (and potentially, Chinese) strategy that has to do little more than move into the crumbling positions on our front lines or jump across into the rotting ones in the rear. Order and moderation used to be organic attributes of the international system, corresponding to domestic conditions within the main states, as well as to the horizontal ties between their diplomatic corps and codes. Today order and moderation tend to be more complex and mechanical, corresponding to necessities of survival and to opportunity costs.

A fourth condition for an effective balance of power system has to do with the international hierarchy. While the world was a much wider field in days of slow communications, the international system was simple: There were few actors, and the writ of the main ones covered the whole field. In Europe, the small powers had no recourse other than to entrust their independence to the balancing mechanism. Outside Europe, the great powers carved up the world. Today, the planet has shrunk, and the superpowers are omnipresent. But there are more than 150 states. The small—thanks to the nuclear stalemate, or by standing on a bigger power's shoulders—have acquired greater maneuverability and often have intractable concerns. Any orderly international system needs a hierarchy. But the relations of the top to the bottom, and the size of the top, vary. In the future, if we want a moderate world, these relations will have to be more democratic, and the oligarchy will have to be bigger. As some of Kissinger's troubles have demonstrated, it is a mistake to treat issues in which third parties are embroiled as if these countries were pawns in a global balancing game, instead of dealing with the issues' intrinsic merits and the nations' interests. The very difficulty of bringing a *theoretical* balancing game no longer sanctioned by the minute of truth to bear on the local situation dooms the old-fashioned approach.

The proliferation of nations in a highly heterogeneous world, like the impact of nuclear weapons, suggests a fragmentation of the traditional scene. The old balance of power system assumed that peace is *ultimately* indivisible—although perhaps not every minute, as pure bipolarity does; more tolerant of minor shifts, it saw any expansion by a great power as a threat to others. Our analysis, however, suggests a greater divisibility of peace and a more evanescent character of influence, as long as the central nuclear equilibrium lasts. What will have to be balanced, so to speak, are that equilibrium and the regional balances. Each one of these has its own features, its own connection with (or disconnection from) the central balance. The contest for influence between Washington, Moscow, and Peking tries to exploit and to shape these balances—we have seen it in Southern Africa and in the Middle East; but their own specificity exposes that contest to their hazards. Thus, in the traditional arena, the *model* of the balance of power provides no real prescription, however wise the *idea* of balance remains. For the model, and the reality on which it was based, essentially rested on the following assumption. A crisis would be kept under control by the mechanism of the balance—i.e., the possibility of a limited war to stop a trouble-maker—and settlements would be ensured or imposed by the great powers. Force was thus both a threat, when used against the balance, and the heart of management, when used by the concert of the great powers. But today, the great powers are hampered by the nature of their rivalry, and demonstrably incapable of imposing their writ (either because they cannot "collude," or even when they do, as the issue of nuclear proliferation shows). This is so, because force in the hands of the great powers is no longer a management technique. Limited war against a superpower is too risky, and there is too much competition between them for joint action against small trouble-makers. The focus of the mechanism was the prevention of forcible action capable of upsetting the delicate balance of the great. Today's balance, being as much one of influence as of might, can easily be upset by domestic, political, and economic trends that neither great-power force nor great-power summits can crush; witness the rise of the Southern European left, which worries Bonn, or the emancipation of South European Communist parties, which troubles Moscow.

Anyhow, the balance of power is not a relevant mechanism in the new arenas of world politics. In games of "complex interdependence," the first or the only imperative of a state is rarely to limit the capabilities or gains of a rival, and even when this is its goal, coalition building is not by itself the most effective method. The rival will have to be restrained, either by building up superior capabilties oneself or

by the coalition's ability to manipulate interdependence, not by threatening the use of force. To be sure, groups are formed as in all politics, for instance, the IEA [International Energy Agency] versus OPEC. But not every form of coalition mongering is a balance of power policy, not every network of bargaining coalitions is a balance of power system. The latter term refers to a system in which military might, and the ambitions carried at the point of the swords, are stopped by equivalent or superior military might. In the realm of interpendence, the excessive power of a state or group of states in one currency (oil, food, technology) is to be neither balanced nor necessarily curtailed, but prevented from reducing others to dependence and turned to mutually beneficial uses, thanks to the assets available to other states or coalitions. These assets usually consist in countervailing but complementary chips. The peril in this realm lies neither in the failure of the balance to beat down the excessive ambitions of one sovereign that even force will not stop, nor in the rigidity of the balance when it splits the world into rival, frozen coalitions that lead to general wars. It lies in anomie: the failure of the groups to agree. To paraphrase Kissinger's style, the essence of the successful balance is stalemate, the essence of successful politics of interdependence is a bargain.

In the golden age of the Concert, the international economy was managed, not by the balance of power, but by largely transnational private markets, in a framework established and preserved by the hegemony of Britain, the guardian of a global system that ran to its advantage. When the rise of rival economic powers, and the beginning of Britain's own decline, put an end to this hegemony, the result was not a balance, but growing chaos.[1] Today, the application of an irrelevant concept to the fields of interdependence would be dangerous. It can, of course, be tried: As we have seen in Chapter Two [*Editor's note:* omitted here.], the Nixon administration's proclamation of the "primacy of national interest" in these matters, and its attempt to link the strategic realm to them to extract advantages from our allies, has had unexpected effects. For the very policies that often succeeded in restoring self-restraint and moderation in the traditional game threaten to breed antagonisms in the new ones. To apply the logic of separateness in

[1] See Benjamin R. Rowland et al., *Balance of Power or Hegemony: The Interwar Monetary System,* New York University Press, New York, 1976.

fields of integration invites disintegration. A universal balancing of power there would actually mean a break-up of the world economy into independent economic blocs with fluctuating relations based on nothing but bargaining strength. This would not be a source of order. The flexibility the world economy needs is not that of shifting alignments and reversible alliances. Such shifts can be beneficial, to be sure, when they prevent a break-up into rigid blocs and facilitate compromises. But once these are struck, rules adopted, and joint regimes set up, one needs committed partners.

QUESTIONS FOR DISCUSSION

1 What information should one have to determine if the balance of power exists?
2 What impact do nuclear weapons have on the balance of power?
3 How has the balance of power changed since the eighteenth century?
4 Does the balance of power have relevance in regional systems?
5 Does the balance of power serve the cause of peace?

SUGGESTED READINGS

Bell, Coral. "Kissinger in Retrospect: The Diplomacy of Power-Concert." *International Affairs* (London) **53** (April 1977): 202–216.

Claude, Inis L. *Power and International Relations.* New York: Random House, 1962.

Cottam, Richard W., and Gerald Gallucci. *Power: The Rehabilitation of Power in International Relations.* Pittsburgh: University Center for International Studies, University of Pittsburgh, 1978.

Daniel, Donald C. (ed.). *International Perceptions of the Superpower Military Balance.* New York: Praeger, 1978.

Dehio, Ludwig. *The Precarious Balance: Four Centuries of the European Power Struggle.* Translation by Charles Fullman. New York: Vintage Books, 1962.

DePorte, Anton W. *Europe Between the Superpowers: The Enduring Balance.* New Haven: Yale University Press, 1979.

Gulick, Edward V. *Europe's Classical Balance of Power: A Case History of the Theory and Practice of One of the Great Concepts of European Statecraft.* New York: Cornell University Press for the American Historical Association, 1955.

Liska, George. *Quest for Equilibrium: America and the Balance of Power on Land and Sea.* Baltimore: Johns Hopkins University Press, 1977.

Quester, George H. *Offense and Defense in the International System.* New York: Wiley, 1977.

Snyder, Glenn H. "The Balance of Power and the Balance of Terror," in Dean G. Pruitt and Richard C. Snyder (eds.). *Theory and Research on the Causes of War.* Englewood Cliffs, N.J.: Prentice-Hall, 1969, pp.114–126.

6 Is Interdependence among Nations Changing the Character of World Politics?

YES

Yoshikazu Sakamoto

Toward Global Unity

NO

John Spanier

"New" Cooperation or "Old" Strife?

Toward Global Unity
Yoshikazu Sakamoto

. . . We can identify three main trends that in varying degrees will modify the nation-state system as it has existed in the last quarter of the century. They are depolarization, denationalization, and increasing interdependence.

Depolarization refers to a political change that has two aspects. First, in terms of the world power structure it involves the transition from a bipolar to a polypolar structure and even to depolarization. That is to say, as there is now a growing rapprochement between the U.S. and the U.S.S.R., and between the U.S. and China (and even Sino-Soviet relations are unlikely to get worse than they are today), the principle of coexistence among the three superpowers is being established. But this does not mean the establishment of a system whereby the world will be partitioned, as in the 19th century, into three segments. In fact, the anticipated detente among the three superpowers will strengthen the demand by other nations for independence both within and without their spheres of influence.

Second, the multipolar coexistence system will undermine the primacy of the issue of military security and thereby decrease the dependence of smaller nations on one or another of the superpowers for such security. The strategic gap between the superpowers and the smaller nations will remain but will count for less. The major issue will shift from military security to socioeconomic security. As the strategic gap diminishes in importance, the developmental gap will become the dominant focus of attention, particularly in the developing areas, although there is the danger of arms races among the developing nations. Depolarization will not, however, lead to a situation in which a large number of self-contained sovereign states coexist. The diffusion of power that will evolve among nation-states will also develop within these states, cutting across them transnationally, that is, there will be denationalization. This process will take place at two levels of society: There will be increasing transnational interactions. The prime mover of transnational interaction is technoeconomic development, of which the obvious example is the multinational corporation

(MNC). The classic notion of the nation-state and national sovereignty is based on the presupposition or myth that the scope of the *national state* coincides with the scope of the *national economy* and the *national culture*. But MNC indicates that the scope of economy has already surpassed, and will increasingly surpass, national boundaries.

The near-exponential increase of the transnational nongovernmental organization (NGO) may be seen in the same light. As most NGOs come into existence by acts of spontaneous organization and cease to exist when unnecessary, they may be considered a much better index of the functional needs of world society than intergovernmental organizations that have a tendency to bureaucratic self-perpetuation.

Another aspect of transnational interactions is increasing transnational social communications, which promote the emergence of a universal culture on the one hand and the reinstatement of subnational ethnocultural communities on the other. Although these communities may be another form of nationalism, while a universal culture is essentially transnational, both tend to erode the authority and legitimacy of the established nation-state as the primary cultural reference group. Even countries in the process of nation-building will not be entirely immune from the twofold impact. Further, as the principle of equality is accepted by an evergrowing majority of mankind to be a component of the emerging world culture, not only specific forms of authority structure such as the nation-state but authority in general will tend to be eroded.

In sum, depolarization and denationalization will contribute to the proliferation of political actors in a variety of dimensions and will not be confined to national governments.

Third, if we were to see only depolarization coupled with denationalization, our image of the world would be one of fragmentation. But as the trend toward increasing transnational interaction indicates, there will also be a growing interdependence. In other words the world is characterized by increasing functional interpenetration, while power is becoming

Yoshikazu Sakamoto, "Toward Global Unity," in Saul H. Mendlovitz (ed.), *On the Creation of a Just World Order.* New York: Macmillan, 1975, pp. 198–200.

more diffuse. Interdependence refers to symmetrical interactions, not to asymmetrical dependence-dominance relations.

Concretely, the over-all political, if not military or economic, relations among the big powers will increasingly become interdependent, taking the form of competition and cooperation rather than confrontation. On the other hand, the relations between North and South will continue to be far from interdependent. Their political relations will however probably become *less* asymmetrical if the developing countries diversify their dependence on the developed countries by taking advantage of the competition, but no longer the confrontation, among the big powers. This change would be aided further if those developing countries endowed with natural resources utilize them as a lever for bargaining to induce the developed countries to provide positive assistance and cooperation and if the developing countries, through reform of their political and socioeconomic structures, reinforce their self-regulatory, shock-absorbing mechanisms, including their systems of regional or subregional integration. . . .

"New" Cooperation or "Old" Strife?
John Spanier

Before we begin our critique of the interdependence model, a preliminary note is in order. The assumption is that humanity is facing critical problems, which will overwhelm it unless nations learn to cooperate to find solutions. We ought to remember, however, that forecasts about the future of humanity are basically guesses, even when based on fairly reliable data about the current world. Who would have believed in 1900 that the 1.5 billion people living then would be increased by 4 billion in less than a century? Thomas Malthus warned 200 years ago that there were too many people then living and that they could not all be fed; already in 1750 Tertullian had advised that "the remedy for nations is to let famine take its course."[1] Who can now say that feeding even 6-7 billion people is out of the question?

In any event, it is ironic that only a few years after the United States was widely criticized—often by current proponents of interdependence—for pursuing a global foreign policy and extending American commitments beyond the nation's alleged capacities, including the costly "adventure" in Vietnam, globalism has reappeared in a new form. Only the agenda has changed, and, as the new welfare issues cannot be managed by single nations, "foreign policy leaders schooled in the old arithmetic of national security will have to learn the formula of economic interdependence, the advanced calculus of planetary bargains and global welfare."[2]

In evaluating interdependence, Robert Paarlberg has raised a fundamental issue when he questioned this emphasis on managing national welfare at the global level, stressing instead that the prerequisite for prosperity is improvement in domestic policy leadership. It may sound convincing to say that global problems require global solutions, but fertility, for example, is hardly amenable to agreement among states. The problem of rapidly growing populations is still primarily a national responsibility. What can foreign governments do in the absence of domestic will to manage this issue? Similarly, emergency food shipments or worldwide food reserves are no substitute for national policies emphasizing agricultural development. Food production and distribution, nutrition, and population control require greater national commitments and shifts of internal priories and resources than most LDCs have been willing to make in the past; for many, painful and difficult structural

[1] Quoted by Alan Berg, "The Trouble with Triage," *The New York Times Magazine,* June 15, 1975, p. 30.

[2] Robert L. Paarlberg, "Domesticating Global Management," *Foreign Affairs,* April 1976, p. 563.

From John Spanier, *Games Nations Play: Analyzing International Politics,* 4th ed. New York: Holt, Rinehart and Winston, 1981, pp. 563–571.

reforms in landowning patterns will also be necessary. Discipline, organization, efficiency in government and administration, and considerable financial investment are all necessary, yet such qualities are in short supply—and not just among the LDCs.

The energy problem may require cooperation with other nations, it is true, but even then the solution will have to begin at home. The United States could go far toward solving its energy problems if its government and people would conserve more oil and act with greater dispatch to find alternative sources of energy. The basic energy problem partly reflects failure to reduce demand, to produce more domestic oil, and to develop other energy sources. Only if these and other measures are undertaken can international cooperation be of some help. "So it is that global welfare cannot be properly managed abroad until it has been tolerably managed at home. Without a prior exercise of domestic political authority, the global welfare crisis will not admit to efficient interstate control."[3]

Indeed, we may add to Paarlberg's comment our own observation that, when the distinction between foreign and domestic policies has been blurred, weak domestic efforts to encourage economic growth and promote prosperity will lead to corresponding tendencies to pin the blame for domestic problems on other nations. The appeal to nationalism and the search for foreign devil figures will increase tensions among the states whose alleged interdependence is supposed to create more harmonious relations. The incentive to externalize domestic failure will surely be very strong if the LDCs do not modernize fairly rapidly. For such failure is very likely to produce more activist, radical, authoritarian regimes that will be more disposed to confrontation than to conciliation. Beleaguered governments, struggling with massive domestic dissatisfaction, may well adopt intensely nationalistic and aggressive policies out of desperation.

A 1976 United Nations report entitled *The Future of the World Economy* declared that, to halve the income gap between rich and poor nations by the year 2000 would require first, "far-reaching internal changes of a social, political and institutional character in the developing countries, and second, significant changes in the world economic order."[4] Each alone would be insufficient; the two types of change must be combined. But it is highly doubtful that the LDCs possess the will or governmental authority and capacity to take the "drastic measures" called for in the agricultural or capital-reinvestment sectors (30–35 percent, even 40 percent, of gross national product is called for). Even more doubtful is their ability to carry out the accompanying "significant social and institutional changes." To read the report is to recognize that its goal is unattainable.

Second, although there can be little doubt that welfare issues have become prominent on the international agenda, the assumption that they have achieved priority because security can be taken virtually for granted is overstated: The threat of global war has not at all vanished because the nuclear balance has so far guaranteed the peace. Both superpowers still use the threat of force and from time to time have precipitated crises that could have gone further. Miscalculation in future crises remains a distinct possibility. In addition, technological innovations in offensive or defensive weapons or the emergence of asymmetrics in force structures may undermine the strategic balance. Or the use of conventional forces may increase in an era of nuclear stalemate. Projecting mutual deterrence into the distant future and assuming that the issue of security is no longer relevant or at least no longer of primary importance may be premature. Most LDCs still believe that they have security problems, and there are few constraints on their use of violence.

Even more fundamental though, is the fact that the "security game" is not some antique remnant from the dark age, which is now best forgotten; the "socioeconomic game," may be more worthwhile, but it is not the only game in the system. The superpowers still give priority to their relations with each other. China pays a great deal of attention to Russia and to Asian security in general. Western Europe must focus on its relations with Russia and the question of Atlantic security. Even in the third and fourth world preoccupation with regional security, competition for leadership, maintenance of military strength, and alignments with extraregional powers typify international politics. The "socioeconomic game" is, in fact, played within the larger framework of the "security game." Instead of economic interdependence generating a new kind of international order that will weaken traditional reliance on forcible means of conflict resolution, it is likely that historical security problems will condition the character of interdependence.

[3] *Ibid.*, p. 571.
[4] *The New York Times,* October 14, 1976.

Indeed, as Robert Gilpin has argued, it was American power that created the conditions for the expansion of American MNCs. Similarly, it can be argued that American postwar security policy, which was focused on alliances with Europe and Japan, established the conditions for the high degree of interdependence that exists today within the European Economic Community (EEC) and between its members and the United States and Japan. Multiple public and private links in trade, investment, and currency bind these highly industrialized states together. But for the American-Soviet security conflict, American protection of Europe, and the European integration movement, the present measure of interdependence might not have come to exist. Symbolically, the chiefs of governments of the major nations of the Atlantic community (which includes Japan) have met regularly at economic summit conferences for years. The degree of interdependence once led West German Chancellor Helmut Schmidt to tell President Gerald Ford bluntly, when the president was thinking of letting New York City go bankrupt, that such an occurrence would have profound international repercussions and could not therefore be allowed.

It may well be, therefore, as John Weltman has said, that

> If major conflagration between the superpowers is avoided, if lesser conflicts are kept from spreading, if indeed governments are able to devote their energies to solving those planet-wide economic, social, and ecological problems which undeniably call for universal cooperation, it will be *because* of successful management of the strategic relationships between the superpowers.[5]

Third, the degree of interdependence among states also varies. The United States is in some ways the least vulnerable of the Western states. Militarily, it provides security for its allies around the world: they are thus dependent upon the United States, which, in turn, is interdependent with the Soviet Union. On economic issues, the United States is comparatively invulnerable, except for oil. It produces abundant food and feeds much of the world. The shortage of global food supplies thus benefits the United States which reaps considerable earnings from exports; a

[5] John J. Weltman, "On the Obsolescence of War," *International Studies Quarterly,* December 1974, pp. 413–414.

crisis for some countries is thus hardly even a threat to the United States. This country is also a major producer of raw materials and, thanks to superior technology, has a significant capacity for making substitution for those raw materials that it lacks. Even in energy, it possesses enormous coal reserves and the technology to develop other sources. Issues like world population growth and the global division between rich and poor have so far had little impact on the United States. They do not at present threaten its national security or well-being; except for OPEC, the American need for the LDCs is not particularly strong. Europe and Japan, for example, are far more vulnerable on the resource issue. Or, to put it in different words: some states are more vulnerable than other states. There is nothing new about that; some states have always been able to use another state's vulnerabilities to influence their behavior. Even if it were granted that military power is less useful today in compelling the latter to do what they might otherwise not do; the fact that economic means are available to achieve the same purpose is surely not an argument that the fundamental nature of international politics has been transformed.

Fourth, the fact that states, while interdependent, may not be equally vulnerable, means that states have some choice of policies to pursue. The United States has pursued a deliberate strategy of *increasing* interdependence with Russia on arms control since 1960; this interdependence has accelerated since 1972 and has been fortified to some degree with agreements on technology and trade. The United States is also seeking to strengthen its ties with Saudi Arabia by helping it to modernize and by supplying it with extensive arms. Conversely, states can also pursue a policy of *decreasing* interdependence, like the various programs proposed by the Nixon, Ford, Carter, and Reagan administrations to make the United States more self-reliant in energy. During the 1970s many LDCs became increasingly concerned about their dependence on the United States for food and began to emphasize their agricultural-development programs, which had previously been secondary to industrialization.

The prospects of too much interdependence may thus provide the incentive for a state to make itself *less* dependent! Few states, if any, seem ready to accept any radical infringement of their freedom of choice and action. Russia still practices selective détente, and there is no available evidence that Soviet leaders have yet given much thought to the problem of interdependence and the supposedly obvious conclusion that their stake in a peaceful and orderly international system is growing for reasons having little to do with nuclear weapons. Indeed, the Russian economy, rich in resources, is less dependent on the rest of the world than are most Western economies. Given the nature of the Soviet regime, it will undoubtedly try to limit the political consequences of importing Western technology. Nor do countries like Libya, Algeria, or Iraq appear very concerned about the effects of their constant push for higher oil prices.

Fifth, as this example shows, political considerations remain primary in international politics. International economic relations have not yet pulled nations so close together that they have displaced politics; rather, economics remains the handmaiden of politics. Events in Iran since the shah's overthrow suggest that "interdependence" among nations is more than simply a matter of mutually beneficial exchanges of specific resources or products. It is also a matter of compatible regimes. The militantly religious Ayatollah Khomeini clearly considers his regime less "interdependent" with the West, especially the United States, than that of the pro-Western shah had been. Indeed, in Iran today there appears to be no awareness of interdependence at all. Khomeini is very much convinced that the United States, and even more Western Europe and Japan, are *dependent* on Iranian oil, and American actions have confirmed this conviction: for example, the refusal to let the shah settle in the United States after he left Iran, as well as continuing shipments of spare parts for American military equipment to help Khomeini's forces crush the Kurds, who were seeking greater autonomy. Before the seizure of the American hostages in late 1979, everything was done to avoid arousing the Ayatollah's wrath and a break in oil shipments. Khomeini could therefore encourage the fanatical Muslim "students" in their invasion of the American embassy and their holding of its personnel as hostages. The fervently anti-American Khomeini regime has wanted little, if anything, from the United States other than the former shah and his money.

Indeed, events in the Middle East illustrate not interdependence but *Western dependence* and vulnerability. The following frightening words are from an editorial in *The New York Times:*

Iran's revolution has stirred up Shiite Moslems

around the Gulf. . . . Saudi Arabia feels a major threat from a Soviet-supported South Yemen. But it also fears revolutionary sentiment that might build up against the ruling dynasty. . . .

In Iraq, meanwhile, a Shiite majority inspired by Ayatollah Khomeini has been seething. The unrest probably accounts for last summer's bloody purge by the new strongman, Saddam Hussein. He has retaliated by encouraging Iran's Arabs in their sabotage and abrogating a border agreement with Iran. Hostile Kurds and other domestic enemies pepper his pot.

A sizable Shiite minority also troubles the sheikdom of Kuwait. Ethnic Iranians have been arrested or deported. Here as elsewhere in the region, anti-American voices call for big cutbacks in oil production to make the national treasure last. . . .

The confederated united Arab Emirates, like Kuwait and Saudi Arabia, rely heavily on foreign workers, including Palestinians. They also confront Iran's claim to three strategic islands near the narrow Strait of Hormuz, a vital oil route. . . .

Finally, in Oman, the ruling Sultan has lost the comforting shield of the Shah's troops against domestic opponents presumably armed by South Yemen. . . .

In sum, a few well-aimed bullets around the Persian Gulf could cause a massive leak of Western-bound oil. There is no real prospect, let alone guarantee, of stability. The region's tensions are rooted in political, religious, national, dynastic and military rivalries only marginally related to the Arab-Israeli conflict and largely beyond American influence. No prudent nation would count on containing them. It would race to escape its dependence.[6]

Interdependence thus appears to be a matter not only of "objective necessity" but of compatible regimes as well. If the governments that sell oil to the West were replaced by anti-Western religious fanatics or radical secular leaders, oil shipments would be endangered. One shudders to think what would happen in the aftermath of a revolution in Saudi Arabia. If there were genuine interdependence, the United States would not have to worry about an overthrow of the Saudi royal house.

[6] *The New York Times,* November 8, 1979.

Is it accidental that the highest degree of interdependence is among the Common Market countries and between them, on one hand, and the United States and Canada, on the other—that is, among primarily industrialized and democratic countries with closely linked political and security interests? Is it surprising that interdependence between the United States and the Soviet Union is much less likely to be successful? And is it really amazing that regimes in conflict with the United States and the West should reject claims of interdependence as attempts to prevent them from advancing their national purposes? Is interdependence not actually the goal of the vulnerable?

Sixth, much of the discussion in favor of interdependence is in fact *prescriptive*. The emphasis is on a strategy of increasing the degree of interdependence among nation-states; the more links there are, the more cooperation will be required, and the greater the restraints on states' freedom of action will be. And this point is really the crux of the interdependence thesis: *placing constraints on the national egotism and assertiveness of states by catching them in a "web of interdependence" in which they will become so deeply enmeshed that, on one hand, they will be unable to extricate themselves without suffering great harm and, on the other, they will be compelled to cooperate for the "good of humanity."* An argument supposedly based on description of the facts of interdependence, whether in security or in economics, thus shifts almost imperceptibly to advocacy of a course of policy intended to suppress conflict in the state system in favor of a focus on the welfare of all human beings. Says Lester Brown, "At issue is whether we can grasp the nature and dimensions of the emerging threats to our well-being, whether we can create an integrated world economy and a workable world order, and whether we can render global priorities so that the quality of life will improve rather than deteriorate."[7]

For those who are not optimistic about the feasibility of supranational integration and a possible new world order, but who despair of the ability of states to solve the security problems of nations in the nuclear age and achieve the welfare of the people living in these nations in an age of apparently declining resources, too many people and too little food, and the pollution of the world's land, sea, and air, interdependence becomes an argument for a "world without borders," a "unified global society," a halfway house. In short, *the advocacy of interdependence tends frequently to become a plea for a world "beyond the nation-state," for transcending the state system and building a better, more cooperative, and more harmonious world order, for subordinating "power politics" to "welfare politics" and national interests to planetary interests, for recognizing before it is too late that humanity shares a common destiny. It is essentially a normative, rather than a functional, argument for a revolutionary shift to a new world order from the current state system in which asymmetrical interdependence equals the capacity to coerce.*

It may be that appeals to global solidarity, moral imperatives, and humanitarian motives are more favorably received today than in the past and that images of a "global village" and "planetary humanism" have been increasingly reflected in world conferences on the environment, population, food, and the new international economic order. But this receptivity does not constitute an

effective consensus on global redistribution of income or wealth, or global guarantees of minimum human needs, or on global equality of opportunity. Those precepts have scarcely achieved a solid footing domestically, even in the most advanced societies, where democratic voting pushes governmental policies toward egalitarianism. At the international level, no corresponding political structure is either in hand or in prospect.[8]

The international cooperation needed to resolve the many issues of low politics depends upon the existence of a sense of community between rich and poor nations at least as strong as that *within* a highly industrialized nation with a tradition of political unity.[9]

Seventh, although these "relevant utopias," the purpose of which is to rescue humanity from becom-

[7] Lester R. Brown, *World Without Borders* (New York: Vintage, 1972), p. 12.

[8] Lincoln Jordon, *International Stability and North-South Relations* (Stanley Foundation Occasional Paper 17; Muscatine, Iowa; 1978), p. 7.

[9] David H. Blake and Robert S. Walters, *The Politics of Global Economic Relations* (Englewood Cliffs, N.J.: Prentice-Hall, 1978), p. 35.

ing an endangered species, are Western and especially American intellectual constructs, with little appeal in the Socialist world or the third world, the latter would presumably be the principal beneficiaries of global reform as a result of a redistribution of wealth. Furthermore, the LDCs are very suspicious of some Western ideas about interdependence. When it is suggested that a major problem is overpopulation in the LDCs, the latter reply that birth control is tantamount to genocide. Supposedly the West is seeking to maintain a favorable ratio of white to colored peoples and to preserve its own high standard of living, which is allegedly based on the LDCs' resources. More people in the third world would mean the LDCs would keep these resources for themselves, thus interfering with Western patterns of consumption. When it is proposed that all nations show more concern for the environment, the LDCs reply that such concern would prevent them from industrializing. After decades of polluting the land, sea, and air freely, the hypocritical West now seeks to persuade the LDCs to remain simply raw-material suppliers. Suggestions that nuclear diffusion is dangerous to all states, are countered with arguments that efforts to limit proliferation of nuclear arms hinder the LDCs' development of nuclear energy for peaceful purposes —even while the nuclear powers continue to build up their arsenals.[10] Nationalism and national interests still appear to be the primary focus of most, if not all, states.

Let us be clear, then, what these examples show— namely, that Western suggestions as to how the LDCs might develop more quickly are not viewed by the LDCs as well-intended, helpful proposals but as a means of holding them down. The energy crisis is bound to accentuate this sense of bitterness, if not paranoia, about the contemporary distribution of wealth in the world. For many LDCs will be hard hit by the ever-increasing price of oil and will go either into further debt if Western banks continue to make them loans, or, more likely, lower their expectations about modernization. This will hardly come easy to regimes whose claim to power is that they will develop their nations. A frustrated "revolution of rising expectations" will intensify the North-South conflict in

two respects: first, between the rich and poor in general, and second, between the rich and OPECs *nouveau riches,* whose wealth and power will continue to grow as oil prices go up and they gradually take over from the oil companies the transportation, refining, and marketing of oil as well.

Eighth, it is not only that the issue of security is neither old-fashioned and out-dated nor guaranteed, but also that economic issues will underline and reemphasize the essentially Hobbesian character of international politics. The reaction to the oil crisis of the 1970s vividly demonstrated the continued stress on national interest, even if close allies and friends were hurt. Thus the United States sought, at least in words, greater energy independence; Canada decided to keep more of its oil and not send it to the United States; the various European states scrambled to make their own oil deals with OPEC countries, including offers of training manpower in nuclear engineering for oil (such as Italy's reported deal with Iraq). Cooperation fell victim to a "me-first" or "beggar thy neighbor" policy among the Western industrial countries. Other nations were hardly wiser or more virtuous, not least the OPEC countries, who regularly raised oil prices. Indeed, OPEC's more radical anti-Western states—whose declarations of policy were generally filled with denunciations of "imperialism" and sympathy for the lot of the poor deprived masses in the underdeveloped world—were frequently in the vanguard of the price "hawks" seeking to maximize their earnings. They "beggared" all their neighbors, Western and non-Western; when oil supplies exceeded demand (which should have lowered oil prices) they simply cut supplies and raised prices further. In both security and economic terms, nations, by and large, continued to fear that another state's advantage was their disadvantage; one state's increase in security and/or wealth was perceived as a loss of security and/or wealth for themselves. To repeat: the energy crisis thus tended to reinforce the essentially Hobbesian nature of international politics, however noble the arguments for a new world order that would improve the lot of all mankind.

QUESTIONS FOR DISCUSSION

1 What information must one have to evaluate the degree of interdependence that exists in the world?
2 Does interdependence promote peace?

[10] *The New York Times,* December 5, 1979.

3 Is interdependence changing the character of world politics from a system based on power considerations of states to one based on cooperation and negotiation?

4 What are the factors that are encouraging interdependence?

5 Do the states control interdependence or are they controlled by the forces of interdependence?

SUGGESTED READINGS

Angell, Robert Cooley. *The Quest for World Order.* Ann Arbor, Mich.: University of Michigan Press, 1979.

Falk, Richard A. *A Global Approach to National Policy.* Cambridge: Harvard University Press, 1975.

Keohane, Robert O., and Joseph Nye, Jr. (eds.). *Transnational Relations and World Politics.* Cambridge: Harvard University Press, 1972.

Mansbach, Richard W., Yale H. Ferguson, and Donald E. Lampert. *The Web of Politics: Non-State Actors in the Global System.* Englewood Cliffs, N.J.: Prentice-Hall, 1976.

Morse, Edward. *Modernization and the Transformation of International Relations.* New York: Free Press, 1976.

O'Leary, James P. "Envisioning Interdependence: Perspectives on Future World Order." *Orbis* **22** (Fall 1978): 503–537.

Rosecrance, R., A. Alexandroff, W. Koehler, J. Kroll, S. Laqueur, and J. Stocker. "Whither Interdependence?" *International Organization* **31** (Summer 1977): 425–471.

Rosecrance, Richard, and Arthur Stein. "Interdependence: Myth or Reality?" *World Politics* **26** (October 1973): 1–27.

Rosenau, James S. *The Study of Global Interdependence: Essays on the Transnationalization of World Affairs.* New York: Nichols, 1980.

Waltz, Kenneth. The Myth of National Interdependence," in Charles P. Kindleberger (ed.). *The International Corporation.* Cambridge: MIT Press, 1970, pp. 205–223.

Chapter Three

Goals

As the primary actors in world politics, states seek a variety of goals, among which are security and ideological and economic objectives. Some of these goals are influenced strongly—some would say determined—by fixed conditions and other goals are set by a wide array of policy choices.

SECURITY

When World War II came to an end, there was much hope that the wartime unity of the allied countries, particularly of the United States and the Soviet Union, could continue into the postwar period. The UN was established with this hope in mind. The UN unit charged with the primary responsibility to maintain international peace and security was the Security Council, and its permanent members consisted of the important states responsible for the World War II victory over the Axis powers: the United States, the Soviet Union, Great Britain, France, and China. These states were given a veto power in the Security Council, which could prevent the UN from taking action on security and other matters when their interests so dictated.

The wartime unity did not last, however, and relations between the Soviet Union and the United States turned hostile. For about a decade, relations between the Soviet Union and the West in general and the United States in particular were so tense that the term "cold war" was used to describe the period. The era was marked by competition in which threats of confrontation were frequent.

For its part, the United States feared the expansion of Soviet power in Europe and elsewhere. The establishment of communist regimes in Eastern Europe was a major cause of contention. Although Czechoslovakia remained a democracy for a few years, a communist regime was implanted in 1948. Failure to decide the future of Germany remained a major source of hostility. Germany had been divided into occupation zones—American, British, French, and Soviet—at the end of the war. West Berlin, which was located in the Soviet zone, became the scene of numerous confrontations in the postwar years. Under a wartime agreement, the Soviets assured the West access to Berlin. When in 1948, the Soviet Union closed off surface transit to the West in an attempt to remove West Berlin from Western control, the United States began its airlift effort to supply the needs of the city's 2.5 million inhabitants. Although the Berlin airlift succeeded in breaking the blockade, it generated much animosity between the Soviet Union and the United States.

In 1949, the communist insurgents achieved victory over the nationalist government in China and established a communist government under Mao Zedong. A treaty of mutual friendship between the new government and the Soviet Union in 1950 appeared, in the minds of many observers in the West, to signify an expansionist trend of world communism: a monolithic movement of communist states committed to fomenting communist revolution everywhere.

In June 1950, communist North Korea invaded South Korea. Under the auspices of the UN, the United States sent its troops along with forces from other UN members to meet the act of aggression. The Korean war was responsible for spurring a major rearmament effort in the West, as it appeared to many people that the real danger was not just in Korea but was worldwide.

For its part, the Soviet Union perceived the United States to be aggressive. The United States was the strongest military power in the world in 1945, and it alone possessed nuclear weapons. It was not willing to share these weapons with the Soviet Union—at least not on terms acceptable to the Soviet Union. American bases in Europe, North Africa, and Asia made the Soviet Union vulnerable to American nuclear attack in a way impossible for the Soviet Union to challenge successfully.

Soviet security concerns were further heightened by the creation of NATO. Although the West asserted that NATO was a defensive alliance, the Soviet Union saw it as a threat to its security.

The cold war had more than political and military causes, however, and chief among these were ideological and economic concerns. In the eyes of many Americans, the Soviet Union represented a threat to the American way of life because of its support of communist ideas. To some observers, the cold war began not in 1945 when the Soviet Union and the United States became the two superpowers of the world, but rather in 1917 when a communist government in Russia committed itself to world revolution. Communist ideas, moreover, were in conflict with Western liberal democratic views focusing on political rights, which the communists regarded as a sham.

The Soviet Union perceived the United States to be the primary imperialist power. Imperialism, in the view of the communist theoreticians, was the highest stage of capitalism. Soviet leaders committed themselves to fighting imperialism as a way to promote communism, which they regarded as a system dedicated to the liberation of human beings from oppression.

Rivalry between the Soviet Union and the United States also had economic causes. The West depended on cheap sources of raw materials from the developing countries of the world. The Soviet Union sought to support independence movements in the world as a way of weakening Western power.

If the cold war is defined as a period of confrontation between the United States and the Soviet Union, it can be said to have ended soon after the death of Stalin in 1953. A policy of peaceful coexistence or détente came to characterize the relations between the Soviet Union and the United States. To be sure, the conflict between the two powers continued, but the harshness and the verbal attacks were often softened.

In 1949, the Soviet Union detonated its first nuclear device. By 1954, it had developed long-range intercontinental bombers. Some scholars believe that this increased Soviet military capacity vis-à-vis the United States, and hence easing of insecurities of the Soviet Union, may have been a factor in helping reduce cold war tensions.

Beginning in the mid-1950s, the Soviet Union improved channels of communication with the United States. Tourism programs and cultural exchanges for citizens of both superpowers were established. Arms control agreements were concluded and remain a continuing topic on the Soviet-American agenda. In its statements, the Soviet Union continued to affirm its commitment to the eventual victory of communism but asserted that military confrontation with the United States would be only suicidal. For its part, the United States sought to improve relations with the Soviet Union by encouraging trade, arms control agreements, and the free movement of peoples across national boundaries.

The nature of Soviet and American objectives remains controversial. Does the Soviet Union seek to dominate the world? Richard Pipes, a Harvard historian and advisor on national security matters in the Reagan administration, argues that it does. According to Pipes, Marxism-Leninism is an inherently militant doctrine emphasizing class war. It is, moreover, an international doctrine that seeks to promote communism everywhere regardless of territorial borders. Soviet leaders lack a legitimate basis for rule and must seek victories over capitalism to justify their rule. Soviet expansionism is further encouraged by a long history of Russian territorial aggrandizement. Soviet foreign policy does not necessarily require conquest of new territory, but it does call for hegemony; that is, the ability of the Soviet Union to assert its interests everywhere either by the threat of coercion or the actual use of coercion.

After describing the Soviet Union's enormous commitment to its military forces, Pipes assesses the motivations behind Soviet policy toward the United States, Western Europe, Japan, and China. He finds that the best way to explain Soviet foreign policy behavior is to see it as one dominated by aggressive impulses. The United States should meet such a danger by not permitting itself to be subjected to Soviet nuclear blackmail, by making NATO a more effective alliance, and by increasing American military strength.

The Pipes hard-line view of Soviet behavior is challenged by Princeton political scientist Stephen F. Cohen. According to Cohen, America is obsessed with cold-war attitudes toward the Soviet Union. This obsession has led to a failure to see realistically what changes have occurred in Soviet society.

Cohen argues that the history of the Soviet Union provides many examples of internal changes. For example, the era of Soviet leader Nikita Khrushchev (1953–1964) ushered in a period of economic and social reforms that ended the mass terror of the Stalin years. Cohen contends that the Soviet leadership faces serious domestic and foreign policy problems. Far from presenting a unified view of the world, Soviet society and the Soviet establishment reflect a great diversity of opinion, political outlook, and proposed solutions to these problems. Soviet society must, however, be understood in the general context of a deep-rooted political and social conservatism. The United States, Cohen asserts, should avoid returning to the cold war and should promote a policy of détente to take into account changing Soviet conditions.

In evaluating the motivations behind Soviet foreign policy, it is essential to understand why there are different perceptions of Soviet behavior. To substantiate the correctness of their views, American hard-liners point to an ever-growing Soviet military establishment, a communist ideology that is anti-United States, and specific Soviet actions, such as the Soviet invasion of Afghanistan and Soviet military support of Cuba. For their part, the more dovish analysts base their opinion on the Soviet quest for arms control, credits, and trade, as well as on a recognition of severe domestic economic and social problems in the Soviet Union. Those who take the hard-line view often perceive any expression of Soviet peaceful intentions as merely tactical and not in contradiction to Soviet long-term objectives of world domination. Those who hold the more dovish position evaluate Soviet efforts for détente as essentially genuine.

Like Soviet foreign policy, American foreign policy lends itself to different interpretations. One group of analysts explains American foreign policy since 1945 as defensive—a reaction to Soviet aggression. Another group explains American foreign policy in terms of American misunderstandings and misperceptions of Soviet government officials and communist ideology.

One important view of the United States focuses on the dominant role of economic groups in influencing American foreign policy. As the most powerful Western nation, the United States, in this outlook, is perceived as an imperialistic nation. Is the United States an imperialistic power? Historian William Appleman Williams argues that empire has been a goal of American history. Defining empire as "the use and abuse, and the ignoring, of other people for one's own welfare and convenience," Williams says that American imperialism is an outreach of Western European imperialism. European imperialism came to dominate the world. What makes America's empire unique is that it was acquired at low cost, produced enormous rewards, and masked its avarice with the rhetoric of freedom. From the eighteenth century to the present, America's political leaders—whether they were founding fathers or post-World War II presidents—found empire a way of life.

Empire was reflected in the nineteenth century by territorial expansion in the continental United States and by political domination of Latin America and Hawaii. The twentieth century saw the United States intervening all over the world. After World War II, the United States sought to expand its empire further, Williams says, in the name of saving the world for democracy. The Korean and Vietnam wars were examples of America's recent quest for empire. The policy of détente advocated by Richard Nixon and Henry Kissinger was designed to strengthen America's empire because it represented an attempt to settle for controlling the world outside Russia and Eastern Europe.

Writer Neal B. Freeman rejects the assertion that America is an imperialistic nation. America has military bases abroad, he says, but their purpose is not imperialistic. American forces overseas are protecting the nation's allies and not victimizing them. America's economic penetration, moreover, is not imperialistic, as America's economic situation reveals. In this regard, American currency is battered by oil-producing countries; and American manufacturing interests are hurt by lack of protection from foreign "dumping" of manufactured goods in the United States. America, too, accepts immigrants from Castro's Cuba. Many of these immigrants are old or infirm, and some of the immigrants are criminals. The United States even permits the new immigrants to retain use of their native languages in their American schooling. The United States should be proud of its nonimperialistic actions in foreign policy, Freeman concludes.

An evaluation of American imperialism should offer some standard of judgment for determining imperialistic actions. One possible standard is interventionism. Since the end of World War II, the United States has intervened around the world in such places as Korea in 1950, the Dominican Republic in 1965, and Indochina in the 1960s and 1970s during international crises. At other occasions, however, such as in China in 1949, Indochina in 1954, and Afghanistan in 1980, it did not. How can one explain American foreign policy in terms of imperialism when there are different responses to similar international situations? Or is the standard of interventionism not a valid one for determining whether the United States is imperialistic?

IDEOLOGY

Two ideologies that have played important roles in world politics in the postwar period are communism and liberalism. Although nationalism has been incorporated into the features of each of these ideologies, both of them possess strong international themes.

To what extent does communist ideology influence the political behavior of Communist Party leaders in communist and noncommunist countries? Not only the Soviet Communist Party but communist parties in other nations pay attention to ideological concerns. Domestically, they often seek to impose ideological orthodoxy to art, music, literature, education, and other aspects of communist society.

In the Soviet Union and other communist nations, pragmatic concerns have forced governments to adapt communist ideologies to the needs of the moment. Such adaptation has been caused by schisms within the communist world and by economic necessity.

According to communist ideology, there is not supposed to be conflict between communist nations. So long as there are no classes, there is no war. Even before World War II, there were, in fact, major differences of view between Soviet communists and leaders of communist parties in other countries. It was not until after World War II, however, that the number of communist nations grew. Stalin was able to manage the communist world by purging opponents in other communist nations. Even while Stalin was alive, however, Soviet domination began to be challenged. In 1948, Josip Broz Tito sought to direct Yugoslavia's foreign policy away from that of the Soviet Union. Later, Tito asserted that there are national roads to communism.

Uprisings that broke out in East Germany in 1953 and in Poland and Hungary in 1956 reflected more challenges to Soviet domination. The most prominent conflict of the communist world developed between Communist China and the Soviet Union, and part of that conflict was based on a central ideological concern: who leads the communist world? Rumania sought an independent course in foreign policy. The influence of Solidarity, the labor union in Poland, threatened in the early 1980s to undermine the basis of communist rule in that communist country.

Communist countries, moreover, have encouraged investment by capitalists in the communist world. Indeed, there is nothing new about that development since Lenin adopted similar pragmatic policies in the 1920s to strengthen the Soviet economy.

The character of communist countries varies considerably. Some are totalitarian political systems with tight controls over their people while others allow for some degree of political liberty. Some communist economies are more centrally directed than others.

One of the most interesting developments in the communist movement of the 1970s was the emergence of "Eurocommunism." The major theme of Eurocommunism is that communist parties could be trusted to maintain democratic processes if they came to political power in Western nations. Western communist parties, moreover, would not follow a Soviet line but would pursue an independent course commensurate with national interests.

The dominant advocates of Eurocommunism were the Italian communists, who saw their electoral strength rising in Italy in the 1970s. Spanish and French communists also supported the Eurocommunist movement.

Does Eurocommunism signal a real change in communist behavior? British writer Edward Crankshaw argues that it does. Writing at the height of Eurocommunism in 1978,

Crankshaw contends that Eurocommunism is a phenomenon that the Soviets have been wrestling with for many years, as the challenges to Soviet domination by Tito in Yugoslavia and by Mao Zedong in China suggest.

According to Crankshaw, we should recognize that communist parties are not alike. The Soviet Union does not approve of displays of independence by communist parties in any nation. Eurocommunism has resulted in a loss of Soviet control over communist parties in Western Europe. The issue of whether the communist parties of West Europe would, on coming to power, retain democratic institutions is an open question, and the answer would be shaped by the character of the people in the countries involved.

Political writer Robert Moss contends that Eurocommunism does not mark a significant change from earlier communist movements. There is no reason to believe that the Eurocommunists accept the rules of political democracy. According to Moss, communist leaders in West European nations have revealed their intention to support the Soviet Union in a European war.

An evaluation of the merits of Eurocommunism should consider the challenges of the movement to both the Soviet Union and the United States. The Soviets denounce the movement and see it as weakening their control of world communism. They fear that Eurocommunist ideas may be infectious and spread to East Europe. Many observers in the West are divided on the subject, and the position of Robert Moss reflects one widely held view of Eurocommunism. Other observers see Eurocommunism as a blessing to the West because of the possibilities of (1) changing the character of communist parties from dictatorial to democratic, and (2) weakening the Soviet Union.

Liberal ideology, like communist ideology, has an impact on world politics. Although there is much disagreement about what liberalism means, nearly every definition includes respect for individual rights as a central feature. In the postwar period the liberal creed of human rights has been advocated frequently by every president of the United States. In 1947, Harry Truman set the tone when he announced the Truman Doctrine. The doctrine called for the United States "to support free peoples who are resisting attempted subjugation by armed minorities or by outside pressures." John F. Kennedy's inaugural address of 1961 had a similar theme: "Let every nation know, whether it wishes us well or ill, that we shall pay any price, bear any burden, meet any hardship, support any friend, oppose any foe to assure the survival and success of liberty."

The Carter and Reagan administrations made human rights an important part of the political agenda. Carter announced in his inaugural address that the United States would promote human rights abroad. Reagan expressed a recognition of the importance of human rights but indicated that the United States would not undermine friendly governments even when those governments violated human rights.

In making foreign policy, the United States has not been evenhanded in supporting regimes that violated human rights. In World War II, it supported the dictator Joseph Stalin because the Soviet Union, like the United States, was fighting Nazi Germany. In the postwar period, the United States aided such dictators as Francisco Franco in Spain, Anastasio Somoza in Nicaragua, and Park Chung Hee in South Korea.

Should the promotion of human rights be a major goal in United States foreign policy? Raymond Gastil, director of the Comparative Survey of Freedom at Freedom House, thinks that it should. Focusing on political rights as human rights, Gastil argues that people everywhere seek freedom to control their own destinies.

In the long run, a strong human rights policy benefits the United States, according to Gastil. In a world of continuing ideological struggle, support for constitutional human rights is one of the few weapons available to a pluralist society. The long-term effect of

American commitment to dictators is to produce popular anti-Americanism. If we expect the people of the world to look to the United States for moral leadership, Gastil says, then the United States must make human rights a goal of foreign policy.

Political scientist Ernest Lefever attacks the notion of a major emphasis on human rights. He is particularly critical of the human rights policy of President Carter. A good human rights policy, he says, should take into account the fact that authoritarian dictatorships are better than totalitarian ones. Totalitarian dictatorship brings total control over all aspects of people's lives. Authoritarian dictatorship, while violating human rights, is concerned with political control rather than restructuring people's lives. American support of authoritarian regimes is often necessary because of security considerations. Authoritarian regimes can evolve into democracies, moreover, whereas totalitarian regimes cannot.

Security should be at the center of foreign policy. As a leader of the free world, Lefever says, the United States should support those countries that strengthen its security position—regardless of the degree of human rights existing in a friendly country.

As the Gastil-Lefever debate suggests, a human rights policy has a bearing on national security. Those who consider the problem may ask not only which of the two views is likely to strengthen security, but also what is the effect of a strong policy on the condition of human rights at home and abroad.

Supporters of a strong human rights policy must determine the specific actions that the United States should take; whether these should include withdrawal of recognition, cessation of diplomatic negotiations, sanctions, or verbal condemnations; and what the consequences of these actions would be for peace. Opponents of a strong human rights policy must weigh the effect of diminishing an important ideological asset on America's moral position in the world.

ECONOMICS

With the rise of new nations in the 1950s and 1960s, the agenda of world politics turned to economic as well as security considerations. Third world countries possessed important resources that the West needed. The West, moreover, had the capital and managerial skills essential for economic development.

The relationship between third world resources and Western needs became an issue in 1973 when the Arab oil-producing countries announced an embargo of oil shipments to the West. From 1973 on, OPEC instituted constant increases in the cost of oil. Oil sold for $3.02 a barrel in September 1973 and was $34 a barrel by the end of 1981.

Most of the third world countries are not fortunate enough to be endowed with rich oil deposits. In general, third world countries are the poor nations of the world. The term "south" is used to refer to these countries because they are located mostly in the southern latitudes. Many third world economies are characterized by low per-capita income, low productivity, high level of illiteracy, high population growth, low status of women, low capital investment, and a predominance of agriculture in their economies. Some countries, such as Bangladesh and Somalia, are so destitute as to be given a separate low classification as the fourth world.

Third world countries have economic development as a primary goal of their policy, both domestic and foreign. In 1974, a number of countries sought help from the advanced industrial nations of the world, principally in the West. They called for the creation of a New International Economic Order (NIEO). The developing nations made several specific proposals through the NIEO that, if implemented, would help them in their quest for economic development. Among the most important were: preferential access to the markets of the developed countries; commodity agreements that would assure them stable prices for their raw material exports; the transfer of loans and grants from industrial to developing nations through multilateral institutions; larger transfers of technology; and more control of multinational corporations by developing nations.

Should there be a new international economic order? Mahbub ul Haq supports the NIEO because the present world order systematically discriminates against the interests of the third world. The market system has not brought prosperity to third world countries but rather has provided benefits to the rich nations. The discrimination is reflected in inequities among which are an imbalance in the distribution of international reserves, unevenness in the distribution of value added to the products traded between the developing and developed countries, protected walls erected by the developed countries, the power of multinational corporations, the minimal third world participation in economic decision making in the world, and the lack of support by the intellectual world of third world ideas on equitable distribution. Haq argues that the Western legacy of imperialism is responsible for third world poverty. To make matters right, there must be a revamping of the entire global economic relationships.

Economist Peter Bauer and journalist John O'Sullivan are opposed to the NIEO. They make the following arguments: (1) Western prosperity is not founded on economic exploitation of Africa and Asia. Some Western countries possessing no colonies became prosperous; others possessing colonies became poor. Third world societies, relatively untouched by the West, are among the poorest in the world. (2) Third world countries pursue policies that impede economic development. Such policies include discrimination in employment, expulsion from the country, and even massacre. (3) Third world countries show a great deal of economic diversity, with some nations being prosperous.

If the NIEO were to become operative, it would be harmful to third world countries, Bauer and O'Sullivan argue. It would mean a transfer of revenues from those who can use them productively to those who cannot. Wealth transfers would go to the third world governments rather than to the population at large, and would, consequently, contribute nothing to economic development. NIEO, moreover, would not itself produce transfers from the rich people to the poor.

In evaluating the wisdom of the NIEO, it is essential to ask: what are the causes of poverty in the world? Why are some states wealthy and others poor? Third world countries are not uniformly poor. What, then, are the reasons for the economic success of such countries as Taiwan and South Korea and for the economic failure of such countries as Tanzania and Uganda? Are there better alternatives than the NIEO for third world prosperity?

Although economic relationships between the West and the third world have achieved prominence, the entire subject of the relationship between economics and politics is an old one. Nineteenth-century liberals argued that free trade encourages peace by promoting economic efficiency and raising the standard of living throughout the world. In the twentieth century, some advocates of interdependence continue to argue in this vein.

Particularly during the Nixon and Ford administrations, there was much attention given to promoting trade between the United States and the Soviet Union. The détente policy was based on improving trade ties, which it was believed, would strengthen interdependence and ease tensions.

Although a great boom in commercial transactions did not occur, trade did increase between the superpowers. In some areas, the Soviet Union has become a major importer of American products. The Russians have, for example, constantly imported wheat when because of climate and production problems they could not produce sufficient quantities to feed their population. They have, moreover, sought high-technology items and have turned to the West for economic cooperation.

Does trade between the United States and the Soviet Union promote peace? Donald M. Kendall, president of Pepsico, says that it does. Trade does not mean that Soviet-American conflict will disappear. Trade, however, will enhance cooperation between the superpowers and will increase the incentives for a peaceful and stable relationship.

Kendall says that trade should not be used to aid Soviet military strength but rather to improve the Soviet civilian sector. The United States benefits from trade with the Soviet Union by finding new markets and by reducing its trade deficit.

As the Soviet economy expands, the Soviet system will become "consumerized" in the direction of the Western models, according to Kendall. This development will lead to a reduction in armaments and a more pragmatic rather than rigid ideological foreign policy.

Social democrat Carl Gershman argues that United States trade with the Soviet Union benefits the Soviet Union but harms the United States. Trade is not a new phenomenon between the two countries. Many American companies flocked to the Soviet Union to help the Soviet Union in the interwar period. Some of their interests in the USSR were confiscated or were forced to close down.

The Soviet Union seeks political advantages from its trade. Its chief priority is the procurement from the West of advanced technology for its heavy industry. The Soviet Union is itself unable to innovate in technology and so needs the West.

Gershman is particularly critical of the one-sidedness of the relationship. Although the Soviets have expected American firms to be forthcoming by providing technical information, they have been secretive in their own plant procedures. The Soviet government has played one capitalist firm off another to get the maximum advantage. Gershman argues that the Soviet market is a small one and will never open opportunities that advocates of détente claim. Western firms that helped the Soviet Union to produce cars and chemicals have found these products being sold in noncommunist countries in competition with the products of those very firms.

Trade does not lead to liberalization, Gershman says. The Soviets suppress Western cultural influences and isolate Westerners who are in the U.S.S.R. Repression and ideological vigilance continue. Western investment in the Soviet Union strengthens a Soviet totalitarian control of the Soviet people. Liberalization would be more likely to occur if the Soviets had to face the necessity of liberalizing their own inefficient economy. That would come about if the West would stop aiding the Soviet Union.

East-West trade, moreover, has not resulted in a reduction of Soviet military spending or in a moderation of Soviet foreign policy; rather it has resulted in more Soviet military buildups and intervention, according to Gershman.

In evaluating the debate on trade, a number of questions arise. Even Kendall, who supports trade, opposes trade that can aid Soviet military strength. Can items considered for trade be clearly distinguished as aiding *either* a civilian or a military sector?

Both Kendall and Gershman believe that the character of the Soviet system can change. Which of the two perceptions of the conditions for change has the greater validity?

From an economic point of view, trade can benefit both the United States and the Soviet Union. Which country has more leverage to use trade for political purposes?

Finally, it is essential to consider whether a cessation of American trade to the Soviet Union would, in fact, harm the Soviet Union to a point where it would have to change its foreign policy. The United States imposed a grain embargo against the Soviet Union in 1980 as a response to Soviet intervention in Afghanistan; yet the Soviet Union was able to obtain the grain it needed from other countries. West Europeans, moreover, have been willing to sell products to the Soviet Union that the United States chooses not to sell. Under what conditions could a cessation of trade by the United States with the Soviet Union have a real impact on the Soviet economy when trade sources in other countries are accessible?

7 Does the Soviet Union Seek To Dominate the World?

YES

Richard Pipes

Soviet Global Strategy

NO

Stephen F. Cohen

Soviet Domestic Politics and Foreign Policy

Soviet Global Strategy
Richard Pipes

In his State of the Union address earlier this year, President Carter at one point addressed himself to the Soviet leadership:

> The Soviet Union must answer some basic questions: Will it help promote a stable international environment in which its own legitimate, peaceful concerns can be pursued? Or will it continue to expand its military power far beyond its legitimate security needs, using that power for colonial conquests?

That the President could seriously raise such questions, with the record of over six decades of Soviet history at his disposal, suggests that while he may have learned by now that the Soviet leaders prevaricate he has yet to find out who they are and what they want.

A few evenings spent with a standard manual of Marxism-Leninism and a good history of the Communist party of the Soviet Union would help the President answer his questions and save him (and the rest of us) from some more costly mistakes. What he would quickly learn—for he is said to be an apt pupil—is that: (1) in the Soviet case, "legitimate" concerns are not synonymous with "peaceful" concerns or "defense"; (2) the Soviet leadership is unable, for sound ideological, political, and economic reasons, to "promote a stable international environment"; (3) its "legitimate security needs" do require "colonial conquests."

These facts are what they are, not because the Soviet leaders will them so but because they themselves are the victims of a system which they lack the power to alter—except at the risk of bringing the whole structure down. The sooner those in charge of our foreign policy abandon their unbearable moralizing and come to grips with the imperatives of the regime which fate has chosen to be our adversary, the better for all concerned.

Here, then, are some rudimentary answers to the questions posed by the President.

To begin with the ideological factors behind Soviet foreign policy: Marxism-Leninism is by its very nature a militant doctrine, the child of the age of Social Darwinism, which views history as the record of uninterrupted class warfare and which advocates the continuation of class war as a means of abolishing, once and for all, classes and the exploitation of man by man. The kind of "stability" of which the President speaks and which he implies to be the desirable objective of all foreign policy can be attained, according to this doctrine, only *after* capitalism has been liquidated. The liquidation of capitalism, however, calls for a long period of instability, including international wars, which, according to Lenin, are an inevitable concomitant of capitalism.

Secondly, Marxism-Leninism is an international doctrine. As it perceives them, the phases in the evolution of mankind are global in scope and cannot be contained (except transitionally) within the limits of the nation-state or served by its "legitimate security needs." The fundamental international, or, rather, supranational, character of the doctrine is symbolized by Communism's permanent slogan since 1847, "Proletarians of all countries, unite!" In 1917, the Bolsheviks (and this held true of the Socialist Revolutionaries and Mensheviks as well) were not fighting for a change of regime in Russia, but for a world-wide revolution. It deserves note that one of the earliest declarations of the Petrograd Soviet (then still firmly in the control of "moderate" socialists), issued in March 1917, was addressed to the "Peoples of the Entire World" and called on them to rid themselves of their "ruling classes." This attitude was never repudiated by Lenin; nor has it ever been repudiated by his successors.

Now it is possible to minimize such ideological considerations with the argument that history is replete with instances of movements which, having laid claim to universality, nevertheless adjusted themselves to more modest roles: several religions, including Islam, provide good examples. But apart from the fact that accommodations of this nature have always occurred as the result of a universalist movement running into resistance that it could not overcome, Communism is not only a faith, it is also the program of a powerful secular government. It is precisely this

From Richard Pipes, "Sovet Global Strategy," *Commentary* (April 1980): 31–39.

fusion of a universalist historical doctrine with the most mundane aspirations of a great imperialist power that lends Communist Russia's global ambitions such force. For behind the lofty ideals of a classless society loom also the very vulgar interests of a ruling elite which finds in them a rationale for power and privilege.

The most painful reality that the Soviet leadership confronts every day of its existence is that it has no generally acknowledged mandate to rule. It lacks the legitimacy of ancient tradition; nor can it derive its authority from the personal charisma of a great living leader. This committee of colorless, self-perpetuating civil servants pretends to rest on a popular mandate and to this end every now and then stages mock elections, but the ritual of choosing without having a choice surely deceives only simpletons. Such mandate as the Bolshevik regime can reasonably lay claim to derives entirely from history, namely, from the assertion that it represents the vanguard of the majestic force of progress whose mission it is to accomplish the final social revolution in human history. Once this particular claim is given up —as it would be were the Soviet government to acknowledge the international status quo as permanent and accommodate itself within its present sphere of influence—the question of legitimacy would at once crop up. For indeed, who has given the Communist party of the Soviet Union the right to monopolize the country's political authority as well as its human and material resources?— none other than the goddess of history who has challenged it to the noblest mission ever assigned to man. The regime, therefore, must press onward and outward, it must win, or at least appear to win, incessant victories against "capitalism" so as to maintain the illusion of a relentless forward movement, commensurate with its mission. The alternative is to risk having its political credentials subjected to scrutiny and possible disqualification.

In addition to its universalist ideology and the ordinary political self-interest of the ruling elite, Soviet expansionism also has solid roots in Russian history. Because of the inherent poverty of Russia, due to adverse climate, soil, and other related factors, the country has never been able to support a population at a level of density common in more temperate zones. Throughout their history, Russians have colonized areas adjacent to their homeland in the northern taiga, sometimes peacefully, sometimes by conquest. Of all European countries, Russia has not only the oldest and most persistent tradition of imperial expansion, but also the record of greatest tenacity in holding on to conquered areas.

Thus, ideology, political survival, and economic exigencies reinforce one another, impelling Russia toward conquest. Each new territory acquired becomes part of the national "patrimony" and is, sooner or later, incorporated into the homeland. Each demands a "buffer" to protect it from real or imaginary enemies, until it, too, becomes part of the homeland, and, in turn, requires its own buffer.

The theory of détente, promoted by the Soviet regime since the mid-1950's, would seem to contradict the thesis that expansionism and international class war are indispensable to Russian Communism. As presented to the West (the matter is handled quite differently within the country), the theory, calling for peaceful coexistence between diverse social systems, seems to accept the prospect of a nonviolent evolution and a common, "convergent" end-product. In reality, détente is merely a tactical adaptation of a general strategy, which does not run contrary to the principles enunciated above. To explain why this is the case, one must say a few words about the essential characteristic of Communist politics as formulated by Lenin and elaborated upon by his epigones.

Lenin's historic achievement is to have militarized politics. It has been aptly said that Lenin stood Clausewitz on his head by making politics the pursuit of war by other means: war is the aim, politics a means, rather than the other way around. This being the case, the application of political strategy and tactics is determined by an essentially military assessment of what is known as the "correlation of forces." The latter, in Communist theory, embraces not only those factors which in Western terminology are included in the concept of "balance of power" but also economic capabilities, social stability, and public opinion, i.e., elements that, although not military in the strict sense of the word, nevertheless have considerable bearing on a nation's ability to wage war.

From this point of view, the decision whether to press one's offensive against the "class enemy," internal as well as external, or to hold back, must be based on a cool appraisal of the contending forces. In a speech delivered in May 1918, in which he reiterated that "final victory is possible only on a world scale," Lenin admonished his followers not to rush headlong into battle under all circumstances:

We possess great revolutionary experience, which has taught us that it is essential to employ the tactics of merciless attack when objective conditions permit. . . . But we have to resort *to temporizing tactics, to a slow gathering of forces* when objective circumstances do not favor a call for a general merciless repulse.[1]

In the eyes of the Soviet leadership, the phenomena which in the West are labeled "cold war" and "détente" and perceived as antithetical are merely tactical nuances of one and the same strategy, alternately applied, depending on "objective circumstances." In the case of the détente policy launched in the mid-1950's, the decisive objective circumstance was the enemy's complete nuclear superiority which placed him in a position to destroy much of the Soviet Union at will. This particular circumstance did not in the least obviate the necessity of waging international class war, but it did call for the adaptation of one's battle plans: confrontation had to be avoided and indirect methods of combat given preference—at any rate, until such time as America's nuclear threat could be safely neutralized.

The end objective of Soviet global policy is, of course, a world from which private property in the means of production has been banished and the constituent states are, with minor variations, copies of the Soviet state. It is only in a world so fashioned that the elite ruling Soviet Russia would feel secure and comfortable.

This objective does not, as is sometimes thought, require that the USSR physically occupy the entire world, a task which is beyond even the capabilities of its large military and security forces. The term "hegemony" conveys very accurately the kind of international arrangement with which the Soviet leadership would be satisfied. The concept is of Greek origin and was originally coined to describe the dominance enjoyed by one or another city state, and especially the Macedonian kingdom, over Hellas. Possession of "hegemony" did not then and does not now entail physical conquest: rather, it signifies the ability of the hegemonial power to assert its interests within the area over which it claims hegemony by the threat of coercion, or, if that fails to produce the desired effect, by its actual application. Britain enjoyed hegemony

over a good part of the globe in the 19th century; the United States had it between the end of World War II and its withdrawal from Vietnam. Germany launched two world wars in an unsuccessful attempt to obtain European hegemony. Andrei Gromyko, the Soviet Minister of Foreign Affairs, stated concisely the ultimate aspiration of Soviet policy in a speech to the 24th Congress of the CPSU in 1971 when he boasted, somewhat prematurely: "Today, there is no question of any significance which can be decided without the Soviet Union *or in opposition to it.*"[2] Implied in this statement is the rejection of the notion that Soviet interests are anything less than global in scope and can be confined within the boundaries of a national state or even a bloc of states. It goes without saying that the assertion of a similar claim by the United States would be rejected out of hand by the Soviet Union (as well as by American liberals) as a manifestation of the crassest imperialism. This is but one of many examples of the Soviet Union laying down the rules of international politics in a manner that entirely favors its own side.

If politics is warfare, then it requires strategic guidance. The strategy that one employs in the pursuit of global objectives cannot involve exclusively military weapons, but must embrace the entire spectrum of instrumentalities. Strategy of this type has been labeled "Grand" or "Total," and it suits a totalitarian country much better than it does a democratic one. The Soviet Union has indeed been organized by Lenin from the beginning for the waging of total war and it is to this end that the Soviet government has taken into its hands a monopoly of national powers and resources. There exists in the Soviet Union a mechanism of vertical and horizontal integration that not only enables but also compels the management of that giant political conglomerate to attempt a coordinated national and international policy. The proprietors of the Soviet Union have to seek to integrate politics, economics, and propaganda (ideology) to an extent inconceivable in the West where each of these realms is controlled by different groups and tends to pull in separate directions.

Let us cursorily survey the ingredients of Soviet Grand Strategy. Space precludes any discussion of the many aspects and nuances of Soviet *political* strategy.

---

[1] V.I. Lenin, *Collected Works*, (London, n.d.), XXVII, pp. 373, 377; emphasis added.

[2] *XXIV S"ezd KPSS: Stenograficheskii otchet* (Moscow, 1971), I, p. 482; emphasis added.

Its guiding principle, however, can be succinctly defined: it is to rely not so much on the forces at one's own disposal (i.e., foreign Communist parties and their "fronts") as on allies one is able provisionally and temporarily to detach from the enemy's camp on individual issues (e.g., nationalism, "racism," "anti-Zionism," etc.). This technique, originated by Russian opposition groups in the Czarist underground, has proved very successful when applied to international relations. Its essence can best be conveyed in the words of Lenin himself. In 1920 the Communist leader was faced with unrest over his cautious foreign policy from hotheads in the Third International. These people wanted a direct assault on the entire capitalist West. To them Lenin said bluntly:

The entire history of Bolshevism, both before and after the October Revolution, is *full* of instances of changes of tack, conciliatory tactics, and compromises with other parties, including bourgeois parties!

To carry on a war for the overthrow of the international bourgeoisie, a war which is a hundred times more difficult, protracted, and complex than the most stubborn of ordinary wars between states and to renounce in advance any change of tack, or any utilization of conflict of interest (even if temporary) among one's enemies, or any conciliation or compromise with possible allies (even if they are temporary, unstable, vacillating, or conditional allies), is that not ridiculous in the extreme? . . .

After the first socialist revolution of the proletariat, and the overthrow of the bourgeoisie in some country, the proletariat of that country remains *for a long time weaker* than the [international] bourgeoisie. . . . The more powerful enemy can be vanquished only by exerting the utmost effort, and by the most thorough, careful, attentive, skillful, and *obligatory* use of any, even the smallest, rift between the enemies, any conflict of interests among the bourgeoisie of the various countries and among the various groups or types of bourgeoisie within the various countries, and also by taking advantage of any, even the smallest, opportunity of winning a mass ally, even though this ally is temporary, vacillating, unreliable, and conditional.[3]

[3] Lenin, *Collected Works*, XXXI, pp. 70-71.

The success of this policy has been in large measure due to the fact that the "international bourgeoisie" not only refuses to acknowledge the manipulative intentions behind Soviet conciliatory policies but feels confident of its own ability to fish in the political waters of the Soviet Union by pitting nonexistent "doves" against equally spurious "hawks."

The Soviet *economic* arsenal is not rich enough to serve as a major weapon of Soviet global strategy. In its expansion, the USSR consequently relies much less on investments and trade as a means of spreading influence than was the case with the other great powers in the classical age of modern imperialism. Soviet economic leverage is exercised mainly through military and economic assistance carefully doled out to countries judged to be of strategic importance. Aid of this kind creates all kinds of dependencies, including the willingness of the recipient to host Communist administrative personnel. It is very instructive to analyze statistics of Soviet economic assistance to Third World countries because the figures give a good insight into the relative importance that Moscow attaches to them. On a per-capita basis, among the greatest beneficiaries of Soviet aid since 1954 have been South Yemen and Afghanistan. More recently, the USSR and its clients have poured vast sums of money into Turkey, a member of NATO, and Morocco. Significant increases in Soviet assistance are usually reliable indicators of Soviet strategic interests in a given area: judging by recent aid patterns, the Mediterranean enjoys very high priority in its mind.

In its relations with the advanced industrial powers, the Soviet Union is at a great disadvantage in attempting to exploit economic leverage, but even so it has had some success in making Western Europe and Japan dependent on its good will.

One form of leverage is the debts incurred in the West by the Soviet bloc during the period of détente. These are estimated today at $60 billion, one-quarter of it owed by the USSR, the remainder by the countries of Eastern Europe. The external indebtedness of the Soviet Union cannot be considered excessive, given that country's natural resources and gold reserves, but the same cannot be said of the "Peoples' Democracies" such as Poland, whose foreign obligations exceed those of its patron state. Western bankers have gladly lent vast sums to Eastern Europe on the assumption that any defaults would be made good by the Soviet Union. In so doing they have chosen to ignore official Soviet statements which repudiate any such obligation. Moscow's position on this issue, recently reiterated at an East-West conference held in Vienna, holds that "every country must repay its own debts."[4] Loans of this magnitude induce among Western bankers solicitude for the economic well-being and benevolence of their Eastern European debtors, and makes them beholden to détente, regardless of its political costs.

The other economic weapon is energy, of whose strategic importance the Soviet leadership had become aware long before it even dawned on Western politicians. In addition to placing itself in a position to impede the flow of Middle Eastern oil (of which more later), the USSR has sought to make Europe and Japan dependent on direct Soviet energy supplies, especially natural gas. To this end, it has established the practice of repaying in gas the costs of transmission pipes supplied by foreign concerns. West Germany is said to rely already for one-quarter of its natural gas on Soviet resources; and if negotiations now in progress for further cooperation in this field are successful, its dependence will increase further. What this development portends became apparent during the October 1973 war when the Soviet Union abruptly suspended gas deliveries to Veba, Germany's largest energy company, apparently in order to pressure that country not to support Washington's pro-Israel policies.

A list of all the other instrumentalities which the Soviet Union employs in its global strategy would be long and diverse. Among them would have to be included such seemingly unpolitical matters as family relations. The broadening of contacts between relatives separated by the border between East and West Germany which followed the Helsinki accords, provides the Communists with useful political leverage, the fear of their disruption being often cited by Bonn circles as a strong reason for preserving détente.

Of all the instrumentalities at the Soviet Union's disposal, it is the military that occupies pride of place. Soviet imperialism (this also held true of Czarist imperialism) is a military phenomenon *par excellence*, and in proportion as Soviet combat power grows, both absolutely and in relation to the West's, it tends to push into the background the political manipulation on which the regime has had heavily to rely earlier. Increasingly, Soviet spokesmen call attention

[4] *Neue Zürcher Zeitung*, October 10, 1979.

to the shift in the military balance in Russia's favor as a decisive fact of the contemporary world, and boast of the ability it gives their country to frustrate America's attempts to respond to Soviet initiatives.

It is sometimes difficult for people who are told of the low living standards of the Soviet Union's population and of the inefficiency of its economy to believe that such a country can present a serious military threat to the West. They ignore the fact that wealth and technical inventiveness, in which the West has an indisputable lead, do not make for military might unless they are harnessed in the service of defense. They further ignore that, conversely, a relatively poor country, as long as it has more than a minimal industrial-technical base, can offer more than a military match for its neighbors once it decides to allocate the necessary resources for war. Japan is an industrial and technological power of the very first rank. Yet because it has chosen to rely for its defense on the United States and forgo a military establishment commensurate with its economic power, its armed forces are one-half in size and a fraction in effectiveness of those of Israel, a country with one-thirtieth of Japan's population and one-fortieth of its GNP. As concerns the Soviet Union's low living standards, it should be obvious that when a country with its huge industrial plant cannot satisfy its population's needs for consumer goods, the reason must be sought not in incapacity but rather in the deliberate diversion of industrial resources to other than consumer needs. In other words, the fact that its population suffers a low living standard attests not to Russia's inability to threaten us militarily but rather to the opposite.

Russia has always tended to devote a disproportionate share of its resources to the upkeep of the armed forces: in the reign of Peter the Great, for example, more than nine-tenths of the state budget was allocated for that purpose. A large military establishment helped conquer new territories for Russia's growing population as well as to maintain order within the empire. High Czarist functionaries were well aware how much of the international influence that imperial Russia enjoyed was due to its ability to threaten small and great powers along its immensely long frontiers.

The principal weakness of pre-1917 Russian armies was a low level of supporting industry and transport, and of all those other non-military factors that World War I revealed to be of decisive importance in modern warfare. The lesson was learned by the

Bolshevik leaders who studied with admiration Germany's extraordinary performance in that war; as soon as they seized power they put into effect the home-front mobilization measures initiated by Germany but made even more effective in Russia by the abolition of private property and the introduction of the universal obligation to render state service. Stalin's Five Year Plans, for all the noise about constructing socialism, were as thoroughly military in their intent as were Hitler's Four Year Plans.

The conglomerate nature of the Soviet regime makes it eminently suitable for purposes of military mobilization. If the Soviet government so decides, it can lavish on the defense sector of the economy manpower and resources in the quantities and qualities required, and let the consumer sector fend for itself. The mightier the industrial base, the more rapid under these conditions can be the expansion of the armed forces, inasmuch as the allocations to the civilian sector can be kept relatively constant while the bulk of the growing surplus is turned over to the military. And, of course, there are no recalcitrant legislatures or inquisitive media to raise questions about the need for such heavy defense outlays.

Thus it happens that neither détente nor the arms-limitation agreements accompanying it, SALT I included, have produced a dent in the upward curve of Soviet defense appropriations. A recent study by William T. Lee, a specialist with long CIA experience, estimates that the share absorbed by the defense sector of the Soviet Gross National Product has grown from some 12-13 per cent in 1970 to perhaps as much as 18 per cent in 1980; and since the Soviet GNP during this decade has also kept on growing, the absolute amounts given to defense have risen yet more impressively.[5] Incidentally, in the same period (1970-79), U.S. defense expenditures as a share of the GNP have declined from 7.5 per cent to 4.6 per cent, and in constant 1972 dollars, from $85.1 to $65.0 billion.

Although the Soviet military seem determined to catch up to and surpass the United States in all the service branches, they assign the central role to strategic-nuclear weapons. These the Soviet military theorists regard as the decisive weapons of modern warfare. All the available evidence furnished by theoretical writings and observable deployments indicates that the Soviet General Staff does not share the prevalent U.S. view that nuclear weapons have no place in a rational strategy except as a deterrent. There exists a high degree of probability that in the event of general war the Soviet Union intends to use a part of its strategic arsenal in a devastating preemptive strike which would make an American retaliatory strike suicidal and possibly inhibit it altogether. The stress on large throw-weight combined with high accuracies of its ICBM's is a good indication that the Soviet Union intends to develop a first-strike capability.

The refusal of the American scientific community, which has been largely responsible for the formulation of U.S. nuclear strategy, to take seriously Soviet nuclear doctrine can charitably be described as an act of grave intellectual and political irresponsibility. Owing to it, in the coming decade the United States will find all three legs of its "triad" under growing threat which will not only make it difficult to respond to aggressive Soviet moves, but will also free the Soviet Union from those restraints which had inspired it to adopt the policy of détente in the first place. Once the nuclear balance will have become highly tilted, American crash programs will likely be discouraged by the same exponents of unilateral restraint who have helped bring the imbalance about, on the grounds that at this point any sudden moves would be "destabilizing" and could provoke the Soviet Union into a preemptive strike.

The strong Soviet commitment to the process of so-called "arms limitation" does not invalidate the contention that it operates on a first-strike doctrine. As has become evident since 1972, SALT I has had no significant influence on the development of Russia's strategic offensive forces. The same may be said of SALT II which, if ratified, would exert only a minimal effect on future Soviet deployments, while inhibiting and in some cases precluding important U.S. responses (such as long-range cruise missiles and protective shelters for the Minutemen missiles). Adopting for negotiating purposes the American "Mutual Assured Destruction" doctrine, the Soviet Union has been able to push through, at a relatively small price to its own deployments, severe restrictions on those of the United States.

Nuclear missiles, however, have not only a military utility: they are equally and perhaps even more useful

---

[5] "Soviet Defense Expenditures in the Era of SALT," United States Strategic Institute Report 79-1 (Washington, D.C., 1979), pp. 10-11.

as a means of political and psychological suasion. Russia's growing nuclear arsenal inculcates in influential Western circles a sense of all-pervasive fear which induces a spirit of accommodation. Once the view gains hold that there is no defense against nuclear weapons, it becomes not unreasonable to advocate avoidance of disagreement with another nuclear power as the highest goal of foreign policy. The following sentiments expressed by Congressman Jonathan Bingham of New York are quite typical of this body of opinion:

Above all, we must remember that the Soviet Union remains the world's only other superpower —the only country in the world capable of destroying us. Maintaining good relations with the Soviet Union must be our *paramount* objective.[6]

I wonder whether Congressman Bingham has thought through the implications of his words. For he is, in effect, urging that we subordinate all our national interests as well as our ideals of freedom and human rights, and whatever else many of us regard as "paramount," to another criterion, namely, survival; and that in line with this criterion, we should seek accommodation with that country which can deny it to us. (Only we: there is nothing in this passage to suggest that the Soviet Union has a similar obligation toward us, the only country in the world capable of destroying it.) When this kind of thinking becomes prevalent, a nation loses the freedom to act in self-defense: psychologically, the white flag of surrender is up and sending unmistakable signals to the adversary. It takes little imagination to picture what effect this kind of thinking must have on the Soviet leaders: it virtually incites them to keep on increasing their nuclear preponderance, given that the greater their theoretical capability to destroy the United States, the louder the voices in the United States demanding that accommodation with the Soviet Union be made the "paramount" objective of national policy.

Soviet global strategy is implemented by means of pressures exerted at various points of the globe in a bewildering succession of shifts that makes it difficult to discern patterns and causes some observers to interpret it as a mere exploitation of random opportunities. But this is not the case. Just as Soviet defense strategy calls for the disposition of forces around the Queen of the chessboard, namely, nuclear-tipped missiles, so its territorial strategy aims at the enemy's King, the United States. The latter is the only country with the wealth and power to frustrate Soviet intentions: the fall or even isolation of that "citadel of international imperialism" would allow the rest of the world to be picked up at will. A world in which the United States carries no weight comes automatically under Soviet hegemony. The reduction of the United States, therefore, is as essential to the Soviet Union as the elimination of Carthage was to Rome.

But this objective cannot quite be achieved by a succession of Punic wars: military conflict with its principal adversary is the least palatable of the alternatives open to Moscow because the U.S. nuclear arsenal can never be entirely suppressed and it is always able to inflict, no matter what the balance of power, devastating punishment. Hence, except in the realm of ideological warfare, to which the United States attaches no importance and where the most venomous hate campaign can be carried on with impunity, assaults on the U.S. must assume indirect forms that undermine America's security without appearing to do so.

This aim is best attained by detaching Europe and Japan from the United States and pulling them into the Soviet orbit: the addition of West European and Japanese industrial capabilities to those of the Soviet bloc would alter immediately and in a most dramatic manner the global correlation of forces in the latter's favor. Here economic statistics speak for themselves. The annual Gross National Product of the Warsaw Pact countries for 1977-78 was estimated at $1 trillion; that of the United States at $2 trillion; that of Western Europe at somewhat above $2 trillion; that of Japan somewhat under $1 trillion. By this yardstick, the present correlation of economic forces is 5-to-1 in favor of the West; but it shifts to 4-to-2 in favor of the Communist bloc once Western Europe's and Japan's links with the United States are severed. Even if one allows for a 50 per-cent decline in European and Japanese productivity as a result of such a change (has it not been said that under Soviet domination the Sahara would promptly experience a shortage of sand?), Moscow could still confront the United States as at least an economic equal.

But an assault on Europe and Japan is risky, because they are protected by forces with large U.S.

[6] Victor C. Johnson, co-author, *Foreign Affairs*, Spring 1979, p. 919; emphasis added.

contingents as well as by the U.S. strategic deterrent. Hence, here too an indirect strategy is preferable.

The Soviet Union may be said to be laying siege to Western Europe and Japan in the same manner in which medieval castles were blockaded prior to the introduction of gunpowder—that is, by a systematic effort to cut off the flow of reinforcements and supplies: reinforcements of manpower and material from the United States, and supplies in the form of fuel and metals from the Middle East and South Africa.

In the event of war, there would be activated a giant sea and air lift pouring troops and material from the United States to the European front. To disrupt this flow, the Russians have constructed a powerful ocean-going navy, centered on submarines and concentrated in ports of the Kola peninsula. This navy would have the task of penetrating the Iceland-Faroes-England gap and striking at American convoys.

As political backing for this naval strategy, the Soviet government exerts relentless pressure on the Scandinavian countries, sometimes directly, sometimes through the agency of Finland. To relieve that pressure, Norway and Denmark have for a long time refused the stationing of NATO troops and nuclear weapons on their territory; this act of self-denial has by now become part of the status quo which the Soviet Union jealously guards and is unlikely to permit to change. . . . The construction in Finland of highways pointing in the direction of Norway strongly suggest[s] that in the event of hostilities the Russians would strike fast to seize Norwegian ports and airfields, as Hitler had done in 1940. Sweden, not a member of NATO, is frequently harassed with accusations of violating its neutral status. It was apparently in response to Soviet browbeating that the Swedes consented to supply the USSR with a floating drydock capable of servicing a giant aircraft carrier presently under construction there. This Soviet activity in Scandinavia is given scant attention by the American media although its strategic implications for Europe are not much less than the more familiar Soviet challenge to the oil routes. Nine-tenths of U.S. war supplies to the European fronts would have to travel by sea, so that a serious Soviet threat to the North Atlantic sea lanes would be bound to have significant repercussions on the progress of European operations. (According to testimony by the recently retired commander of the Atlantic Fleet, Admiral Isaac Kidd, the Allied navies could maintain control of the North Atlantic sea lanes in face of this threat but only at a very high cost.)

The other Soviet pincer is directed toward the Middle East and aims at cutting off, in the event of hostilities, fossil fuels and minerals without which the economies of America's allies would not be able to function. The task here is much more difficult to accomplish than in the north, if only because the Red Army lacks naval and air bases in this area, but the intensity of the effort bespeaks the strategic design. Soviet forces have been positioning themselves over the years near three principal choke-points through which Middle Eastern oil supplies must travel en route to their destinations in Europe and Japan. One of these is the Straits of Bab el Mandeb which guard access to the Red Sea and the Suez Canal. Soviet and pro-Soviet forces stationed in South Yemen and Ethiopia would undoubtedly attempt to seize this waterway in the event of war. To the east lie the Straits of Hormuz, at the entrance of the Persian Gulf. The Soviet Union has a long way to go to gain a stranglehold on these straits, but it should be noted that its occupation of Afghanistan has cut in half (from 1,100 to 550 kilometers) the distance Soviet planes must traverse to reach them. Finally, in Southeast Asia, where it has a friendly client in Vietnam, the Soviet Union is within reach of the Straits of Malacca, a major route for oil tankers on their way to Japan.

European and Japanese dependence on South African minerals, though less well known than their reliance on Middle Eastern oil, is nevertheless considerable. America's allies derive a high proportion of such industrial minerals as chrome, platinum, vanadium, and manganese from Rhodesia and South Africa. The intense involvement of the Soviet Union in the so-called "national-liberation" movements in sub-Saharan Africa, the quick exploitation of opportunities offered by the dissolving Portuguese empire, indicate the intention to deny these resources to the West.

The flanking movement directed at Europe through Africa and the Middle East brings the USSR into contact with Third World countries and demands the formulation of a Third World political strategy. In the immediate post-Stalin years, the Soviet Union relied on alliances with so-called "national-bourgeois" movements, that is, movements that shared with the

Soviet Union a common hostility toward the "capital-ist" and "imperialist" West without being pro-Communist or socialist. They provided the kind of "temporary" allies whose utilization Lenin had rec-ommended. The policy called for the exploitation of the anti-Western, anti-colonial sentiments of charis-matic national leaders, some of them tainted with pro-Axis collaboration, as a means of eliminating the many strands of Western influence which remained in place even after formal colonial ties had been cut.

This strategy proved, by and large, disappointing. The Third World leaders whom the Soviet Union cultivated and supported with munificent aid turned out to enjoy too narrow a power base to serve as reliable allies: the sudden death of one or a successful coup against another could change the political cli-mate in a given country overnight, turning it from a friend into an enemy and, in the process, sending billions of rubles' worth of aid down the drain. Such disagreeable reversals occurred in 1965 in Indonesia with the overthrow of Sukarno and a year later in Ghana with the removal of Nkrumah. Even worse were the consequences of the change in political orientation accomplished by Sadat after the 1973 war during which the Soviet Union had given him invalu-able help. Once Sadat concluded that the concessions he desired from Israel could be procured for him by the United States but not by the Soviet Union, and that to qualify for U.S. support he needed to assume an anti-Soviet stance, the days of Soviet influence in Egypt were numbered. Moscow had to stand by helplessly while its immense investment in Egypt went to naught.

The defection of Egypt was the unkindest blow to Soviet policies in the Third World. Egypt was the linchpin of Soviet Middle Eastern strategy, the political-military base from which Moscow hoped to expand its influence both into East Africa and into the Arabian peninsula. It was the recipient of unstinting Soviet aid. To save its armies from impending disas-ter, the Soviet Union had engaged in a serious confrontation with the United States. And all this proved in vain once the "bourgeois-nationalist" dicta-tor decided to reorient his foreign alliances.

Following Egypt's defection, Moscow seems to have undertaken a reappraisal of its Third World strategy, the results of which are becoming increasing-ly apparent. The new strategy calls for smaller reli-ance on "bourgeois-national" leaders like Sukarno, Nkrumah, and Sadat, in favor of minor political

figures who owe their political status to Soviet back-ing. Such new Soviet friends in the Third World as the recently deceased Neto of Angola, Colonel Mengistu of Ethiopia, and Taraki and Karmal of Afghanistan are not national heroes with their own power base, however narrow, but small-time politicians dependent on Moscow's support. To place them in power—or to remove them from it once they have proven inconvenient—the Russians have not hesitated to resort to gangster-type "executions" by their military or security services. To buttress their influence, they bring in large numbers of permanent Soviet military "advisers," Cuban mercenaries, and security services from the USSR and Eastern Europe. Once these forces are installed, an infrastructure is created which is fairly impervious to sudden changes in native leadership. Because of the presence of Soviet, Cuban, and East European military and police personnel within their borders, it is unlikely that either Angola or Ethiopia will slip out of Soviet control as easily as Indonesia or Egypt did. To solidify their hold further, the Russians have assisted their hand-picked heads of state in carrying out mass murders of the opposition: according to the late Amin, the Taraki government in Afghanistan during its brief tenure in office executed 13,000 political prisoners. Massacres on a similar scale have been perpetrated in Ethiopia.

Promising as the new Third World strategy is, it is not without drawbacks. In countries in which it intervenes so heavily, the Soviet government assumes deeper commitments and finds it even more difficult to accept with equanimity the prospect of the area's slipping out from under its control, as its recent actions in Afghan-istan have demonstrated. Here even the advanced type of control—hand-picked candidate, surrounded by Soviet military and police advisers, and made secure by extensive bloodletting of opponents—did not suffice and a full-scale occupation was deemed necessary.

It is doubtful whether the Soviet Union would have dared to intervene in the Caribbean as it is now doing were it not for a fortunate accident. In 1962, in what he seems to have regarded as a major diplomatic coup, President Kennedy agreed to guarantee Cuba from American invasion in return for the Soviet removal from there of its medium-range ballistic missiles. This guarantee proved so valuable to the Soviet Union, by providing it with a secure base for political subversion and military action in the Western hemisphere, that one is tempted to suspect that the USSR had planted the missiles in Cuba precisely in order to wrest just such an agreement. Cuba provides limited but potentially valuable air and naval bases to Soviet forces. It also furnishes troops and political cadres to carry out Soviet missions in the Middle East, Africa, and Central America. It is altogether the most dependable Third World ally, headed by a megalomaniac whose self-defined historic mission requires him to lean heavily on Soviet assistance.

There remains China. In regard to that country, the Soviet Union seems to have settled, after a certain hesitation, on a defensive strategy. In the early years of their quarrel, some Soviet leaders seem to have desired a quick, preemptive strike against China, but in the end cooler heads prevailed. The prospect of fighting another totalitarian regime, thousands of miles away, in an area poorly served by transport, was not appealing to a regime which, if it is to fight at all, must win quick, decisive victories. Soviet forces presently deployed in the Far East are formidable, to be sure, but they do not appear designed for offensive operations. The Chinese military estimate that in order to present a credible threat to them, the Russians would have to mass along their frontier between 2 and 3 million troops, which is several times the number they have there at present. Soviet missiles, too, are deployed mainly against NATO.

To frustrate Soviet global strategy, it is necessary, first and foremost, to acknowledge that it exists. We must get rid of the notion, widespread among America's educated and affluent, that the Soviet Union acts out of fear, that its actions are invariably reactions to U.S. initiatives, and that it seizes targets of opportunity like some kind of international pickpocket. We are dealing with an adversary who is driven not by fear but by aggressive impulses, who is generally more innovative in the field of political strategy than we are, and who selects his victims carefully, with long-term objectives in mind.

Secondly, it is essential to overcome an attitude toward nuclear weapons which leaves us increasingly vulnerable to subtle forms of psychological and political blackmail. We once had a similar attitude toward cancer: it used to be thought that the mere mention of this disease brought it about. In fact, however, open discussion of cancer has led to early diagnosis and treatment, and considerably reduced the danger of

death from it. Nuclear weapons are a kind of cancer of the international body politic. Awareness of their actual (rather than imaginary) dangers can lead to sensible measures being taken to reduce the risk of nuclear war breaking out and to keep casualties low should it nevertheless happen. Unless we are prepared to confront this danger, the growing Russian preponderance in strategic weapons will leave us in a position where we shall have no choice but to capitulate to Soviet demands whenever they are backed with the threat of war.

Thirdly, we should take an honest look at our alliance system which has deteriorated to the point where its utility seems more psychological than real. For some time now NATO has been a one-way street: the United States underwrites the security of Western Europe against Soviet attack, but its West European allies feel no particular obligation to support the United States in its confrontations with the Soviet Union in any other part of the world. This holds true even of the Middle East where Europe's interests are, if anything, yet more directly involved. Such behavior encourages the Soviet leaders to act aggressively in the Third World, in the knowledge that here the United States will be confronting them alone, and that such confrontations serve to exacerbate America's differences with its allies.

Fourthly, we must correct as rapidly as possible the skewed military balance, especially where strategic and naval forces are concerned. If a commensurate effort is undertaken by Western Europe and Japan, and if the mutual obligations of our alliance are made more equitable than they now are, then Soviet expansion into the Middle East and Africa ought to prove costlier and therefore less attractive.

The ultimate purpose of Western counterstrategy should be to compel the Soviet Union to turn inward —from conquest to reform. Only by blunting its external drive can the Soviet regime be made to confront its citizenry and to give it an account of its policies. It is a well-known fact of modern Russian history that whenever Russian governments suffered serious setbacks abroad—in the Crimean war, in the 1904-05 war with Japan, and in World War I—they were compelled by internal pressure to grant the citizenry political rights. We should help the population of the Soviet Union bring its government under control. A more democratic Russia would be less expansionist and certainly easier to live with.

Soviet Domestic Politics and Foreign Policy
Stephen F. Cohen

Soviet Russia has been on our minds—a virtual obsession—for exactly sixty years. During these sixty years, far more has changed in the Soviet Union, and in the world, than in our perceptions and ideas. Even now, as a new American debate on Soviet domestic and foreign policy unfolds, it seems clear that much of our thinking still bears deep traces of that narrow consensus once admired as "bipartisanship," and that in many quarters cold-war attitudes and misconceptions are as firmly lodged as ever. This should alarm us, not only because of the sterile foreign policies this kind of thinking once produced, but because of the way these cold-war attitudes have distorted our own domestic values and priorities.

Any rethinking about Soviet intentions and behavior abroad must begin with an understanding of Soviet domestic politics and society. Indeed, American thinking about Soviet foreign policy over the years has almost always emphasized this connection; and, by the same token, most of our misconceptions of Soviet intentions abroad have derived from misconceptions of the character and direction of Soviet domestic factors. In particular, the tenacious view of a continuously revolutionary and militantly expansionist Soviet Union, a view that dominated American thinking for so long and has now, after a short decline, reappeared in opposition to detente, is based on a static, ahistorical image of a fundamentally unchanged and unchanging Soviet system. Just as observed alterations in Soviet foreign policy are dismissed, in this view, as merely tactical maneuvers in a relentless drive for world conquest, so too are internal changes said to be secondary to the basic continuities that determine the real nature of the Soviet Union and its intentions abroad.

No informed person will deny that the Soviet political system continues to be a highly authoritarian and often repressive one, which systematically deprives its citizens of elementary political liberties, or that the USSR is a formidable international adversary with great power ambitions around the world. Nor will a careful student any longer argue either of two once-popular extremes—that there is an immutable irreconcilability between the Soviet Union and the United States; or, on the other hand, that modern history is somehow moving toward a "convergence" between the two systems. The rejection of these two excessive perspectives should be our starting point, the minimal consensus from which different perspectives proceed. Beyond this, however, there is an almost unlimited potential for disagreement among knowledgeable people.

We have learned a great deal about Soviet life in recent years, but this knowledge has demonstrated mainly that none of our conceptions or models of the Soviet Union are adequate—that all are far too simplistic. The main thing we have learned is that behind the crumbling facade of political and social conformity, there is a tremendous diversity and complexity of reality at every level of Soviet life. Students of Soviet economics, for example, have begun to speak less of an omnipotent centralized planned economy and more of a "multicolored" economy of official and unofficial components, state and private enterprises, controlled and free transactions, of red, white, grey, and black markets.[1] We need the same kind of "multi-colored" approach to Soviet reality in general, which conforms as little to our models as it does to official Soviet ones, whether we are discussing the high politics of the Communist Party or the everyday life of ordinary citizens.

In this connection, I want to make four very general points about Soviet politics and society. They concern realities often obscured but which influence Soviet intentions and behavior abroad in important ways. First, the history of the Soviet Union provides many examples of internal change, and there is no reason to exclude the possibility of further change in the future. Second, the Soviet leadership today faces —as will its successor—an array of serious domestic and foreign problems; and while these problems should not be construed as crises that seriously enfee-

[1] See, for example, A. Katsenelinboigen, "Coloured Markets in the Soviet Union," *Soviet Studies*, January, 1977, pp. 62-85.

From Stephen F. Cohen, "Soviet Domestic Politics and Foreign Policy," in Fred Warner Neal (ed.), *Detente or Debacle: Common Sense in U.S.-Soviet Relations*. New York: Norton, 1979, pp. 11–28.

ble or endanger the system, neither should they be minimized. Third, there is within both Soviet society and the establishment itself a great diversity of opinion, political outlook, and proposed solutions to these problems. And fourth, this diversity of opinion must nonetheless be understood in the general context of a deep rooted political and social conservatism, which is widespread among Soviet officials and ordinary citizens alike.

CHANGE IN THE SOVIET SYSTEM

To understand that Soviet history has witnessed periodic and far-reaching internal changes is to reject the popular view of an immutable Soviet system. The fact that the main institutions of the political system—the Communist Party, the official Marxist-Leninist ideology, the planned state economy, the political police, and so forth—have continued to exist over the years says little. It is a commonplace of political history that deep changes in the working and nature of a political system often occur within a continuous institutional framework, and in this process the institutions themselves are inwardly changed. The American Presidency and the English Parliament continue to exist; but they are not the same institutions they were in the 19th century. Nor do the American and English political systems function just as they did a hundred years ago. Even the names that historians customarily give to the main periods in Soviet political history bespeak the deep changes that have recurred since 1917: War Communism, the New Economic Policy, Stalinization, de-Stalinization.

The most recent of these great changes in the Soviet Union must be kept in mind when we talk about the present and the future. Our focus on the continuing authoritarianism and political abuses in the Soviet Union obscures the fact that during the Khrushchev years there occurred in that country an authentic political and social reformation. Virtually every area of Soviet life was affected by the changes, however contradictory and ultimately limited, of 1953-1964, from the end of mass terror and freeing of millions of prison camp victims, the measures introduced to limit at least some of the worst bureaucratic abuses and privileges, the civic awakening and growing political participation of educated society, and the array of economic and welfare reforms, to revisions in Soviet foreign policy that led to what we now call detente.

For our own thinking, the significance of this reformation (sometimes called de-Stalinization), which changed the Soviet Union for the better in many fundamental ways, is threefold. First, it reminds us that current Soviet abuses of power and violations of civil rights, however deplorable, are far more limited and less severe than in the Stalinist past. Second, it is evidence that a short time ago there existed inside the Soviet Union, within the Soviet political establishment, and apart from international pressures, significant forces for reform. There is no reason to assume that such forces do not still exist. And third, it helps us to understand the conservative reaction that followed the overthrow of Khrushchev in 1964 and continues today. In another society, this reaction would be considered normal. In American and English politics, for example, it is thought to be virtually axiomatic that periods of reform are followed by conservative backlashes.

Some of the major problems faced by the Soviet leadership today are common to industrial societies, but many are the direct legacy of Soviet historical development, the limitations of the reforms of 1953-1964, and the conservative reaction after 1964. Western specialists disagree as to which problems are the most serious, much depending on the specialist's own interests. Suffice it to itemize a few that Soviet citizens themselves emphasize.

At home, there is a chronic decline in industrial and technological development and persistently low labor productivity; a collective agricultural system which still cannot reliably feed the population; widespread consumer grumbling and housing shortages; a politically restive intellectual class; disenchantment with official values among young people; growing birth rates and nationalist sentiments among the major non-Slav groups, and a declining birth rate among Russians; a small but defiant dissident movement along with a large readership of uncensored (*samizdat*) literature; and, in the realm of political authority, the still unresolved, and pertinent, question of the terrible crimes of the Stalin era. More generally, I would stress the overarching administrative problem of a centralized bureaucratic system created in the very different conditions of the 1930's, which still prevails in all areas of Soviet life—political, economic, social, cultural, scientific—and which generates and institutionalizes a multitude of inefficiencies, Catch 22's, and popular resentments. On another level, I would stress the manifestations of rampant alcoholism and family disintegration, and, from the party's viewpoint, the revival of religious belief, because they reflect or impinge upon so many other problems.

At the same time, the Soviet leadership, for all its gains as a great power since 1945, can find little solace in foreign policy achievements. There is the perceived menace of China; the recalcitrant empire in Eastern Europe, which has been the scene of a major crisis every decade; the advent in Western Europe of so-called Euro-communist parties, whose success threatens to complete the de-Russification of international communism; the familiar problem of third-world "allies," who become fickle or difficult to control, as in Egypt and India; and the staggering costs of a global competition, however peaceful, with the United States.

The main thing to be said about these problems is not that they portend an imminent crisis, but that they represent long-term and hopelessly intertwined dilemmas and impose severe constraints on domestic and foreign policy, and that there is no real majority view as to their solution.[2] In part, this is because no majority consensus has been allowed to develop through an uncensored public discussion. But, equally, it is because of the deep divisions on every major issue and problem, even among Soviet officials and party members.

For many years, misled by the silence and conformity imposed by Stalin's terror, we imagined something

that did not exist—a homogeneous Soviet officialdom and even society. The complex reality is now clear: the diversity of Soviet opinion is probably equal to that in any "open" society (though more private, of course), ranging from orthodox Marxism-Leninism to Russian Orthodox religion, from democratic to authoritarian, liberal to neo-fascist, from left to right. More important for our purposes, variations of this diversity exist within the political establishment and even inside the ruling Communist Party.

This will surprise those who take seriously official claims of a "monolithic" party, who continue to speak meaninglessly of "the Soviets," "the Communist mind," and "ideological blueprints," and who imagine an unbridgeable gulf between the party-state and society-at-large. In fact, it may be that a monopolistic political party inescapably acquires a more diverse membership than do parties in multiparty systems simply because there is no organized alternative.[3] Whatever the case, it makes no sense to think of the Communist Party, with its more than 15 million members, or the Soviet state, which employs virtually the entire population, as somehow remote or apart from society. At the very least, we must understand that while the party-state seeks to direct and control society, it is permeated by the diverse, conflicting attitudes of that society.

It is in this context that we can gain a better perspective on the dissident movement, which has come to figure so prominently in American thinking and, alas, is in danger of becoming the hostage of our foreign policy. Western specialists have trouble reconciling two seemingly contradictory truths. On the one hand, we know that the emergence and persistence of open dissent is an important development in Soviet history. On the other hand, we know that the active dissidents are very small in numbers and political impact.

How can we reconcile these truths? By realizing, I think, that most of the different trends of thought expressed openly by dissidents are to be found, in at least some subterranean form, within Soviet officialdom. This does not mean that dissident activists are spokesmen for real or potential oppositionists inside the establishment, but simply that dissident views

---

[2] As an example of how these problems are related and create interlocking constraints, consider the following. Beginning with the Khrushchev period, the Soviet leadership has made repeated promises, and unfolded several unsuccessful campaigns, to satisfy the consumer desires of the population. This is, I think, a genuine commitment, deriving partly from ideological tenets of communism, which sounds in official statements increasingly like the Welfare State plus consumerism, and partly from a need to counter political demands of the intelligentsia. But this commitment to a mass consumer-goods program is inseparable from other areas of domestic and foreign policy. It involves a restructuring of economic life and thus raises the question of reforms in the planning, industrial, and agricultural sectors. It involves new techniques of economic decision making and thus the problem of centralized power. It involves capital investments and allocations incompatible with escalating military budgets and grandiose commitments abroad. Meanwhile, Soviet consumerism is part of the leadership's concept of a peaceful competition abroad with the United States, as well as its anxiety that working-class discontents over prices and wages in Eastern Europe could be replicated in the Soviet Union.

[3] Ilya Erenburg, the late Soviet writer, once remarked, complaining about some of his fellow party members, that the problem with having only one party is that anybody can get in.

reflect in significant measure, however obliquely, the array, and disarray of attitudes among officials as well.

Most important for our thinking about future Soviet and American policy are the competing political trends inside the Communist Party, and particularly at its middle and upper levels. Our knowledge here is imprecise, and this advises caution and against speculation. But it is safe to say that the three main trends, which have formed and struggled over the past 25 years, may be termed reformist, conservative, and reactionary or neo-Stalinist.[4] I use these terms loosely to designate amalgams of party opinion, not single-minded groupings.

Party reformers, who are certainly now the weakest in number and influence, include some advocates of authentic democratization, but many more administrators, managers, or technocrats who only want more initiative, and hence some liberalization, in their own areas of responsibility, be it the economy, science, culture, or international affairs. The conservatives, who have predominated almost everywhere in Soviet politics since the mid-1960's, also include various types, from sincere believers in the virtues of the *status quo* to cynical defenders of vested bureaucratic interests. Some lean toward the moderate reformers, some toward the neo-Stalinists. The party's neo-Stalinist wing can only be called reactionary. Its solutions to contemporary problems are couched in an extreme Russian chauvinism and nostalgia for the more despotic ways of the Stalin days, though short of the mass terror which, as they know, victimized Soviet officials capriciously, regardless of political outlook.

Although these party trends are part of the power struggles that range more or less continuously across all the important policy areas, it would be wrong to think that they have nothing in common. All are proud of the Soviet Union's achievements at home and abroad, nationalistic and patriotic in one way or another, loyal to the party system, and, to take a specific example, fearful about China. Nor are they incapable of collaboration in various areas of policy-making. Like politics elsewhere, much of Soviet politics involves compromises and coalitions. Most reformers and conservatives seem now to favor, for example, detente and expanding economic relations with the West, though for different reasons; reformers hope it will promote economic reform at home, while conservatives hope it will enable them to avoid it. At the same time, there has been a growing conservative-neo-Stalinist coalition in cultural and intellectual policy in recent years.

Future change in the Soviet Union will depend in large measure on the struggle between these trends in the party. Change can be for the better or the worse, of course, toward liberalization or back toward a harsher authoritarianism. Since its inception in 1964, and especially since 1966-68, the conservative or centrist, Brezhnev government has turned increasingly toward the party's neo-Stalinist wing, particularly in domestic affairs. The bleak prospect of still greater neo-Stalinist influence, or even a leadership dominated by these party elements, cannot be excluded. I personally, however, have not yet succumbed to the chronic pessimism that seems eventually to come over many Western Specialists on the Soviet Union. I do not rule out the possibility of another wave of reform, during or in the aftermath of a leadership succession.

SOVIET REFORM AND CONSERVATISM

Any genuine reform requires, however, two conditions, both of which concern us. First, it must be reform with a Soviet face. Those among us who argue that Soviet reform must be patterned on Western examples or imposed from abroad understand little about Russia or the process of reform in general. No reform movement anywhere, but especially in a country as historically self-conscious as the Soviet Union, can be successful estranged from its own history and culture. It must find inspiration, roots, and ultimately legitimacy within its native—in this case, Russian *and* Soviet—political and historical traditions. A Soviet reformism couched in Westernism, or encumbered by foreign sponsors, would be tainted and doomed. For this reason alone, the best hope are those Soviet innovators who reason in terms of the existing system, whether they call themselves liberal socialists, communist reformers, democratic Marxist-Leninists, or

---

[4] There are several informed accounts of these trends, though categories and labels sometimes vary. See, for example, Roy A. Medvedev, *On Socialist Democracy* (New York, 1975), chap. iii; and Alexander Yanov, *Detente After Brezhnev: The Domestic Roots of Soviet Foreign Policy* (Berkeley, California, 1977). Much first-hand information on reformers and neo-Stalinists is available in the *samizdat* journal *Politicheskii dnevnik* (2 vols; Amsterdam, 1972 and 1975). Since the 1950's, these trends have been associated with, and articulated in, various official journals.

simply doers of small deeds, and not those who repudiate the whole Soviet experience since 1917.

Second, much will depend upon the international environment, and thus American policy and behavior. Soviet reform has a chance only in conditions of a progressive relaxation of tensions between the USSR and its foreign adversaries. Worsening international relations will drive the Soviet Union back into her isolation and past, strengthening reactionaries and further diminishing reformers of all stripes. Or to take a different example, a complete break between the Soviet Communist Party and the Euro-Communist parties of Italy, France, and Spain would be an unfortunate development. These European parties have been a source of some restraint and liberal influence on the Soviet leadership, and a break would only further reduce this kind of Western influence and strengthen hard-line tendencies in the Soviet Union.

If this perspective on the future is one of guarded optimism, my last general point about the Soviet domestic scene is different. Despite the diversity of Soviet opinion, the predominant outlook, again both among officials and ordinary citizens, is a profound conservatism. This conservatism is strongest, of course, among the older generation, which still dominates middle and upper levels of officialdom, but it also appears to play a role in the attitudes of the younger generations.

By "Soviet conservatism" I mean the everyday gut sentiments that characterize socal and political conservatism elsewhere, including in our own country. It is a deep sentimentality about one's own past, about the commonplace and familiar, an instinctive preference for existing routines and orthodoxies (however obsolete), and a fear of things new as somehow threatening and potentially chaotic. Politically, it is not always a flat rejection of any change; but it is an almost prohibitive insistence that change be very slow, tightly controlled, based on "law and order" (which is also a Soviet catchphrase) lest "things will be worse," and hence it is an instinctive, though often conditional, deference to political authorities that guard the present against the future, including the armed forces and the police.

That a system born in revolution and still professing revolutionary ideas should have become one of the most conservative in the world may seem preposterous. But history has witnessed other such transformations, as well as the frequent deradicalization of revolutionary ideologies.[5] Moreover, there are specific, and mutually reinforcing, sources of this Soviet conservatism. All of those factors variously said to be the most important in Soviet politics have contributed to it: the bureaucratic tradition of Russian government before the revolution; the subsequent bureaucratization of Soviet life, which proliferated conservative norms and created an entrenched class of zealous defenders of bureaucratic status and privilege; the geriatric nature of the present-day elite; and even the official ideology, whose thrust turned many years ago from the creation of a new social order to extolling the existing one.

Underlying all the factors making for Soviet conservatism is the Soviet historical experience, which is still for a great many citizens the story of their own lives. If few nations have achieved so much in so short a time, none has suffered such a traumatic history. In sixty years, man-made catastrophes have repeatedly victimized millions of Soviet citizens—the first European war, revolution, civil war, two great famines, forcible collectivization, Stalin's great terror, World War Two. Every family has lost someone dear, often more than once. These memories live with an intensity that is hard for us to imagine. The victims have often been the essential elite of any nation's progress —the young, the strong, the enterprising, the gifted. No less remarkable than the Soviet Union's achievements is the fact that they were accomplished in the face of these colossal losses. Out of this experience in living memory have developed the underlying joint pillars of Soviet conservatism—a sense of great national pride and earned prestige from the achievements, together with an anxiety that the next disaster forever looms and must be guarded against.

Because we are slow to recognize this conservatism, we have yet to calculate fully its influence on either Soviet domestic or foreign politics. At home, it is an important bond—a truly collective sentiment— between the government and the majority of the people. It affects all areas of policymaking, all segments of the population, high and low, and even political dissidents, who fear internal turmoil as much as they object to the government.

Its influence on foreign policy cannot be easily exaggerated. Above all, this conservatism informs

[5] See Robert C. Tucker, *The Marxian Revolutionary Idea* (New York, 1969), chap. vi.

Soviet leaders' acute sense of national prestige, a crucial element in their outlook obscured by our rival notions that they are either aggressive ideologues or cynical realists. When offended, this prestige factor can cause them to postpone, or even jettison, international relations that they otherwise desire, be it economic, trade or arms limitation agreements. On the other hand, when they perceive a ratification of Soviet prestige and status, it can lead them to join in international agreements that included provisions not to their liking, such as the Helsinki accords of 1975.

To put this differently, we usually discuss Soviet policy in military terms of "strategic parity." This is important, of course. But the larger Soviet striving in recent times has been for political parity, equal respect as the other super-power—full recognition of its achievements and rightful place in the world. As with the United States, this striving means both conserving and where possible enhancing the Soviet Union's status in a changing world. It is manifest in the Soviet infatuation with traditional diplomatic protocol, global meddling, and obsessive counting of everything from Olympic medals to strategic weapons. And nothing is more insulting than persistent suggestions in the West that the achievements and power status of the Soviet Union are somehow illegitimate.

Righteous indignation about foreign "interference in our internal affairs" is often a hypocritical dodge. But when a Soviet official complains, to take a recent example, that "James Carter has assumed the role of mentor to the USSR,"[6] we hear the voice of hurt pride and genuine resentment. The "surprising adverse reaction in the Soviet Union to our stand on human rights," which President Carter now acknowledges, should have surprised no one. It proved to be "a greater obstacle to other friendly pursuits, common goals, like in SALT, than [President Carter] had anticipated"[7] because, contrary to American spokesmen, there was for Soviet leaders a "linkage." Perceiving a direct affront to their self-esteem, they reacted—as they did when confronted by the Jackson-Vanik and Stevenson Amendments in 1974—accordingly, and predictably.

The ways that this conservatism can influence Soviet behavior are too numerous to explore here. A

last example must suffice. American critics of detente and SALT see aggressive military intentions in the circumstance that "Americans think in terms of deterring war almost exclusively. The Soviet leaders think much more of what might happen in such a war."[8] Given the Soviet unpreparedness and loss of perhaps 20 million people in the last war, we should be surprised if it were otherwise. Indeed, a Soviet government that did not make some efforts in this direction, for example the civilian defense programs in which our anti-detente lobby sees such ominous implications, would hardly be a Soviet government at all.

NO ALTERNATIVE TO DETENTE

What does all this tell us more concretely about Soviet foreign policy and prescribe for American policy? For me there is no sane or moral or otherwise desirable alternative to what is now called, somewhat loosely, detente. If we begin with the simplest literal meaning of the word—a relaxation of historical tensions between Washington and Moscow—and with its foremost objective—a reduction of the possibilities of war through strategic arms control—the alternative, an "Era II of the Cold War," is plainly unacceptable in the nuclear age. Those Americans, and their Soviet counterparts, who insist that detente is a "one-way street," that "we have nothing to gain from it," or that the two countries share no basic interests, should say openly that they prefer a world of escalating arms races, nuclear proliferation, and mounting risks of mutual destruction by design or mishap.

Reducing the risks of nuclear war is the first, indispensable, and irreproachable reason for detente. There is, however, even among its American (and Soviet) advocates, a spectrum of thinking about the desirable nature and scope of detente. Some advocate a narrow policy centered almost exclusively on military issues. While this position is preferable to the flatly anti-detente one, it is one-dimensional and unrealistic. Cooperation in the area of military safeguards is inseparable from broader forms of cooperation that promote stable relations between the two countries. I favor a policy of detente that can go

[6] *The New York Times*, June 9, 1977.
[7] *Ibid.*, June 26, 1977.

[8] Paul Nitze quoted in Charles Gati and Toby Trister Gati, *The Debate Over Detente* (Headline Series, No. 234; New York, 1977) p. 27.

beyond relaxation of tensions to full relations on all levels, but one consistent with intractable realities and free of extravagant expectations. For this we need an understanding of detente considerably broader than today's events.

Just as the history of the cold war did not begin in 1947-48, but in 1917, what we now call detente did not begin in 1972. Leaving aside early milestones such as our belated recognition of the Soviet Union in 1933, the contemporary history of detente began in the Eisenhower-Khrushchev era, and not with the Nixon-Brezhnev phase. In short, detente is a historical process with previous stages of development that include both progress and setbacks. At different stages, quite different issues have been in the forefront and have defined the status of detente at the time—pullbacks from military confrontation, cultural exchanges, summitry, Berlin, Cuba, the Middle East, arms talks, trade, Jewish emigration, human rights.

It is therefore essential that detente as an ongoing and future process not be understood as something ultimately determined by one or more current events. This kind of political gimmickry, practiced sometimes by the opponents of detente as well as Nixon-Kissinger proponents of detente, can only produce unrealistic expectations and needless disillusionment, as we are now witnessing. A durable detente policy must be both historical and long-sighted.

Even in the best circumstances, there will be tough bargaining, resentment, serious misunderstandings, sharp disagreements, and open conflicts of national interests between the United States and the USSR. The goal is to reduce these elements progressively at each stage. We are, after all, talking about "detente" between long-standing rivals with very different social systems, political traditions, and orthodoxies, and not about Anglo-American relations. To imagine that these differences will disappear, or even diminish notably, in an appointed time because of proclamations is dangerous nonsense.[9] To promise detente without conflict, or to reject detente because of the

conflict, is silly illogic. It is like saying that the job of diplomacy is only to formalize what already unites nations, and not to reconcile what divides them.

Two primary conditions for a progressively broadening detente are already present. First, there are substantial domestic forces for detente in both countries, despite parallel controversies about its dangers, strong opposition, and fluctuating internal conditions. Alarmist warnings about secret Soviet "intentions" and strategic "blueprints" fly in the face of the realities. Escalating military expenditures, the danger of mutual destruction, economic problems, and other domestic factors have brought a sizable part even of the conservative Soviet establishment away from old autarchic habits to acceptance of fuller relations with the West.

In other words, the main thrust of Soviet conservatism today is to preserve what it already has at home and abroad, not to jeopardize it. A conservative government is, of course, capable of dangerous militaristic actions, as we saw in Czechoslovakia and Vietnam; but these are acts of imperial protectionism, a kind of defensive militarism, not a revolutionary or aggrandizing one. It is certainly true that for most Soviet leaders, as presumably for most American leaders, detente is not an altruistic endeavor but the pursuit of national interests. In one sense, this is sad. But it is probably also true that mutual self-interest provides a more durable basis for detente than lofty, and finally empty, altruism.

The second existing condition is a shared philosophy of detente. Both sides now officially define detente as including both cooperation and competition, in peaceful conditions, between the two countries. If cooperation through SALT eliminates or significantly reduces military competition, we have no reason to fear the other kinds of competition, assuming we have confidence in our system. If American business firms cannot be allowed to trade freely with Soviet agencies, it speaks poorly for the capitalism the United States claims to profess. If the Soviet leadership's refusal to give up what it calls "ideological struggle," which so alarms our critics of detente, deters us, this speaks poorly for our own ideology, which emphasizes the virtue of conflicting ideas.

Without exaggerating or blinking away the competitive and conflictual aspects, we should pursue the cooperative component of detente vigorously and imaginatively. Global areas of cooperation, such as strategic arms control, ecology, and food shortages, may require protracted negotiations and the partici-

[9] Historians will find some whimsy, or at least understatement, in the following: "Two years is a relatively short time in which to alter the long-standing practices of sovereign nations, either in regard to one another or to their citizenries." The Commission on Security and Cooperation in Europe, *Report to the Congress of the United States on Implementation of the Final Act of the Conference on Security and Cooperation in Europe: Findings and Recommendations Two Years After Helsinki* (Washington, August 1, 1977), p. 5.

pation of other nations. But there is a wide range of immediate opportunities for fuller bilateral relations in the areas of trade, education, culture, science, sports, and tourism, to name a few.

Detente is too important to be left to governments alone. A variety of nongovernmental American organizations and citizens have been pursuing these kinds of relations, sometimes in the face of official American indifference and even obstructionism, for many years. They should be encouraged, and their ideas and expertise solicited, so that detente will become not merely fuller government-to-government relations, but institution-to-institution, profession-to-profession, citizen-to-citizen relations, both as a buffer against leadership changes in both countries and as a way of building popular support here and in the Soviet Union. Meanwhile, the American government should make its own direct contribution by, among other things, promoting trade by granting to the Soviet Union favorable tariff and credit provisions,[10] funding larger and more diverse exchanges of people, and pressing for liberalized entry-visa procedures and fewer travel restrictions in both countries.

American policy alone cannot, of course, guarantee the future of detente. This requires no less a pro-detente Soviet leadership with sufficient support in its own high establishment to withstand the inevitable setbacks in Soviet-American relations. And this returns us to the Soviet domestic scene.

Supporters of the Jackson-Vanik Amendment and other restrictions on detente have, so to speak, a half-idea. They argue, correctly, that the future of detente must be related to change inside the Soviet Union. Unfortunately, they seem not to understand that domestic change can also be for the worse, and that liberalizing change depends upon the respective political fortunes of trends and groups inside the Soviet establishment. These proponents of a kind of remote American interventionism in Soviet politics violate what should be our first axiom: We do not have the wisdom or the power, or the right, to try

directly to shape change inside the Soviet Union.[11] Any foreign government that becomes deeply involved in Soviet internal politics, or for that matter in Soviet emigre politics (whose many different "ambassadors" will continue to appeal to us), will do itself and others more harm than good.

What the United States can and should do is influence Soviet liberalization *indirectly* by developing a long-term American foreign policy, and thereby an international environment, that will strengthen reformist trends and undermine reactionary ones inside the Soviet Union. This means a further relaxation of tensions, increasing contacts on all levels, and drawing the Soviet Union into full, stable relations with the Western countries—in short, detente. This is not, in the lingering rhetoric of another generation, "appeasement." Such a policy allows for hard bargaining for our own national interests and private demands for certain kinds of Soviet behavior. But it is predicated on an American conduct that takes into account the nature of Soviet conservatism and is not calculated to offend needlessly the self-image and prestige of the Soviet establishment. Our new interventionists fail on all counts. Bombastic ultimatums, discriminatory congressional restrictions, and condescending preachments addressed publicly to the Soviet leadership offend the conservative majority, vivify the xenophobic prophecies of the reactionaries, and make meaningful reform suspect, if not impossible, as a concession to outside pressure.

THE "HUMAN RIGHTS" CAMPAIGN

This brings us, finally, to the issue of political rights[12] in the Soviet Union, which (for better or worse) has become a central focus in our current debate over

---

[10] This means, of course, reviving the Trade Act of 1972 by repealing the Jackson-Vanik Amendment and the Stevenson Amendment, which severely restricted Export-Import Bank credits to the USSR. For a persuasive argument in favor of expanding trade, see Daniel Yergin, "Politics and Soviet-American Trade: The Three Questions," *Foreign Affairs*, April, 1977, pp. 517-38; and on the more general aspects of detente, Marshall D. Shulman, "On Learning to Live With Authoritarian Regimes," *ibid.*, January, 1977, pp. 325-38.

[11] An unfortunate example of this lack of wisdom and potential for mischief was Senator Jackson's attack on the well-known dissident Roy Medvedev as "nothing but a front man, a sycophant for the leadership." Senator Jackson went on to liken Medvedev to "certain Jews [who] fronted for Goering, Goebbels, and Hitler." *The New York Times*, January 28, 1975. Expelled from the party, subjected to periodic searches, and out-of-work, Medvedev is a democratic Marxist who tries to speak to and for reformers inside the party.

[12] The Carter Administration has defined this issue in terms of Soviet "human rights," which is inexact. The issue is political rights or liberties. The term "human rights" includes a whole range of economic and other welfare problems, in which the Soviet Union, in the world context, can boast considerable achievement.

detente. The question is terribly complex, even agonizing, especially for people with first-hand knowledge of the Soviet Union. And like other issues that are translated superficially into a Manichean choice between morality and immorality, it creates acrimonious divisions and false illusions.

Our own disagreements about American policy toward Soviet political rights should be among Americans equally committed to political liberties as a universal principle. The real question is not the validity of this principle, but whether specific American policies actually promote political liberties and safeguard dissent in the Soviet Union. There are, for example, knowledgeable Westerners who have had extensive contact with Soviet dissidents over the years, who admire them as courageous individuals and as representatives of a noble cause, but who have deep misgivings about recent American measures in this area. Furthermore, speaking for myself, it is fully consistent to want a larger moral aspect in American foreign policy, especially after our immoral and even criminal commissions in Vietnam and Chile, and still disapprove of certain American measures directed against Soviet violations of political rights. This does not reflect, as is sometimes charged, a bias in favor of left-wing dictatorships and against right-wing ones, but concern for the actual consequences of a specific policy.

American proponents of a hard-line policy exhort us to rally behind "our friends, the Soviet dissidents." But the Soviet dissident community is itself deeply divided into at least three groups on the question of American policy.[13] The larger group does insist that a tough American line on behalf of Soviet political rights has been, and will continue to be, only beneficial. They want more, and stronger, of the same. A second group acknowledges that recent American actions have caused the democratic movement setbacks and hardships, but insists that they will be beneficial in the long-run—how and when is left unclear. The third group argues that tougher American policies, from Senator Jackson's to President Carter's, have had, and can only have, a negative impact because, by going beyond diplomatic pressure to open confrontation, they galvanize Soviet conservative and reactionary opposition and jeopardize both active dissidents and reformers inside the Soviet system.

General references to "the Soviet dissidents" are therefore meaningless. Dissident opinion is far too diverse. Indeed, there are even Orthodox nationalist dissidents who dislike both detente and American interference in Soviet affairs. But even the numerical fact that most dissident activists want a hard-line American policy does not prove its wisdom. It reflects instead the fact that since 1972 many Soviet protesters have increasingly lost hope in internal sources of change and thus, for reasons of politics and morale, have looked increasingly to pressure from outside and specifically from the United States. We can understand this psychological development; but good sense tells us that it is bad for us and for them.

The proof is, as we say, in the pudding. President Carter's human rights campaign of early 1977 (insofar as it was directed at the Soviet Union), like earlier measures linking trade and detente to levels of Jewish emigration, has done more harm than good. It may be inexact to call President Carter's campaign a policy since, as Andrew Young has stated, it "was never really set down, thought out and planned."[14] It may even be that the campaign originated as much with domestic American political concerns.

Whatever the case, the "adverse reaction in the Soviet Union" was unanticipated. Though it is possible that a new Soviet crackdown on dissidents was planned even before President Carter took office, the nature and dimensions of the crackdown were made worse by American statements and actions. Each dramatic act of the Carter Administration's campaign — sharp warnings on behalf of Soviet dissidents in late January, the President's personal letter to Andrei Sakharov in early February, his White House meeting with exiled dissident Vladimir Bukovsky in early March—was followed by new acts of Soviet repression at home, from the arrests of Aleksandr Ginzburg and Yuri Orlov in February to the interrogation of American correspondent Robert Toth in June. We must see clearly what ensued—a dangerous game of political chicken, reminiscent of the cold war, played at the highest levels. ("We're not going to back down," declared President Carter.)[15] The victims were both our "common goals" and Soviet dissidents themselves.

[13] For a full examination of this subject, see Frederick C. Barghoorn, *Detente and the Democratic Movement in the USSR* (New York, 1976).

[14] *The Washington Post*, June 6, 1977.
[15] *The New York Times*, January 31, 1977.

Why did the Carter Administration's campaign become counterproductive? I do not think that the reason is to be found in the President's general statements on human rights and Helsinki. In signing these accords, the Soviet leadership must have reconciled itself to something along these lines, particularly from a new American administration, as part of the "ideological struggle." The reason was rather the way in which the campaign directly assaulted, even if only inadvertently, all those aspects of Soviet conservatism I discussed earlier. Two highly publicized episodes— the President's letter to Sakharov and the White House invitation to Bukovsky—are vivid examples.

The Carter campaign began in January, 1977, and thus coincided with the sixtieth anniversary year of the Russian revolution, when Soviet conservatism and official self-esteem are in continuous celebration and at their most acute. The Administration's first statements and President Carter's letter then came on the heels of an extraordinary event and one of Sakharov's rare mistakes—his public suggestion that Soviet authorities themselves were responsible for the fatal bombing in a Moscow subway in early January. Scarcely any dissidents took this suggestion seriously, and Sakharov himself later seemed to regret it.[16] More important, the bombing was an exceptional event that greatly alarmed and embarrassed Soviet authorities. The decision to issue a Presidential statement on Soviet civil rights in the form of a letter to Sakharov on this unusual occasion was, to be kind, very bad judgment. Nothing could have been more offensive to official Soviet sensibilities or to have assured a stronger reaction. (It may also have confirmed doubts among some Soviet officials about the authenticity of American concern for Soviet political rights.)

The Bukovsky affair raises similar questions of judgment. In December 1976, the Soviet government exchanged Bukovsky, a defiant and brave dissident then in his eleventh year of prison camps and mental hospitals, for the jailed Chilean Communist leader Luis Corvalan. This, too, was an extraordinary development. The Soviet Union not only dealt equally with what it calls a "fascist dictatorship," it also acknowledged for the first time its own political prisoners.

International publicity had made Bukovsky's personal fate an embarrassment. But it seems likely that the Soviet decision to risk its prestige in this dramatic way also had the larger purpose of weighing the feasibility, and political costs, of future agreements for the release of other Soviet prisoners.

Any such possibility was aborted, at least for the time, by President Carter's invitation to Bukovsky. Their meeting, which had the earmarks of a public relations coup against former President Ford's rebuff to Aleksandr Solzhenitsyn, allowed Bukovsky to denounce the Soviet government from the White House, implied that his release was a triumph of American policy, and thereby probably persuaded Soviet leaders that the political costs of such releases were too high. If our real concern is the plight of people, and not a propaganda victory, where is the morality in this outcome?

The same criticism applies to earlier American campaigns, culminating in the Jackson-Vanik Amendment of 1974, to make trade and detente dependent upon levels of Soviet Jewish emigration. The net effect was, as we know, to diminish that emigration considerably. But other questions were similarly ignored during the presidential primary season, when the issue of Jewish emigration came to the fore. Did the almost exclusive focus on Jews who wished to leave, with scant regard for other groups, reflect a moral commitment to the principle of open borders or the political power of Jewish lobbies in this country? How much thought was given to the frightful backlash that this campaign was certain to have on Soviet Jews who did not wish to emigrate? And how can monthly or annual quotas, and Soviet compliance, be determined when no one knows how many Jews actually want to leave?

The case against these kinds of short-sighted, highly publicized, and politically volatile campaigns that link American policy to specific events, issues, or prominent dissidents inside the Soviet Union is, I think, overwhelming. They involve us in complexities and ramifications beyond our control and in moral ambiguities beyond our resolution. Inside the United States, they encourage a revival of cold-war attitudes which could again distort our own domestic priorities, while undermining public support for detente. Internationally, they generate tensions and confrontations between Moscow and Washington detrimental to our mutual interests, endanger private concessions already granted by Soviet and East European authori-

[16] Various explanations of the bombing circulated in Moscow. The most frequent theory linked it to food shortages, poor living conditions, rumors of price increases, and other discriminatory practices in provincial towns outside Moscow. This theory viewed it as a Polish-style protest.

ties (in the area of family reunification, for example),[17] and, perhaps most important, they create an atmosphere unconducive to Soviet liberalization. Inside the Soviet Union, they arouse the conservative majority against American "interference," taint both dissidents and reformers as "Western agents," abet the party's neo-Stalinist wing, and further divide and misguide the dissident community.[18]

Indeed, the most ominous of recent Soviet reactions is neither the new arrests, which arguably would have come anyway, nor the setbacks in SALT negotiations, which after a decent interlude will move ahead, but the official Soviet campaign linking dissidents, and potentially any reformer, to the American government and specifically to the CIA. The emptiness of this charge is matched only by its grim revival of one of the worst themes of the Stalinist past. It seems to be, alas, a response to the Carter Administration's own campaign and plain evidence that the neo-Stalinists have gained new influence in Soviet affairs.[19]

THE LESSONS TO BE LEARNED

The lessons to be learned are not all negative. They teach us that whatever potential the American government has for influence on the Soviet leadership in the area of political rights must be exercised in private negotiations and not through public ultimatums, sermons, and other confrontations of national prestige.

[17] Prime Minister Trudeau and Chancellor Schmidt have expressed concern, for example, that increased movement of people from Eastern Europe to Canada and West Germany may be jeopardized. *The New York Times*, July 17, 1977. Austrian Chancellor Kreisky expressed similar concerns earlier. *The International Herald Tribune*, March 16, 1977.

[18] On February 7, 1977, the prominent dissident Yuri Orlov said publicly, "I think after the State Department statement on Ginzburg I will not be arrested." He was arrested three days later. This is, of course, subject to different interpretations, one being that Orlov's own statement made certain his arrest.

[19] On March 21, 1977, in a speech little noted outside the Soviet Union, Brezhnev made an unusual distinction between internal critics. Constructive critics were to be thanked; mistaken but "honest" critics were to be forgiven; but "anti-Soviet" critics, who had Western support and were often "imperialist agents," were to be punished. In the Soviet context, these distinctions suggested some flexibility and even a little "liberalism." My guess is that Brezhnev was trying to guard against neo-Stalinist excesses in the anti-dissident campaign. See *Komsomol'skaia Pravda*, March 22, 1977.

Since "quiet diplomacy" appears to have acquired a sinister connotation, let us call it simply "diplomacy."

The Soviet leadership wants detente and the various agreements that it encompasses. In the proper place and manner, American respresentatives, from the President to State Department officials, can and should make clear that American public support for these relations depends significantly upon the status of political rights in the Soviet Union. Modest concessions and achievements are possible, certainly at first in the areas of emigration and family reunification. Despite its abominations in other areas, the Nixon-Kissinger administration did in fact achieve a great deal in this way. If our purpose is to help people, why scorn it?

At the same time, the American government should push for fuller relations at all levels with the Soviet Union. Not only because this will promote a general international environment more conducive to Soviet liberalization, but because these diverse contacts create additional opportunities for direct influence. The Soviet Union has demonstrated its desire for expanded, regularized transactions with, for example, American business, scientific, and other academic groups, which in turn gives these groups some influence on their Soviet counterparts and thus indirectly on Soviet policy-makers.

Moreover, it is at this profession-to-profession level that outcries against specific violations of political rights can be most effective. A good example is the campaign on behalf of Academician Sakharov waged successfully by the American Academy of Sciences in 1973. An organized protest by a professional association and directed to its Soviet counterpart is more effective because it does not directly confront the Soviet government's prestige, it allows the Soviet leadership at least the fiction of referring the matter to a lesser Soviet body, and it thus draws a broader (and frequently more liberal) segment of Soviet officialdom into the deliberations. In brief, unlike official campaigns by the American President or Congress, it leaves room for concessions.

The final guideline simply reiterates the axiom I tried to formulate earlier. Any policies that involve the American government deeply in the quite different world of Soviet domestic (or emigre) politics will end badly. It is neither indifferent nor platitudinous to emphasize that the Soviet future must be decided by people in the Soviet Union and in their own way. I believe that even modest reform within the existing system would be good for them, for us, and for the world, and that this remains a real possibility. But the main contribution our government can make is more concern for our own problems at home, and a calm policy of restraint and detente abroad.

QUESTIONS FOR DISCUSSION

1 What motivates Soviet foreign policy behavior?
2 What are the Soviet Union's legitimate security interests?
3 What actions would the Soviet Union have to take before United States policymakers accepted the proposition that the Soviet Union was not expansionistic?
4 How have American actions promoted insecurity in the minds of Soviet political leaders?
5 Are there actions that could be taken by the West to produce changes in Soviet society and policies that the West would find desirable?

SUGGESTED READINGS

Aron, Raymond. "From Yankee Imperialism to Russian Hegemony?" *Encounter* (August 1979), pp. 10–21.

Barnet, Richard J. *The Giants: Russia and America.* New York: Simon & Schuster, 1977.

Gray, Colin S. "The Most Dangerous Decade: Historic Mission, Legitimacy, and Dynamics of the Soviet Empire in the 1980s." *Orbis* **25** (Summer 1981): 13–28.

Hoffmann, Stanley. "Reflections on the Present Danger." *New York Review of Books*, Mar. 6, 1980, pp. 18–24.

Kaiser, Robert G. "U.S.-Soviet Relations: Goodbye to Detente." *Foreign Affairs* **59** (Fall 1980): 500–521.

Lens, Sidney. "But Can We Trust the Russians?" *Progressive* (July 1980): 19–20.

Solzhenitsyn, Alexsandr. "Misconceptions About Russia Are a Threat to America." *Foreign Affairs* **58** (Spring 1980): 797–834.

Valenta, Jiri. "The Soviet Invasion of Afghanistan: The Difficulty of Knowing Where to Stop." *Orbis* **24** (Summer 1980): 201–218.

Vernon, Graham D. "Controlled Conflict: Soviet Perceptions of Peaceful Coexistence." *Orbis* **23** (Summer 1979): 271-297.

Yergin, Daniel. *Shattered Peace: The Origins of the Cold War State and the National Security State.* Boston: Houghton Mifflin, 1977.

8 Is the United States an Imperialistic Power?

YES

William Appleman Williams

Empire as a Way of Life

NO

Neal B. Freeman

Colonial America

Empire as a Way of Life
William Appleman Williams

I

From the beginning, our imperial way of life seduced us into assuming that we could go on forever projecting the present into the future: that we could start over again and again and again. F. Scott Fitzgerald understood that when he had Jay Gatsby speak these lines: "Can't repeat the past," he cried incredulously. "Why of course you can."

That traditional assumption was elevated into a blind faith by the tremendous absolute and relative power that we Americans enjoyed after 1945. We came to think of ourselves as being beyond history— *beyond being human.* Secretary of State Dean G. Acheson expressed the feeling perfectly in his attitude that "only the United States could get hold of History and make it conform." It was not simply our military and economic power over other societies; it also, and perhaps more importantly, involved the way that we allowed our technological accomplishments to fragment the essential continuity—the process—of life. The most obvious example is television, which defines experience as disconnected episodes without significant relationships or consequences. A terrifying distortion of reality certified by Walter Cronkite's daily Hail Mary: "And that's the way it is." But in truth it is extremely difficult to imagine anything further from the way it is.

We can see that dramatically illustrated by our response to events in Iran, the West Bank, Afghanistan and in America itself. Our intellectual, political and psychological confusion is the result of our *a*historical faith that we are not now and never have been an empire. Yet there is no way to understand the nature of our predicament except by confronting our history as an empire. That is the only way to comprehend the Iranian demand that we acknowledge our long term interference in their affairs, the widespread anger about our acquiescence in the progression of Israel's settlements on the West Bank, the Russian charge that we apply one standard to them and another to ourselves and the deep resentment of us among the peoples of poor countries. The only way we can come to terms with those matters is to look our imperial history in the eye without blinking, flinching or walking away into the wonderland of Woodrow Wilson's saving the world for democracy.

EMPIRE DEFINED

Let us start with a workable definition of empire: the use and abuse, and the ignoring, of other people for one's own welfare and convenience. Now in truth, America was born and bred of empire. That does not mean that we are unique; indeed, just the opposite. We are part and parcel of the imperial outreach of Western Europe that came to dominate the world. But therein lies the irreducible cause of our present predicament. We have from the beginning defined and viewed ourselves as unique. The differences between ourselves and other nations are not incidental but they are irrelevant to the fundamental issue. We are different only because we acquired the empire at a very low cost, because the rewards have been enormous and because until now we have masked our imperial truth with the rhetoric of freedom.

But we do have a bench mark. Once upon a time, about a century before America was rediscovered by Christopher Columbus, at least the fifth time someone had done it, the Chinese sent seven massive fleets westward to Africa and perhaps on into the Atlantic Ocean. The ships measured between 400 and 500 feet, and there were enough of them to carry upward of 37,000 people. Their so-called junks were impressive intercontinental missiles. The Chinese came, they traded, they observed. They made no effort to create an empire or even an imperial sphere of influence. Upon returning home, their reports engendered a major debate. The decision was made to burn and otherwise destroy the great fleets and concentrate on developing Chinese society and culture.

The point is not to present the Chinese as immaculately disinterested, or whiter than white. It is simply to note that we now know that the capacity for empire does not lead irresistibly or inevitably to the reality of empire. The Chinese, driven south by the Mongols and other invaders, could easily have rationalized

From William Appleman Williams, "Empire as a Way of Life," *The Nation* (August 2–9, 1980): 104–107 and 110–119.

empire as necessity. They chose instead to defeat the invaders and develop their own culture in its almost infinite variations on the two themes of Confucianism and Taoism.

Not so with Western Europeans, including our English forefathers. They were not content with exploration and nonviolent intercourse with other cultures. From the beginning, the Western Europeans went for global empire. We Americans were conceived and born and bred of that imperial conception and way of life. We can explain that, even defend it, but we cannot deny it.

That phrase, that idea—*way of life*—puzzles some people and upsets other people. A way of life is the pattern of assumptions and perceptions, and values, methods and objectives, that characterize and guide the actions of a culture. Here are three amplifications of that definition:

"We stabilize around a set of concepts . . . and hold them dear. At each moment of each day we make the same mistakes."

"Those unconsciously accepted presuppositions which, in any age, so largely determine what men think about the nature of the universe and what can and cannot happen to it."

"*Ideas that we do not know we have, have us.* And they shape our experiences from behind, unbeknown."

THE PRICE OF FREEDOM

Within that framework, let us examine certain ideas that guided the development of our imperial way of life. Christianity was once a vital part of Western European expansionism. It provoked and justified all kinds of imperial activity; accumulating capital by conquest, striking terror into the hearts and minds of the heathens who wanted to keep their wealth for themselves and forcibly changing other peoples' ways of life the better to convert them to the true religion. I am more concerned here, however, with three ideas developed by secular British leaders that came to define so much of our own imperial outlook.

John Locke provided a fine summary of two of them in one classic paragraph. Wealth, he explained, was not defined by having what one needed but by having more than one's neighbor; hence it was permissible, even desirable, to take riches away from one's neighbor. That neatly doubled the relative advantage. The third proposition was most strikingly formulated by Sir Francis Bacon. The worst kind of

domestic disorder was caused by "the rebellions of the belly." Expansion was the only sure way to prevent that kind of threat to the social order. It not only generated economic growth but it dispersed potential troublemakers and thus decreased the density of discontent.

The American leaders who made the Revolution and the Constitution were familiar with all those imperial ideas. And in Virginia, for example, men of property had realized the value of imperial expansion for controlling the white poor long before Patrick Henry began talking about liberty or death. Indeed, the dialogue between other Virginians provides an excellent insight into the development of an imperial way of life. . . .

II

Make no mistake about it: the imperial way of life produced the promised rewards. It generated great economic wealth and effectively limited the scope and intensity of social discontent. By the time that James Monroe had left the White House, the United States had asserted its predominance throughout the Western Hemisphere and was well entrenched in Hawaii.

But we must also report the costs. I do not for a moment dismiss the people killed and the property stolen, but I would suggest that the greatest price was paid in the coin of our sensitivity about what we were doing and how that was understood by other peoples. We were already far down the road of *believing* that we were not an empire, and viscerally resenting any suggestion that we were an empire. And already far down the road, as Prof. Arthur K. Weinberg pointed out many years ago, of assuming that our right to security transcended the traditional right to defend what we had and had become the right to perfect security in any imaginable future contingency. We began to define security as the natural right to empire.

MORE FREEDOM: MORE EMPIRE

There was another cost. Americans became so habituated to empire as the price of freedom that they demanded ever more freedom and ever more empire. Andrew Jackson was at once a prime mover and the symbol of that new enthusiasm for the imperial way of life. More freedom at home and more expansion elsewhere. People like the Cherokees who could create and sustain a representative government within fixed spatial limits were clearly backward—and so a threat to the American Way. Move them out and force them to adapt to surplus space. People like the inhabitants of the northern half of Mexico, who used surplus space to relax and live a balanced and ecologically responsible life, were backward for another reason. They did not exploit the surplus space. So move them out or aside. And all the while other Americans, the merchants, the shippers, the sealers, the whalers and the Navy, were busy defining the sea to itself as another frontier to be penetrated, controlled and exploited. . . .

IMPERIAL FARMERS

. . . I suggest that American farmers of the nineteenth century provide us with a revealing illustration of the dynamic evolution of our imperial way of life. They began by defining empire as ever more free or cheap land and concluded by demanding strong government action to help them penetrate and hold foreign markets. All in the name of freedom and security. . . .

Nobody knows, or ever will know, what form the vigorous expansionism of the agricultural majority would have taken if William Jennings Bryan (or another agrarian leader) had won one or more of the elections of 1892, 1896 and 1900. But we do know what most of them did in response to the actions of their opponents, and that does not suggest that they would have mounted a frontal assault on the imperial way of life. They supported the annexation of Hawaii, demanded a tough line against Great Britain during the Venezuelan boundary crisis, agitated militantly for intervention in Cuba and cheered Adm. George Dewey's victory in the Philippines. As for Bryan, he shifted back and forth between reform at home and educating the Mexicans and other Latin Americans without dropping a note or mixing a metaphor.

BATTLESHIPS AND BIBLES

The agricultural spokesmen were defeated by urban commercial, financial and industrial leaders who accepted the importance of overseas markets and resources. Indeed, Lincoln's successors in the Republican Party increasingly stressed the martyred President's line of argument in building their constituency in the West. Ulysses S. Grant, James G. Blaine, Benjamin Harrison and William McKinley all responded to the rising demand for markets and sought to reform various heathens while challenging Europe's global power. . . .

BULLY POLICEMAN

During those three decades [1890–1920]. . . , the United States evolved and acted upon a coherent and dynamic imperial outlook. The image of themselves that Americans developed in those years is best characterized as one of the United States as a benevolent, progressive policeman. That view was classically expressed by Theodore Roosevelt and Woodrow Wilson: the former in his famous corollary to the Monroe Doctrine and the latter in his cry to make the world safe for democracy. . . .

Leaders like Hoover, Morrow and Secretary of State Charles Evans Hughes were not isolationists. They did not propose to refrain from using American power and influence. But they did entertain grave doubts about the imperial policies of Theodore Roosevelt and Woodrow Wilson. They wanted to reduce armaments and avoid military interventions, and they manifested a far more relaxed attitude toward the various movements for social change throughout the world. They also enjoyed a sense of history that gave them a perspective on the limits of empire and the counterproductive consequences of trying to control everything that happened around the globe. . . .

Given the approach that those leaders were attempting to put into operation, and the dynamics of their dialogue with more explicitly anti-imperial spokesmen, it is clear that the United States was beginning to come to terms with empire as a way of life. But that process was aborted when, for the fourth time in a century, the capitalist political economy collapsed in a massive depression. The Great Depression of the 1930s was a vast social trauma of great intensity, and the culture proved incapable of dealing with the crisis by evolving an alternative way of life.

SAVING AMERICA FIRST

The debate about foreign policy continued, but the talk rather quickly focused on its role in saving the system and on the question of going to war against Germany and Japan. The overriding concern with saving the system meant that serious talk about alternatives was lost in the scramble to find and apply traditional remedies. From the outset, for example, President Franklin Delano Roosevelt and his associates viewed expanded foreign trade and rearmament as central features of the New Deal.

Neither those nor other programs proved effective.

One does not have to cite radical critics. Harry Hopkins and Adolph A. Berle candidly admitted at the end of the 1930s that the New Deal had failed to restore the health of the political economy. There were still ten to twelve million unemployed, and the recession of 1937 was the most devastating one in the history of the country.

And so to war. But not a war to defend a functioning, equitable society—not even a new vision of such a society. And so into the dissembling and the lying; and into the stretching of the letter as well as the spirit of the Constitution—and the related weakening of the principles and practices of representative government. I say those things with great anguish because I thought then and I think now that we should have stood with England against Hitler.

But we should have done it at the end of an open, honest debate. And if the decision had been to wait and see, or to go to war only with a clear commitment to basic structural reforms, or to fight Germany but not Japan (or vice versa)—then so be it. What nags my soul in the sunshine on the Oregon beach is not that I was shot at and hit but that my leaders lied to me and never faced the real issue inherent in the imperial way of life. . . .

CHURCHILLIAN CHALLENGE

At that point, a disinterested observer from another galaxy might reasonably have expected Americans to face up to the price of their imperial way of life, perhaps even to consider an alternative. Now Winston Spencer Churchill was hardly disinterested, but he did his best to educate Americans about the elementary facts of imperial life. The fascinating and revealing part of our response to Winnie's tutorials is how we accepted his recommendation to stand firm while ignoring his advice—indeed, his pleas—to negotiate a clear, explicit and rational imperial settlement.

There are two primary explanations for that response. On the one hand, we simply could not confront the truth that we were an empire and so act responsibly as an empire. On the other hand, we could not imagine any alternative to empire as a way of life. Hence we revived Lincoln's policy of containment, extended Theodore Roosevelt's corollary to the Monroe Doctrine and set out once again to save the world for democracy—get hold of History and make it conform.

Nothing documents that as clearly as National Security Council Document No. 68, approved by President Harry S. Truman in April 1950. Notice first two things about that date: it is before the eruption of the Korean War and it is more than two years after Churchill almost begged us to come to terms with reality. Furthermore, NSC-68 is a reaffirmation and extension of NSC-20/4 of November 1948, which also came after Churchill's efforts to save us from ourselves.

NSC-68 begins with a disturbed review of how all the old empires have collapsed. It summarizes that overview with this revealing conclusion: "*Even if there were no Soviet Union we would face the great problem . . . [that] the absence of order among nations is becoming less and less tolerable.*" Then, defining the United States as the only nation capable of imposing such order, it makes the Soviet Union the focus of the effort. It candidly admits Churchill's main point: the United States and its allies possess greater power—enough to deter any direct attack.

But, unlike Churchill, American leaders concluded that such power must be further increased and deployed to "foster a fundamental change in the nature of the Soviet system"; "foster the seeds of destruction within the Soviet system," and foment and support "unrest and revolt in selected strategic satellite countries." As for means: "any means, covert or overt, violent or nonviolent." Then, pointing to the experience of World War II, the policy makers confidently predicted that the increase in military spending would prevent the possibility of any socially and politically explosive "real decrease in the standard of living."

III

In a rare moment of candor, Secretary of State Dean Acheson admitted in 1953 that he and Truman might not have been able to sustain their grandiose imperial policy if the North Koreans had not "come along and saved us."

On balance, however, it was simply one of those wars that anybody could have counted on to erupt sometime. Both halves of that divided country were dying to go to war to unite themselves. That old deb'l nationalism had been raised to fever pitch by very strong shots of mutually exclusive theology. In any event, the debate about who bears ultimate responsibility obscures the fundamental issue of the response by Truman and Acheson.

Clearly, when the Secretary acknowledged that Korea "saved us," he did not mean in the sense of preventing the defeat or the destruction of the United States. He meant only that it allowed the Government to implement the apocalyptic imperial strategy of NSC-68. Primed and ready, armed (or driven) psychologically as well as with the heady rhetoric of that document, they simply went to war. They bypassed the Congress and the public and confronted both with an accomplished fact. A few phone calls, and it was done. Go to bed at peace and wake up at war.

It was even more dramatic than the subsequent intervention in Vietnam as a demonstration of the centralization of power inherent in empire as a way of life. The State had literally been compressed or consolidated into the President and his like-minded appointees. In a marvelously revealing description, underscoring Truman's earlier lecture to the Cabinet, the war without a declaration of war was called a "police action." Ironically, the most succinct commentary applicable to Truman's remark was provided by an early editor of *The New York Times*. "We are the most ambitious people the world has ever seen," noted Henry J. Raymond on May 30, 1864, "—& I greatly fear we shall sacrifice our liberties to our imperial dreams."

EMPIRE AT BAY

The military containment and subsequent rout of North Korean forces (by the end of September 1950) created a moment of imperial euphoria. American leaders were high on NSC-68. The United States undertook to liberate North Korea by conquest and integrate it into the American empire. It was assumed in Washington that such action would accelerate the process of disintegration within and between Russia and China and so finally create an open door world. Then came the moment of truth, and the empire suddenly found itself at bay. The Chinese entered the war with massive force on October 26 and drove the Americans southward to the line that originally divided Korea.

Once again one thinks of the way American leaders failed to comprehend the willingness of black citizens to settle for promises of future equality and freedom at home. They had first misread and misapplied that episode in their dealings with the Russians, then with the Chinese and, finally, with increasing frequency, in Latin America, Africa, Southeast Asia and the Mid-

dle East. The mistaken assumption that other poor and demeaned peoples would display similar forbearance almost seemed like the cosmic cost of such prejudice and racism.

The Roosevelts, the Trumans and the Achesons, and most of their successors, fundamentally misconceived the deeply patriotic—even loving—commitment of American blacks to what Martin Luther King Jr. called The Dream of America. And because they could not acknowledge the existence of an American empire, they could not comprehend—let alone understand—that other so-called inferiors felt the same love for their cultures; and that, viewing America as an empire that threatened the integrity and existence of their cultures, they would ultimately fight rather than accept indirect destruction.

The empire had been brought to bay. Dwight David Eisenhower understood that essential truth, and further realized that the future character of American society depended upon how the culture responded. His first objective after he became President in 1952 was to end the Korean police action before it spiraled into World War III. That accomplished, he set about to calm Americans, cool them off and refocus their attention and energies on domestic development. He was a far more perceptive and cagey leader than many people realized at the time—or later.

The image of a rather absent-minded, sometimes bumbling if not incoherent Uncle Ike was largely his own shrewd cover for his serious efforts to get control of the military (and other militant cold warriors), to decrease tension with Russia and somehow begin to deal with the fundamental distortions of American society. He clearly understood that crusading imperial police actions were extremely dangerous, and he was determined to avoid World War III. When Britain, France and Israel attacked Egypt in 1956 over the nationalization of the Suez Canal, the President called British Prime Minister Anthony Eden and scolded him sharply: "Anthony, you must have gone out of your mind."

When the moment came, Eisenhower could be just as blunt with Americans. A good many of them were probably shocked when, in his farewell address of 1961, he spoke candidly and forcefully about the military-industrial complex that since 1939 had become the axis of the American political economy. That was such a catchy phrase that not many of them noticed that he went on to assault the distortion of education involved in that consolidation of power. The historically free and critical university, he noted, "the fountainhead of free ideas and scientific discovery, has experienced a revolution in the conduct of research. . . . A governmental contract becomes virtually a substitute for intellectual curiosity."

The speech was not an aberration: Eisenhower had become ever more deeply concerned with those issues after retiring from the Army. Thus, while it is true that he was not an intellectual, and was conservative in many ways, it is also true that he had a firm sense of how the State had gradually taken over the very process of creating and controlling basic ideas—the ways of making sense of reality. Or, in a different way, how the State used its extensive control of information, and its ability to make major decisions in the name of security, to create an ideology ever more defined in content as well as rhetoric as an imperial way of life.

Eisenhower's most serious weakness did not lie in his fidelity to a rudimentary version of marketplace economics, or even in his excessive caution about how quickly and how far he could move the American citizenry away from its imperial obsessions with Russia, China and other revolutionary movements. It was defined by his unwillingness to translate his valid perceptions into strong policies and active, sustained leadership. He lacked Hoover's (or even Churchill's) toughness about accepting the limits of American power and the former President's knowledge that the only way to deal with the costly and unhealthy consequences of empire was to begin creating a different way of life. Given his charisma, Eisenhower could have initiated that process and perhaps even created an irreversible momentum.

ENTER THE NEW FRONTIER

Failing to do that, he left no dynamic legacy. The militant advocates of the global imperial way of life quickly reasserted their power and policy. They, too, recognized that the Chinese counterintervention in Korea had brought the empire to a critical juncture. Their response was to reassert American power and get on with policing the world in the name of benevolent progress. Led by John Fitzgerald Kennedy, and calling themselves the New Frontiersmen, they perfectly expressed the psychopathology of the empire at bay and its consequences. Onward and outward in the

spirit of NSC-68. "Ask not what your country can do for you," intoned Kennedy in his 1961 inaugural address, "ask what you can do for your country." By country, of course, they meant *their* Government.

Kennedy and his advisors had the brilliant perception to talk about the empire in the classic idiom of the frontier. That propaganda gem is of itself almost enough to justify honoring them as the cleverest imperial leaders of their generation. The best that Henry Kissinger could do a few years later, for example, was to blurt out a crude reference to the same idiom—presenting himself as Gary Cooper in *High Noon*. The excessively self-conscious Dr. Cowboy will ride on stage in good time, but for the moment let us concentrate on those Kennedy hands who were born and bred to empire.

"Our frontiers today," cried Kennedy, "are on every continent." America has "obligations," he explained, "which stretch ten thousand miles across the Pacific, and three and four thousand miles across the Atlantic, and thousands of miles to the south. Only the United States—and we are only six percent of the world's population—bears this kind of burden." He understandably neglected to mention that the burden on the metropolis was somewhat eased by the benefits of controlling a grossly disproportionate percentage of the world's resources. He was more concerned with creating the psychological mood of impending doom: "The tide of events has been running out and time has not been our friend."

The failure of the effort early in 1961 to overthrow Fidel Castro's revolution in Cuba intensified that trauma. Not only did the rhetoric become ever more apocalyptic ("this time of maximum danger") but Kennedy immediately began a massive military build-up in the spirit of NSC-68 (three special requests for extra funds during 1961). Then he indulged himself in a truly arrogant and irresponsible act. Knowing that the United States enjoyed a massive superiority in strategic weapons. Kennedy publicly goaded, even insulted, the Soviet Union about its gross inferiority.

He scared the Russians viscerally, and in the process not only prompted them to launch a desperate effort to correct the vast imbalance but very probably touched off the internal Soviet dialogue that led to the confrontation in 1962 over Russian missiles in Cuba. The more evidence that appears about that moment on the edge of the abyss, the more it seems probable that the Russians never had any intention of going to war. Taken with all appropriate skepticism, for example, Premier Nikita Khrushchev's account very likely contains the essence of the truth: Moscow was less concerned with the possibility of a second invasion of Cuba than with somehow—even at sizable risk—jarring Washington into a realization that, if pushed to the wall, the Russians would fight rather than surrender. Given their grave inferiority, the only way they could make that point was by creating a situation that would dramatize for Americans the threat as experienced daily by the Soviet Union.

Kennedy's understanding of that message was limited. He spoke of the need to avoid further such crises, but he clearly felt that America had regained the initiative, that he was now free to deploy American forces to prevent or control further change that might weaken the American empire. He did talk about accepting diversity among the poor and developing nations, and about programs to facilitate some social and economic improvements in Latin America and other countries. And he did make some efforts, as in the Alliance for Progress and the Peace Corps, to act on that rhetoric. But he also embarked upon an obsessive campaign to murder Castro, and he deployed between 15,000 and 20,000 American troops (many of them in the field as advisers) to intervene in the revolutionary civil war in Vietnam. Those frontiers on every continent were going to remain frontiers in the traditional American meaning of a frontier—a region to penetrate and control and police and civilize.

WHAT HATH IMPERIALISM WROUGHT

This essay, an effort to review our development as an empire and to encourage a searching dialogue among ourselves about the character of our culture, does not attempt to offer a detailed reconstruction of American foreign policy. Hence it would be a contradiction in terms to wander off into a blow-by-blow account of recent events. But it does seem useful to explore some of the contemporary aspects of our imperial way of life.

Let us begin with the relationship between NSC-68 and the civil rights movement of the 1950s and 1960s; and let us assume that American leaders, whatever their prejudices or racism, believed that the empire would provide blacks and other disadvantaged groups (including poor whites) with greater opportunities and rewards. Their most popular euphemism for

empire—*growth*—was invoked on the ground that even the same share of an ever larger pie would produce improvement for everyone. And elitists like Acheson had reason to believe that the minorities and other poor would continue to be patient until the fruits of empire were harvested.

But the war in Korea, and the related increase in military spending, revealed the true priorities of the empire and hence dramatized the discrepancy involved in talking about empire in terms of liberty, freedom, equality and welfare while denying those benefits to large numbers of people at home. That contradiction was further highlighted by the nonviolent nature of black protest against being denied elementary equity on the buses of Montgomery, Alabama, in 1955 and in the eating places of Greensboro, North Carolina, in 1960. Some white Americans recognized and became upset about that contrast, but neither Eisenhower nor Kennedy devised an effective response. The former was socially and politically too conservative and cautious, and the latter was more concerned with standing up to the Russians all along America's global frontier.

L.B.J.'S TRAGEDY

But Lyndon Baines Johnson did make a brave—and in the end tragic—effort to resolve that visceral contradiction in the imperial way of life. He tried to make major improvements in the quality of life for the poor and disadvantaged of all colors (and therefore for all other Americans) and at the same time secure the frontier in Indochina. That proved to be impossible because by 1964–65 the dynamics of empire as a way of life left him no room to maneuver. Given the legacy of prejudice and racism, and the global definition of America's political economy and its security as formulated in NSC-68, Johnson was trying to swim in the sky. But at least he tried.

Stated bluntly, the President could not muster the votes to help the poor at home unless he honored the imperial ethic in Vietnam. He simply did not enjoy the personal and political advantages that enabled Eisenhower to move quietly toward a less grandiose foreign policy. That meant that any effort to make structural reforms at home would provoke a militant reaction around the classic imperial theme of "Who Lost Whatever Wherever?"

Johnson first tried to finesse the war issue. Therein lies the stuff of great drama. A modern Shakespeare might well do it this way: If only Johnson had gone with his instinct as a Southerner to recognize in the Vietcong the American blacks driven to violence, then he might—just might—have begun the process whereby Americans said no to empire and yes to the vision of community. But the imperial North had forever scarred the South. Left it resentful and determined to prove its valor and its equality. There is a great play in that old fear of the South transformed into a recognition of the truth that one either frees the slaves or confronts a rebellion. But the North had failed to learn that lesson during Reconstruction after the Civil War, and so Johnson had no allies to help him redefine the truth of America.

So from finessing the war Johnson moved to lying about the war. His effort to stand firm on the frontier while effecting reforms at home led him to create enormous inflationary pressures within the economy and to engage in ever more serious self-deception and public dissembling to sustain popular support for the imperial war. In the end, that is to say, Johnson was the victim of the basic fear, so candidly expressed in NSC-68, that America was fundamentally threatened by *any* disorder in the world (a fear also revealed in the President's intervention in Santo Domingo).

That fog of trepidation and dread continued to influence the conduct of foreign affairs by President Richard Milhous Nixon and Secretary of State Henry Kissinger. Their bone-marrow anxiety provides the key to resolving the apparent paradox in a diplomacy that sought to stabilize relations with the Russians while simultaneously recognizing the Communist Government of China, falsifying official records to hide an illegal and devastating expansion of the Vietnamese war into Cambodia, launching an effort to subvert an *elected* socialist Government in Chile and supporting a dictatorship in Iran that was instrumental in raising oil prices.

KISSINGER'S GEOPOLITICS

No one yet knows the precise nature of the relationship between Nixon and Kissinger. But Kissinger could not have functioned as he did without the support of the President. The Secretary of State has provided the most information about the assumptions that underlay their policies, and it seems apparent that they recognized that the grand objective of NSC-68—the subversion of the Soviet Union—was no longer realistic. Kissinger had long agreed with Churchill, for example, that the United States should have negotiated a broad settlement with the Russians in 1947–48, and concluded during the 1950s that American policy had "reached an impasse."

Thus it was necessary to stabilize the existing balance between the two superpowers. The first step on that road, at least in their view, was to assert their power over the bureaucracies in the State Department and other branches of Government—a task Kissinger undertook with great relish as an exercise of his own ego in the service of his great-man interpretation of history. That done, Kissinger could begin the effort to order and balance the world.

He now and again admitted the impossibility of doing that without a clear conception of such a system, and likewise spoke of the importance of justice, but he never provided either the vision or the definition of justice. Indeed, Kissinger had little patience with anyone who was concerned with the character of the world order he invoked so often. In one classic instance, for example, he dismissed such people for "confusing social reform with geopolitics." Yet his favorite word to define geopolitics was "equilibrium"—little more than a fancy synonym for order. As for justice, Kissinger might usefully have remembered the rabbi's wisdom about Deuteronomy 16:20: "Justice, justice shalt thou pursue." Asked why the word justice is repeated, the rabbi explained that it was done to emphasize the necessity of pursuing justice *with* justice.

Given the Nixon-Kissinger willingness to settle for controlling nothing more than the world outside Russia and Eastern Europe, their policy of détente and strategic arms control was a rational first step toward that objective. And it is certainly arguable that their approach to China (despite their tactics of secrecy and shock) was on balance a positive and stabilizing maneuver as long as it was not allowed to become a part of a new strategy of containment designed to destabilize the Soviet Union. And that caveat applies to subsequent American leaders as well as to Nixon and Kissinger.

The weaknesses of the Nixon-Kissinger approach became clear in their dealings with the rest of the world. On the one hand, they defined stabilization as allowing the United States to decide what was permissible and impermissible beyond the Soviet sphere. But, on the other hand, they lacked any significant comprehension or understanding of the dynamic, causal interrelationships between economics, politics and social affairs within the poor regions of the world, or between the global rich and poor. Hence they mistakenly linked any changes not approved or controlled by the United States to the influence of the Russians. The unhappy results became most apparent in Cambodia, Chile and Iran.

The unconstitutional bombing of Cambodia, which clearly did more to destroy the fabric and morale of that society than the incursion of the North Vietnamese which Kissinger used to justify the monstrous act, is in some respects less revealing of their diplomacy than their actions in Chile and Iran.[1] The American Ambassador to Chile began his report on that nation's Presidential election of 1970 with these words: "Chile voted *calmly* to have a Marxist-Leninist state, the first nation in the world to make this choice *freely and knowingly*." [Italics added.] In keeping with the primary responsibility of a foreign service officer, that is an essentially factual report; although adding the term *Leninist* to Marxist has long been the routine ploy used by those in power in America to turn an avowed socialist into a Communist pawn of the Kremlin. The ambassador then offered, in a wholly legitimate way, his evaluation of the evidence: it was in his view "a grievous defeat" for the United States.

Kissinger's account of America's subsequent efforts to prevent Salvador Allende from becoming President of Chile, and later to destabilize and subvert his Government, is remarkable for its conscious and unconscious revelations about the Nixon-Kissinger conduct of foreign affairs. Before Allende became President, for example, Kissinger presents the man as a doctrinaire Communist in a Russian mold. Once Allende becomes President, however, Kissinger talks about the *possibility* that he will *become* such a puppet. In a similar way, the former Secretary of State stresses Allende's narrow plurality in 1970 without once noting, even in a footnote, that Allende increased his vote in the next election, which was held in accordance with Chile's constitution.

All that tells us more than Kissinger intended us to

know, but he is even more illuminating when he insists that "our concern with Allende was based on national security, not on economics," and proceeds to emphasize "American interests in the hemisphere." There are three responses. First, Kissinger cannot seriously expect the observer to believe that Washington was worried about the Russians' turning Chile into a base for a strategic—geopolitical—military attack on the United States. Even he admits that the matter had been settled during the Cuban missile crisis, and, for that matter, refined during his tenure in the basement of the White House.

Second, if Kissinger did in truth not consider economic interests as an integral part of national security ("American interests in the hemisphere"), then one must conclude that he was stunningly obtuse and probably not qualified to be Secretary of State in the world's premier capitalist political economy.[2]

Third, in view of Kissinger's presentation of himself as a realist, he wholly ignores the feasibility of working with an elected socialist government as a hardheaded as well as moral strategy to counter the Soviet appeal in the Third World and to give hope to all democratic reformers in the poor nations. American leaders seem to be limited in their sight to the left by benevolent dictators like Marshall Josip Tito of Yugoslavia.

The Secretary's performance in dealing with Iran offers support for all those criticisms. Give him his due: he has quietly and cryptically admitted that his comprehension of the relationships between economic, political and social development was less than sophisticated. Hardly even rudimentary. But that is only part of the explanation of his failure in Iran. For it is extremely doubtful that anyone could control events in the non-Soviet world. Asked for his comment on the matter, Karl Marx would have laughed aloud in the reading room of the British Museum.

Still and all, it is difficult to imagine how anyone of Kissinger's intelligence could combine more errors of perception, understanding, analysis and policy in dealing with Iran. Neither he nor Nixon exhibited any sense of that nation's history, or even of its intensely

---

[1] Although everyone concerned with the Cambodian matter is indebted to William Shawcross's *Sideshow: Kissinger, Nixon and the Destruction of Cambodia* (New York: Simon & Schuster, 1979), it is important to remember that the House of Representatives Judiciary Committee raised and defined the issue during its consideration of the bill of particulars for the impeachment of Richard Nixon.

[2] It is possible, of course, that Kissinger made his disavowal in the hope of defusing the criticism that economic concerns were involved in the effort to subvert an elected government. If so, his sensitivity to the charge is revealing in its own right; and, in any event, he would have been better advised to be candid to avoid the thought that he was incompetent.

religious and nationalistic pride. And they obviously assumed that Iranians had accepted or forgotten that the United States had grossly intervened to control the resources and the government of that country even before overthrowing an elected government in the 1950s.

Given all that, it is not surprising that they embarked upon a policy doomed to failure. In embracing and arming the Shah, in truth a petty despot, they committed America's geopolitical interests to a government guaranteed to generate ever growing internal opposition to its pretensions. And in supporting, even encouraging, the despot to raise the price of oil to pay for his Tinkertoy regime they undercut the foundation of the American imperial way of life they sought to preserve.

The oil crisis is not a simple matter of the poor determined to become rich. It defines far more important issues. It asks to what lengths the United States is prepared to deny its commitment to self-determination, to freedom and liberty, in order to preserve its imperial way of life. The Palestinians are as much human beings as the Israelis. And so we come ever closer to the dangers inherent in lying to ourselves about our imperial way of life.

THE OIL-FIRED EMPIRE

America began to produce oil near Titusville, Pennsylvania, on August 27, 1859. Fifty years later the United States pumped more than the rest of the world combined. The political economy of capitalism shifted away from coal and neglected to explore other sources of energy. There was a short but intense oil scare between 1917 and 1924, a hullabaloo created by the Navy shifting to oil-fired turbines, the Mexican revolution, the boom in automobiles and airplanes, the beginnings of the petrochemical industry and the struggle for market supremacy (and survival) among American petroleum corporations.

That crisis disappeared in the cloud of confidence puffed up by the finding of new reserves abroad (as in Venezuela), by new discoveries at home (as in Texas), by more efficient exploration and production at home and—most particularly—by gaining access to the vast reserves in Saudi Arabia and other poor and weak countries in the Middle East. No better example ever of the rewards of empire as a way of life. But make no mistake, we also came to rely on other cheap materials from the provinces.

The United States continued to produce half the world's oil until, in 1948, it became a net *importer* of oil. True imperial dependency upon the natives. But a statement by John McCloy that we *should* "have our cake and eat it too" perfectly captures the euphoria of the imperial way of life as applied to oil. Americans, citizens as well as leaders, simply assumed that they could sell their oil abroad for a good profit while importing it from the provinces at *pennies a barrel.*

The imperial way of life was disrupted by the Organization of Petroleum Exporting Countries in 1973–74. But the oil-fired empire, once symbolized by the Navy and now by intercontinental bombers, could not talk about the problem in a realistic way simply because it had never come to terms with its imperial way of life. The euphemisms began to dissolve. The United States supported the creation of Israel for three reasons: a commitment to the principle of self-determination, the financial and political power of Jews in domestic American politics and the imperial usefulness of Israel as a client state in the oil-rich Middle East. The problem was that the Palestinians also had a right to self-determined nationhood, and oil was a most effective way to make that point.

And so the crisis deepened. Kissinger said it all in one sentence: The United States must somehow "shape events in the light of our own purposes." A marvelously subtle definition of empire. But not particularly that *somehow.* What a wonderful way of avoiding any coming to terms with the reality of empire. But to evade that moment of truth means again going to war.

No candor, more flight from reality. More flight, no peace. No chance finally to confront the central challenge:

Is the idea and reality of America possible without empire?

IV

We come full circle. History never provides programmatic answers. But it does guide one to ask the right questions—and that is crucial to developing the right answers.

It all calls to mind, once again, the wise observation offered by Carl Becker. We Americans must "be always transforming the world into [our] idea of it." Such a culture, "knowing that it is right, . . . wishes only to go ahead. Satisfied with certain conventional premises, it hastens on to the obvious conclusion." More than a bit like Wright Morris—we do duck off.

What are the right questions? I suggest that they are the same ones that Eugene Debs and Charles Beard—even Herbert Hoover—began to ask two generations ago. Asking the right questions is what we are about. I do not think that even Debs, let alone Beard or Hoover, have given us the right answers. Those people are important because they asked the right questions.

The best thing that can be said for our American empire is that we produced some very good questions. Now is the time to begin answering those questions.

Say regional socialism: push through the implications of the Tennessee Valley Authority, for example; or . . . whatever you have given serious thought to developing into a program.

I like to return to the question raised by our history.

Is the idea and reality of America possible without empire?

Can you even imagine America as not an empire?

I think often these days about the relationship between those two words—imagination and empire—and wonder if they are incompatible.

The truth of it is that I think they are incompatible.

So there we are.

Do you want to imagine a new America or do you want to preserve the empire?

Now, as surely we all know, preserving the empire is an exercise in futility. We will sizzle or suffocate.

So let us get on with imagining a new America.

Once we imagine it, break out of the imperial idiom, we just might be able to create a nonimperial America.

Colonial America
Neal B. Freeman

We are indebted to Philip Dunne, of all people, for his insight into the nature of our current leadership. A longtime writer and producer and on the side a Hollywood political activist, as the euphemism still has it. Dunne records a synecdochic incident in his recently published memoirs, *Take Two: A Life in Movies and Politics*. The scene is a plush tinseltown studio, a story conference is in progress, and the atmosphere is charged with—well, what else? Electricity! Darryl Zanuck—the irrepressible, autocratic Zanuck—takes command. Swinging the polo mallet that was his trademark prop, Zanuck cruises the room, talking, reaching, creating. "And now, and *now* her love turns to hate," Zanuck intones. The group of screen-writers absorbs this wisdom silently. Then a lone voice pipes up, "Why, Mr. Zanuck? Why does her love turn to hate?" Zanuck pauses, then leaves the room. A few moments later a flushing toilet can be heard. Then Zanuck strides back into the room, points the mallet at the questioner, and says, "All right, her love *doesn't* turn to hate."

That, my friends, is leadership in the Carter mode.

Consider our position in the world today. It has become the rhetorical twitch not only of our elected officials but also of the public disclaimers to describe our role in imperial terms. Our military bases are far-flung. Our economic penetration is deep. Our cultural presence is ubiquitous. We are a Superpower, of which there are no more than two. The rhetoric is high-blown, but it does in fact reflect how most of us feel most of the time. The pertinent question, however, is this: Do these words describe the actuality of the American role in the world today? Do they capture the essence of the current situation? Suppose, for the purposes of argument, that our mind-set is not imperial but rather colonial. What symbols and images would we employ to describe our condition?

Take our military bases. To be sure, in the geographical sense they are far-flung. Year-end editions of pretentious newspapers still run maps with forests of pins representing planes and ships. Those pins stretch from one border of the map to the other. But

From Neal B. Freeman, "Colonial America," *National Review* (October 17, 1980): 1246.

what is the *function* of those far-flung bases? Are they entrusted with an imperial mission? The enforcement of moral-legal codes? Collecting taxes? Consolidating gains won on the fields of military or economic battle? Or could it be said that they are protecting, and *in extremis* fighting for, the Germans, the Japanese, and the genuinely strong economies of the world? Are they, in a word, serving as colonial troops, fighting wars in which the indigenous peoples prefer to remain uninvolved? Is the apposite metaphor a nuclear umbrella or a Hessian troop?

Or take a look at the structure of economic relationships. It is the bias of our educational system, and fundamental to the hierarchy of civilizational beliefs, that the American economy is the best in the world. We carried the industrial revolution to its glistening conclusion; we honored the entrepreneurial spiral; we went multinational with a vengeance. The business of America *was* business. But a quick trip through the financial section of the paper confirms that the veritable sea-changes have set in. We now find our currency manipulated by forces beyond our own borders. The dollar, the Godalmighty dollar, can be yanked around by a few guys wearing sheets in a Vienna hotel lobby. Our central manufacturing enterprises—those firms whose corporate names are synonymous with American economic might—go begging to the government for protection against foreign dumping, never risking to inquire how Panasonic and VW and Michelin can sell their products below cost and still make a handsome profit. (The minimanagers of Detroit would no doubt answer: They make it up in volume.) The only entry that begins to balance our national checkbook is raw materials, which in classic colonial style we trade for the lower-priced, higher-quality manufactured goods we now import. (Scanning the stats for hopeful signs, the business press has invested great promise in another emerging export industry. *Textiles!*)

Liberate yourself from imperial rhetoric and you can see something of the same pattern in the developing problem of immigration. Traditionally, it has been a source of national pride that foreigners seek America as a new home. They come here, we like to believe, because they have recognized the superiority of American life, the siren opportunity of the free society. What has happened in recent months, however, is sharply at variance with the sampler-philosophy. Castro is not letting the best and the brightest of Cuban society slip through his fingers to south Flori-

da. He is sending us, instead, his old, his infirm, and, in especially generous amounts, his criminal elements. As the rash of hijackings has made clear, these are not your budding capitalists yearning to be free. These are social undesirables who are being sent to the great penal colony to the north. Shipped out from the home country, as it were, to the remote outpost from which return passage is a forlorn, desperate hope. Next stop Devil's Island.

It was with some of these notions in mind that we wrote in this space about bilingual education. That pernicious program is very much of a piece with the progressive colonialization of America. When a foreign power first stakes its claim to a new territory, the agenda can take many forms but it always begins with a single item: the waxing power imposes its own language on the waning, subjected peoples. (And taxes them, of course, for the privilege of diluting their own culture.)

It goes without saying, but perhaps shouldn't, that we are not arguing here for a new American imperialism. In the present circumstance, such an argument would be irrelevant. We have neither the will nor the force of arms to restore the *status quo ante*. But we think it is neither too much nor too late to ask of our national leadership that they conduct our affairs with a semblance of pride, with prudence, and with a decent respect for the greatness that was America.

QUESTIONS FOR DISCUSSION

1 What information is necessary for one to have to describe accurately a country's behavior as imperialistic?

2 Compare the nature of, and motivations behind, Soviet and United States interventions beyond their borders.

3 What purposes or aims are United States worldwide involvements and commitments designed to serve?

4 What is the relationship between America's foreign policy and social reform and justice at home?

5 Compare American foreign policy in the post-World War II period with the imperialism of Britain and France in the nineteenth century.

SUGGESTED READINGS

Ambrose, Stephen E. *Rise to Globalism*. Baltimore: Penguin, 1980.

Aron, Raymond. *The Imperial Republic: The United States and the World, 1945–1973*. Cambridge: Winthrop, 1974.

Bailey, Thomas A. *A Diplomatic History of the American People*, 8th ed. New York: Appleton-Century-Crofts, 1968.

Isaak, Robert A. *American Democracy and World Power*. New York: St. Martin's Press, 1977.

Liska, George. *Career of Empire: America and Imperial Expansion Over Land and Sea*. Baltimore: Johns Hopkins University Press, 1978.

Magdoff, Harry. *Imperialism: From the Colonial Age to the Present*. New York: Monthly Review Press, 1977.

May, Ernest R. *American Imperialism: A Speculative Essay*. New York: Atheneum, 1968.

McCarthy, Eugene J. "Is America the World's Colony?" *Policy Review* No. **17** (Summer 1981): 120–124.

Paterson, Thomas G. (ed.). *American Imperialism & Anti-Imperialism*. New York: Crowell, 1973.

Steel, Ronald. *Pax Americana*, rev. ed. New York: Viking, 1970.

9 Does Eurocommunism Signal a Real Change in Communist Behavior?

YES

Edward Crankshaw

Europe's Reds: Trouble for Moscow

NO

Robert Moss

The Spectre of Eurocommunism

Europe's Reds: Trouble for Moscow
Edward Crankshaw

Change in the Communist world is so slow that only a specialist can make it out. It goes on all the same, though as a rule, and for quite long periods, hidden from the outside view.

Once in a while there is an earthquake that brings about a radical change even though it may take the outside world years to believe the evidence of its own eyes. A Yugoslav Communist called Tito, who is also a patriot and a natural leader in his own right, throws down the gauntlet to Stalin refusing to be ordered about, and, ultimately "survives"—thus exploding forever the illusion that Soviet power is limitless (1948). Mao Tse-Tung leads his Chinese Communists to victory in the teeth of Stalin's disapproval and establishes what must inevitably become a rival base to Moscow (1949). Stalin dies in 1953, and his death sets off a chain reaction, beginning with the abandonment of wholesale terror inside the Soviet Union and continuing to this day.

The latest manifestation of this chain reaction is the emergence of a phenomenon called Eurocommunism, and as usual, a certain kind of skeptic insists that it does not mean a thing, that Communism is what it always has been and always will be, that any changes in the professed beliefs or goals of the Communist party are nothing but deception. Unenlightened skepticism is as dangerous as and much sillier than exaggerated credulity. There are still people who believe that the great quarrel between Russia and China is not real. We should not make the same sort of mistake about the Eurocommunists.

The term Eurocommunism is now used to include all those Western European Communist parties that have come to reject total subservience to Moscow. This, as far as I can discover, means *all* the Western European parties, though one or two, like the British Communist Party, have split, with a minority group setting itself up as the repository of the true faith, wholly loyal to Moscow. But Eurocommunism implies more than simple refusal to obey the Kremlin's orders blindly and to all particulars. If this were all, then, Marshal Tito would be a Eurocommunist, but he is not. So would Nicolae Ceausescu of Rumania,

who most decidedly is not. Certainly Eurocommunism includes a strong element of nationalism, but its really distinguishing feature is that it stands for the victory of Marxism by parliamentary means and, furthermore (at least in some cases), the throwing overboard of the very idea of the dictatorship of the proletariat—i.e., the dictatorship of the innermost circle of the Communist Party.

This gives the Russians much pain. But the interesting thing is that although the term Eurocommunism was invented only two or three years ago and has become fashionable over the past year, and although the conflict between Moscow and the Eurocommunists was dramatized conspicuously for all to see only last June in the historic clash between the Kremlin and the Spanish Communist leader Santiago Carrillo, the Russians have been wrestling with it in vain for the last 20 years. It is no sudden growth. And it is here to stay.

The decision to seek power not through violent revolution but openly, by parliamentary means, by persuasion and maneuver, is important for the time being only in those countries that have strong Communist parties—that is, in Italy and France. Obviously, the prospect of Communist parties in NATO countries attaining even a share in government let alone control of it, is bound to alarm the more nervous spirits in the West, regardless of the fact that there have been Communists in the Icelandic Cabinet for some time now.

The immediate worry over France has been relieved by the collapse of the electoral alliance among French Socialists, radicals and Communists, a bonus for Giscard d'Estaing. The breakdown may inject new vitality into the moderate Socialists, but it is certainly not the end of the Communist Party's attempt to work its way to power in France, as in other West European countries, by what it likes to call parliamentary means. It is obvious that Georges Marchais, the French Communist leader, has himself forced the break for tactical reasons, almost certainly because he has decided that his Communists are not yet strong enough to dominate any coalition. Making a virtue of

Edward Crankshaw, "Europe's Reds: Trouble for Moscow." *The New York Times Magazine*, February 12, 1978, pp. 18–20, 46, 48, 50, 51, and 56.

necessity, he has reverted to his old line of rather bad-tempered intransigence.

The Communists in Italy, on the other hand, have recently become much more demanding. Instead of continuing to lend their support to Giulio Andreotti and his Christian Democratic Party, they precipitated a Government crisis by insisting on Cabinet representation. Now Enrico Berlinguer declares that rather than call a general election, the Communists should be invited to form a government.

It is still too early to draw conclusions from these developments. What seems to me certain is that the first major rift in the image of reconciliation between the Socialists and Communists of Western Europe cannot possibly be seen as the end of a process that has struck deep roots. It is no more than a check, a check useful and salutary to use if only because it brings home certain valuable lessons.

First, we are reminded how hard it is for Communists to change their spots, even when they are trying. But perhaps the most important point, which we are forever forgetting, is that no two Communist parties are alike. Thus, for decades, the French Communist Party has been a byword for intransigence and suspicious secretiveness. Exhibiting in its relations with other Communist parties (to say nothing of the non-Communist world) something of that touchy, chauvinistic disdain seen at its most extreme in de Gaulle, it reflects aspects of the French national temperament no less than the Italian Communists reflect the subtlety and quicksilver flexibility so characteristic of their countrymen at large.

By insisting that Communists, of whatever country or color, are all the same, Western states only succeed in driving them into each other's arms. Communists are all different. They were different in the days when, by insisting that Russia and China were indivisible, the Western world actively helped to keep those two countries together. They are very different now.

In Moscow's eyes, the only good foreign Communist is one who obeys the Kremlin's instructions without question, as in East Germany, in Bulgaria and in Czechoslovakia since the 1968 invasion; in Poland, Hungary or Rumania, Giereck, Kadar and Ceausescu are all awkward customers in their very different ways. At the same time, Moscow is never really happy about the Communists of any country that is not adjacent to the Soviet Union—and thus not immediately accessible to Soviet tanks—or that is not permanently garrisoned by Soviet troops.

A successful show of independence on the part of any Communist party beyond the immediate reach of the Soviet Army is something the Russians regard with apprehension, alarm and even fear, for its disruptive effect on their Eastern European satellites. Ever since 1948, Titoism has been regarded by the Russians as an open wound in the body of the Soviet bloc, inviting infection and corruption. And, of course, they have been right to see it so. Without the example of Yugoslavia, there would have been no attempt in Czechoslovakia, just 20 years later, to let in light and air. As we know that poor Dubcek had to be put down with a public display of brute force that sickened the world—not only because the East Germans and other Soviet-bloc Communists were stricken by the fear that their own people might start to follow the Czechoslovak example, but also because the Russians feared that their own non-Russian peoples (most dangerously, the Ukrainians) might be similarly inspired.

From Moscow's standpoint, the first duty of a foreign Communist party is not to conduct experiments in revolution or succor the working class but to underwrite the security of the Soviet Union. And the Soviet Union, like Czarist Russia, is always uneasy with an independent ally and has no idea how to handle a dependent one with tact and flexibility. Leonid Brezhnev hauling some fraternal comrade over the coals for betraying the sacred cause of Lenin is reminiscent of Nicholas I reproaching his brother-in-law, King Frederick William IV of Prussia, for being soft toward the revolutionaries in 1848, bitterly accusing him of betraying his royal trust.

The Russians, of course, are right in a way. They can no longer believe in the victory of a world revolution effortlessly presided over by Moscow. (What would happen to Moscow if America went Communist and started throwing its weight about? There's a nightmare for the Kremlin!) So, to the Russians, the Communist parties of Europe have only one use—to keep the Western allies individually and collectively vulnerable to subversion, without going too far and plunging the whole continent into chaos at a time when Russia still requires help from the advanced economies. Above all, the Russians need to use the foreign parties to make Western governments feel the potential power of Communism. And Western governments, alas, all too often play into the Russians' hand by exaggerating that power.

In order that they may use foreign parties for their

own ends, the Russians have to keep the strictest possible control over their movements. Once this control is lost, anything may happen. It seems to me that Eurocommunism has already gone so far that Moscow has lost not merely control but also understanding of where the European comrades are going. I am also fairly sure that the European comrades hardly know where they are going themselves. With the exception of the Spanish Party, and to a slightly less emphatic degree, the Italians, they are still, to all appearances, tied to Moscow. But do they really believe in Moscow, or is this bond no more than a habit of mind or even, a matter of expediency? And, in particular, are they so conditioned that their first thought, if they should come to share secrets of state, would be to pass on those secrets to the Kremlin?

It is useful at this point to go back a little. Last summer, the Spanish Communist Santiago Carrillo publicly declared that the Soviet Union could no longer be regarded as a Socialist state (presumably he shared the view of most non-Communists that the Russian system is only a form of state capitalism). Although assailed sharply by Moscow, he was not disowned by any of the West European parties and was treated sympathetically by Poland, Hungary and Yugoslavia. How did this become possible?

It all began with Khrushchev. In his public address (as opposed to his secret speech) to the 20th Soviet Party congress in January 1956, he solemnly revised the Leninist canon. Lenin had insisted that there was only one way of making a true revolution in Russia—the Bolshevik way, his way; all others were vain imitations, and criminal into the bargain. In due course, the Bolshevik way, Lenin's way, hardened into a model for the world. At the same time, he categorically laid down the canon that world revolution could be achieved only through a series of major wars.

In Lenin's day, this sounded grand and apocalyptic, if one liked that sort of thing. But in the atomic age, it made no sense at all. Stalin, just before he died, was cautiously starting to revise the canon in the light of the nuclear facts of life; there must be wars, he said, but the Soviet Union should be able to keep out of them. Malenkov, as soon as he took over, went much further and said that war in the atomic age was unthinkable. Khrushchev, for his own purposes, attacked Malenkov violently for his heresy. Yet as soon as Malenkov was down, Khrushchev appropriated the idea, as Stalin had appropriated some of Trotsky's ideas when the great demagogue was down.

Khrushchev's contribution at the 1956 party congress was that war was no longer "fatally inevitable." He went further—mostly to please Marshal Tito, to whom he had rather clumsily apologized the year before for Stalin's savage treatment of Yugoslavia in 1948 when he went as far as he could go, short of war, to bring the Yugoslav party to heel. Different countries, Khrushchev declared, might take different ways to Socialism. And he went further still. There were those among the Western Communists who even then were privately airing doubts as to whether Russian- or even Balkan- or South American-style revolutions were applicable to the advanced industrial countries. To reassure these faint hearts, Khrushchev acknowledged that in certain lands and in certain circumstances, revolution might be achieved by peaceful means.

For the world at large, these pronouncements were soon overshadowed by the revelations of Khrushchev's secret speech, with its story of Stalin's crimes, but they were not forgotten by the European Communist parties. And before long those statements were being exploited in a manner not at all foreseen by Khrushchev himself.

Quite soon after the party congress, the veteran Italian Communist leader Palmiro Togliatti took Khrushchev to task for blaming all the evils that had befallen the Soviet Union on Stalin. This was nonsense he said, in effect: It was perfectly obvious that there must be something wrong with a system that had permitted a Stalin to flourish unopposed, and it was high time the Moscow comrades pulled themselves together and tried to improve that system very radically indeed. But that was only one voice.

The first major occasion for a general airing of Western European Communist thinking on the subject was provided by the celebrated Moscow conference of 81 Communist parties in December 1960. Curiously enough, it was the Chinese who gave the Europeans the chance to tell the Russians with perfect impunity something of what they thought of them.

The conference will go down in history as a grand climacteric. It was the last time that almost all the Communist parties of the world got together, meeting in secret and presenting to the outside world a monolithic image. That image was about as far from the truth as it is possible to imagine. The great quarrel between Russia and China had started up in earnest nearly a year earlier, and had been revealed to a chosen few at a meeting in Bucharest the previous summer. Now delegates from all the parties were treated to the unnerving spectacle of Khrushchev and Teng Hsiao-ping shouting each other down like fish-wives in the Great Hall of the Kremlin. At this stage, the outer world knew nothing of the quarrel or of Moscow's desperate need for support against Chinese pretensions.

What happened was that the Chinese attacked Khrushchev as the betrayer of Leninism not only for his condemnation of Stalin but especially for his reconciliation with Marshal Tito, his acceptance of different paths to Socialism and his rejection of the "fatal inevitability" of war. All this, they insisted, was nothing less than "revisionism," the most deadly sin in Bolshevik eyes.

Revisionism, for all practical purposes, meant the concept of evolutionary (as opposed to revolutionary) Socialism, as proposed at the turn of the century by the distinguished German Socialist Eduard Bernstein, who was consigned to outer darkness by Lenin for holding that society might be transformed, capitalism abolished and Socialism enthroned by peaceful means. Now, in Moscow, in the winter of 1960, a very paradoxical situation arose. The Chinese were quite correct in accusing Khrushchev of revisionism, but the Europeans, in coming to his support and accusing Peking of obscurantism, were able to compound that very sin and thus push the case for their own independence much further than the Russians liked.

The Europeans were in a mood to do this because, in private, most of them had been critical of Moscow ever since the 1956 Hungarian uprising; and, on the very eve of the great conference, they had been deeply upset by the crudely high-handed manner in which their Soviet hosts had tried to stage-manage the whole affair, briefing the visitors in an obviously equivocal and tendentious way and worse, treating the various delegations almost like prisoners under house arrest and keeping them rigidly apart so that it was impossible for them to meet and compare notes.

Now they had their chance, and they took it. The Russians could do nothing to curb them without appearing to take China's side. Thus, they had to sit and listen in their own Moscow stronghold to the Swedish party secretary, Hilding Hagberg, declaring that there was no sense in parroting Lenin without taking note of the changes since his time. Further-more, the Swedish as well as the Swiss comrades announced that they found all talk about the dictator-ship of the proletariat (still a sacred and unquestioned phrase) anachronistic and distasteful. Even Maurice Thorez of France, hitherto grimly loyal to Moscow, if only because of his hatred of the Italians, agreed with this.

Luigi Longo, the Italian representative, continued the Togliatti line with considerable panache, blazing the reformist and revisionist trail under cover of support for Moscow against the Chinese heresy hunt-ers. But it was the Swede, once again, who declared less equivocally than any of his colleagues that the hatchet must be buried between the Communists and their most hated opponents, hated far more than any right-wing party—the Social Democrats. The Swedish Communist Party, he said, had decided to give up fighting the ruling Social Democrats once and for all. They were now working for the day when the two parties would be fused into one.

Here the Swedish party was on the most treacher-ous ground imaginable. For Soviet Communism as we know it today arose from Lenin's bitter quarrel with some of his closest colleagues—fellow members of the Russian Social Democratic Labor Party, which he split irrevocably into two wings, Bolshevik and Men-shevik.

The last attempt to restore the unity of the party— and of the Second International, to which it belonged —was made in 1914 by Rosa Luxemburg, the Polish revolutionary who came to dominate the German Socialists. In despair over Lenin's dictatorial ways, she tried to bring the Russian Socialists together in July of that year—on the eve of World War I. When war broke out, all the European Socialists surprised themselves, and each other, by putting country before the international ideal.

In 1919, with the Bolshevik faction in power in Russia, Lenin founded the Third International, which in no time at all became the instrument of Russian state power. With Rosa Luxemburg murdered in Germany that same year, there was no foreign Social-ist strong and determined enough to stand against Russian hegemony. Ever since Lenin's day, Social Democrats all over the world have been anathema-tized by the Communists and pursued with the unre-lenting hatred reserved for heretics.

Now in 1960, 41 years after the foundation of the Third International, reunion with the heretics was being proposed all over again, this time by the Communist Party of Sweden, with the seeming ap-proval of the other Western European Communist delegates.

As I have said, the outside world knew nothing at the time of what went on at the Moscow conference, which was presented as a show of solidarity and force and was accepted as such by most outsiders. A few months later, I was able to reveal in some detail the story of the Sino-Soviet quarrel, but it was not until 1963 that a number of the other Communist parties, most notably the Italian, French and Belgian, began to publish in their journals accounts of their own contributions.

The following year, Khrushchev was overthrown, and Communist affairs stagnated while his successors sorted themselves out, attended to urgent domestic matters and found their bearings. But in 1968, when the Russians reacted with such characteristic brutality to the Czechoslovak party's attempt to civilize itself, the Western European parties for the first time came out in open and public condemnation of Moscow's action.

It is not too much to say that, since 1968, one of Brezhnev's main preoccupations has been to bring those Europeans under stricter control. He has failed. One measure of his failure was their stubborn resistance to an idea behind which he was putting all his weight—a conference of European parties to affirm and formalize total unity, a unity presided over by the Communist Party of the Soviet Union.

The European Communists resisted, first, to the holding of a conference at all; then, when the meeting was held in 1976, to Soviet attempts to rig it in Moscow's favor; and after that to Moscow's renewed attempts, despite a rebuff at the conference, to reassert Soviet hegemony over the whole Communist world and excommunicate China. And it was during the organization of this resistance that the term Eurocommunism began to come into use.

A still more striking measure of Brezhnev's failure has been Carrillo's scathing criticism and the way in which the West European comrades rallied to his support when Moscow opened up on him with its big guns, including a blast from the Soviet foreign-policy weekly New Times. Indeed, they forced the Russians to withdraw. In a second article, New Times declared that it was all a misunderstanding arising from slanders in the bourgeois press; that Moscow had nothing against the respected Spanish party, only against Carrillo personally. This line was promptly denounced by the French as an impermissible attempt by Moscow to make trouble between a fraternal party and its chosen leader. And there the matter rests—but not, I think, for long.

What does all this amount to? As we all know, the lie is a most favored weapon in the Communist armory, and the techniques of deception and softening up are highly developed. It has also to be remembered that the Communist parties of Western Europe contain some extremely tough individuals. The men who are now speaking out against some of Moscow's policies and attitudes include some who, for a very long time, accepted Stalin as their master, holding him up to the rest of the world as a great and benevolent leader and pursuing anyone who tried to tell the truth about his crimes (e.g., the present writer) with a sustained venom hard for anyone who has not been the object of it to imagine.

Even more interestingly, in spite of Stalin, in spite of Hungary, in spite of Prague, in spite of Brezhnev's continuing persecution of so many brave and distinguished men and women who ask only for the chance to help the Soviet system approximate more closely the ideals it professes (to say nothing of the Jews), in spite of the sadly obvious fact that in Poland, Hungary, East Germany, Czechoslovakia and even Rumania, Soviet rule means domination of the more advanced by the more backward—in spite of all this and more besides, Carrillo is so far the only Eurocommunist leader to pronounce the simple truth well known to all the fraternal comrades—namely, that the Soviet Union cannot be called a Socialist country—and to take the logical next step—namely, to urge the Eurocommunists to set themselves up against Moscow as the champions of real Socialism. Italy's Berlinguer, in a speech before his Party's Central Committee last month, seemed to have implied the same message, but his words were ambiguous. All the others, however sharply they may criticize some of the Kremlin's activities, preserve their links with Moscow as the acknowledged headquarters of the world Communist movement.

Why? Is it because, in spite of their reservations about the Russian way of doing things, they are still working for the Kremlin, as they most certainly did in the past? Do they dream of the day when, by whatever means, they win power to their own countries and will then proudly announce to whoever is then sitting at the top of the pile in the Kremlin: "Sire! Italy (or France, or Luxembourg) is at your feet!" And the Brezhnev of the day will then smile and say, "Well done, good and faithful servant! Go thou and rule in my name in just the way you think best." Will they then show themselves as being aliens in their own countries and among their own people—become Russian puppets, like Ulbricht in Germany, Gottwald in Czechoslovakia, Rakosi in Hungary, and the rest?

That seems improbable to me. It seems far more

likely that the present links with Moscow, varying in strength from party to party, are being maintained partly for what can be gotten from the Soviet Union in the way of material and moral support but far more from habit, for the sake of a feeling of solidarity with some sort of world movement, even if the chairman is not all that might be desired.

When all is said, they have come very close to endorsing Carrillo's most extreme statements by the very act of not condemning them as outrageous and criminal. And a further sign of the times may be found in the reaction of some of the Soviet-block parties to the first New Times article. The Czechs, as would be expected from a Government installed by Marshal Grechko after the destruction of "Socialism with a human face," were abusive to the point of hysteria in their condemnation of the Spaniards. But the Poles managed to get by without saying anything at all, simply publishing the New Times article rather belatedly and without comment. While the Hungarians, following Kadar's familiar line, expressed continued sympathy with Eurocommunism, upheld the idea of different paths to Socialism, and only very gently urged good Communists to refrain from questioning the "victorious path" taken by other Socialist countries in the past.

It is important to remember two things. The first is that the original bosses of the Eastern European parties were nothing but Stalin's puppets, installed and protected by the Soviet Army, without which they would never have attained power. The one Communist head of state who fought his own way to power and had next to no help from Moscow— Marshal Tito—soon made it clear that he proposed to remain his own master. Should we expect Western European Communists, who have also had to make their own way to forget their nationality any more than Tito? Or to subdue their very much more advanced economies and cultures to the backward, unattractive, uncomprehending parvenus in the Kremlin?

The second thing to remember is the nature of the Communist voters in the Western European countries. In Britain, these tend to be fanatical, but they are pathetically few. In Italy and France, they are counted in millions, and they include some fanatics, of course, but the vast majority are not Communists at all, in the sense of being disciplined ideologues: They are radical protesters, very much French and Italians first, but disillusioned with the older parties. It is inconceivable to me that even if he so wished, a

Marchais in France or a Berlinguer in Italy could carry his countrymen into the Soviet camp and hand them over to Brezhnev, or whomever, without provoking a civil war.

And it is no answer to retort that the Italians and the Germans between the wars had no difficulty in delivering themselves into slavery at the hands of Mussolini and Hitler. The appeal of both these creatures, in their very different ways, was precisely to the spirit of nationalism—chauvinistic and unashamed. Carrillo declared that if Moscow had attacked him sooner, it would have been worth many more votes to him at the recent Spanish election, and this is the sort of factor that Communist leaders in other lands must bear in mind.

It could be argued that the Eurocommunists are exhibiting measured antagonism to Moscow and appealing to reason and common sense simply to deceive and attract more voters to their side. Even if that were so, and they win those additional voters, will it make them, in the long run, any stronger? I think not. I think that the very existence of Eurocommunism has weakened the Soviet position irretrievably. Further, that a point will soon be reached at which the success and growing influence of the Communist parties, and their involvement with the established parties will turn the scales against them. Rather than frightening away their moderately inclined supporters, they will have disgusted their more radical supporters and driven them into splinter groups, to Maoism or Trotskyism—anything but Brezhnevism, which is Russian imperialism writ very large and in red letters, and of use to self-respecting revolutionaries only insofar as it can be persuaded to back them with arms or hard cash.

The Russians may not understand all this, but I think they have grasped the central fact—the weakening of their own power by the reduction of their fifth column influence in Western Europe. The decline of Soviet Communism does not, by any means, imply the decline of revolutionary activities in the West. Far from it. And one of the questions it is necessary to ask is whether we are not allowing ourselves to be dangerously diverted by thinking too much about Eurocommunism and not enough about the various militant extremists—terrorists of various colors, anarchists, so-called Maoists and Trotskyites—whose activities are already too familiar and who are dedicated to the overthrow of the established order.

There is, of course, another question to be asked about the Eurocommunists. If they attain power—

even in ideological opposition to Soviet Communism —what sort of government are they likely to provide? Can the freedoms West Europeans now enjoy hope to survive?

There is no straight answer. Berlinguer of Italy has said that his party, if it came to power, would tolerate opposition parties, and, furthermore, would be prepared to hold elections and to surrender office if voted out. There is no way of knowing how true this is. My own idea is that just as the Soviet Communist Party was colored, conditioned and shaped by the character of the backward, cunning, ignorant, suspicious peasants who came to dominate it once the revolution had succeeded, so Communism in Italy and France has already been colored and shaped by the character of the people of those countries, who would go on behaving very much as in the past. I believe that unless the Communist parties can rally the Italians and the French with patriotic war cries, they will fail. I believe that a resurgence of some sort of right-wing extremism is more likely than the victory of Moscow-led Communism. This means that European Communism must either go on transforming itself, or fall apart.

It seems to me fairly obvious that with any sort of Communist party in power in any country, there would be a great deal more authoritarianism than exists at present in the Western democracies which vary among themselves on that score. But this problem of the authoritarian state transcends the problem of Communism. If the Soviet Union were swallowed up tomorrow, we would still be faced with the problem of how a world of rapidly increasing populations dependent on relatively dwindling resources can be organized and held together without resort to totalitarian methods, moderate or extreme, left or right. One of the most unfortunate consequences of Lenin, it seems to me, is that the bogy of Russian Communism has effectively prevented us from thinking straight about this very problem.

In other words, the growth of Eurocommunism, and its appeal, owes far, far more to the failures of the Western world than to Moscow. I mean, for example, our failures to deal adequately with such continuing scandals as excessive unemployment, and the failure of people who pass for leaders of our societies to find a language to share with the idealistic young, who in frustration turn, at best, to cynicism and apathy; at worst to violence.

The Spectre of Eurocommunism
Robert Moss

The visit of Chancellor Helmut Schmidt to the White House on July 13 and 14 and that of Prime Minister Giulio Andreotti on July 26 and 27 will include a "hidden agenda" according to *The New York Times* of July 12, 1977.

"At the highest level of the Carter Administration," wrote *Times* reporter Bernard Gwertzman, "officials are expressing deep concern over what they see as a political and economic deterioration in many Western European countries."

The "hidden agenda" to be discussed privately includes primarily "the swing toward the left" and "the trend known as Eurocommunism", which, says *The New York Times*, has "created mixed feelings" in Washington.

There can be little doubt, that from a European standpoint (and ultimately for the interests of the West as a whole) the "trend toward Eurocommunism" is indeed serious. Let us begin with Spain which recently transformed itself into a democracy.

The results of the Spanish elections on June 15th were less than a triumph for the Communist Party (which gained only 20 seats out of 350 in the Cortes) but the Communist Party leader, Santiago Carrillo, could put a braver face on it than the leaders of the traditional right which fared even worse. The Communist Party emerged as the third largest party in a situation where party allegiances are still very fluid.

Superficially, the election results seemed to have opened the way for a two-party system in Spain, with a center-right party of government clustered around the prime minister, Adolfo Suarez, and a socialist party of opposition (the PSOE) led by Felipe Gonzales. Could it be that, despite the Communist Party's

From Robert Moss, "The Spectre of Eurocommunism," *Policy Review* No. 1 (Summer 1977): 7–26.

role in Spain as the focus for secret opposition to Franco and its *avant-garde* role, since 1968, in developing a "Eurocommunist" image of independence from Moscow and tolerance towards other parties, it will now be condemned to the sidelines?

Such a conclusion would be rash. First of all, it is worth recalling that the Spanish Communist Party polled only 191,000 voters in the first legislative elections of the Spanish Republic in June, 1931—not enough to capture a single seat in parliament—and only slightly more in the elections in 1933. The Communist Party's lack of a significant electoral following did not, however, make it a negligible force when the Republic fell victim to its internal conflicts.

Second, the PSOE is a Marxist, not a social democrat, party, and has attracted the votes of many of the people who might well have voted for the CP in Italy or France. The Soviets—as well as West European Socialist parties—gave considerable encouragement to the PSOE in the run up to the elections. This was no doubt related to their distrust of Carrillo's "Eurocommunist" pretensions, but also to the calculation that the PSOE was the most worthwhile cause—in an *electoral* sense—since its foreign policy completely coincides with Soviet interests, while it has already earned the approval of Socialist governments in Europe.

Finally, the Communist Party's organized membership (it claims 150,000 members) and trade union support, steeled by the long years of underground resistance, will be a force to be reckoned with in any future political crisis: while its mastery of conspiratorial techniques is evident from the way that the party has rapidly moved to assume dominant influence over the major news magazines—and even the recently-legalized girlie magazines.

So, while it may be concluded that the net result of Spain's elections was to expose the limited popular support for the Communist Party, it does not follow that the Communist Party has suffered some irreversible setback. It can count on mobilizing union discontent in a deepening economic recession in Spain, and of continuing to try to build a broad "popular front" combining the Communist, Socialist and left-wing Christian Democratic forces. Meanwhile, the specter of Eurocommunism is more immediate to the north and east: in Italy, where the Communist Party gained 34.4 percent of the votes in the elections of June 1976 and controls all the major urban centers; and in France, where recent opinion polls suggest that the

Communist Party-Socialist alliance (the Union of the Left) has a chance of winning next year's legislative elections.

One of the most striking features of the advance of Communism in Southern Europe is the widespread assumption that the nature of Communism has somehow changed. The postwar leader of the French Communist Party, Maurice Thorez, coined the celebrated phrase that his party was "*pas comme les autres*." Yet when the pollsters recently asked (in a poll that appeared in *Paris-Match*) whether people thought that the Communist Party had become "a party like the others," an astonishing 43 per cent of those interviewed said yes. Only 35 per cent continued to believe that the French Communist Party was different from other parties. The rest were undecided.

Even more striking, perhaps, was the response to another question, "Would the Communist Party be favorable to press freedom?" Of those interviewed, 35 per cent thought the Communist Party would respect press freedom; only 32 per cent thought that it would not.

Has the nature of Communism changed in Western Europe? Is "Eurocommunism" different in kind from Soviet Communism or merely an electoral charade played by shrewd tacticians who know that their chances of winning votes will be lessened if they are identified with the repression of Soviet dissidents or the invasion of Czechoslovakia?

A NEW WORD IS COINED

It should not be forgotten that the word "Eurocommunism" only came into circulation in 1975, and has only started to be used by Communist Party leaders—after much initial hesitation—over the past year or so. (Carrillo recently published a book with "Eurocommunism" in the title.) One Soviet critic of "Eurocommunism," V.V. Zagladin, has suggested that the term was invented by Zbigniew Brzezinski. More probably, it is the invention of journalists: a convenient, but misleading, bit of shorthand used to describe some tendencies that seem to be common to several CPs in Western Europe, rather than a description that they initially applied to themselves.

The "Eurocommunist" parties have set out to demonstrate the following points:

1 That a Communist victory in a West European country would not mean domination from Moscow.

2 That Western Communist Parties are not responsible for the crimes of Stalinism and the contemporary treatment of dissidents within the Soviet bloc; and are capable of taking a critical attitude toward what their Soviet patrons do.

3 That Communism is compatible with political liberty and the survival of parliamentary institutions.

In pursuit of (1), the Eurocommunists have dropped one of the key phrases in the Marxist-Leninist lexicon: "proletarian internationalism," a euphemism for Soviet control of the world Communist movement.

In pursuit of (2), some Western Communist Parties make regular—but highly selective—criticisms of the Stalinist past and the Soviet present, usually on occasions when there are no Russians present.

In pursuit of (3), some Western Communist Parties have abandoned one of the key phrases from Marx, the "dictatorship of the proletariat," in an effort to imply that "socialist" revolution can be brought about by peaceful democratic means in conditions of political pluralism. It is not always observed that when Marx wrote of the "dictatorship of the proletariat," he was not discussing a political strategy, but setting out what he conceived as an historical inevitability— a stage of social and political evolution that would have to be undergone during the transition from capitalism to socialism. The house style-sheets for *L'Humanite* and *L'Unita* (the organs of the French and Italian Communist Parties) may be revised, but no genuine Marxist can abandon the underlying conception of history.

The three major Communist Parties that it is now customary to group together as "Eurocommunist" are those of Italy, France and Spain. Each is pursuing a strategy of tactical alliance with other parties, whose success will partly depend on convincing evidence of "de-Stalinization" within the Communist Party. It is equally important to note that each of these parties is also responding to recent historical events in other parts of the world which are interpreted as particularly relevant to the success or failure of Communism in these three countries. Thus it was in September-October, 1973, after the fall of Allende in Chile, that the Italian Communist Party leader, Enrico Berlinguer, mapped out his plan for a "historic compromise" between the Communist Party and the Christian Democrats. He had clearly drawn the lesson from Chile's coup that Communist Party success in Italy

would hinge on drawing together a broader coalition of political forces than Allende was able to bring about.

While the Communist-Socialist alliance in France came about in 1972, it was after the defeat of Portugal's Communist Party in the fall of 1975 that Georges Marchais, the French Communist Party leader (and until then a staunch defender of the hardline Stalinist approach of Alvaro Cunhal) apparently drew the conclusion that he must take steps to avoid the possibility that his party could be similarly isolated and identified as an anti-democratic force. From that time, the French Communist Party joined the Eurocommunist chorus. The decisive event for Carrillo came earlier—in 1968, when Soviet tanks ended the "Prague spring."

The French, Italian and Spanish Communist Parties are the strongest in Western Europe. But beyond their ranks, "Eurocommunism" has not proved notably infectious.

The degree of agreement and co-ordination between Berlinguer, Marchais and Carrillo themselves should not be exaggerated. Their meetings have been bilateral, rather than trilateral, with the Italian Communist Party taking the lead—by inviting Carrillo to Livorno in July, 1975 and to Rome in September, 1976, and by inviting Marchais to Rome in November, 1975 and May, 1977. The only "Eurocommunist summit" that has taken place was the meeting in Madrid on March 2–3 this year, and it was notable that Berlinguer was extremely reluctant to attend and that the conference ended with a relative anodyne statement.

MYTHS OF EUROCOMMUNISM

Those who argue that Eurocommunism is a qualitatively new form of Communism, shorn of some of the Leninist terrors, rather than a mere tactic for acquiring power via the ballot-box in advanced industrial democracies, derive most of their ammunition from the statements that are put out for public consumption by the Communist Party leaders themselves. Those who maintain that, whether or not Communism in Southern Europe is likely to prove different in kind from Communism elsewhere in the world, it will pose major problems for the Russians, also cite the statements of Soviet bloc leaders who attack "revisionism" and "anti-Sovietism" in the Western parties. Let us single out the major assertions that are made by those who believe that the West can live with

Eurocommunism, and see whether any of them stand up:

1. "Eurocommunist parties are independent from Moscow."

Marchais declared early this year that "there is not, there cannot be, it is totally impossible that the Communist movement could again be directed from any center, whether it is an international center or a regional center." (*L'Humanite*, February 14, 1977). The theme is constant in recent statements from Communist Party leaders in France, Italy and Spain.

It was during the run up to the conference of European Communist Parties in East Berlin in June 1976 that the Russians began to engage in direct criticism of the Eurocommunist parties. Spanish Communist leaders like Carrillo and Manuel Azcarate had, of course, long been targets for Soviet propaganda attacks; the Russians had actually tried to cut the ground from under Carrillo's feet by sponsoring rival Communist parties.

But Soviet attacks on Eurocommunism in general in late 1975 and early 1976 seemed to have been largely inspired by the new line of the French Communist Party. The Russians evidently found this harder to swallow than the attitude adopted by the Italian Communists long before. The reason may be that the Russians had always understood that the Italian Communist Party had its own path to tread. Unlike the French Communist Party, the Italian Communists began in the 1920s with the backing of a majority of the socialist movement in Italy, and the decay of the Italian Socialist Party since 1945 has left the Italian Communist Party in the singular position where it can plausibly claim to represent the Left as a whole—in the absence of a serious Socialist rival. While the Russians have always been sensitive to criticism of their behavior towards dissidents at home, such attacks seemed to sting them more when they started to be made—however hypocritically and erratically—by Marchais and his supporters than when they came from Berlinguer.

In any event, in the months before the Berlin summit, a series of heavyweight attacks on "anti-Sovietism" (meaning any and all criticism of Soviet policy) and on "revisionist" tendencies in the Western Communist Parties appeared in the Soviet press. One such attack was that of A. Viktorov (*Pravda*, March 1, 1977). Viktorov took up an earlier critique of the concept of "arithmetic democracy"—in other words,

the idea that political decisions should be taken on the basis of one man, one vote. According to Viktorov "experience has shown that it is impossible to achieve socialism in the framework of a bourgeois state, of bourgeois democracy. History offers numerous examples, the latest of them being Chile."

Russian displeasure has also been expressed indirectly—and frequently in more abusive language—by the leaders of satellite states in Eastern Europe and by hardline pro-Soviet Communists from the Third World and Portugal. Thus the Bulgarian leader, Todor Zhivkov, has been a bitter critic of Eurocommunism, while a member of the Central Committee of the Czech Communist Party wrote in *Rude Pravo* last month that Eurocommunism represents an oblique attack on genuine socialism.

Similarly, hardliners like Alvaro Cunhal from Portugal or Luis Corvalan, the Chilean Communist leader who was released from detention in exchange for Vladimir Bukovsky, have been wheeled out to criticize the errors of Eurocommunist parties.

How are we to interpret these Soviet outbursts? Are such criticisms merely a smokescreen, intended to increase the credibility of claims by Western Communist Party leaders that they are genuinely independent from Moscow?

French and Italian Communist Party leaders continue to attend closed meetings with the Soviet leaders in Moscow, although Marchais goes less frequently than before. Their tone tends to be far more moderate when they are speaking in the presence of senior Soviet officials than when they are speaking for internal consumption, while the party newspapers in both France and Italy regularly censor statements—including those of their own party secretaries—which are deemed too critical of the Soviets. Furthermore, there has been a noticeable retreat towards a more cautious position in the first half of 1977. This was evident at the Madrid meeting in March. In speeches in Budapest and Milan in January, Berlinguer praised the revolution of October, 1917, the "superiority" of the Soviet system over the West, and the "irreversibility" of socialism in the East. He also lauded the principle of "democratic-centralism." On April 5th, the Italian Communist Party spokesman, Asor Rosa, declared that democratic centralism and the leading role of the Communist Party of the Soviet Union remained the bases of international communism.

But there are three simple reasons for doubting whether a Communist Party in government in Western Europe would be able to pursue policies that conflicted with basic Soviet interests. The first, quite simply, is that the debate between Moscow and the Eurocommunist parties has been, so to speak, a discussion within the church. Criticisms of the Soviet Union from Western Communist Parties involve only the internal life of the world Communist movement, and do not affect broader Soviet interests. Thus Western Communist Parties have automatically adopted the Soviet line on international crises such as the Middle East, Angola and Southern Africa. The world view of the Western Communist Parties is a manichean view of a global conflict between "socialism" and "imperialism."

Second, the only genuine example of what Togliatti was describing back in the mid-1950s as "polycentrism" is China, which is big enough and powerful enough to sustain its own version of Communism in the face of Soviet pressures.

Third, the ultra-orthodox pro-Soviet factions inside Western Communist Parties remain very strong, and unregenerate Stalinists are frequently found to have their hands on the levers of power.

Thus, even if it were possible to believe that a leader like Marchais is sincere in what he now says, it remains very doubtful whether the structures of his own party—and the existence of clandestine networks of Soviet agents responsible to the International Department of the Central Committee of the Communist Party of the Soviet Union—would allow him to do anything that ran seriously counter to Soviet policy.[1]

[1] A newly-published essay for the London-based Foreign Affairs Research Institute by Mr. Ronald Waring is skeptical indeed (and with reasons) of a "change-of-heart" on the part of Europe's Communists. Mr. Waring in his article, entitled "Eurocommunism and Italy," notes that: "It is inconceivable that Moscow could permit a new form of Communist heresy which would be so immensely attractive to the peoples of the Eastern European countries such as Rumania, Hungary and Poland, not to mention the Russian people themselves. Both Russian imperialism and international Communism themselves would be in mortal danger. Moscow has already attacked Carrillo for splitting Communism by supporting the concept of Eurocommunism, but this condemnation is a tactic to give greater credence to the acceptable "independence" of Eurocommunism and it is worth noting that La Passionara—a creature of the Soviets if ever there was one—voted for Carrillo. The Soviet Union would have the military force to crush such a dangerous situation should it arise, and could easily be called in by a hard core within the Party, after the overthrow of Berlinguer and his adherents, to restore order in the interests of "proletarian internationalism" and the upholding of the Brezhnev Doctrine."

The fact that the Chinese are publicly skeptical about the credentials of Eurocommunist parties is revealing, since leading figures in the Italian Communist Party have called for a detente between Russia and China. However, the Chinese have not failed to notice that leading advocates of this approach—such as Alberto Jacoviello—have had their wings clipped by the Party. Their primary concern appears to be that the victory of Western Communist Parties would undermine NATO's defenses, and so strengthen the Soviet Union in its conflict with China.

2. "If Eurocommunism is independent from Moscow, NATO could live with it."

It is often argued, by those who maintain that there is some real difference of kind between Western and Soviet Communism, that the election of a Communist Party to government in Paris or Rome could create more headaches for the Russians than for the West. The argument is that this would have a contagious effect on Eastern Europe, encouraging new attempts to produce "socialism with a human face."

Secretary of State Cyrus Vance has employed this argument in what must be taken as the definitive attitude of the Carter administration (at least to date) on Eurocommunism. Speaking recently in the rambling prose style—interspersed with the calculated naivete which seems to be the mark of the new American government—Mr. Vance thought out loud using the following phrases from the *U.S. Department Stock Phrase Book* (Washington, D.C., 1977).

We have said that in dealing with our Western allies on vital issues we would prefer to be dealing with countries who have the same fundamental values, the same democratic concerns that we have, and if the Communists were to take a dominant role in those governments, that could present serious problems insofar as we are concerned. We have gone on to say that we think the question, the political question of whether or not Communists should or should not play a part in the government of a particular country is a political issue to be decided by the people of that country and one in which we should not interfere. However, at the same time I say again that does not mean we are indifferent to the fact that they may.

He added that it "is a possibility" that Communists in NATO governments would lead to new problems for the Soviets, possibly outweighing any difficulties endured by the West. He concluded in *Il Tempo*, incisively with the sentence: "I think it depends on how Eurocommunism develops."

This possibility should not be hastily ruled out. However, it is equally true that the more attractive and independent Communism in one Western country is made to appear, the more likely it is to take root somewhere else. The domino effect of a Communist electoral victory in Paris would be felt in Rome more quickly than in Prague or Warsaw.

The key question for NATO remains: which side would the Eurocommunists take if war broke out between the Soviet Union and the West? The question was put to Lucio Lombardo Radice in a revealing interview in *Encounter*, published in its May, 1977 issue. In the original tape-recorded version of the interview, Radice said "we would choose the Soviet side, of course, and we would do so on grounds of principle. . . ." In the edited version of the interview, the passage was altered at Radice's request to read as follows: "It depends. If there is an imperialist aggression with the avowed objective of rolling back socialism, we would feel entirely absolved of any obligation of loyalty to the defensive character of NATO and take the side of the Soviet Union." Whichever version is deemed more authentic, it is plain that in a war between "socialists" and "imperialists," the Italian Communist Party would find it hard to stand with the "imperialists."

3. "Eurocommunists will respect the rules of the Democratic game."

Assurances from Western Communist Parties that their brand of Communism has become compatible with political liberty would be more plausible if they did not totally subscribe to the doctrine of democratic centralism—which means that all key decisions are taken at the top, and that as soon as the background discussion has taken place, no differences of opinion will be tolerated. In short, while Western Communist Parties attack the historical errors of Stalinism in Russia, they continue to practice Stalinism within their own parties.

The supposedly "liberal" Italian Communist Party, for instance, gave an assurance at its conference in Bologna in February, 1969, that it would tolerate internal differences of opinion. Later that year, after a Stalinist-style show trial, it exiled the supporters of *Il Manifesto*, a magazine of New Left tendencies, for exceeding the "tolerable" limits of dissent. If Eurocommunist parties cannot tolerate differences of opin-

ion within their own ranks, how is it possible to believe that they will allow political freedom for rival parties if they manage to take power?

The typical reply from Eurocommunist leaders to the question—would they be prepared to bow out peacefully if they lost their popular support?—is that such a situation is impossible to imagine. Thus Lombardo Radice said: "once the working class has acquired hegemony . . . it would be difficult to envisage anyone wanting a regression from a better state of society to a worse state." In the same interview, he allowed that "it is in the logic of our policy" that the Italian Communist Party should give up power if it suffered a defeat under the democratic system.

However, his comments on the Soviet intervention in Budapest in 1956 do not encourage confidence that this would happen, and raise the specter of the ultimate instrument that a Communist government in Western Europe could employ to maintain itself in power: the Red Army. Radice admitted that he was in favor of Soviet action in Hungary because "Socialism in Hungary was a weak plant, only some seven years old, and there was a danger of a regression to capitalism . . . socialism was as yet without roots, therefore the roots had to be protected." Is it impossible to conceive of a Communist Government in Rome several years hence appealing to the Russians to defend it against the dangers of "a regression to capitalism"?

So how should we interpret statements like Marchais' declaration last year that "there is no democracy and liberty if there is no pluralism of political parties, if there is no freedom of speech"? (He added that "we have a disagreement with the Communist Party of the Soviet Union about this problem.")

A helpful guide is Lenin, who wrote, in a notorious letter to Chicherin, that "to tell the truth is a bourgeois prejudice. On the other hand a lie is often justified by our ends." There is further evidence for thinking that pluralism would not last long under a Communist government in Paris or Rome. Look at the way the French and Italian Communist Parties deal with the press.

The Italian Communists have been trying to silence a television station that is outspoken in its criticism of them, Tele-Monte-Carlo, under Clause 40 of the recent law on Italian broadcasting, which seeks to restrict material transmitted to Italy from abroad. Tele-Monte-Carlo broadcasts an Italian service with a special news program produced by Indro Montanelli, the distinguished conservative journalist and co-founder of *Il Giornale Nuovo*, the Milan newspaper which has systematically exposed the inside workings of the Italian Communist Party. (Montanelli was shot in the legs by terrorists of the "Red Brigades" on June 2nd.) In their communique, they denounced him as "a servant of the bourgeois State and the multi-national companies."

Tele-Monte-Carlo has been a tremendous popular success in Northern Italy, as an alternative to the increasing left-wing bias of the State television network inside the country. So it is no real surprise that the Communist Party, which noticed no illegality about broadcasts from Yugoslavia and Switzerland to Italy, should now be seeking a pretext to gag a formidable critic.

In the case of the French Communist Party, it is even clear that its attitude to press freedom will be based on its ancient philosophy that the truth is what it is expedient to say. When Costa-Gavras' film about the Prague show trials, *L'Aveu*, was first screened, it was attacked by *L'Humanite* as the "exploitation of a bad cause." The film touched a sensitive nerve, not least because it was not forgotten that the French Communist Party forwarded material on members of the International Brigade who had fought in the Spanish Civil War to Prague, to help in preparing the case against Slansky and others.

When *L'Aveu* was screened on French television last December, Jean Kanapa, one of the most pro-Soviet figures in the party leadership, joined a panel to discuss it. He tried to absolve the French Communist Party from the charge that it had tried to cover up the crime of Stalinism by pleading ignorance. "If we had only known," he said, "we would have shouted our indignation."

Within a few days, however, Kanapa's argument of ignorance was demolished by the appearance of a two-part article in *Le Monde* by a Communist Party historian, Jean Ellenstein. He revealed that the French delegation at the 20th Congress of the CPSU, when Khruschev gave his celebrated "secret speech" denouncing Stalin, had been shown the text of the speech the morning after—but decided not to make public what it contained; Communist Party spokesmen, including Kanapa, had always denied that this had happened.

A *gauchiste* weekly, *Politique Hebdo*, followed up by publishing the personal reminiscences of an ex-member of the Communist Party's Central Commit-tee, Jean Pronteau, who had traveled to Warsaw shortly after the 20th Congress. He was also shown a copy of the Khruschev speech. On his return he went to see Maurice Thorez, the leader of the French Party. Pronteau promptly opened his briefcase and began to read from the text he had brought back from Warsaw. Thorez's response was a classic, "Alright then. You've got it. You could have said so right from the beginning. But remember one thing, this secret speech does not exist."

If the French Communist Party goes to such lengths to conceal the past, would it really be prepared to allow frank discussion of the present if it gained a position of power?

But there is a still broader reason for believing that "Eurocommunism"—like any brand of Marxism-Leninism—is incompatible with the survival of political liberties. The radical changes in economic and social structures that the Communists propose to bring about are not only designed to be irreversible, but are incompatible with political pluralism.

A final cautionary note is that, for every reassurance that a Western Communist Party leader makes about guarantees for political pluralism under a future popular front, it is possible to dredge up a dozen or more from the recent past that say precisely the opposite. One example will have to suffice. It is from Georges Marchais, in *L'Humanite* on December 23, 1970: "We do not believe that the struggle for socialism should be inspired by the system of alternative government (*politique d'alternance*) that, as in England, allows the Conservatives and the Socialists to take turns in power to inflict the worst possible injuries on the workers."

SCENARIOS FOR TAKEOVER

Despite the similarities in their recent public posturing, the Communists in France, Italy and Spain face very different political situations and their tactics for acquiring power will diverge in important ways.

In Italy, the Communist Party tactic is to support a lame-duck Christian Democrat government with only minority support in Parliament while the Communists themselves expand their power within regional government, the media and the labor unions.

While the structural power—and the broad spread of support—that the Italian Communist Party can command make it the most serious long-term threat to NATO, it is the French Communist Party that appears to have an immediate chance of participating in government. With the forces of the center and the right in France divided, against a backdrop of rising unemployment, the Union of the Left has a fair chance of taking control of the French National Assembly in the 1978 elections.

Without doubt, the accession of the Communists to power in Paris would have two inevitable consequences. The first would be financial panic, with huge sums of money being transferred or smuggled abroad, bringing in its train the collapse of the French currency and the fatal weakening of France as a partner in the EEC. Economic crisis would inevitably spill over into a political crisis, in which the claimed necessity to impose import controls and other state regulations could be used to rapidly expand the powers of a left-wing central government. Second, the possibility of any continued, though limited, French involvement in NATO would vanish.

In Spain, the Communists have a long march ahead of them, but will stand to gain from any deepening of the economic crisis (the Suarez government has been running a deficit of some $4 billion) and can count on consolidating their alliance with other groups on the left. What would no doubt suit Communist Party interests based in Spain would be some abortive attempt at a coup from the right that would enable them to posture once again as the defenders of the republic. They have expressed their reluctant acceptance of the monarchy for the time being, but would seek to abolish it as soon as they gained any position of influence.

Communist Party tacticians in all three countries must have been studious readers over the past three years of the series of blue-prints for Communist takeovers that have been issued from Moscow, mostly in the guise of re-appraisals of what went wrong in Chile.

Since Boris Ponomarev published his celebrated article on the lessons of Allende's downfall in *World Marxist Review* in 1974, the Russians have not ceased to lecture the world Communist movement on the tactics that future Allendes, in Western Europe, will need to adopt in order to avoid the same fate. The most authoritative recent statement on this theme comes from two Soviet specialists called M.F. Kudachkin (who is a senior officer of the International Department of the Central Committee of the CPSU, which Ponomarev controls) and N.G. Tkachenko. They have co-authored a book entitled *The Chilean*

Revolution—its Experience and Meaning and an article in the November/December 1976 issue of the Soviet historical journal *Novaya i Noveishaya Istoriva*.

Kudachkin's main conclusion is that Allende failed to understand soon enough that he would be unable to achieve full socialism in Chile by legal means. He observed that the strategy of the Chilean Communist Party—in contrast to that of ultra-leftist groups which demanded a more revolutionary policy—was based on the belief that it was possible to avoid an armed conflict. He maintains that this was the right approach but that the Chilean Communists committed a serious error in overestimating the democratic character of the armed forces and the bourgeois state system.

Kudachkin, following Lenin, insists that in similar situations the Communists must be prepared "to take all necessary steps, such as armed suppression of insurrection, measures against sabotage, controls and other means of compulsion" in order to maintain themselves in power. The danger of over-commitment to the peaceful road to socialism, in his view, is that it will allow time for the "reactionary" forces to organize themselves and will encourage the emergence within the Socialist camp of "elements of right-wing opportunism."

He regrets that in Chile, the Allende government allowed the opposition considerable freedom, so that the "reactionaries" were able to use their strength in the National Assembly, the Civil Service, the courts and the security forces to prevent the government from carrying through fundamental revolutionary changes. By implication, Kudachkin's advice to the Eurocommunist parties is that, once elected to power, they should not feel inhibited by the constitution which enabled them to assume office but to proceed as rapidly as possible to purge the armed forces and the Civil Service of politically unreliable elements and to clamp down on opposition parties.

Kudachkin insists that the Marxist experiment in Chile again demonstrated that the decisive factor in any revolutionary process is the leading role of the Communist party. The message to the Eurocommunists is plain: It is that no Western Communist Party should allow itself to get into a position where it may have to play second fiddle to its tactical allies. It could also be read as a warning not to seek political responsibility, before the Communist Party has acquired sufficient power throughout society as a whole, to bring about those radical transformations which it advocates.

WHEN OPEN-MOUTH DIPLOMACY WORKS

The policy of many Western governments, that do not have to deal with strong Communist Parties, toward the advance of Eurocommunism can be summed up as accommodation in advance. It was not an uplifting spectacle to see the Socialist governments of Western Europe dropping heavy hints to the Spanish government that it would never gain entry to the EEC or be recognized as fully democratic unless it legalized the Communist Party.

But it is the attitude of the U.S. government that is all important. It is worth noting the effects of the major policy changes that have taken place since Dr. Kissinger left the State Department. Instead of warning against the effects of Communist successes in Southern Europe, President Carter compliments his team on having lost the "inordinate fear of Communism" and declares that "European citizens are perfectly capable of making their own decisions in the free election process." American diplomats trot along to see Jean Kanapa at the French Communist Party's palatial headquarters at 2, Place Colonel-Fabien; Italian Communists like Elio Cabbugiani, the mayor of Florence, are given U.S. visas and invited to speak before the Council on Foreign Relations.

And, as a former Labor Party Member of the Greater London County Council, Dr. Stephen Haseler, points out in another article in this journal, there is now increasing pressure upon the U.S. State Department to grant visas to so-called Soviet "trade-unionists" to visit the U.S. in their false capacity as elected representatives of workers. This, of course, lends credence to their pronouncements and gives them an acceptability they do not deserve. The AFL-CIO, to its lasting credit, has staunchly opposed such visas for any Communist "trade-unionists" and in a forthcoming article in the Summer 1977 issue of *The Journal of International Relations* (Washington, D.C.), Mr. Jay Lovestone, a senior foreign policy adviser to George Meany, explains why the trade unions have taken this stand.

It is striking that while Carter's spokesmen on foreign affairs are enthusiastic practitioners of open-mouth diplomacy in relation to anti-Communist governments in the Third World, they fall strangely silent when it comes to discussing the possible consequences of Eurocommunism. Dr. Kissinger recently warned that "we do our friends in Europe no favor if we encourage the notion that the advent of Communists and their allies into power will make little or no difference to our own attitudes and policies."[2]

Kissinger is right on this. It makes no sense to criticize the policies of governments in sympathy with the U.S. if the U.S. administration is not also prepared to speak out in favor of the democratic, pro-western forces in Europe. While it might be argued that, by criticizing the Communists in France or Italy, the U.S. may risk being accused of intervention in the internal affairs of those countries, there is a far greater danger that, by letting it seem that the election of Communists to Government would *not* produce far-reaching economic and political reactions, the U.S. will assist European Communist Parties to re-assure their own electorates that they would be able to comfortably co-exist with the rest of NATO.

This is *not* the case, and there is no reason for not making it crystal clear that this is so. The reluctance of some West European governments to point out the dangers of a Communist victory helped the Italian Communist Party to make major gains in the June elections last year. Comments made by the late British foreign secretary, Anthony Crosland (in a supposedly off-the-record press conference) about how the Italian Communist Party did not—in his view—pose any major problem for NATO were given major exposure in the Communist press in Rome.

Is it too much to ask that Mr. Carter, and the non-Marxist governments of Europe, should publicly dissociate themselves from parties that are biologically opposed to the survival of a mixed economy and parliamentary institutions? No NATO member can offer to adopt a posture of studied neutrality on the eve of the 1978 elections in France. This is one of those occasions when open-mouth diplomacy is not only acceptable; it becomes a necessity.

[2] Dr. Kissinger in the same speech lucidly analyzed the credibility of the French Communist Party's new-found belief in democracy: "We are entitled to certain skepticism about the sincerity of declarations of independence which coincide so precisely with electoral self-interest. One need not be a cynic to wonder at the decision of the French Communists, traditionally perhaps the most Stalinist party in Europe, to renouce the Soviet concept of dictatorship of the proletariat without a single dissenting vote among 1,700 delegates, as they did at their party congress in February 1976, when all previous party congresses had endorsed the same dictatorship of the proletariat by a similar unanimous vote of 1,700 to nothing."

POST-DISASTER POLICY OPTIONS FOR NATO

The emergence of a "popular front" government including Communists anywhere in Western Europe would pose a major challenge to Western security interests. The argument that the Communists' coalition partners would be able to "domesticate" them is not entirely plausible; it is salutary to remember the rapid moves that were made by the French Communist Party, in an earlier post-war coalition, to colonize those sections of the civil service that came under its control—and notably the ministry of aviation. It would be impossible to avoid giving Communist Party members key cabinet portfolios if a coalition including Communists emerged in France or Italy.

What options would be open to NATO in such an event? The question would be most acute in the case of Italy, since—unlike France—Italy remains a full member of the military alliance, including the NATO Nuclear Planning Group, and the home for important NATO facilities, as well as the NATO Defense College in Rome. It is clearly impossible to devise general guidelines that could be applied in situations as diverse as Italy (a full member of the military alliance), France (which was removed from NATO's integrated command structure in accord with De Gaulle's strategy of *tous azimuts* in 1966) and Spain (until now kept outside NATO itself, but the site of important U.S. air and naval bases). But it may not be too misleading to suggest some of the alternatives that might well be considered in the case of a Communist Party victory in Italy, some of which might also apply in the case of France—or even Spain. Five post-disaster options may be summarized as follows.

1. The "so-what" policy

This is actively canvassed in Washington by two contrasting schools of thought. Thus it is argued either that NATO could live with Eurocommunism (and that, in view of the uncertain future of neighboring Yugoslavia and possible fear of Soviet disciplinary action, Berlinguer may be serious in his desire to keep Italy in NATO) or that Southern Europe is as good as "lost" anyway, and was never vital to U.S. interests. The second argument can be extended to justify the withdrawal of U.S. forces from Western Europe on the grounds that "it is not the business of the United States to defend Communists against Communists." The isolationist option does not need to be seriously discussed, except by those who imagine that the U.S.

could live with a Communist international world order.

2. Quarantine within NATO

A Communist Party government in Rome would be excluded from sensitive NATO discussions, but base facilities would be maintained and Italy would remain a formal NATO member. This could be extended to the doctrine that *countries* may remain members of NATO even if their governments are excluded—the so-called "empty chair" policy. In the event of a continued radicalization of the new government, the NATO bases might be retained rather as Guantanamo in Cuba has been retained by the U.S.

3 Expulsion from NATO

Either by formal vote of the other members, or by making it plain to the suspect country that it was no longer wanted, so that it would finally withdraw.

4. A new defense pact

As an alternative to NATO in its present form. This would include the remaining countries in Western Europe that are unequivocally anti-Soviet. It might also embrace countries farther afield that share the same security interests—e.g., Iran and Brazil.

5. The carrot-and-stick approach

A system of incentives (e.g., economic aid, debt-rescheduling, EEC tolerance for import restraints) and deterrents (e.g., denial of credits, trade restrictions) to induce a further "Eurocommunist" government to respect the political liberties of its own citizens as well as Western security interests. This might involve strict instructions on the exclusion of Communists from sensitive posts in the cabinet and the civil service, notably the defense and interior ministries.

This seems to me the most promising approach, and one that might be applied in the case of either Italy, France or Spain, It would involve drawing detailed lists of the areas of political and social life that could provide an index of how democratic or "European" the new government was proving to be. One of the easiest gauges would be its attitude toward freedom of the press—which, according to the Ponomarev school of thought, is a dangerous weapon of the bourgeoisie which must be taken away as quickly as possible.

It would be useful for the Carter Administration and for private study-groups to undertake in-depth research into how such guidelines might be established and how a subsequent policy of sanctions and rewards might be put into effect. It would be foolish to expect that the EEC would continue to function for long in its present form in the event of a Communist triumph in France or Italy.

There is, of course, a further option: direct intervention on behalf of the anti-Communist forces in a country threatened with revolution via the ballot-box. But after Chile, it looks as if the U.S. has little appetite for covert action to support anti-Communists. The Soviets are not troubled with scruples of this kind. Not only are the Russians prepared to use the Red Army to maintain ideological purity on their side of the Iron Curtain, but they are making a heavy investment in subversion and espionage in Western Europe. The French and Italian Communist Parties are less directly dependent on Soviet financing than in the past, since they are in a position to make sizable profits through their privileged position as brokers for East-West trade and through their control of local government councils. But the arm of the Soviet Union is always there to lean on.

Raymond Aron ends his most recent book, *Plaidoyer pour L'Europe Decadente*, with a chapter entitled "Two Specters Haunt Europe—Liberty and the Red Army." Eurocommunism is not a middle choice. There is no reason to believe that it would prove compatible with liberty. And there is no reason to believe that it would not be overshadowed by the Red Army.

QUESTIONS FOR DISCUSSION

1 Is it possible to have political democracy in a communist-run government?

2 How independent are Eurocommunist parties from the Soviet Union?
3 What impact has Eurocommunism had on United States and Soviet interests in West Europe?
4 Are NATO and Eurocommunism compatible?
5 Should the United States look at Eurocommunism as a threat or an opportunity?

SUGGESTED READINGS

Carrillo, Santiago. *Eurocommunism and the State*. Westport, Conn.: Lawrence Hill, 1978.

"The Case of the Vanishing Eurocommunists." *Economist* (Jan. 12, 1980): 51–52.

Childs, David (ed.). *The Changing Face of Western Communism*. New York: St. Martin's Press, 1980.

Godson, Roy, and Stephen Haseler. *Eurocommunism: Implications for East and West*. New York: St. Martin's Press, 1978.

Hardi, Peter. "Why Do Communist Parties Advocate Pluralism?" *World Politics* **32** (July 1980): 531–552.

Kriegel, Annie. *Eurocommunism: A New Kind of Communism?* Translation by Peter S. Stern. Stanford: Hoover Institution Press, 1974.

Leonhard, Wolfgang. *Eurocommunism: Challenge for East West*. New York: Holt, Rinehart and Winston, 1978.

Mandel, Ernest. *From Stalinism to Eurocommunism: The Bitter Fruits of "Socialism in One Country."* Translation by Jon Rothschild. New York: Schocken Books, 1978.

Tökés, Rudolf L. (ed.). *Eurocommunism and Detente*. New York: New York University Press, 1978.

Urban, G.R. *Eurocommunism: Its Roots and Future in Italy and Elsewhere*. New York: Universe Books, 1978.

10 Should the Promotion of Human Rights Be a Major Goal in United States Foreign Policy?

YES

Raymond D. Gastil

Human Rights and U.S. Policy

NO

Ernest W. Lefever

Human Rights and United States Foreign Policy

Human Rights and U.S. Policy
Raymond D. Gastil

The aspirations associated with the concept of human rights are inseparable from the history of Freedom House. Formed immediately before America's entry into World War II as a nongovernmental, voluntary organization, Freedom House helped mobilize American support in the struggle against the Axis powers and the repressions they represented. In succeeding decades Freedom House's programs have emphasized the hazards to freedom originating in repressive and totalitarian societies of both the left and the right.

Through conferences, studies, and publications Freedom House focuses public attention on countries that restrict human rights. The organization has played a part in monitoring compliance with the Helsinki Accords of 1975. For several years our Comparative Survey of Freedom has examined the level of political rights and civil liberties in all countries. We judge actual behavior rather than constitutional guarantees that may or may not be honored. For each country we try to determine the degree to which the citizen has a choice of parties (or factions within a single-party system); elections are fair and frequent, and result in the assumption of power by a properly selected victor; political choices are possible at local as well as national levels; mass communications systems are independent, and if so, free of pressuring by the regime; the judiciary is independent; and voluntary association and freedom of assembly and speech are protected. To the extent a country is free its people will be able to determine the priorities to be given economic, social, and symbolic desires, and the balance between their individual or collective expression.

Against this background, I will address two questions of human rights policy: What do we mean by human rights? and, How should the American commitment to human rights be expressed?

Three definitions of human rights are current today. The first restricts our attention to political execution or murder, torture, and imprisonment, especially when these are carried out by a government. This restrictive definition is that used by Amnesty International and found in Section 116 of the Foreign Assistance Act of 1975. The second is the inclusive definition contained in the Universal Declaration of Human Rights. According to the State Department's limited formulation of the Universal Declaration human rights can be grouped into violations of the integrity of the person (the focus of the restrictive definition above), rights to other civil and political liberties (press, thought, assembly, religion, and travel, as well as that to participate in the political process), and rights to fulfill such human needs as shelter, food, health, and education. A third definition focuses on "constitutional," or civil and political, human rights. It includes the first two groups of rights in the State Department's formulation and deemphasizes or eliminates the third group of "human needs."

Although U.S. policy reflects, and will reflect, all three definitions of human rights, policy guidelines should emphasize political and civil liberties, the constitutional definition.

The restriction of human rights concern to violations of the integrity of the person has the advantage of sharp delimitation and concentration of interest; it serves well the purposes of organizations that mobilize public opinion such as Amnesty International. However, a well-run totalitarian state need have little resort to the crudities of imprisonment to enslave its people. America's traditional concern for democratic rights and the expectation of much of the world that we stand for these rights also suggest that national policy should be based on one of the two broader definitions of human rights.

In developing U.S. policy there are several reasons we are not bound to accept the Universal Declaration as our guideline. There was no serious discussion of its terms by the people of the world when the Declaration was developed, nor did a majority of the world's peoples have elected representation to affirm it. Most importantly, neither the United Nations nor major nations other than the United States take the Declaration or the subsequent Covenants as a serious guide for action. The communist world's lack of interest in such documents is suggested by the fact that the Final Act of the Helsinki Accords of 1975

From prepared statement of Raymond D. Gastil, U.S. Congress, House of Representatives, *Human Rights and Foreign Policy*, Hearings before the Subcommittee on International Organizations of the Committee on Foreign Affairs, 96th Cong., 1st Sess., 1979, pp. 262–272.

referred only to the constitutional human rights in our tradition, ignoring through inattention the concept of human rights as human needs that is supposedly of special concern to the socialist countries. It appears that if we are to have a human rights policy, its emphases must be ours to define.

In expressing our international concern for human rights we have properly focused on how governments respond to and behave toward their people or peoples. We are saying, in effect, that Americans have identified certain fundamental principles of human dignity and equality that all governments should respect; we are expressing a faith that when given an adequate chance all peoples will desire their governments to obey these principles. We cannot be so arrogant in our human rights advocacy as to claim that we have a right to tell other peoples what to do. We are only hoping to establish standards by which peoples can effectively control their governments.

If so, then the fundamental focus of human rights policy must be to advance the day when the peoples of the world are in charge of their own affairs, when all adult individuals have a fair chance in every country to establish majorities to formulate or change policies in a democratic manner. The political and civil rights with which we are concerned are directly or indirectly supportive of this goal. Free and competitive elections choosing, affirming, or replacing government leaders are necessary. Freedom of the press, thought, assembly, organization, and travel are essential to meaningful opportunities to form new majorities or coalitions around new issues. Freedom from political imprisonment, torture, execution, or exile are essential to an ability to oppose a system politically. More indirectly, freedom for religion, labor, business, or education allow those material and symbolic allegiances and organizations to be maintained or develop that are necessary for the average person to deal on a basis of equality with his government.

Our national role in promoting human rights in other countries is to act as a proxy for what we believe to be the desire of all peoples to control their own affairs. As a proxy we must be careful to restrict our role, first, to promoting the rights of peoples to determine the nature of their society, and, second, to protecting the rights of subnational peoples or minorities against dehumanizing discrimination, including expulsion and genocide, that cancels the rights of a majority over them. Beyond this we have the right to tell a people what decisions they should make once they attain control over their own affairs. Unfortunately, the inclusion of human needs as rights forces us to cross over this boundary by defining what the responsibilities of majorities must be. It may be that most majorities will demand that their governments provide all persons with a level of nutrition, education, health care, and housing that is acceptable to American consciences. But some majorities may decide that because of the demands of economic growth, they can afford neither the diversion of capital nor the reduction in incentive such programs might produce. They may decide like Medieval Europeans to build cathedrals instead of schools. In any event it cannot be a responsibility of the American government to set social standards of this kind, particularly when there continue to be unsettled questions in our own society as to how large a role government should play in guaranteeing minimums or what minimums are adequate.

It is simply wrong to say that human rights means constitutional rights to the people of wealthy nations but means human needs to the poor. Representatives of countries making this claim are generally not representatives elected by their people. Naturally this argument appeals to petty tyrants or one-party bureaucrats wishing to justify their refusal to test their decisions at the polls or in the press. It is an argument too easily believed by wealthy Americans who cannot conceive of living at the material levels of most of the world. But poor people living within the assumptions of their poverty have the spiritual, aesthetic, and political desires common to humanity. Primitive tribesmen living below the standards of landless peasants often devote less time to securing a living than Americans. Democratic institutions were developed by people in Greece, Switzerland, Iceland, and colonial America with standards of health care, education, and housing that would hardly be acceptable today. In Asia the poor people of the cultural area represented by India, Sri Lanka, and Bangladesh have repeatedly shown deep attachment to constitutional human rights, far deeper than the wealthy people of many countries. In Africa the three most democratic states are among the smallest and poorest. In the face of this evidence we should not allow the repressors of countries such as Argentina, Chile, Uruguay, Cuba, Indonesia, China, or Czechoslovakia to get away with this argument. All peoples may not have the organization, knowledge, or experience to achieve or maintain fully democratic systems today, but it is demeaning to imagine that they are so engrossed in materialism that they do not desire the basic equality and dignity represented by constitutional human rights.

It should also be remembered that many poor people want political rights because they see them as the only way to guarantee their material wants. Democratic countries with constitutional human rights are less likely to divert money away from meeting fundamental needs than those without rights. In particular, developing Third World democracies are less likely to spend a nation's resources on military equipment or warfare against their neighbors: sufferings of war are seldom popular. Whether for ideological goals, vainglory, or personal profit, only tyrants are likely to institutionalize such diversions. Democracies, however, will differ on the degree to which they believe governments should use their taxing power to directly supply social needs.

Human needs can be thought of as human rights, but the responsibility for meeting them can be placed legitimately on the individual adult, the family, the local community, the national government, or the international community. To this extent they fall into a different area of attention than the constitutional human rights that can be defined unequivocally as responsibilities of governments in regard to their peoples.

Practically, including the degree of satisfaction of human needs in the evaluation of progress weakens the ability of human rights policy to establish international standards of government behavior. Let me give as an example the discussions of Cuba and South Korea in the report prepared last year for this Subcommittee by the Library of Congress on "Human Rights Conditions in Selected Countries and the U.S. Response." For many readers the significance of the denial of civil and political liberties in these countries may be seriously diluted by their success in achieving economic progress and equality, that is, in meeting basic human needs. I am not arguing that meeting these needs was not important, but only that such accomplishments should not be seen to modify our concern with political imprisonment or the stifling of dissent.

The inclusion of human needs progress in the discussion of human rights achievement also leads to an unjustified expectation or claim that there are moral trade-offs between constitutional human rights and human needs. An examination of economic and social performance around the world will suggest that there are as many poor tyrannies that fail to meet basic needs as there are poor democracies. Often, as in recent revelations from China, the apparent material progress of totalitarian states is more a figment of managed news and access than a reality. Even if empirically there were a trade-off, we should resist the averaging of socioeconomic performance with constitutional performance. Nazi Germany and *Brave New World* made good provisions for basic needs, but this should not affect the intensity of our condemnation.

In suggesting this emphasis for human rights policy I am not suggesting that the United States lessen its interest in meeting international human needs. Long before the current flurry of interest under the human rights rubric American foreign aid policies were concerned with these needs; the United States has often used the leverage of foreign aid to improve the performance of particular governments in meeting human needs. The most important aspects of American policy in meeting human needs are trade policy, technical assistance, emergency relief, and efforts to reduce the prices of basic commodities such as petroleum or wheat. In other words, the human needs area is one we approach primarily through American control over its material resources and its influence over international actions rather than through prescribing standards of conduct for governments of countries that have not, often cannot, meet socioeconomic minimums.

I conclude that it might be useful for future legislation in this area to emphasize more explicitly the constitutional definition of human rights as political and civil liberties.

In Freedom House's first two yearbooks of Freedom *(Freedom in the World 1978* and *Freedom in the World 1979)* I have developed the case for emphasis on freedom or constitutional human rights in U.S. foreign policy and briefly reviewed the first year of the implementation of this policy under the Carter administration. Although public emphasis on asserting human rights appears to have declined in 1978-79, the policy may at the same time have become increasingly institutionalized. Certainly one hears complaints of its continued operation by those who question it. This institutionalization is one in which Congress has played an important part. One would hope the policy is expressed consistently and is characterized by a coordination rather than opposition of interests. Yet the extent to which Congress should further specify government action for human rights is problematic, as long as legislation is sufficient to assure the policy's continuity.

America's human rights concerns must necessarily compete for attention with the many other material and ideological interests of the United States. As in World War II, we must at times be allied with tyrannies to defeat even worse tyrannies. Nevertheless, a relatively consistent concern with human rights should characterize American policy. Although in the short run this policy may have mixed results, in the longer run it represents our best claim to legitimacy. In a world of continuing ideological struggle, support for constitutional human rights is one of the few weapons available to a pluralist society.

In the most recent yearbook I write:

In the past the tendency of Western leaders and "responsible" publics has been to emphasize short-term material and military interests, and to resolutely stand up for freedom only when there is little conflict with these interests. This is commitment to freedom by exception. However, to win the ideological struggle and ultimately therefore the struggle for freedom everywhere we need to reverse these priorities and stand up for freedom regularly. With this priority we would ignore freedom only when this is demonstrably in our long- as well as short-run interest.

The strength of free institutions everywhere has been weakened when we as citizens or governments have failed to criticize the Pinochet regime of Chile, General Somoza in Nicaragua, the Shah in Iran, and the whites in South Africa, just as it has been weakened when we ignored the recent inhumanities in Indochina or Uganda, or the suppression of intellectual dissent by the cruel fabrications of Soviet courts. Consistency is justice, it builds, one case upon another, toward an international consensus that by its nature leaves totalitarianism out in the cold. Inconsistency makes all our actions, idealistic or Machiavellian, appear insincere, to be merely the manipulation of the pain of others for short-term advantage. For this reason a strategy for freedom must employ inconsistency most sparingly.

Commitment to human rights by exception allowed us to support repressive military rule in Greece for ostensible (but short-sighted) security reasons: the collapse of military rule left a heritage of anti-Americanism. Although so far this history has not destroyed our relationship with Greece, it has weakened NATO, and the case is one not soon forgotten by the younger generation of Greeks or Western Europeans. Elsewhere we have not been so lucky. We became identified with Ethiopia's feudal repression to such an extent that its replacement was almost sure to be viciously anti-American. Even clearer has been the case in Iran. We had the exceptional opportunity of educating a whole generation of Iran's secular leaders in our universities. And yet by seeming to condone the imprisonment, torture, censorship, and misappropriation of the Shah's government we laid the basis for a revolutionary Iran that from left to right has few principles of foreign policy other than anti-Americanism. For years we seemed to condone Portugal's African Empire and the repressive Portuguese regime that maintained it. Again, when the system collapsed we were likely to find few friends in the new countries of Angola, Mozambique, Guinea-Bissau, Cape Verde Islands, and Sao Tome and Principe. Our very long association with President Somoza may well bear similar fruit.

These examples are not only important because they represent setbacks to our narrower national interests. They are important because when peoples see the United States as their enemy they are more likely to see the systems and rights identified with the United States as questionable, and thereby to accept the legitimacy of those anti-American elites that fundamentally deny human rights. The old policy of human rights by exception will in the end have hurt most profoundly the interests of those whose human rights we have overlooked.

The examples also illustrate the proposition that the chief reward of a more consistent commitment to human rights will be in the reidentification of the United States and the principles it represents with the hopes and aspirations of peoples everywhere.

Although we have as a nation been concerned with Jews in the USSR, Chinese in Vietnam, and blacks in South Africa, we have been reluctant to take a creative interest in the causes of many oppressed peoples searching for political identity. This is perhaps the thorniest area of human rights concern, for responsible support of self-determination is extremely difficult. Our sometime support of the Kurds under a previous administration turned into their betrayal. Yet the right of a people to self-determination is another side of the right of a people to rule itself; this right cannot be evaded in the human rights dialogue.

If we want the peoples of the world, national and non-national, to look to the United States for moral support in their struggles for respect and dignity, we must respond to their faith.

To be used as policy criteria human rights must be regarded as standards of behavior to be expected of all governments in regard to their citizens. High standards should be applauded and low standards condemned. All else being equal, material benefits, arms, and other assistance must be seen to flow more easily to the governments with the higher standards. The question becomes more difficult when we add the necessity to reward or punish gains or losses in human rights. On the one hand, it is important to see the significance of small moves, such as a limited release of political prisoners or the lifting of direct censorship. Substantial, lasting change often occurs in small increments. On the other hand, too much attention should not be paid to small advances within a generally unchanging pattern of oppression or to small declines in the level of rights, due perhaps to particularly violent conditions, as recently occurred in Turkey. We should not too quickly label positive changes as merely cosmetic, but should avoid the appearance of giving excessive praise to minor changes by regimes that remain repressive, as happened last year in Nicaragua. More effort to consult with opposition circles as we make attempts to reward incremental advance could reduce this danger.

When the principle of human rights becomes established as a part of U.S. policy, its application will become more sophisticated. A more successful and responsible human rights policy might place as much emphasis on the management of human rights progress as on expressions of American approval or disapproval. American policy was largely responsible for the triggering of repressed forces in Iran that led to revolution, anarchy, and traditionalist revenge. The result has served some Iranians well; the new regime comes closer to majority rule than the Shah's, but the advance in human rights is surely partial and endangered. We must learn how to deal with the fact that it is very hard for a repressive regime to relax its oppression without unleashing violence and renewed repression. Too often countries trying democratic experiments, such as Afghanistan in the 1960's or Thailand in the early 1970's find liberalizing experiments canceled by the reimposition of tyranny. In the communist world the Party found in Hungary, Poland, Czechoslovakia, Yugoslavia, and China that relaxing oppressive practices to achieve a higher standard of human rights often threatened to destroy the system; thus, human rights progress has again and again been arrested by one or another communist agency in the interest of communist self-preservation.

If our human rights policy could become the basis for planning transitions to democracy with the aid of local government, military, and opposition representatives, advances in human rights would be undertaken more often and they would be more lasting. The hatreds engendered by oppressive regimes are not easily set aside, but as Spain demonstrates, and Brazil may be demonstrating, these hatreds can be overcome. We must develop a human rights policy based on conciliation, communication, and a concern for the interests of every people as they express them. Respect for human rights is respect for the rights of all individuals and all groups. It cannot be promoted without searching for compromises that encompass the full range of the conflicting interests that characterize societies.

Human Rights and United States Foreign Policy
Ernest W. Lefever

THE CURRENT HUMAN RIGHTS CAMPAIGN

. . . The current wave of concern for human rights around the world is a Western phenomenon foreshadowed by several developments, notably Woodrow Wilson's crusade for "self-determination" and the Universal Declaration of Human Rights adopted by the United Nations in 1948.

The U.S. campaign to make the advancement of human rights abroad an objective of foreign policy is

From statement of Ernest W. Lefever, U.S. Congress, House of Representatives, *Human Rights and U.S. Foreign Policy,* Hearings before the Subcommittee on International Organizations of the Committee on Foreign Affairs, 96th Cong., 1st Sess., pp. 222–232 and 235–237.

more recent, but it did not start with President Jimmy Carter. He simply built on the lively interest developed in Congress during the past several years which has been expressed largely in Foreign Aid legislation designed to prohibit or restrict economic or military assistance to any government "which engages in a consistent pattern of gross violations of internationally recognized human rights, including torture or cruel, inhumane, or degrading treatment or punishment, prolonged detention without charges, or other flagrant denial of the right to life, liberty, and the security of person" (Foreign Assistance Act, Section 502B, adopted in 1974). Most of the congressional human rights activists have limited their advocacy of punitive measures to Chile, South Korea, and Iran, and belatedly Southeast Asia. A somewhat different group has focused attention on Soviet emigration policy.

Human rights was a natural cause for President Carter. As a born-again Baptist and a latter-day Wilsonian, he repeatedly stated his intention to restore integrity and compassion to American domestic and foreign policy. In his Notre Dame University address on May 22, 1977, Mr. Carter deplored our "intellectual and moral poverty," illustrated by our past Vietnam policy, and our "inordinate fear of Communism which once led us to embrace any dictator who joined us in that fear." He called for a "new" American foreign policy, "based on constant decency in its values and on optimism in its historical vision." The most conspicuous manifestation of his new policy is the effort to promote human rights in other countries by means of U.S. statecraft, including private diplomacy, public preaching, and measures to deny or threaten to deny economic, military or nuclear assistance.

The human rights campaign had received mixed reviews at home and abroad. In a *New Yorker* article in July 1978, Elizabeth Drew reported that Mr. Carter's people "are pleased, and some even a bit awestruck, at the impact that the human-rights campaign has had thus far. 'I think' says one, 'that the mulish world has noticed the two-by-four.'"

There is no doubt that the threatening plank has been noticed, and probably in isolated cases it has accomplished some good. But it should be recorded that some un-mulish elements in the world, including friendly and allied governments, have also seen the two-by-four and are not convinced that its whack, however well intended, has always been redemptive. There is no doubt that it has harmed relations with

some allies and has both irritated and comforted adversaries.

It is by no means clear that the campaign has resulted in any significant relaxation of Soviet restrictions against emigration or political dissent. There is evidence that the opposite may be the case. On December 30, 1977, a *New York Times* page-one story reported: "The small Soviet human rights movement . . . is at its lowest point in years after a campaign of arrests, threats, and forced exile."

It is clear, however, that a score of allies have been unhappy with a policy they regard as arrogant and unfairly applied. Brazil, Argentina, Uruguay, and Guatemala have been alienated to the point where they have refused military assistance from Washington. And Brazil has served notice that it wishes to withdraw from its Security Assistance Agreement of 25 years standing. This alienation of allies gives aid and comfort to Moscow which more than offsets the minor embarrassment the Soviets suffer from Mr. Carter's conspicuous "intervention" in behalf of prominent dissidents.

SIX FLAWS IN THE CARTER POLICY

Far more serious, however, the Carter campaign has confused our foreign policy goals and trivialized the concept of human rights. It both reflects and reinforces serious conceptual flaws in the worldview of its most articulate spokesmen. These flaws, if permitted to instruct foreign policy, or even influence it unduly, could have catastrophic consequences for the security of the United States and the cause of freedom in the world. Six interrelated flaws deserve brief mention:

1. Understimating the Totalitarian Threat

Human dignity and freedom are under siege around the world. It has been ever so. The islands of community protected by humane law have been contracting ever since postwar decolonization began. The citizens of most of the newly independent states in Asia and Africa now experience less freedom and fewer guaranteed rights than they did under Western colonial rule.

The greatest threat to human rights comes from messianic totalitarian regimes whose brutal grip brooks no opposition. Their self-anointed and self-perpetuating elites have become the arbiters of orthodoxy in every sphere—politics, economics, education, and arts, and family life. The ruling party even usurps the place of God. In totalitarian states like the Soviet

Union, Cuba, Cambodia, and Vietnam, countervailing forces are not permitted to challenge the power, will, or policies of the entrenched elite.

In spite of notable exceptions, the general political situation in the Third World is characterized by chaos and authoritarian regimes. Democratic and antidemocratic ideas and institutions are competing for acceptance. In this struggle, we should not underestimate the attraction of the totalitarian temptation to leaders who are grappling with the perplexing problems of holding onto power while they attempt to move their traditional societies into the modern world.

The human rights activists tend to underestimate the totalitarian threat to the West and the totalitarian temptation in the Third World. Hence, they neglect or trivialize the fundamental political and moral struggle of our time—the protracted conflict between forces of total government based on coercion and the proponents of limited government based on popular consent and humane law. In their preoccupation with the minor abridgment of certain rights in authoritarian states, they often overlooked the massive threat to the liberty of millions. They attack the limitation of civil rights in South Korea and at the same time call for the United States to withdraw its ground forces, an act that may invite aggression from North Korea. It would be a great irony if Washington in the name of human rights would adopt a policy that would deliver 35,000,000 largely free South Koreans into virtual slavery.

2. Confusing Totalitarianism with Authoritarianism

In terms of political rights, moral freedom, and cultural vitality, there is a profound difference between authoritarian and totalitarian regimes. Most Asian, African, and Latin American countries are ruled by small elites supported by varying degrees of popular consent. Some are run by brutal tyrants, others by one-party cliques, military juntas, or civilian-military committees. Most authoritarian regimes permit a significantly greater degree of freedom and diversity than totalitarian ones in all spheres— political, cultural, economic, and religious. Authoritarian rules often allow opposition parties to operate and a restrained press to publish. Foreign correspondents usually can move about freely and send out uncensored dispatches. They often permit and sometimes encourage relatively free economic activity and freedom of movement for their citizens.

There is far more freedom of choice, diversity of opinion and activity, and respect for human rights in authoritarian South Korea than in totalitarian North Korea. There is also far more freedom and cultural vitality in Chile—even under its present military rule—than in Cuba. There have been political prisoners in Chile and there may be a handful now, but there are an estimated 15,000 to 60,000 political detainees in Cuba. These facts are noted, not to praise Chile or condemn Cuba, but to emphasize the consequential difference of human rights under the two profoundly different kinds of regimes.

Another crucial difference is the capacity of authoritarian rule to evolve into democratic rule. This has happened recently in Spain, Portugal, Greece, and India. In sharp contrast, a Communist dictatorship has never made a peaceful transition to more representative and responsive rule.

3. Overestimating America's Influence Abroad

If the human rights zealots do not indulge in what Denis Brogan once called "the illusion of American omnipotence," they tend to overestimate the capacity of our government to influence the external world, particularly domestic developments in other countries. America is powerful, but it is not all powerful. Our considerable leverage of the 1950s and even our diminished leverage of the 1960s has been seriously eroded by OPEC, the great leap forward in Soviet military might, and our abandonment of Vietnam.

Quite apart from our limited capacity to influence intractable realities abroad, there is and should be a profound moral constraint on efforts designed to alter domestic practices, institutions, and policies within other states. Neo-Wilsonian attempts to make the world safe for human rights seem to be rooted in the naive view that the rest of the world is malleable, responsive to our wishes, and vulnerable to our threats.

The extravagant rhetoric of a Carter or a Wilson, with its crusading and paternalistic overtones, draws upon a persistent idealistic stream in the American character. But there is another and quieter stream, equally honorable, but less pushy and perhaps more persuasive—symbolized by the Biblical parable of a candle upon a candlestick or a city set upon a hill, an example to the "lesser breeds without the law," as it was put in a more candid era.

John Quincy Adams expressed this more modest understanding of America's external responsibility: "We are the friends of liberty everywhere, but the custodians only of our own." Thirty years later, Abraham Lincoln spoke of "liberty as the heritage of all men, in all lands everywhere," but he did not claim that the United States was the chosen instrument for fulfilling this heritage.

4. Confusing Domestic and Foreign Policy

Many human rights crusaders confuse the fundamental distinctions between domestic and foreign policy which are rooted in international law, the U.N. Charter, and common sense. They do not take seriously the limits in authority and responsibility that flow from the concept of sovereignty which underlies the modern state system. Our President and all other heads of state have authority to act only in their own states, within the territory of their legal jurisdiction. They are responsible only for the security and welfare of their own people, including their citizens living or traveling abroad.

There are, of course, multiple modes of interaction and cooperation between states based on mutual interest, ranging from trade, investment, and cultural exchange to military assistance and alliance ties. These activities are consistent with the concept of sovereign equality and non-interference in internal affairs. But short of a victorious war, no government has a right to impose its preference on another sovereign state. The mode and quality of life, the character and structure of institutions within a state should be determined by its own people, not by outsiders, however well intentioned. The same is true for the peace and direction of social, political, or economic change.

U.S. foreign policy toward a particular state should be determined largely by the foreign policy of that state. Domestic factors and forces are significant determinants only if they bear on external realities. Washington is allied with Taiwan, Thailand, South Korea, and a dozen Latin American states whose governments are authoritarian, not because they are authoritarian, but because they are regarded as important in maintaining a semblance of world order in the face of chaos and the expansion of Soviet or Chinese power. We have, therefore, provided economic or military assistance to them, even though they do not hold regular elections or conduct open trials.

5. Ignoring the Perils of Reform Intervention

The impulse to impose our standards or practices on other societies, supported by policies of reward and punishment, leads inevitably to a kind of reform intervention. We Americans have no moral mandate to transform other societies, and we rightly resent such efforts on the part of the totalitarians. There is more than a touch of arrogance in our efforts to alter the domestic behavior of allies, or even of adversaries.

In addition to the human rights clause in the Foreign Assistance Act noted above, Title IX of the Act specified that U.S. aid should be used to encourage "democratic private and local government institutions" within the recipient states. The implications of this seemingly innocent phrase are disquieting. Should U.S. assistance be used to alter domestic institutions? Should we insist on an ideological or reform test before providing economic or military aid? Is this not a form of uninvited interference in domestic matters? If we take sovereign equality seriously, we will recognize that the people of every state should determine their own system of political authority, justice, and security.

Other states may request assistance from friendly governments on mutually agreed terms. But external forces, however nobly motivated, cannot impose justice, human rights, or freedom on other states without resorting to direct or indirect conquest. It may be possible to "export revolution"—as the phrase goes—but we cannot export human rights or respect for the rule of law. Freedom and justice are the fruit of long organic growth nurtured by religious values, personal courage, social restraint, and respect for law. The majesty of law is little understood in traditional societies where ethnic identity tends to supersede all other claims on loyalty and obedience.

6. Distorting Foreign Policy Objectives

A consistent and single-minded invocation of a human rights standard in making U.S. foreign policy decisions would subordinate, blur, or distort other essential considerations. After all, our foreign policy has vital but limited goals—national security and international peace—both of which have a great impact on human rights. Aggressive war and tyranny are the two chief enemies of freedom and justice. Our efforts to deter nuclear war and nuclear blackmail are calculated to protect the culture and free institutions of Western Europe and North America. In the Third World we seek to maintain a regional stability conducive to responsible political development and mutually beneficial economic intercourse among states. Economic productivity alleviates stark poverty and thus broadens the range of cultural and political choice.

Therefore, our policies of nuclear deterrence should be determined by our understanding of the Soviet nuclear threat and our trade policies toward Moscow should be determined by our economic and security interests. Neither should be significantly influenced, much less determined, by the extent of human rights violations in the Soviet Union. Likewise, in dealing with Third World countries, their foreign policy behavior should be the determining factor, not their domestic practices. Even though South Korea has an authoritarian government, we should continue our security support because it is a faithful ally under siege from a totalitarian neighbor and because its independence is vital to the defense of Japan and Japan's independence is vital to the U.S. position in the Western Pacific and the world.

THE PITFALLS OF SELECTIVE APPLICATION

These six conceptual flaws which underlie the human rights crusade have already led to unwise policies and, if carried to their logical conclusion, could end in disaster. . . .

WHAT IS AMERICA'S RESPONSIBILITY?

In a formal and legal sense, the U.S. Government has no responsibility—and certainly no authority—to promote human rights in other sovereign states. But this is hardly the whole story. Because of our heritage, our dedication to humane government, our power, and our wealth, we Americans have a moral responsibility, albeit ill defined, in the larger world consistent with our primary obligations at home and commensurate with our capacity to influence external events. We are almost universally regarded as a humanitarian power and as the champion of freedom and decency. We should be proud of our humane occupation policies in Germany and Japan. But we enjoy no occupation rights now, and the role of our government abroad is less clear. Saying this, the American people and their government can make two major contributions to the cause of human rights in other countries.

First, in the spirit of John Quincy Adams and Lincoln, we can be worthy custodians of the freedom bequeathed us by the Founding Fathers and thus continue to give heart to the aspirations of peoples

everywhere. We can give hope to those in bondage by illustrating what the late Reinhold Niebuhr has called "the relevance of the impossible ideal." We can never fully realize our own ideals, but we can strive toward them. In most other cultural settings, full respect for human rights cannot be expected in the foreseeable future. A quick change in government will not enshrine liberty or justice. The message of our example is subdued, but not without hope—the struggle for a bit more freedom of choice or a better chance for justice is a never-ending one and after small gains have been made, eternal vigilance is vital to avoid sliding back into bondage. Serving as an example of decency, then, is our most effective way to nudge forward the cause of human dignity.

Second, our government can advance human rights by strengthening our resolve and our resources to defend our allies who are threatened by totalitarian aggression or subversion. This requires security guarantees, military assistance, and in some cases the presence of U.S. troops on foreign soil. Our combined effort to maintain a favorable balance of power has succeeded thus far in preserving the independence of Western Europe, Japan, and South Korea. But because of our half-hearted commitment, we failed in Vietnam, Cambodia, and Laos, and in a different sense, in Angola. . . .

Beyond serving as a good example and maintaining our security commitments, there is little the U.S. Government can or should do to advance human rights, other than using quiet diplomatic channels at appropriate times and places. Moscow and other governments should be reminded of their pledges in the United Nations Charter and the Helsinki Agreement. Public preaching to friend or foe has limited utility. As we have already seen, it is both embarrassing and counter-productive to threaten punitive measures against friendly, but less than democratic, regimes which are attempting to achieve a reasonable balance between authority and freedom at home, often under severely trying circumstances, and are pursuing constructive policies abroad. . . .

QUESTIONS FOR DISCUSSION

1 Should human rights be a goal of American foreign policy?
2 Should the United States pursue an activist human rights policy even toward those of its allies who violate those rights?

3 Does a strong United States human rights policy impede improved relations between the United States and the Soviet Union?

4 What rights ought to be included in any basic list of fundamental human rights?

5 Does it make sense to attempt to develop policies and institutions at the international level designed to promote and protect human rights?

SUGGESTED READINGS

Berger, Peter L. "Are Human Rights Universal?" *Commentary* (September 1977): 60–63.

Buckley, William F., Jr. "Human Rights and Foreign Policy: A Proposal." *Foreign Affairs* **58** (Spring 1980): 775–796.

"Human Rights and American Foreign Policy: A Symposium." *Commentary* (November 1981): 25–63.

Laqueur, Walter. "The Issue of Human Rights." *Commentary* (May 1977): 29–35.

McDougal, Myres, Harold D. Lasswell, and Lung-Chu Chen. *Human Rights and Public Order.* New Haven: Yale University Press, 1980.

Moynihan, Daniel P. "The Politics of Human Rights." *Commentary* (August 1977): 19–26.

Thompson, Kenneth W. (ed.). *The Moral Imperatives of Human Rights: A World Survey.* Washington, D.C.: University Press of America, 1980.

U.S. Congress. Senate. *Nomination of Ernest W. Lefever.* Hearings before the Committee on Foreign Relations, 97th Cong., 1st Sess., 1981.

Utley, T. E. "A Reappraisal of the Human Rights Doctrine." *Policy Review* No. **3** (Winter 1978): 27–34.

Vogelgesang, Sandy. *American Dream/Global Nightmare: The Dilemma of U.S. Human Rights Policy.* New York: Norton, 1980.

11 Should There Be a New International Economic Order?

YES

Mahbub ul Haq

A Lingering Look at the Old Economic Order

NO

Peter Bauer and John O'Sullivan

Ordering the World About: The New International Economic Order

A Lingering Look at the Old Economic Order
Mahbub ul Haq

The vastly unequal relationship between the rich and the poor nations is fast becoming the central issue of our time. The poor nations are beginning to question the basic premises of an international order which leads to ever widening disparities between the rich and the poor countries and to a persistent denial of equality of opportunity to many poor nations. They are, in fact, arguing that in international order—just as much as within national orders—all distribution of benefits, credit, services, and decision-making becomes warped in favor of a privileged minority and that this situation cannot be changed except through fundamental institutional reforms. This thinking appears to underlie their demand for a "New International Economic Order."[1]

When this is pointed out to the rich nations, they dismiss it casually as empty rhetoric of the poor nations. Their standard answer is that the international market mechanism works, even though not too perfectly, and that the poor nations are always out to wring concessions from the rich nations in the name of past exploitation. They believe that the poor nations are demanding a massive redistribution of income and wealth which is simply not in the cards. Their general attitude seems to be that the poor nations must earn their economic development, much the same way as the rich nations had to over the last two centuries, through patient hard work and gradual capital formation, and that there are no short cuts to this process and no rhetorical substitutes. The rich, however, are generous enough to offer some help to the poor nations to accelerate their economic development if the poor are only willing to behave themselves.

In reviewing this controversy, we must face up to the blunt question: Does the present world order systematically discriminate against the interests of the Third World, as the poor nations contend? Or is the demand for a new order mere empty rhetoric against imagined grievances, as the rich nations allege?

[1] U.N., *Declaration and Program of Action on the Establishment of a New International Economic Order*, A/RES/3201 and 3202 (S-VI), May 1, 1974.

FAILURES OF MARKET SYSTEM

There is sufficient concrete evidence to show that the poor nations cannot get an equitable deal from the present international economic structures—much the same way as the poorest sections of the society within a country and for much the same reasons. Once there are major disparities in income distribution within a country, the market mechanism ceases to function either efficiently or equitably since it is weighted heavily in favor of the purchasing power in the hands of the rich. Those who have the money can make the market bend to their own will. This is even more true at the international level since there is no world government and none of the usual mechanisms existing within countries which create pressures for redistribution of income and wealth. Barbara Ward quite succinctly summarized the case against the workings of the international market mechanism in a situation of gross inequalities in world income:

To rely solely on the market system [in such a situation] has wider consequences for society in general and for resource use in particular. The capacity to sell, to have responsive buyers, becomes the overriding criterion for producing goods. This raises a number of problems. Production is geared to those who can effectively buy. Internationally, that means richer countries rather than poorer countries, and nationally it means middle and high income groups rather than the poorer people. Within most developed societies, social mechanisms—public ownership, redistributive income tax, welfare schemes, social insurance—try to offset this trend. No such institutions are at work at the world level, nor in a number of developing countries. In such conditions, market mechanisms are linked, by their own logic, to the affluent, making resources available to those who can buy them and not necessarily to those who need them. This fact generates a series of backward linkages. It determines the nature of the technology needed to maintain the consumption of the more affluent. It guides the allocation of resources in research and

From Mahbub ul Haq, *The Poverty Curtain: Choices for the Third World.* New York: Columbia University Press, 1976, pp. 153–168.

development. This in itself creates a demand for certain types of professional know-how, rather than for others.[2]

. . . It is only recently that new perceptions on development strategies are beginning to be accepted within national orders. It is being increasingly realized that economic growth does not automatically filter down to the poorest sections of the society; that the distribution of all credit, investment resources and public and private services gravitates towards the richest sectors unless there is a conscious intervention in the market by the government; that equality of opportunity cannot automatically be ensured when vast inequalities in the distribution of income and wealth prevail; that the essence of new development strategies in such a situation is to make resources and opportunities available to increase the productivity of the poor on a permanent basis, not to place the poorest people on a short-term dole; that fundamental institutional reforms are required to remedy the situation, not marginal adjustments in the price system; and, finally, that a restructuring of political and economic power takes place either through revolutions or when the rich realize that the political risks of rebellion far outweigh the economic costs of reform.

Evolution of thinking at the international level generally follows that at the national level, though with a time lag of several decades. This is likely to be true in the case of the thinking on the new international economic order as well. There is a remarkable parallelism between the situation of the poorest sections within a society and that of the poorest nations (particularly those below $200 per capita income currently, containing over one billion people) within the international community. This parallelism has been only dimly perceived at present. It is ironic at times to witness that some of the developed countries, which so eagerly advocate the new development strategies to the developing countries, suddenly develop a case of schizophrenia when it comes to a discussion of a new economic order at the international level.

And yet the poorest nations within the international community face many of the same crippling handicaps as do the poorest people within a nation. The world economic growth does not automatically filter down to these nations. Their initial poverty becomes a major handicap in obtaining either short-term credit or long-term investment resources as they are regarded, in the fashionable parlance of international life, simply "uncreditworthy." All international mechanisms, structures and decision making get mortgaged to the interests of the rich nations. The income disparities between the poor and the rich nations, in such a situation, are bound to increase unless a conscious attempt is made by the international community to reduce them.[3] The heart of such an attempt lies in increasing the productivity of the poor nations —through their own efforts and through an automatic transfer of resources to them—rather than in any marginal adjustments in the present flow of foreign assistance. This requires the evolution of many of the same institutions and mechanisms which have been gradually accepted at the national level—including the acceptance of the concept of international taxation and establishment of an international central bank. And just as in national orders, the short-term costs of reform to the rich nations are likely to be outweighed by the long-term benefits to the entire international community in terms of more harmonious economic growth and greater political stability.

But this is still a case at a level of generality which is neither convincing nor helpful unless it is backed up by concrete evidence. It is here that the Third World has not helped its cause much since it did not undertake the detailed homework that was necessary to demonstrate that the poorest nations were being consistently denied equality of opportunity. It is time, in fact, that the research institutions of the Third World should do some serious work in documenting specific instances of inequities in the world order.

In undertaking such a serious analysis, the two staple diets that the Third World has used so often in the past must be discarded. First, the poor nations cannot keep the rich nations feeling either guilty or

---

[2] Barbara Ward, Report on the UNEP-UNCTAD Symposium on *Patterns of Resource Use, Environment and Development Strategies*, Cocoyoc, Mexico, May 1975.

[3] This is as true of the income gap between the developed and the developing countries as between the poorest and the richer developing countries. For instance, the absolute disparity in per capita income (in constant U.S. dollars) increased from $2,700 to $4,000 between developed and developing countries during 1960 to 1974 while the income disparity between the poorest (below $200) and other developing countries (above $200) also went up during the same period from $330 to $625.

uncomfortable by simply pointing out that three-quarters of income, investment, and wealth are in the hands of one-quarter of its population. The rich nations are increasingly turning around and saying: "So what? We worked for it and so should you." The world income disparities are not an issue, *per se*. It must also be demonstrated that the prevailing disparities are creating major hurdles for the poor nations in carrying out their own development programs and are denying them the basic equality of opportunity to which they ought to be entitled.

Second, the Third World has often used the argument of instability of commodity prices and worsening terms of trade to illustrate their uncertain plight in the present world order. This argument has been overdone and is certainly not the heart of the matter. . . . If low earnings are stabilized, they would still remain low. The Third World needs higher earnings, not only more stable earnings. In any case, worsening terms of trade and commodity price instability are mere symptoms, not the root cause of the problem of unequal relationships. Ultimately, the reasons for this inequality in relationships must be sought in international economic structures and mechanisms which put the Third World at a considerable disadvantage and which require thorough-going institutional reforms. It is worthwhile to explore some of these areas in a more concrete fashion, even though the necessary background research work is not fully available at present.

EVIDENCE OF INEQUITIES

First, there is a tremendous imbalance today in the distribution of international reserves. The poor nations, with 70 percent of the world population, received less than 4 percent of the international reserves of $131 billion during 1970–74 . . . simply because the rich nations controlled the creation and distribution of international reserves through the expansion of their own national reserve currencies (mainly dollars and sterling) and through their decisive control over the International Monetary Fund. For all practical purposes, the United States has been the central banker of the world in the post-World War II period and it could easily finance its balance-of-payments deficits by the simple device of expanding its own currency. In other words, the richest nation in the world has had an unlimited access to international credit facilities since it could create such credit through its own decisions. This has been less true of other developed

countries, though Britain and Germany have enjoyed some of this privilege at various times. This has certainly not been true of the developing countries which could neither create international credit through their own deficit financing operations nor obtain an easy access to this credit because of the absence of any genuine international currency and because of their limited quotas in the Fund.[4] The heart of any economic system is its credit structure. This is controlled entirely by the rich nations at the international level. The poor nations merely stand at the periphery of international monetary decisions. This is nothing unusual. Like in any normal national banking system, the poor get very little credit unless a concerned government chooses to intervene on their behalf.

Second, the distribution of value-added in the products traded between the developing and the developed countries is heavily weighted in favor of the latter. The developing countries, unlike the developed ones, receive back only a small fraction of the final price that the consumers in the international market are already paying for their produce,[5] simply because many of them are too poor or too weak to exercise any meaningful control over the processing, shipping, and marketing of their primary exports. As a very rough estimate, the final consumers pay over $200 billion (excluding taxes) for the major primary exports (excluding oil) of the developing countries (in a more processed, packaged, and advertised form) but these countries receive back only $30 billion, with the middlemen and the international service sector—mostly in the hands of the rich nations—enjoying the difference. On the other hand, the rich nations have

[4] For a very perceptive analysis of the international monetary system, see Robert Triffin, *New Structures for Economic Interdependence*, Richard N. Gardner, ed., Rensselaerville, N.Y., Institute on Man and Science, September 1975.

[5] Unfortunately, few detailed studies have been undertaken so far on individual commodities to document the margins between producer's return and the consumer's price. One of these studies is on bananas (see Jean Paul Valles, *The World Market for Bananas: 1964–1972* (New York: Praeger, 1974), where the empirical evidence shows that the producers obtain less than 10 percent of the final price. A detailed commodity-by-commodity study of the margins between producer's and consumer's price can illuminate concretely the areas where policy action is most needed and could yield the most promising results. The U.N. Special Session in September 1975 has directed UNCTAD to carry out such a study.

the resources and the necessary bargaining power to control the various phases of their production, export and distribution—often including their own subsidiaries to handle even internal distribution within importing countries. In fact, if the poor nations had been able to exercise the same degree of control over the processing and distribution of their exports as the rich nations presently do and if they were to get back a similar proportion of the final consumer price, their export earnings from their primary commodities would be closer to $150 billion. Again, there is a parallel here between national and international orders: within national orders as well, the poor receive only a fraction of the rewards for their labor and a high proportion of the value-added is appropriated by the organized, entrenched middlemen unless the national governments intervene.

Third, the protective wall erected by the developed countries prevents the developing world from receiving its due share of the global wealth. The rich nations are making it increasingly impossible for the "free" international market mechanisms to work. In the classical framework of Adam Smith, the cornerstone of the free market mechanism is the free movement of labor and capital as well as of goods and services so that rewards to factors of production are equalized all over the world. In fact, world inequalities can simply not persist in such a framework. Yet immigration laws in almost all rich nations make it impossible for any large-scale movement of unskilled labor in a worldwide search for economic opportunities (except for a limited "brain drain" of skilled labor); not much capital has crossed international boundaries, both because of poor nations' sensitivities and the rich nations' own needs; and additional barriers have gone up against the free movement of goods and services—e.g., over $20 billion in farm subsidies alone in the rich nations to protect their agriculture and progressively higher tariffs and quotas against the simple consumer goods exports of the developing countries, like textiles and leather goods. . . . The rich, in other words, are drawing a protective wall around their life styles, telling the poor nations that they can neither compete with their labor nor with their goods, while paying handsome tribute at the same time to the "free" workings of the international market mechanism. Unfortunately, while the rich can show such discrimination, the poor cannot by the very fact of their poverty. They need their current foreign exchange earnings desperately, just in order to survive

and to carry on a minimum development effort, and they can hardly afford to put up discriminatory restrictions against the capital good imports and technology of the Western world. There is again a parallel here between national and international orders. Within national orders as well, the poor generally have very little choice but to sell their services to the rich at considerable disadvantage just in order to earn the means of their survival.

Fourth, another area in which the unequal bargaining power of the poor and the rich nations shows up quite dramatically is the relationship between multinational corporations and the developing countries. Most of the contracts, leases, and concessions that the multinational corporations have negotiated in the past with the developing countries reflect a fairly inequitable sharing of benefits. In many cases, the host government is getting only a fraction of the benefits from the exploitation of its own natural resources by the multinational corporations. For instance, Mauritania gets about 15 percent of the profits that the multinational corporations make from extracting and exporting the iron ore deposits in the country. Similarly, in Liberia the foreign investors export nearly one fourth of the total GNP of the country in terms of their profit remittances. Such examples can be multiplied.[6] In fact, it would be useful to tabulate all the concessions, contracts, and leases which have been negotiated between the multinational corporations and the developing countries and to present to the world an idea of what the present sharing of benefits is between host governments and multinational corporations in case after case. Such a factual background will not only illustrate the concrete and specific fashion in which the poor nations are now discriminated against but could also be a very useful prelude to the necessary reforms.

Fifth, the poor nations have only a *pro forma* participation in the economic decision making of the world. Their advice is hardly solicited when the big ten industrialized nations get together to take key decisions on the world's economic future; their voting strength in the Bretton Woods institutions (World Bank and International Monetary Fund) is less than one third of the total; and their numerical majority in the General Assembly has meant no real influence so

[6] See, for instance, Richard J. Barnet and Ronald E. Muller, *Global Reach: The Power of the Multinational Corporations* (New York: Simon & Schuster, 1974).

far on international economic decisions. In fact, it may well be an indicator of the sense of accommodation that the rich nations are willing to show that they have started protesting against the "tyranny of the majority" at a time when the majority resolutions of the poor nations within the United Nations carry no effective force and when the Third World countries are not being allowed to sit even as equals around the bargaining tables of the world.

Finally, to take an example from the world of ideas, these unequal relationships pervade the intellectual world and the mass media as well. The developing countries have often been subjected to concepts of development and value systems which were largely fashioned abroad. While economic development was the primary concern of the developing countries, so far it has been written about and discussed largely by outsiders. The mass media, which greatly shape world opinion, are primarily under the control of the rich nations. The Nobel Prize, which is presumably given for excellence of thought, is given to so few in the Third World, even in nontechnical fields such as literature. Is it because the poor nations are not only poor in income but also poor in thought? Or is it because their thought is being judged by standards totally alien to their spirit and they have no organized forums for either projection or dissemination of their thinking?[7] The answer is quite obvious. There is no international structure, including intellectual endeavor, which is not influenced by the same inequality between rich and poor nations.

HISTORICAL PERSPECTIVE

The basic reasons for this inequality between the presently developed and developing nations lie fairly deep in their history. In most parts of the Third World, centuries of colonial rule have left their legacy of dependency. Political independence has often not succeeded in eliminating either economic dependence or intellectual slavery. On the contrary, the big powers have sometimes cultivated their spheres of political and economic influence with ruthless determination in the mistaken notion that it is in their long-term interest. They have at times purchased the shifting alliance of various leaders and governments

in the Third World, confusing this with an alliance with their people and often ignoring the strong underlying forces of nationalism within these countries. Many Third World countries have been willing victims in this game because of a complex of motives, ranging from the narrow, personal self-interest of a few individuals to the inferiority complex of new nationhood, from hopes of temporary gains to fears of national survival. The international scene has often been dominated by relationships based on outmoded concepts of feudalism, where political or economic assertions of independence were met by swift retribution by the super-powers so as to prevent any further insubordination in the ranks.

The international economic life in such a situation became organized around principles which man had learnt from tribal days onwards. The industrialized countries, with their enormous economic and political power, stood at the center of this world order. The developing countries stood at the periphery, supplying their raw materials and services to the metropolitan center and being grateful for whatever little return they could get from the benevolence of the rich. It is not that the rich deliberately exploited the poor. It is merely that this pattern was based on concepts of feudalism, not democracy; on unequal relationships, not equality of opportunity. As such, it was inherently unstable. The first dent came with the movements for political liberation. The second stage—for economic liberation—is being set by the demand for a new international economic order. And accompanying it all is an intellectual ferment in the Third World, sweeping aside the cobwebs of inferiority complex and bringing into power a new generation of people, confident of themselves and their countries, believing in their own culture and their manifest destiny, and willing to deal with the industrialized world only on a basis of equality.

In this context, a net bilateral transfer of about $12 billion of official development assistance to the poor nations every year is neither adequate nor to the point: the quantitative "loss" implicit in the previously quoted examples of maldistribution of international credit, inadequate sharing of benefits from the export of their natural resources, and artificial restrictions on the movement of their goods and services (not to speak of labor) would easily amount to $50–100 billion a year. More pertinently, the poor nations are seeking greater equality of opportunity, not charity from the uncertain generosity of the rich.

[7] Mahbub ul Haq, "The Third World Forum: Intellectual Self-Reliance" in *International Development Review,* 1(1975):8–11.

The demand for economic equality must be seen, however, in its proper historical perspective. It is a natural evolution of the philosophy already accepted at the national level: that the governments must actively intervene on behalf of the poorest segments of their populations ("the bottom 40 percent") who will otherwise be bypassed by economic development. In a fast-shrinking planet, it was inevitable that this "new" philosophy would not stop at national borders; and, since there is no world government, the poor nations are bringing this concern to its closest substitute, the United Nations.

At the same time, the developing countries must recognize the intimate link between the reform of the national and international orders. If national economic orders in the poor nations remain unresponsive to the needs of their own poor and if they continue to benefit only a privileged few, much of the argument for a fundamental reform in the international order would disappear, as any benefits flowing from such a reform would go only to a handful of people who currently wield political and economic authority. Moreover, when the international and national orders are dominated by privileged minorities, the possibilities of a tacit collusion between their natural interests are quite unlimited. The developing countries have to learn, therefore, that reforms in their own national orders are often the critical bargaining chip that they need in pressing for similar reforms at the international level.

The reforms in the national orders of the poor nations, however, are a necessary but not a sufficient condition for a major improvement in the economic conditions of their masses. According to a recent World Bank study,[8] if the present internal and external policies continue unchanged, the poorest developing countries, below a per capita income of $200, face the prospect of virtually no increase in this low level of income during 1975–80.[9] A major change will be required in the internal policies (in saving and investment policies and in the distribution of rewards of economic growth) if such a grim prospect is to be

[8] World Bank, *Prospects for Developing Countries: 1976–80,* July 1975.

[9] The developing countries above $200, because of their better opportunities in the export of manufactured goods and their better access to the international capital market, are expected to pull away further from the poorest less developed countries by experiencing a per capita growth of about 3 percent per annum during the same period.

averted. But a good part of this effort will be frustrated if these countries cannot import the needed machinery and technology and if critical foreign exchange shortages persist because of their limited access to the international market either through trade or through international resource transfers. The solution for this is not piecemeal reforms—via selective trade "concessions" or somewhat larger foreign assistance—since these achieve exactly the same purpose, and provide as temporary a relief, as limited social security payments to the poor within a national system. The long-term solution is to change the institutional system in such a way as to improve the access of the poor to economic opportunities and to increase their long-term productivity, not their temporary income. . . .

PRINCIPLES FOR CHANGE

The basic principles for such a change can be easily established and follow logically from the analysis of institutional imbalances cited above. For instance, any long-term negotiating package should include:

- revamping of the present international credit system by phasing out national reserve currencies and replacing them by an international currency;
- gradual dismantling of restrictions in the rich nations on the movement of goods and services as well as labor from the poor nations;
- enabling the developing countries to obtain more benefit from the exploitation of their own natural resources through a greater control over various stages of primary production, processing, and distribution of their commodities;
- introduction of an element of automaticity in international resource transfers by linking them to some form of international taxation or royalties from the commercial exploitation of international commons or international reserve creation;
- negotiation of agreed principles between the principal creditors and debtors for an orderly settlement of past external debts;
- renegotiation of all past leases and contracts given by the developing countries to the multinational corporations under a new code of conduct to be established and enforced within the United Nations framework; and
- restructuring of the United Nations to give it greater operational powers for economic decisions

and a significant increase in the voting strength of the poor nations within the World Bank and the International Monetary Fund.

In fact, some of these negotiating principles can be left deliberately vague in the first instance to gain general acceptance for them and to give both sides sufficient room to maneuver during the actual negotiations. This has already happened to some extent in the Seventh U..N. Special Session. . . . But no amount of adroit drafting or skillful negotiations can hide the fact that whenever such fundamental reforms in the international order are attempted, they are likely to change the world balance of power in no uncertain terms. The existing power structures may not accept that without a major fight.

The debate on the establishment of a new international economic order has only recently begun. The battle lines are still being drawn; the battle plans of the rich and the poor nations are hardly clear at present. Our world may well be "poised uneasily between an era of great enterprise and creativity or an age of chaos and despair,"[10] between a grand new global partnership or a disorderly confrontation. Unfortunately, there are very few examples in history of the rich surrendering their power willingly or peacefully. Whenever and wherever the rich have made any accommodation, they did so because it had become inevitable since the poor had become organized and would have taken away power in any case. The basic question today, therefore, is not whether the poor nations are in a grossly unfavorable position in the present world order. They are, and they will continue to be, unless they can negotiate a new world order. The basic question really is whether they have the necessary bargaining power to arrange any fundamental changes in the present political, economic, and social balance of power in the world. . . .

---

[10] Henry A. Kissinger, "Global Challenge and International Cooperation," a speech delivered to the Institute of World Affairs, University of Wisconsin, July 14, 1975.

Let me conclude this part of the discussion with three main observations.

First, a tremendous responsibility rests on the universities, research institutions and various intellectual forums of the Third World. It is for them to work out carefully concrete instances of systematic discrimination built into the existing economic order—whether it be the inadequate return from raw material exports, or inequitable sharing of gains from multinational corporations, or unequal distribution of world liquidity. This should be done in a spirit of serious, objective analysis so that there is concrete documentation available to the negotiators from the Third World to press this point in international forums. There is no excuse for the Third World not to produce a sufficient number of factual and convincing studies on this subject since they have a legitimate case and since, in the last analysis, facts are always more powerful than words.

Second, the Third World must keep stressing, as often as it can, that the basic struggle is for equality of opportunity, not equality of income. The Third World is not chasing the income levels of the rich nations. It does not wish to imitate their life styles. The Third World is only suggesting that it must have a decent chance to develop, on an equal basis, without systematic discrimination against it, according to its own value systems and in line with its own cultural traditions. The Third World is not asking for a few more crumbs from the grand table of the rich. It is asking for a fair chance to make it on its own.

Finally, the Third World has to make it quite clear in its future negotiations that what is at stake is not a few marginal adjustments in the international system: it is its complete overhaul. The Third World should also make it clear that it is not foolish enough to think that a new international order can be established overnight. It is willing to wait. And it is willing to proceed in a step-by-step manner. But it is not willing to settle for some inadequate, piecemeal concessions in the name of a step-by-step approach. Short-term tactics can vary so long as they do not mortgage the long-term goals.

Ordering the World About: The New International Economic Order

Peter Bauer
John O'Sullivan

In 1975, to mark Somalia's commitment to the ideals of the International Women's Year, the President announced that in the future women would enjoy equal rights of inheritance with men. Twelve Muslim religious leaders protested that this violated Koranic law. Whereupon they were shot.

This instructive tale should warn us that the liberal ideas and phraseology of the West, once transplanted to the Third World, often assume fantastic and distorted forms. We might bear this in mind when assessing the interminable discussions on the establishment of a "New International Economic Order" (NIEO) at the "North-South Dialogue" in Paris, The Commonwealth Conference in London and the numerous United Nations Conferences on Trade and Development (UNCTAD) and other UN gatherings in Geneva, New York, Nairobi, Delhi and wherever else luxury hotels are to be found.[1]

For, on the face of it, the NIEO boasts an impeccably Western, indeed English, genealogy. It is the most far-reaching application of Fabian socialist theories of wealth distribution, state control and economic planning to international economic relations yet attempted by Third World governments and their Western cheerleaders. In no sense, of course, is it new. Its Fabian inspirations apart, the various UN and other declarations, in which the NIEO is embodied, contain wearisomely familiar demands for still greater foreign aid; comprehensive schemes for "stabilizing" (i.e. raising) commodity prices, transferring technology and cancelling debt repayments by developing countries; and even hazy notions of restricting Western production of synthetic substitutes for Third World products.

But some little novelty is introduced in the argu-

ments justifying these claims. No longer is foreign aid solicited as an act of charity. Indeed, charity is indignantly rejected as demeaning. Nor is it still justified principally as the means of ensuring economic development in less developed countries—though that remains a secondary argument. Today, in international forums, the large-scale transfer of resources from the West to the Third World is demanded as a *right*. It is presented as some small recompense for the West's unjust economic exploitation, past and present, which is alleged to have caused the poverty of the developing world. But the NIEO goes beyond even this. Its demands clearly imply that everyone everywhere should be entitled to a substantial income by virtue of being alive, regardless of economic performance.

Dr. Julius Nyerere, the austeritarian Tanzanian dictator, put these arguments succinctly during his 1975 state visit to Britain:

> In one world, as in one state, when I am rich because you are poor, and I am poor because you are rich, the transfer of wealth from rich to poor is a matter of right; it is not an appropriate matter for charity.
>
> The objective must be the eradication of poverty and the establishment of a minimum standard of living for all people. This will involve its converse—a ceiling on wealth for individuals and nations, as well as deliberate action to transfer resources from the rich to the poor within and across national boundaries.

Endlessly and sanctimoniously repeated, almost never rebutted, such arguments have not been without effect. Mr. Callaghan told Commonwealth statesmen that 650 million people had *per capita* incomes of less than $34 a year and that this was "the most serious challenge to our age and to our leadership." At the recent Paris Conference, the West, alias the "North," agreed to set up a commodity stabilization

---

[1] For a restrained and relatively reasonable statement of the views of the proponents of the NIEO see a new book by a UN civil servant of Indian nationality: Jyoti Shankar Singh, *Toward a New International Economic Order*, N.Y., 1976.

From Peter Bauer and John O'Sullivan, "Ordering the World About: The New International Economic Order." *Policy Review* No. 1 (Summer 1977): 55–69.

fund and to grant more aid, beginning with another $1,000,000,000 to the hardest-hit poor countries. And, expressing a general journalistic consensus, Mr. Keith Richardson of the *London Sunday Times* admits that the West enjoys a "disproportionate share of the world's wealth" (does it not also have a disproportionate share in creating that wealth?) and doubts if we can keep our present ill-gotten living standards.[2]

But are the arguments in support of the NIEO valid? And would the consequences of implementing it be those desired by the Third World's Western sympathisers? Or those experienced by the Somalis?

WAS LENIN RIGHT?

Is it, first, really true that Western prosperity is founded on the economic exploitation of Asia and Africa? For this seems to be plainly contradicted by common observation. Sweden and Switzerland, two of the world's richest nations, had no colonies at all and few direct economic contacts with the Third World. Portugal, on the other hand, which relinquished large colonies only recently, is the poorest nation in Western Europe.

Nor can the extreme poverty and backwardness of aborigines, pygmies, nomads and African tribesmen be due to exploitation in international transactions since these groups have almost no links with the rest of mankind. Indeed the usual relationship is between material backwardness and *lack* of external contacts. If we examine the "Fourth World" countries listed in UN agency documents as least developed, namely Burundi, Chad, Lesotho, Ethiopia, Rwanda, Afghanistan, Bhutan, Nepal and Sikkim, we find that they are scarcely involved in trade with the West. Certainly, their trading links are fewer and less extensive than those between the West and Malaysia, Hong Kong, Venezuela, South Korea, Singapore, Mexico and Taiwan—all relatively prosperous and developing rapidly in flat contradiction to NIEO reasoning.

Such examples clearly support the traditional pre-Leninist view of international trade, namely that it benefits both parties. In more modern jargon, it is not a "zero-sum game" in which one man's gain is necessarily another's loss. Western nations undoubt-

edly benefited from the access to raw materials brought by trade. Yet did not developing nations also obtain access to markets, to a variety of goods, to new ideas and information and to such complementary resources as capital, enterprise and specific skills? Without these, would not the Third World be much poorer today?

Moreover, even amongst developing countries with equal access to trade opportunities, some have prospered more than others.[3] Why? Surely the principal reason is that nations, peoples, tribes, communities and ethnic groups are not equally endowed with those qualities which mainly determine economic achievement. These are not, as is commonly supposed, plentiful raw materials and the supply of capital on easy terms, but aptitudes, social customs, motivations, modes of thought, social institutions and political arrangements. For it is these qualities which influence people's willingness to save, work hard, take risks, and to seek and develop the economic opportunities, however limited, that are available.[4]

How else can we explain the many startling group

---

[3] Edwin F. Feulner, Jr. in *Congress and the New International Economic Order*, Washington, D.C., 1976, provides a brief and incisive comparison of two island economies, Sri Lanka and Taiwan:

Another comparison is between the island nations of the Republic of Sri Lanka (Ceylon), a nation of 14 million and the Republic of China (Taiwan) a nation of 15 million inhabitants. Foreign capital was a major factor in the early post war development of both Taiwan and Sri Lanka. Then the government of the latter started a widespread nationalization program in 1961 and strengthened this in 1970 to form a national plan for a socialist society. The effect of these policies has been to limit the investment of new private funds in Sri Lanka. Per capita output has dropped from $128 in 1963 to $110 in 1974.

The Republic of China was also essentially an agrarian economy but they have followed a policy of industrialization encouraging private investment by a liberalization of government control and tax concessions. Today Taiwan is one of the fastest growing economies in Asia. In 1967 output per capita was $209, in 1974 it had jumped to $700, second only to Japan among Asian countries. Even allowing for the possibility that significant error is present in the figures, the correlation between economic freedom (including private foreign investment) and successful development (and improved personal well-being) is vividly illustrated by these comparisons.

[4] A full-length analysis of the underlying conditions and of their economic importance is provided in Peter Bauer and B.S. Yamey, *The Economics of Under-Developed Countries*, Chicago, 1957. For a debate on some of these issues, see Barbara Ward and Peter Bauer, *Two Views on Aid to Developing Countries*, London, 1966.

[2] Two recent articles in *Commentary* further elucidate a more critical view of the NIEO. See Peter Bauer, "Western Guilt and Third World Poverty," *Commentary*, January 1976 and Peter Bauer and B.S. Yamey, "Against the New Economic Order," *Commentary*, April 1977.

differences in economic performance where economic opportunities have been identical, or broadly similar, or even relatively unfavorable to the successful group —the Chinese, Indian and Malays in Malaya, the Asians and Africans in East Africa and the Greeks and Turks in Cyprus? Have not some groups 'failed' in the narrowly economic sense because of such factors as a preference for the contemplative life over the active; a reluctance to undertake profitable tasks traditionally regarded as demeaning; and a social hierarchy in which mere economic success is not particularly esteemed? Why should such preferences necessarily be condemned?

HUMAN RIGHTS IN THE THIRD WORLD

In recent years, however, a less justifiable influence favoring poverty and economic backwardness has made its appearance—namely, the economic and other policies pursued by Third World governments. Everyone is well-informed about the expulsion of Asians from East Africa which, incidentally, at a stroke reduced *per capita* income in those countries and widened the gap between them and the heartless West. But, in general, Western liberal opinion has been strangely and culpably blind to the extent of the persecution of economically productive, perhaps relatively well-off, but politically unpopular minorities.

It ranges in kind from discrimination in employment to expulsion and even massacre, and geographically from Algeria to Burma, Egypt, Ghana, Indonesia, Iraq, Kenya, Malawi, Malaysia, Morocco, Nigeria, Sri Lanka, Tanzania, Uganda, Zaire and Zambia. So much for the theory that wealth is synonymous with power.[5]

And when such groups as the enterprising Indian community in Burma are driven out, they take with them scarce skills, the ability to generate capital locally and often an indispensable service to the local community. President Mobutu's expulsion of Greek

and Portuguese traders from Zaire, for instance, caused a breakdown in the bush trading and distribution system. Farmers were thus unable to market their products effectively: in some cases, planting stopped altogether.

Some regimes do not stop at persecuting minorities. Dr. Nyerere's government in Tanzania has in the last decade forcibly moved millions of people into collectivized villages, and sometimes simply into the bush. Among the methods of encouragement employed are the destruction of existing homes, physical force and barring recalcitrant elements from such social facilities as communal transport, beer shops, ceremonial dances and cattle auctions. The number of people subjected to this new life certainly runs into millions. Some estimates are as high as six to eight million (*The Washington Post*, May 6, 1975) and even thirteen million (*The Times*, April 20, 1977) out of a total population of fifteen million.

It is hardly likely that agricultural prosperity will be improved by this disruptive move to a variant of the collective farming that has been a disaster everywhere else. Another article in *The Washington Post* (February 7, 1977) reports that both food production and rural living standards have in fact declined. Is that perhaps the reason there is so little official data on the economic achievements of *ujamaa* policy, as a sympathetic official of the World Bank lamented?

Tanzania's general economic failure, relative to less ideological neighboring countries, is unmistakable. It has indeed provoked Dr. Nyerere into sour complaints that Kenya's prosperity is merely the tawdry jewelry of the harlot. He can hardly claim, however, that Tanzania aims at a higher goal than wealth—equality, spartan virtue, African socialism, or whatever. For, like a quiz contestant who asks both to open the box *and* take the money, President Nyerere demands that nations which have successfully sought enrichment should subsidize his nation's austerity.

That is only one, admittedly glaring, example. Other government policies, which have served to impoverish further the people in developing countries, include restrictions on the inflow of foreign capital and on the activities of expatriates; the establishment of costly and inefficient state monopolies in trading, transport, banking and industry; widespread restrictive licensing on economic activity; penal taxation of small-scale farmers; the political diversion of resources to state-sponsored enterprises that cannot survive unassisted; and the suppression of private firms that inconveniently compete with them.

---

[5] In order to carry out such policies a tame press is, of course, highly desirable. There has been much discussion among Third World nations (who disagree on many points but who tend to agree on this one) on the best means of insuring a controlled flow of information. The Fall 1977 issue of *Policy Review* will include an article by the American journalist, Jeffrey St. John, on this increasing tendency toward organized suppression of a free press. For a broad view of the decline of human rights around the world, see Robert Moss, *The Collapse of Democracy*, New Rochelle, N.Y., 1976.

HOW POOR IS THE THIRD WORLD?

But the Third World is far from being a homogeneous, uniform group of countries, all sunk in an identical poverty that is irremediable without foreign aid. Numerous regions and groups there are actually more prosperous than some in the West—compare Chinese communities in South-East Asia with much of rural Ireland and Southern Europe. And among Third World countries which have enjoyed rapid economic growth are South Korea, Taiwan, Hong Kong, Malaysia, the Ivory Coast, Kenya, Brazil, Colombia, Mexico, Venezuela and, of course, the oil states of the Middle East which were treated as less developed until 1973 despite high *per capita* incomes.

Properly considered, then, the Third World is little more than an arbitrary classification covering half the world's population and including societies ranging from millions of aborigines to populous cities—the composition of which is occasionally altered with an arbitrariness bordering on caprice. The developed world is only slightly more homogeneous. It would make little sense to talk of an income "gap," especially a "widening gap," between two such shifting classifications, even if the statistical bases for comparison were otherwise valid. Of course, they are nothing of the sort.

Professor Oscar Morgenstern, in his book, *On the Accuracy of Economic Observations*, quotes an unnamed civil servant as admitting: "We shall produce any statistics that we think will help us to get as much money out of the United States as we can. Statistics which we do not have, but which we need to justify our demands, we shall simply fabricate." His light-hearted approach is certainly not contradicted by the black comedy of the Nigerian population estimates. When Professor Peter Kilby, a leading independent American scholar, put the population at 37.1 million, the official 1963 census produced an estimate of 55.6 million—a figure not unconnected with the then government's need for inflated parliamentary representation. Even today, when parliamentary representation is of little moment in Nigeria, the UN's estimate of its population is ten million less than the Nigerian government's.

Honest statistics, however, would be only marginally less inaccurate. National income comparisons, for instance, are rarely adjusted for differences in age composition. Yet the proportion of children is much larger in developing countries than in the West. And both the incomes and requirements of children are lower than those of adults—not to allow for age composition in such statistics is to transform age differences into income differences.

Another major flaw arises from how changes in life expectation are interpreted statistically. In the last 25 years, mortality has declined substantially in the Third World. Since most people like to live longer and to see their children survive, this is surely an improvement. Without much doubt the standard of living of those who would otherwise have died has improved. But there are, as a result, more children and old people in the population. So this improvement is registered in national income statistics as a decline in *per capita* income and a widening of the gap.

The aggregate effect of these and other flaws is to exaggerate, often wildly, the poverty of developing countries and hence the gap between them and the West. In an article published in 1963, subsequently expanded into a book, Professor Dan Usher, who lived and worked for several years in Thailand, estimated on the basis of personal observation and sophisticated statistical analysis that living standards there were approximately one-third of those in Britain. Yet, as Professor Usher points out, calculations based on conventional statistics put *per capita* income in Britain *at fourteen times that of Thailand*, where accordingly the people must be "desperately, if not impossibly, poor." It is such Laputan estimates which form the basis of NIEO declarations, of presidential demands for "reparations" from the West and of Mr. Callaghan's conviction that 650 million people have to subsist each year on less than the goods and services that £20 would purchase in Britain or $34 in the United States, or one breakfast every three weeks with nothing left over for other meals, accommodation, clothing, medicine or any other goods and services.

So much for the arguments justifying the NIEO. What of its likely effect?

IS FOREIGN AID ENOUGH?

Let us first deal with two general points. Were the NIEO to be implemented seriously, it would clearly mean a transfer of resources from groups in the West to groups in the Third World. If people's aptitudes, motivations and economic capacities were everywhere the same and official policies broadly favorable, this could be achieved without a reduction in the wealth and income of mankind as a whole. NIEO documents often assume tacitly that this is so.

Yet we have already noticed that people's abilities to take advantage of economic opportunities differ very radically. And, paradoxically, this is confirmed by one of the NIEO's principal demands—namely, debt cancellation. For the arguments that debtors face great, even insurmountable, difficulties in repaying loans means that the borrowed capital has been wastefully employed. Otherwise the incomes in recipient countries would have increased by more than the cost of the capital. This is further confirmed by the fact that the great proportion of Third World government debt arises from foreign aid loans on concessionary terms. Often the grant element in these loans has been over half the nominal value, sometimes over 90 percent. Moreover, the burden of debt has *already* been much reduced by inflation and by various disguised forms of substantial default.

The NIEO, therefore, especially in the form of debt cancellation, represents a transfer of resources from those who can use them productively to those who cannot. World income as a whole must therefore either fall or fail to rise as it otherwise would. If this effect were concentrated in the West, some NIEO advocates would presumably count it as a gain—a step towards a more egalitarian, if poorer, world. But, insofar as the West's income is reduced, so is its capacity to trade with developing countries, some of which in consequence share in this virtuous impoverishment.

Secondly, official wealth transfers go to Third World governments, not to the population at large. Inevitably, this increases the power of the ruling groups over their peoples—an effect often reinforced by the preferential treatment accorded to governments establishing state-controlled economies.[6] To Western supporters of aid programs, there is nothing

objectionable in this. They enthusiastically urge vigorous state action to promote development and social and economic equality.

But this is where the Somali distorting mirror effect intrudes. For between the intentions of Third World governments and those of their Western sympathizers, there is a wide and widening gap.

It is the over-riding aim of almost all Third World governments to consolidate and extend their own power over their subjects. Surely this is patently clear from the policies they consistently pursue? Monopolies, valuable licenses and other privileges are granted to those who support the government, often very prosperous people. Quite small properties and businesses, on the other hand, are often confiscated wholesale. Small-scale producers of export crops have often been singled out for penal taxation at the hands of state export monopolies. And there have been countless instances of massive discrimination against poor members of ethnic minorities distinct from the ruling group, even though they may sometimes be indigenous to the country—such as Tamil plantation workers in Sri Lanka and Ibo clerks and laborers in Nigeria.

What have such policies got to do with promoting either equality or development? Very little. In fact, they hold development back. But they have a great deal to do with placating government supporters, winning over entrenched groups, making more and more people dependent upon government decisions for their economic success or failure, and depriving potential opponents, or merely disfavored groups, of power, advantages and even of their livelihood. Indeed, a Burmese cabinet minister was candid enough to admit privately that, although the expulsion of foreigners damaged the economic interests of the Burmese, he favored the policy simply in order to rid his country of aliens.

And, as for equality, some conspicuous beneficiaries of aid are relatively well-to-do, even very rich. They are rulers, politicians, civil servants, members of Westernized *elites*, businessmen close to the government and the more politically astute local academics—not to mention foreign economic advisers and employees of international organizations.

Would not the large-scale transfer of resources under the NIEO strengthen such governments in power, keep them financially solvent, help to conceal the disastrous results of their policies, and generally increase state power and politicization of society? And, in a contemporary politicized society, the re-

---

[6] A clear-cut example of how government-to-government aid programs often enrich the ruling class at the expense of the needy is given in an article entitled "Food Bungle in Bangladesh" by Donald F. McHenry (Ambassador Andrew Young's deputy at the UN) and Kai Bird (a journalist for *Newsweek International*). Writing in the Summer 1977 *Foreign Policy* they relate in detail how approximately 90% of the U.S. food aid to Bangladesh went to favored groups in the cities (bureaucrats, the armed services, rich businessmen, etc.). Practically none went to the starving people in the countryside. This sort of activity is not confined to the Third World, of course, *The Washington Post* on July 7, 1977, reported that a substantial amount of Small Business Administration funds intended to help minorities actually went to white (and prosperous) businessmen using blacks as fronts.

wards of political power rise proportionately; but the penalties of exclusion rise exponentially.

During Mrs. Gandhi's rule in India, well over ten million people were sterilized, very many forcibly, sometimes with great brutality and fatal results. According to an academic Indian report, which forms the basis of an article in *New Scientist* (May 5, 1977) the compulsory sterilization campaign included such methods as: organized manhunts; dawn police raids to catch people, physical force to hold down the victims; entire villages fleeing from sterilization squads; refusal to admit unsterilized people to hospitals; the withholding of licenses from taxi-drivers, rickshaw drivers and others unless they could produce sterilization certificates; and the use of economic policy and civil service pay and promotion to foster the program "voluntarily." And the report noted significantly that compulsion was exercised on a partial basis. Administrators, the urban elite and local politicians were able to avoid it, even when they had more than the usual quota of children; whereas an almost random brutality was employed against poor people, village-dwellers and minorities like the Muslims, who rioted in consequence and were shot down.

It is, of course, commonplace in societies that are both multi-racial and highly-politicized for minorities to find themselves economically ruined and even physically threatened. Who controls the government becomes a life-and-death matter, sometimes literally so. Asians have been expelled from East Africa, Ibos massacred in Northern Nigeria and the Chinese subjected to various degrees of discrimination all over South-East Asia. Naturally they suffer most. But such struggles, expulsions and civil wars also inflict extreme hardship on the rest of the population as, for instance, food shortages when the trading system breaks down.

Does all this sound a far cry from bland World Bank communiques hymning "partnership in development"? Well, in November 1976, at the very height of the compulsory sterilization campaign, Mr. Robert McNamara, the President of the World Bank and a large supplier of finance to India, congratulated the Indian Health and Family Planning Minister on his government's "political will and determination" in popularizing family planning. It is the Somali distortion again—some spice being added by the report that Somalia is Mr. McNamara's "second favorite African country." His "real African favorite," however, is Tanzania where he doubtless imagines an exciting

development in rural democracy is spontaneously erupting.

Third World governments have nonetheless taken precautions against Mr. McNamara and others suddenly realizing what Somalia is really like. Into one of the NIEO declarations they have written the condition that: "Every country has the right to adopt the social and economic system that it deems most appropriate for its own development and not to be subjected to discrimination of any kind as a result." Discrimination here is broadly defined; it includes failure to provide aid.

DO THE POOR REALLY BENEFIT?

We have so far assumed that the NIEO will actually transfer resources from the rich to the poor. But will it do so? Take, for instance, one specific and widely-canvassed proposal to which Western countries have now reluctantly agreed—commodity agreements to maintain stable prices. If these are intended to transfer wealth from rich to poor, then they are inefficient to the point of perversity.

To begin with, primary producers of raw materials are by no means necessarily poor. The OPEC countries are an extreme example of the opposite—and were so long before 1973. Rich countries, in fact, are net exporters of major primary products and their close substitutes. Moreover, within the less developed world, those countries which export such products are generally to be found among the most prosperous. And, within the exporting countries themselves, the main beneficiaries of commodity agreements and higher prices are likely to be existing producers, the scheming administrators and politicians—all relatively prosperous people already.[7]

And how will such schemes work in practice? Commodity agreements can normally be maintained only if they exclude potential producers from entering the market. Only thus can supply be restricted and prices raised. Yet the excluded producers are usually poorer than those inside the cartel—and than those who otherwise gain, both internationally and within exporting countries. Their poverty is thus perpetuated.[8]

[7] William Schneider, Jr., of the Hudson Institute, has written a useful book on this subject, *Food, Foreign Policy and Raw Materials Cartels*, N.Y., 1976.

[8] See Peter Bauer, "Foreign Aid Forever?" *Encounter*, March 1974.

It is also noteworthy that most of the suggested agreements cover commodities (e.g., tea, rubber, copper) that are subsequently used in mass consumption products. Poor Third World countries are net importers of many of these. So the contrived increase in prices will tax consumers, often regressively, in rich and poor countries alike, at a time of world-wide inflation. And the experience of the OPEC cartel suggests that poor people will not be protected against these price rises by anything more substantial than rhetoric.

But commodity agreements also tend to be unstable. If the incomes of those inside the cartel are to be kept up, then not only must the supply of the commodity reaching the market be controlled effectively; so must the supply of its close substitutes. Yet the resulting high price itself stimulates the search for new sources and the development of new substitutes. So, save in very exceptional circumstances where control of a scarce and indispensable resource is confined to a few countries, any commodity scheme will succeed in raising prices for a prolonged period only at the cost of large sums of the money being tied up in unsold stocks.

In the meantime, while prices remain high, potential producers and excluded countries will grow increasingly hostile and restive. Why should they not be allocated export rights and quotas? Why should they be denied this arbitrary and guaranteed "license to print money"? Only massive international pressure could prevent them from undermining the agreement by introducing or expanding their competing supplies. International tensions far more destructive than those exhibited in the North-South dialogue would thus be stimulated by the scheme's continuance; and, should it eventually collapse, incomes and prices would fall through the floor.

It is clear, therefore, that commodity agreements would harm many poor people, benefit few poor people and enrich quite a number who are already prosperous. Some relatively rich people in the West might also be discommoded, but that is surely an insufficient benefit for so much waste, conflict and distress. So much for this cornerstone of the NIEO. Debt cancellation, as we have already shown, specifically benefits the improvident and affects the poorest least of all. And the transfer of technology, as expounded in NIEO documents, is a notion too vague and mystical for systematic assessment.

WOULD A NIEO WORK IN PRACTICE?

But all this does not justify dismissing the NIEO as unimportant. If the "eradication of poverty" and the confining of income differences, both within and between countries, to within a narrow band were to be seriously pursued, then a far-reaching, intensive and persistent coercion would be required. Nothing less would remove or overcome the wide and deeply rooted variety of attributes, motivations, values, customs, social institutions, living conditions and political arrangements of different countries, societies, groups and individuals which lie behind income differences.

NIEO advocates admit, for instance, that the use of substitutes and the application of new inventions in Western industries would need to be limited in order to protect commodity agreements and to maintain Third World export earnings. What else is this but the internationalization of industrial restrictive practices, maintaining high-cost production and thus harming the poorest everywhere? Yet if Western governments fail to enforce such luddite interventions, will they not be pressed to step up direct tax-financed wealth transfers by way of compensation? Indeed, Dr. Nyerere has obligingly made clear that they will be required to step up such transfers in any event—until world economic equality has been substantially achieved or, in practice, indefinitely.

But who will enforce these policies and transfers? Western governments acting voluntarily? Hardly. National governments acting under pressure from a combination of other governments, or from international organizations, in accordance with agreements they had thoughtlessly endorsed? Perhaps, but for how long? Would policies that substantially depressed or retarded the living standards of Western voters survive more than a few democratic elections? Again, hardly. Only a world government with extensive, or indeed almost totalitarian, powers would stand a reasonable chance of enforcing such an economic order indefinitely.

And such powers would need to be exercised indefinitely. As with the commodity agreements, the exercise of some powers would perversely create and reinforce economic differences rather than reduce them. They would thus be continually manufacturing the justification for their own existence: and if, for whatever reason, economic differences were to be reduced within and between countries, this would not abate egalitarian demands one whit. As Tocqueville observed, when social differences have narrowed, those that remain appear particularly offensive.

And, finally, the commitment to the NIEO is by its very nature open-ended. Third World incomes, as we have already seen, depend principally upon domestic factors, not on external donations. So any obligation to establish minimum living standards in the Third World, or to reduce international income differences substantially or to any specified extent, implies a completely open-ended Western commitment, determined by the Third World's performance. At the very least, international redistributive taxation would be required. Attempts to enforce this permanent, worldwide standardization, then, would lead to increasing international tension, a Hobbesian war of all against all, the spread of totalitarian powers and to further erosion of the West's power and influence.

Is it unreasonable, in the light of these considerations, to regard Dr. Nyerere's call for a world "ceiling on wealth" as "first and foremost a matter of political will and determination" as something more, and more sinister, than harmless cant? Or to hope that, when Western leaders warmly endorse the NIEO's objectives, they are simply indulging in the political equivalent of singing "Auld Lang Syne" on New Year's Eve?

In summation, the objective of the NIEO is, of course, quite unattainable. There is no prospect whatever of transforming the Third World into a series of prosperous, socially just, high-income Swedens by the methods proposed. But we might well create one, two, three, many Somalias.

QUESTIONS FOR DISCUSSION

1 What information must one have to evaluate the responsibility of the West for third world poverty?
2 Will the establishment of the NIEO result in more equitable distribution of economic resources throughout the world?
3 Will the NIEO lead to an increase in economic development in the third world?

4 Should the Soviet Union be considered an advanced industrial nation similar to Western nations if NIEO is implemented?
5 What are the prospects for NIEO?

SUGGESTED READINGS

Amacher, Ryan C., Gottfried Haberler, and Thomas D. Willett (eds.). *Challenges to a Liberal International Economic Order*. Washington, D.C.: American Enterprise Institute for Policy Research, 1979.

Bauer, P. T., and B. S. Yamey. "Against the New Economic Order." *Commentary* (April 1977): 25–31.

Bedjaoui, Mohammed. *Towards a New International Economic Order*. New York: Holmes & Meier (for UNESCO), 1979.

Bhagwati, Jagdish N. (ed.). *The New International Economic Order: The North-South Debate*. Cambridge: MIT Press, 1977.

Cox, Robert W. "Ideologies and the New International Economic Order: Reflections on Some Recent Literature." *International Organization* **33** (Spring 1979): 257–302.

Denoon, David B. H. (ed.). *The New International Economic Order: A U. S. Response*. New York: New York University Press, 1979.

Laszlo, Ervin, Jorge Lozoya, A. K. Bhattacharya, Jaime Estevez, Rosario Green, and Venkata Raman. *The Obstacles to the New International Economic Order*. New York: Pergamon Press, 1980.

Rothstein, Robert L. "The North-South Dialogue: The Political Economy of Immobility." *The Journal of International Affairs* **34** (Spring/Summer 1980): 1–17.

Tinbergen, Jan (ed.). *Reshaping the International Order: A Report to the Club of Rome*. New York: Dutton, 1976.

Tucker, Robert W. *The Inequality of Nations*. New York: Basic Books, 1977.

12 Does Trade with the Soviet Union Promote Peace?

YES

Donald M. Kendall

U.S.-Soviet Trade Relations: A Time to Re-Examine and Re-Think Our Positions

NO

Carl Gershman

Selling Them the Rope: Business & the Soviets

U.S.-Soviet Trade Relations:
A Time to Re-Examine and Re-Think Our Positions
Donald M. Kendall

It's no secret that I am a long-term supporter of expanded East-West trade. As a private businessman I have been promoting commerce between the United States and the Soviet Union for nearly 20 years— much longer than the idea of "detente" has been fashionable in either country.

It's also a matter of public record that PepsiCo has a mutually beneficial commercial agreement with the Soviet Union. We opened our first Pepsi-Cola plant in the Soviet Union in 1973. I was there last fall for the opening of our second plant and we presently have three more under construction. The first two plants are located in the Black Sea area and the ones under construction are located in Moscow, Leningrad and Talin.

Also, as you undoubtedly heard, last month we signed an agreement which will double the number of plants from five to ten by 1980, by which time we will be selling 30 million cases of Pepsi-Cola in the Soviet Union. I am also happy to say that we are doing very well on our importing arrangement for Stolichnaya Russian vodka. U.S. sales have increased from 18 thousand cases in 1972 to nearly 200 thousand in 1977, and are still growing at a rapid rate.

So much for my credentials as a capitalist doing business with the Soviet Union.

It will take a little bit longer to explain why I believe the promotion of broader East-West trade should be a high-priority plank in the national trade policy of the United States. That's what I want to talk to you about today.

I believe we need a more realistic understanding— in government, in the press and among the general public—of what detente involves, and how to apply the principle more skillfully and imaginatively. Above all, we need to adjust to the reality that detente means continuing East-West competition, risks, and times of confrontation—as well as patient efforts to reduce tensions and expand cooperation.

Ups and downs in Soviet-American relations are nothing new. We have been going through hot and cold cycles ever since the death of Stalin, a quarter century ago. Following those bleak Cold War years, and the changes in leadership in the Soviet Union, both sides—including a few of us in the private sector on this side—began looking for practical ways to moderate our mutual hostilities, and reduce the danger of a Cold War neither side wanted.

The Khrushchev era, you will remember, gave us the word "coexistence," which was a forerunner of detente. The basic idea was simple enough: How can the world's two most powerful nations, fundamentally opposed to each other in ideology and global aims, nonetheless learn to live together peacefully on the same planet?

In this last quarter century, we have gone to the brink once or twice, but we have avoided nuclear war. We have also made some progress on limiting nuclear tests, placing ceilings on strategic-arms stockpiles, and inhibiting the spread of nuclear weapons.

East West scientific and cultural exchanges have expanded considerably, especially in the 1970's. So has East West trade. However, since 1974 the chief beneficiaries of that trade expansion have been Western Europe and Japan, rather than the United States —except, of course, for some unusually large U.S. agricultural shipments to the Soviet Union.

I needn't remind you that 1974 was the year Congress denied Ex-Im Bank credits to the Soviet Union, and insisted that Most Favored Nation (or MFN) status for the Soviets be linked to their making explicit declarations about free emigration. As a result, U.S.-Soviet trade began to stagnate, and emigration slowed to a trickle.

That experience is a reflection of how difficult it is for the American people—and for successive American administrations of both parties—to conduct a consistent diplomacy of *both* competition and cooperation.

As professor George Kennan, one of the most respected American authorities on the Soviet Union, says, this problem is complicated by the two views

From Donald M. Kendall, "U.S.-Soviet Trade Relations: A Time to Re-Examine and Re-Think Our Positions." *Vital Speeches of the Day* **44** (April 1978): 389–392.

that are held in this country about Soviet leadership. In one of these views, the Soviet leaders appear as a terrible and forbidding group of men—monsters of sorts, really, because lacking in all elements of common humanity—men totally dedicated either to the destruction or to the political undoing and enslavement of this country and its allies—men who have all internal problems, whether of civil obedience or of economic development, essentially solved and are therefore free to spend their time evolving elaborate schemes for some ultimate military showdown—men who are prepared to accept the most tremendous risks, and to place upon their people the most fearful sacrifices, if only in this way their program of destruction or domination of ourselves and our allies can be successfully carried forward. That is one view.

In the other view, these leaders are seen as a group of quite ordinary men, to some extent the victims, if you will, of the ideology on which they have been reared, but shaped far more importantly by the discipline of the responsibilities they and their predecessors have borne as rulers of a great country in the modern technological age. They are seen, in this view, as highly conservative men, perhaps the most conservative ruling group to be found anywhere in the world, markedly advanced in age, approaching the end of their tenure, and given to everything else but rash adventure. They are seen as men who share the horror of major war that dominates most of the Soviet people, who have no desire to experience another military conflagration and no intention to launch one—men more seriously concerned to preserve the present limits of their political power and responsibility than to expand those limits—men whose motivation is essentially defensive and whose attention is riveted primarily to the unsolved problems of economic development within their own country.

They are seen as men who suffer greatly under the financial burden which the maintenance of the present bloated arsenals imposes on the Soviet economy, and who would like to be relieved of that burden if this could be accomplished without undue damage to Russia's security and to their own political prestige.

They are seen, finally, as men who are, to be sure, seldom easy to deal with, who care more about appearances than about reality, who have an unfortunate fixation about secrecy which complicates their external relations in many ways, but who, despite all these handicaps, have good and sound reason, rooted in their own interests, for desiring a peaceful and constructive relationship with the United States within the area where that is theoretically possible.

Attitudes of the broader American public are seesawed between these two views as the continuing rivalry between the two superpowers heats up or cools off.

I would add, that is why American public opinion is so confused about the nature and purposes of detente.

The architects of detente never promised that the ideological conflict between the United States and the Soviet Union would disappear, nor that the political struggle between us would become any less vigorous because of detente diplomacy.

All they promised was a difficult, patient, step-by-step process toward a less dangerous and more manageable competition between us. The purpose of detente is neither convergence nor conversion.

There is no evidence the two societies are moving toward some common ground in structure or beliefs, nor would most of us find that a desirable aim. Neither is there any reason to expect we can convert Soviet leaders and the Russian people to *our* values and world outlook.

No, the competition is going to go on for some time, because the ideological differences which divide our two systems are very deep, and because our roles as the world's only two superpowers are inherently competitive.

Despite these differences, however, the people of the United States and the Soviet Union—and our two governments—share many important overlapping interests. Cooperation in these areas can benefit both sides, while reducing mutual suspicion and hostility. Avoiding a mutually catastrophic war is only the most obvious of our shared interests.

Managing this aspect of our competition is the function of arms-control agreements, political understandings, and mutual restraint in the ways we use our deadly power.

Our two peoples and governments also have a common stake in developing and expanding cooperation in those fields, such as commercial trade, where both sides can benefit from the exchanges. By deliberately weaving a denser web of economic cooperation and mutual benefit, we can create additional incentives for keeping the overall relationship stable and peaceful.

It's common knowledge that the Soviet economy is suffering from problems of inefficiency, low productivity, uneven quality, faulty distribution and shortages of supply—especially in consumer industries and, of course, agriculture. Other, more privileged sectors of the Soviet economy receive top priority in the allocation of resources. These are the most advanced industrial sectors, which define Soviet national power.

Many of the Soviet Union's economic problems are the result of this uneven development. Others, I believe, are inherent in the centralized planning structure. For these reasons, I think it is unfortunate that the decentralizing economic reforms of the 1960's were abandoned.

In any event, Soviet leadership is keenly conscious of the need for expanding trade with the West in order to compensate for current production shortfalls and, over the long run, to update lagging sectors of the economy.

Innovation will have to be induced by imports of advanced technology and high-technology machinery and systems from the West. Hence, the Soviet economic plan for 1971–75, which they called a plan for "efficiency and quality," mandated a 35 percent increase in foreign trade.

The actual growth during those years was 186 percent, and in the final year of the plan, over 30 percent of that trade was with the capitalist West, especially Japan, Italy, West Germany and France. Each of these nations, unlike the United States, offers nondiscriminatory trade terms and credits to the Soviet Union.

The potential market is enormous. Substantial imports of capital and consumer goods, as well as agricultural commodities, will be needed for some time to fill gaps in current Soviet production. Over the long run, imports of entire factories, fertilizer plants, petroleum and natural gas facilities, power-generating systems, transport and distribution systems, high-technology hardware and software in nonmilitary areas, and managerial know-how, will be needed to spur industrial modernization.

Some of this needed infusion is coming from Eastern Europe. More of the higher-technology production and know-how is coming from Western Europe and Japan. A growing share is coming from foreign affiliates of U.S. firms with the jobs going to foreign, rather than American workers.

But what the Soviet Union needs and wants is advanced-technology goods, equipment and know-how available here in the United States—if we are willing to sell it to them on the same commercial terms and credits we offer to nearly every other trading partner in the world.

I repeat, I am not talking about defense-related technology and equipment. I am talking about industrial goods of commercial value, which are the leading and most profitable edge of trading among all the great industrial nations of the West.

What about American interests in expanding trade? The American economy, you need not be reminded, is also experiencing some problems. We are suffering from a weakening dollar, inflation, unemployment, and a whopping trade deficit that reached $27 billion last year.

The principal cause of that trade deficit was, of course, the $45 billion we had to pay out last year for oil imports. Since that import dependence is not going to shrink in a hurry, it is very much in the U.S. self-interest to expand our exports wherever we can. A sizable export growth is the only arithmetic that will reduce our intolerable trade and payments deficits, and will salvage the value of the dollar in world money markets.

The Soviet Union offers us an opportunity to expand our exports, cut our trade deficit, and reduce unemployment. However, these opportunities are not going to be realized unless we normalize our trade relations with the Soviets, grant them Most-Favored-Nation status, and give them access to Ex-Im Bank credits on the same terms as our other valued trading partners.

For the foreseeable future that trade will not only be profitable for the American firms engaged in it, but will also contribute positively to our national accounts, since *their* capacity to absorb our exports greatly exceeds *our* capacity to absorb theirs.

From 1971 to 1976, the U.S. surplus in trade with the Soviet Union was $2.5 billion. Based on Department of Commerce calculations, which estimate that $25,000 in U.S. manufactured exports and $42,000 in agricultural exports provide one American job in each of these sectors, it is easy to see how much employment in this country has already been stimulated and how much more could be through expanded Soviet-American trade.

Another opportunity for trade is in the area of badly needed raw materials for the future. I refer particularly to oil and gas. It is in our own self-interest to help the Soviet Union develop their vast resources of oil and gas. We should do everything possible to keep them a net exporter of oil and gas. The more oil and gas on the world market, the greater the likelihood of stable supply and prices. With our domestic oil supplies decreasing, it is imperative that we help develop new sources.

The question of Soviet creditworthiness is sometimes raised, often on the basis of prejudice rather than facts. Both by Soviet official accounting, and by the best independent analysis in the West, the current hard-currency foreign debt of the Soviet Union is now $15 billion. That represents about one quarter of the value of the Soviet Union's annual foreign trade. I'd call that a pretty good risk.

The record also shows that the Soviet Union has yet to default on any commercial foreign debt. In short, whether in terms of private American business interests, or in terms of U.S. and world economic interests, I can see no sensible grounds for denying ourselves, or the Soviet Union, the two-way benefits of expanding commercial trade with each other.

At the same time, I do not wish to encourage any exaggerated expectations. Even a flourishing U.S.-Soviet trade will not change the Soviet political system—although it can hardly help having a constructive impact on their economic structure.

I am confident there will be other constructive effects, as the Soviet economy modernizes and adjusts itself to wider world influences. Person-to-person contacts between East and West will broaden at all levels of both societies, labor as well as administration, management and bureaucracy.

Some of the insulation which isolates the entire Soviet society will have to peel away. The Soviet economy will begin to interact with—and integrate into—the dynamic technological revolution that is under way in the West. Pressures will build on the Soviet system to "consumerize" it in the direction of Western models.

Pressures may even build for the Soviet economy to compete in the benign, commercial sense with the West, in world markets, a competition infinitely preferable to arms races.

Most important, their leadership may begin to define Soviet self-interest more in the direction of pragmatism than ideology—more in terms of cooperation in commercial and other peaceful fields, and less in terms of competition in the strategic and political arenas.

This is by no means inevitable, but if we see signs of it, we should be receptive and responsive. The trade avenue won't even be open to us until we live up to the terms we agreed to in the now-suspended 1972 trade pact.

This means wiping the Jackson-Vanik and Stevenson Amendments off the books. It means treating the Soviet Union commercially on the same terms as other great nations, without tacking on unrelated demands which would be embarrassing or demeaning to any proud people.

If we expect a quid pro quo in, for example, the human rights area, let's be more subtle about it, and we're likely to get better results. The Soviet leadership is learning, at some cost, the intricacies of negotiating with this democracy. They have also demonstrated they are more responsive to hints than to being hit over the head. And it should not surprise us that they want to be treated as equals.

Besides, who knows what the future holds if we are wise and humble enough to approach it with hope instead of fear?

George Kennan spelled out the challenge last year. Kennan pointed out that profound changes have been taking place internally in the Soviet Union, and that a generational change in Soviet leadership is about to take place. Yet there is very little scholarship in this country covering what has happened and what is happening.

Too many of us are still reading the Soviet Union in terms of a Stalinist or other stereotype. We need, Kennan said, to "check our existing views at the door, together with our hats," and then reexamine and rethink our relations with that other superpower.

"Nothing could be more unfortunate, surely," Kennan said, "than that a new and inexperienced team of leaders should come into power in the Soviet Union confronting what would appear to be a blank wall of hostility and rejection at the American end—a situation in which they would see no choice but to look for alternatives other than those of good relations with the United States. This is no time to foreclose other people's options."

I warmly endorse Ambassador Kennan's caution. I urge that we reopen *our* options, so we may fairly test the chances for peaceful cooperation with the Soviet Union, even as our competition continues.

Selling Them the Rope: Business & the Soviets
Carl Gershman

I must say that Lenin foretold this whole process. Lenin, who spent most of his life in the West and not in Russia, who knew the West much better than Russia, always wrote and said that the Western capitalists would do anything to strengthen the economy of the USSR. They will compete with each other to sell us goods cheaper and sell them quicker, so that the Soviets will buy from one rather than from the other. He said: they will bring it themselves without thinking about their future. And, in a difficult moment, at a party meeting in Moscow, he said: "Comrades, don't panic, when things go very hard for us, we will give a rope to the bourgeoisie, and the bourgeoisie will hang itself."

Then, Karl Radek, . . . who was a very resourceful wit, said: "Vladimir Ilyich, but where are we going to get enough rope to hang the whole bourgeoisie?" Lenin effortlessly replied: "They'll supply us with it."

—Aleksandr Solzhenitsyn,
June 30, 1975, in a speech to the AFL-CIO

The issue of trade has figured prominently in relations between the United States and the Soviet Union ever since the Nixon administration initiated the policy of détente almost a decade ago. Already in 1969, even before détente had become the central theme of the Nixon administration's foreign policy, the President signed into law the Export Administration Act, replacing the Export Control Act which had been adopted two decades earlier. The new act greatly liberalized restrictions on the export of goods and technology to the Soviet Union. While continuing to prohibit exports that would "make a significant contribution to the military potential" of the Soviet Union, it lifted the ban against those that would strengthen the Soviet Union's "economic potential." The change grew out of pressure from American corporations anxious to do business with Moscow and fearful of losing contracts to competitors in Europe and Japan. But to President Nixon and his principal foreign-policy adviser, Henry Kissinger, the change had chiefly political, not economic, significance. They saw increased U.S.-Soviet trade as an essential component of détente.

The idea of using trade to promote détente with the Soviet Union did not originate with the Nixon administration. President Johnson too had expressed the desire to "build bridges" to the Communist world through trade. A special committee he appointed to look into the matter had concluded that trade could be "one of our most powerful tools of national policy," since it would enable us to "influence the internal development and the external policies of European Communist societies along paths favorable to our purpose and to world peace." Kissinger's version of this general view was the concept of linkage, according to which increased U.S.-Soviet trade would help to establish "a web of constructive relationships" that would give the Soviet Union a stake in peace by making it "more conscious of what it would lose by a return to confrontation." Finally, increased trade might also, in Kissinger's words, "leaven the autarchic tendencies of the Soviet system" and eventually lead to the integration of the Soviet Union into the world economic system and thus to the gradual liberalization of Soviet society.

The Nixon administration's eagerness to embark on this new course was evident in the terms of the trade agreement reached with Moscow on October 18, 1972. It provided both for the financing of Soviet purchases with long-term loans through the Export-Import Bank, and for a request to Congress to grant most-favored-nation tariffs for Soviet imports. Congress, however, reacting to the Yom Kippur War and the continuing harassment of Sakharov, Solzhenitsyn, and other Soviet dissidents, was in no mood to grant Moscow such generous terms. It added the Jackson amendment to the Trade Reform Act, making freer emigration from the Soviet Union the condition for lowering tariffs and qualifying for Export-Import Bank loans. Subsequently, Congress adopted the Stevenson amendment limiting Export-Import Bank credits to $300 million without further congressional approval. The Russians objected to these amendments—especially the credit ceiling, for they had been willing to compromise on the emigration

From Carl Gershman, "Selling Them the Rope: Business & the Soviets." *Commentary* (April 1979): 35–45.

issue—and in early 1975 canceled the whole agreement.

The issue of U.S.-Soviet trade became a point of controversy once again last summer when President Carter, in response to the trials of Soviet dissidents Anatoly Shcharansky and Aleksandr Ginsburg, blocked the sale of a Sperry-Univac computer system to the USSR and placed the export of oil and gas technology to the Soviet Union under government control. Moscow immediately charged that the President was taking a "path of confrontation," and a U.S. Commerce Department official warned that the trade curbs would have "a substantial chilling effect on exports." The Carter administration quickly backed off, and approved all 74 of the applications submitted for the export of oil technology to the Soviet Union. Last December, the President dispatched Commerce Secretary Juanita M. Kreps and Treasury Secretary Michael Blumenthal to Moscow with the message that the administration wanted more trade between the two countries and was in favor of removing some of the obstacles standing in its way—presumably the Stevenson and Jackson amendments.

It appears, then, that another round is looming in the ongoing battle over the trade issue. Once again it is being argued that the United States, with its balance-of-payments deficit running at record levels, has a vital economic stake in trade with the Soviet Union and a vital political stake as well, since closer economic ties will promote the liberalizing tendencies inside the Soviet Union and establish a foundation for improved U.S.-Soviet relations. William Verity, the chairman of Armco Steel Corporation and co-chairman of the U.S.-USSR Trade and Economic Council, said recently that "a policy of holding trade hostage for political reasons is self-defeating." And Averell Harriman, at a luncheon meeting of U.S. business leaders in Moscow, blamed U.S. congressional leaders for the "outrage that for all these years we cannot have normal trade relations with the second greatest nation in the world." In Harriman's view, which is shared by many businessmen, U.S.-Soviet trade would blossom were it not for anti-Soviet forces in this country.

And yet from a strictly economic point of view, trade with the Soviet Union hardly merits the attention that has been lavished upon it by U.S. businessmen and trade officials. In 1978, for example, the volume of trade with the USSR was $2.8 billion, an all-time high, but just over one-third the amount of trade that was carried on with Taiwan last year. One would hardly know this from comparing the sheer volume of congressional studies, books, conferences, and news articles devoted to the two subjects; and yet in a sense it is beside the point. It is not the present level of trade with the Soviet Union that excites U.S. businessmen, but the possibility of exploiting the vast, hitherto forbidden Soviet market. "Otherwise cautious executives," Marshall I. Goldman has written, "all but trample over one another in their effort to establish a foothold on this new frontier."[1]

But how new is this frontier? When the question of trade is debated, it is frequently forgotten that there are many historical precedents for the current efforts to expand trade with the Soviet Union, and while they explain why Russia is so interested in trade, they do little to justify business's continuing optimism.

There was substantial Western investment in Russia during the half-century preceding the Bolshevik revolution. The coal, iron, and steel-producing region of southern Russia was developed with capital and technical assistance from British, French, and Belgian companies, and German and Dutch firms helped develop these industries in the north. The "iron king" of Russia was an Englishman, John Hughes, who built the mining and metallurgical factories of Yuzovka—named in his honor—in the Donets Basin. The Swedish Nobel brothers developed the oil fields of Baku on the shores of the Caspian Sea, which helped make Russia the world's leading oil producer by 1901. The Trans-Siberian railway was built with Western (principally French) capital and technology, and the parallel telegraph line was built and operated by the Danes. Many American firms, too, participated in Russia's industrial development during this period. International Harvester was the largest manufacturer of agricultural equipment in pre-war Russia and Singer Sewing Machine had holdings worth over $100 million and employed a sales force in Russia of over 27,000 people in 1914.

When the Bolsheviks seized power in 1917, all this came to an end, as the new regime expropriated all Western capital investment and financial assets. But even this unprecedented act of industrial theft did not discourage Western business interests, eager to regain

[1] *Détente and Dollars: Doing Business with the Soviets*, Basic Books, 1975, p. 5.

access to the alluring Russian market. The opportunity came soon enough. Just three years after the revolution, with the Russian economy in a state of total wreckage, Lenin invited Western firms back to Moscow and asked them to set up concessions. In the West this new policy was welcomed as a sign of moderation and a move toward "peaceful coexistence," but Lenin, as it turned out, had not ceased to be a Bolshevik. "Concessions—," he told a meeting of the Soviet Communist party in 1920, "these do not mean peace with capitalism, but war on a new plane." Lenin's sole objective was to revive Soviet industry, and, as subsequent events revealed, he had every intention of expropriating the concessions after production had been organized and sufficient capital, equipment, and skills had been brought into the country.

Nevertheless, Western firms, oblivious to the risks involved, flocked to the Soviet Union once more, bringing with them technicians, machinery, technology, and capital. From Germany came such major companies as Krupp, Thyssens, Otto Wolff, Siemens, the AEG, Junkers, Telefunken, and I. G. Farben; from the United States, General Electric, Westinghouse, International Harvester, RCA, Alcoa, Singer, Du Pont, Ford, and Standard Oil of New York. Concessions were also established by important English, French, Swedish, Danish, and Austrian companies. All told, the government granted about 350 concessions, and their impact on the Soviet economy was extraordinary. A recent study, which analyzes in painstaking detail the impact of the concessions on each sector of the Soviet economy, concluded that by 1930 there was not a single important industrial process—from mining, oil production, metallurgy, chemicals, transportation, communications, textiles, and forestry to the production of industrial and agricultural equipment and the generation of electrical power—which did not derive from transferred Western technology.[2]

If the advantages to the Soviets from all this are obvious, one is hard-pressed to identify any benefits accruing to the Western firms involved. By 1933,

[2] See Antony C. Sutton's *Western Technology and Soviet Economic Development 1917–1930*, Hoover Institution Publications, 1968. Two subsequent volumes by Sutton describe the transfer process and assess its contribution to Soviet economic development for the periods 1930–45 and 1945–65.

there were no foreign manufacturing concessions left in the Soviet Union, even though many firms had signed contracts covering periods of thirty and even fifty years. Some of the concessions were closed down by force, but the more common methods were punitive taxation, breach of contract, legal harassment, and disruptions by workers. The largest concession of all, the British mining company Lena Goldfields Ltd., had assembled its technicians, invested almost $80 million in equipment, and completed its surveys when it was attacked as a "weed in the socialist system." The OGPU raided its units, threw out many of its personnel, and jailed several of its leading technicians on charges of "industrial espionage."

In only a handful of special cases was compensation granted. Armand Hammer, who represented 38 large American firms in their dealings with Moscow and was a political sympathizer (his father had been a member of the steering committee that founded the U.S. Communist party in 1919), was compensated for the liquidation of his asbestos and pencil-manufacturing concessions. (Interestingly, these were also the only concessions to earn significant profits.) The Soviet authorities also agreed to compensate Averell Harriman for the liquidation of his manganese concession in Chiaturi in 1928, but only after Harriman had agreed to arrange a long-term loan for them in the United States (aimed both at demonstrating Soviet credit-worthiness and undermining official U.S. policy against such loans). Most firms were not so lucky, however, and those which had lost their holdings once before in 1917 had the dubious distinction of being expropriated twice.

Far from signaling the end of Western business involvement in the Soviet Union, the liquidation of foreign concessions marked the beginning of the most massive transfer of Western technical resources yet undertaken in the form of American assistance to the first Five-Year Plan (1928–33). The plan, still thought by many to have been a remarkable Soviet achievement, turns out to have been largely the work of American management and engineering, as Stalin acknowledged in 1944, when he told Eric Johnston, the president of the U.S. Chamber of Commerce, that two-thirds of the large industrial projects in the Soviet Union had been built with American assistance.

America's leading industrial-architecture firm, the Albert Kahn Company, was contracted to design and supervise the major units of the plan, as well as to organize Gosproektstroi, the Soviet Design Bureau.

Kahn's engineer, G.K. Scrymgeour, directed Gosproektstroi and also chaired the Building Commission of the Supreme Council of the National Economy, while various other American companies got individual contracts to build the mammoth separate projects outlined in the plan.[3] Du Pont built two nitric-acid plants at Kalinin and Shostka; the Arthur G. McKee Company of Cleveland managed the construction of the steelworks of Magnitogorsk, a replica of U.S. Steel's Gary Indiana plant and the largest steel complex in the world; Colonel Hugh Cooper, the builder of the great Wilson Dam at Muscle Shoals, supervised the construction of the even larger Dniepr Dam, for which he received the Order of the Toilers of the Red Banner. In addition, General Electric built and installed the massive generators at the Dniepr and also designed the Kharkov turbine works which had a manufacturing capacity two-and-a-half times greater than its own central plant in Schenectady. The Austin Company, builder of Ford's River Rouge factory, constructed the great auto plant at Gorki (known as "the Detroit of Russia"), while the USSR's other auto plants, at Moscow and Yaroslavl, were built respectively by the A.J. Brandt Company of Detroit and the Hercules Motor Corporation of Canton, Ohio. Austin's John Calder (whom Maurice Hindus called "Russia's miracle man" at the time) managed the construction of the Stalingrad Tractor Plant, Europe's largest, which was first built in the United States, then dismantled and shipped to Russia, where it was put together again. For this achievement (and for salvaging the construction of another plant at Chelyabinsk after an abortive effort by a Russian team of engineers) Calder received the Order of Lenin, as did his colleague, Leon A. Swajian, who was chief engineer for the construction of an identical tractor plant at Kharkov.

In 1930, *Business Week* proclaimed that Russia, though unrecognized politically, had "come to the aid of depressed American industry." American businessmen, delighted with these Russian contracts, looked forward to a period of expanding U.S.-Soviet

trade. Unfortunately, the benefits that American business actually derived from this unprecedented burst of commercial activity proved to be meager and short-lived—as well as absurdly disproportionate to what the Russians gained. In 1930, U.S. exports to Russia reached the all-time high of $230 million, but it was still only a small fraction of total U.S. exports. By 1932, exports had dropped to less than $28 million, and the following year they dropped still further to $14 million. The Soviet government (which had sold grain to finance imports while millions of Russians starved) had simply run out of money.

But even after the Export-Import Bank had been set up in 1934, primarily to finance Soviet purchases, exports still did not increase significantly. The main reason for this was that Russia had by then attained a considerable degree of industrial self-sufficiency, made possible by the willingness of American companies to construct finished plants and assist in their duplication, and to transfer essential technology to the USSR. To its $30-million sale of auto parts, for example, the Ford Motor Company threw in an extra bonus in the form of an agreement to send its technicians to Gorki to introduce Ford production methods[4] and to bring Soviet engineers to its River Rouge plant for training. (Of the 1,039 Soviet nationals arriving in the U.S. between January 1, 1929 and June 15, 1930, 81 per cent came for industrial-training programs.)

America's wartime alliance with the Soviet Union produced still another wave of euphoria at the prospects of trade with the USSR. In 1944, soon after his meeting with Stalin, Eric Johnston wrote in *Nation's Business* that "Russia will be, if not our biggest, at least our most eager customer when the war ends." The following year *Fortune* published a poll showing

---

[3] Antony C. Sutton, in this context, defines the phrase "built by Western companies" to mean not just the management of construction and equipment installation, but also the supply of technology, patents, engine-test results, and operator training, as well as supervision of the plant during its initial period of operation. The Russians supplied labor, semi-fabricated materials, and middle-level engineers whose chief job was to learn from the Americans.

[4] One of these Americans, Victor Herman, has just published an extraordinary memoir of his experiences in Russia (*Coming Out of the Ice*, Harcourt Brace Jovanovich, 369 pp., $12.95). At the age of sixteen, Herman accompanied his family from their home in Detroit to Gorki, where they were planning to stay for three years working in the auto plant. He ended up spending forty-five years in Russia, eighteen of them in the Gulag, where he encountered many Americans. Herman describes his ordeal with an austerity that makes it all the more horrifying. He claims to be the only survivor of all the men, women, and children from the American village at Gorki who were sent to the Siberian camps—forgotten victims of an earlier period of Soviet-American "cooperation."

business leaders to be the "most friendly" toward the USSR of all American groups and also the most hopeful about postwar relations—annual exports to Russia, the magazine predicted, would be between $1 billion and $2 billion. Alas, in 1946 annual U.S. exports to Russia, though still financed by Lend-Lease credits, totalled only $236 million, and even that level would not be reached again for more than a quarter of a century.

While the export controls imposed by the U.S. in 1949 played a part in delaying a new round of Soviet purchases, they had nothing to do with the initial drop in exports after 1946. What happened to cause this drop was precisely what had happened fifteen years earlier when Russia reverted to autarchy immediately after having absorbed an enormous amount of Western technology and equipment. Under Lend-Lease, Russia had received $2.6 billion worth of nonmilitary goods from the U.S. (in addition to $8.5 billion in military hardware), including $1.25 billion of the latest American industrial equipment. Even more significant, however, was the more than $10 billion worth of industrial and military equipment dismantled in Germany and shipped to Russia in the greatest and most systematic looting of a defeated country in the history of war.[5] From the Soviet Zone the Russians acquired several thousand plants representing 41 per cent of Germany's 1943 industrial capacity, and still more was removed from the Western Allied zones under an agreement allocating 25 per cent of the plants there to the Russians. The booty included such plants as the famous Karl Zeiss factory at Jena which manufactured optical precision instruments, and the Opel autoworks at Brandenburg. (Small wonder that the 1947 Moskvich 401 was a replica of the 1939 Opel Kadett!) Berlin's entire electrical-equipment industry was removed, as was two-thirds of Germany's aircraft and rocket industry, including the enormous underground V-2 rocket plant at Nordhausen which provided the foundation for the Soviet Union's Sputnik program.

Since specialists were needed to bring this new

industrial capacity into operation and to develop it further, technicians were also shipped off to Russia. On a single night—October 22, 1946—6,000 German scientists, engineers, and aviation experts, along with 20,000 dependents, were placed on trains and transported to various points throughout the Soviet Union where German industry had been reassembled. Once again Russia had become "self-sufficient."

Contemporary champions of U.S.-Soviet trade[6] view this historical background as relevant only to the extent that it helps to explain why psychological barriers to the unrestricted expansion of commercial relations with the USSR still exist in the United States. Fears based on past experience are groundless, they argue, since the Soviet Union is a vastly different country today—less oppressive, more stable, and more committed to consumerism—than it was after the devastations of World War II, not to mention during the periods of revolutionary consolidation and forced industrialization. Samuel Pisar, for example, a leading trade advocate, is confident that the American and Soviet economic systems, at one time diametric opposites, are now "actually creeping toward convergence," a process that will accelerate if there is increased trade.[7]

But how different *is* the Soviet Union today? Like every other country in the world, the USSR has of course changed over the past thirty years, but nothing has happened to alter the nature of its economic relations with the West in any fundamental way. The Soviet Union's chief priority is still the procurement from the West of advanced technology for its heavy industry (machine-building, metalworking, chemicals, and so forth). Though the new emphasis on consumer needs in the ninth Five-Year Plan (1971–75) raised hopes that the Soviet Union would enter the market for consumer goods, this emphasis was dropped when the plan was actually implemented, and the current Five-Year Plan restores producer goods to their traditional preeminence.

The continuing Soviet need for Western technology results directly from the weaknesses of its centralized, state-run, command economy. Much has been written about the inefficiencies of the Soviet economy which

[5] Germany was not the only country looted by Russia. A U.S. mission headed by Ambassador Edwin Pauley in the spring of 1946 concluded that Russia had dismantled and removed $895 million worth of industrial equipment from Manchuria. In addition, $400 million worth of equipment was taken from the Soviet Zone in Austria, while peace treaties with Finland and Rumania resulted in the transfer of $600 million of equipment.

[6] See, for example, *The Psychology of East-West Trade*, by Zygmunt Nagorski, Jr., Mason & Lipscomb, 1974.

[7] *Coexistence and Commerce: Guidelines for Transactions Between East and West*, McGraw Hill, 1970, p. 8.

produces about half the American GNP using a larger workforce (and which now suffers from a labor shortage). What is not sufficiently appreciated is the degree to which the system, because of its stifling rigidity, is structurally resistant to technological innovation. This problem became acute in the 1960's with the slowdown in the Soviet growth rate and with the realization by Soviet leaders that the country could not keep pace with the West, let alone catch up with it, if it did not obtain access to revolutionary Western innovations in computers and electronics. There is no question that the need for such access was a critical factor in the Soviet conversion to détente.

Indeed, the one change that can be detected in the pattern of Soviet trade relations with the West involves the absorption of Western technology, which no longer occurs at fitful intervals, as it did in the 30's and 40's, but appears, at the moment at least, to have become an uninterrupted process.

Still, the importance of this development should not be exaggerated. It is not the result of changes that have taken place inside the Soviet Union, nor is it evidence that Russia has been drawn into "the disciplines of international economic life," as the original linkage policy had hoped. It merely means that Soviet leaders are satisfied with an economic relationship in which, according to the Soviet journal *Foreign Trade* (1977), the USSR "efficiently uses the benefits of the international division of labor and constantly imports technically advanced plant and the latest licenses and know-how."

And why indeed should they not be satisfied with an arrangement which virtually guarantees greater advantages to the USSR than to its Western partners? If for no other reason, the Soviet Union stands to benefit simply by virtue of its technical backwardness. During the early years of détente, for example, the Nixon administration encouraged top American firms to sign "technological-exchange" agreements with Moscow. The firms had nothing to gain technologically from such agreements, but went along with them in the hope that "exchanges" of this sort might eventually lead to large contracts. The contracts rarely materialized, but the Russians received valuable technology in the meantime. A spokesman for Control Data Corporation, which signed a ten-year agreement with the Soviet Ministry of Science and Technology that included a plan for the joint development of a new super computer, admitted not long ago that the Russians gained fifteen years in research and

development by spending just $3 million over three years. And government-to-government exchange agreements, another by-product of the early euphoria over détente, have had the same result. The Apollo-Soyuz space program, one of the better known examples, has been called by Zbigniew Brzezinski "a vehicle for the one-sided transfer from the United States to the USSR of a technology that has obvious military applications."

The asymmetry of the technological "exchange" relationship is reinforced by the Soviet Union's obsession with secrecy and by its unabashedly predatory approach. While American firms are expected to be forthcoming with technical information, especially if they hope to win contracts, the Russians have been extremely reluctant to divulge information on plant operations, let alone to allow American technicians to visit the plants for which they have been asked to design systems.

At the same time, American firms have trained hundreds of Soviet technicians in the U.S., and teams of Soviet specialists—ostensibly looking into possible purchases—have been allowed to tour defense-related American plants. A member of one such group, which closely inspected the Boeing, Lockheed, and McDonnell Douglas factories in 1973 and 1974, admitted privately to a Boeing official that purchases had never been contemplated—meaning, of course, that the group's real purpose had been industrial espionage. Within the FBI, concern has been expressed that Moscow's espionage efforts have expanded in recent years owing to the sharp increase in the number of Soviet citizens here on official business and to the treaty arrangement allowing Soviet ships to call at 40 American ports.

Still another factor that works to the USSR's advantage is that Soviet foreign trade is a state monopoly. As the sole buyer in a situation where there are many sellers—competing American firms as well as firms from Europe and Japan—it has unequal bargaining leverage which it uses not only to bring down prices but also to secure maximum technological benefits that include the provision of technical data and licenses, extensive training of Soviet personnel, and increasingly, long-term arrangements for the continuous supply of new technology. American firms in high-technology fields like computers, aerospace, and automotives are willing to agree to such arrangements in order to compensate for the high cost of research and development. But the end results favor the Russians, as exemplified in the Soviet purchase not too long ago of space suits for $150,000 which had cost the Americans $20 million apiece to develop.

There have even been some instances where American firms have provided valuable technology in the hope of landing a major contract, only to lose the contract to a competitor. In 1973 the Raytheon Corporation, seeking direct contact with the USSR's Ministry of Civil Aviation to promote the sale of an advanced air-traffic control system (ATC), mounted an elaborate exhibition in Moscow in cooperation with the U.S. Federal Aviation Administration. After Raytheon had invested $220,000 in the exhibition and presented plans for an ATC system more advanced than the one in the United States, the Russians asked for competing bids from four other American and two European companies. They also indicated in the course of the negotiations that an American bid would receive more favorable attention if it were accompanied by an offset purchase of Soviet-made YAK-40 jet aircraft, and if the U.S. granted increased landing rights to Aeroflot. In all, the U.S. companies spent over $500,000 and provided the Russians with quite a lot of valuable technical work before the contract was awarded to a Swedish-Italian consortium.

Not all the American firms dealing with Moscow have been quite so unsuccessful as Raytheon, but according to a prominent U.S. businessman quoted in a recent report in the *Wall Street Journal*, "Nobody is doing the business he expected." (Even the modest U.S. export figures—$2.26 billion in 1978—overstate the amount of trade carried on by high-technology firms, since agricultural products account for more than 75 per cent of U.S. exports to the Soviet Union.) In addition, U.S. businessmen stationed in Moscow have had to work under extremely trying conditions: the enormous, impenetrable Soviet bureaucracy; the bugging of their offices, conference rooms, and private residences by what the *Journal* report called "the omnipresent official eavesdroppers"; the fear for their personal safety, as pointed up by the arrest last June of International Harvester's F. Jay Crawford.

Still, it is all worth it in the opinion of Harold B. Scott, the former president of the U.S.-USSR Trade and Economic Council, for the Soviet Union "will one day be the largest market in the world. The

systems put in place there now will determine the patterns of trade. Now is the time when it is crucially important to put our technology there."

With all due respect to Mr. Scott, it is hard to believe that this perpetually alluring Russian market really exists, or if it does exist, that it will one day be ours, especially if we continue to "put our technology there," as he urges. Why should such a market come into being when by selling whole factories (called "turnkey" plants) and training Soviet personnel, we help Russia produce by itself what it might otherwise have to buy from us or from other Western countries? Ironically enough, the way trade has been conducted with the Soviet Union not only does not discourage those autarchic tendencies Kissinger was talking about, but actually reinforces them, even as Soviet purchases of Western technology continue.

Many businessmen claim that the chief obstacle to more U.S.-Soviet trade is the Jackson amendment tying lower tariffs to freer emigration. But even if the USSR were granted most-favored-nation tariffs, Soviet exports to the U.S. would still not increase significantly (which means that its ability to import American goods would also not increase by very much). Even now, the great bulk of Soviet exports consists of raw materials and semi-manufactured goods which are not subject to discriminatory tariffs. The only exports which would be affected if the Jackson amendment were withdrawn are manufactured goods, and there just is not very much of a market in the U.S. for Soviet products.

The congressional limitation on Export-Import Bank credits is far more important in this connection since the Soviet Union simply does not have the hard currency to finance its purchases. The amendment limiting credits, adopted in 1974 in the climate of growing disillusionment with détente, resulted in the U.S. government's withdrawal from a reckless economic venture, the financing of the huge Soviet-bloc debt. This debt was about $8 billion at the end of 1970. By the end of 1975, it had mushroomed to $38 billion, according to an estimate by the Chase Manhattan Bank, and by 1976, it had increased still further to $48 billion. Today it has reached $55 billion and is still growing. At a ministerial meeting of the OECD in June 1976, Henry Kissinger described the debt surge as "sudden" and "striking" and went on to raise questions about its economic and political implications. Kissinger also voiced concern that the debtor countries had acquired substantial leverage over the creditor countries through the latter's fear of default.

The Soviet Union's lack of hard currency has led to another practice which also skews the trade relationship in its favor. This is the so-called compensation agreement whereby a Western firm builds a plant in a Communist country and supplies equipment and know-how in return for part of the plant's eventual output. Once again, the advantages of this arrangement to the Soviet Union and its satellites are considerable. They not only increase their production with Western financing and advanced machinery and technology, but are also given access to Western markets in the course of "repayment"—and all this without spending any hard currency. The advantages to Western firms are cheap, strike-free labor (which, however, means a loss of jobs in the West) and access to untapped sources of raw materials. At the same time, however, they risk substantial losses if the market is glutted at the time of repayment, which is what happened to Armand Hammer's Occidental Petroleum, for instance, in its $20-billion fertilizer deal with the USSR.

Furthermore, they have no protection against repayment in substandard products, or against market disruption if the Communists, seeking hard currency or market penetration, choose to dump goods in the West. Fiat, for example, had no idea that it was creating a trade rival when it built the Volga Auto Plant at Togliatti (since it was assumed that Soviet domestic needs would easily absorb the plant's production). But the Fiat-like Lada is being sold right now in Europe and Canada at well below the cost of production. Similarly, unions throughout Europe's depressed chemical industry have expressed alarm that the products of the massive petrochemical plants to be built with Western support at Tomsk and Tobolsk will one day flood the European market.

In addition to the problems of market disruption and job displacement, Western firms run the added risk—always present when dealing with Communist countries—that political relations may deteriorate before compensation has been received. In some agreements the payback period is twenty years, a longer time than "détente" (by any prudent estimate) can be expected to hold up. If the Russians, for whatever reasons, should decide to cancel the compensation

agreement at any time during that period, it will not do a Western firm much good to know that its collateral consists of oil pipelines buried beneath the Siberian steppes, or industrial machinery installed in Tobolsk. The knowledge that their investments have made them hostages to political circumstances could well turn Western businessmen into fervent defenders of appeasement.

Among votaries of U.S.-Soviet trade, however, the idea that political relations might deteriorate even in the face of expanded trade is virtually ruled out, since it is taken as axiomatic that trade will strengthen the liberalizing, peaceful tendencies in the Soviet Union. This is an old notion. In 1922, British Prime Minister Lloyd George said that trade "will bring an end to the ferocity, the rapine, and the crudity of Bolshevism surer than any other method." In our own time it is widely believed that trade, in Daniel Yergin's words, "draws the Soviet Union into the community of advanced industrial nations." From this point of view, of course, trade with the Soviet Union is valuable even if it does entail certain economic disadvantages. But is there any evidence so far of this happy outcome?

The view that trade will lead to liberalization in Russia is partly based on the not illogical belief that exposure to the West will encourage the development of Western norms and values in the USSR. Unfortunately, the present Soviet leaders, like the Czars before them, are as mindful of this possibility as anyone else, which is why they take great care to shut out Western cultural influences even while helping themselves to Western products and technology. To realize how far the Soviet authorities are willing to go to prevent any contacts from taking place outside of very tightly controlled official channels, one need only think of the confiscation of follow-up cards passed out at a seminar in Moscow conducted by Singer personnel, or the removal of subscription forms from all copies of *Aviation Week and Space Technology* distributed at the Raytheon exhibition, or the totally self-contained office, hotel, and apartment complex for foreigners that is being constructed in Moscow—the modern equivalent of the *Nyemetskaya Sloboda*, or "foreigners' quarter" (literally, "German Quarter") built by Vassily III almost 500 years ago.

But the Soviet regime not only isolates Westerners, it also tightens internal controls to prevent Western influences from seeping through. Particularly during periods of détente—the last decade is a good example —there seems to be an increased tendency for the regime to step up repression and ideological vigilance. All of this would seem to suggest that trade does not promote liberalization, and may actually have the opposite effect.

The fact, too, that trade is used as a way to obtain the technology needed for rapid modernization means, in the context of a command economy, that it is frequently associated with forced industrialization and the use of slave labor. The program of Westernization under Peter the Great was achieved at the cost of immense sacrifice and suffering imposed on the Russian people. Two centuries later, Stalin's first Five-Year Plan, which marked another period of intense absorption of Western technology, took an even greater toll in freedom and human life.[8]

The argument is also made—again to show the link between trade and freedom—that the Soviet Union must liberalize its system in order to solve its economic problems, and that increased exposure to our superior economic methods will encourage Soviet leaders to take this course. This argument might be valid if the Soviet leaders were interested in nothing more than promoting economic efficiency and technological innovation. But they also have a stake in maintaining their totalitarian system, a system which is inherently inefficient and uncreative. If this funda-

mental contradiction were allowed to work itself out, it might conceivably lead to real reforms inside Russia, but Soviet leaders have been able to avoid the choice between reform and stagnation precisely by turning to the West for totalitarianism's "missing dynamic." (It is instructive to recall that Brezhnev's decision to import Western technology on a large scale followed a brief but politically costly experiment in the 60's with economic decentralization.)

Thus trade, by injecting into the Communist system the technological innovations without which it could not survive but which it cannot achieve on its own, actually helps to sustain totalitarianism.

The strategic as well as the moral implications of this fact have thus far been ignored. The idea that trade promotes East-West peace, central to the thinking of those who shaped the policy of détente, remains basically unchallenged among U.S. policymakers today, despite evidence that the increase in trade since 1970 has not been accompanied by reduced Soviet military spending or greater moderation in the Middle East, Africa, or elsewhere. In fact, increased trade (or, more specifically, the increased pace of technology transfers) has been accompanied by the continuing build-up of Soviet military forces and by a greater Soviet readiness to intervene in local conflicts.

Pre-revolutionary Russian history offers numerous examples of the rulers of Russia importing technology from the West to strengthen their country's military capacity. And far from ending the practice of importing Western technology for military use, the Bolshevik rulers have simply recast it into revolutionary terms. Occasionally these acquisitions have been accomplished by theft—as in the case of the atomic espionage of the 40's—but more often the same result has been achieved through political and trade agreements, in accordance with Lenin's famous statement that the capitalists "will supply us with the materials and technology which . . . we need for our future victorious attacks upon our suppliers."

In the 20's Germany was the main foreign source of military assistance. Thereafter, the United States took over, becoming the main supplier of military-related technology, along with Germany and Britain, until the cold war. Fertilizer plants supplied by the West were used to produce explosives, machine plants turned out gun barrels, and—most important—the automotive industry which had been set up by U.S.

---

[8] The American-Russian Chamber of Commerce, whose board included representatives of the top American corporations doing business in Moscow, did what it could to whitewash the Soviet Union on charges of forced labor during this period. In a speech at the Bankers Club in New York in 1932, Colonel Hugh Cooper said that "The Chamber has made a real study of these charges. It has obtained signed statements from many leading American businessmen, who have actually been to Russia and have personally observed labor conditions there, and I am glad to say that not one of these men think labor in Russia is forced." Since American firms instructed their engineers not to discuss conditions in the USSR, only the apologists were heard from. Alcan Hirsch, who supervised the construction of the Du Pont nitric acid plant at Chernorechenski, claimed in his book, *Industrialized Russia* (1934), that while the Soviet Union had "not as yet reached unprecedented eminence in the arts, science, or industry, . . . sociologically it is far ahead of the rest of the world." With all the attention paid to intellectual fellow-traveling with Stalinism in the 30's, it appears that the subject of business complicity has been sorely overlooked.

firms produced tanks and armored trucks.[9] For years after World War II, Lend-Lease transfers and the dismantling of German industry were providing the Soviet Union with the foundation for military production.

This process is still going on today. Indeed, there is now a growing concern in the United States that the technology we have already supplied to the Soviet Union, particularly in the computer field, has contributed to Soviet advances in strategic weaponry and strengthened the USSR's overall economic and military capability. The president of Texas Instruments, J. Fred Bucy, who chaired the Defense Science Board Task Force on the Export of U.S. Technology, told a Senate panel in 1977 that "the transfer of militarily significant technology has been of major proportions," and that the full consequences of this development "will become evident over the next five years."

Presumably the U.S. government approves only technology transfers which have no military significance, but the problem is that most modern technologies have both civilian and military uses. The air-traffic control system, for example, can also be used for air defense and vectoring fighter aircraft; the semiconductor technology used in computers has numerous military applications, including missile-guidance systems; technology for the manufacture of wide-body aircraft and high-bypass turbofan jet engines can be used in the production of military aircraft. And while precision ball bearings certainly have many industrial uses, they are also essential for the production of the guidance mechanism in MIRV warheads.

The problem is further complicated by the fact that the technologies of greatest interest to the Soviet Union are first developed by the private sector in the U.S. for commercial use, and are only later adapted to military programs. As Bucy pointed out, this means that "increased pressures for commercial trade with the USSR and its Comecon partners may result

in the flow of significant technologies before similar technologies are applied to advanced weapon systems in the U.S."

To add to the problem, many Soviet factories have both civilian and military lines of production. It would be most surprising, for example, if the Western-built Kama River truck factory, which is slated to be the largest industrial complex in the world, did not produce military vehicles upon its completion, in addition to diesel trucks and engines. This has been standard procedure in Soviet motor plants for some time, and, given the regime's obsessive secrecy— which is not, after all, a psychological aberration but has a rational purpose—it will be impossible to verify whether or not the Kama plant is producing for the military. Indeed, when one considers for a moment that military production is the first priority of the centralized Soviet economy, and that it is the sector in which the best available technological and human resources are concentrated, the notion that imported Western technology will *not* be used for military purposes seems rather farfetched.

Nor need this technology be directly used by the military in order for it to be "militarily significant." Even if applied to industry, it serves the purpose of freeing scarce research talent for military work. It seems perfectly obvious that if foreign technology relieves the labor shortage by modernizing Soviet industry, it makes it easier for Moscow to maintain a standing army of 4 million men. And if this modernization is financed with Western credits, it reduces the burden of a military budget that now consumes somewhere between 11 and 15 per cent of the Soviet GNP.

An example of how technological transfers to Russia of great strategic importance can take place with the approval of the U.S. government is provided by the recent controversial sale by Dresser Industries of a $144-million turnkey plant for the manufacture of deep-well drilling equipment. This particular deep-well technology is needed by the Soviet Union if it is to develop major new oil reserves, an urgent priority since it is now expected to become a net importer of oil by the mid-1980's. Lacking adequate energy sources, the Soviet economy's growth rate could slow to about 3 per cent, which would make it exceedingly difficult for Moscow to continue to increase military spending by 4 to 5 per cent every year, or to finance

---

[9] Much of this was known to American officials. In 1933, for example, the American engineer, Zara Witkin, who supervised construction of some of the "secret industry" plants in Russia (Eugene Lyons called this task "the most important given to any single foreign specialist"), told a U.S. Consul in Poland that every tractor plant "is of course a tank factory and an automobile plant [is] a factory which may at any time produce mobile artillery."

Cuban expeditions to Africa. Hence the Soviet interest in American oil technology.

Nevertheless, last summer, only weeks after President Carter announced that the government would assume control over all sales of oil technology and equipment to the Soviet Union, the administration approved the Dresser sale. Its reasoning, summed up by the Washington *Post* in an approving editorial, was that "the technology is widely available" outside the U.S., and that in view of the energy shortage "it serves American interests to get the maximum number of explorers into operation as soon as possible."

The administration appears to have given no consideration at all to the strategic significance of this sale, which greatly enhances the USSR's oil-production capabilities by giving it the capacity to manufacture premium rock-drill bits equal to the entire U.S. output, and greater than the Soviet Union's anticipated deep-well drilling requirements for the 1980's!

In the controversy surrounding the sale, attention was focused on only two items of the manufacturing equipment which were thought to have possible military application. These two items were subsequently approved by the Defense Department, despite expert opinion which held that one of them could produce armor-piercing projectiles. Senator Jackson, chairman of the Senate subcommittee which investigated the sale, cited pressure by both the Commerce Department and Dresser Industries as a factor that "may have contributed to what appears to have been a less than thorough assessment of national-security questions."

Following protests by Energy Secretary Schlesinger and members of the National Security Council, approval of the sale was suspended pending a review by a special task force of the Defense Science Board. The task-force report concluded that the deep-well technology in question "has strong strategic value in its application to Soviet energy needs of the 1980's" and that it is "wholly concentrated in the U.S.," thus giving this country effective control over its export to the Soviet Union. The report also pointed out that the transfer of this technology to the Soviets would allow them "to enter world markets with advanced drilling capabilities," thereby enabling them to increase their presence and influence in the Middle East and other oil-producing areas of the world. On the question of the two supporting technologies which the Defense Department had previously approved, the report

concluded that both would contribute significantly to the Soviet Union's military potential.

Despite these warnings, the President approved the Dresser sale a second time. Subsequently, he told a news conference that the administration takes adequate precautions "to be sure that we are not deliberately or inadvertently giving to [Communist] countries a means by which their military capability would be greatly escalated. This would be contrary to the existing law."

But what exactly did the President mean when he used the words "greatly escalated" here? The ambiguity of the formulation cannot be attributed only to the informal conditions prevailing at a news conference. It also serves to point up the fact that the United States does not at present have an effective or even coherent policy governing the export through commercial trade of strategic technology to the Soviet Union. The agency authorized to control commercial exports affecting national security is the Commerce Department, and since this department is interested primarily in promoting trade and reducing the U.S. balance-of-payments deficit, these considerations play a great part in influencing judgments on what is "militarily significant."

But the fundamental reason for the absence of a sound policy in this area is political. As long as it is assumed that trade promotes peace, no matter what is being traded, the problem of the flow of strategic technology to our principal adversary is not likely to be given serious consideration.

The argument heard most often—that controls cannot work since other nations will export what we embargo—is a rationalization for having no policy at all. In the Dresser case, for instance, there was no foreign producer the Russians could have turned to if we had denied the sale, but we approved it nonetheless. It is hard to see how the U.S. can expect to gain the cooperation of its allies in denying strategic technology to the Soviet Union if we ourselves continue to supply it in abundance. In fact, the relaxation of U.S. controls over the last decade is a major reason for the diminishing effectiveness of CoCom, the international body established in 1950 to regulate the export of strategic items to Communist nations.[10]

---

[10] CoCom's full name is Coordinating Committee of the Consultative Group of Nations, and its membership consists of NATO nations (except Iceland) and Japan. It maintains a common list of embargoed strategic items.

Only a rigorous control policy can be expected to shore up the faltering CoCom arrangement and win broad support in the U.S. The objective of such a policy need not be to restrict trade with the Soviet Union, but only to shut off the flow of strategic technology in accordance with the Defense Science Board's crucial distinction between products and technology—that is, between the item produced and the know-how required to produce it.

This distinction did not matter so much thirty years ago, when the U.S. and its CoCom allies first attempted to work out a control policy for trading with the Soviet Union. At that time a favorite Soviet method of acquiring technology was to copy Western prototypes which had been procured through single-item purchases. But as technology became more complex and the pace of technological change increased, this kind of "reverse engineering" became less feasible—by the time a process had been mastered and brought to production the product would have become obsolete. So the Russians naturally dropped their interest in individual products, and turned instead to the direct acquisition of critical technologies and production capability.

Control policies, however, have been oblivious to these changes and are still focused on the regulation of product transfers, so that items of secondary importance to the Soviet Union are now regulated while the U.S. and other Western countries actually encourage the transfer of what the Russians want most. We now have a policy, in other words, which allows Western firms to build whole production facilities in the Soviet Union, transfer vital manufacturing information, and train Soviet personnel, while withholding one particular item in the sale because it is on the CoCom list of embargoed goods. Small wonder that our allies are cynical about it.

It seems clear that this must change. While controls on selected critical products should be maintained, policy must be revised to take account of the central importance of technology transfers which contribute in any way at all to the Soviet Union's military and industrial strength. To be sure, in a world where technology is widely diffused, a policy aimed at denying the Soviet Union access to such technologies cannot be airtight. But as Fred Charles Iklé, the former director of the Arms Control and Disarmament Agency, has observed, "gradual seepage is one thing. It is quite another matter to expedite the spillage of some of the most advanced and complex technologies." And even if Soviet acquisition of such technologies cannot be prevented, it can at least be delayed, which may serve to maintain and perhaps extend what is called "the strategic lead time" of the United States over the Soviet Union. Our present lead in strategic technologies, estimated at three to ten years, is smaller than it was before "détente," but it is still a factor that restores some stability to the growing imbalance between U.S. and Soviet military forces.

Despite the current avidity for trade, it should be possible to win at least a measure of business support for a policy of stricter controls on technology transfers to the Soviet Union. In his new book, *A Time for Truth*, former Treasury Secretary William E. Simon traces the history of U.S. business aid to the Soviet Union by way of demonstrating the economic superiority of capitalism over Communism. But except in a footnoted afterthought in which he calls the whole enterprise "desperately unwise," Simon never comes to grips with the basic question of who stands to benefit most from current U.S.-Soviet trade ventures. Lenin put it rather succinctly in his famous question, *"kto kogo?"* ("Who [will defeat] whom?"), and perhaps it is time this question was asked by more than a small handful of business leaders. Capitalism is indeed more efficient than Communism, but if this very efficiency is used to sustain and fortify the enemies of free society, does this not, in the words of Seymour Martin Lipset, constitute "the ultimate failure of capitalism"?

But business need not even bother about such ultimate conclusions in order to support a policy of controls on the transfer of technology to the Soviet Union—it need only recognize its own economic self-interest. The transfer of production capability will dry up markets and create competitors far sooner than it will enhance trade or profits. All it takes is one firm—poorly managed, perhaps, and needing a Soviet deal to balance its books—to transfer the technology of an entire industry; surely this consideration should provide sufficient incentive for business to *demand* an effective policy of controls. Then, too, there is the question of the competitive disadvantage individual firms now face in negotiating with the Soviet state trading monopoly. Should not businessmen see the need for a central clearing house for U.S.-Soviet trade to offset this disadvantage?

A policy of control on technology transfers differs

significantly from the so-called policy of "economic diplomacy" which has stirred up so much pointless controversy in recent months. The former would shut off technology transfers to the Soviet Union while the latter would offer technology as an incentive to moderation and deny it as punishment for hostile acts. But "economic diplomacy" is no substitute for a policy of military deterrence, and common sense should dictate that anything the Russians might want badly enough to forgo opportunities for expansion is probably something they should not have in the first place. A policy of controls, on the other hand, would not be tied to politics, but for reasons that should already be clear, it could in the long run limit the Soviet Union's ability to threaten the security of the West.

The denial of foreign technology might very well succeed—where the present policy has failed—in bringing about a greater degree of decentralization and liberalization within the Soviet Union, but such a policy should not be aimed at changing the Soviet system. Nor should controls be loosened in response to favorable Soviet gestures on human rights. Technology is too valuable to be turned into a pawn in a game which the Soviet Union could easily manipulate in its favor. (This criticism, incidentally, does not bear upon the Jackson amendment, which in any case does not offer technology in exchange for freer emigration but only a modest amount of hard currency in the form of credits and lower tariffs on Soviet imports. There is nothing wrong with buying people's freedom, which is what the Jackson amendment amounts to. On the contrary, it is an objective worthy of a democratic society.)

It is difficult to speculate on future trends inside the Soviet Union and more difficult to influence them from the outside. If we have learned anything at this late date in our relations with the USSR it is that interaction with the West does not necessarily yield helpful results, and that the rich creations of a free system become distorted when absorbed by a system that is not free. Those who wish to build bridges to the East through trade might recall that Brezhnev, on the eve of détente, observed that "scientific-technical progress has now become one of the main bridgeheads of the historical struggle of the two systems."

It would be ironic if the one system able to generate such progress lost the struggle because it lacked the wisdom to understand its advantage and the will to protect it.

QUESTIONS FOR DISCUSSION

1 What information should one have to evaluate whether trade among nations promotes peace?
2 What are the likely consequences for the United States and the Soviet Union of increased trade between the two?
3 Can trade be used as a useful weapon in foreign policy?
4 Should trade be used as a weapon of foreign policy?
5 If the United States were not to trade with the Soviet Union, would the Soviet Union be able to obtain what it needs from other nations?

SUGGESTED READINGS

Agnelli, Giovanni. "East-West Trade: A European View." *Foreign Affairs* **58** (Summer 1980): 1016–1033.

Goldman, Marshall I. *Detente and Dollars: Doing Business with the Soviets*. New York: Basic Books, 1975.

Levinson, Charles. *Vodka Cola*. London: Gordon & Cremonesi, 1978.

Nove, Alec. *East-West Trade: Problems, Prospects, Issues*. The Washington Papers **6**, no. 53. Beverly Hills, Calif.: Sage, 1978.

Pisar, Samuel. *Coexistence and Commerce: Guidelines for Transactions Between East and West*. New York: McGraw-Hill, 1970.

Randolph, R. Sean. "Trading with the Enemy: A Happy Way to Die?" *National Review* (Sept. 19, 1980): 1132–1133 and 1136–1137.

"Trading with Russia: A Dangerous Game?" *U.S. News & World Report*, Dec. 18, 1978, pp. 22–25.

U.S. Congress. House of Representatives. *Review of Implementation of Basket II of the Helsinki Final Act*. Hearings before the Subcommittee on International Economic Policy and Trade of the Committee on Foreign Affairs and the Commission on Security and Cooperation in Europe, 96th Cong., 2d Sess., 1980.

U.S. Congress. Senate. *Suspension of United States Exports of High Technology and Grain to the Soviet Union*. Hearings before the Committee on Banking, Housing, and Urban Affairs, 96th Cong., 2d Sess., 1980.

Watts, Nita G. M. (ed.). *Economic Relations Between East and West*. London: Macmillan, 1978.

Chapter Four

Instruments of Power

Even when objectives of a nation's foreign policy are clear, there are often differing views among policymakers about what instruments of foreign policy should be used. When, in 1979, the revolutionary Iranian government sanctioned the action of Iranian students in seizing the American Embassy in Teheran and in holding American diplomatic and military officials as hostages, President Carter faced the policy problems of deciding what instruments of power the United States should use to get the hostages released with the least risk to their lives and to the security interests of the United States. He relied on diplomatic efforts, such as gaining support of other countries in an appeal for the release of the hostages. He brought the issue to the attention of the International Court of Justice. He approved a plan to rescue the hostages through a commando raid in Iran, but the raid was aborted because of technical problems once the American force landed in Iran.

Although the hostages were eventually released, Americans continued to debate whether or not the Carter administration manipulated the correct levers of power to meet the challenges of the crisis. The United States, of course, has not been the only country to face problems in deciding what to do in different troubling situations. The Soviet Union, for example, contemplated taking military action against the Chinese Communist government as tension between the Soviet Union and China intensified during the 1960s. Israel considered actions, such as war, reprisals, and negotiations, to meet challenges from its Arab enemies. North Vietnam pondered the kinds of steps it could take to rid Indochina first of the French and then of American military forces in southeast Asia.

This chapter deals with the use of military and economic levers of power since the end of World War II. Subjects involve nuclear weapons, NATO, terrorism, and foreign aid.

NUCLEAR WEAPONS

World War II ended with the use of two nuclear bombs against Japan. Since 1945, nuclear weapons have not been used in warfare although several nations now possess them. As indicated in Chapter 2, the United States has been joined by the Soviet Union, Great Britain, France, Communist China, and India as members of the nuclear-weapons club. Other nations are expected to produce nuclear weapons in the coming decades.

Not only has the number of nuclear-weapons states grown, but so, too, has the variety of nuclear weapons. Nuclear weapons have been tested with yields measured in megatons (millions of tons of TNT). In 1961, the Soviet Union tested a nuclear weapon estimated to be between 57 and 100 megatons. Weapons have been made smaller than that—down to the low kiloton range. Today, there are atomic mines and atomic cannons deployed in West Europe ready for use against invading Soviet forces. There are also nuclear warheads that can be carried over short and long distances by missiles, bombers, and submarines.

When the United States had a monopoly of these weapons, it chose not to use them after World War II. When it had superiority in such weapons—a situation that may have lasted into the early 1960s—it again chose not to use them. It accepted a stalemate in the Korean war rather than employ such powerful weapons. It saw Vietnam overrun by communism rather than risk the devastation of nuclear warfare.

Although the superpowers have not used nuclear weapons, they have threatened to use them on varying occasions. In 1956, the Soviet Union warned that it would use nuclear weapons if Great Britain and France did not withdraw their forces from the Suez Canal area when those countries sought to end Egyptian control over the canal. The United States went on alert in 1962 when the Soviet Union prepared to install missiles capable of launching nuclear weapons in Cuba. In spite of the threats, other measures were taken to achieve political goals.

Nuclear weapons are so powerful and the means to deliver them so swift and relatively protected that the superpowers have relied on deterrence (the prevention of war) to provide for their security. Deterrence is based on the premise that the nuclear forces of either superpower are so strong that neither side would be a victor in a nuclear war. *Mutual assured destruction*, commonly known by its acronym MAD, is generally regarded as the basis for keeping the nuclear peace. Through MAD, each superpower has the capability of destroying the other even if the other side launches a sneak attack. Sufficient retaliatory nuclear forces would survive a nuclear attack to make MAD credible.

Although MAD has proved effective, superpowers still devise plans to use these weapons. Attention has often been given to theories of counterforce and countervalue. Counterforce is a strategy that directs nuclear forces at the other side's nuclear arsenal. Countervalue directs nuclear forces at the other side's cities and industrial targets. Although it is difficult to assume pinpoint accuracy against targets in either of these strategies, counterforce is generally regarded as the most threatening. A country that aims its nuclear weapons at an adversary's nuclear forces is perceived as preparing for a first-strike capability: one in which a sneak attack would cripple the attacked country's nuclear retaliatory capability. A countervalue strategy, in contrast, would not have such an outcome.

Military analysts and political leaders have talked about the possibility of engaging in limited nuclear war. In 1980 President Carter issued Presidential Directive (PD) 59. It called for the possible use of controlled precision nuclear attacks directed at Soviet military and political targets in the event of war. Even before 1980, however, NATO devised its military strategy based on the use of theater nuclear weapons to meet a Soviet conventional attack on West Europe. (See below.)

Nuclear-weapons states other than the superpowers have their own plans for the use of nuclear weapons. France, for example, relies on a *force de frappe*—a nuclear organization that would be strong enough to cause severe damage to a country launching a nuclear attack against France although not powerful enough to achieve victory. As more countries obtain nuclear weapons, they will devise their own uses for such weapons not always consistent with superpower objectives.

Although the destructive power of conventional weapons has become greater since the end of World War II, there is general acceptance of the use of such weapons in warfare. Even nuclear powers have made a distinction between conventional and nuclear weapons. There is, however, no stated agreement distinguishing small from large nuclear weapons, or tactical from strategic nuclear weapons.

During most of the nuclear age, those who thought about nuclear strategy in the West focused on deterrence and the avoidance of nuclear war. It was assumed that nuclear war between the United States and the Soviet Union would inevitably produce a nuclear holocaust. Since the late 1960s, there has been some active attention given to the possible use of nuclear weapons with less than total war results.

Is it likely that nuclear war can be controlled? As Secretary of Defense in the Carter administration, Harold Brown defended such a possibility in speaking in support of PD 59. The United States should have selective nuclear options, Brown declares, so that it will not have to choose between a nuclear holocaust or doing nothing. Brown notes that such a policy is not new for the United States since former defense secretaries Robert McNamara and James Schlesinger defended similar strategies during their terms in office.

Military analyst Desmond Ball argues that it is unlikely that nuclear war can be controlled. Command and control systems are inherently relatively vulnerable. Uncertainties in the effect and accuracy of weapons mean that collateral casualties can never be calculated precisely. Ball contends that decision makers would be likely to prevent initiating nuclear strikes no matter how limited or selective the options available to them.

In evaluating the wisdom of relying on the controlled use of nuclear weapons, a number of questions arise. How would a country that is hit by a few limited weapons be certain that its adversary is not engaged in an all-out war? What kinds of targets make a controlled response credible? Does a doctrine accepting controlled nuclear war make nuclear war more or less likely to occur?

NATO

NATO was formed in April 1949 because of a fear by its original signatories—Belgium, Canada, Denmark, France, Iceland, Italy, Luxembourg, the Netherlands, Norway, Portugal, the United Kingdom, and the United States—that the Soviet Union posed a major threat to their security. Its central provision is Article 5, which states: "The parties agree that an armed attack against one or more of them in Europe or North America shall be considered an attack against them all."

NATO is a grand alliance. It is, however, a grand alliance different from earlier alliances. Where grand alliances were formed in the past—such as those that put down Napoleon, Kaiser Wilhelm, and Adolf Hitler—they were formed after an act of aggression occurred. The purpose of NATO is twofold: deterrence and defense. The very act of forming a peacetime alliance, it was believed, would serve to deter aggression by the Soviet Union. If deterrence failed, however, the alliance would be politically united and militarily strong so as to protect its members from a Soviet victory.

Certain factors underlay the formation of NATO. These involved the supremacy of the United States as a nuclear power, the fear of Soviet policies, and the economic condition of the Europeans. First, in April 1949, the United States had a monopoly of nuclear weapons. The United States could carry those weapons to the Soviet Union itself by relying on its air bases in West Europe and Africa. NATO members could believe that the American nuclear forces offered a credible deterrent to Soviet aggression.

Second, it seemed to NATO members that the Soviet Union in particular and communism in general posed a threat to Western security. The post-World War II period was characterized by such apparent threats as a civil war in Greece, communist political strength in France and Italy, a Soviet-inspired communist takeover of Czechoslovakia in 1948, and a blockade of Allied surface routes to Berlin in 1948.

Third, West Europe was devastated by World War II. It depended on the United States for its economic support. The Marshall Plan of 1947 in which the United States committed nearly $15 billion of economic aid to its West European allies was a reflection of that economic bond.

In the more than three decades since NATO came into existence, there have been many changes in the conditions underlying NATO and in the character of the alliance itself. Most important, no longer does the United States possess a monopoly of nuclear weapons. Even after it lost that monopoly in 1949, the United States maintained a superiority of nuclear weapons, which extended into the 1960s. During the Cuban missile crisis of 1962, the Soviet Union had about seventy long-range missiles that took 10 hours to fuel. This situation made Soviet missiles easily vulnerable to an American attack before they could be launched. Even as late as the Yom Kippur war of 1973, the United States had a superiority of about 8 to 1 in nuclear warheads. The United States had maintained through this period a superiority in theater nuclear forces, as well.

Starting in the 1960s, however, the Soviet Union began a massive nuclear program. It reached nuclear parity in the 1970s in strategic and tactical weapons. Strong evidence indicates that it now leads in both strategic and theater nuclear forces. Whether equal or superior, however, the rising Soviet military strength has led to changed military relationships and political uncertainties.

As the Soviet nuclear arsenal grew after 1949, West Europeans became increasingly doubtful that the United States would risk an attack against its own cities to defend its NATO partners. In 1951, the United States sent additional troops to West Europe as an added assurance that if there were a war, the United States would become involved. Later, theater nuclear weapons were deployed in Europe to strengthen the West's deterrent forces. In spite of the deployment of these weapons, fears are continually expressed that if a war does break out, it will be fought on European rather than American soil. Such a feeling has led to a growing movement of neutralism and disarmament expressed through demonstrations and parades in West Europe in late 1981.

Changes have occurred not only in nuclear aspects of the alliance, but in other areas, as well. Since the 1950s, the Soviets have engaged in various peace offensives. Soviet leader Nikita Khrushchev became identified with a policy of "peaceful coexistence." Leonid Brezhnev, Khrushchev's successor, advocated a policy of détente.

The West European economy experienced continuing improvement. West Europeans rid themselves of their African and Asian colonies, which had become indefensible and economically debilitating. The establishment of the European Economic Community served to strengthen the economies of West European countries. Trade between West

Europe and East Europe increased. No longer was West Europe dependent on the United States, so that West European nations could more readily pursue an independent course in foreign policy.

In its more than three decades, the NATO alliance experienced many changes. Its membership grew. Greece and Turkey joined the alliance in 1952, and West Germany entered in 1955. West German entrance into NATO was the immediate cause of the establishment in 1955 of the Soviet equivalent alliance defense organization—the Warsaw Pact. In 1982, Spain became the sixteenth member of NATO.

In spite of its increased membership, the NATO alliance faces many difficulties of a political, military, and economic nature. Foremost among its political problems is the choice that NATO's European members make between focusing on European solutions or casting their lot with the United States: that is to say, Europeanism versus Atlanticism. In 1965, France withdrew from the military arrangements of NATO, although it remained a formal member of the alliance. French President Charles de Gaulle hoped to create a French-led Europe dominated by neither the United States nor the Soviet Union.

Militarily, two key NATO issues have been the role of American forces in Europe and the use of nuclear weapons. American forces were sent to West Europe after World War II and are there today so as to provide assurance that the United States will become involved if a war breaks out in Europe. Medium-range theater nuclear weapons were first deployed in NATO in the early 1950s to strengthen the alliance. NATO strategy provides for the use of nuclear weapons in case of a successful Soviet strike across West Europe. Although West Europeans were anxious for the United States to deploy tactical nuclear weapons in West Europe, a growing opposition to such deployment has arisen. The fear is expressed that in the event of war with the Soviet Union, the United States will use Europe as a nuclear battlefield rather than risk the destruction of its own cities.

The economic condition of West Europe has an impact on the alliance. How strong NATO is depends on the contributions that member states make to NATO. Particularly through the 1970s, a time of economic decay, NATO's military contributions did not keep up with Soviet military strength in Europe. Peace movements and demands for expenditures in the welfare sector served to limit defense expenditures.

Because West Europe was more dependent on Middle East oil for its industrial development, it became more responsive to Arab demands in 1973, when the Arab oil boycott was announced, and in later years. The objectives of the United States and West Europe continued to differ on Middle East matters in the 1970s.

Because of the changing character of the alliance, some observers have had to reassess the value of the alliance in the 1980s. Does NATO deter aggression? Sir John Killick, a former Ambassador and United Kingdom Permanent Representative to NATO, argues that NATO continues to be relevant for the West's security. Even in an age of détente, NATO is important. A Soviet perception that the West has fallen behind in the preservation of the military balance will encourage Soviet interventionism. A strong NATO will stimulate cooperation between the U.S.S.R. and the West.

Irving Kristol argues that NATO has ceased to be a living reality and will soon die. NATO made sense when the United States possessed nuclear superiority. As the Soviet Union achieved nuclear parity and perhaps nuclear leadership, nuclear weapons ceased to be a credible deterrent against a Soviet attack of West Europe. In the event of Soviet aggression in West Europe, Kristol argues, the United States will *not* initiate a strategic nuclear exchange. The only purpose of America's strategic nuclear weapons is to deter a Soviet first strike against the United States itself. Even if a Soviet invasion of West Europe produced a NATO response in the form of tactical nuclear weapons, the spirit of NATO resistance would quickly give way to a spirit of negotiation.

Kristol assesses why the Soviet Union has not attacked West Europe. First, once nuclear weapons are used, the future is unpredictable. The use of nuclear weapons could result in a nuclear holocaust or produce internal tensions within the Soviet system itself. Second, the Soviet Union may not be much interested in achieving a Soviet-occupied Western Europe. It may be the case that the Soviets feel they have enough trouble with their East European communist nations or that West Europe would fall under their influence without armed attack. Third, West Europe is no longer so central to the foreign policy of either of the two superpowers. The Middle East and Latin America are at least of equal importance.

Since the NATO alliance was formed in 1949, not a single NATO member has been attacked by the Soviet Union. In considering the Killick-Kristol debate, we may ask: what criteria should be used to evaluate the effectiveness of NATO in the survival of its members? If, in fact, Soviet aggression in West Europe was deterred not by NATO but by other factors, what would be the consequences of a termination of the NATO alliance to the security of its members?

TERRORISM

The use of troops by one state to fight in wars against the military forces of another state constitutes a traditional application of force in international politics. The post-World War II period, however, has been characterized not only by conventional warfare but also by a different form of force: terrorism.

Terrorism lacks a precise definition. The term "terror" was first used in a political sense during the French Revolution. The Terror referred to the period between June 1793 and July 1794 in which a dictatorship promoted terror through its policies of political repression. The uncontrolled use of coercion by a government against its people continues to be a practice of governments. Stalin and Hilter in the 1930s are modern examples of political leaders who engaged in terror against their own peoples. Pol Pot in Cambodia in the 1970s is a more recent example, as that Cambodian communist leader was responsible for the liquidation of millions of his own people.

Terrorism has another meaning: the use of violence by substate actors against civilians and political figures for the purpose of ending a regime's rule and establishing a new government. Terrorism, in this sense, is a form of unconventional war. Because nongovernmental terrorists are militarily weak, they cannot hope for any success by confronting government forces in set battles. Rather, they must engage in activities that are unexpected, secret, and newsworthy.

Terrorist actions have become global—and particularly prominent in the 1970s—and have involved the hijacking of aircraft, assassination of political leaders, bombing of government buildings, and kidnapping of business leaders who work in multinational corporations.

Organizations, such as the Black September Movement, the Irish Republican Army (IRA), the Symbionese Liberation Army, and the Red Brigade, have engaged in major terrorist plots. The actions of these organizations are diverse, but some of the more prominent are the following:

In 1972, Black September members entered the Olympic grounds in Munich and held Israeli athletes as hostages. As a result of their operation, some Israeli hostages were murdered, and the terrorist squad got away in airplanes that took them out of West Germany and into a friendly Arab country.

The IRA was responsible for the assassination of Lord Mountbatten, British Queen

Elizabeth's uncle. It has been involved in placing bombs in British cities in locations where ordinary citizens congregate.

The Symbionese Liberation Army, an American-based organization of revolutionaries, kidnapped heiress Patricia Hearst and held her hostage at the same time that they made public threats about killing her. They forced Miss Hearst's father, publisher William Randolph Hearst, to provide funds to distribute food to people living in poor neighborhoods. While under terrorist control, Miss Hearst engaged in illegal activities alongside the group's members.

The Red Brigade in Italy was involved in numerous kidnappings of political leaders and journalists. It kidnapped Aldo Moro, the former Italian premier, and held him for weeks before killing him.

Terrorists have received media publicity of their exploits. They have, moreover, succeeded in creating fear among a nation's population made aware of terrorist acts.

It is useful in analyzing terrorism by substate actors to distinguish among the different kinds of terrorist groups. Are their objectives nationalistic or revolutionary? Do they receive support from states or are they independent? Had it not been for terrorism, would world public opinion be less knowledgeable about the goals of such groups as the IRA and the PLO? Do terrorist goals justify terrorist methods?

One central question about terrorism is: is terrorism an effective instrument? Writer Paul Johnson thinks that it is. He argues that terrorism poses an enormous threat to our civilization. Johnson defines terrorism as "the deliberate systematic murder, maiming and menacing of the innocent to inspire fear in order to gain political ends." He points to seven reasons why terrorism is dangerous. (1) Terrorism is the deliberate and cold-blooded exaltation of violence over all forms of political activity. (2) It is the deliberate suppression of the moral instincts in man. (3) It rejects politics as the normal means by which communities resolve conflicts. (4) It actively, systematically, and necessarily assists the spread of the totalitarian state. (5) It poses no threat to the totalitarian state. (6) It exploits the apparatus of freedom in liberal societies, and thereby endangers freedom. (7) It saps the will of a civilized society to defend itself. These evils of terrorism make it a threat to the peace and stability of all legitimate states.

Political analyst Walter Laqueur argues that the power of terrorists to compel major political changes is negligible. Terrorists are able to attract headline attention but media spotlight is not the same as political power.

Guerrilla wars have been successful only against colonial rule, and the age of colonialism is over, Laqueur observes. He adds that there is no known case in modern history of a terrorist movement seizing political power. Dangers of nuclear terrorism, moreover, are no greater than dangers from individuals, madmen, or criminals in blackmailing society. Terrorism is a danger, but society is resilient enough to deal with it and has more serious problems to resolve.

FOREIGN AID

Foreign aid is an instrument of foreign policy not only for wealthy countries but for poor countries, as well. To some observers, foreign aid is nothing more than "giveaways" that states would do well to avoid. To other observers, foreign aid is a necessary instrument of foreign policy in a world where nations need allies.

Superpowers have provided enormous assistance to friendly countries. The United States established the Marshall Plan after World War II to get Europe on the path to economic recovery from the devastation of that war. The United States has extended aid to third world countries in every presidential administration since that of Harry Truman. The Soviet Union has provided economic assistance to other communist nations and to neutral countries. The People's Republic of China provided funds to help build the Tanzam railway—the train link between Tanzania and Zambia. Many advanced industrial nations have aid programs in third world countries.

Foreign aid is provided for many purposes. The intent of donors includes strengthening allies, bolstering unstable governments, assisting states to be strong enough to defend themselves, making governments dependent on loans, and promoting economic development. States also offer aid for purely humanitarian purposes, such as during a famine or earthquake, or after a war.

A central issue about aid involves the utility of foreign aid in promoting economic development and stability. As Secretary of State in the Carter administration, Cyrus Vance justified the importance of foreign assistance to developing nations. In the statement below taken from testimony before a congressional committee. Vance makes the following points: (1) less-developed countries have a growing importance to America's security needs in both economic and political aspects; (2) the United States should respond in different ways to the varying needs of developing nations. United States foreign assistance programs serve a variety of objectives in the third world: e.g., providing help for the poor, giving loans for large-scale infrastructure projects, financing technical assistance, and promoting human rights. American foreign assistance will be directed to increasing food supplies, aiding population planning programs, improving health conditions, assisting education efforts, and engaging in other matters. Aid will also take the form of military assistance to strengthen security forces of friendly nations.

Economist P. T. Bauer and journalist John O'Sullivan criticize the use of foreign aid as an instrument of foreign policy. They argue that aid is not necessary for development. The West did not rely on aid for its own development but rather drew on vast external markets, an abundant supply of capital, and a more primitive technology than is available today. Aid based on criteria of poverty has little impact on economic progress. Aid goes generally to government officials and the more powerful segments of society, not to the poor.

According to Bauer and O'Sullivan, aid from the West to the third world would not lead to redistribution of the wealth from the rich to the poor. The recipients of aid would be the affluent in their countries. The West, moreover, is under no obligation to provide reparations for the poverty of the third world since Western involvement in the third world helped rather than hindered economic development. Aid does not serve security and economic interests of the donor countries.

An evaluation of aid programs reveals successes and failures in economic development. Many commentators argue that the Marshall Plan was a success, but point to other aid programs that failed or were even harmful to the recipients. It is essential to consider why some aid programs are successful and others failures, whether developing nations would obtain capital if aid were denied them, and whether, if aid is granted, it is best to give it through multilateral agencies than directly from one government to another. It is also worth considering the role of foreign aid in third world countries that have made enormous economic gains. Did these countries prosper because of aid?

13 Is It Realistic to Believe That Nuclear Weapons Are Likely to Be Used in Warfare in a Controlled Manner?

YES

Harold Brown

American Nuclear Doctrine

NO

Desmond Ball

Can Nuclear War Be Controlled?

American Nuclear Doctrine
Harold Brown

As a complement to our [nuclear] force modernization efforts and our arms control negotiations, for the
past three years we have been working intensively to
make deterrence more certain and more effective,
through better planning and a more cogent statement
of our strategic doctrine. In this process, we have
taken a number of important analytic and operational
steps.

In the summer of 1977, President Carter ordered a
fundamental review of our targeting policy. Over the
course of the next 18 months, that study was conducted by military and civilian experts taking into account
our forces, plans, problems, and capabilities as well as
Soviet perspectives, strengths, and vulnerabilities.

Since my report to the President on that analysis,
we have been moving deliberately to implement its
basic principles. I outlined the major precepts of this
countervailing strategy in my Defense Report in early
1979, and in more detail in January of this year.

At a meeting of the NATO Nuclear Planning
Group in June of this year, I briefed our allies on the
conclusions we reached and the actions we are taking.
They fully support the need for the United States to
have a wide range of strategic nuclear options. Our
countervailing strategy is fully consistent with
NATO's flexible response and indeed indicates our
determination to carry out that Alliance strategy.

President Carter has recently issued an implementing directive—Presidential Directive No. 59—
codifying our restated doctrine, and giving guidance
for further evolution in our planning and systems
acquisition.

Obviously, the details of our planning must remain
a closely guarded secret. Nonetheless, the basic premise of our policy can be stated publicly without
compromise to our security. In fact, it is very much in
our national interest that our deterrence policy—and
the consequences of aggression—are clearly understood by friend and adversary alike.

At the outset, let me emphasize that PD 59 is not a
new strategic doctrine; it is not a radical departure
from US strategic policy over the past decade or so. It
is, in fact, a refinement, a codification of previous
statements of our strategic policy. PD 59 takes the

same essential strategic doctrine, and restates it more
clearly, more cogently, in the light of current conditions and current capabilities.

Moreover, one purpose of my own exposition of
the subject today, as of my previous statements along
these lines, is to make clear to the Soviets the nature
of our countervailing strategy. This is to assure that
no potential adversary of the United States or its allies
could ever conclude that aggression would be worth
the costs that would be incurred. This is true whatever
the level of conflict contemplated.

Deterrence remains, as it has been historically, our
fundamental strategic objective. But deterrence must
restrain a far wider range of threats than just massive
attacks on US cities. We seek to deter any adversary
from any course of action that could lead to general
nuclear war. Our strategic forces also must deter
nuclear attacks on smaller sets of targets in the US or
on US military forces, and be a wall against nuclear
coercion of, or attack on, our friends and allies. And
strategic forces, in conjunction with theatre nuclear
forces, must contribute to deterrence of conventional
aggression as well. (I say 'contribute' because we
recognize that neither nuclear forces nor the cleverest
theory for their employment can eliminate the need
for us—and our allies—to provide a capable conventional deterrent.)

In our analysis and planning, we are necessarily
giving greater attention to how a nuclear war would
actually be fought by both sides if deterrence fails.
There is no contradiction between this focus on how a
war would be fought and what its results would be,
and our purpose of insuring continued peace through
mutual deterrence. Indeed, this focus helps us achieve
deterrence and peace, by insuring that our ability to
retaliate is fully credible.

By definition, successful deterrence means, among
other things, shaping Soviet views of what a war
would mean—of what risks and losses aggression
would entail. We must have forces, contingency
plans, and command and control capabilities that will
convince the Soviet leadership that no war and no
course of aggression by them that led to use of nuclear
weapons—on any scale of attack and at any stage of

From an address by U.S. Secretary of Defense Harold Brown, Aug. 20, 1980.

conflict—could lead to victory, however they may define victory. Firmly convincing them of that fundamental truth is the surest restraint against their being tempted to aggression.

Operationally, our countervailing strategy requires that our plans and capabilities be structured to put more stress on being able to employ strategic nuclear forces selectively, as well as by all-out retaliation in response to massive attacks on the United States. It is our policy—and we have increasingly the means and the detailed plans to carry out this policy—to insure that the Soviet leadership knows that if they chose some intermediate level of aggression, we could, by selective, large (but still less than maximum) nuclear attacks, exact an unacceptably high price in the things the Soviet leaders appear to value most—political and military control, military force both nuclear and conventional, and the industrial capability to sustain a war. In our planning we have not ignored the problem of ending the war, nor would we ignore it in the event of a war. And, of course, we have, and we will keep, a survivable and enduring capability to attack the full range of targets, including the Soviet economic base, if that is the appropriate response to a Soviet strike.

At the President's direction, the Department of Defense has, since 1977, been working to increase the flexibility of our plans to make use of the inherent capabilities of our forces. We are also acting to improve our ability to maintain effective communications, command and control of our forces, even in the highly uncertain and chaotic conditions that would prevail in a nuclear war. These actions greatly strengthen our deterrent.

This doctrine, as I emphasized earlier, is not a new departure. The US has never had a doctrine based simply and solely on reflexive, massive attacks on Soviet cities. Instead, we have always planned both more selectively (options limiting urban-industrial damage) and more comprehensively (a range of military targets). Previous administrations, going back well into the 1960s, recognized the inadequacy of a strategic doctrine that would give us too narrow a range of options. The fundamental premise of our countervailing strategy is a natural evolution of the conceptual foundations built over the course of a generation, by, for example, Secretaries McNamara and Schlesinger, to name only two of my predecessors who have been most identified with development of our nuclear doctrine.

This Administration does not claim to have discovered the need for broad scale deterrence, or for improved flexibility, or for secure and reliable command and control of our own forces should deterrence fail, or for effective targeting of military forces and their political leadership and military control.

This evolution in our doctrine enhances deterrence, and reduces the likelihood of nuclear war. It does so because—like our nuclear modernization programs—it emphasizes the survivability of our forces and it conveys to the Soviets that any or all of the components of Soviet power can be struck in retaliation, not only their urban-industrial complex.

What we have done in the past three and a half years is to look more closely at our capabilities, our doctrine and our plans in the light of what we know about Soviet forces, doctrine, and plans. The Soviet leadership appears to contemplate at least the possibility of a relatively prolonged exchange if a war comes, and in some circles at least, they seem to take seriously the theoretical possibility of victory in such a war. We cannot afford to ignore these views—even if we think differently, as I do. We need to have, and we do have, a posture—both forces and doctrine—that makes it clear to the Soviets, and to the world, that any notion of victory in nuclear war is unrealistic.

Implementing our strategy requires us to make some changes in our operational planning, such as gradually increasing the scope, variety and flexibility of options open to us should the Soviets choose aggression. Some of this has already been done since 1977. More needs to be done. We must also improve the survivability and endurance of our command and control.

This is not a first strike strategy. We are talking about what we could and (depending on the nature of a Soviet attack) would do in response to a Soviet attack. Nothing in the policy contemplates that nuclear war can be a deliberate instrument of achieving our national security goals, because it cannot be. But we cannot afford the risk that the Soviet leadership might entertain the illusion that nuclear war could be an option—or its threat a means of coercion—for them.

In declaring our ability and our intention to prevent Soviet victory, even in the most dangerous circumstances, we have no illusions about what a nuclear war would mean for mankind. It would be an unimaginable catastrophe.

We are also not unaware of the immense uncertainties involved in any use of nuclear weapons. We know that what might start as a supposedly controlled, limited strike could well—in my view would very likely—escalate to a full-scale nuclear war. Further, we know that even limited nuclear exchanges would involve immense casualties and destruction. But we have always needed choices aside from massive retaliation in response to grave, but still limited provocation. The increase in Soviet strategic capability over the past decade, and our concern that the Soviets may not believe that nuclear war is unwinnable, dictate a

US need to more—and more selective—retaliatory options.

The doctrinal and planning measures we are taking —coupled with our force modernization programs— improve the effectiveness of our strategic nuclear forces across the full range of threats. They make clear our understanding that the surest way to avoid a war is to insure that the Soviet leadership can have no illusions about what such a war would mean for Soviet state power and for Soviet society . . .

Can Nuclear War Be Controlled?
Desmond Ball

CONCLUSIONS

A strategic nuclear war between the United States and the Soviet Union would involve so many novel technical and emotional variables that predictions about its course—and especially about whether or not it could be controlled—must remain highly speculative.

To the extent that there is a typical lay image of a nuclear war, it is that any substantial use of nuclear weapons by either the United States or the Soviet Union against the other's forces or territory would inevitably and rapidly lead to all-out urban-industrial attacks and consequent mutual destruction. As Carl-Friedrich von Weiszacker recently wrote, 'as soon as we use nuclear weapons, there are no limits'.[1]

Among strategic analysts on the other hand, the ascendant view is that it is possible to conduct limited and quite protracted nuclear exchanges in such a way that escalation can be controlled and the war terminated at some less than all-out level. Some strategists actually visualize an escalation ladder, with a series of discrete and clearly identifiable steps of increasing levels of intensity of nuclear conflict, which the respective adversaries move up—and down—at will. Current US strategic policy, although extensively and

carefully qualified, is closer to this second position: it is hoped that escalation could be controlled and that more survivable command-and-control capabilities should ensure dominance in the escalation process. Indeed, reliance on the ability to control escalation is an essential element of US efforts with respect to extended deterrence.

Escalation is neither autonomous and inevitable nor subject completely to the decision of any one national command authority. Whether or not it can be controlled will depend very much on the circumstances at the time. The use of a few nuclear weapons for some clear demonstrative purposes, for example, could well not lead to further escalation. However, it is most unrealistic to expect that there would be a relatively smooth and controlled progression from limited and selective strikes, through major counter-force exchanges, to termination of the conflict at some level short of urban-industrial attacks. It is likely that beyond some relatively early stage in the conflict the strategic communications systems would suffer interference and disruption, the strikes would become ragged, unco-ordinated, less precise and less discriminating, and the ability to reach an agreed settlement between the adversaries would soon become extremely problematical.

There is of course no immutable point beyond which control is necessarily and irretrievably lost but

[1] Carl-Friedrich von Weiszacker, 'Can a Third World War be Prevented?', *International Security* (vol. 5, no. 1). Summer 1980, p. 205.

From Desmond Ball, *Can Nuclear War Be Controlled?* Adelphi Paper No. **169**. London: International Institute for Strategic Studies, Autumn 1981, pp. 35–38.

clearly the prospects of maintaining control depend to a very great extent on whether or not a decision is taken deliberately to attack strategic command-and-control capabilities.

Command-and-control systems are inherently relatively vulnerable, and concerted attacks on them would very rapidly destroy them, or at least render them inoperable. Despite the increased resources that the US is currently devoting to improving the survivability and endurance of command-and-control systems, the extent of their relative vulnerability remains enormous. The Soviet Union would need to expend thousands of warheads in any comprehensive counterforce attacks against US ICBM [Intercontinental Ballistic Missile] silos, bomber bases and FBM [Fleet Ballistic Missile] submarine facilities, and even then hundreds if not thousands of US warheads would still survive. On the other hand, it would require only about 50-100 warheads to destroy the fixed facilities of the national command system or to effectively impair the communication links between the National Command Authorities and the strategic forces.

This figure would permit attacks on the National Military Command Center, the major underground command posts (including the Alternative National Military Command Center and the NORAD [North American Air Defense] and SAC [Strategic Air Command] Command Posts), the critical satellite ground terminals and early-warning radar facilities, the VLF [Very Low Frequency] communication stations, etc., as well as 10 or 20 high altitude detonations designed to disrupt HF [High Frequency] communications and generate EMP [Electro-Magnetic Pulse] over millions of square miles. Any airborne command posts and communication links that survived the initial attack could probably not endure for more than a few days. Soviet military doctrine suggests that any comprehensive counterforce attack *would* include strikes of this sort. US strategic targeting plans involve a wide range of Soviet command-and-control facilities, and, while attacks on the Soviet national leadership would probably only be undertaken as part of an all-out exchange, it is likely that attempts would be made to destroy the command posts that control the strategic forces, or at least to sever the communication links between the Soviet NCA [National Command Authorities] and those forces at a much earlier stage in the conflict.

In fact, control of a nuclear exchange would become very difficult to maintain after several tens of strategic nuclear weapons had been used, even where deliberate attacks on command-and-control capabilities were avoided. Many command and control facilities, such as early-warning radars, radio antennae and satellite ground terminals would be destroyed, or at least rendered inoperable, by nuclear detonations designed to destroy nearby military forces and installations, while the widespread disturbance of the ionosphere and equally widespread generation of EMP would disrupt HF communications and impair electronic and electrical systems at great distances from the actual explosions. Hence, as John Steinbruner has argued, 'regardless of the flexibility embodied in individual force components, the precariousness of command channels probably means that nuclear war would be uncontrollable, as a practical matter, shortly after the first tens of weapons are launched'.[2] Moreover, any attack involving 100 nuclear weapons that was of any military or strategic significance (as opposed to demonstration strikes at isolated sites in northern Siberia) would produce substantial civilian casualties. Even if cities were avoided, 100 nuclear detonations on key military or war-supporting facilities (such as oil refineries) would probably cause prompt fatalities in excess of a million people.

The notion of controlled nuclear war-fighting is essentially astrategic in that it tends to ignore a number of the realities that would necessarily attend any nuclear exchange. The more significant of these include the particular origins of the given conflict and the nature of its progress to the point where the strategic nuclear exchange is initiated; the disparate objectives for which a limited nuclear exchange would be fought; the nature of the decision-making processes within the adversary governments; the political pressures that would be generated by a nuclear exchange; and the problems of terminating the exchange at some less than all-out level. Some of these considerations are so fundamental and so intemperate in their implications as to suggest that there can really be no possibility of controlling a nuclear war.

The origins of a nuclear exchange are relevant because, for example, a strategic nuclear strike by the United States or the Soviet Union against targets in the other's heartland—no matter how limited, precise, or controlled it might be—is most unlikely to be

[2] John Steinbruner, 'National Security and the Concept of Strategic Stability', *Journal of Conflict Resolution* (vol 22, no. 1). September 1978, p. 421.

the first move in any conflict between them. Rather, it is likely to follow a period of large-scale military action, probably involving substantial use of tactical nuclear weapons, in an area of vital interest to both adversaries, and during which the dynamics of the escalation process have already been set in motion. Some command-and-control facilities, communications systems and intelligence posts that would be required to control a strategic nuclear exchange would almost certainly be destroyed or damaged in the conventional or tactical nuclear phases of a conflict. And casualties on both sides are already likely to be very high before any strategic nuclear exchange. In the case of a tactical nuclear war in Europe possible fatalities range from 2 to 20 million, assuming extensive use of nuclear weapons with some restraints, up to 100 million if there are no restraints at all.[3] The capabilities of the Warsaw Pact forces (using large and relatively 'dirty' warheads) and the Warsaw Pact targeting doctrine make it likely that the actual figure would lie at the higher end of this range.

A war involving such extensive use of nuclear weapons in Europe would almost inevitably involve attacks on targets within the Soviet Union. Indeed, it has long been US policy to use nuclear weapons against the Soviet Union even if the Soviet Union has attacked neither US forces nor US territory. As Secretary Brown expressed it in January 1980, 'We could not want the Soviets to make the mistaken judgment, based on their understanding of our targeting practices, that they would be spared retaliatory attacks on their territory as long as they did not employ strategic weapons or attack US territory.'[4] The US would attempt to destroy the Soviet theatre nuclear forces, including the MRBMs [Medium-Range Ballistic Missile], IRBMs [Intermediate-Range Ballistic Missile] and bombers based in the western USSR, the reserve forces, and POL [Petrol, Oil, and Lubricants] and logistic support facilities. Soviet casualties from these attacks could amount to several tens of millions. The prospects for controlling any subsequent strategic exchange would not be auspicious.

In addition to these technical and strategic considerations, the decision-making structures and processes of large national security establishments are quite unsuited to the control of escalatory military operations. The control of escalation requires extreme decisional flexibility: decision-makers must be able to adapt rapidly to changing situations and assessments, and must have the freedom to reverse direction as the unfolding of events dictates; their decision must be presented clearly and coherently, leaving no room for misinterpretation either by subordinates charged with implementation or by the adversary leadership.

These are not attitudes that are generally found in large national security establishments. In neither the United States nor the Soviet Union are these establishments unitary organizations in which decisions are made and executive commands given on the basis of some rational calculation of the national interest. They are made up of a wide range of civilian and military individuals and groups, each with their own interests, preferences, views and perspectives, and each with their own quasi-autonomous political power bases; the decisions which emerge are a product of bargaining, negotiation and compromise between these groups and individuals, rather than of any more rational processes. The heterogeneous nature of the decision-making process leads, in the first instance, to a multiplicity of motives and objectives, not all of which are entirely compatible, and resolving them generally involves the acceptance of compromise language acceptable to each of the contending participants. The clarity of reception among the adversary leadership is consequently generally poor, and the reactions invariably different from the responses initially sought.

The 'fog of war' makes it extremely unlikely that the situation to which NCA believe themselves to be reacting will in fact correspond very closely to the true situation, or that there will be a high degree of shared perception between the respective adversary leaderships. In these circumstances it would be most difficult to terminate a nuclear exchange through mutual agreement between the adversaries at some point short of all-out urban-industrial attacks.

Of course, the pressures to which decision-makers are subject do not come only from within the national security establishment. In the event of a nuclear exchange, the national leadership would also be subject to the pressures of popular feelings and demands.

[3] Alain C. Enthoven, 'US Forces in Europe: How Many? Doing What?', *Foreign Affairs* (vol. 53, no. 3), April 1975. p. 514; Alain C. Enthoven and K. Wayne Smith, *How Much is Enough?: Shaping the Defense Program, 1961-1969*, (New York: Harper and Row, 1971), p. 128.

[4] Harold Brown, *Department of Defense Annual Report Fiscal Year 1981* (29 January 1980), p. 92.

The mood of horror, confusion and hatred that would develop among the population at large as bombs began falling on the Soviet Union and the United States and casualties rose through the millions would inevitably limit the national leaderships' freedom of manoeuvre. Whether the horror would force them to recoil from large-scale attacks on urban-industrial areas or the hatred would engender rapid escalation must remain an open question—but neither mood would be conducive to measured and considered actions.

The likelihood that effective control of a nuclear exchange would be lost at some relatively early point in a conflict calls into question the strategic utility of any preceding efforts to control the exchange. As Colin Gray has argued, it could be extremely dangerous for the United States 'to plan a set of very selective targeting building blocks for prospective rounds one, two and three of strategic force application' while rounds four and five entailed massive urban-industrial strikes.[5] Implementation of such a plan, no matter how controlled the initial rounds, would amount 'in practice, to suicide on the instalment plan'.[6]

The allocation of further resources to improving the survivability and endurance of the strategic command-and-control capabilities cannot substantially alter this situation. Command-and-control systems are inherently more vulnerable than the strategic forces themselves, and, while basic retaliatory commands would always get to the forces eventually, the capability to exercise strict control and co-ordination would inevitably be lost relatively early in a nuclear exchange.

Furthermore, the technical and strategic uncertainties are such that, regardless of the care and tight control which they attempt to exercise, decision-makers could never be confident that escalation could be controlled. Uncertainties in weapons effects and the accuracy with which weapons can be delivered mean that collateral casualties can never be calculated precisely and that particular strikes could look much less discriminating to the recipient than to the attack planner. The uncertainties are especially great with

respect to the operation of particular C³ [Command, Control, and Communications] systems in a nuclear environment. The effects of EMP and transient radiation on electrical and electronic equipment have been simulated on many components but rarely on large systems (such as airborne command posts). Moreover much of the simulation of nuclear effects derives from extrapolation of data generated in the period before atmospheric nuclear tests were banned in 1963.

Given the impossibility of developing capabilities for controlling a nuclear exchange through to favourable termination, or of removing the residual uncertainties relating to controlling the large-scale use of nuclear weapons, *it is likely that decision-makers would be deterred from initiating nuclear strikes no matter how limited or selective the options available to them.* The use of nuclear weapons for controlled escalation is therefore no less difficult to envisage than the use of nuclear weapons for massive retaliation.

Of course, national security policies and postures are not designed solely for the prosecution of war. In both the United States and the Soviet Union, deterring war remains a primary national objective. It is an axiom in the strategic literature that the criteria for deterrence are different from those for war-fighting, and capabilities which would be deficient for one purpose could well be satisfactory for the other.[7] The large-scale investment of resources in command-and-control capabilities, together with high-level official declarations that the United States would be prepared to conduct limited, selective and tightly controlled strategic nuclear strikes (perhaps in support of extended deterrence), could therefore be valuable because they suggest US determination to act in limited ways—the demonstrable problems of control notwithstanding. However, viable deterrent postures require both capabilities and credibility, and it would seem that neither can be assumed to the extent that would be necessary for the concept of controlled nuclear war-fighting to act as a deterrent. Rather than devoting further resources to pursuing the chimera of controlled nuclear war, relatively more attention might be accorded to another means of satisfying the

---

[5] Colin S. Gray, 'Targeting Problems for Central War', *Naval War College Review* (vol. 33, no. 1), January-February 1980, p. 9.

[6] *Ibid.*, p. 7.

[7] See André Beaufre, *Deterrence & Strategy*, (London: Faber & Faber, 1965), p. 24; and Glenn H. Snyder, *Deterrence & Defense: Toward a Theory of National Security*, (Princeton NJ: Princeton University Press, 1961), pp. 3-6.

objectives that limited nuclear options are intended to meet. This is likely, in practice, to mean greater attention to the conditions of conventional deterrence.

QUESTIONS FOR DISCUSSION

1 What is the logic behind the notions of a limited nuclear war and a nuclear war-fighting capacity?

2 What are the distinctions between tactical and strategic nuclear weapons? Would these distinctions be important in wartime?

3 Does PD 59 make the use of nuclear weapons in war more likely?

4 Is it possible to win a nuclear war?

5 Is the use of nuclear weapons ever morally justifiable?

SUGGESTED READINGS

Ericson, John. "The Chimera of Mutual Deterrence." *Strategic Review* **11** (Spring 1978): 11–17.

The Future of Strategic Deterrence: Part I. Adelphi Paper No. **160**. London: International Institute for Strategic Studies, 1980.

Jensen, John W. "Nuclear Strategy: Differences in Soviet and American Thinking." *Air University Review* **30** (March/April 1979): 2–17.

Jervis, Robert. "Deterrence Theory Revisited." *World Politics* **31** (January 1979): 288–324.

——. "Why Nuclear Superiority Does Not Matter?" *Political Science Quarterly* **94** (Winter 1979–1980): 617–633.

Morgan, Patrick M. *Deterrence: A Conceptual Analysis.* Beverly Hills, Calif.: Sage, 1977.

Russett, Bruce, and Bruce G. Blair (eds.). *Progress in Arms Control?* San Francisco: Freeman, 1979.

Smoke, Richard. *War: Controlling Escalation.* Cambridge: Harvard University Press, 1978.

Steiner, Barry H. "On Controlling the Soviet-American Nuclear Arms Competition." *Armed Forces and Society* **5** (Fall 1978): 53–71.

Thaxton, Richard. "Directive Fifty-Nine." *Progressive,* (October 1980.): 36–37.

14   Does NATO Deter Aggression?

YES

Sir John Killick

Is NATO Relevant to the 1980s?

NO

Irving Kristol

Does NATO Exist?

Is NATO Relevant to the 1980s?

Sir John Killick

Asked to define the problems of the next decade, any thinking member of a 'Western' industrialized society would probably list socio-economic and socio-political questions like housing, urban living, education, health and welfare, traffic in drugs, law and order, terrorism, unemployment, recession, inflation and industrial relations; and in the international field, the energy crisis, the North-South dialogue and, conceivably, other raw materials aspects of the world environment. It is by no means self-evident that European security in the traditional sense would feature high on this list, if at all.

Yet, as NATO enters its fourth decade, it is worth considering its relevance to the agenda for the 1980s. It is a truism that NATO has become the victim of its own success. While the Alliance is perhaps taken for granted and accepted as necessary for the foreseeable future, defence spending and military preparedness are seen at best as necessary evils, militating against the allocation of resources to the solution of our other difficulties and in no way making any positive contribution to dealing with them.

The familiar phrases fall easily from the lips of political leaders. In face of the 'Soviet threat' we must not 'lower our guard'. The Alliance stands for 'détente and defence' and we must 'negotiate from strength'. We must strive for 'undiminished security at a lower level of armaments and armed forces'. These propositions are all entirely sound and valid, but what do they mean in practice for those concerned with the day-to-day conduct of affairs in the Alliance?

One naturally starts with the military equation. Here the 'Soviet threat' is perhaps best used as a Staff College term of art, related solely to the observable and quantifiable facts of the Soviet military build-up, which are common knowledge. The essentially speculative and unquantifiable problem of assessing Soviet intentions is another matter. Soviet military writings are not of much assistance. They throw light on how a war might be fought—not on whether the Soviet leadership intends to embark on deliberate aggression. The chances of a military take-over in the Soviet Union are very small, and it should in any case not be assumed that the Soviet military

leadership would go in for high-risk policies. It is true that a new political leadership looms on the horizon. It is no less unpredictable—probably more so—than in the past. The possibility of deliberate aggression, whatever present intentions may be, cannot therefore be ruled out, given the military capability which the new leadership will inherit. But, in Central Europe at least, I find it extremely difficult to envisage any credible or rational political scenario or objective for such a course of action. The flanks may be a different matter, but even there, provided the cohesion of the Alliance holds and there is no question of "decoupling" (whose avoidance is no less vital in this context than in the field of nuclear deterrence), the risk of escalation to general war must surely remain the prime factor governing Soviet decision-making. At all events, in addition to political resolution, the maintenance of an adequate perceived Alliance military capability and strategy remains the sine qua non of deterrence of aggression. I believe that deterrence still holds, and greatly regret the kind of self-doubt which is being expressed on this score, for example in the debate on the ratification of SALT II [Strategic Arms Limitation Treaty]. We should never forget that deterrence is not a matter of convincing Moscow 100 per cent that, if attacked, we will fight, ultimately with all the weapons at our disposal, but of leaving Moscow as near to 100 per cent as possible uncertain that we will not.

SOVIET VULNERABILITY AND ITS IMPLICATIONS

In any case, deliberate aggression is by no means all we have to deter. By common consent, the much more probable threat is of the implied or explicit use of military power for political purposes. Mr. Brezhnev has said 'The Soviet Union does not need war', and indeed it would undoubtedly prefer to attain its objectives without it. It may well be that those objectives do not at present envisage the physical occupation or control of further territory in Europe. I suggest it is not excessively charitable to assume that they arise from a feeling of vulnerability, but not to Western military might or aggressive intentions.

From Sir John Killick, "Is NATO Relevant to the 1980s?" *The World Today* (January 1980): 4–10.

Marxism-Leninism, as practised in the Soviet Union and imposed, so far as possible, throughout the Warsaw Pact and Comecon, is a failure. A failure in economic and agricultural terms, in management and productivity. A failure in ideological terms. Furthermore, the problems looming for the Soviet Union in the 1980s are daunting and liable to demonstrate more sharply than ever the inability of the system to cope. They are well enough known, and include demographic trends which portend both internal political and labour force difficulties; technological backwardness; extraction problems in regard to the exploitation of raw materials, particularly oil; political and economic problems throughout Comecon which reflect the underlying instability of what the Chinese would call Soviet hegemony throughout Eastern Europe. It is worth noting, incidentally, that where individual East European Governments have done better, politically or economically, than the Soviet Union, this has been in areas where Soviet theses of Marxism-Leninism have been modified or discarded.

In this situation, it is only Soviet power that continues to prevail, and the sole decisive manifestation of that power is military. Thus, while in Western society political and economic difficulties have important and adverse effects on military spending, to the leadership in Moscow the exact opposite must appear to be true. That is why the Soviet military effort has remorselessly continued at 11 to 13 percent of GNP, increasing by 5 per cent year on year, despite the "era of détente". It is rather because of, and not in spite of, political and economic failure that the military effort remains necessary, if the destabilizing consequences of failure are to be contained. And they are contained because every East European leadership, not to mention the peoples of the Soviet Union itself, know, from past experiences and without the need for explicit threats, what would happen to them if they sought radical change.

The sense of vulnerability of the system is further exacerbated when, on the very borders of Eastern Europe, there exist states with different political and economic systems with which, in these days of increasing flow of information and knowledge, comparisons can be made. There can be no doubt which the peoples of Eastern Europe would choose, if they had the choice, despite the manifestations of the "crisis of capitalism" for which the propagandists in Moscow are always on the lookout. The Soviet leadership must consequently be concerned to mitigate the effects of this constant comparison. In the ultimate this can only logically involve a desire to achieve the establishment of Marxist-Leninist regimes everywhere, owing allegiance to Moscow as the guiding centre. Such an objective is obviously wildly unrealistic in any foreseeable circumstances, and no student of Soviet affairs would believe that any scenario or master-plan for its achievement exists. But the next best thing—indeed an essential and urgent requirement if a "crisis of Communism" is to be avoided—must be to work for a Western Europe whose military, economic and political strength and potential are weakened to the greatest possible extent. A Europe whose bonds with the United States are loosened and undermined, whose own unity and cohesion are impaired, whose freedom of choice, collective or otherwise, is circumscribed and inhibited by sensitivity to Soviet interests and policies and ultimately intimidated by the perception of Soviet military strength.

This year's "Strategic Survey" of the IISS [International Institute for Strategic Studies] spoke of 'the Soviet Union's traditional tendency to define her security in a way that often implies insecurity for others', adding that 'Perhaps her intentions were defensive, rather than aggressive or expansionist, but the way in which she pursued them often constituted a threat to her neighbors and to those seeking a more stable international order'.[1] This seems to me a very considerable understatement. I eschew words like 'Finlandization', although they have a certain validity. One has only to follow the course of relations between Norway and the Soviet Union on such issues as fisheries and the demarcation of the Continental Shelf to see the point. What could be a cruder illustration than the deliberately-timed firing of rockets into the Barents Sea with the obvious purpose of intimidating the other side in a negotiation? Indeed, I fear we may still have further unpleasant experiences in store with the use of the new Soviet maritime capability in relation to maritime issues like fisheries and navigation.

We have only seen the attempted beginnings of this process. If it is expanded and extended, it will affect our freedom of decision-making in regard to the international, and conceivably even the domestic, issues on our agenda for the 1980s. Even if it reflects a kind of perverted Soviet view of 'deterrence', a sort of defensive reaction to perceived vulnerability, a

---

[1] International Institute for Strategic Studies, *Strategic Survey 1978* (London: IISS, 1979).

search for security on the basis that attack is the best form of defence, politically no less than militarily; and even if this helps us to understand Soviet motives, the process cannot by its very definition be acceptable to us since it ultimately involves our survival in terms of the protection of our legitimate interests as we wish to remain free to define them. It is not a matter of 'Better Red than dead' or the reverse, but of ensuring that we never have to make such a stark choice. It is, above all, a matter of avoiding situations which involve the risk of war by miscalculation.

WESTERN OBJECTIVES

The only defence against this aspect of the 'threat' must be to stand firm politically and to continue to do what we judge best and right—to refuse to be dictated to in terms of what we may not do or even what we must, against our better judgement, do. But the lesson of the 1930s is surely that political fairness will prove an empty bluff or a dangerous invitation to miscalculate unless it is backed by adequate perceived military power. Moscow will continue to pitch its policies and behaviour at the limit of what its calculation of the 'correlation of forces' will prudently bear. In that correlation, the West has the advantage politically, economically, technologically and even ideologically; we must not allow the military element in the equation to become the decisive factor in Soviet favour. NATO is the only vehicle for maintaining the necessary safeguard in military terms as the foundation on which the equally necessary lines of political action can be harmonized to the greatest possible extent—amongst the Europeans themselves, and between them and the Transatlantic partners.

It would be idle to deny that in the present world situation the major threats of instability present themselves outside the area of the North Atlantic Treaty. They are not necessarily instigated by the Soviet Union and its proxies, but are certainly being exploited by them opportunistically, if not always with success. This is not a zero sum game, however, and even where equal and opposite Soviet gain cannot be identified, there is undoubtedly net loss to legitimate Western interests. The Alliance recognized in the Ottawa Declaration that developments outside the Alliance area could have implications for the interests of the Allies. But the fact must be faced that political consensus does not now exist in favour of the expansion of the responsibilities of the Alliance as such. Even if it did, it is surely unrealistic to envisage the

extension of the Treaty boundaries to cover other countries which do not wish to come formally under the Alliance umbrella.

These extra-Alliance situations must therefore remain the responsibility of those member countries, acting individually or in consortium, who are willing and able to take action—political, economic or even military—if, indeed, there are circumstances in the fragmented and confused outer world with which we are now confronted in which military action seems useful or practicable. The Allies concerned will not be acting under a NATO label, but NATO must continue to provide the forum for the monitoring and exchange of information about extra-Alliance developments and their implications, for the explanation by those directly involved of their policies and intentions, and thus ultimately for the generation of broad Alliance understanding and support. Failure in this can lead to divisions and disputes, as happened in 1973, and to the consequent undermining of the cohesion which is vital to the safe and successful conduct of the East-West relationship in the Treaty area itself.

In short, my submission is that NATO is not just *necessary* for the 1980s, as a kind of backdrop against which other problems are grappled with, but directly *relevant* to the handling of them. These other problems have not superseded or become a substitute for the basic issue of European security; they are additional to it and in many ways intertwined with it. The proposition that "détente must be indivisible" is not just an empty phrase. Such progress as has been made in détente, let alone further progress along the road, will be jeopardized if Soviet behaviour in the outside world continues to be inconsistent with co-operation in the Transatlantic area.

DÉTENTE AND SECURITY

As regards the détente process itself, despite current disenchantment it must certainly continue to be the Western objective to try for an improved relationship with the East in which underlying political problems can be solved, as the Harmel Report defined it in 1967. It is also the professed Soviet objective to extend détente, and there is an identifiable Soviet interest in economic and technological cooperation. The East talks also of "expanding détente in the military field", but it is far from clear whether Soviet objectives in this respect match those of the West. Prospects for significant reductions of armaments and armed forces do not look very promising, and perhaps the best we can hope for is the maintenance of a degree of stability through the medium of arms control. We must not forget that the main stated objective of Mr. Brezhnev's *Westpolitik* was 'to draw a line under the results of the Second World War', and in most respects he has achieved this. While nobody should minimize what has been attained in other respects (e.g. Berlin, the German Eastern Treaties) through détente in the 1970s, it would be illusory to extrapolate from this and assume that the agenda for the 1980s offers similar prospects of progress on matters of concern to the West. In any case, technological change, as has been cogently pointed out in Adelphi Papers in 1978,[2] has put the problem of right line arms control and disarmament into very different perspective for the years ahead, because of the difficulty of verification and the multi-mission roles of new weapons systems.

The role of NATO in the field of arms control and disarmament is nevertheless a growing one. It has never been clearer that security is a single coin of which one side is defence posture and the other arms control/disarmament. What is done, or left undone, on one side may have important effects, for good or ill, on the other. The two sides must be looked at as an integrated whole if stability is to be maintained. NATO is the only forum in which the military as well as the political aspects and implications of developments can be properly considered together. This seems bound to be a "growth industry" as a development of the existing role of the Alliance in harmonizing policy on such things as CSCE [Conference on Security and Cooperation in Europe], MBFR [Mutual and Balanced Force Reductions] and, increasingly, SALT, as and when SALT III develops.

So détente itself must be part of the 1980s' agenda, and NATO's role in it could not be more directly relevant. But historical experience tends to show that, during periods of leadership change in the Soviet Union, there is usually a period of some years' consolidation, normally collegial in nature, before a new leader or leaders feel able to embark on meaningful new initiatives in foreign policy. The feeling of vulnerability is enhanced during such periods, and the support of the Soviet military-industrial complex is assured by the continuing and even increased provision of resources to the Soviet armed forces. This may

[2] Christoph Bertram (ed.), *The Future of Arms Control, Part I: Beyond Salt II*, Adelphi Paper No. 141, and Christoph Bertram, *Part II: Arms Control and Technological Change*, AP No. 146 (London: IISS, 1978).

well again be the case, and it would mean that serious negotiation and progress would be delayed for several years. Yet the Soviet military build-up will continue meanwhile, so that when negotiation is resumed from the Soviet side, it will be from the platform of an even greater military capability than that which confronts us today. In the Soviet calculation of the "correlation of forces" this will weigh heavily on the prospects for fruitful progress; a Soviet perception that the West has fallen behind in the preservation of the military balance will only encourage the belief in Moscow that the accretion and exploitation of military power is the course that pays; on the other hand, visible evidence that the West is capable of holding the position will contribute, probably decisively, to the painful and lengthy process of convincing the Soviet leadership that true co-operation and constructive relations are the only sensible course to follow, as a matter of Soviet national interest.

DEFENCE SPENDING

On the face of it, this may seem to militate against arms control and disarmament. That is why some people suggest the *reductio ad absurdum*, particularly with reference to the modernization of the NATO inventory of theatre nuclear weapons, that 'it is ridiculous to introduce new weapons systems in order to take them away'. In fact, that is more or less what must be done if there is to be any incentive for Moscow to negotiate realistically—confronted with the evidence that the Alliance is capable of keeping pace with the Soviet effort.

Very well, others say, but will the cost not ruin our economies and exacerbate our social problems? Certainly, it will be an expensive business, and increasingly so. So is the payment of insurance premiums! But it is not a matter of matching the Soviet Union in percentage of GNP devoted to defence. The Allies need only do fractionally more than they are doing already—albeit probably better than 3 per cent increases in defence budgets, year on year. Even so, practically all of them, save the United States, which is a global power, spend well below 5 per cent of GNP. It is doubtful in the extreme whether savings on defence spending contribute to the solution of domestic problems; that was certainly not the experience of the United States after the ending of the Vietnam war. Defence spending, in fact, makes a certain contribution to economic health, at least in terms of employment. I have never seen it suggested that

Sweden, spending 4 per cent of GNP on defence, is ruining its economy or its social fabric, let alone Yugoslavia, at about 7 per cent. The defence efforts of such European neutrals (who know perfectly well that their national independence is crucially dependent not only on what they do themselves, but on the maintenance of a stable overall military balance in Europe) are surely proof of the fact that, whether we like it or not, the standing and influence of the nation-state in Europe or in the world at large remains a function of its observed power, military no less than economic, political or ideological.

There is perhaps here a final observation which needs to be addressed to Britain. Sitting in Brussels, the headquarters of the EEC as well as NATO, and looking at this sometimes rather too tight little island, one wonders whether it has dawned fully on the British consciousness that the Defence Review of 1974,[3] leaving 95 per cent of our defence effort devoted to NATO, was as significant a historical watershed as our accession to the European Commu-

[3] See A.S.B., "British Defence Review", *The World Today*, April 1975.

nities. It really provided the final answer to Dean Acheson's assertion that we had lost an Empire but not yet found a role. Our national security is no longer a matter of throwing our weight, in the form of some temporary 'expeditionary force', into the European scales to prevent the emergence of a dominant European power. We now have to live permanently with the challenge of Russia, as a global power, and one which we must assume is here to stay. This challenge can only be met by a permanent European, indeed transatlantic, coalition. In committing forces permanently to the continent of Europe, against centuries of historical tradition, we are not just doing the Germans or the Europeans a favour; not just legalistically fulfilling a Brussels Treaty commitment; but defending ourselves as far to the East as possible. Conversely, the defence of these islands is no longer a matter of sole concern to ourselves, since we constitute the Western flank of integrated European defence. Our security is now totally immersed in that of the Alliance in the broadest possible sense—not just as a military matter, but as part of the essential fabric of our policies in East-West relations through the years ahead.

Does NATO Exist?
Irving Kristol

I have not chosen this title out of intellectual perversity or a willful desire to shock or provoke. It is a question that many Americans are only too likely to ask in the course of the 1980s. True, at the moment the opinion polls show that NATO is quite popular among Americans. But this positive response is little more than a vague benevolence towards nations that are understood to be our allies. As the nature and depth of this alliance is put to the test, however, those attitudes will surely change.

Indeed, by putting the title in the form of a question I believe that, in a spirit of moderation, I am giving NATO the benefit of the doubt. For in a very real sense the NATO alliance has already been tested —and has been found wanting. It is my own sad

conviction that, after an initial decade of quite vigorous existence, NATO ceased to be a living reality some years ago. I also anticipate that, sometime in the not too distant future, the appropriate formal funeral services will occur.

In retrospect, one can see that NATO was programmed to self-destruct. As the late Martin Wight acutely remarked: "It may be noted, as a melancholy law of coalitions, that they are designed to avert the last war." NATO was designed as if to avert World War II, the only difference being that (1) it was now the Soviet Union rather than Germany which was to be deterred from aggression against its European neighbors, and (2) the United States was now, from the beginning, a full partner in this coalition. The

From Irving Kristol, "Does NATO Exist?" in Kenneth A. Myers (ed.). *NATO, the Next Thirty Years: The Changing Political, Economic, and Military Setting*. Boulder, Colo.: Westview Press, 1980, pp. 361–371.

lessons of the 1930s were well learned, if somewhat belatedly, and were applied to the 1950s. And because there were genuine resemblances between the situation of Western Europe in the 1930s and 1950s— but only to the degree that there were such resemblances—this response was quite effective.

It is important, however, to note one crucial difference between the hypothetical coalition of the 1930s and the actual coalition of the post-World War II period. This difference involves the nature of the military deterrent. While deterrence in the 1930s involved what we now call "conventional" weaponry, NATO was originally entirely dependent on the strategic nuclear "umbrella" of the United States. This "umbrella," of course, was only aggression-proof to the extent that the United States had a clear superiority over the Soviet Union in strategic nuclear weaponry. The retaliatory threat was simple: if Soviet troops were overtly to move against Western Europe, the Soviet Union would be annihilated. That is "deterrence" with a vengeance.

But as the Soviet Union gradually acquired its own strategic nuclear capability, this mode of deterrence became less and less credible. It then became reasonable to wonder just how much destruction and loss of life the United States would be willing to accept on behalf of Western Europe, in a massive nuclear exchange. And as the Soviet Union moved inexorably toward something approaching strategic nuclear equivalence—in short, as the terms of the equation became steadily less favorable to the United States— the very notion of such "deterrence" became ever more preposterous. In the 1980s, according to practically all military analysts, the strategic nuclear balance will actually have tilted somewhat in favor of the Soviet Union. Under these circumstances, the idea of strategic deterrence will have slid from the merely preposterous to the patently absurd.

It is still the official military doctrine of the United States and NATO that the use of strategic nuclear weapons is not excluded, in a case of Soviet aggression with conventional military forces— or, *a fortiori*, using tactical nuclear weapons—against Western Europe. There may even be American and NATO generals who believe this is so. They, and anyone else who believes it, are living in a world of fantasy. Under no conceivable circumstances—I repeat: under *no* conceivable circumstances—will an American government respond to such Soviet aggression in Western Europe by initiating a strategic nuclear exchange.

That deterrence has ceased to exist, whatever some military men or politicians may officially say. The function of America's strategic nuclear weaponry today is to deter a Soviet first strike against the United States itself—that and nothing but that.

Indeed, it was in implicit recognition of this fact that NATO, in the course of the 1950s and 1960s, began to place an ever greater reliance on *tactical* nuclear weapons. These could inflict such enormous losses on Soviet troops that, even though NATO troops (and civilians) were suffering comparable losses from Soviet tactical nuclear weapons, there would be a genuine deterrent effect. This is certainly a far more credible deterrent than the (by now) empty threat of a strategic nuclear exchange. But one wonders: Just how credible *in fact* is it, now that the Soviets have effective parity (at the least) in such weapons? Here again, the official point of view is so insistent, even adamant, that one suffers twinges of conscience in engaging in private, skeptical speculation. Still, one cannot help but wonder . . .

Let us assume the following, perfectly plausible, scenario: Soviet troops, together with East German troops, move massively against West Germany on several fronts. Given their clear superiority in numbers, as well as in tanks, artillery, etc., they will certainly achieve some breakthroughs. The NATO troops will then, presumably, duly employ their tactical nuclear weapons, inflicting substantial casualties on the enemy. The enemy replies in kind, inflicting large casualties in turn—not only against NATO troops but, inevitably, against some of NATO's urban centers and their civilian population. What then? Will the governments and peoples of Western Europe grit their teeth, fighting on tenaciously in the face of huge casualties and mass suffering, until the Soviets agree to withdraw? Will the NATO nations of Western Europe accept the devastation of their own lands in stoical, heroic, and perhaps ultimately successful resistance to Soviet domination?

The official doctrine is that they will. I, for one, do not believe it, and I have met precious few observers of the European scene who do believe it. It seems clear to me that, as things stand today, such a martial spirit, a spirit of patriotic self-sacrifice, does not exist in any European country (with the possible exception of Switzerland). Yes, initial resistance there certainly would be—this is practically built in to the present military structure of NATO, is well-nigh automatic— and the enemy would doubtless suffer many casualties. But after that initial response? After some NATO divisions have been decimated and some NATO cities ruined? Then, I think, the spirit of resistance will quickly give way to a spirit of negotiation and accommodation. Whereas in the 1930s resistance followed appeasement, in Europe today it is likely to be the other way around.

The reasons why the governments and peoples of Western Europe can, in my opinion, be expected to react in this way has to do with their political experience and formation since World War II. Perhaps one can sum it up, roughly and vaguely, by saying that, in the intervening three decades, the social-democratic temper, the inward-turning politics of compassionate reform, has largely replaced the patriotic temper, the politics of national self-assertion. I shall enlarge on this theme in a moment, but would like first to address myself to the obvious question: If strategic nuclear weapons are no longer a credible deterrent, and if tactical nuclear weapons are a less than convincing deterrent, what *does* deter the Soviet Union from a takeover of Western Europe?[1]

One possible answer is that the Soviet Union simply doesn't realize how feeble a deterrence they are confronted with; they apparently at least half-believe the solemn, official declarations as to our resolute will to resist at any cost. There may be some truth in this. It is possible that the Soviet leaders really do believe that there are "ruling circles" in the West who will fight to the death to maintain their power and prerogatives. (If this is the case, it would be nice to figure out a way to keep this illusion alive.) But it seems to me that there are three better explanations for Soviet behavior, explanations which give more credit to Soviet realism than to Soviet self-deception.

There is, to begin with, the factor of unpredictability. Once any kind of nuclear conflict begins, no one can be absolutely sure how it will evolve. It just might end up with nuclear holocaust. And it just might provoke new and devastating tensions within the

Soviet system itself. The Soviet leadership has generally revealed itself to be cautious and prudent (if persistent) in its aggressiveness. There would seem to be no reason, under the circumstances existing today, for it to engage in the kind of desperate action that overt military aggression in Europe would represent. It may, at some point, feel forced to such action should this appear necessary to preserve the regime. It is hard to imagine it taking such action, however, simply because cold-blooded military calculations imply a favorable outcome.

Perhaps more important is the fact that the Soviet leadership may actually not be much interested in achieving a Soviet-occupied Western Europe. Whatever the paranoid fears of a rearmed and aggressive Germany which once existed, these have surely been dispelled by the progress of Soviet nuclear capability over the past 15 years. And the satellite nations of Eastern Europe, after all, are not exactly secure and profitable assets—one doubts very much that the Soviet leadership is eager to expand this portion of their portfolio. To be sure, it would like to see something approaching the "Finlandization" of Western Europe. But it has many reasons to think that, with patience, this goal can be achieved without resorting to armed conflict. After all, the very existence of Soviet military superiority at all levels, with its prospects for intimidation, is itself a long step in that direction.

A third reason—in my opinion the most important —is that Western Europe itself is no longer so central to the foreign policy of either of the two superpowers. Other areas of the world—the Middle East and Latin America especially—are of at least equal importance to those foreign policies. Some kind of armed confrontation between the United States and the Soviet Union in the Persian Gulf is far more probable than such a confrontation in Central Europe. It would be a wild exaggeration to say that Western Europe has shrunk to insignificance on the world scale where foreign policies are weighed and measured. But what *is* true is that the nations of Western Europe who are America's NATO allies have, since World War II, become increasingly "isolationist." They have no coherent foreign policy that looks beyond the geographical confines of Western Europe. To an ever-increasing degree the foreign policies of the United States and the Soviet Union, as these great powers maneuver for position and advantage, can and do ignore Western Europe as a factor in their reckonings.

---

[1] The United States is now trying to persuade its NATO allies to participate in a Theatre Nuclear Force (TNF)—i.e., missiles whose capability lies somewhere between the tactical and the strategic. As of this writing, the nations of Western Europe are demonstrating a great reluctance to permit any such force to be located on their territories. This suggests to me that a TNF will be but another fictitious deterrent, born of the union of two older fictitious deterrents.

Western Europe, in turn, seems perfectly content that this should be the case.

And it is this situation, I believe, that will guarantee the eventual demise of NATO. Not only are the *military* assumptions on which NATO is based highly problematic today, but the key *foreign policy* assumption—that Western Europe is, as it were, the "world's cockpit," the critical locus of world conflict —is rapidly being emptied of substance. These two assumptions remain as *fables convenus*, duly reiterated by the NATO governments. But no one outside the diplomatic corps takes them seriously anymore. And in this context, a growing divergence between the United States and its NATO allies is inevitable. For the United States is and will—despite the current disarray in Washington—remain a great power, profoundly enmeshed in world politics. The nations of Western Europe, in contrast, seem to have opted out of the strenuous game of world politics in order to pursue the comforts of domestic life.

One might say, in retrospect, that NATO at birth was predestined to suffer such a dissolution. A purely defensive coalition; having neither the intention nor the will to defeat the enemy in case of conflict, nor to achieve larger goals of its own, but only successfully to resist overt military aggression, has assumed a posture which, sooner or later, will give rise to acute tensions and strains. But it is also true that when NATO was formed, it was widely hoped that something more than a contingent, purely defensive coalition had taken shape. There was the thought that the nations of Western Europe together with the United States would develop a "foreign policy for the Free World." That thought has all but vanished from memory.

To a considerable degree, the United States must bear a large share of the responsibility for the way things turned out. We still do not have (in my opinion) an adequate intellectual history of American foreign policy in the postwar world, and it is not entirely clear just how we Americans ended up being so besotted with callow, even childish, notions of what foreign policy is all about. But it is clear that our State Department, over these years, blandly forgot the first principles of foreign policy as these pertain to a great power. Above all it forgot that, to quote Martin Wight once again, "a Foreign Minister is chosen and paid to look after the interests of his country and not be a delegate for the human race." To put it another way: what one might call "the global

point of view" is appropriate enough for the scholar and philosopher, or even for the statesman who is out of office—but not for the statesman in office. Nevertheless, it is this "global point of view," the legacy of a debased and vulgarized Wilsonianism, which to this day permeates our foreign policy establishment, and leads to a posture and actions in foreign affairs which future scholars will have difficulty taking at face value. But, alas, they will be wrong, for in this case, face value conceals nothing more substantial.

One clear sign of this "global point of view" is the way in which the United States has retained a solemn commitment to the United Nations as an international institution, long after it became clear that the majority of the UN's members were and would remain hostile to the basic purposes of American foreign policy. Indeed, it is not too much to say that the idea of NATO having any kind of "foreign policy for the Free World," while its members are loyal members of the United Nations, has become a flat contradiction. This would not be the case if the nations of NATO were disloyal members of the UN, using that institution cynically where and if this served their purposes. This, of course, is exactly the way communist nations or Third World nations use the UN. But they can only do this precisely because the NATO nations, and most especially the United States, do *not* behave with a corresponding cynicism. Were everyone to be purely manipulative of the UN, it would soon cease to exist. That prospect, oddly enough, is regarded as alarming, even unthinkable, by the American foreign policy establishment, which is firmly committed to a "global point of view," to the utopian notion that the ultimate and governing purpose of American foreign policy is to establish a world community of nations all living amiably under the rule of law.

It may be difficult for Europeans, with their long and disenchanting experience in foreign affairs, to believe that our State Department is actually intoxicated with this vision. They are likely to think that it is little more than sanctimonious, self-serving rhetoric. They are quite wrong to think this. Sanctimonious it may be, self-serving it is not. Indeed, all too often it is self-destructive.

Nothing exemplifies this better than the Suez imbroglio of 1956, when the United States, having to choose between the ideals of the United Nations and the reality of NATO, firmly and disastrously chose the former. I am convinced that this incident was the turning point in the history of NATO, and perhaps even a watershed in the diplomatic history of this century. Until that point, it was possible to think that NATO, for all the original flaws in its conception, might yet develop into an authentic force in world affairs. After the event, that prospect could not seriously be entertained.

Obviously one cannot know with any assurance what the world would be like today if the United States had not frustrated the Anglo-French occupation of the Suez Canal. Perhaps such an occupation could not have endured for long, in any case. Or perhaps it could have—and we might have been spared the 1967 Israeli-Arab conflict, OPEC, and sundry other unfortunate happenings. But one thing is clear: after Suez, the idea of a NATO foreign policy, one applicable to troubled areas of the world as well as to the defense of Western Europe, had vanished from the realm of possibility. What survived is the actuality of today: an American foreign policy that tries to cope, on its own, with noxious eruptions all over the globe, and a Western Europe only too anxious to avoid overseas responsibilities or even involvement, whose foreign policy has degenerated into a desperate reliance on the "NATO shield" to protect it against the Soviet Union, while moving toward nervous appeasement of all other enemies everywhere else. I note that the Atlantic Institute has called for a "new partnership" between NATO and OPEC—one hardly knows whether to laugh or cry at such hypocrisy.

It may be that this decline of Western Europe as a force in world affairs, even if the United States had not provided such inadequate leadership, was inevitable—and there are doubtless numerous observers who, without hesitation, would be happy to give us an appropriate philosophic explanation for the "decline of the West." The trouble with such explanations, however, is that they mystify more than they explain. Anyone who, looking at Western Europe after World War II, could be impressed mainly by signs of decline would have to be working with a very peculiar notion of "decline." Never had Western Europe shown more rapid economic growth accompanied by significant population growth—the two indicators one ordinarily looks at first when discussing national decline. Even today, Western Europe as a whole possesses the economic and demographic preconditions for matching the Soviet Union in conventional military strength, thereby placing on the latter the risk of first-use of nuclear weapons—a risk it is not

likely to underestimate. These same preconditions make it possible for Europe as a whole, in the abstract, to rank as a great power. What is lacking is, quite simply, the motivation.

I have already referred to the "social democratization" of Western Europe—and to a far lesser degree, of the United States as well—as explaining the absence of a will to self-assertion. By this I mean the increasingly intense focus on satisfying the demands of a "risk aversive" society, demands which in themselves are natural enough but which are magnified many times over by politics that inflames them even as it seeks to satisfy them. More and more, the politics of Western European nations centers on the provision of more complex and expensive social services, more complex and expensive subsidies to practically every group and subgroup, not merely to those whom we have conventionally deemed to be "needy." All political parties, and not only those which designate themselves as social-democratic, seem to be captive (in varying degrees) to this conception of what national politics is all about. Among contemporary European leaders, only Charles de Gaulle had a vision that rose above this level of prosaic domesticity—the nation as one vast household, whose daily problems have now been transformed into the stuff of politics. But he, most unfortunately, thought that France alone, not Western Europe in coalition, could re-emerge as a major power. This was and is a chimera. Had he been able to think in European terms, had he been able to bring himself to imagine a strong NATO consisting of European powers alone, his anti-Americanism would have served a positive end—one, indeed, that would have suited American ends (in spite of American objections) better than the NATO that survives today. His legacy, however, is merely a France which indulges in the rhetoric of national pride and power, but which in international affairs engages merely in independent strategies of appeasement.

One hears it said that this "social-democratization" of politics—the movement from a mere welfare state to a truly paternalistic (or maternalistic?) state—is an inevitable end product of democracy itself, and that it would have been futile to contemplate any other destiny for the Western democracies. Perhaps. Or perhaps this is a rationale for ideologists whose utopian vision of a good society has no place for foreign policy, with all its moral ambiguities. (It is surely no accident that one cannot even mention a socialist work on foreign policy worth the reading. Socialism in any community is supposed to conquer the hearts and minds of men, everywhere, simply by its inspiring example.) Or perhaps it is our democratic politicians, as distinct from our democratic peoples, who prefer this type of political order, since it offers seemingly endless opportunities for quarrelsome self-advancement. I myself think there is much to be said in favor of this last thesis. After all, at the time of Suez it was not the British or French people who suffered a failure of nerve, but their political establishments. And while it is often said that a democratic people will almost always incline toward a higher budget for social services and a lower budget for military expenditures, it is remarkable how infrequently they are ever candidly offered such a choice. Of course, no one will vote for higher military expenditures unless he perceives ways in which these expenditures are likely to be put to productive use. It may well be that, so far from an acceptable level of military expenditures defining one's foreign policy, it is the nature of one's foreign policy that sets limits to the acceptable level of military expenditures.

In any case, there can be little question that the democracies of Western Europe seem today to be far more interested in relatively marginal increments in "welfare" than in playing any significant role in world affairs. The impulse toward the welfare state, in its origins very naturally and properly seeking a program of collective insurance for all citizens in a dynamic, often turbulent, if affluent society, has degenerated into a fierce internal struggle between proliferating interest groups for particular advantage, a struggle usually fought under the banner of "equality." The economic consequences are already highly visible: a rate of taxation that frustrates economic incentives, and an inexorable decline in productivity and economic growth—the same thing, really—so that each new generous gesture can be financed only by inflation. This, in turn, results in collective impoverishment which eventually makes every particular gain more and more illusory. It is not the case, as some lament, that this kind of "welfare-state politics" transforms life in a liberal democracy from a game in which, in the longer run, everyone (as a consequence of economic growth) wins (if to unequal degrees), to a zero-sum game in which there are arrogant winners and embittered losers. It transforms liberal democracy into a process of conflict in which everyone loses, although unequally.

And the political consequences are predictable. So far from achieving greater social and political stability, accompanied by more universal tranquility, "social-democratization" generates discontent, cynicism, and "alienation" among the citizenry. Those of us of a certain age can easily remember the hopes, which we may have shared, for a new and better world that accompanied the impulse to reform after World War II. The reforms have been effected, and the reality is disillusioning. This has a terribly important implication which we are only now beginning to perceive: *modern social democracy is an inherently unstable system.* It generates a momentum for "equality"—in the bizarre sense of special privileges for all—which, unless firmly controlled, creates an overbearing, bureaucratic state confronting a restless and "ungrateful" citizenry. And such firm control appears extraordinarily difficult to attain, except intermittently for relatively brief periods.

So the nations of NATO and Western Europe—social-democracies all, in their different ways—are at the point of realizing that they will have to drift either to the "Left" or to the "Right" (to use the conventional terminology which is as indispensable as it can be confusing). This realization has already spread so rapidly in the leading NATO nation, the United States, that even the American government of today, which when elected two years ago had expected to proceed along familiar social-democratic lines, finds itself out of phase with a popular opinion that is moving massively to the "Right." It is trying somewhat desperately (if most reluctantly and ineffectually) to catch up.

As it pertains to foreign policy, I would say that this shift of American opinion represents the initial stages in the burgeoning of a new American nationalism. It is "new" in a crucial respect: it is in the process of transcending the older isolationist-internationalist polarity that has hitherto established the parameters for all controversies over foreign policy. Oddly enough—odd certainly by European standards—it is the isolationist current of thought that has always been nationalistic in temper, while the internationalists have always operated with the "global point of view." The new nationalism, however, is based on the proposition that the United States should be *the* major and most influential world power, and as it gathers ideological momentum—some would say *if*, I venture to say *as*—it is going to place a strain on NATO which it can hardly cope with.

Thus, the United States is not only now increasing

its military budget (over the objections of an administration which hangs grimly on to an enfeebled version
of the older "internationalist" conception of America's role in the world), it is also now forming, at the
insistence of Congress and the military, something
called a "unilateral force"—a small army of 100,000
rigorously trained men with a "logistics tail" that will
permit it to operate anywhere in the world
independently of support from any existing ally. One
would have to be maddened with optimism to think
that no occasion will arise—in the Middle East, the
Indian Ocean, Africa, perhaps South America, perhaps even Southern Europe—for this force to be
used. And what happens to NATO when it is used,
when it is engaged in combat somewhere, with someone? If, as now seems most probable, our European
allies simply stay aloof, discreetly approving or sullen-
ly disapproving, what will the consequences be? One
certain consequence, I predict, would be overwhelming support in Congress and in public opinion for the
removal of American troops from Western Europe.
Such a movement of opinion could already be dis-
cerned during the Vietnam War. Another such situation and it will be irresistible. Indeed, NATO officials
are already quietly discussing the mechanisms whereby the United States may be given "permission" to
withdraw its troops "temporarily," in case of need.
But no one is going to be asking their permission.

The message for Western Europe is clear: *il faut
choisir*. If American military operations abroad are
executed entirely by a "unilateral force," a corresponding unilateral foreign policy will emerge. From
having been the centerpiece of American foreign
policy, NATO will become an afterthought, and then
a mere memory. Not that the United States will ever
repudiate a very keen interest in the defense of
Western Europe. But the European partners in
NATO will discover the partnership to have been
dissolved, and that they are now allies of convenience
—"client states"—on the order of South Korea, let us
say. And unless they sharply increase their own
defense expenditures and efforts—again, let us say, to
the South Korean level—they could end up as allies of
inconvenience. It is also worth noting that, though
the United States is committed in a general way to the
defense of South Korea against aggression from the
North, it is most definitely *not* committed to the initial
use of nuclear weapons in such a defense. Presumably
that would also hold true in the case of Western
Europe. There are some who would claim that, de
facto, it already holds true.

I should like to make it clear that I am *not* saying
that Western Europe faces the choice between becoming "client-states" of the United States or of the
Soviet Union. There is indeed a third alternative: for
Western Europe to begin thinking of itself as a world
power in its own right, and to take the painful steps
necessary to make that thought a reality. The first
such step is to move toward parity with the Soviet
Union in conventional military strength. The second
is to begin thinking (once again) in terms of world
power and world politics, as against merely Western
European power and politics. It is possible that such
a new "great power" will so define its interests,
and conduct its foreign policy, in a way that occasionally makes the United States unhappy. *Tant
pis*. The world, in my opinion, would still be much
better off if Western Europe were to become an independent and effectual force in world affairs. For
these nations share a legacy of civilization that, however shaky it may be at the moment, the world very
much needs.

QUESTIONS FOR DISCUSSION

1 Does NATO promote Western security?
2 What impact do nuclear weapons have on the unity
of NATO?
3 What relationship should exist between United
States military strategy and planning and NATO?
4 Would disarmament prospects improve if NATO
were disbanded?
5 Have the conditions that shaped the formation of
NATO changed in such a way as to destroy the
justification for perpetuating NATO?

SUGGESTED READINGS

Aron, Raymond. *In Defense of Decadent Europe*.
South Bend, Ind.: Regnery/Gateway, 1979.
Bertram, Christoph (ed.). *New Conventional Weap-
ons and East-West Security*. New York: Praeger,
1979.
Buchan, Alastair F. "The United States and the
Security of Europe," in David S. Landes (ed.).
Western Europe: The Trials of Partnership. Lexing-
ton, Mass.: Lexington Books, 1977, chap. 9.
Davis, Jacquelyn K. "Theater-Nuclear Force Moder-
nization and NATO's Flexible Response Strategy."
*The Annals of the Academy of Political and Social
Science* **457** (September 1981): 78–87.

DePorte, A. W. *Europe Between the Superpowers: The Enduring Balance*. New Haven: Yale University Press, 1979.

Frye, Alton. "Nuclear Weapons in Europe: No Exit from Ambivalence." *Survival* (May/June 1980): 98–106.

Greenwood, David. "NATO's Three Per Cent Solution." *Survival* (November/December 1981): 252–260.

Grosser, Alfred. *The Western Alliance: European-American Relations Since 1945*. New York: Continuum, 1980.

U.S. Congress. House of Representatives. *United States-West European Relations in 1980*. Hearings before the Subcommittee on Europe and the Middle East of the Committee on Foreign Affairs, 96th Cong., 2d Sess., 1980.

Windsor, Philip. *Germany and the Western Alliance: Lessons from the 1980 Crises*. London: International Institute for Strategic Studies, 1981.

15   Is Terrorism an Effective Political Instrument?

YES

Paul Johnson

The Seven Deadly Sins of Terrorism

NO

Walter Laqueur

The Futility of Terrorism

The Seven Deadly Sins of Terrorism
Paul Johnson

Before identifying the correct approach to the terrorist problem, let us look at the wrong one. The wrong
approach is to see terrorism as one of many symptoms
of a deep-seated malaise in our society, part of a
pattern of violence which includes juvenile delinquen-
cy, rising crime rates, student riots, vandalism and
football hooliganism, and which is to be attributed to
the shadow of the H-bomb, rising divorce rates,
inadequate welfare services and poverty. This analysis usually ends in the meaningless and defeatist
conclusion that society itself is to blame: 'We are all
guilty.'

The truth is, international terrorism is not part of a
generalised human problem. It is a specific and identifiable problem on its own; and because it is specific
and identifiable, because it can be isolated from the
context which breeds it, it is a remediable problem.
That is the first point to get clear.

But to say it is remediable is not to underestimate
the size and danger of the problem. On the contrary:
it is almost impossible to exaggerate the threat which
terrorism holds for our civilisation because, unlike
many other current threats, it is not being contained.
Quite the reverse, it is increasing steadily, and one
reason is that very few people in the civilised world—
governments, parliaments, journalists and the public
generally—take terrorism seriously enough.

Most people, lacking an adequate knowledge of
history, tend to underestimate the fragility of a civilisation. They do not appreciate that civilisations fall as
well as rise, that they can be and have been, destroyed
by malign forces. In our recoverable history, there
have been at least three Dark Ages. One occurred in
the third millennium B.C., and smashed the civilisation of the Egyptian Old Kingdom—the culture which
built the pyramids. Another occurred towards the end
of the second millennium B.C., and destroyed Myce-
naean Greece, Minoan Crete, the Hittite Empire, and
much else. We are more familiar with the third, which
destroyed the Roman Empire in the West in the fifth
century A.D.: it took Europe 800 years to recover, in
terms of organisation, technical skills and living standards. The great catastrophes had varying causes, but
there was a common factor in all of them. They

occurred when the spread of metals technology, and
the availability of raw materials, enabled the forces of
barbarism to equal or surpass the civilised powers in
the quality and quantity of their weapons, for in the
last resort, civilisations stand or fall, not by covenants, but by the sword.

ENEMIES OF SOCIETY

Edward Gibbon, at the end of his great book, *The
Decline and Fall of the Roman Empire*, wrote: 'The
savage nations of the globe are the common enemies
of civilised society, and we may well inquire with
anxious curiosity whether Europe is still threatened
with a repetition of those calamities which formerly
oppressed the arms and institutions of Rome.' Writing in the 1780s, on the threshold of the Industrial
Revolution, Gibbon thought he could answer his own
question with a reasonably confident negative. He
rightly estimated the strength of the civilised world to
be increasing, and he believed the scientific and
rational principles on which that strength was based
were becoming more firmly established with every
year that passed.

Now nearly 200 years later, we cannot be so sure.
The principles of objective science and human reason,
the notion of the rule of law, the paramountcy of
politics over force, are everywhere under growing
and purposeful challenge; and the forces of savagery
and violence, which constitute this challenge, are
becoming bolder, more numerous and, above all,
better armed. The arms available to terrorists, the
skills with which they use them and, not least, the
organisational techniques with which these weapons
and skills are deployed, are all improving at a fast and
accelerating rate—a rate much faster than the countermeasures available to civilised society.

Take one example—Northern Ireland. In August
last year members of the Provisional IRA killed Lord
Mountbatten and other members of his party, and, in
another attack that same day, killed 18 British soldiers. They suffered no casualties themselves, a pattern of success which is all too familiar. There are two
reasons for this. The first is the replacement of the old

From Paul Johnson, "The Seven Deadly Sins of Terrorism," *NATO Review* (October 1980): 28–33.

amateurish IRA structure by what the BBC Defence Correspondent has called, 'a modern clandestine force, well-organised and well-equipped, with a classic cellular structure which is strong and almost impossible to penetrate or break.' During a single night, for instance, they were able to plant 49 bombs in 22 towns throughout Northern Ireland which, again according to the BBC, 'must have meant staff work of a very high standard.' The second is that the range and quality of weapons now used by Irish terrorists are becoming very formidable.

These menacing improvements in weaponry and organisation have been brought about by the international availability of terrorist support, supply and training services. Terrorism is no longer a purely national phenomenon, which can be destroyed at national level. It is an international offensive—an open and declared war against civilisation itself—which can only be defeated by an international alliance of the civilised powers.

To the argument that terrorists are not enemies of civilisation in that they are often idealists pursuing worthy ultimate aims, I would answer that the terrorist can never be an idealist, and that the objects sought can never justify terrorism. For what is terrorism? It is the deliberate, systematic murder, maiming and menacing of the innocent to inspire fear in order to gain political ends. By this definition, the impact of terrorism, not merely on individuals, not merely on single nations, but on humanity as a whole is intrinsically evil, necessarily evil and wholly evil. It is so for a number of demonstrable reasons—what I call the Seven Deadly Sins of Terrorism.

EXALTATION OF VIOLENCE

First, terrorism is the deliberate and cold-blooded exaltation of violence over all forms of political activity. The modern terrorist does not employ violence as a necessary evil but as a desirable form of action. There is a definite intellectual background to the present wave of terrorism. It springs not only from the Leninist and Trotskyist justification of violence, but from the post-war philosophy of violence derived from Nietzsche through Heidegger, and widely popularised by Sartre, his colleague and disciple. No one since 1945 has influenced young people more than Sartre and no one has done more to legitimise violence on the Left. It was Sartre who adapted the linguistic technique, common in German philosophy,

of identifying certain political frameworks as the equivalent of 'violence,' thus justifying violent correctives or responses. In 1962 he said: 'For me, the essential problem is to reject the theory according to which the Left ought not to answer with violence.' Note his words: not 'a problem,' but 'the essential problem.'

Some of those influenced by Sartre went much further—notably Franz Fanon. His most influential work, *Les Damnés de la Terre*, which has a preface by Sartre, has probably played a bigger part in spreading terrorism in the Third World than any other tract. Violence is presented as liberation, a fundamental Sartrean theme. For a black man, writes Sartre in his preface, 'to shoot down a European is to kill two birds with one stone, to destroy an oppressor and the man he oppresses at the same time.' By killing, the terrorist is born again—free. Fanon preached that violence is a necessary form of social and moral regeneration for the oppressed. 'Violence alone,' he writes, 'violence committed by the people, violence organised and educated by its leaders, makes it possible for the masses to understand social truths and gives the key to them.' The notion of 'organised and educated violence,' conducted by elites is, of course, the formula for terrorism. Fanon goes further: 'At the level of individuals, violence is a cleansing force. It frees [the oppressed] from his inferiority complex and from his despair and inaction.'

It is precisely this line of thought, that violence is positive and creative, which enables the terrorists to perform the horrifying acts for which they are responsible. Of course the same argument—almost word for word—was used by Hitler, who repeated endlessly, 'Virtue lies in shedding blood.' Hence the first deadly sin of terrorism is the moral justification of murder not merely as a means to an end but for its own sake.

MORAL INSTINCTS SUPPRESSED

The second is the deliberate suppression of the moral instincts in man. Terrorist organisers have found that it is not enough to give their recruits intellectual justifications for murder: the instinctive humanity in us all has to be systematically blunted, or else it rejects such sophistry. In the Russia of the 1870s and 1880s, the Neznavhalie terror group favoured what it called 'motiveless terror' and regarded any murder as a 'progressive action.' Once indiscriminate terror is adopted, the group rapidly suffers moral dis-integration—indeed the abandonment of any system of moral criteria becomes an essential element in its training. The point is brilliantly made in Dostoevsky's great anti-terrorist novel, *The Possessed*, by one of the gangsters, who argues that the terror-group can be united only by fear and moral depravity: "Persuade four members of the circle to murder a fifth," he says, "on the excuse that he is an informer, and you will at once tie them all up in one knot by the blood you have shed. They will be your slaves." This technique is undoubtedly used by some terror groups today, on the assumption that neither man nor woman can be an effective terrorist so long as he or she retains the moral elements of a human personality. One might say, then, that the second deadly sin of terrorism is a threat not merely to civilisation but to humanity as such.

REJECTION OF POLITICS

The third, following directly from the first two, is the rejection of politics as the normal means by which communities resolve conflicts. To terrorists, violence is not a political weapon, to be used *in extremis*: it is a substitute for the entire political process. Middle East terrorist groups, the IRA, the Bader-Meinhoff gang, Red Armies or Brigades in Japan, Italy and elswhere, have never shown any desire to engage in the demo-cratic political process. The notion that violence is a technique of last resort, to be adopted only if all other attempts to obtain justice have failed, is rejected by them. In doing so, they reject the mainstream of civilised thought, based, like so much of our political grammar, on the social-contract theorists of the 17th century. Hobbes and Locke rightly treated violence as the antithesis of politics, a form of action characteris-tic of the archaic realm of the state of nature. They saw politics as an attempt to create a tool to avoid barbarism and make civilisation possible: politics makes violence not only unnecessary but unnatural to civilised man. Politics is an essential part of the basic machinery of civilisation, and in rejecting politics, terrorism seeks to make civilisation unworkable.

SPREADS TOTALITARIANISM

Terrorism, however, is not neutral in the political battle. It does not, in the long run, tend towards anarchy: it tends towards despotism. The fourth

deadly sin of terrorism is that it actively, systematical-ly and necessarily assists the spread of the totalitarian state. The countries which finance and maintain the international infrastructure of terrorism—which give terrorists refuge and havens, training-camps and bases, money, arms and diplomatic support as a matter of deliberate state policy—are, without excep-tion, totalitarian states. The governments of all these states rule by military and police force. The notion that terrorism is opposed to the "repressive forces" in society is false—indeed, it is the reverse of the truth. International terrorism, and the various terrorist movements it serves, are entirely dependent on the continuing good will and active support of police states. The terrorist is sustained by the totalitarian paraphernalia of tanks, torture, and the secret police. The terrorist is the direct beneficiary of the Gulag Archipelago and everything it stands for.

ENEMY OF DEMOCRACY

Which brings us to the fifth deadly sin. International terrorism poses no threat to the totalitarian state. That kind of state can always defend itself by judicial murder, preventative arrest, torture of prisoners and suspects, and complete censorship of terrorist activi-ties. It does not have to abide by the rule of law or any other consideration of humanity or morals. Hence, the fifth deadly sin is that terrorism can destroy a democracy, as it destroyed the Lebanon, but it cannot destroy a totalitarian state. All it can do is to trans-form a nation struggling towards progress and legality into a nightmare of oppression and violence.

EXPLOITS FREEDOM

This leads us to another significant generalisation about terrorism. Its ultimate base is in the totalitarian worlds—that is where its money, training, arms and protection come from. But at the same time, it can only operate effectively in the freedom of a liberal civilisation. Terrorists are the advance scouts of the totalitarian armies. The sixth deadly sin of terrorism is that it exploits the apparatus of freedom in liberal societies, and thereby endangers it.

In meeting the threat of terrorism, a free society must arm itself. But that very process of arming itself against the danger within threatens the freedoms, decencies and standards which make it civilised. Ter-rorism then—and it is this we must get across to intelligent young people who may be tempted to sympathise with it—is a direct and continuous threat to all the protective devices of a free society. It is a threat to the freedom of the press and television to report without restraints. It is a threat to the rule of law, necessarily damaged by emergency legislation and special powers. It is a threat to *habeas corpus*, to the continuous process of humanising the legal code and civilising our prisons. It is a threat to any system designed to curb excesses by the police or prison authorities or any other restraining force in society.

INDUCEMENT TO SUICIDE

Yet the seventh deadly sin of terrorism operates, paradoxically, in the reverse direction—and is yet more destructive. A free society which reacts to terrorism by invoking authoritarian methods of repression necessarily damages itself. But an even graver danger—and a much more common one today—is of free societies, in their anxiety to avoid authoritarian excesses, *failing* to arm themselves against the terrorist threat, and so abdicating their responsibility to uphold the law. The terrorists succeed when they provoke oppression: but they triumph when they are met with appeasement.

The seventh and deadliest sin of terrorism therefore is that it saps the will of a civilised society to defend itself. We have seen it happen. We find governments negotiating with terrorists—negotiations aimed not at destroying or disarming them, for such negotiations may sometimes be necessary—but negotiations whose natural and inevitable result is to concede part of the terrorists' demands. We find governments providing ransom money to terrorists— or permitting private individuals to do so, even assisting the process whereby such funds reach terrorist hands. We find governments releasing convicted criminals in response to terrorist demands, according terrorists the status, rights and advantages, and above all, the legitimacy, of negotiating partners. We find governments conceding to terrorist convicts the official and privileged status of political prisoners. We find governments yielding to demands—an invariable and well-organised part of terrorist strategy—for official enquiries, or international investigations, into alleged ill-treatment of terrorist suspects or convicts. We find newspapers and television networks—often, indeed, state networks—placing democratic governments and the terrorists on a level of moral equality. We find governments failing, time and again, in their duty to persuade the public—that terrorists are not misguided politicians: they are criminals, extraordinary criminals indeed, in that they are exceptionally dangerous to us all and pose a unique threat not merely to the individuals they murder without compunction but to the whole fabric of society—but criminals just the same.

In short, the seventh and deadliest sin of terrorism is its attempt to induce civilisation to commit suicide.

These seven mortal dangers must be seen in the light of the fact that terrorism is not a static threat but a dynamic one. Not only is the international infrastructure of terrorism becoming better organised and more efficient, but the terrorists' own sights are being raised by their successes. We must expect and prepare for yet further improvements in the types of weapons which they deploy. We cannot rule out the possibility that terrorists will obtain access to nuclear devices or even to their production process.

Terrorism, in short, is no longer a marginal problem, something to be contained and lived with, a nuisance. It is a real, important and growing threat to the peace and stability of all legitimate states—that is, all those states which live under the rule of law. It is an international threat—therein lies its power. That power can only be destroyed or emasculated when there is international recognition of its gravity and international action by the united forces of civilisation to bring it under control.

The Futility of Terrorism
Walter Laqueur

A few days before Christmas a group of terrorists broke into the OPEC building in Vienna; the rest of the story is still fresh in the memory and need not be retold. Coming so soon after the attacks of the South Moluccan separatists in the Netherlands, the incident occasioned great hand-wringing and tooth-grinding among editorialists all over the globe with dire comments about the power concentrated in the hands of a few determined individuals and harrowing predictions as to what all this could mean for the future. Because the significance of terrorism is not yet widely understood, such a nine days' wonder could be regarded as an action of world-shaking political consequence. Yet, when the shooting was over, when the terrorists had vanished from the headlines and the small screen, it appeared that they were by no means nearer to their aims. It was not even clear what they had wanted. Their operation in Vienna had been meticulously prepared, but they seemed to have only the haziest notion of what they intended to achieve. They broadcast a document which, dealing with an obscure subject and written in left-wing sectarian language, might just as well have been broadcast in Chinese as far as the average Austrian listener was concerned.

The Vienna terrorists claimed to be acting on behalf of the Palestinian revolution, but only some of them were Arabs and it is not certain that there was a single Palestinian among them. Their leader was the notorious "Carlos," a Venezuelan trained in Moscow and supported by Cuban intelligence in Paris—a branch of the Soviet KGB. Yet the operation, according to the Egyptian press, was paid for by Colonel Qaddafi. The working of modern transnational terrorism with its ties to Moscow and Havana, its connections with Libya and Algeria, resemble those of a multinational corporation; whenever multinational corporations sponsor patriotic causes, the greatest of caution is called for.

Similar caution is required if one is to avoid exaggerating the importance of terrorism today. It is true that no modern state can guarantee the life and safety of all of its citizens all of the time, but it is not true that terrorists somehow acquire "enormous power" (to quote our editorialists) if they kidnap a few dozen citizens, as in Holland, or even a dozen oil ministers, as in Vienna. If a mass murder had happened in Vienna on that Sunday before Christmas, long obituaries of Sheik Yamani and his colleagues would have been published—and within twenty-four hours, ambitious and competent men in Tehran and Caracas, in Baghdad and in Kuwait, would have replaced them. Terrorists and newspapermen share the naive assumption that those whose names make the headlines have power, that getting one's name on the front page is a major political achievement. This assumption typifies the prevailing muddled thinking on the subject of terrorism.

In recent years urban terrorism has superseded guerrilla warfare in various parts of the world. As decolonization came to an end there was a general decline in guerrilla activity. Furthermore, rural guerrillas learned by bitter experience that the "encirclement of the city by the countryside" (the universal remedy advocated by the Chinese ten years ago) was of doubtful value if four-fifths (or more) of the population are city dwellers, as happens to be the case in most Western industrialized countries—and quite a few Latin-American countries too. With the transfer of operations from the countryside to the cities, the age of the "urban guerrilla" dawned. But the very term "urban guerrilla" is problematical. There have been revolutions, civil wars, insurrections, and coups d'etat in the cities, but hardly ever guerrilla warfare. That occurs in towns only if public order has completely collapsed, and if armed bands roam freely. Such a state of affairs is rare, and it never lasts longer than a few hours, at most a few days. Either the insurgents overthrow the government in a frontal assault, or they are defeated. The title "urban guerrilla" is in fact a public-relations term for terrorism; terrorists usually dislike being called terrorists, preferring the more romantic guerrilla image.

There are basic differences between the rural guerrilla and the urban terrorist: mobility and hiding are the essence of guerrilla warfare, and this is impossible in towns. It is not true that the slums (and the rich

From Walter Laqueur, "The Futility of Terrorism," *Harper's Magazine* (March 1976): 99–105.

quarters) of the big cities provide equally good sanctuaries. Rural guerrillas operate in large units and gradually transform themselves into battalions, regiments, and even divisions. They carry out political and social reforms in "liberated zones," openly propagandize, and build up their organizational network. In towns, where this cannot be done, urban terrorists operate in units of three, four, or five; the whole "movement" consists of a few hundred, often only a few dozen, members. This is the source of their operational strength and their political weakness. For while it is difficult to detect small groups, and while they can cause a great deal of damage, politically they are impotent. A year or two ago anxious newspaper readers in the Western world were led to believe that the German Baader-Meinhof group, the Japanese Red Army, the Symbionese Liberation Army, and the British Angry Brigade were mass movements that ought to be taken very seriously indeed. Their "communiqués" were published in the mass media; there were earnest sociological and psychological studies on the background of their members; their "ideology" was analyzed in tedious detail. Yet these were groups of between five and fifty members. Their only victories were in the area of publicity.

TERRORIST MYTHS

The current terrorist epidemic has mystified a great many people, and various explanations have been offered—most of them quite wrong. Only a few will be mentioned here:

Political terror is a new and unprecedented phenomenon It is as old as the hills, only the manifestations of terror have changed. The present epidemic is mild compared with previous outbreaks. There were more assassinations of leading statesmen in the 1890s in both America and Europe, when terrorism had more supporters, than at the present time. Nor is terrorist doctrine a novelty. In 1884 Johannes Most, a German Social Democrat turned anarchist, published in New York a manual, *Revolutionary (Urban) Warfare*, with the subtitle "A Handbook of Instruction Regarding the Use and Manufacture of Nytroglycerine, Dynamite, Guncotton, Fulminating Mercury, Bombs, Arson, Poisons, etc." Most pioneered the idea of the letter bomb and argued that the liquidation of "pigs" was not murder

because murder was the willful killing of a human being, whereas policemen did not belong in this category.

It is sometimes argued that guerrilla and terrorist movements in past ages were sporadic and essentially apolitical. But this is not so; the Russian anarchists of the last century were as well organized as any contemporary movement, and their ideological and political sophistication was, if anything, higher. The same goes for the guerrilla wars of the nineteenth century. The guerrilla literature published in Europe in the 1830s and 1840s is truly modern in almost every respect. It refers to "bases," "liberated areas," "protracted war" as well as the gradual transformation of guerrilla units into a regular army. The basic ideas of Mao and Castro all appeared at least a hundred years ago.

Terrorism is left-wing and revolutionary in character Terrorists do not believe in liberty or egality or fraternity. Historically, they are elitists, contemptuous of the masses, believing in the historical mission of a tiny minority. It was said about the Tupamaros that one had to be a Ph.D. to be a member. This was an exaggeration but not by very much. Their manifestos may be phrased in left-wing language, but previous generations of terrorists proclaimed Fascist ideas. Nineteenth-century European partisans and guerrillas fighting Napoleon were certainly right-wing. The Spanish guerrilleros wanted to reintroduce the Inquisition, the Italian burned the houses of all citizens suspected of left-wing ideas. Closer to our own period, the IRA and the Macedonian IMRO at various times in their history had connections with Fascism and Communism. The ideology of terrorist movements such as the Stern gang and the Popular Front for the Liberation of Palestine encompasses elements of the extreme Left and Right. Slogans change with intellectual fashions and should not be taken too seriously. The real inspiration underlying terrorism is a free-floating activism that can with equal ease turn right or left. It is the action that counts.

Terrorism appears whenever people have genuine, legitimate grievances. Remove the grievance and terror will cease The prescription seems plausible enough, but experience does not bear it out. On the level of abstract reasoning it is, of course, true that there would be no violence if no one had a grievance or felt frustration. But in practice there will always be disaffected, alienated, and highly aggressive people claiming that the present state of affairs is intolerable and that only violence will bring a change. Some of their causes may even be real and legitimate—but unfulfillable. This applies to the separatist demands of minorities, which, if acceded to, would result in the emergence of nonviable states and the crippling of society. It is always the fashion to blame the state or the "system" for every existing injustice. But some of the problems may simply be insoluable, at least in the short run. No state or social system can be better than the individuals constituting it.

It is ultimately the perception of grievance that matters, not the grievance itself. At one time a major grievance may be fatalistically accepted, whereas at another time (or elsewhere) a minor grievance may produce the most violent reaction. A comparison of terrorist activities over the last century shows, beyond any shadow of doubt, that violent protest movements do not appear where despotism is worst but, on the contrary, in permissive democratic societies or ineffective authoritarian regimes. There were no terrorist movements in Nazi Germany, nor in Fascist Italy, nor in any of the Communist countries. The Kurdish insurgents were defeated by the Iraqi government in early 1975 with the greatest of ease, whereas terrorism in Ulster continues for many years now and the end is not in sight. The Iraqis succeeded not because they satisfied the grievances of the Kurds but simply because they could not care less about public opinion abroad.

Terror is highly effective   Terror is noisy, it catches the headlines. Its melodrama inspires horror and fascination. But seen in historical perspective, it has hardly ever had a lasting effect. Guerrilla wars have been successful only against colonial rule, and the age of colonialism is over. Terrorism did have a limited effect at a time of general war, but only in one instance (Cuba) has a guerrilla movement prevailed in peacetime. But the constellation in Cuba was unique and, contrary to Castro's expectations, there were no repeat performances elsewhere in Latin America. The Vietnam war in its decisive phase was no longer guerrilla in character. There is no known case in modern history of a terrorist movement seizing political power, although terror has been used on the tactical level by radical political parties. Society will

tolerate terrorism as long as it is no more than a nuisance. Once insecurity spreads and terror becomes a real danger, the authorities are no longer blamed for disregarding human rights in their struggle against it. On the contrary, the cry goes up for more repressive measures, irrespective of the price that has to be paid in human rights. The state is always so much stronger than the terrorists, whose only hope for success is to prevent the authorities from using their full powers. If the terrorist is the fish—following Mao Tse-tung's parable—the permissiveness and the inefficiency of liberal society is the water. As Regis Debray, apostle of the Latin-American guerrillas, wrote about the Tupamaros: "By digging the grave of liberal Uruguay, they dug their own grave."

The importance of terrorism will grow enormously in the years to come as the destructive power of its weapons increases   This danger does indeed exist, with the increasing availability of missiles, nuclear material, and highly effective poisons. But it is part of a wider problem, that of individuals blackmailing society. To engage in nuclear ransom, a "terrorist movement" is not needed; a small group of madmen or criminals, or just one person, could be equally effective—perhaps even more so. The smaller the group, the more difficult it would be to identify and combat.

Political terrorists are more intelligent and less cruel than "ordinary" criminals   Most political terrorists in modern times have been of middle- or upper-class origin, and many of them have had a higher education. Nevertheless, they have rarely shown intelligence, let alone political sophistication. Larger issues and future perspectives are of little interest to them, and they are quite easily manipulated by foreign intelligence services. As for cruelty, the "ordinary" criminal, unlike the terrorist, does not believe in indiscriminate killing. He may torture a victim, but this will be the exception, not the rule, for he is motivated by material gain and not by fanaticism. The motivation of the political terrorist is altogether different. Since, in his eyes, everyone but himself is guilty, restraints do not exist.

Political terror therefore tends to be less humane than the variety practiced by "ordinary" criminals. The Palestinian terrorists have specialized in killing children, while the Provisional IRA has concentrated its attacks against Protestant workers, and this despite their professions of "proletarian internationalism." It is the terrorists' aim not just to kill their opponents but to spread confusion and fear. It is part of the terrorist indoctrination to kill the humanity of the terrorist—all this, of course, for a more humane and just world order.

Terrorists are poor, hungry, and desperate human beings Terrorist groups without powerful protectors are indeed poor. But modern transnational terrorism is, more often than not, big business. According to a spokesman of the Palestine "Rejection Front" in an interview with the Madrid newspaper *Platforma*, the income of the PLO is as great as that of certain Arab countries, such as Jordan, with payments by the oil countries on the order of $150 million to $200 million. Officials of the organizations are paid $5,000 a month and more, and everyone gets a car as a matter of course; they have acquired chalets and bank accounts in Switzerland. But the "Rejection Front," financed by Iraq, Libya, and Algeria is not kept on a starvation diet either. The Argentine ERP and the Montoneros have amassed many millions of dollars through bank robberies and extortion. Various Middle Eastern and East European governments give millions to terrorist movements from Ulster to the Philippines. This abundance of funds makes it possible to engage in all kinds of costly operations, to bribe officials, and to purchase sophisticated weapons. At the same time, the surfeit of money breeds corruption. The terrorists are no longer lean and hungry after prolonged exposure to life in Hilton hotels. They are still capable of carrying out gangster-style operations of short duration, but they become useless for long campaigns involving hardship and privation.

All this is not to say that political terror is always reprehensible or could never be effective. The assassination of Hitler or Stalin in the 1920s or 1930s would not only have changed the course of history, it would have saved the lives of millions of people. Terrorism is morally justified whenever there is no other remedy for an intolerable situation. Yet it seldom occurs, and virtually never succeeds, where tyranny is harshest.

THE TERRORIST'S FRIENDS

Events in recent years offer certain obvious lessons to terrorists. These lessons run against the terrorist grain, and have not yet been generally accepted. For example, terror is always far more popular against foreigners than against one's own countrymen. The only terrorists in our time who have had any success at all are those identifying themselves with a religious or national minority. It is sectarian-chauvinist support that counts, not drab, quasirevolutionary phraseology; Irish, Basques, Arabs, and the rest have found this out by trial and error. The media are a terrorist's best friend. The terrorist's act by itself is nothing. Publicity is all. Castro was the great master of the public-relations technique, from whom all terrorists should learn; with less than 300 men he created the impression of having a force of overwhelming strength at his disposal. But the media are a fickle friend, constantly in need of diversity and new angles. Terrorists will always have to be innovative; they are the super-entertainers of our time. Seen in this light the abduction of the OPEC ministers rates high marks.

The timing of the operation is also of paramount importance, for if it clashes with other important events, such as a major sports events or a natural disaster, the impact will be greatly reduced. Whenever terrorists blackmail governments, it is of great importance to press realistic demands. Democratic authorities will instinctively give in to blackmail—but only up to a point. The demand for money or the release of a few terrorist prisoners is a realistic demand, but there are limits beyond which no government can go, as various terrorist groups have found out to their detriment.

Psychiatrists, social workers, and clergymen are the terrorist's next-best friends. They are eager to advise, to assuage, and to mediate, and their offer to help should always be accepted by the terrorist. These men and women of goodwill think they know more than others about the mysteries of the human soul and that they have the compassion required for understanding the feelings of "desperate men." But a detailed study of the human psyche is hardly needed to understand the terrorist phenomenon; its basic techniques have been known to every self-respecting gangster throughout history. It is the former terrorist, the renegade, who has traditionally been the terrorist's most dangerous opponent. Once again, the terrorist should never forget that he exists only because the authorities are prevented by public opinion at home and abroad from exercising their full power against him. If a terrorist wishes to survive, he should not create the impression that he could be a real menace, unless, of course, he has sanctuaries in a foreign country and strong support from a neighboring power. In this case political terrorism turns into surrogate warfare and changes its character, and then there is always the danger that it may lead to real, full-scale war.

Recent terrorist experience offers some lessons to governments too. If governments did not give in to terrorist demands, there would be no terror, or it would be very much reduced in scale. The attitude of Chancellor Bruno Kreisky and his Minister of the Interior, who virtually shook the terrorist's hands, is not only aesthetically displeasing, it is also counterproductive. It may save a few human lives in the short run, but it is an invitation to further such acts and greater bloodshed. However, it would be unrealistic to expect determined action from democratic governments in present conditions. In wartime these governments will sacrifice whole armies without a moment's hesitation. In peace they will argue that one should not be generous with other people's lives. Western politicians and editorialists still proclaim that terrorism is condemned "by the whole civilized world," forgetting that the "civilized world" covers no more than about one-fifth of the population of the globe. Many countries train, equip, and finance terrorists, and a few sympathetic governments will always provide sanctuary. Western security services may occasionally arrest and sentence foreign terrorists, but only with the greatest reluctance, for they know that sooner or later one of their aircraft will be hijacked or one of their politicians abducted. Ilyich Ramírez Sánchez ("Carlos"), the Venezuelan terrorist, is wanted in Britain for attempted murder, yet Scotland Yard decided last December not to press for his extradition from Algiers. For, in the words of the London *Daily Telegraph*, "the trial of an international terrorist could lead to political repercussions and acts of terrorist reprisals." A good case could be made for not arresting foreign terrorists in the first place but simply deporting them. The European governments on a West German initiative have had some urgent deliberations in recent weeks as to how to collaborate in combating terror. But, according to past experience, it is doubtful whether international cooperation will be of much help unless it is worldwide.

These observations do not, of course, refer to the South Moluccans, the Kurds, and other such groups in the world of terrorism. They fight only for national independence; they are on their own because they fulfill no useful political function as far as the Russians and the Cubans are concerned. The Libyans and Algerians will not support them because they belong to the wrong religion or ethnic group, and even South Yemen will not give them shelter. They are the proletariat of the terrorist world.

Terrorism is, of course, a danger, but magnifying its importance is even more dangerous. Modern society may be vulnerable to attack, but it is also exceedingly resilient. A plane is hijacked, but all others continue to fly. A bank is robbed, but the rest continue to function. All oil ministers are abducted, and yet not a single barrel of oil is lost.

Describing the military exploits of his Bedouin warriors, Lawrence of Arabia once noted that they were on the whole good soldiers, but for their unfortunate belief that a weapon was dangerous in proportion to the noise it created. Present-day attitudes toward terrorism in the Western world are strikingly similar. Terrorism creates tremendous noise. It will continue to cause destruction and the loss of human life. It will always attract much publicity but, politically, it tends to be ineffective. Compared with other dangers threatening mankind, it is almost irrelevant.

QUESTIONS FOR DISCUSSION

1 Is terrorism ever justified?
2 What is the difference between a terrorist and a freedom fighter?
3 What causes terrorism?
4 Are there differences between acts of violence by governments and by terrorist groups?
5 What impact has terrorism had on international politics?

SUGGESTED READINGS

Alexander, Yonah, David Carlton, and Paul Wilkinson (eds.). *Terrorism: Theory and Practice.* Boulder, Colo.: Westview Press, 1979.

Bishop, Joseph W., Jr. "Can Democracy Defend Itself Against Terrorism?" *Commentary* (May 1978): 55–62.

Clutterbuck, Richard. *Guerrillas and Terrorists*. London: Faber and Faber, 1977.

Horner, Charles. "The Facts About Terrorism." *Commentary* (June 1980): 40–45.

Kupperman, Robert, and Darrell Trent. *Terrorism: Threat, Reality, Response*. Stanford: Hoover Press, 1979.

Laqueur, Walter. *Terrorism*. Boston: Little, Brown, 1977.

Lineberry, William P. (ed.). *The Struggle Against Terrorism*. New York: H. W. Wilson, 1977.

Parry, Albert. *Terrorism: From Robespierre to Arafat*. New York: Vanguard Press, 1976.

Stohl, Michael (ed.). *The Politics of Terrorism*. New York: Marcel Dekker, 1979.

Wilkinson, Paul. *Terrorism and the Liberal State*. New York: Wiley, 1977.

16 Does Foreign Aid Promote Economic Development
and Stability?

YES

Cyrus Vance

U.S. Foreign Assistance Programs

NO

P. T. Bauer and John O'Sullivan

Foreign Aid for What?

U.S. Foreign Assistance Programs
Cyrus Vance

I am delighted to present the Administration's foreign assistance programs for the fiscal year 1979. We are requesting an authorization of $1.6 billion for our bilateral development assistance progam, $2.7 billion for our security assistance program, and $282 million for programs of the United Nations and the Organization of American States. Although we do not require authorization in FY 1979, we are planning to contribute $3.5 billion to the international financial institutions (IFI's) and to undertake a $1.4 billion program in P.L. 480 Food for Peace for that year.

Today, I would like to explain to you the goals which the Carter Administration seeks to achieve with these programs.

This is the first foreign assistance budget which fully reflects the policies and priorities of the Carter Administration. It was developed after an extensive Administration review of our relations with less developed countries (LDC's) generally and of our foreign assistance programs in particular.

I would like to summarize for you the results of our assessments.

LESS DEVELOPED COUNTRIES

First, our review highlighted the growing importance of less developed countries to U.S. interests. The cooperation of Third World countries is essential in helping to resolve pressing global problems that affect all nations: economic instability or stagnation, rapid population growth, adequate food and energy production, environmental deterioration, nuclear proliferation, terrorism, and the spread of narcotics.

The less developed countries are increasingly important to the economic welfare of the United States. Last year, for example, the non-oil producers alone accounted for 23% of our imports, including a very high percentage of our critical raw materials. They were also the market for 25% of our exports and 25% of U.S. direct investment abroad.

Earnings from U.S. direct investment in these countries in 1975 amounted to $7.4 billion—more than our total foreign assistance that year. Moreover, in recent years, non-oil-producing less developed

countries have bought more from us than we have from them, thereby improving our trade balance and helping to sustain American production and jobs during the recent recession.

The developing countries are central participants in our quest for peace. Their cooperation is essential to regional stability and peace in the Middle East and southern Africa, to name the most obvious cases. Moreover, we need to work closely with these countries on other security issues as well: in deploying our armed forces effectively and in maintaining access to straits, ports, and aviation facilities, for example.

Second, our review of American relations with the less developed countries also emphasized that their interests and needs vary enormously and require differing responses by the United States. The developing world is really several worlds:

- The OPEC nations with substantial financial surpluses and the ability to pay in full for technical assistance;
- The rapidly industrializing "upper tier" countries such as Brazil and Mexico with access to private capital but with large pockets of poverty;
- The "middle-income" nations like the Dominican Republic or Tunisia which still require some concessional assistance to help the poor; and
- The low-income nations, such as the Sahel countries, which rely heavily on concessional aid to finance their development programs.

Despite their differences, however, the developing countries have worked closely together to support a series of ideas which found expression in their call for a new international economic order. These have included proposals for price stabilizing commodity agreements, automatic debt relief, and permanent trade preferences. The United States has endeavored to respond positively where such efforts would actually promote development. We have also made our own proposals—for example, in negotiations on a common fund for buffer stock financing and on a sugar agreement.

However, we cannot respond favorably to a num-

From Cyrus Vance, "U.S. Foreign Assistance Programs," *Department of State Bulletin* (April 1978): 24–30.

ber of LDC demands, especially their desires to use commodity agreements or blanket debt relief as instruments of resource transfer. Yet we share the aspirations of less developed countries for economic growth and development and understand their need for additional resources.

It has become clear to us that foreign assistance is among the most important and effective instruments we have for promoting economic development as well as other U.S. interests in LDC's. It addresses problems of development directly. It supports an open international economy. And, as the last years demonstrate, international development efforts have contributed substantially to the growth and well being of the LDC's.

• The per capita gross national product of LDC's as a group grew at an average rate of 3.4% per year during 1950–75, faster than any group of countries in any comparable period prior to 1950.

• In the past 3 decades LDC's have experienced increases in life expectancy which took the industrialized world a century to achieve.

• Significant progress has been made in expanding shelter, education, nutrition, and food production.

We are also encouraged by the fact that a number of countries—for example, Brazil and Taiwan—have made such rapid and sustained economic progress that they have outgrown the need for our bilateral assistance.

Much has been accomplished, but a great deal more still needs to be done. There remain profound problems of poverty and underdevelopment in many parts of the world; over 1.2 billion people—30% of the world's population—do not have access to safe drinking water or to any public health facility; 700 million are seriously malnourished; 550 million are unable to read or write; over half the children in LDC's suffer from debilitating diseases. These are difficult problems; their solution will require a sustained effort over many years. Our foreign assistance programs are a critical element in this effort.

FOREIGN ASSISTANCE PROGRAMS

Having reviewed our relations with less developed countries generally, let me now turn to our review of U.S. foreign assistance programs.

First, it affirmed that these programs serve a variety of objectives in the Third World.

• Our bilateral economic assistance programs are aimed at insuring that the benefits of development reach the poor and serve their basic human needs.

• U.S. contributions to international financial institutions, in addition to supporting projects specifically designed to benefit the poor, also provide loans for larger scale infrastructure projects crucial to development. These institutions provide loans on very soft terms to the poorest countries and on nearly commercial terms to LDC's which are better off but still need additional resources to support continued growth and development.

• Our voluntary contributions to U.N. programs help finance technical assistance to poor countries which lack the skills essential to their development. These programs also provide direct humanitarian assistance to children, refugees, and other groups in need of particular relief.

• Finally, our security assistance programs serve the cause of peace in the troubled areas of the Middle East and southern Africa and strengthen the military capabilities of friendly developing countries.

Second, our review of U.S. foreign assistance gave special attention to the importance of improving the condition of political, economic, and civil rights worldwide and of integrating these basic considerations more fully into our decisions on foreign assistance programs.

• Under the chairmanship of the Deputy Secretary of State [Warren Christopher], an interagency group has been established to review all economic development assistance decisions for their human rights impact.

• In accordance with our laws, we have opposed loans by the World Bank and other international financial institutions to countries that engage in flagrant violations of human rights. Consistent with legislation, we have also made exceptions when proposed loans would address the needs of poor people.

• We have also assessed our security assistance programs in light of human rights considerations.

I would like to say an additional word on our experience with implementing our human rights policies. We have made progress in our efforts to persuade and influence other governments, sometimes in private communication, sometimes with changes in our assistance relationships.

However, we recognize that there is no automatic

formula for the application of each possible diplomatic tool, including the use of our foreign assistance programs. Human rights conditions along with governmental attitudes and other local factors in individual countries differ greatly. If U.S. efforts to improve human rights abroad are to be successful, our policies must take into account the needs of differing situations.

I believe that any additional legislative restrictions should be reviewed carefully to insure that they achieve the desired effect of promoting human rights goals as well as not undermining the essential functions of the multilateral institutions. If and when additional amendments are contemplated, we will work with you to develop provisions which serve these ends. We believe that the provisions of last year's legislation calling on us to undertake wide international consultation on this complex subject were helpful, and we have begun those consultations. The initial responses were sympathetic.

Third, our policy review has led to the firm conclusion that the effectiveness of our foreign assistance programs must be improved. As noted below such efforts are underway—in the internal reorganization of the Agency for International Development (AID) and in our efforts to make IFI's more efficient. In addition the Administration is now studying several proposals which involve the overall organization of our foreign assistance programs. These include the proposals contained in the Humphrey bill under consideration in the Senate and House.

We in the executive branch share with the Congress the goal of bringing greater coherence to a more effective foreign assistance effort. We expect to have a Presidential decision on aid organizational issues by the middle of March and will discuss our views with Congress at that time.

Fourth, based upon our review of foreign assistance, the President made several decisions on the future size and direction of our foreign assistance programs.

• Our bilateral development assistance should focus even more sharply on helping poor people, largely in poor countries. In some instances, it is appropriate to fund projects which benefit poor people in middle-income countries if the governments of those countries demonstrate a major commitment to meet the needs of their people.
• We should seek substantial increases in our foreign assistance during the 1979–82 period, at the same time insuring that such aid can be effectively and efficiently used.

I would like to turn to our foreign assistance programs for FY 1979 and relate them to the review I have described.

BILATERAL ASSISTANCE

We are requesting an authorization of $1.6 billion for our bilateral development assistance program for 1979. This would mean a 15% increase over the FY 1978 program. In accordance with the President's decision to focus our bilateral program more specifically on the poorest countries, 85% of our bilateral grants and loans are planned for countries with annual per capita incomes of less than $550. This would continue the growing emphasis in our aid program toward these countries.

The principal purpose of this program is to meet the basic human needs of poor people in the developing world. It directly addresses global problems of hunger and malnutrition, population pressure, disease, and ignorance. When we talk about meeting basic human needs we are not talking about an international welfare program. We are talking about giving the poor a chance to improve their standard of living by their own efforts, to rise above the extreme poverty levels that degrade and brutalize human existence.

Food and Nutrition Reflecting this focus, $673 million, or over 50% of the FY 1979 loans and grants under this program are planned for activities involving food and nutrition. These programs are designed primarily to help small farmers by providing them with the means to expand their production, such as credit, better seeds, technical advice, farm-to-market roads, small-scale irrigation, and a host of other activities.

We have had some encouraging successes in helping poor farmers expand their production and improve their standard of living. For example, one of the principal causes of food shortage in many areas is loss due to poor storage. In Rwanda, grain losses from inadequate storage have run around 25%. Small-scale grain storage facilities financed by AID have helped reduce losses for some small farmers to about 3%. AID and the Government of Rwanda will expand this project to provide the same benefits to others.

Another problem is the lack of good quality seed

which farmers can use. The Tanzanian Government, with AID support, has established a successful seed multiplication organization that provides improved seed for the main crops grown by poor people throughout that country.

In many places, research is needed to develop and adapt improved crops which will provide greater yields when used in small farmers' fields. In Guatemala AID helped to establish an effective research agency which works in small farmer areas and produces improved varieties of basic crops such as corn and beans and more productive planting techniques which small farmers can utilize. In the Philippines the International Rice Research Institute, which is partly funded by AID, has developed high yielding varieties of rice which are now planted on 70% of the rice acreage and thus benefit some 9 million Filipino farmers. Through its greatly increased production, the Philippines has become virtually self-sufficient in rice, a major food staple in that country.

Still another difficulty faced by small farmers is inability to obtain and to pay for the inputs needed to raise their production. In Pakistan small farmers are now able to use about the same amount of fertilizer per acre as large farmers, in part because of an AID loan to finance fertilizer imports as well as Pakistan Government efforts to improve distribution and use of agricultural imputs to small farmers.

Population Planning A second major focus of AID funding is population planning. Bilateral population programs in 32 LDC's currently finance the training of paramedics to provide family planning information and contraceptives. AID also funds continued research to develop simple but effective means of fertility control, the collecting and analysis of fertility and other demographic data, and the development of improved delivery systems.

Recent statistics on declining birth rates in Korea, Taiwan, Indonesia, and Colombia are encouraging. We have had substantial family planning projects in each of these countries. It must be recognized, of course, that many economic and social factors influence a country's birth rate. What is important is that these countries are having significant success in achieving their objective of reducing birth rates. We are hopeful of similar successes elsewhere.

Health Conditions A third important objective of our bilateral assistance is improving health conditions, especially among the rural poor. U.S. health assistance is targeted mainly on low-cost basic health care for rural areas, clean water and sanitation, and projects to control parasitic diseases.

Let me cite three recent successes in this field.

• An experimental project in Thailand has brought health, nutrition, and family planning services to 60% of the population in a province where only 15% were previously covered. It has done this at costs affordable by the Thai Government which now plans to extend the approach to the entire country.

• In Africa AID is helping to finance the successful suppression of the disease of river blindness in the Volta River basin in Sahel countries. People are already beginning to resettle there and to farm these fertile areas which before were virtually abandoned.

• In Tanzania the government has, with AID assistance, set up and equipped 18 regional centers to teach personnel to provide health, nutrition, and family planning services to the rural poor. By 1982, when this project is completed, these and other rural health centers will provide the Tanzanian Government with a strong rural health delivery system.

Education The fourth major focus of AID funding is education. Assistance in this area centers on providing basic skills to the poor, enabling them to earn a better living and improve their lives generally. AID projects finance expanded elementary education in LDC's and nonformal education projects, such as radio programs on agricultural techniques.

An evaluation of one such radio project in Guatemala indicates that agricultural practices have improved and yields are substantially higher in the areas served by the broadcasts. Another example is AID's radio math project in Nicaragua which has resulted in substantial gains in arithmetic skills among primary school-age children and significant reductions in grade repetition.

Other Programs Other AID programs address problems of energy, environmental decay, technology transfer, and urban development. AID is giving particular attention in all sectors to the development and use of appropriate technologies in LDC's. AID projects in Haiti, Guatemala, and Pakistan finance the development and distribution of technology appropriate to small-scale farming and rural enterprises.

For example in Honduras the small-farmer technology loan and grant program of $7.2 million is designed to provide small farmers with technical assistance, training, and investment credit so they may benefit from such light capital technology as a successful hand seeder. Seventy-five hundred farm families will benefit from this project over the next 4 years.

Improving Programs Of course, not all of our projects have been successful. Poor planning, unexpected delays in obtaining personnel and equipment, inadequate knowledge of local factors affecting our projects, and a number of other problems have limited the effectiveness of some of our projects. But we are trying to evaluate our programs better and learn from our past mistakes.

Our successes are encouraging. But we regard them as a beginning, not an end, in insuring that our aid is effectively and efficiently managed.

Reflecting the high priority this Administration puts on improving the effectiveness of our assistance effort, AID Administrator John Gilligan has taken the following steps:

• The Agency for International Development has been reorganized and the number of bureaus has been reduced, resulting in fewer administrative units and more direct lines of responsibility.
• AID has decentralized, shifting greater authority to its field officials to speed its responsiveness.
• Finally, AID has improved its programming procedures by eliminating unnecessary paperwork and improving the budgeting for operating expenses.

Aid plans further improvements over the coming year. The agency is enhancing its capability to review and analyze the impact of AID programs. This effort —while a long-term program—will include a much more active and consistent evaluation of the extent to which individual aid programs make a difference to the wellbeing of the people to whom they are directed. It will also assist us in translating our experience into future programming and budgeting.

These are first steps in what we believe must be an ongoing effort to improve the efficiency and effectiveness of our bilateral assistance programs.

P.L. 480 FOOD ASSISTANCE

We are planning a program of $1.4 billion for the Public Law 480 food assistance program in FY 1979 to finance shipments of approximately 6.7 million tons of agricultural commodities to less developed countries. This is the same tonnage as planned for FY 1978.

Our food aid program under P.L. 480 Title I provides agricultural commodities at concessional terms to developing countries. The Title II program provides free food, primarily through American private voluntary agencies and the World Food Program, directly to the poor for feeding and food-for-work programs, as well as for emergency disaster assistance. Last year 5.5 million poor people in 83 countries benefited from the Title II program.

Our project to feed school children in Egypt is an example of how this program can be effective—32,000 children are receiving school lunches as a result of American grant food aid; the Egyptian Government is committed to taking over this program entirely by 1982. These programs illustrate the way in which our food aid can stimulate a growing commitment by governments in developing countries to meet the nutritional needs of the most vulnerable groups in their population.

In the Philippines a similar program is reaching about 1 million primary school children and about 600,000 pre-school children and pregnant or lactating mothers. In Brazil a national school feeding campaign which received similar support for 10 years up to 1973 has since continued effectively and now operates almost entirely with national resources.

We share congressional concerns that the developmental impact of food aid should be improved. We are currently implementing the new Title III legislation which we believe will help to accomplish this. This new program can support development efforts in poor countries by providing them with assured supplies of food aid on concessional terms for periods of up to 5 years. In addition, payment for the food aid can be waived when proceeds from the sale of the food aid in the recipient country are used to finance additional development projects. One Title III program has been approved for Honduras, and several possible programs are under active review.

FINANCIAL INSTITUTIONS

We are planning contributions of $3.5 billion to fulfill U.S. pledges to the international financial institutions, of which $1.4 billion is callable capital and, as such, highly unlikely ever to result in budget outlays. Thus, actual government expenditures will be considerably smaller than our total request.

These institutions are a vital element in our overall effort to support development in the Third World. While no authorizing legislation is being sought this year, a description of the Administration's foreign assistance programs would be incomplete if it did not spell out why this is a critical component of our FY 1979 program.

The international financial institutions are the principal, and often only, source of financing for large-scale loans for critical infrastructure projects in LDC's such as roads, dams, and irrigation facilities. These projects are both crucial to a country's overall development effort and to improving the lives of poor people, for example:

• A $50 million World Bank irrigation project in the Philippines to improve and expand irrigation facilities in some of the poorest regions of the country will benefit about 250,000 people;
• A $48 million rural electrification project in Egypt will bring electricity for the first time to 2 million people;
• A $35 million road construction project in Honduras will connect the interior with the main port.

The IFI's increasingly serve basic human needs.

• In Pakistan a $15 million International Development Association (IDA) loan will improve access to primary and secondary education—particularly for females in rural areas—by increasing the number of qualified teachers. This project will also reach 96,000 adult villagers through a literacy program.
• In Burma a $26 million Asian Development Bank loan will increase fish production for domestic consumption, thus raising the low protein intake of the population. The project will substantially improve the lot of 900 fishermen and will directly or indirectly create 6,000 jobs.
• In El Salvador a $1.5 million loan by the Inter-American Development Bank is providing potable water to 102 impoverished rural communities with an average annual per capita in 1971 of $55; 73,000 people will benefit.

The IFI's facilitate a more equitable sharing of the development burden among donor countries. For example, for every dollar the United States provides to IDA, other countries provide two.

IFI's encourage recipient countries to adopt sound economic policies often essential to their development. As relatively nonpolitical institutions, they can exert an influence for domestic policy reform more persuasively and effectively than can bilateral donors.

In their role as financial intermediaries they play a crucial role in the world economy. In 1977, for instance, the World Bank borrowed a total of $4.7 billion from world capital markets for ultimate relending to LDC's which often do not yet have adequate access to world capital markets.

We are facing two fundamental problems in our relationship to these important institutions: insuring that their nonpolitical, multilateral character is maintained and fulfilling our pledged contributions.

The multilateral character of the IFI's has important advantages.

• They can mobilize and coordinate large amounts of capital for development.
• They can build consensus between aid donors and recipients on development goals.
• They can act as especially effective sources of advice for needed policy reforms in developing countries.

In performing these functions, these institutions serve both U.S. interests and those of developing countries. If these institutions are to continue to make an effective contribution to development, they must maintain their multilateral, nonpolitical character. Restrictive legislation, which prohibits U.S. contributions to the IFI's from financing loans for individual countries or projects, would be a first step in politicizing these institutions. If the U.S. Government takes this step, other governments may do likewise. This would undermine the effectiveness of these institutions and their value to us in multiplying our own contributions and strengthening the international economy.

The second major problem facing us is fulfilling our pledges to the IFI's. Our contributions for the IFI's this year fall into two categories: funding to fulfill past pledges which were earlier authorized but not appropriated by the Congress and appropriations which we are seeking for the first time this year.

It is critical that the United States satisfy its past pledges to these institutions in order to maintain institutions to function smoothly in supporting development in less developed countries. Our past pledges amount to $835 million, nearly one-half for the fourth replenishment of IDA, the soft loan window of the World Bank.

We are now 1 year behind in fulfilling this pledge. IDA has already committed all the funds it was pledged under this replenishment. Without the U.S. contribution, IDA may have difficulties in completing these projects. If this happens, the smooth operation of the banks will be disrupted and the beneficiaries of these projects in poor countries will suffer.

Other unfunded past pledges include the selective capital increase of the World Bank and the capital increase of the International Finance Corporation. If we do not fulfill these pledges, the capital increases of these institutions will be smaller due to a reduced U.S. contribution. Also, the U.S. voting strength and influence in these institutions inevitably will be reduced.

In both cases, our failure to contribute our full share means that we are repudiating the principle of equitable burden sharing. Without replenishments, the role in world development of these institutions will diminish at a time when the need for their skills and investments is greater than ever.

To fulfill our current pledges to IFI's we are planning a contribution of $2.6 billion, including $800 million for the fifth replenishment of IDA and $1.8 billion for U.S. pledges toward the World Bank selective capital increase, the International Finance Corporation, the Inter-American Development Bank, the Asian Development Bank and Fund, and the African Development Fund.

INTERNATIONAL PROGRAMS

In the same multilateral context, we are also requesting the authorization of $282 million for U.S. voluntary contributions to U.N. assistance programs and the Organization of American States.

Our contributions to U.N. programs support the principles of multilateral cooperation and burden sharing and reinforce the constructive trend in our relations with the developing countries within the United Nations. Moreover, they represent a U.S. response through the U.N. system to the real needs of people in the developing countries.

These contributions support programs in four major areas: developmental technical assistance, humanitarian needs, international scientific cooperation, and education and training. Let me discuss these major programs briefly and give examples of what they do.

We propose $133 million for the U.N. Development Program (UNDP). As the largest multilateral source of grant technical assistance, UNDP projects benefit over 130 nations. In Sri Lanka, for example, UNDP experts have developed an integrated water basin plan that is expected to raise agricultural production by $200 million. In Central America, UNDP experts are working in four countries to develop energy from volcanic steam.

To meet humanitarian needs, we are requesting $35 million for the U.N. Children's Fund (UNICEF), one of the best managed and most effective U.N. programs. UNICEF provides children and mothers opportunities for a more productive life. It also works to meet basic subsistence needs. In India, for example, UNICEF is working to restore and improve potable water sources in the areas hardest hit by the November 1977 cyclone and tidal wave.

We propose $52 million for the U.N. Relief and Works Agency (UNRWA) which provides needed assistance to over 1.5 million Palestinian refugees. It supplies rations, medical services, and, most importantly, secondary educational and vocational training programs. It is essential that UNRWA be adequately funded in order to continue its present level of services while negotiations proceed for a political solution to the conflict in the Middle East.

In the field of scientific cooperation, the $12 million contribution proposed for the International Atomic Energy Agency will support its role in our efforts to stop nuclear proliferation, through its safeguards system which monitors nuclear materials in many countries to insure that they are used for peaceful purposes. The $10 million requested for the U.N. Environmental Program will sustain its continued effort to encourage international actions to reduce damage to the natural environment.

As with the international financial institutions, we are concerned with improving the effectiveness of the U.N. programs. The U.N. system has grown rapidly in its scope and responsibilities. As this has occurred, the coordination, management, and budgeting procedures have become matters of increasing concern.

We and other nations have urged broad management reforms, and some important steps have been taken to address these problems. The General Assembly has created the new position of Director General for Development and International Economic Cooperation with particular responsibility for providing effective leadership and coordination of economic and social activities. In addition, new efforts will be made to establish maximum uniformity in administrative, budgetary, personnel, and planning procedures within the U.N. development system. . . .

CONCLUSION

I would like to conclude my testimony where I began—on the review which this Administration has made of our interests in the Third World and the role foreign assistance can—and should—play. Our examination convinced us that our programs are a critical element in relations with developing countries generally and in our efforts to promote peace and improve individual well-being worldwide. We strongly believe that at the levels requested these programs can be effectively implemented. . . .

Foreign Aid for What?
P. T. Bauer
John O'Sullivan

"Do not attempt to do us any more good. Your good has done us too much harm already."
    —SHEIK MUHAMMED ABDUH, an Egyptian in London, 1884

Foreign aid[1] is perhaps the only item of public expenditure in the West which is never criticized in principle. It is, of course, often said to be insufficient. *Past* aid programs too are sometimes denounced as inappropriate—in particular, aid which has financed obviously wasteful investment, or aid to oil-rich countries with a high per-capita income. But this criticism is itself merely the basis for advocating that aid should be directed to more appropriate targets as well as increased.

Nor is this advocacy confined to mere rhetoric. Of all forms of public expenditure, aid is the last to be cut in times of crisis, even when the crises are caused by balance-of-payments deficits to which aid contributes far more directly than, say, domestic welfare pro-

grams. And when aid has been cut *in extremis*, as in Britain during the unusually severe 1976 sterling crisis, those reductions have been the first to be made good.

In public discourse, those whose views reach the general public—with a few notorious exceptions—have an almost umbilical attachment to extensive and continuing aid. That aid is virtuous and desirable is no longer the conclusion of an argument; it is the starting point of *all* arguments, an axiom. The implications of this axiomatic status were crisply summarized in a 1972 editorial in the scientific journal, *Nature:* "If 1 per cent, in total, is the present target, what is wrong with 2 per cent?" And if 2 per cent, why not 4, or 8, or 16? For you can never have too much of a good thing.

But the validity of an axiom is independent of what occurs in the real world. Whatever happens in recipient countries can therefore be adduced to support maintenance or extension of aid. Progress is evidence of its efficacy and so an argument for its expansion; lack of progress is evidence that the dosage has been insufficient and must be increased. Some advocates argue that it would be inexpedient to deny aid to the speedy (those who advance); others, that it would be cruel to deny it to the needy (those who stagnate). Aid is thus like champagne: in success you deserve it, in failure you need it.

Accordingly, and with perfect logic, the terms "increase" and "improvement" are synonymous in aid discussions. Thus, according to an official OECD

---

[1]Throughout this article, all references to "aid" and to "foreign aid" are to official, government-to-government economic aid, whether bilateral or channeled through international organizations. Aid also includes the grant element in subsidized loans, debt cancellations, and certain kinds of international commodity schemes. We generally follow the common practice of referring to "aid" when the primary emphasis is on development or the relief of poverty, and to "wealth transfers" when it is on global redistribution or restitution.

From P. T. Bauer and John O'Sullivan, "Foreign Aid for What?" *Commentary* (December 1978): 41–48.

report in 1972: "In these GNP terms, the biggest *increases* were made by Sweden, Denmark, Portugal, France, with the United Kingdom also doing quite well. Belgium, Germany, Italy, Norway, and the United States also *improved* their performance . . ." (emphasis added).

So familiar are we with terminology in which giving more is unhesitatingly equated with doing better that we may not notice how perverse it is. It equates benefits with costs. Of course, benefits *may* accrue to someone. But we cannot simply assume that this is so. Nor can we assume that the beneficiaries, if any, will necessarily be the *peoples* in less developed countries (LDC's) rather than their governments. Still less can we take it for granted that their benefit will vary in line with our sacrifice. Yet we make this very assumption without realizing it when we equate greatly increased expenditures with improvement and a smaller increase with "doing quite well."

In short, if one starts from the axiom that aid is a good thing, not even an avalanche of evidence will produce any other conclusion. Yet to dispense altogether with arguments and evidence would amount to a social and intellectual solecism. Numerous rationalizations are therefore deployed. The most familiar are that aid is indispensable for development; that it is necessary for the relief of poverty; that it is an instrument for international redistribution of income; that it represents restitution for past wrongs; and that it serves the political and economic interests of the donors. Aid advocates shuffle these arguments freely —primarily in response to the shifting demands of intellectual and political fashion. There were few appeals to the restitution argument in the 1950's, for example, when the West had not yet built a religion out of the White Man's Guilt.

Development   It used to be argued in the early days of foreign aid that it was indispensable for the development of poor countries. Without aid, incomes would be too low to generate the capital required for investment and thus higher incomes. This argument was popularized as "the vicious circle of poverty."

Yet we know that *all* the present developed societies began poor and subsequently progressed without external aid. Large areas of what are now LDC's also progressed rapidly long before foreign aid—for instance, Southeast Asia, West Africa, and Latin America. Moreover, Western societies made great progress in the past under conditions far more difficult than

those which face LDC's today. These latter can draw on vast external markets, on an abundant supply of capital, and on a wide range of technologies which were not available in the early stages of Western development. It is plainly not true that aid is indispensable for development.

A more sophisticated version of this argument holds that external subsidies are required because, without them, LDC's will run into balance-of-payments difficulties, supposedly inherent in the early stages of development. Professor Gunnar Myrdal, in his book *An International Economy*, argued that ". . . there must be something wrong with an underdeveloped country that does not have foreign-exchange difficulties." Hong Kong, Singapore, and Malaysia, among others, then, are presumably guilty of succeeding in the face of the best professional opinion. And, of course, contrary to Professor Myrdal's prescription, all Western countries developed and enjoyed rapid economic progress without running up against payments deficits.

Might it be, however, that the West was able to advance without alms but that LDC's today cannot do so? There is just this much truth in the argument: namely, that economic achievement depends principally on people's attitudes, motivations, mores, and government policies. People in LDC's may place a high value on factors that obstruct material progress. They may be reluctant to take animal life, they may prefer the contemplative life over an active one, they may oppose paid work by women, or they may simply be fatalistic. If, on account of such factors, they are uncongenial to material progress, then external doles will not promote development. For if the conditions for development other than capital are present, the capital required will either be generated locally or be available commercially from abroad. If the required conditions are not present, aid will be ineffective and wasteful.

It might be argued in reply that aid, while not indispensable for progress, is nonetheless likely to accelerate what would otherwise be a very slow rate of development. This contention, which differs substantially from the vicious-circle-of-poverty argument, is inconclusive. Aid means at most that some capital is supplied more cheaply than if it had been obtained commercially. But in the context of development, this benefit is offset by at least two disadvantages. Capital supplied commercially has to be adjusted to market factors and to general local conditions much more closely than official gifts and loans (which can be, and often are, written off). It is therefore much more likely to be productive. And, as we shall see, aid inflows set up a whole host of unfavorable repercussions on the basic determinants of development.

Poverty To reduce poverty and distress is an irreproachable and unambiguous aim. That is perhaps one reason why this justification has come to loom large in aid propaganda. But there are certain moral and practical anomalies concealed here.

Aid to relieve poverty is not merely unconnected logically with aid as a spur to development; it is largely at variance with it. These two objectives differ in much the same way as alms to a beggar differ from scholarships to promising students, or assistance to an invalid from loans to establish young people in business. The poorest people in any society are unlikely to have, to the same extent as the better off, the aptitudes and motivations that encourage economic achievement. Aid based upon the criterion of poverty, therefore, will have little impact on the economic progress of the recipient society as a whole.

This confronts donors with a dilemma familiar to 19th-century social reformers. Are they simply to dispense aid and do nothing more? If so, they run the risk of transforming poor people into paupers permanently dependent on the dole. But the alternative is hardly more attractive. It is that donors should intervene extensively to instill in the recipient poor those qualities conducive to economic success.

In many Asian and African societies, such godlike intervention would require wholesale reform of local social institutions and cultural values and therefore large-scale coercion of the alleged beneficiaries. This stern necessity is recognized, indeed almost welcomed, by some of the more clearsighted supporters of development aid like Professor Myrdal. In his vast tome, *Asian Drama* (1968), he specifies what would be required in India if "the government were really determined to change the prevailing attitudes and institutions and had the courage to take the necessary steps and accept their consequences." His proposed measures include the abolition of caste, a rational policy for husbandry, including the killing of cows, and "in general, enactment and enforcement, not only of fiscal, but also of all other obligations on people that are required for development."

But as Professor Myrdal tentatively admits else-

where in the book, ". . . institutions can ordinarily be changed only by resort to what in the region is called compulsion—putting obligations on people and supporting them by force." Is such social upheaval justified by the aim of relieving poverty? And even if it is, would aid be accepted by the recipients if they understood the terms? And would such measures even relieve poverty—or would they intensify it, by transforming a living society into a dejected, inert, apathetic mass?

Perhaps it is fortunate that official aid in reality has little to do with the relief of poverty. It goes to governments and is spent by politicians and civil servants. Its allocation is inevitably influenced by their personal interests, and by the political objectives of the groups to which they belong. Is it surprising then that the beneficiaries of aid usually turn out to be those same politicians and civil servants, academics and businessmen close to them, and social groups which are connected to the government in some way, perhaps through tribal, family, or ideological links, or whose support is considered valuable? Only by rare accident are the poorest likely to come into any one of these categories. Indeed, the most indigent groups in the LDC's are largely outside the orbit of aid—for instance, aborigines, pygmies, and desert peoples. These groups contain many millions of people, but they are practically never mentioned in the literature.

Many of the schemes now being canvassed as an extension of Third World aid—commodity agreements covering primary products, for instance—can benefit the poor only haphazardly, if at all. Exporters of primary products are by no means always poor. Many developed countries are net exporters of primary products—as, of course, are the very rich OPEC countries. And quite apart from OPEC, primary producers are often the more prosperous LDC's—for instance, Malaysia, the Ivory Coast, Colombia, and Brazil. Within the exporting countries, moreover, it is the well-off, in particular established producers as well as politicians and administrators, who stand to benefit from commodity agreements.

If anything, the poor are likely to be harmed by such arrangements. They raise the price of necessities to poor people in both rich and poor countries. And to maintain prices, which is the *raison d'être* of such schemes, suppliers have to be restricted by excluding potential producers who are generally much poorer than those who benefit.

Finally, many governments receiving aid have pursued policies which have *reduced* per-capita incomes in their countries and aggravated the lot of the poorest. The expulsion of small traders from Zaire, for instance, had both these results. But if the criterion of the relief of poverty were to be applied uncritically, then such governments would qualify for more aid. Paradoxically this would encourage policies of impoverishment.[2]

Redistribution Since the UN General Assembly declared its support for a new international order in 1974, the redistribution of world income has become a leading aim of foreign aid. But this is a misleading phrase. When "world income" is "redistributed," what happens is that a proportion of incomes in developed countries is confiscated and handed over to the governments of recipient countries and the administrators of aid agencies.

Foreign aid is thus seen by many of its advocates as the natural extension of progressive taxation onto the international plane. Even the British humor magazine, *Punch*, traditionally known for its insular conservatism, wrote some years ago in an editorial: "In a sane world, the rich countries would be required to surrender a proper fraction of their productive resources to an international body charged with the duty of assisting the economic programs of the needy nations: progressive taxation at the international level."

But this is again misleading. Aid is a transaction between governments. Unlike progressive taxation, it cannot be even imperfectly adjusted to the personal and family circumstances of payers and recipients. Indeed, many people in donor countries are far poorer than many in recipient countries, especially those in recipient countries who actually benefit from aid. Hence, in the now familiar formation, aid takes money from the poor in rich countries, and gives it to the rich in poor countries.

Another argument for international "redistribution" is the need to contain an allegedly widening gap between the rich and poor countries. Yet the concept of such a widening gap is arbitrary, and the evidence for it nebulous. It is based on faulty statistics and comparisons which overlook differences of physical and social context.[3]

There is, however, one gap between the West and the Third World which is more significant and precise than the nebulous gap in living standards. This is the difference in life expectancy between LDC's and the developed world. It declined sharply between 1950 and the early 70's. Life expectancy in LDC's rose from 35–40 years in 1950 to 52 years by 1970—an increase of between 30 and 50 per cent. By comparison, the developed-world increase was from 62–65 years to 71 years over the same period. This represents a fall in the ratio between the two aggregates from 1.7 to 1.3–1.4 and a decline in the absolute difference from about 26 to about 19 years.

Here then is a gap, relatively free from conceptual ambiguity, which has not widened but narrowed recently. And (as Macaulay insisted in his review of Southey's *Colloquies on Society*), "We might with some plausibility maintain that the people live longer because they are better fed, better lodged, better clothed, and better attended in sickness. . . ."

The idea of world redistribution is thus full of ambiguities and defects. At the same time, it inspires policies which are both futile and destructive. For policies of world redistribution are usually based on the tacit assumption that people's attitudes, motivations, and mores are essentially uniform and that, accordingly, differences in incomes and wealth are somehow abnormal results of accident or exploitation. Yet, as we have seen, these factors are the underlying causes of visible differences in incomes and living standards. Three clear conclusions follow. First, any serious attempt to realize international equality by wealth transfers would have a purely temporary effect. The underlying factors would soon reassert themselves to produce visible income differences. So the process would need to be repeated endlessly.

---

[2] For a fuller discussion of this point, see "Against the New Economic Order," by P. T. Bauer and B. S. Yamey, *Commentary*, April 1977.

[3] Some doubts about the significance of the widening gap, especially as a ratio of incomes, have recently crept into the aid literature. According to a World Bank study, the average per-capita GNP of the collectivity of LDC's (excluding China) grew in recent decades at a faster rate than that of the collectivity of developed countries. *25 Years of Economic Development* 1950–75, by David Morawetz, World Bank, 1977, Chapter 2. See also, for a detailed analysis of the fallacies involved in the concept of a widening gap, "Against the New Economic Order," *op. cit.*

Secondly, once this was grasped and the leveling process extended to reduce the underlying differences, a wide-ranging and persistent coercion would be required. Just how much coercion might be needed would depend on the degree of standardization sought and the strength of a given people's attachment to their established customs. But the process of coercion would certainly have to include much heavier taxation on all Western countries; additional taxes on relatively prosperous groups in LDC's; and the ruthless uprooting of all customs and attitudes standing in the way of material progress. Obviously such a forcible remolding of both individuals and nations could not even be attempted by democratic national governments. Some international authority with near-totalitarian powers would be required.

Thirdly, unless a uniform ability to take advantage of economic opportunities were to be instilled into the various peoples of the earth, wealth transfers would reallocate resources from those who use them more productively to those who use them less so. This result would come on top of any disincentive effective, or other adverse repercussion, of the transfers in the West or the Third World. So the exercise is bound to reduce total world income.

Restitution   When other arguments fail, appeals are addressed to the West's guilty conscience and foreign aid is urged as restitution for past wrongs inflicted on the Third World. In fact, some of the poorest Third World countries were never colonies. And such victims of colonialism as there were (people killed or maimed in colonial wars, tribal farmers dispossessed by colonists, slaves, etc.) are now dead and beyond the reach even of the World Bank.[4] Their descendants have gained greatly from being born into the modern colonial and post-colonial world rather than into the circumstances of pre-colonial Africa and Asia. Indeed, millions of people, who would otherwise have died, have survived because of Western techniques and ideas, notably medicine and public security, imported by colonial governments. Would the rest really have preferred a low life expectancy,

continued poverty, disease, slavery, and incessant wars in order to retain undisturbed control of mineral resources they were unable to develop adequately?

Even if it could be established that colonialism was on balance harmful to the colonized, any theory of restitution would still fail because of the obvious impossibility of righting historical wrongs. What date would we fix after which crimes might be considered for compensation? Any choice would be arbitrary and therefore unjust. How would we identify the victims and the beneficiaries? Not, surely, on racial grounds alone with their primitive implication of collective guilt ("his blood be on us, and on our children"). And would all historical crimes be brought to book (Arab slave trading, pre-colonial wars of aggression in Asia and Africa), or only Western and colonial crimes? A statute of limitations on historical wrongs is more than just; it is unavoidable.

More often, however, is it not the past but the very existence of international income differences in the present which is denounced as a Western crime on the grounds that such differences necessarily reflect Western economic exploitation. Thus, in *Christianity Today*, an influential evangelical journal, Professor Ronald J. Sider wrote, under the heading "How We Oppress the Poor": "It would be wrong to suggest that 210 million Americans have sole responsibility for all the hunger and injustice in today's world. All the rich developed countries are directly involved. . . . We are participants in a system that dooms even more people to agony and death than the slave system did" (July 16, 1976). And Jill Tweedie, a prominent British journalist, wrote in the *Guardian* (London): ". . . a quarter of the world's population lives, *quite literally*, by killing the other three-quarters" (emphasis added).

In recent years, such virulent allegations have been commonplace in the advocacy of wealth transfers. Yet they are absurd and unfounded, as can be seen from the single fact alone that in the Third World today the poorest nations are those with the fewest Western contacts, the richest those with the most extensive links. Conversely, some of the richest Western countries, notably Sweden and Switzerland, had until recently little economic contact with the Third World.

These baseless assertions of Western responsibility for poverty in the Third World have received some ostensible academic stiffening from the argument that the Third World has been held back by Western

[4] A more detailed account of the many absurd and false allegations against the West by those anxious to stimulate its considerable feelings of guilt will be found in "Western Guilt and Third World Poverty," by P. T. Bauer, *Commentary*, January 1976.

manipulation of the terms of trade. Yet even if it were true (which in point of fact it is not) that the terms of trade were unfavorable to LDC's or deteriorating, it would not follow that they are damaged by trading links with the West, merely that they do not derive quite as much benefit as they would under more favorable terms. They would be even worse off if there were no trade to have terms about.

Self-interest Finally, there is the suggestion— frequently put forward by aid advocates with Machiavellian pretensions—that aid serves the political strategy of the donors and that it promotes exports.

Yet to serve Western interests, aid would need to have clear conditions attached to it, and to be adjusted to the conduct of the recipients. Such criteria have been notably absent from its operation. (Only recently the European Economic Commission assured the Marxist government of Angola that EEC aid would be free of political conditions.) Multinational aid, a large and increasing proportion of the total, is specifically supported on the grounds that it does not lend itself to arm-twisting or blackmail—a curious use of the concept in which it is the payers and not the recipients who engage in blackmail.

But in practice, Western interests are also largely ignored in bilateral aid. Many, possibly most, recipients of aid, especially in Asia and Africa, have confiscated Western enterprises and yet have continued to receive aid. Examples include Algeria, Ghana, India, Mozambique, Sri Lanka, Tanzania, Zaire, and Zambia. The hostility of many aid recipients to Western donors and their friendliness toward the Soviet bloc are also a familiar feature of the international scene.

The anomalous and baffling absence of conditions to protect or promote the interest of the Western donors paradoxically arouses suspicion in the recipient countries. It suggests that aid is a covert attempt to buy influence, that it is only partial restitution for past wrongs, or that it is an instrument for dumping unsellable goods on the recipient countries. Such allegations are advanced even by aid recipients friendly to the West.

Very recently, it has come to be argued that aid could serve a wider political interest by promoting human rights in the recipient countries. In practice, however, expressions of concern about human rights are determined by the vagaries of political fashion and by the talents for propaganda of different groups. How else can we explain the absence of protest at, or even the explicit tolerance of, such large-scale brutality and inhumanity by aid recipients as the forcible sterilization of hundreds of thousands, probably millions, of people (predominantly the poorest) in India under Mrs. Gandhi, or the enforced herding of millions into collectivized villages in Tanzania, as well as massacres in Burundi, Ethiopia, Nigeria, Tanzania?

If a strict and disinterested criterion of human rights were to be applied to foreign-aid programs, there would be very little aid granted to LDC's: President Carter himself recognized this implicitly last year when he asked Congress to remove human-rights restrictions on U.S. funds for the World Bank. So much for aid as an instrument of human rights.

When addressing domestic politicians, labor leaders, and businessmen, advocates of aid often urge that aid promotes exports and employment. In its crudest form, the argument is that aid funds are used to buy exports, and thus sustain employment. But aid is taxpayers' money. It therefore reduces the domestic demand for other goods which the taxpayers would have bought if their taxes had been lower. To argue that aid helps domestic employment is like saying that a shopkeeper benefits from being robbed if the burglar spends part of the money in his shop. Direct subsidies to export industries would simplify the process. This method would also generate more employment, because less money would "leak" abroad— in the sense of not being spent on the exports of the donors—to the detriment both of employment and the balance of payments.

According to another version of this argument, aid benefits the donor economies and sustains employment by promoting the long-term development of the recipients. As we have seen, this argument prejudges the issue by assuming that aid is necessarily effective, which is doubtful at best. The argument also ignores the alternative and more productive use of aid funds in the donor countries and elsewhere. That such uses exist is suggested by the fact that aid programs and policies have to be financed by taxes. Were they as attractive as alternatives, they could be financed through the market. And there is also the difficulty aid recipients have in servicing even very soft loans, which indicates that much of the capital supplied has been wasted.

II

If aid were like manna which simply descended from heaven, both costless and enriching everyone equally, producing no unlooked for and damaging consequences, then it could only be beneficial. But mundane aid is not at all like manna. It unleashes a host of repercussions, damaging to economic performance and development, which can easily outweigh the marginal effect of an inflow of subsidized resources.

Aid promotes the widespread politicization of life in the Third World. This is because it goes to governments, not to the people at large—a distinction obscured by conventional terminology which identifies a government with the people. Aid therefore necessarily increases the power, resources, and patronage of government in the society. This result is reinforced by preferential treatment of governments which try to establish state-controlled economies—a preference supported by the spurious argument that comprehensive state planning is necessary for material progress. In fact, economic controls introduced in the name of so-called development planning divorce output from consumer requirements and generally waste resources and obstruct their growth. These effects are particularly pronounced and damaging in poor countries where there are rarely enough trained and experienced administrators to fulfill the essential functions of government, let alone embark on sophisticated economic tasks which have baffled the British Treasury for thirty years. Indeed, an important economic effect of development planning is the waste of that scarce resource—administrative talent.

Aid also enables Third World governments to extend these economic controls and to manipulate them for purely political aims. Such controls—state monopolies in major sectors of the economy, including imports, exports, and the purchase of farm produce; ubiquitous state enterprises in trade, industry, banking, and transport; extensive licensing of economic activity; and special taxation of particular groups—serve to strengthen the grip of rulers over their populations, to reward or placate their supporters, to undermine their opponents, and even to confiscate their incomes and property. Mrs. Gandhi, during the Indian "emergency," was able to intimidate and suppress a great many political opponents, especially in the press and business world, without recourse to legislation or administrative measures of a nakedly repressive character. She simply manipulated long-standing economic controls, which had been granted to the government ostensibly for quite different purposes (e.g., import licenses and price controls), against them and their suppliers or customers. Such manipulation of economic controls is taken for granted in most of the Third World. It evokes resistance or criticism only if it leads to economic breakdown or if some victims are unexpectedly intractable or become visible, as, for instance, the Asians expelled from East Africa.

The beneficiaries are politically effective groups, especially politicians, but also the military, civil servants, and politically acceptable businessmen. The victims are such unpopular groups as landowners, small traders, or members of particular tribes like the Ibo in Nigeria. Large sections of the rural population are often severely harmed, sometimes directly, more often because measures against minorities disrupt the trading system on which their livelihood largely depends. Ethnic minorities are often the worst affected; in the Third World, economic controls are used widely and sometimes explicitly against the Indians in Burma, or against the Chinese in Malaysia.

In a politicized society, economic success or survival, and often even the physical survival of large numbers of people, come to depend on political developments and administrative decisions. This diverts the energies and activities of ambitious and resourceful men from economic life to politics, to the civil service and the politicized military—to the detriment of economic prosperity and progress. All this inevitably raises the political temperature and provokes acute political tension, especially in multiracial, multi-cultural, and multi-tribal societies—that is, practically all LDC's.

What has all this to do with aid? Much state brutality and political instability would occur in any event. But in various ways, aid has encouraged or even made them possible. It has increased the stakes of political power. Are not well-rewarded and relatively secure political posts more attractive than striving after economic success that probably depends anyway on the arbitrary and uncertain will of politicians? Altogether, the flow of aid, the criteria of its allocation, and the dominant ideology of aid advocates and administrators, have served to further the politicization of life throughout the Third World, especially in Asia and Africa.

Apart from promoting or helping along this disas-

trous politicization, aid has other adverse economic repercussions. It encourages restrictions on the
inflow and deployment of private capital and enterprise. Such restrictions are imposed by most aid
recipients—an evident anomaly, as a shortage of capital is the avowed ground for aid. But this anomaly
becomes readily understandable when it is recognized that, whatever they say about development or
equality, the prime purpose of most aid-recipient
governments is to strengthen their hold over the
societies they rule.

Aid also often supports projects so wasteful that
they not only incur losses year after year, but absorb
more domestic resources than the value of their
output. Yet they are continued for such political
reasons as the reluctance of the government to lose
prestige at home, or contacts with the donors, especially when these are politically congenial, or a desire
to appear technologically up-to-date. To mention but
one of the many examples, some years ago Tanzania
received bush-clearing equipment under a Yugoslavi-
an aid scheme. This was designed for use in temperate
climates. Much labor and scarce water were necessary
for cooling to keep it going somehow in the tropics. It
was only after protracted pressure from external
advisers that the Tanzanian government agreed to
abandon the equipment.

Aid often biases social and economic policies toward inappropriate Western models. In many Asian
and African countries Western-style universities have
been financed with aid when there is neither adequate
personnel to staff them nor suitable jobs for their
graduates who become a discontented intellectual
proletariat. Western-inspired trade unions are another instance of inappropriate external models in aid-
recipient LDC's: if they are effective, they inflate
costs and thus impair both competitiveness and local
employment opportunities. But the most familiar and
most inappropriate external prototypes are prestige
industries and activities such as engineering complexes, steel works, and airlines. Even Laos and Ethiopia
have, or at least had, their own national airlines
(operated for them by foreign airlines who supply
personnel, organization, and equipment).

Aid also encourages balance-of-payment crises because these can be used as a ground for demanding
more aid. If a deficit occurs in the course of development planning, it may even be regarded by people like
Gunnar Myrdal as the outcome of laudable efforts.
Not unnaturally, this encourages Third World govern-

ments to pursue inflationary policies, to run down
their exchange reserves, and to generate payments
deficits. These in turn inhibit private saving and
investment and encourage the flight of capital. Both
the policies and their consequences justify the imposition of further economic controls and create an
atmosphere of crisis. All of which stimulates requests
for more aid—and so on *ad infinitum*.

Major psychological repercussions of aid also deserve notice. Aid encourages the delusion that a
society can progress from indigence to prosperity
without the intermediate stage of economic effort and
achievement. Insistence on the need for external
donations obscures the necessity for the people of
poor countries themselves to develop the faculties and
attitudes and to adopt the conduct and the mores
required for sustained material progress—if this is
what they wish to do. (Of course, they may reasonably prefer to remain poor and to hold on to their
traditional ways.) Aid also subtly confirms and per-
petuates ideas and modes of conduct which obstruct
economic development—notably the idea that an
improvement in one's fortunes depends on other
people, the state, the rich, one's superiors, local
rulers, or foreigners.

Some observers have emphasized the profoundly
disturbing effects of the sudden impact of Western
contact in LDC's. Official aid is much more likely
than commercial contacts to produce such effects.
Whereas the success of those who stake their own
resources depends on estimating correctly the appropriate local conditions, those who direct taxpayers'
funds from far away are under no such constraint.
Hence the British government's celebrated East African groundnut scheme of 1947–50, in which huge
sums were spent with virtually no regard to local
conditions and which finally produced no groundnuts
at all. By contrast, those who invest or work in LDC's
often have to recognize not only local resources and
mores, but local customs, susceptibilities, and hierar-
chies as well.

Moreover, the disturbing effect of Western commerce is partial, gradual, tentative, and almost casu-
al, as against the sudden and coercive modernization
of traditional society so often associated with foreign
aid. Thrust between two cultures, neither directed by
traditional customs nor inspired by Western incentives, the people in aid-recipient countries are probably less able to take advantage of economic opportunities than they were before.

III

How did it happen, then, that such a far-reaching and momentous policy was advanced on the slender basis of negligible rationalizations; that it was nonetheless supported by public men and prominent academics with a notable lack of caution or skepticism; and that, despite plentiful evidence of its perverse and harmful consequences, it finally achieved the status of an undeniable axiom?

"In the beginning was the word." The concept of a less developed world, eventually to become the Third World, was forged after World War II, largely under U.S. auspices, to denote the whole of Asia other than Japan; Africa, except occasionally South Africa and Rhodesia; and Latin America. The less developed world or Third World is thus in effect the whole world outside the West and Japan, and it includes some two-thirds of mankind.[5]

But "the word" was less a description of reality than an attempt to change it. Phrases like "the less developed world" served to provide a spurious veneer of unity to a vast aggregate of radically different, deeply divided, and often mutually antagonistic or bitterly hostile components. What is there in common between, say, Papua New Guinea and Algeria, or between Malaysia and Argentina, or between Thailand and Botswana, or between Sri Lanka and Ecuador, or between Chad and Peru? In most LDC's even today, the majority of people do not even know of the existence of other less developed countries, let alone feel a common solidarity. Some are in a state of uneasy truce with their neighbors, as for instance India and Pakistan, as well as many African states. Others, like Algeria and Morocco, are in a state of intermittent hostilities: yet others are engaged in deadly combat, as are Ethiopia and Somalia.

In one respect only are these various countries at all united—in distinction to and, as time has progressed, in *opposition* to the West (from which they nevertheless demand and receive aid). But this invented and theoretical unity has served an important practical purpose. For Third World governments, and agencies, and certain groups within the West, it has become a source of ideological and even financial advantage.

Ideologically, the invention of the Third World both reflects and promotes the radical-equalitarian belief that economic and social differences perform no useful function and are therefore abnormal and reprehensible. By this standard the West stands condemned both for its internal arrangements, which permit of such differences, and also because it is more prosperous than most of the Third World. Removing resources from or otherwise undermining the position of this corrupt metropolis thus becomes an instrument for promoting international equality, reducing the power of the West, and encouraging state-controlled economies in Asia, Africa, and Latin America.

In giving practical effect to these ideas, international organizations, notably the UN and its affiliates, have been a major force. Prominent staff members within these bodies—occupying highly paid and prestigious positions—have discarded even the appearance of neutrality to become, in effect, union organizers for the Third World. Thus, Dr. Mahbub ul Haq, director of the Policy Planning Department of the World Bank, an influential speech writer for Robert McNamara, wrote in his book, *The Poverty Curtain: Choices for the Third World*:

> A major part of the bargaining strength of the Third World lies in its political unity. This unity is going to be even more important in the struggle ahead. One of the essential tactics of the Third World should be to proceed through the process of collective bargaining so that whatever bargaining strength its individual members possess is pooled together.

Such distinguished *apparatchiks* have done much to popularize the idea of a homogeneous less developed world with a common interest, and to organize concerted action by the most diverse countries against the West.[6]

Social scientists and academic economists form

---

[5] The treatment of the oil states and of the Communist countries is often ambiguous. Until 1973 the oil states were invariably classified as less developed countries even though some already had very high per-capita incomes. In political discourse they are still often included in the Third World. The position of the Soviet bloc is apt to be left undefined. Such practice illustrates the political nature of the division of the world into developed countries and less developed countries, or the West and the Third World.

[6] Note, incidentally, one pertinent aspect of aid. From its earliest days to the present global egalitarianism, Western countries have largely financed the spokesmen who assail them, the organizations which shelter these spokesmen, and the platforms for their attacks.

another pressure group which advocates—and benefits from—official aid. Before World War II, indeed, development economics did not exist as a well-defined academic subject. It owes its birth very largely to the emergence of foreign aid, which led to a proliferation of posts in universities and foundations. Those who toil in the vineyard of development economics can aspire to well-paid and prestigious posts with aid agencies and international bodies or in organizations supported by them.

But there are more subtle advantages to be gained from the extension of aid. For if we try to see the world as aid advocates would wish us to do, it appears to be divided into two sharply distinct categories. The one category is represented by the people of the Third World, sunk in poverty, helpless and at the mercy of their environment, exploited by the West, caught in a vicious circle of poverty, unable to control their own fertility, devoid of will and with little capacity for individual action. In short, they are like paupers or children. On the other side of a vast gulf are the prosperous people in the West, partly conditioned by their environment but with a will of their own, active but villainous, responsible for the plight of the world's poor, but refusing to take the actions required to improve it.

There is no doubt which is the superior in this scenario. We emerged from poverty; they cannot. Their poverty is the result of our past exploitation; their chance of a better future rests with us. Whatever happens to the people of the Third World is determined by us. In short, what poses as compassion comprises much condescension. And this condescension readily leads to coercion by enlightened guardians who will act in everyone's best long-term interests. Thus, writes Dr. ul Haq (Kings College, Cambridge; Yale; Pakistan Planning Commision; the World Bank):

> The Third World can help its cause a great deal by establishing a substantive secretariat to serve the needs of its own forums . . . manned by the best people from the Third World and its main task should be to produce well-researched, well-documented, specific proposals which harmonize the political and economic interests of the Third World.

Can anyone doubt that the "best people" will be drawn from such institutions as Cambridge, Yale, the Pakistan Planning Commission, the World Bank, and their surrogates in the Third World? And is it therefore any wonder that such people are fervent believers in aid and in the kind of future it contributes to creating?

QUESTIONS FOR DISCUSSION

1 Is foreign aid a useful instrument of foreign policy?
2 Would third world countries be harmed if the United States eliminated its foreign assistance?
3 How can it be argued that foreign aid is a form of imperialism?
4 Should aid be dispensed to third world countries regardless of their internal political character?
5 Who benefits from aid? Who is hurt?

SUGGESTED READINGS

Bauer, P. T. *Dissent on Development*, rev. ed. Cambridge: Harvard University Press, 1976.

Harrington, Michael. *The Vast Majority: A Journey to the World's Poor*. New York: Simon and Schuster, 1977.

Hopkins, Raymond F., and Donald J. Puchala. *Global Food Interdependence: Challenge to American Foreign Policy*. New York: Columbia University Press, 1980.

Independent Commission on International Development Issues. *North-South: A Program for Survival* (*The Brandt Report*). Cambridge: MIT Press, 1980.

Kindleberger, Charles P. *America in the World Economy*. New York: Foreign Policy Association, 1977.

Leontief, Wassily et al. *The Future of the World Economy*. New York: Oxford University Press, 1977.

Packenham, Robert A. *Liberal America and the Third World: Political Development Ideas in Foreign Aid and Social Science*. Princeton: Princeton University Press, 1973.

Sumberg, Theodore A. *Foreign Aid as a Moral Obligation?* Beverly Hills, Calif.: Sage Publications, 1973.

Wall, David. *The Charity of Nations: The Political Economy of Foreign Aid*. New York: Basic Books, 1973.

White, John. *The Politics of Foreign Aid*. New York: St. Martin's Press, 1974.

Chapter Five

Constraints on War

From ancient times to the present, mankind has known both war and the need to impose constraints on war. Various proposals—some frivolous and others realistic—have been put forward to regulate war. In the fifth century B.C., Aristophanes's play *Lysistrata* called on the women of Greece to refuse sex with their husbands if war continued. In the 1970s, anti-Vietnam war protesters chanted: "Make love, not war." In a time span of almost 2400 years, the world has experienced a bountiful amount of both war and sex, as it has resisted attempts to regulate each of them.

The regulation of war by controlling the use of force is but one way that governments have constrained power. Governments have also relied on other methods, such as international law, diplomacy, and moral considerations to constrain power. In the nineteenth and twentieth centuries, in particular, there have been developments in the law of war. Military forces are not legally permitted to torture prisoners or deliberately harm innocent civilians, and the use of certain weapons in war has been made illegal.

Disarmament and arms control agreements have limited the kinds of weapons that can be employed. Disarmament is the abolition or reduction of armaments and armed forces; arms control is the regulation of armaments for the purpose of promoting stable relationships among potential adversaries. An example of disarmament is the Allied effort through the Versailles Peace Treaty to reduce sharply the armed forces of Germany after World War I. An example of arms control is the agreement by the Soviet Union and the United Sates in 1972 to limit the number of antiballistic missile (ABM) installations to two each.

International law, like arms control, may serve as a constraint on power. International law consists of principles and rules that states and other international entities feel bound to observe. International law was developed in the past four centuries to regulate state behavior in a predictable and orderly manner. Some of the essential areas deal with the protection of diplomats, jurisdiction in disputes involving nationals of different countries, maritime law, and peaceful settlement of disputes.

Diplomacy is the art of peaceful negotiations among states. Diplomatic efforts involve government-to-government interactions in both state and multinational forums.

Moral considerations may limit the use of force. The British felt constrained to allow peaceful protests against British rule in India rather than to execute independence activists. Evidence indicates that in the Cuban missile crisis of 1962 John Kennedy chose to quarantine Cuba by United States naval forces rather than to bomb Cuban missile sites because of moral considerations of saving Cuban lives.

This chapter deals with two matters that have served to constrain war in the postwar period: arms control agreements and legal regulation of terrorism.

ARMS CONTROL

The regulation of armaments has been on the agenda of nations for centuries, but the nuclear age has made the subject more vital than ever before. As indicated in Chapter 4, the world has become a more dangerous place in the 1980s because of the growth of both nuclear and conventional weapons.

States have raised the level of defense expenditures for many reasons. First and foremost is the uncertainty of living in an international system in which states feel that they alone must provide for their own security. Second, the character of technology is so rapidly changing that states must keep up with research and development of new weapons systems so as not to lose the advantages of their existing arsenals. Third, states have formed strategic doctrines that have required ever larger numbers of nuclear weapons. Fourth, states have been encouraged by bureaucratic agencies charged with providing security and by interest groups that are the beneficiaries of big military establishments to increase defense spending. In this latter regard, some observers point to a military-industrial complex composed of generals who favor military action for their promotion, politicians who support military action for their popularity and reelection, and private firms with vested interests in a large military establishment, such as defense contractors.

The attempt to control nuclear weapons has involved not only the United States and the Soviet Union but many other countries, as well. The earliest effort to regulate nuclear weapons was the Baruch plan, which called for the establishment of an international atomic energy agency with broad powers of inspection within all the nations of the world and the turning over to that international agency of weapons systems and production facilities once inspection had been assured.

The Soviet Union rejected this plan but called instead for the United States to turn over its weapons to an international agency. It insisted, however, that there be no compulsory inspection system. Neither the United States nor the Soviet Union trusted each other, and no substantial progress was made on arms control for years to come.

There have, however, been arms control successes, and these have taken different forms: test-ban treaties, geographical disengagement, and nonproliferation.

With the widespread recognition that nuclear tests in the atmosphere posed dangers to health, a movement emerged in the 1950s to end testing of nuclear weapons. In 1963, the United States, the Soviet Union, and other nations concluded the Partial Test Ban Treaty (PTBT), which prohibits nuclear weapons tests or any other nuclear explosions in the atmosphere, in outer space, and under water. Underground tests were not covered by this agreement. Efforts to bring about a comprehensive test ban treaty (CTBT) in which all nuclear tests would be forbidden have been unsuccessful. The Soviet Union and the United States, however, signed a Threshold Test Ban Treaty (TTBT) in 1974 and a Peaceful Nuclear Explosion Treaty (PNET) in 1976, and these two treaties are awaiting ratification.

The TTBT establishes a nuclear "threshold" by prohibiting tests having a yield exceeding 150 kilotons. Under the PNET, both powers agreed not to carry out any individual nuclear explosions having an aggregate yield of 1500 kilotons. The PNET was concluded because of the belief that nuclear explosions would be useful in digging canals and in other nonmilitary projects.

In addition to test bans, a geographic approach to arms control was adopted in the postwar period. The principle of geographic disengagement is to place certain regions off limits for the storage or testing of nuclear weapons. The Antarctica Treaty (1961) prohibits nuclear explosions and the disposal of radioactive wastes in Antarctica. The Outer Space Treaty (1972) mandates that no signatory place nuclear or any other weapons of mass destruction in orbit around the earth, install them on the moon or any other celestial body, or otherwise station them in outer space. The Seabed Treaty (1972) prohibits parties from emplacing nuclear weapons or other weapons of mass destruction on the seabed and the ocean floor beyond a 12-mile coastal zone. The Treaty for the Prohibition of Nuclear Weapons in Latin America, known as the Treaty of Tlatelolco (1967), attempts to limit the spread of nuclear weapons by preventing their introduction into areas of Latin America hitherto free from them.

Some arms-control proposals with a geographic approach have been put forward that have not been adopted. In 1958, Polish Foreign Minister Adam Rapacki suggested that a denuclearized zone be placed in Central Europe. Other advocates of arms control have suggested nuclear-free zones for the Middle East and for Africa.

Another approach to arms control deals with nonproliferation. Both nuclear and nonnuclear powers were concerned with the spread of nuclear weapons to more countries. In 1967, a nonproliferation treaty was concluded. The principal terms of this treaty require the nonnuclear weapons states that ratified the treaty not to produce nuclear weapons. It also called on the nuclear-weapons states to reduce their nuclear weapons arsenals. The United States and the Soviet Union agreed to enter into negotiations on the matter, consequently.

Spurred on by the pressure of the small powers, voices for arms control within the United States and the Soviet Union, and a realization that the nuclear force was becoming so large that the security of both sides was being threatened, the two superpowers entered into negotiations to limit the size of their strategic nuclear forces. The process, which is a continuing one, is known as the Strategic Arms Limitation Treaty (SALT) talks. Since 1972, the United States and the Soviet Union have concluded one accord, SALT I, but have been unable to ratify a SALT II agreement.

SALT I deals only with strategic weapons and contains two principal elements. First, an ABM treaty limited the number of ABM sites to two that each superpower could possess. Two years later, both sides agreed to reduce the number to one ABM site apiece.

The second part of the SALT I accord was an interim agreement, to last for a 5-year period, which would limit the size of strategic nuclear delivery systems—bombers, intercontinental ballistic missiles (ICBM), and submarine launched ballistic missiles (SLBM). The agreement froze at existing levels the number of strategic ballistic missile launchers, operational or under construction, on each side and permitted an increase in SLBM launchers up to an agreed level for each party only with the dismantling or destruction of a corresponding number of older ICBM or SLBM launchers.

In 1974, American President Gerald Ford and Soviet leader Leonid Brezhnev agreed to a framework for a SALT II accord. A total of 2400 offensive strategic vehicles was set as the limit of the strategic forces for each side. Of the 2400 vehicles, 1320 could be equipped with multiple independently targetable reentry vehicles (MIRV). A MIRV is a missile capable of carrying more than one warhead to different targets. United States Secretary of State Henry Kissinger referred to the interim agreement as "putting a cap on the arms race."

In 1979, the United States and the Soviet Union seemed close to a SALT II agreement. The new agreement would have required each superpower to reduce its strategic nuclear vehicles from 2400 to 2250 before 1985. A limit of 1320 of these vehicles could be the MIRV type. It also limited deployment of the cruise missile for a period of 3 years. The cruise missile is a pilotless bomb that is guided by computers and can move in a preprogrammed, nonballistic-type trajectory. The cruise missile can be fitted with nuclear weapons. The SALT II accord, moreover, called for a SALT III agreement, which would reduce the strategic arsenals further. After the Soviet Union invaded Afghanistan in December 1979, SALT II was held in abeyance, its prospects ruined by rising Soviet-American tensions. In 1981, President Reagan called for the beginning of new negotiations, which he named Strategic Arms Reduction Talks (START), although no specific details were mentioned in his initial statement on the subject.

In spite of the numerous arms control agreements concluded since 1945, there is still controversy about the effectiveness of these agreements. The arms race continues throughout the world. Do arms control agreements slow down the arms race?

G. B. Kistiakowsky, who was Special Assistant for Science and Technology to President Eisenhower from 1959 to 1961, believes that the negotiated arms control agreements have resulted in the expansion of the nuclear stockpiles of the superpowers. Without these agreements, however, the nuclear weapons situation would be worse. Possibly without these agreements, Antarctica would not be demilitarized, nuclear mines would be deployed on oceanic areas, and H-bombs would be orbiting the earth. Nuclear weapons atmospheric tests, moreover, would pollute the atmosphere, antiballistic missiles would be deployed, man-made satellites would be destroyed, and the hotline that provides a communication link between Soviet and American political leaders probably would not have been established. On net, Kistiakowsky asserts, the arms control treaties probably have moderated the rate of growth of arms budgets. On balance, arms control agreements serve to improve the relations between the United States and the Soviet Union.

Edward N. Luttwak, an associate of the Georgetown Center for Strategic and International Studies, believes that arms control agreements exacerbate the arms race. According to Luttwak, arms control has value in theory but fails in practice. In theory, it offers a fully equivalent degree of security, and a higher degree of security in many cases, at a much lower risk of instability and war.

In practice, there are obstacles to the effectiveness of arms control. When more than two countries are involved, arms control agreements become most complex. Countries are not identical: There are variations in political will, economic resources, and popular support for military objectives. Weapons, too, are not identical, and it is difficult to compare weapons systems of different countries. Geographic and demographic differences further compound the problem. Information about the other side's compliance with arms control is often uncertain, moreover.

Luttwak contends that the most that arms-control efforts can achieve is to prohibit the deployment of specific weapons and forces. Arms control will not bring strategic competition to an end. Successful arms control agreements will direct the efforts of states to develop weapons not covered by agreements.

An evaluation of the merits of arms control should consider the technological and political problems that modern weapons systems create. Attention should be given to the effectiveness of agreements in a rapidly changing military technology, the difficulty in finding a formula that would equate somewhat similar weapons systems in different countries, and the problems of concluding agreements that do not include every state in the world.

TERRORISM

Terrorism as an instrument of foreign policy is described in Chapter 4. Among the methods used to thwart terrorist acts are international legal controls. Does international law serve as a constraint on terrorism? Political scientist Alona E. Evans notes that each state has a stake in the control of terrorism lest it find itself controlled by terrorists or engaged in continuing conflicts to contain them. States have resorted to many methods of dealing with terrorism. International legal controls have been particularly evident in two kinds of terrorism: aircraft hijacking and attacks on internationally protected persons. States are awakening to the threat of terrorism to all members of the international community. According to Evans, "Everyone loses when terrorism goes unchecked." There is increasing movement toward development of international controls through international legislation, national legislation, and international cooperation in the enforcement of this legislation.

Legal scholar L. C. Green finds that international law of the post-World War II period sanctions acts of terrorism. The UN Charter mentions respect for the principle of equal rights and self-determination for people. In 1960, the UN General Assembly issued a Declaration on the Granting of Independence to Colonial Countries and Peoples. According to Green, many UN members saw this declaration as legalizing and making respectable any act of terrorism committed by any dissident in a respected independence cause. UN members have accepted terrorism in the name of self-determination when applied to countries they do not like, such as Israel, South Africa, and Rhodesia (now Zimbabwe), but not to those places where self-determination is opposed, such as the countries who are members of the Organization of African Unity (OAU) in which tribalism and secessionism are constant problems. Although opposed to hijacking, UN members failed to condemn terrorists who hijacked a plane terminating in the Israeli rescue at Entebbe in Uganda. Even a 1974 convention to protect diplomats adopted by the General Assembly recognized that the principle of self-determination is superior to terrorist acts against diplomats. The PLO, an organization that has engaged in terrorism, has been granted respectability and legalization by the UN. So long as terrorism is justified and legitimized by states committed to the principle of national self-determination, it has little chance of ever being controlled, according to Green.

An evaluation of legal controls on terrorism may consider under what conditions states are likely to support such controls. Also to be considered is whether states are hypocritical when they condemn terrorists; whether international law against terrorism is enforceable in a world in which political necessity sometimes requires state support of terrorists; and whether international law against terrorists is more or less likely to be enforced than international law in other areas, such as the law of the sea and the protection of citizens in foreign countries.

17 Do Nuclear Arms Control Agreements Slow Down the Arms Race?

YES

G. B. Kistiakowsky

The Good and the Bad of Nuclear Arms Control Negotiations

NO

Edward N. Luttwak

Why Arms Control Has Failed

The Good and the Bad of Nuclear Arms Control Negotiations

G. B. Kistiakowsky

Negotiations between the superpowers on strategic nuclear forces under the auspices of the United Nations began a few years after the acquisition of nuclear warheads by the Soviet Union: Now, about a quarter century later and after the investment of thousands of man-years of effort in seeking arms controls, the superpowers have expanded their nuclear warhead stockpiles a hundredfold in numbers and a thousand-fold in megatonnage, meanwhile reducing warhead delivery time from hours to minutes. More than once, arms control negotiations have directly stimulated nuclear forces' build-up.

• In 1963, Senator Henry M. Jackson, in return for supporting the partial nuclear test ban treaty, received from President John F. Kennedy a commitment to increase the rate of nuclear warhead testing once the treaty came into force and the commitment was carried out.
• President Richard M. Nixon, pleading that he needed a bargaining chip for the SALT I negotiations in 1971, persuaded Senator John Stennis to switch his vote to assure the passage of a bill accelerating the development of the Trident submarine.
• After the signing of the SALT I Treaty and Agreement, the Nixon administration authorized development of the first cruise missile, while Henry Kissinger publicly stated that he supported this project because it would serve as a bargaining chip in the next round of SALT negotiations.
• For about a year negotiations for the SALT II treaty, as well as the Comprehensive Test Ban treaty, seem to have been stalled. At the same time, President Carter appears to have been making commitments to the Senate hawks which, if carried out after the treaty's ratification, would effectively negate its intended purpose of relaxing the arms race.
• The military section of the budget for fiscal 1980 is to be greatly increased, in contrast to the civilian part. Development of MX, the new intercontinental ballistic missile, will be intensified. This missile, with ten large warheads and very precise guidance, will be

a highly provocative counterforce weapon; the MX will threaten Soviet missile silos, which constitute the bulk of Moscow's strategic forces, in contrast to U.S. reliance on a weapons triad.
• Reinforcing this implication of increased provocation is the language in a recent posture statement by the Secretary of Defense, indicating that future emphasis in our strategy is to be on counterforce rather than on deterrence. A retired Army general, recently made head of the Arms Control and Disarmament Agency, was, until his appointment, a member of an offshoot of the American Security Council. Upon assuming his new post he promptly announced that our nuclear forces must be "modernized."
• The expenditures on civil defense are to be increased to devise ways to evacuate our cities in a crisis.
• Another step toward the deployment of the neutron bomb has been taken, and development of assorted cruise missiles is to be pushed, as is the Trident II missile (the twin of the MX).

The veil of secrecy over the Kremlin's internal debates prevents me from identifying the Soviet Union's moves to devise bargaining chips. Nevertheless, the reported massing of Soviet tanks and the addition of some 100,000 men to its forces in Eastern Europe are difficult to dissociate from the bargaining on mutual force reductions (MBFR) that has been long underway in Vienna.

The foregoing illustrates that the protracted arms control negotiations, including SALT, have not, up to now, reversed or stopped the nuclear arms race; and on occasion they have even exacerbated it and might do so again. Before making a final judgment on the negotiations, however, we should consider the alternative.

What might have happened if several existing agreements had not been in force, and if only fiscal strictures and deliberate self-denial were impeding ever-increasing armaments? This, of course, has been the case with conventional arms relative to which only

From G. B. Kistiakowsky, "The Good and the Bad of Nuclear Arms Control Negotiations," *The Bulletin of the Atomic Scientists* (May 1979): 7–9.

token efforts for international controls have been made. What we discover is very grim. Annual world expenditures have risen above $300 billion. Nearly 25 million men and women are under arms. The yearly trade in arms exceeds $20 billion, mostly to the underdeveloped nations. With great sophistication of firepower becoming available to even the poorest nations local military have been able to grab political control over a large portion of the globe and, with tanks and helicopters at their command they have felt secure from popular revolts—or at least they did until the extreme case of Iran.

Compared with conventional arms, the proliferation of nuclear weapons might almost be called restrained, thanks perhaps to past agreements on nuclear arms limitations. It is quite likely that without these agreements the continent of Antarctica would not be demilitarized; there would be nuclear mines deployed in strategically important oceanic areas; and man-made heavenly bodies loaded with H-bombs would be flying overhead, ready to pounce on the opponent if he were to undertake a suspicious move.

Without the 1963 Test Ban treaty, atmospheric pollution by radioactive fall-out from nuclear testing would have continued on a large scale, facilitating further study of the effects of nuclear explosions on military structures and permitting exploration of new concepts invented by the fertile minds of American and Soviet weaponeers.

Without the 1972 ABM treaty, which effectively eliminated ballistic missile defenses, research into the destruction as well as the protection of incoming warheads would continue to provide a rationale for further atmospheric nuclear tests. Moreover large deployments of ABM defenses would have been practically assured. This, besides consuming vast resources (the Grand Forks ABM Safeguard installation alone cost about $5 billion), would have triggered a continuing expansion of offensive missile forces, justified by the need to maintain the capacity for assured destruction of the opponent in a retaliatory strike on which the state of mutual nuclear deterrence depends. This expansion of offensive forces is being prevented now by the SALT I Agreement, however ineffective it is in restraining qualitative "improvements" such as precision-guidance and MIRVS, which tend to undermine the stability of the mutual deterrence equilibrium.

SALT I formalized a tacit U.S.-U.S.S.R. agreement, already in effect during the 60s, not to interfere

with the non-instrusive "national technical means of verification," such as intelligence satellites. The contrast between the Soviets' shooting down of an RB47 reconnaissance plane 50 miles off-shore over the White Sea in 1960, and their recent mild action against a South Korean airliner that flew directly over their nearby defense installations, signals a dramatic change in Soviet attitude away from "secrecy at any cost." The reasons for this change are unclear but I suggest that strategic arms control negotiations have had much to do with it. Soviet leaders must gradually have recognized that means for verification of agreements was a non-negotiable issue with the United States.

Although the U.S.S.R. regarded all variants of "on-site" inspections unacceptable, the "national technical means of verification" may have appeared to them as a harmless compromise. One can be sure that at the time they did not foresee the extraordinary richness of military information which modern technology has provided via these national means, when coupled with the SALT I agreement not to resort to camouflage, and so forth. The recent development of satellite killers by the Soviets perhaps indicates that they have had second thoughts about that agreement and want to be prepared in case of a breakdown in further SALT negotiations.

Had the nuclear arms race progressed without restraint, the Soviet Union probably would long ago have taken harsh steps against our satellites (as it did against the U2 in 1960) and would have rendered them ineffective. From the bald military point of view, they gain more by shrouding their military activities in secrecy than we do.

Moreover, the hotline between the White House and the Kremlin is an indirect result of arms control negotiations and probably would not have been established had there been an unrestrained strategic arms race.

Somewhat more conjectural is the effect of arms control negotiations on military budgets. There is no concrete evidence that arms control treaties have brought about lasting reductions in military spending. Yet the aggregate effect of these agreements probably has been to moderate the rate of growth for arms budgets. Had the cold war continued unabated into the 70s, it is likely that by now we would have had an even more powerful and costly "military-industrial complex."

Does the process of arms control negotiations

enhance mutual confidence and understanding, or is it the other way around? This is really a variant of the old question about the chicken and the egg: The earliest meetings and exchanges after World War II between U.S. and Soviet scientists took place before the start of any successful arms control negotiations. Since the conclusion of the SALT I agreements, however, not only scientific but also cultural and business exchanges have greatly expanded. The negotiations of the 50s and early 60s were severely hindered by mutual suspicions: the Americans insisted on absolute and total verification of compliance, which would have involved intrusive activities, while the Soviets asserted that American verification proposals were a screen for military intelligence gathering.

Both attitudes have greatly mellowed during the last decade of expanded communication and now it is largely the individuals comprising the Committee on the Present Danger and their like who assert that "Russians are Cheating" (see *Literary Digest*, December 1977). The changed attitudes have made arms control negotiations much more fruitful.

In sum, these negotiations and the state of mutual confidence and understanding would seem to be closely coupled, but which is the cause and which the effect is not at all clear.

Some thoughtful individuals have asserted that the avoidance of nuclear war between the United States and Russia during the last 30-odd years has been as much a matter of luck as design. Because I share that view I do not suggest that it was the arms control negotiations which saved us. But I am sure that a collapse of the arms control agreements would enhance the probability of a nuclear conflict. While the immediate cause of war is political rather than technological, technology does play a role in events leading to war. Thus Kaiser Wilhelm I is known to have taken an adamant position in August 1914 because he had just completed the modernization of German field artillery, while France and Russia were only starting that process. Hitler was convinced of the invincibility of Blitzkrieg tactics based on advanced design German tanks and Stuka bombers. Certainly, the cessation of negotiations and the consequent decay of current agreements on arms controls would hamper the superpowers in limiting some future local armed conflict and in that sense could be a cause of war.

On balance, it would appear that however feeble, and perhaps even negative, the results of arms control negotiations may be, they do not exacerbate the arms race, and they serve to ameliorate the U.S.-U.S.S.R. relations.

Why Arms Control Has Failed
Edward N. Luttwak

Over the last decade, the strategic competition between the United States and the Soviet Union has been transformed. From a clear American superiority, by all criteria of measurement, the balance has tilted to an increasingly precarious parity. A net American inferiority, in *all* dimensions of capability, is projected by 1985. At the same time, the strategic-nuclear arsenals of both the Soviet Union and the United States have increased very greatly in power, and expenditures on strategic forces and their ancillaries have grown considerably. All these changes have taken place under the aegis of an American strategic policy dominated by arms-control objectives. Clearly something must be very wrong with our

pursuit of arms control, especially in the Strategic Arms Limitation (SALT) negotiations. But what?

I

Whatever is wrong with arms control, it is not the essential theory, whose logic is perfectly sound.

Imagine a world of two identical countries, X and Y, whose array of forces is also identical. Let X make preparations to build a new weapon, say, a bomber. Faced with an emerging bomber force in X, the leaders of Y can choose between two instruments of strategic statecraft, force-building or arms control.

One force-building response is defensive; in this

From Edward N. Luttwak, "Why Arms Control Has Failed," *Commentary* (January 1978): 19–28.

case, it would mean deploying fighters and anti-aircraft weapons capable of intercepting the new bombers. The other response is competitive; country Y could build a bomber force of its own (or some other offensive force) to offset whatever political or military gains X hoped to achieve with its new bomber force.

As Y reacts to X and vice-versa, an additional and purely mechanical source of tension will arise between the two countries, even if each has good information about the actions of the other (so that surprises and overreactions can both be avoided). If, for example, Y's progress in building air defenses lags behind X's bomber effort, Y will be faced with an interval of vulnerability. At worst, it may be tempted to launch a preventive attack to destroy X's nascent bomber force before it becomes ready to operate. Even less drastic alternatives, such as the accelerated deployment of bombers or other offensive weapons, to offset by competition what cannot be negated by defense, will open new channels of force-building, which will unfailingly generate their own instabilities. If the information that each side has about the other is *not* good, with odd glimpses of truth or falsehood dimly perceived through walls of secrecy, action and reaction could be altogether more dangerous. But this case is irrelevant here, since without good information, arms control is not feasible either.

Even if no preventive wars break out, the best result that the force-building response can yield, is that the two countries will acquire a matched set of bombers and anti-bomber defenses. While they are reaching this new equilibrium, scarce resources will have been expended, new weapons will have come into existence to add to the violence of an eventual war, and the military and military-industrial interests in each country will have been strengthened, thus making it that much more likely that there will be yet more military competition between X and Y. And when the new offensive and defensive weapons are fully deployed, neither country will have gained any lasting advantage in physical security or political power. Moreover, any *temporary* advantage gained by either along the way will have entailed a corresponding risk of conflict, generated precisely by the imbalance which yielded that advantage in the first place.

The force-building approach guarantees these grim results, while also increasing the risk of war. Arms control, by contrast, offers the possibility of a zero-cost and low-risk solution to the same predicament.

Provided with early information of X's bomber-building intentions, let Y open negotiations. Assuming that the leaders of X are rational, and assuming further that they do believe that Y will react to their bomber effort with equivalent force-building of their own, the leaders of both X and Y should be able to agree in principle that the best course for both would be to foreclose the new channel of competition. At this point, matters can proceed to detailed technical negotiations, in order to agree on precise descriptions of the bombers to be prohibited, and to define the means of inspection which will be used by both sides to verify compliance. If the difficulties of drafting can be overcome, and mutually acceptable verification arrangements can be made, both sides will have avoided the costs of building new forces, as well as the risks they generate. The two countries will also have averted a further increase in the overall destructive potential of the military forces that any war might unleash, and, moreover, they will have prevented an increase in the role of the military and industrial interests of each society.

The same happy result may be achieved without any actual negotiations, through unilateral or tacit arms control. For example, country X may be initiating its bomber program in reaction to some tentative weapons-building plans being discussed in Y. If so, Y may pursue unilateral arms control by formally renouncing any intention of acquiring the weapons being considered, so long as X exercises similar restraint. Or else, to avoid provoking X with an offer of mutual restraint that could easily be misinterpreted as a polite ultimatum, Y may practice tacit as well as unilateral arms control by demonstratively abandoning plans to build the weapons which were triggering X's bomber effort, while leaving the conditions of its restraint implicit.

To some ears, unilateral arms control has defeatist connotations, but whether arms control is negotiated or unilateral, declared or tacit, is in fact of little consequence; the different methods can yield exactly the same beneficial results.

II

In this elementary and abstract formulation, the merits of arms control as a tool of national strategy are compelling. As compared to force-building, it offers a fully equivalent degree of security, and indeed a higher degree of security in many cases, at a much lower risk of instability and war, at no cost, without any increase in the ultimate destructive potential of war arsenals, and also without the deformations of society caused by the artificial growth of military-industrial interests. Whatever is wrong with arms control, then, it is clearly not its logic.

To be sure, this model of the basic theory is highly artificial, assuming, as it does, only two identical countries, with identical weapons-building capabilities and also good information. When these artificial assumptions are waived, practical obstacles arise.

For example, once the real world of many powers is accepted into the model, the scope of arms control may diminish. Country X may be deploying its bombers against country Z rather than against country Y; as far as Y is concerned, the threat to its security is real nonetheless, but in this case it cannot hope to dispose of the problem by negotiating a bilateral arms-limitation agreement with X, and still less can it hope to dissuade X by unilateral restraint and tacit bargaining. There does remain the possibility of multilateral arms control, with Z being brought in along with X and Y, but that would complicate matters severely, and might fail (even with ample good will all around) simply because of the sequence and phasing of the various force-building efforts. If, for instance, X is building its bombers in response to some effort by Z, undertaken by Z in the first place to react against the weapons being deployed by yet another country, by the time Y moves to negotiate limitations, X may be confronting weapons already being produced in country Z, and it in turn may be facing a force already deployed in country A.

And then, of course, countries are not identical, and neither are their weapons. In our model, the decisive argument that Y advances to persuade X to agree to bomber limitations is that Y can and will nullify whatever military or political gains X may be hoping to obtain from its new bombers. But if X is richer and more advanced than Y, its leaders may remain unpersuaded, and may calculate instead that Y will not be able to afford the resources needed to nullify their bomber effort. Alternatively, the leaders of X may concede that Y does have the resources needed to make their bomber program unprofitable, but they may also believe that Y's rulers lack the political will to react, or that Y's populace may refuse to make the necessary sacrifices. In either case, arms control may be impossible.

Variety in weapons characteristics is as great a problem as variety in the countries that build them. If X is planning to build weapons of a given type, and Y of another, the two countries may disagree about their respective capabilities, thus failing to agree on criteria for reciprocal limitations. It is enormously difficult to find any objective standard to measure the capabilities of dissimilar weapons: strategic bombers may have more payload than strategic missiles, but the performance of the latter may be more reliable, especially if anti-bomber defenses are deployed while anti-missile defenses are not. Even within the same category of weapons, comparisons are very difficult. (Until quite recently there was disagreement on the capabilities of the new Soviet Backfire bomber even within different agencies of the same U.S. government.) In practice, each side may privately believe that its own weapons are superior, while arguing the opposite in arms-control negotiations. ("If you are allowed to build fifty of your large-payload bombers, then our side must be allowed to build a hundred of our little missiles.")

Even if there is no deliberate manipulation—which the internal politics of arms control does tend to encourage—there is much scope for honest disagreement. Prudent defense planners must be conservative in assessing the performance of their own forces (thus evaluating downward) while being equally conservative in estimating the enemy's strength (thus evaluating upward). In their calculations, prudent country Y planners must accordingly assume that all the bombers of country X are fully operational when needed, and that very few would be intercepted by Y's defenses, while at the same time making all due allowance for technical failures, enemy intercepts, and maintenance rotation when estimating the capabilities of their own weapons. And of course country X planners must make the opposite assumptions. With prudent evaluation on both sides, there is therefore a systematic difference in the weight that each side gives to the forces of the other.

Geographic and demographic differences compound the difficulty of evaluating weapons and forces. If the forward bases of country Y are quite close to the main cities of X, then the two sides may disagree on what is a "strategic" weapon at all. From the X-country point of view, Y's light bombers might as well be heavy since they only have a short way to travel. But it may be very difficult to secure an agreement in which Y's light bombers are counted on the same footing as Y's heavies: any departure from clear-cut parities is likely to meet much resistance.

Differences of demographic structure are of particular importance in today's world of nuclear forces aimed at entire national populations. If country X is largely urban, with some high proportion of its population in a few large city areas, while Y's population is significantly more dispersed, then the destructive potential of identical nuclear forces will be correspondingly different. Country X is not likely to agree to a treaty that limits each side to, say, fifty identical missiles, if Y's fifty missiles can kill 70 per cent of X's population while X's identical force can only kill, say, 7 per cent of Y's population. Of course, a formula that equalizes vulnerability rather than the forces themselves could be written into a treaty. But again, as matters are made more complicated, agreement becomes correspondingly less likely.

And then there is the still greater problem of information. Nowadays, the superpowers have reliable observation satellites, and indeed much of the whole arms-control phenomenon has been brought into existence by their development. It is well known that TV and film cameras carried into space by orbiting satellites can produce very precise images of the ground below for immediate transmission, or in a more accurate and secure form, the data can also be recovered on film. (Capsules released from orbiting satellites in space are caught at low altitudes in a rather spectacular manner by transport aircraft equipped with nets.) But if satellite observation is available for arms-control inspection, it is equally available to find targets for a disarming "counterforce" attack. This provides an automatic incentive to build exactly those types of strategic weapons (mobile and/or concealed) which *cannot* be reliably located by satellite observation, and the qualities which protect against attack must also prevent inspection for arms control.

In retrospect, it seems clear that the advent of satellite observation in the 1960's did not truly abolish strategic secrecy, thus assuring the information needed for arms control forever after; satellites merely opened a temporary window in the wall of secrecy because of the sheer coincidence that the weapons of the 1960's happened to be large and easily identifiable. Satellite observation came along precisely when the weapons that the cameras could identify and count were being deployed. Nowadays, by contrast, we have new types of weapons, including both cruise and ballistic missiles, which are mobile or small, or both, and thus easily concealed from satellite obser-

vation. While it is virtually impossible to hide fixed-site ballistic missiles, properly housed in their concrete "silos," or the yards in which submarines are built, thousands of cruise missiles could be kept fully concealed quite easily. It is true that the scrutiny of the satellites, and all the incidental knowledge of industry which they provide, would undoubtedly allow us to determine whether or not some large number of mobile missiles had been built, but satellite cameras could not be used to count these weapons with any precision, any more than they could help us to fix their position for a disarming counterforce attack.

This brings to the surface the peculiar paradox of arms control over the cruise missile. The qualities of the cruise missile which subvert the procedures of negotiated limitations are precisely the qualities which also achieve the substantive purposes of arms control. Because cruise missiles are small, inherently mobile, and therefore easily concealed, it is a hopeless task to devise any treaty to limit them that would rest on any serious assurance of verification. But their small size is also the reason that cruise missiles are relatively cheap. Further, since these small and easily concealed weapons are not vulnerable to disarming counterforce attacks, rival cruise-missile forces should be quite stable: neither side could hope to disarm the other in a surprise attack, so that both sides can be secure. Thus not only the costs, but also the risks generated by these weapons, are inherently smaller than those of the fixed-site ballistic missiles now deployed. It follows that as far as cruise missiles are concerned, the best form of arms control may be no control at all.

But the nexus between arms control and the information needed to draft treaties and to verify compliance entails a deeper and ultimately more sinister paradox. If all obstacles are overcome and arms-control treaties are duly negotiated to constrain all that *can* be constrained with adequate verification, the ironical result might be to displace the strategic competition from the large weapons of classic form that are easily identified and counted, to weapons that have neither attribute. In a world of many powers, each with its own distinct internal politics of resource-allocation, and each with its own circle of friends and enemies, it is entirely unlikely that arms-control efforts, however successful, can achieve more than to prohibit the deployment of specific weapons and forces. The hope, sometimes expressed, that arms control may in itself bring the strategic competition to an end is supported neither by the pure logic of arms control nor by the experience of its practice.

Successful arms-control efforts will therefore channel the competition for military power into the development of those weapons which are not subject to limitations because they cannot be identified and counted. In this way, the very success of arms control may eventually create a situation of the most dangerous instability, in which all sides are working on small and easily concealed weapons which can suddenly appear fully operational to confront unready opponents. With each side knowing that it may be faced by strategic surprise at any time, maximum incentives for competition, and for preventive war, will have been created.

It is true that even at present the imponderable results of research efforts conducted in the secrecy of military laboratories entail a permanent danger of instability. But the large-scale force-building efforts now conducted openly (because arms control is not effective) provide a double guarantee against destabilizing surprise. First, the sheer scale of the visible efforts implies a corresponding limitation on the resources flowing into secret force-building activities; second, the large and diversified forces now deployed provide a high degree of insurance that the sudden emergence of any revolutionary new weapon will not undermine stability. This indeed is the logic of current American deployment. The land-based missiles, the submarine systems, and the long-range bombers could all be neutralized quite suddenly by the emergence of revolutionary devices. But simultaneous breakthroughs in all the very different scientific areas involved are most unlikely.

Neither guarantee can survive in the wake of prolonged and successful arms-control efforts, through which the forces in place will have been greatly reduced in size and diversification, and through which *overt* force-building efforts will have been greatly diminished or even eliminated, thus releasing abundant resources for less visible activities. True, secrecy is much more easily maintained in laboratory research than in engineering development, when weapons are taken out to be tested, but this does not dispose of the problem. Even if the tests of some revolutionary new weapon that threatens to undermine stability were duly observed and properly understood, it might take years for development to catch up, and in the meantime the prospect of unilat-

eral vulnerability will be an incentive to preventive war. This, then, is the ultimate irony: the inherent limits that information sets on the scope of arms control may mean that the final reward of sustained success in arms control will be the utter defeat of its goals.

Still, even when all these practical problems and all these dangers of varying likelihood are taken into account, arms control remains in principle a much more desirable alternative than force-building.

Bilateral arms control is undoubtedly easier to achieve than arms control in the real world of many powers, but then multilateral agreements are scarcely an impossibility, either. Negotiations will be more complicated when many parties are involved, but on the other hand, the existence of alliances may offer solutions denied in the pure bilateral case of country X and country Y. For example, alliances can help to overcome the difficulties that emerge when the artificial assumption of identical countries is waived. Country Y may be too poor, or too irresolute, effectively to discourage X from opening a new channel of competition by building its bombers, but an alliance of Y and Z may together dissuade X by convincingly threatening to nullify the gains of its bomber program through a joint force-building effort of their own.

As for differences in weapons characteristics, and the built-in asymmetry caused by conservative evaluations on each side, these certainly create many difficulties, but they are after all of a purely technical character, and patient negotiations by technical experts should in principle be able to overcome such problems.

Much the same goes for geographic and demographic differences between the parties. Given good will, or rather a rational appreciation of the mutual advantages of restraint, there is no reason why formulas could not be found to equalize the asymmetries. If Y's light bombers can reach the main cities of X as easily as X's heavy bombers can travel the much greater distance to Y's cities deep inland, then the two physically different forces can be evaluated by their actual effectiveness against their respective targets, and then limited accordingly in a treaty. Similarly, if X is inherently more vulnerable to nuclear bombardment because of its higher population densities, Y's weapons can be more severely restricted so as to yield equality in destructive power under an arms-limitation treaty.

Even the paradox of visibility and vulnerability, as well as the long-term effects of arms control over the more visible weapons which release resources for more unstable invisible weapons, does not make arms control futile. If cruise missiles inherently achieve the substantive aims of arms control, let the negotiations focus on the many other costly and destabilizing weapons now being built. As for the long-term problem, it may well be argued that in the presence of today's luxuriant force-building, the immediate gains of economy and safety that arms control can yield are of much greater consequence than the remote dangers which successful arms control may eventually cause in the very long term. Certainly these hypothetical dangers need not deter the modest efforts now under way.

III

Whatever is wrong with arms control, therefore, it is not the various practical difficulties, each of which can be overcome, at least in part.

If our arms-control model is brought still nearer to reality by substituting the Soviet Union and the United States for X and Y, a new set of difficulties immediately arises. The Soviet Union undoubtedly lacks the attributes of an ideal partner for arms control; indeed, some might say that it is grotesquely miscast for the part.

The first obstacle is the Soviet negotiating style. If a unilateral concession is made to Soviet negotiators for the sake of "generating a positive atmosphere," the Soviet side will take what is given but will under no circumstances volunteer a reciprocal concession. It is not that Soviet diplomats are necessarily tougher than Western negotiators or even that their conduct is a symptom of inflexibility. It is merely a question of method. Soviet negotiators insist on treating each issue quite separately, making the best bargain they can in each case. They do not try to smooth the path to agreement by yielding on lesser points for the sake of the common interest in the outcome of the negotiations as a whole.

There is training and tradition behind this method; there may also be fear, personal fear. Soviet diplomats must clearly remember what happened to their colleagues during the earlier stages of the purge period under Stalin, when very many were killed or deported on the charge that they had betrayed the Soviet side in international negotiations by making unnecessary concessions. (In the later stages of the great purge, this was no longer the case: mere contact with foreigners was then often sufficient evidence of treason.) But whatever the reason, Soviet negotiators invariably seek to make each bargain as specific as possible, and far from trying to create a good "negotiating climate," will sometimes deliberately stage episodes of uncivil conduct as a bargaining tactic, to intimidate the other side or just to distract attention.

None of this need matter very much in negotiations where single issues must be decided by straightforward bargaining. One can certainly agree on the price of a shipment of apples with Soviet traders as well as one can with their British or French counterparts. But in trying to negotiate significant arms-control measures, one must almost invariably trade *across* the issues, since the variety of weapons characteristics and all the other asymmetries make issue-by-issue bargaining very difficult.

In Western diplomatic practice, negotiators often make "good-will" exchanges to one another to help overcome technical complexities and other intractable obstacles to agreement. If Britons and Americans are negotiating on the price of apples today and will move on to determine the price of pears tomorrow, and there is sharp disagreement on both, one side may well yield on the price of the apples in the expectation that the other side will feel duty-bound to show flexibility when negotiations move on to pears. In dealing with Soviet negotiators, by contrast, the full difficulty of resolving the apple issue will have to be confronted, and when the discussions move on to the pears, the process must begin all over again, with neither side having good-will points in hand to make an agreement any easier. Given the inherent complexities of arms-control negotiations, and the great scope for sharp disagreements on hard technical questions, it is evident that issue-by-issue bargaining may sometimes make agreement quite impossible.

A second and more serious obstacle to arms control with the Soviet Union is the very nature of its politics. The logic of arms control depends on the recognition of a common interest in avoiding force-building which can bring no *national* advantage. In our initial example, country X refrains from building its planned bomber force because it calculates that after Y has duly reacted, it will have gained no net benefit, "it" being the country as a whole, rather than its soldiers and weapons builders. But if country X is the Soviet Union, then the logic may not apply at all.

In American politics, arms contractors have some political leverage, especially on Capitol Hill, since they employ quite a few constituents. (In fact, the arms industry seems to have more influence than the soft-drink bottlers, though of course much less than the dairy farmers.) But in the Soviet Union the "metal eaters," as the party leaders who run the military industries are known, are not just one interest group among many, as in the United States, but rather core members of the major coalition of Soviet politics. The key to the ability of the "metal eaters" to claim such a large proportion of Soviet economic resources seems to be their alliance with the secret police at one end—whose calls for "vigilance" and whose repressions are justified by the fancied menace of NATO and of the Chinese—and, at the other, with the armed forces, which of course have a direct consumer interest in military production.

The politics of the Kremlin are poorly understood, but virtually all our experts agree that the coalition of the KGB, soldiers, and military-production managers is a major force in shaping policy. It follows that within the Soviet Union there is powerful and systematic pressure for more force-building—in fact, there is every reason to believe that the coalition only allowed Brezhnev to embark upon the policy of détente on condition that the military build-up would continue as before, if not actually accelerate. This state of affairs naturally restricts the scope of arms control, since the common interest on which it must be based cannot be the Soviet "society-wide" interest in economy and safety. Instead, there is only the much narrower overlap between the general U.S. interest on the one hand, and the highly specialized interests of the Soviet military-production coalition on the other. American SALT negotiators were given some idea of the peculiar autonomy of the "metal eaters," even at a fairly high level in the Soviet government, when a senior Russian delegate privately asked his American counterpart to persuade his colleagues to stop discussing the details of Soviet forces in front of the *Soviet* foreign-ministry types in the delegation.

Another serious obstacle to arms control is the traditional Russian passion for secrecy. Even after many years of supposedly intimate negotiations on strategic forces, the Russians refuse to disclose any meaningful information about the characteristics of their weapons and the structure of their forces, let alone about their force-building plans; there is not even any substitute discussion of Soviet strategy and

doctrine. It has been reported that in SALT both delegations use only American data, for Soviet as well as for American forces; apparently the Soviet delegates have not even disclosed the proper designations of their weapons (that is why the terminology of the 1972 SALT-1 accords is so vague, with references to "ballistic-missile launchers of older types" and so on, in lieu of any precise designation). Of course, satellite observation can provide a reliable count of strategic weapons, so long as they are fairly large, of classic form, and actually deployed. However, not even the magic of high-resolution cameras, scanning computers, and electronic intelligence can reveal weapons until after they have been tested, and sometimes not until they are actually deployed. Unfortunately, the success of arms control often depends on information at the earliest possible stage of the force-building cycle and certainly before production is under way. If country Y finds out about X's bombers only when the prototypes begin to appear on the testing airstrip, it will usually be too late to negotiate limitations. Within country X, the bomber effort will have acquired momentum, if only because much of the total cost will have been paid already, and Y on the other hand cannot have much confidence in a limitation treaty if X already has developed prototypes, ready for large-scale production at any time. The Soviet refusal to publish future deployment plans—as the United States does—or indeed anything at all specific about its military forces, past, present, or future, therefore restricts the scope of arms control rather seriously.

The Russian passion for secrecy also diminishes the scope of arms control by making verification extremely difficult. Satellite observation is once again crucial, but for all the remarkable detail of the photography, and the valuable performance data that can be obtained from electronic intelligence, the information may nevertheless be too ambiguous to give sufficient confidence for proper verification: data which are technically very good may be worthless because Soviet secrecy denies the wider circumstantial knowledge that can give them meaning. When Soviet satellite cameras photograph a missile-like object on some American testing site, Soviet analysts can usually identify the missile quite easily and they can then consult an abundance of published information on the exact specifications of the missile, its particular mission, the number to be built, and so on. By contrast, American analysts provided with a similar photograph can do no better than guess the mission of the weapon and make very tentative estimates of its range and payload. Usually the numbers to be built cannot be estimated at all: the counting can begin only when the weapons are actually being deployed. Even then, doubts may remain; for all we know, there could be hundreds of uncounted strategic missiles kept in concealed places other than the characteristic operational launchers easily recognized in satellite photographs. In practice, this means that in dealing with the Soviet Union, standards of verification must be relaxed, or else many arms-control hopes must be abandoned. In either case, the scope for genuine—that is, properly verified—arms control is considerably restricted. Arms control without high-confidence verification is a contradiction in terms. It does not lessen the risks of conflict but increases them, and it does not diminish incentives to force-building but makes them stronger. Low-confidence verification is not a substitute for proper inspection procedures, and it is not even a good device to mask unilateral disarmament.

Another peculiarity of Soviet statecraft which affects arms control, or rather the observance of its agreed limitations, is the Soviet penchant for the use of probing tactics. Like the hotel thief who will not break a lock but who will walk down the corridors trying each door in the hope of finding one carelessly left open, Soviet policy constantly probes such arms limitations as there are, to exploit any gaps in American vigilance, as well as any loopholes in the agreed texts. For example, under the terms of Article IV of the 1967 Outer Space Treaty, no nuclear weapons may be placed in orbit around the earth. The Russians are not known to have sent up weapon satellites equipped with nuclear warheads, but they have continued to test the so-called FOBS version of the SS-9 heavy missiles since signing the treaty; with FOBS delivery, these large nuclear-capable missiles do not quite complete a full orbit around the earth, but rather descend to earth just before doing so. In this way, the Russians have tested a weapon (which may or may not have carried a nuclear warhead) without precisely violating the terms of the agreement, which defines space vehicles as those completing at least one *full* orbit around the earth.

An altogether more serious probing operation also failed to evoke firm American reaction. The 1972 ABM treaty, actually the only really significant arms-control measure in force at present, prohibits not only the deployment but also the development and testing of mobile systems designed to intercept ballistic mis-

siles (Article V). In a "common understanding" appended to the treaty on April 13, 1972, the Soviet Union further agreed that the development and testing of *any* non-fixed ABM component was forbidden by the treaty. However, for the last five years there have been persistent reports from authoritative intelligence sources that the Soviet Union has violated the treaty by testing components of mobile ABM systems at the Kapustin Yar and Shary Sagan ranges. It seems that there have been intermittent American complaints about these tests but no really determined action. It appears to be Soviet diplomatic doctrine that if the injured party does not resist such probing, it is actually giving its tacit consent, so that the violations are thereby virtually legitimized.

There are no doubt many observers who would dismiss each of these separate points as trivial, arguing quite simply that the Russians cannot be trusted to keep the agreements they sign, least of all important arms-control agreements. It is certainly true that the constant duplicity of Soviet public discourse scarcely inspires confidence. The Soviet press, radio, and television and all the overseas outlets of Soviet propaganda, do not merely slant the news and distort history, as many others do, but also disseminate a great quantity of outright falsehood, obviously quite deliberately. In the Soviet media, one may read stories full of circumstantial details about secret American cooperation in South African nuclear-weapons efforts, about the Nazi experts who instruct the Israeli General Staff, about CIA payoffs to Soviet dissidents, about West German plots against Czechoslovakia's independence [*sic*], and so on. At a more prosaic level, there is constant lying in newspaper articles which compare the Soviet and the Western standards of living, and these are lies known to be such by those who write them, by the typesetters, the proofreaders, the censors, and all but the most ignorant readers. All governments engage in lying, but in the Soviet Union deliberate and massive public falsehood is very much a normal circumstance, by now no doubt widely accepted as such. This naturally inspires doubts about the sincerity of any Soviet statements, and about the reliability of any Soviet undertakings, including those written into the texts of treaties.

Nevertheless, although the Soviet Union has violated many treaty commitments, this has mostly occurred in its dealings with the weak. There have been few outright violations of agreements signed with the United States, and of these violations, most have been quite small, in accordance with the slow tempo of Soviet probing tactics. (A recent outright violation was an exception. Article 4 of the Agreement on the Prevention of Nuclear War of June 22, 1973 required the Soviet Union to inform the United States of Arab preparations for the 1973 war, about which the Russians clearly knew a great deal. A mere 104 days passed between the signature of the agreement and its clear-cut violation.) Naturally the Soviet Union does not live up to the "spirit" of international understandings, but there is no duplicity at all in this case because Soviet diplomacy explicitly rejects that concept. In fact, Soviet leaders have been frank in stating that only the actual language of treaties is binding, so that everything not explicitly disallowed will be treated as fair game by them. It has been *Western* statesmen who have insisted that this or that summit, or treaty, has generated a binding "spirit" of cooperation.

A nation of lawyers such as ours should hardly be incapable of dealing with this particular problem. The Soviet refusal to accept voluntary inhibitions for the sake of the "spirit" of things merely requires that arms-control agreements be drafted very carefully indeed, in all necessary detail. The Soviet position is in fact quite traditional; Russians accept the necessity of fulfilling treaties (*pacta sunt servanda*) but they also maintain the hidden conditional clause, "so long as conditions do not change"—as do many others who will also break treaties if their interests are no longer served by them. This does not mean that the Soviet Union is not a fit party for arms control by treaty. It merely requires the United States to be ready at all times to make violation unprofitable.

None of the other obstacles to effective arms control caused by the peculiarities of Soviet conduct is decisive either. For example, it is true that the Soviet negotiating style, with its refusal to make good-will exchanges from issue to issue, greatly prolongs the process, but on the other hand, Soviet negotiators are very patient, and Soviet policy does not lack persistence. There is therefore plenty of time to overcome the additional complications created by ferocious haggling on each point. Certainly it should not be beyond the tenacity of our diplomats to suffer prolonged bargaining.

The structural obstacle of Soviet party politics is not so easily dismissed. Now that Ustinov, defense minister and former chief of military production, is overtly identified as a top-level leader, it is evident that the coalition of the "metal eaters" with the secret police and the armed forces is more powerful than ever. Even the traditionally optimistic analysts of the CIA concede that the Soviet Union is now allocating between 11 per cent and 13 per cent of its gross national product to military purposes, as compared to roughly 5.5 per cent for the United States; other reputable observers reject the CIA estimates as too low and argue for 15 or even 17 per cent, almost three times the American proportion. All seem to agree that Soviet defense expenditure has been increasing at a steady rate of roughly 4.5 per cent per year, for many years, and this too is much higher than the American rate, which was actually negative between 1968 and 1972, and which even now, when outlays on strategic weapons have increased, stands at *less* than 3 per cent, net of inflation.

The contrast in these figures suggests that the Soviet interest in equitable arms control is bound to be rather limited. But even this obstacle is not insurmountable. First of all, experts on the Soviet Union assure us that the coalition is not entirely dominant in the top echelon of the Soviet leadership. While it is true that the earlier plans for a major expansion of consumer-goods production have been dropped, the present leadership is making really huge investments in agriculture and it is steadily increasing the effort going into light industries. Such considerations must moderate in some degree the claims of the "metal eaters" on Soviet resources, and this in turn suggests that there may be room for successful arms control. Of course this is only true of weapons systems and forces that are particularly costly—as opposed to those that are particularly destabilizing or destructive—but that still leaves plenty of scope for arms control.

Nor should the obstacle of secrecy be overestimated. True, it is most unfortunate that the Soviet government insists on denying to its own citizens and to the outside world all manner of information, military or not, even when it gains no possible advantage from doing so. It would be much better for all concerned if the Soviet Union were to adopt the practices of most civilized states and publish its force-building plans in advance. The lack of advance information does mean that the huge advantage that comes from negotiating over force-building *plans*, as opposed to actual deployments, is irremediably lost. But the need to wait until weapons are brought out into the open to be tested need not utterly preclude successful arms control. Even if it would be preferable

to negotiate before the momentum of such investments has had an opportunity to develop, a rational
calculation of mutual advantages should still serve to
limit armaments, at least in those cases when *further*
outlays still to be made are sufficiently great, and the
likelihood of a determined American response is
sufficiently credible.

The effect of Russian secrecy on verification is not
decisive either. It must be conceded that the lack of
truthful budget data, the lack of a Soviet technical
press on military production, and the lack of other
sources of circumstantial knowledge make it very
difficult to interpret visual and electronic data to
verify compliance with arms-control agreements. But
on the other hand, verification ultimately requires
positive proof rather than circumstantial evidence. If
a violation must be proved to American and world
opinion as well as to Soviet delegates in consultative
meetings, generic evidence will not suffice in any case;
in fact, usually only the photography matters.

Nor does the Russian fondness for probing tactics
to create gaps in limitation agreements while fully
exploiting bona-fide loopholes make a stable arms-
control regime impossible. It does mean that the
United States must expect probing operations to
begin as soon as an agreement is signed, and that it
must be ready to take firm action to stop violations—
any violations, however small— as soon as they are
detected. It is of course fatal to mute protests and to
refrain from sanctions in order to preserve the "atmosphere of détente," and it is quite useless to
complain in general terms; unless appropriate retaliation is convincingly threatened for each specific violation, complaints will simply be ignored. It should be
normal American practice, for example, to suspend
all U.S.-Soviet negotiations, on *all* issues, military or
not, as soon as there is fully reliable evidence of the
deliberate violations of any prior agreements still in
force. Failure to do this may harden the Soviet
position in general, and it certainly invites further
probing: unless there is a prompt and forceful reaction, those Soviet officials of moderate views who had
counseled prudence in the pre-violation internal policy debate will be undermined, and the hardline
advocates of further probing will be strengthened.
Inaction tends to legitimize the prior gains of probing
operations while inviting new ones, and since each
small step leads to the next, any violation, even if
quite inconsequential in itself, must be resisted in full
force. For example, when the United States failed to

react adequately to the visits of Soviet ballistic-missile
submarines to Cuban ports (in violation of an executive agreement), these visits were gradually length-
ened until the presence of the submarines became a
commonplace. Next, supporting facilities were established. American protests led to the removal of
non-critical crew facilities, but technically essential
maintenance items remained. This situation has now
been inherited by the Carter administration as a
reality no longer open to challenge. Similarly, the
Russians used probing tactics in implementing the
SALT-1 accords by taking new submarines out for sea
trials before scrapping equal numbers of pre-1964
land-based missiles (or converting older submarines)
as required by "agreed interpretation" K appended to
the 1972 "interim agreement." Again, American
complaints on the matter were belated and not forceful. It seems that the Russians blamed the poor
weather for the overlap, and that the feeble excuse
was accepted. If a new SALT treaty includes similar
provisions, "slippages" will no doubt become quite
routine.

At a time when the Soviet Union has more than
2,500 nuclear weapons of intercontinental range, it
may be difficult for an outsider to understand why its
military and civil officials would try so hard to cheat
on the rules to deploy a few more weapons here and
there, which can add nothing of substance to overall
Soviet capabilities. It is hard to resist the impression
that for these men there are rewards to be had for
cheating successfully, rewards political or bureaucratic. All this is of course very unpleasant, and also at
first quite unsettling for those who come to deal with
the Soviet Union from the relatively innocent atmosphere of American academia or even American public life. However, so long as the United States acts
correctly,—that is, promptly and forcefully—probing
tactics can be defeated, or at least contained so as to
make their results insignificant from the arms-control
viewpoint.

IV

It is therefore clear that none of the peculiarities of
Soviet conduct is a decisive obstacle to successful
arms control. Whatever is wrong with arms control, it
is not the fact that dealings with the Soviet Union
must loom large in its pursuit.

The process of elimination has left only one possible culprit: the United States.

While arms control can only be effective in limiting specific deployments under specific arrangements, serving thereby as an alternative to force-building, the United States has consistently misused arms control in pursuit of the abstract goal of "strategic parity." When that concept was challenged, it was redefined by the White House as "essential equivalence," which is equally vague. Neither set of words has any meaning in the reality of weapons or forces. Neither set of words can define negotiating objectives.

While arms control can only be effectively pursued if negotiated limitations are defined with extreme precision, the United States has consistently tolerated ambiguities in its urgent pursuit of agreement for its own sake. As a result, a new and entirely artificial source of U.S.-Soviet tensions has been created. Changes in the Soviet strategic forces that would otherwise have passed almost unnoticed have excited suspicion and resentment when seen in high contrast against the poorly drafted texts of the 1972 Moscow accords. One side-benefit of each arms-control agreement should be to build confidence for the next, but the tension-creating ambiguities of SALT-1 have utterly defeated this purpose.

While effective arms control requires that high standards of compliance be enforced, the United States has consistently allowed Soviet probing to develop without effective challenge. This permissive stance was a natural consequence of the attempt to use SALT as a general sedative in U.S.-Soviet relations. The attempt has undoubtedly failed, SALT having become, on balance, a further source of friction. But in the process, arms control itself has been discredited, since negotiated agreements have been enforced far too loosely in deference to the atmospherics of détente.

Above all, the United States has misused arms control in the attempt to dampen the strategic competition in itself, as if the growth of strategic arsenals were the cause of Soviet-American rivalry rather than merely one of its symptoms, and incidentally a much less dangerous symptom than the growth of non-nuclear forces, whose warlike use is much more likely.

Who are the men in this country who have brought about these consequences that may yet prove to be catastrophic? Some, including a former Secretary of Defense, are essentially technicians, who have nevertheless been allowed to shape strategic policy as if its essence were technical rather than political. Unable to define the benefits of superior strategic-nuclear forces with technical precision, in mathematical terms, entirely unable to comprehend the diffuse political meaning of military capabilities, these technicians who imagine themselves to be strategists see no reason why the United States should strive to keep a strategic superiority which they believe to be meaningless. After all, they can prove with their mathematical models that there is no middle level of capability between the minimum of strike-back deterrence and the unattainable maximum of a disarming counter-force capability. Under attack for having waged war in Indochina, these men have embraced the cause of unilateral arms control with much enthusiasm; the activity has a pleasantly humanitarian connotation and also some intellectual appeal (arms-control models can be interesting) while supposedly entailing no loss in "real" American strength.

Others, sometimes very influential but mostly outside government, advocate arms control because it is a respectable vehicle for an isolationist foreign policy. After all, the logical result of abandoning additional forces and retaining only a strike-back capability is to uncouple American nuclear forces from NATO and the other alliances. The United States will still be able to deter any direct nuclear attack upon its own soil, and only the nuclear protection offered to its allies will be sacrificed.

For still others, by no means devoid of influence, arms control is a substitute for disarmament, which to their regret the American people still entirely reject. More or less convincing arms-control arguments can always be invoked, along with technical, economic, and now environmental objections, to oppose any and every strategic weapon that the services want to build. Some of these unilateral disarmers camouflaged as arms controllers simply believe that strategic-nuclear weapons are so destructive that their use cannot ultimately serve any rational purpose, military or political. Some are driven by a passionate desire to change the course of world history, so largely characterized by the dismal consequences of force-building, and they do not accept the prosaic objection that wars are most frequently brought about by the failure to make aggression unprofitable. Others among them oppose American weapons because they are American, and remain quite undisturbed by the huge increase in all forms of Soviet military power; believing America to be an essentially evil force in the affairs of mankind, they necessarily regard all instruments of American power as instruments of evil. And some arms-control advocates share none of these beliefs but have merely made arms control their profession, having found work in the dozens of anti-Pentagon lobbies which are now active. Seeing themselves in unequal combat with the vast defense bureaucracy and the still greater military bureaucracies, and forced to contend with a public which obstinately continues to believe that the richest country on earth should also be the most powerful, these professional advocates of arms control concentrate their energies on fighting the Pentagon.

Arms control can be no more than a tool of national strategy if it is to be effective. It is an alternative to the other tool, the deployment of weapons, and it can be the superior alternative. But this is only true when its goals are the same, that is, the goals of national strategy: to enhance security at the lowest possible cost and risk. In American policy, arms control has usurped the function of strategy and has become an end in itself. The consequences are now manifest: the unilateral arms control pursued by the U.S. since at least 1964, and the bilateral efforts that culminated in the 1972 Moscow agreements, have diminished rather than enhanced American security; they have not contained the growth of the arsenals of both superpowers; they have increased rather than diminished outlays on U.S. strategic forces; and they have now begun to compromise strategic stability, since the increasing obsolescence of an old bomber force and the approaching vulnerability of American land-based missiles will soon leave the submarine-missile force exposed to undivided Soviet counter-force efforts. As a result of these unhappy trends, we may be approaching a new period of acute instability in which we will be forced to undertake very expensive build-up programs on a crash basis. One consequence is already with us: the trust that allies can place in American nuclear protection has been sharply diminished, the bonds of alliance have been weakened, and powerful incentives have been created for nuclear proliferation.

American strategic policy has been dominated for more than a decade by the overwhelming desire to bring the Soviet-American competition to an end. Arms control could never serve such an unstrategic purpose, and its use to mask a renunciatory passivity

in the face of the Soviet build-up has merely served to compromise a perfectly respectable tool of strategic policy.

QUESTIONS FOR DISCUSSION

1 What are the factors inhibiting real reductions in defense expenditures? Can these be overcome?

2 Do arms races cause wars?

3 Do negotiated arms control agreements promote détente, peace, and better relations among nations?

4 Is disarmament possible? Is it desirable?

5 What is the impact of technological innovation on arms control?

SUGGESTED READINGS

Beer, Francis A. *Peace Against War: The Ecology of International Violence.* San Francisco: Freeman, 1981.

Blechman, Barry M. "Do Negotiated Arms Limitations Have a Future?" *Foreign Affairs* **59** (Fall 1980): 102–125.

Blechman, Barry M., and Stephen S. Kaplan. *Force Without War: U.S. Armed Forces as a Political Instrument.* Washington, D.C.: Brookings, 1978.

Carlton, David, and Carlo Schaerf (eds.). *Arms Control and Technological Innovation.* London: Croom Helm, 1977.

Epstein, William. *The Last Chance: Nuclear Proliferation and Arms Control.* New York: Free Press, 1976.

Friedberg, Aaron L. "What SALT Can (And Cannot) Do." *Foreign Policy* No. **33** (Winter 1978–1979): 92–100.

Johansen, Robert C. "Arms Bazaar: SALT Was Never Intended to Disarm." *Harper's Magazine* (May 1979): 21, 24, and 28–29.

Lord, Carnes. "The ABM Question." *Commentary* (May 1980): 31–38.

Luttwak, Edward N. "Ten Questions About SALT II." *Commentary* (August 1979): 21–32.

Myrdal, Alva. *The Game of Disarmament: How the United States and Russia Run the Arms Race.* New York: Pantheon Books, 1976.

18 Does International Law Serve as a Constraint on Terrorism?

YES

Alona E. Evans

Perspectives on International Terrorism

NO

L. C. Green

The Legalization of Terrorism

Perspectives on International Terrorism
Alona E. Evans

INTRODUCTION

Recent terrorist incidents in Tehran, Islamabad, Bogota, Mexico City, Ankara, London, San Salvador, Misgav Am, Hebron, Sarafand, Nablus-Ramallah, Washington, Rome, and Athens demonstrate—if we need the proof— that international terrorism is a part of modern life. In this context, little solace is found in the thought that there is nothing new about the kind of behavior and frame of mind manifested in the violence, usually directed against unwitting victims, which characterizes terrorism. History is replete with examples, and the French Revolution cannot be held responsible for initiating the personal or factional power struggles which erupt into terrorist acts.

What is new, however, is a growing disposition on the part of a wide variety of states to recognize that international terrorists are no respecters of persons, places, governments, international organizations, or international communications systems. In the long run, each state has a stake in the control of international terrorism, lest it find itself controlled by terrorists or, at least, enthralled in an unending struggle to contain them. "Control" is the word, not "eradication," for international terrorism is an inevitable part of the international scene, at least for the foreseeable future. Terrorism is inevitable if people are unwilling to recognize that, as Mr. Justice Brandeis once observed, some questions can be decided, if not answered. In the international community, many questions must be decided in the short run because the answer can be found only through experience over an extended period. In this context, states are beginning to face the problem of control in international terrorism. Control is formulated within the framework of legal measures, focusing upon prevention of terrorist acts, upon consultation and negotiation in the resolution of terrorist incidents, and upon the apprehension and prosecution of terrorist offenders.

"International terrorism" is defined here as comprehending acts of violence undertaken by private persons, factions, or groups with the intent of intimidating or harming internationally protected persons, endangering public safety, interfering with the activities of international organizations, damaging or destroying internationally protected property, or disrupting international transportation or communications systems for the purpose of undermining friendly relations among states or among the nationals of different states.[1] The subject is considered in terms of the following questions: (1) what are the dimensions of international terrorism today; (2) what impact do legal measures have upon control of international terrorism; and (3) what problems of legal control should be in prospect for this decade.

I. THE DIMENSIONS OF INTERNATIONAL TERRORISM

Experience over the past two decades shows that international terrorists are as diverse in nature as the states in which they operate. Terrorists may act for real or for ostensibly political reasons or for no discernible reasons at all. They may be members of organized political groups of long standing, such as the Croatian separatist movement or the Irish Republic Army (IRA). They may be splinter factions of organized groups. Examples of splinter factions include the Provisional Wing of the IRA (Provos) and the Popular Front for the Liberation of Palestine, which has a tenuous connection with the Palestine Liberation Organization. Terrorists may be ideological mercenaries, such as the Japan Red Army. They may be random actors, such as the Eagles of the Revolution who attacked the Egyptian Embassy at Ankara last July, the terrorists who seized the American Embassy at Tehran last November, or the M-19 *soi-disant* "soccer players"[2] who seized the Domini-

---

[1] COMMITTEE ON INTERNATIONAL TERRORISM, INTERNATIONAL LAW ASSOCIATION, REPORT OF THE FIFTY-SEVENTH CONFERENCE, MADRID 1976 art. I(1), at 143-44 (1978)(Draft Outline of Single Convention on Legal Control of International Terrorism).

[2] Newsweek, Mar. 17, 1980, at 57.

From Alona E. Evans, "Perspectives on International Terrorism," *Willamette Law Review* **17** (Winter 1980): 151–164.

can Embassy at Bogota in February 1980. They may be "hired guns" of a regime, as in the recent wave of attacks upon Libyan exiles in a number of countries. To this motley collection, there must be added individuals who engage in international terrorist acts for personal reasons—to escape from trial or prison, from family, or from a psychotic condition. From these individuals typically develop the aircraft hijacker or mad bomber.

The victims may be anyone because terrorists are no respecters of persons: male or female, old or young, infants or school children, diplomats or businessmen, tourists or housewives. For terrorists the ends justify the means, and the means must, of necessity, be violent. Geographically, terrorism is widespread. It occurs in states in which there is political turmoil as well as in those in which there is political stability. The nature of the incumbent government appears to have little relevance, for international terrorism is found in states with democratic governments, authoritarian governments, and in countries which are close to or have achieved anarchy. The factor of an effective government is significant, however, where hostages are concerned. For instance, compare the unhappy situation at the American Embassy in Tehran with the successful conclusion of the situation at the Dominican Embassy in Bogota[3] or with the vigorous but successful conclusion of the situation at the Iranian Embassy in London.[4]

International terrorists focus upon certain types of targets. Internationally protected persons and premises are fair game for a variety of reasons. The diplomat or embassy may be seen as a symbol of foreign domination or of objectionable ideas; a diplomat or embassy may be attacked as a way of embarrassing the incumbent government of the territorial state to which the terrorists are opposed by creating strained relations between that government and the country which the embassy represents; or the act may be done to accomplish the terrorists' objectives by overriding the policies of the incumbent government or by acting in the absence of a government. Whatever the rationale, the fact remains that the inviolability of internationally protected persons has been established in customary international law for several millenia or

through international conventions and agreements. Examples of the latter are the Vienna Convention on Diplomatic Relations of 1961,[5] the United Nations Convention on the Prevention and Punishment of Crimes against Internationally Protected Persons,[6] and a number of bilateral agreements such as the Treaty of Amity, Economic Relations, and Consular Rights between the United States and Iran of 1955.[7]

Terrorist attacks upon international civil aviation in the form of aircraft hijacking began to flourish in 1968. To date, these attacks are unabated. There also have been many acts of sabotage against aircraft and a variety of attacks upon aviation facilities, including urban airline offices. The rationale for these acts seemingly is the immediate interruption of international communications and publicity for the terrorists' causes.

In recent years, multinational corporations are frequent targets of international terrorists. These attacks are directed against high managerial personnel, both foreign nationals and nationals of the territorial state, who are kidnapped and held for ransom.[8] The object of these acts is either to make a point about the alleged economic exploitation of a country by the foreign corporation or to embarrass the government that allowed the corporation to operate within its territory. The consequences of these acts are strained international relations and domestic unrest.

Another form of international terrorism is reflected in the efforts by terrorists to advance their causes in the home state by violent action abroad. The Croatian separatist movement is active in this way. For example, the movement hijacked an American aircraft to Paris and distributed manifestoes en route.[9] Similarly, the Baader-Meinhof gang mounted an attack upon the Embassy of the Federal Republic of Germany at Stockholm.[10] The ultimate political effect of these acts in the home state is not marked by success. Conse-

---

[3] Christian Sci. Mon., Apr. 29, 1980, at 4, col. 3.
[4] N.Y. Times, May 7, 1980, § A, at 1, col 3; *id.* May 9, 1980, § A, at 3, col. 1.

[5] 23 U.S.T. 3227, T.I.A.S. No. 7502, 500 U.N.T.S. 95.
[6] Dec. 14, 1973, 28 U.S.T. 1975, T.I.A.S. No. 8532.
[7] 8 U.S.T. 899, T.I.A.S. No. 3853, 284 U.N.T.S. 93.
[8] *E.g.*, Williams F. Niehous, Operations Manager of Owens-Illinois, Inc., in Venezuela who was kidnapped and held by terrorists for three and a half years until his escape in July 1979. N.Y. Times, July 2, 1979, § A, at 3, col. 1.
[9] *Id.* Sept. 22, 1976, at 22, col. 2.
[10] KEESING'S CONTEMPORARY ARCHIVES, 27261A (1975); *id.* 28922 (1977).

quently, terrorists find themselves subject to prosecution and imprisonment.[11]

The assassination of a national in exile whose existence is perceived to be inimical to the interests of a government is becoming more common. This is a form of state terrorism because the act is apparently carried out under the overt or covert auspices of a foreign government. The ramifications of state terrorism are not discussed here. Yet, the international dimensions of the assassinations of Orlando Letelier[12] in the United States, the Libyan exiles in Italy, the Federal Republic of Germany, Greece, and the United Kingdom[13] warrant mention of this form of terrorism. The rationale for these acts apparently is internal political conflicts involving insecure governments. The effect, however, is international and can be detrimental to the relations between the state in which the acts occur and the state which instigated or condoned them.[14]

These few instances suggest something of the scope of international terrorism. The possibility of new directions[15] for international terrorism is a gloomy prospect. It is obvious that modern refinements in explosive and incendiary devices, not to speak of chemical and biological weapons, could yield critical effects if used upon the populations of both developed and developing states. These high-potential weapons also have some significance for purposes of extortion. The highly developed industrial states, such as the United States, Japan, and the Western European states, display ready vulnerability to terrorist attacks, relying as they do upon sophisticated economic processes heavily dependent on the use of computers in business, banking, and government. One can expound upon the future targets of international terrorism, possibly running the risk of the self-fulfilling prophecy. But an analysis of the current habits of international terrorists suggests that a well-placed molotov cocktail may be more effective than the threat of botulism poisoning or of nuclear explosion.

II. THE IMPACT OF LEGAL CONTROLS UPON INTERNATIONAL TERRORISM

Having sketched some manifestations of current and prospective international terrorism, it may be asked whether the legal controls developed in the past decade have demonstrated any success in such highly political situations. Any answer must be based upon the premise that political ends do not justify illegal means; law provides the frame of reference for any response to terrorist acts. A government which chooses to fight terrorism with terrorism runs the risk of outdoing the terrorists by destroying the fabric of the state itself.

International legal controls have been particularly evident in two kinds of international terrorism: aircraft hijacking and attacks upon internationally protected persons. Aircraft hijacking reached its zenith in 1969 with eighty-nine incidents. Since then, there has been a gradual decline in incidence, twenty-seven hijackings having been reported for 1979.[16] Looking at the total number of passenger kilometers flown in any given year, the number of hijackings is statistically unalarming. Indeed, this undoubtedly contributed to lethargic state recognition that hijacking was a serious matter and that it was here to stay. What remains troublesome is that aircraft hijacking continues ten years after the 1970 Convention for the Suppression of Unlawful Seizure of Aircraft at The Hague.[17] Becoming, in a sense, the prototype for multilateral antiterrorist conventions, The Hague Convention established the offense of seizing or attempting to seize control of an aircraft in flight. The states that are parties to the Convention committed themselves to extradite hijackers or to submit them to prosecution. Any state which is a party to the Con-

---

[11] See note 9 supra. A jury found four of the five Croatian hijackers guilty of aircraft piracy; the fifth pleaded guilty to this charge. N.Y. Times, May 3, 1977, § B, at 4, col. 2.

[12] Id. Sept. 22, 1976, at 1, col. 2 (late city ed.).

[13] Id. May 23, 1980, § A, at 4, col. 2; Christian Sci. Mon., Oct. 5, 1978, at 5, col. 1 ("umbrella murders" of Bulgarian exiles in London).

[14] The United States ordered six Libyan diplomats to leave the country because of their harassment of Libyan exiles. N.Y. Times, May 5, 1980, § A, at 10, col. 3. The United Kingdom has expelled four Libyan diplomats on similar grounds. Id. May 13, 1980, § A, at 5, col. 1.

For a discussion of the jurisdictional implications of the litigation concerning the Letelier assassination, see 17 Willamette L. Rev. 291 (1980).

[15] See Legal Aspects of International Terrorism (A. Evans & J. Murphy eds. 1978)[hereinafter cited as Evans & Murphy].

[16] Office of Civil Aviation Security, Federal Aviation Administration, Department of Transportation, Worldwide Significant Criminal Acts Involving Civil Aviation, January-December 1979, at 1 (1980).

[17] 22 U.S.T. 1641, T.I.A.S. No. 7192.

vention has universal jurisdiction over a hijacker. Today, 108 states are bound by The Hague Convention. There are also seven bilateral agreements on hijacking.[18] Even though hijacking continues, the Convention is effective in curbing it because the Convention's standards have been widely implemented by statutes carrying out its provisions or by related statutes establishing preventive measures. There is ample evidence that hijackers have been submitted to prosecution either in the states in which they have been found or in the states to which they have been extradited or expelled.[19] The offense continues because hijacking is appealing not only to terrorists but also to other disgruntled or mentally unbalanced persons. Also, despite the most careful preventive measures, magnetometers and security personnel can slip up at times. As a consequence, hijackers succeed in their objectives.

Internationally protected persons have been subject to a growing number of attacks in the past decade. Indeed, the Department of State is reported to have "list[ed] 254 significant terrorist attacks against U.S. diplomatic installations or individuals" in this period.[20] As mentioned above, both customary and conventional international law establish the inviolability of the diplomat. This principle has been enforced through the prosecution of offenders in many states. These states include the United States, the United Kingdom, the Federal Republic of Germany, Italy, and Turkey. Territorial states have acknowledged and, presumably, have paid damages for their failure to protect embassies or consulates. This principle is recognized in the International Court of Justice's decision that Iran must pay damages to the United States for the seizure of the American Embassy at Tehran.[21]

The hostage situation in Iran demonstrated recourse to a variety of legal measures, ranging from submission of the case to the International Court of Justice to the assertion of unilateral and multilateral diplomatic and economic measures by the United

States, Japan, and the European Community.[22] The impact of these actions in the current context of the hostage situation is open to speculation. The situation appears to be sui generis. In other terrorist situations, as in the United Kingdom and in Ireland, vigorous enforcement of legal measures has served to contain and reduce the pressure of terrorist activity.

Considering the reaction of states to international terrorism during the past two decades, two trends are discernible. First, there is an awakening of states to the threat of international terrorism to all members of the international community. Enlightened self-interest, if nothing else, suggests that everyone loses when terrorism goes unchecked. Second, there is an increasing movement toward development of international legal controls over terrorism through the development of international legislation, related national legislation, and international cooperation in the enforcement of this legislation. This development is evident in the growing network of treaties which are designed to identify international terrorist offenses. Multilateral conventions open to all states include the Convention on Offenses and Certain Other Acts Committed on Board Aircraft of 1963 (Tokyo Convention),[23] together with four punitive conventions: The Hague Convention of 1970,[24] the Convention for the Suppression of Unlawful Acts Against the Safety of Civil Aircraft of 1971 (Montreal Convention),[25] the United Nations Convention on Protection of Diplomats of 1973 (U.N. Diplomats Convention),[26] and the United Nations Convention Against the Taking of Hostages of 1979 (Hostages Convention).[27] To these may be added the regional conventions such as the Organization of American States' Convention on Terrorism of 1971,[28] and the European Convention on the Suppression of Terrorism of 1976 with the Dublin Supplement of 1979.[29] Bilateral agreements against

[22] See N.Y. Times, Apr. 23, 1980, § A, at 12, col. 1; id. May 23, 1980, § A, at 5, col. 1.
[23] 20 U.S.T. 2941, T.I.A.S. No. 6768, 704 U.N.T.S. 219.
[24] See note 17 supra.
[25] 24 U.S.T. 565, T.I.A.S. No. 7570.
[26] See note 6 supra.
[27] U.N. Doc. A/34/819, at 5 (1979). See also G. A. Res. 34/145 (1979).
[28] 27 U.S.T. 3949, T.I.A.S. No. 8413.
[29] Europ. T.S. No. 90; 15 I.L.M. 1272 (1976); Agreement Concerning the Application of the European Convention on the Suppression of Terrorism among the Member States, 1979, 12 BULL. EUROPEAN COMMUNITIES 90-91 (1979); 19 I.L.M. 325 (1980).

[18] Cuba has agreements with Canada, Mexico, Venezuela and Columbia; the Soviet Union has agreements with Iran, Finland and Afghanistan. See Evans & Murphy, supra note 15, at 21-25.
[19] See id.
[20] Time, Mar. 17, 1980, at 29.
[21] Case Concerning United States Diplomatic and Consular Staff in Tehran (United States of America v. Iran), 19 I.L.M. 553 (1980).

aircraft hijacking include those between Mexico and Cuba of 1973 and between the Soviet Union and Finland of 1974.[30] A recent extradition treaty between the United States and Canada provides that the political defense is not available to a person accused of aircraft hijacking or of an attack upon an internationally protected person.[31] Apart from the treaties, there have been unilateral actions under national legislation, such as the United States refusal to supply spare parts for military aircraft, telecommunications equipment, and computers to Libya because of that country's continued support of international terrorism. Notably, Libya's support of terrorism has begun to decline.[32]

The 1979 Hostages Convention encompasses both of the trends mentioned. It demonstrates how many members of the United Nations have come to recognize that the taking of hostages, for whatever reason, is a violation of human rights and is no more justifiable in a struggle for national liberation than it is in international warfare. The conclusion of this convention suggests that a distinction must be drawn between national liberation movements and international terrorism. This is a distinction which was not evident in the thinking of many members of the United Nations in 1972 when the United States initiative for a convention on terrorism failed.

III. PROSPECTIVE PROBLEMS OF LEGAL CONTROL

Treaties, laws, security measures, and prosecutions have not eliminated international terrorism, but they have blunted its thrust. The need in this decade is to provide for further measures of legal control. A few possibilities are suggested.

A. Expansion of International Antiterrorist Legislation

The present five general multilateral conventions which define the international terrorist offenses should be adopted, establishing a firm base in conven-

tional international law for national action against persons charged with these offenses.[33] At the same time, there should be widespread adoption of present treaties which prohibit the use of bacteriological, toxin, and chemical weapons.[34]

Several areas of legislation could be usefully developed. For example, attacks upon aviation facilities are frequent, but security standards for such facilities are determined by national or local law. International standards are needed for the physical protection of nuclear facilities and nuclear materials. The sale of arms and other destructive devices should be subject to international legislation which would provide for nuclear tagging of such arms so that their presence could be easily detected. Some other possible subjects for international legislation are noted in connection with the next two points.

B. Controls on the Apprehension and Prosecution of Offenders

The current multilateral antiterrorist conventions include the common requirement that states "extradite or submit to prosecution" persons accused of the proscribed offenses. State practice indicates that extradition processes are resorted to less often than expulsion for the purpose of international rendition. If this is an acceptable alternative to extradition, then it is desirable to recognize expulsion as a legal method of rendition and to provide some minimum standards for its use either by a separate convention or by provision in a general convention on international terrorism.

The political defense (the plea of an accused that the act was committed for political reasons) is a potential obstacle to the extradition of persons charged with offenses other than those proscribed in the multilateral antiterrorist conventions. Resort to the political defense is limited or barred under these conventions. A problem arises with respect to the

---

[30] See note 18 supra.

[31] Treaty on Extradition between the United States and Canada, June 28 & July 9, 1974, 27 U.S.T. 983, T.I.A.S. No. 8237.

[32] Hearings on Omnibus Antiterrorism Act of 1979 Before the Senate Comm. on Governmental Affairs, 96th Cong., 1st Sess. (1979) (statement of Ambassador Anthony Quainton, Director, Office for Combatting Terrorism).

[33] As of June 2, 1980, the number of states bound by these conventions were as follows: Tokyo Convention, 103 states; Hague Convention, 108 states; Montreal Convention, 105 states; U.N. Diplomats Convention, 45 states. There were 19 signatories to the Hostages Convention. See notes 6, 17, 23, 25, and 27 supra.

[34] E.g., the Convention on the Prohibition of the Development, Production and Stockpiling of Bacteriological (Biological) and Toxin Weapons and on their Destruction, Apr. 10, 1972, 26 U.S.T. 583, T.I.A.S. No. 8562, is binding on 78 states.

terrorist act which is classifiable as a common crime but which is allegedly motivated by political considerations and for which extradition is sought pursuant to a bilateral extradition treaty containing the usual exception for the political offense.

The problem can be solved in several ways. First, extradition treaties can be written to bar resort to the political defense with reference to selected offenses, as in the United States Extradition Treaty with Canada of 1971. The political defense may be proscribed in judicial practice as in two recent extradition cases. In *In re Eain*,[35] a United States court found no evidence that the act of placing a bomb in a trash can in a marketplace was directed against the Israeli government. In *In re Piperno*,[36] a French court held that the accused's complicity in the kidnapping and assassination of former Premier Aldo Moro of Italy was an act of odious barbarism to which no political defense could be made. The judicial approach to the problem has the disadvantage of being subject to a case by case interpretation. Moreover, in some countries a court's finding that extradition should be granted may be overruled by the Executive who has the final decision on surrender of the accused.[37] A third, and more constructive approach, would be an international agreement delimiting the scope and use of the political defense. When prosecution is preferred to extradition, such a convention could provide for a bifurcated trial in which the common crime and the political factor (here a request for political asylum) would be treated separately. Political asylum could be granted following the acquittal of the accused or, if convicted, the completion of a prison sentence. This approach would meet the needs of those states that historically support the right of an accused to invoke the political defense as well as the growing commitment of the international community to prosecution of international terrorists.

C. Protection of the Interests of Victims of Terrorism

Responses to international terrorism cannot be limited to the dimensions of criminal law or to measures of public policy. There is a civil law dimension, a recognition that victims of international terrorist acts should not suffer the unrecompensed consequences of the acts. The concern here is for compensation other than the reparations which might be ordered pursuant to international litigation as in the recent judgment of the International Court of Justice in the case between the United States and Iran. A few examples from private litigation suggest the appropriate direction.

Increasingly, international air carriers are held liable to their passengers for failure to control a terrorist attack upon an aircraft or in an air terminal. The basic international legislation apposite here is the Convention for the Unification of Certain Rules Relating to International Transport by Air of 1929 (Warsaw Convention).[38] That legislation is supplemented by the Montreal Interim Agreement of 1966[39] between the United States and the international carriers who do business in this country. The Convention provides *inter alia* for carrier liability for the death or injury of a passenger resulting from an accident occurring either on board an aircraft or in the process of boarding or leaving an aircraft.[40] The carrier can invoke the affirmative defense of contributory negligence on the part of the passenger[41] or try to show that it had endeavored without success to avoid the injury.[42] Under the Montreal Interim Agreement, the limit of recovery on the theory of absolute liability is $75,000. The Second Circuit has held that the Convention creates a right of action,[43] a view which conforms to that of other states which are parties to the convention.[44]

Litigation in the United States and France, by passengers who have been the victims of aircraft hijacking, has established that since the carrier is responsible for the safety of its aircraft, the carrier is liable where its aircraft is hijacked.[45] Recently, a

---

[35] No. 79-M-185 (N.D. Ill. Dec. 18, 1979).

[36] Judgment of Oct. 11, 1979, No. 1343-79, Cour d'appel, Paris, Cass. acc. Ire.

[37] *E.g.,* Jhirad v. Ferrandina, 536 F.2d 478 (2d Cir.), *cert. denied,* 429 U.S. 833 (1976)(Secretary of State disagreed with court on interpretation of statute of limitations; extradition was denied); *see* McDowell, *supra* note 18, at 114-16).

[38] 49 Stat. 3000, 137 L.N.T.S. 11.

[39] 17 U.S.T. 201, T.I.A.S. No. 5972.

[40] *Id.* art. 17.

[41] *Id.* art. 21.

[42] *Id.* art. 20.

[43] Benjamins v. British European Airways, 572 F.2d 913 (2d Cir. 1978).

[44] *E.g.,* Judgment of Oct. 25, 1976, Trib. di Milano, *cited in* 4 AIR LAW 175 (1979).

[45] Husserl v. Swiss Air Transport Co., 351 F. Supp. 702 (S.D.N.Y. 1972), *aff'd,* 485 F.2d 1240 (2d Cir. 1973); Judgment of Apr. 28, 1978, Trib. gr. inst., Paris, *cited in* 3 AIR LAW 180 (1978).

French court held that when the preboarding security measures provided by local authorities were inadequate, the carrier had a duty to supplement them and was liable for a hijacking resulting from poor security.[46]

An American court has held that a carrier was liable to passengers injured by terrorist action while standing at the departure gate in a transit lounge waiting to board an aircraft.[47] On the other hand, where disembarked passengers were waiting in the luggage claim area and were subjected to terrorist attack, the carrier was not found to be liable for damages because it was not in control of the passengers.[48]

A different type of issue was raised by the heirs of victims of a terrorist assassination which was engineered by a foreign government. In *Letelier v. Republic of Chile*,[49] a United States district court held that a foreign state cannot protect itself from liability for damages for aiding and abetting an assassination by claiming that its tortious act fell within the "discretionary function" exception in the Foreign Sovereign Immunities Act of 1976.[50] *Letelier* appears to set the course for personal injury suits under this Act. Recently, it has been reported that ten persons, relatives of two current hostages and eight former hostages, have filed claims against the Government of Iran, the Ayotollah Khomeini, and 500 terrorists who held or are holding them hostage at the Embassy.[51]

Obviously, these latter actions can only be undertaken in a country in which the appropriate legislation is available. There is a need, however, for international legislation providing for the payment of compensation to victims of international terrorist offenses when states have failed to implement antiterrorist conventions, to extradite or expel offenders, to submit offenders to prosecution, or when states have temporized with international terrorists. Such a provision could be made in a separate convention or be part of a general convention setting broad standards for the control of international terrorism.

CONCLUSION

International terrorism is a part of modern life. It has been demonstrated in the past decade, however, that governments and peoples do not have to submit to international terrorism. Some have argued that the targets and style of terrorism will change in the future, but current experience does not indicate that this is happening. Terrorists use the old methods against the established targets and seem likely to continue the same in the 1980s.

The past decade has been a learning experience for a wide variety of states faced with the menace of international terrorism. The significant lesson of that experience, and the one which should dominate the 1980s, is the recognition that measures to control international terrorism are effective only if they are founded on law and are carried out through cooperative state action.

---

[46] Bornier v. Air Inter, Trib. gr. inst., Paris, *cited in* 4 AIR LAW 168 (1979).

[47] Day v. Trans World Airlines, 528 F.2d 31 (2d Cir. 1975), *cert. denied*, 429 U.S. 890 (1976), *rehearing denied*, 429 U.S. 1124 (1977).

[48] Martinez Hernandez v. Air France, 545 F.2d 279 (1st Cir. 1976).

[49] No. 78-1477 (D.D.C. Mar. 11, 1980). Two persons were convicted of murder in the criminal case and a third pleaded guilty to conspiracy to murder a foreign official. N.Y. Times, Feb. 15, 1979, § A, at 1, col. 1; Boston Globe, Aug. 12, 1978, at 2, col 2. The civil aspect of *Letelier* is noted in 17 Willamette L. Rev. 291 (1980).

[50] 28 U.S.C. § 1605(a)(5)(A)(1976).

[51] N.Y. Times, May 21, 1980, § A, at 11, col. 1.

The Legalization of Terrorism
L. C. Green

Murray's Oxford English Dictionary defines terrorism as "Government by intimidation as directed and carried out by the party in power in France during the Revolution of 1789-1794; the system of the 'Terror.' A policy intended to strike with terror those against whom it is adopted; the employment of methods of intimidation. . . ." This definition is not very helpful and is perhaps somewhat circuitous, although it gives those with a knowledge of history a picture of unrestricted violence and horror, involving arbitrary executions on a large scale. More practically motivated is the Terrorists Order propounded by the British authorities to deal with the situation in Northern Ireland. This document defines terrorism as "the use of violence for political ends [including] any use of violence for the purpose of putting the public or any section of the public in fear."[1] However, this definition, too, is open to criticism and is somewhat extensive. Moreover, it is wide enough not only to embrace the atrocities against which it is directed and the victims of which are alleged to be innocent bystanders, but also to include within its ambit almost every case of one-to-one criminal confrontation as well as governmental oppression directed against the national population.

It must not be overlooked that those organizations that are commonly regarded as terrorist, such as the Weathermen, the Baader-Meinhof group, the Japanese Red Guard, the Tupamaros, and urban and street guerrillas, as well as those radical and libertarian movements that tend to support them (often completely ignorant of their true purpose but devoted to liberalism *in abstracto*) frequently maintain that such governmental oppression is the only true terrorism, for what the majority of the "establishment" regards as terrorism is nothing but the reaction to such governmental abuse. For this reason, these movements sympathize with those who are not anxious to see international cooperative action directed at suppressing terrorism, for the end justifies the

means and if the causes of terrorism were dealt with, the manifestations would disappear. The definition of governmental terrorism tends to be somewhat subjective as is evident from the decision of the European Court of Human Rights in the dispute between Ireland and the United Kingdom. While the European Commission of Human Rights found that certain practices indulged in by Britain amounted to "torture" and, to some extent at least, may be considered to have "terrorized" some portions of the public, the court itself, regardless of the British decision not to contest this finding, held that the practices in question did not amount to torture, but only to cruel and degrading punishment. From this, one may assume that what the recipient regards as terrorism may not be so considered by the administrator. In any case, to the extent that governmental authority permits such intimidatory activity, it may be presumed that it is legalized terrorism, and it matters little that the world community or individual states condemn it as outrageous conduct.[2]

However, the world, and especially the public at large, is not excessively interested in governmental terrorism, which tends to be accepted as unavoidable and is often viewed as inevitable if a government is to retain its authority against threats emanating from woolly-headed or vicious revolutionaries. For the public, such acts of terrorism, if such they be described, are only likely to be condemned by revolutionaries (potential or active), idealists, libertarians, starry-eyed academics, and similar radicals. What the man in the street has become concerned about are acts that are officially directed against a government or some political movement and that work themselves out against innocent bystanders or are executed in the territory of a third state that is in no way directly involved in the conflict between the actor and the alleged object of his action. It is this sort of activity that he expects his and other states to take action to

---

[1] See Ireland v. United Kingdom (1978, European Court of Human Rights, official text, para. 85).

[2] See, e.g., 1978 report of United States State Department on governmental derogation of human rights, *The Times* (London), 10 February 1978.

From L. C. Green, "The Legalization of Terrorism," in Yonah Alexander, David Carlton, and Paul Wilkinson (eds.), *Terrorism: Theory and Practice*. Boulder, Colo.: Westview Press, 1979, pp. 175–197.

control. He is not concerned with the legality of Israel's raid upon Entebbe airport[3] nor the Egyptian commando operation in Cyprus. In his eyes, such actions are morally correct activities directed towards the suppression or frustration of terrorist acts.

It would appear that states and their governments tend to take a somewhat similar hands-off approach towards terrorism alleged to have been committed by the authorities of a fellow member of the family of nations. International law has long since recognized the right of a state to do what it desires with its own nationals and the principle of nonintervention in domestic affairs is perhaps one of the oldest, even though incursions into its ambit may have taken place in the last twenty or thirty years. Perhaps the most notorious examples of state-directed terrorism are to be found in the practices of Stalin's Russia, Hitler's Germany, or the so-called psychiatric hospitals of Brezhnev's Soviet Union. Nevertheless, to a very great extent, the world adopts the view that was exemplified by Great Britain just prior to World War II. While H. A. Smith was denouncing Nazi Germany for activities that, in his view, placed that country outside the orbit of civilized society,

In practice we no longer insist that States shall conform to any common standards of justice, religious toleration and internal government. Whatever atrocities may be committed in foreign countries, we now say that they are no concern of ours. Conduct which in the nineteenth century would have placed a government outside the pale of civilised society is now deemed to be no obstacle to diplomatic friendship. This means, in effect, that we have now abandoned the old distinction between civilised and uncivilised States.[4]

This statement is equally applicable to many of the activities of the United Nations, its Human Rights Commission, and many of the so-called human rights and civil liberties organizations that now exist and that are highly eclectic in their choice of countries and activities for condemnation. At the time Smith was writing, the governments of Europe were maintaining

either that what was alleged to be occurring in Germany was not in fact taking place, or that if the allegations were true then the events in question were within the domestic jurisdiction of the German government and, by international law, therefore outside the scope of third party criticism. Of course, as today, when political convenience demanded, the attitude changed. Thus, immediately upon the outbreak of World War II, Britain's reservations disappeared and His Majesty's Stationery Office issued a White Paper entitled the Treatment of German Nationals in Germany.[5] This "new" approach to domestic activities is reflected in the words of Sir Hartley (now Lord) Shawcross at Nuremberg:

the right of humanitarian intervention on behalf of the rights of man trampled upon by a state in a manner shocking the sense of mankind has long been considered to form part of the recognised law of nations.[6]

This is in line with the views of Grotius, who stated in his *De Jure Belli ac Pacis*,

Kings and those who are invested with a Power equal to that of Kings, have a Right to exact Punishments, not only for Injuries committed against themselves, but likewise, for those which do not particularly concern them but which are, in any Persons whatsoever, grievous violations of the Law of Nature or Nations. For the Liberty of consulting the Benefit of Human Society, by Punishments, . . . means that War is lawful against those who offend against Nature.[7]

While, in the nineteenth century, there were many attempts by the more powerful states—who described themselves as the guardians of civilization—to assert their right to intervene in the name of humanity, it is now little doubted that these claims were nothing but ideological covers for predatory assertions.[8] It is

---

[3] See, e.g., Green, "Rescue at Entebbe—Legal Aspects," 6 *Israel Yearbook on Human Rights* (1976), 312; Strebel: Nochmals zur Geiselbefreiung in Entebbe, 37 Z.A.Ö.R.V.R. (1977), 691.

[4] 19 *The Listener* (1938), 183.

[5] Cmd. 6120 (1939).

[6] Concluding Speeches by the Chief Prosecutors (H.M.S.O., 1964), 63-4.

[7] (1625) Lib. II, cap. 20, ss. 40 (1,4), Eng. tr. 1730, 436-7, 438 (Carnegie tr. 504, 506).

[8] See, e.g. (Sir Wm. Harcourt) *Historicus on International Law* (1863), 6, 14; Lauterpacht, "General Rules of the Law of Peace," 1 *Collected Papers* (1970), 3-4 (English trans. of "general course" delivered at the Hague Academy, 1937).

difficult, therefore, to perceive on what legal authority Shawcross made his assertion.

Since 1948, when the Universal Declaration of Human Rights[9] was adopted, the potential has existed for protests, if not action, against state-directed terrorism; but as such incidents as the Russian Wives case[10] (the United States and Australia condemned Soviet refusal to allow Russian women to join their husbands, at a time when some states in the United States were still punishing miscegenation and Australia was refusing to allow the Japanese wives and children of Australian servicemen to join their husbands and fathers in Australia) indicates the basis of such criticism is frequently nothing but the gaining of advantage points in the political confrontation. At the same time, these developments with regard to the paper protection of human rights have encouraged various organizations like the International Commission of Jurists and Amnesty International to organize mass publicity and condemnation campaigns against states that pursue policies of political terror against their own nationals, although there is some evidence in the publications and operations of such organizations that their targets are often somewhat one-sidedly selected. Moreover, the Charter of the United Nations clearly precludes[11] "intervention" into matters that are essentially within domestic jurisdiction unless there is a threat to peace. In the first place, it would be difficult for a politician to persuade his people that "terror" directed by a state against its own nationals really constitutes a threat to peace and warrants the imposition of international sanctions (the situation in South Africa is a case apart and cannot be taken as a precedent). Second, it must never be forgotten that no state is an isolated island unto itself. Each has a protector among the great powers. If its smaller friends fail it, and criticism of its policies should figure on the agenda of the Security Council, a state may rest assured that it will ultimately be protected by the veto of a friend among the Big Five.

The type of issue that has aroused concern is, for example, the hijacking of aircraft and the holding of passengers and crew, the kidnapping of diplomats, the use of the international mails for the dispatch of explosive materials, and the activities of dissident movements involving extreme violence allegedly under the guise of a campaign for political independence or reform. In the past, movements opposed to a government have tended to restrict themselves to individual acts of political assassination, organized rebellion, or civil war. While the latter have frequently been accompanied by acts of terror, perhaps due to the paucity of effective media cover, the protesters have not found it essential to indulge in isolated acts of outrage directed against the population or private nongovernmental establishments, with the aim of securing publicity for their alleged cause. In fact, when acts of individual terror were perpetrated during the nineteenth century, governments tended to react by describing them as anarchist and denying them the political protection[12] that they were inclined to offer to those whose activities were directed at governmental takeover.[13] While it is true that some of these acts might well have incurred general opprobrium, there was a feeling that John Stuart Mill's view that a political offense was "any offence committed in the course or furthering of civil war, insurrection, or political commotion"[14] had much to commend it, this went too far for a nineteenth century establishment to adopt, although there was sufficient sympathy for those committing violent acts that were politically motivated for the view to develop that if the act was committed in the course of an organized attempt to overthrow and replace the government, then international customary law, while not necessarily legalizing such acts of terrorism, should afford the offender protection from extradition.[15] There was, however, no attempt to embody this as a principle confirmed by a general or universal treaty.

When this attitude was developing during the nineteenth century, acts of terrorism, whether committed by a government under the umbrella of legislation or by dissidents acting on their own or in unison, remained territorial. The place of the act, normally speaking, was within the territory of the government concerned, while the victims were within the national

[9] G.A. Res. 217A (III).
[10] (1949) Res. 285 (III), see Green, "Human Rights and the Color Problem," 3 *Current Legal Problems* (1950), 236, 245 et seqq.
[11] Art. 2(7).

[12] See, e.g., *Re Meunier* [1894] 2 Q.B. 415.
[13] See, e.g., *Re Castioni* [1891] 1 Q.B. 149.
[14] House of Commons, 6 Aug. 1866, 184 Hansard (3rd Ser.), col. 2115.
[15] See, e.g., U.S. practice in absence of a treaty reservation, 4 Moore, *Digest of Int'l Law* (1906), 332 et seqq.; see also, British Despatch re Kossuth, 1849, 6 *Br. Digest of Int'l Law* (1965), 44.

territory. Private acts of terrorism tended to be committed against government institutions or official personalities. The situation has now changed. The modern terrorist seems to be completely unconcerned with the geographic location of his act and equally reckless as to the nationality of his victim. In fact, it would appear at times as if, perhaps in the hope of securing publicity or pressure upon his government, the terrorist intends to internationalize his act. This has become particularly true since resolutions of the United Nations concerning the right of self-determination appear to have given this right a status in law and morality that is not accorded to any other right or principle. It is not difficult today, in view of this, to echo the words of Mme. Roland on passing the statue of Liberty on her way to the scaffold during the Reign of Terror in 1793: *Ô Liberté! Ô Liberté! que de crimes on commet en ton nom.*

The Charter of the United Nations talks rather nebulously of respect for the principle of equal rights and self-determination for peoples, without making any attempt to define what was meant by peoples or self-determination. However, responding to the upsurge of anticolonialism, the General Assembly in 1960 adopted a Declaration on the Granting of Independence to Colonial Countries and Peoples,[16] declaring that "all peoples have the right to self-determination; by virtue of that right they freely determine their political status . . . ," but pointing out that "any attempt at the partial or total disruption of the national unity and the territorial integrity of a country is incompatible with the purposes and principles of the Charter of the United Nations." A committee was established to supervise the implementation of this right. It soon became clear that the concept of decolonization was amenable to differing interpretations, while the meaning of self-determination was political in the extreme, with some states conceiving it to be no more than the withdrawal of a former European colonial power[17] and others as an exhortation to independence and self-government, regardless of whether the entity in question would be viable or whether its inhabitants were in favor of this interpretation of their destiny.[18] It was not long, however, before it became clear that in the eyes of many members of the United Nations, this declara-

tion had heralded in what many might consider as an inevitable slide towards legalization and respectability for any act of terror committed by any dissident, provided the right ideological jargon was employed.

To emphasize the importance of the idea of self-determination and to remind the world that it was more than a political concept, the United Nations embodied this principle into the Covenant on Economic, Social, and Cultural Rights and the Covenant on Civil and Political Rights.[19] Article 1 of each of these covenants proclaims, "all peoples have the right to self-determination." To highlight the importance of this principle, it is included as one of the seven principles appearing in the Declaration on Principles of International Law Concerning Friendly Relations and Cooperation Among States in accordance with the Charter of the United Nations.[20] The declaration places this "principle of equal rights and self-determination of peoples" on the same level as the principles

> that States shall refrain in their international relations from the threat or use of force against the territorial integrity or political independence of any State, or in any other manner inconsistent with the Purposes of the United Nations . . . of sovereign equality of States . . . [and] that States shall fulfil in good faith the obligations assumed by them in accordance with the charter.

The elevation of the principle ensconces it as a basic principle of international law equal in importance to such traditionally recognized basic principles as sovereignty—a fact that is reiterated in the declaration when it states that all seven principles are interrelated and "constitute basic principles of international law," which should be strictly observed.

The declaration explains what it means by the principle of self-determination. It adds little when it states that by virtue of this principle "all people have the right freely to determine, without external interference, their political status," but it goes on to impose upon every State

> the duty to promote . . . realization of the principle . . . in order . . . to bring a speedy end to colonialism, having due regard to the freely expressed will

---

[16] Res. 1514 (XV).
[17] E.g., Indonesian and West Irian.
[18] E.g., Spain and Gibraltar.

[19] Res. 2200, Annex.
[20] Res. 2625 (XXV).

of the peoples concerned, and bearing in mind that subjection of peoples to alien subjugation, domination, and exploitation constitutes a violation of the principle, as well as a denial of fundamental human rights, and is contrary to the Charter.

Stated baldly in this fashion, the declaration might be considered as nothing but a pious invocation. However, it goes on, to affirm

> every state has the duty to refrain from any forcible action which deprives peoples . . . of their right to self determination and freedom and independence. In their actions against, and resistance to, such forcible action in pursuit of their right to self-determination, such peoples are entitled to seek and to receive support in accordance with the purposes and principles of the Charter.

Presumably, it is in acknowledgment of these purposes and principles that the declaration, having apparently sanctified the use of force in the search for self-determination, proclaims that it is not to

> be construed as authorizing or encouraging any action which would dismember or impair, totally or in part, the territorial integrity or political unity of sovereign and independent States conducting themselves in compliance with the principle of equal rights and self-determination of peoples . . . and thus possessed of a government representing the whole people belonging to the territory without distinction as to race, creed or color.

Critics might be forgiven if they feel that this caveat tends to reduce the meaning of the principle of self-determination or else has little intrinsic meaning of its own. Further, as if to reduce the obligation of support placed upon third states, the declaration affirmed "every state shall refrain from any action aimed at the partial or total disruption of the national unity and territorial integrity of any other state or country"—a further caveat that would, if it meant anything, reduce the value of the commitments in the declaration almost to vanishing point. In fact, if one looks at the modern world to ascertain where movements on behalf of self-determination appear legitimate, it would seem that this is true only in regard to the Republic of South Africa, regardless of the fact that it is a member of the United Nations; or Zimba-

bwe where the local inhabitants have reached an agreement for temporary sharing of power with their white rulers prior to complete independence under a black majority; or Israel where a number of fellow members of the United Nations are providing arms, men, and other supports to the Palestine Liberation Organization, which claims to be engaged in a struggle for self-determination which, according to the movement's own charter, is aimed at the liquidation of a member of the United Nations. On the other hand, the Organization of African Unity has made it clear that, no matter what the complaints of any ethnic or tribal community within an African state may be, no support will be given to any movement for self-determination directed against a member of that organization, for Article 3 of the Addis Ababa Charter listed as one of the principles of the organization "respect for the sovereignty and territorial integrity of each state and for its inalienable right to independent existence."[21]

When condemning colonial regimes and approving struggles for self-determination, international organizations have tended to avoid any specific recommendation or expression of approval that might indicate support for terrorism or violence as such. On the other hand, the form of words used has been sufficiently wide to embrace such activities. Thus, in 1972, when the Security Council met in Addis Ababa to discuss African problems, its resolution condemning apartheid[22] recognized "the legitimacy of the struggle of the oppressed people of South Africa in pursuance of their human and political rights as set forth in the Charter of the United Nations and the Universal Declaration of Human Rights," without making any reference to the nature or modalities of that struggle. On the same day it adopted another resolution[23] condemning Portuguese attempts to suppress the rebellious independence movements in Portugal's African colonies, recognized the "legitimacy of the struggle of [those] liberation movements," but again made no reference to the manner in which those movements sought to achieve their ends.

While the United Nations was concerned with the right of non-self-governing peoples to achieve their independence by whatever means they considered suitable, acts of terrorism (the despatch of letter

---

[21] 1963, 2 Int'l Legal Materials 766.
[22] Res. 311 (1972).
[23] Res. 312 (1972).

bombs, attacks on diplomats, deviation of aircraft on international flights, and violent attacks on civilians) were being committed and were frequently explained away on the basis of national sef-determination and the logical conclusion to the denial by a political opponent of the rights claimed by those committing the acts. There was a growing tendency among those sympathetic to the actors to suggest that the end justifies means, or that there was no point in seeking to suppress terrorist activities until the causes of such activities had been eradicated. From a practical point of view, it would seem that political problems that had proved well nigh insoluble through the years, such as the achievement of majority rule in South Africa, solution to the Middle East problem, and the like, were of more immediate concern that the question of releasing civilian hostages, rescuing kidnapped diplomats, or suppressing interference with air transport. Presumably all such incidents could continue pending the solution of the insoluble. This attitude is well illustrated by the General Assembly Resolution on measures to prevent international terrorism.[24] True, the assembly expressed

> deep concern over increasing acts of violence which endanger or take innocent human lives or jeopardize fundamental freedoms [and urged] States to devote their immediate attention to finding just and peaceful solutions to the underlying causes which give rise to such acts of violence.

The motivation of this wording perhaps becomes clear from other clauses of the resolution. Thus, the General Assembly found it necessary immediately to

> reaffirm the inalienable right to self-determination and independence of all peoples under colonial and racist regimes and other forms of alien domination and uphold the legitimacy of their struggle, in particular the struggle of national liberation movements, in accordance with the purposes and principles of the Charter and the relevant resolutions of the organs of the United Nations [and] condemn the continuation of repressive and terrorist acts by colonial, racist and alien regimes in denying peoples their legitimate right to self-determination and independence and other human rights and fundamental freedoms.

[24] Res. 3034 (XXVII).

Reminding itself that the resolution opens by stating that the General Assembly is "deeply perturbed over acts of international terrorism which are occurring with increasing frequency and which take a toll of innocent human lives"—and perhaps recalling that only three months earlier the United States had submitted a draft convention[25] embodying

> measures to prevent international terrorism which endangers or takes innocent human lives or jeopardizes fundamental freedoms and study of the underlying causes of those forms of terrorism and acts of violence which lie in misery, frustration, grievance, and despair and which cause some people to sacrifice human lives, including their own, in an attempt to effect radical changes

—the assembly went on to "invite States to become parties to the existing international conventions which relate to various aspects of the problem of international terrorism . . . [and] to take all appropriate measures at the national level with a view to the speedy and final elimination of the problem." However, this imprecation to states had attached to it a proviso reminding them that they were to "bear in mind" the provisions relating to "the inalienable right to self-determination and independence . . . in particular the struggle of national liberation movements."

By wording its resolution in this fashion, the General Assembly has clearly elevated the right to self-determination above human life. Moreover, while apparently condemning acts of terrorism, it has bluntly asserted that if undesirable acts—which some might describe as terrorism—are undertaken in the name of self-determination or national liberation, then such acts are beyond the scope of condemnation and are legal.

The international conventions to which the General Assembly was referring are those of Tokyo, The Hague, and Montreal in regard to aerial hijacking. After the Tokyo Convention of 1969,[26] which condemned acts jeopardizing the safety of aircraft and which made no reference to self-determination, the General Assembly itself condemned acts of hijacking as well as those which might "endanger the life and health of passengers and crew in disregard of com-

[25] UN Doc. A/C/6/L.850 (11 Int'l Legal Materials 1382).
[26] 2 Int'l Legal Materials 1042.

monly accepted humanitarian considerations,"[27] and saw no need to add a caveat in respect of self-determination. Similarly, the Security Council expressed concern at international hijackings and called for the release of all passengers and crews "without exception"[28] (a provision that appears to have been forgotten when the Security Council failed to support a United Kingdom–United States proposal to condemn the hijacking that was terminated by the Israeli rescue at Entebbe with some members more concerned with condemning Israel's act of "aggression,"[29] while the General Assembly by a resolution adopted *nemine contradicente*[30] condemned "*without exception whatsoever*, all acts of aerial hijacking" and urged states to deter and punish all such acts. In neither case was it deemed necessary to introduce political exceptions based on ideological sympathy for self-determination or national liberation. It was only after the Hague and Montreal conventions of 1970 and 1971[31] had widened the scope of condemnation, extended the nature of criminal jurisdiction (apparently making aerial hijacking and the like subject to universal jurisdiction), introduced the concept *aut dedere aut punire* ("extradite or prosecute"), and seemed to call for local criminal prosecution even when extradition might not be possible because the local legislation recognized the exception based on the political character of the offense,[32] that the General Assembly found it necessary to introduce its "safeguards" with regard to self-determination and national liberation.

These conventions, aimed at the suppression and punishment of aerial hijacking, were drawn up under the auspices of the International Civil Aviation Organization. But there is one international convention dealing with terrorism which is a United Nations Convention. In the past few years, a number of attacks have been made against diplomats (usually those of third countries) by terrorist activists seeking to apply pressure against their own government,

anticipating that the diplomat's home country will add to this pressure in an attempt to ensure the safety of the diplomat in question. In addition, embassies abroad have been attacked and diplomats murdered sometimes merely to ensure publicity for the terrorist group concerned. This appears to be the difference between the attack upon the Israeli embassy in Thailand in 1972 and that upon the Saudi Arabian embassy in the Sudan in 1974, both of which were committed by the Black September group of Palestine terrorists. Since all countries make use of diplomats, and since the kidnappings of such persons by, for example, urban guerrillas in South America indicates that all are equally at risk, it is perhaps not surprising that the General Assembly in 1974 adopted by consensus a Convention on the Prevention and Punishment of Crimes against Internationally Protected Persons, including Diplomatic Agents.[33] Taken by itself, this convention appears to provide for making such offenses as much crimes by international law as is piracy *jure gentium*. However, the resolution to which the convention is annexed expressly provides that its provisions are "related" to the convention and "shall always be published together with it." Paragraph 4 of the resolution makes crystal clear the reason for this proviso. While the purpose of the resolution and the convention annexed thereto is to prevent and punish such crimes "in view of the serious threat to the maintenance of friendly relations and cooperation among States created by the commission of such crimes," paragraph 4

recognizes that the provisions of the annexed Convention could not in any way prejudice the exercise of the legitimate right to self-determination and independence, in accordance with the purposes and principles of the United Nations and the Declaration on Principles of International Law concerning Friendly Relations and Cooperation among States in accordance with the Charter of the United Nations, by peoples struggling against colonialism, alien domination, foreign occupation, racial discrimination and apartheid.

Thus, once again we find that an act of terrorism that is considered likely to affect international relations and friendly cooperation among states, and that therefore might be considered contrary to the purpos-

---

[27] Res. 2551 (XXIV).

[28] Res. 286 (1970).

[29] For a summary of debate and texts of draft resolutions, see 15 Int'l Legal Materials 1224 et seqq.

[30] Res. 2645 (XXV) (italics added).

[31] 10 Int'l Legal Materials 133, 1151, resp.

[32] See, e.g., Green, "Hijacking and the Right of Asylum," in McWhinney, *Air Piracy and International Law*, 1971, 124 et seqq.; "Piracy of Aircraft and the Law," 10 *Alberta Law Rev.*, 1972, 72 et seqq.; Joyner, *Aerial Hijacking as an International Crime*, 1974, 201-16.

[33] Res. 3166 (XXVIII), Annex.

es and principles of the United Nations and of any Declaration of Principles in such a field, is sanctified and no longer regarded as a crime if it is committed in the sacred name of twentieth century holy writ: self-determination.

This same concern for the new gospel is to be found in the General Assembly Resolution defining aggression.[34] Since the days of the League of Nations, attempts have been made to define aggression and the International Military Tribunal at Nuremberg held "to initiate a war of aggression . . . is the supreme international crime differing only from other war crimes in that it contains within itself the accumulated evil of the whole."[35] After much debate and study, the General Assembly eventually, in 1974, came upon a definition that was adopted without a vote, pointing out that *no consideration of whatever nature, whether political*, economic, military, *or otherwise*, may serve as a justification for aggression. A war of aggression is a crime against international peace." Nevertheless,

> nothing in this definition . . . could in any way prejudice the right to self-determination, freedom and independence, as derived from the Charter, of peoples forcibly deprived of that right and referred to in the Declaration on Principles of International Law concerning Friendly Relations and Co-operation among States in accordance with the Charter of the United Nations, particularly peoples under colonial and racist regimes or other forms of alien domination; nor *the right* of these peoples *to struggle to that end and to seek and receive support*, in accordance with the principles of the Charter and in conformity with the above-mentioned Declaration.

It is clear, therefore, that not only does the General Assembly recognize the plea of self-determination as justification for an act of terrorism which thereby ceases to carry such an obloquious description, but it goes further and the General Assembly concedes that under the claim of seeking self-determination the "supreme international crime," condemned as such by the assembly itself in 1946,[36] is in fact lawful and

should "receive support." Can anything be a better example of "diplomatic double talk"[37]?

One of the main problems that arises in connection with these various measures legalizing terrorism is the definition of self-determination and national liberation. As yet, there is no accepted definition of either of these terms, although a number of rebellious organizations have described themselves as national liberation movements. It is clear, however, that such autonomous assumptions of this title are not adequate. Thus, the Biafran movement in Nigeria, the Eritrean and Somali national liberation movements in Ethiopia, or the Front de Libération Québécois in Canada have not been accepted as such by anybody, so that the latter's kidnapping of a British diplomat in 1970 would fall within the ban of the convention. Current practice, as illustrated by events in Angola, South Africa, and the Middle East, suggest that the test of whether an organization is entitled to describe itself as a national liberation movement, and thus entitled to carry out acts that would otherwise be condemned as terrorism or international crimes, is recognition by the local regional organization—a test that would ensure that a movement on the North American continent or in Europe would almost certainly never qualify.

In the eyes of most states and perhaps of the majority of the people in the world, the organization that has been responsible for most acts of international terrorism, and that in fact has not hesitated to claim responsibility for such, has been the Palestine Liberation Organization (PLO) or one or other of its dependent groups. This is the organization, moreover, that has been granted respectability and legalization by the United Nations. Despite its commitment to the overthrow and destruction of Israel, and despite their undertakings with regard to that member of the United Nations by its fellow members, the PLO has been afforded, by the General Assembly, a status of acceptability as a national liberation movement that authorizes it to commit virtually any act of terror with impunity, since the General Assembly has opened the door of the organization to claim that all its activities are directed towards self-determination and as such legalized by the United Nations. The first indication that this might occur is to be found in the Resolution on Basic Principles of the Legal Status of the Combatants Struggling against Colonial and Alien

---

[34] Res. 3314 (XXIX) (italics added).
[35] H.M.S.O., Cmd. 6964 (1946), 13; 40 *Am. J. Int'l Law* (1946), 186.
[36] Res. 95 (I).

[37] Schwarzenberger, *Power Politics*, 1951, 716-20.

Domination and Racist Regimes.[38] Ostensibly, this resolution was based on recognition of the need to apply the basic humanitarian principles to all armed conflicts, and it reaffirms

> that the continuation of colonialism in all its forms and manifestations . . . is a crime and that *colonial peoples have the inherent right to struggle by all necessary means at their disposal* against colonial Powers and alien domination in exercise of their right of self-determination.

It goes on to assert that such struggles are

> legitimate and in full accordance with the principles of international law [and that] *any attempt to suppress the struggle* against colonial and alien domination and racist régimes are [sic.] incompatible with the Charter of the United Nations, the Declaration on Principles of International Law concerning Friendly Relations and Co-operation among States in accordance with the Charter of the United Nations, the Universal Declaration of Human Rights, the Declaration on the Granting of Independence to Colonial Countries and Peoples and *constitutes a threat to international peace and security*.

As such, therefore, the attempt is amenable to the application of enforcement measures by the Security Council. This has the effect of placing such activities whatever the means employed by the independence seekers under the protection of the United Nations and entitled to full support by all its members. Moreover, such a struggle is declared to be an "international armed conflict," so that those committing acts of terror in its name cannot be tried for such crimes, since they are entitled to treatment as prisoners of war and immune from criminal action unless their acts constitute war crimes.

All that now remained was for the United Nations to declare that the Palestine Liberation Organization was in fact a national liberation movement and that the State of Israel was a colonial, alien, or racist regime. It did not take long for the United Nations to adopt such measures. On November 22, 1974,[39] the General Assembly by majority vote, "taking into consideration the Universality of the United Nations prescribed in the Charter," invited the Palestine Liberation Organization "to participate in the sessions and the work of the General Assembly in the capacity of observer," and, in a related resolution, recognized "that the Palestinian people is entitled to self-determination . . . [and appealed] to all States and international organizations to extend their support to the Palestinian people in its struggle to restore its rights."[40] It should be pointed out that the charter does not provide for any entity to enjoy observer status with the General Assembly. Moreover, insofar as the charter looks to the universality of the organization, it must be remembered that membership is restricted to states, and it is difficult to see how the participation as observer or otherwise of a nonstate organization committed to violence and the extinction of an existing member of the United Nations can in any way contribute to the universality of membership. The resolution went on to declare that the Palestine Liberation Organization "is entitled to participate as an observer in the sessions and the work of all international conferences convened under the auspices of the organs of the United Nations." This resolution on observer status for the Palestine Liberation Organization was only one of a number relating to the status of national liberation movements vis-à-vis the United Nations and must be read in conjunction with that on Participation in the United Nations Conference on the Representation of States in Their Relations with International Organizations.[41] This resolution provided for invitations to "all states," and "the national liberation movements in their respective regions recognized by the Organization of African Unity and/or by the League of Arab States in their respective regions to participate as observers in the Conference, in accordance with the practice of the United Nations." This resolution indicates the highly selective approach of the General Assembly to bodies claiming to be national liberation movements and clearly reflects the present voting power in the assembly. Consequent upon this resolution, the Palestine Liberation Organization has been invited to conferences of the International Labor Organization, though it is difficult to see in what way, whether as observer or anything else, it can contribute to that organization's activities, and of the International Civil

---

[38] Res. 3108 (XXVIII) (italics added).
[39] Res. 3237 (XXIX).

[40] Res. 3236 (XXIX).
[41] Res. 3247 (XXIX).

Aviation Organization, although it has no aircraft (its activities in this sphere having been directed against the interests of that organization as expressed in the antihijacking conventions).

The activities of the General Assembly in legalizing the operations of the Palestine Liberation Organization culminated in the adoption of a resolution allegedly concerned with the Elimination of All Forms of Racial Discrimination[42] in furtherance of the Declaration of 1963 on this subject.[43] Having already condemned zionism for its "unholy alliance" with South African racism,[44] which, as everyone knows, is "a crime against humanity . . . violating the principles of international law . . . and constituting a serious threat to international peace and security,"[45] the General Assembly now saw fit to "determine that zionism is a form of racism and racial discrimination." This resolution only just achieved the requisite two-thirds majority needed for adoption, receiving seventy-two votes in favor, thirty-five against, and thirty-two abstentions. It is interesting to note that a number of African, Latin American, and non-aligned states generally were among those opposing or abstaining, for the resolution in its preambular phrases notes that, in 1975, the Assembly of Heads of State and Government of the Organization of African Unity at their meeting in Uganda considered

> that the racist regime in occupied Palestine and the racist regimes in Zimbabwe and South Africa have a common imperialist origin, forming a whole and having the same racist structure and being organically linked to their policy aimed at repression of the dignity and integrity of the human being

and that in the same year, the Conference of Ministers for Foreign affairs of Non-Aligned Countries meeting in Peru "severely condemned zionism as a threat to world peace and security and called upon all countries to oppose this racist and imperialist ideology." Having come to this world-shattering conclusion, the General Assembly by its resolution has placed Israel, as a state based on zionist philosophy, in the same class as states committed to colonialism, racism, and alien domination. The Palestine Liberation Organization as a national liberation movement committed to its overthrow and the achievement of self-determination for the Palestinians is thus now fully authorized to indulge in whatsoever acts of violence it may please, without any fear of condemnation that the acts in question constitute terrorism or any offense against international law.

It should not be assumed that the Palestine Liberation Organization is the only one that has been accorded recognition by the League of Arab States or the Organization of African Unity. The same status has been accorded to the South West African People's Organization, the Pan-Africanist Congress, the African National Congress, the African National Congress of Zimbabwe, and the Patriotic Front of Zimbabwe. All of these, therefore, are authorized to commit terrorist acts against the Republic of South Africa and Rhodesia with equal impunity. In fact, we now find that even though the representative organizations within Namibia and Zimbabwe appear to be satisfied with arrangements for the achievement of self-determination through cooperation with the former white rulers, the Organization of African Unity, the United Nations, and the president of the United States are not prepared to accept this and apparently would prefer to see the continuance of terrorism, so that the particular organization that enjoys favorite son status in the eyes of the local regional organization may assume power, regardless of the attitude or wishes of the local population in whose name the movement in question purports to be seeking self-determination. Once again, could there be clearer evidence of the legislation of terrorism and the application of diplomatic double talk?

While one may deplore the methods employed by *soi-disant* or recognized national liberation movements, it has to be remembered that some of these are engaged in actual armed conflict and their views may therefore be of significance in conferences related thereto. Little criticism can be made of the United Nations for resolving that the Palestine Liberation Organization should be involved in talks concerning peace in and the future of the Middle East. Nor can criticism be leveled at those who call for the involvement of the South West Africa People's Organization or the Patriotic Front in discussions concerning the future of Namibia and Zimbabwe. Equally, one can appreciate why the Geneva Conference on Humani-

---

[42] Res. 3379 (XXX).
[43] Res. 1904 (XVIII).
[44] Res. 3151 G (XXVIII).
[45] International Convention on the Suppression and Punishment of the Crime against *Apartheid*. Art. 1, Res. 3068 (XXVIII), Annex.

tarian Law in Armed Conflict agreed to the demand that certain national liberation movements should be invited to participate, and since they were actively engaged in hostilities, it is perhaps understandable that they received a status between that of observer and full participant. What is perhaps not quite so acceptable was the decision of the conference to be controlled by the views of regional organizations, for this meant that invitations, as in the case of the United Nations, were not based on any objective standards but on the political predilections of a numerical voting majority. The resolution of the conference as it appears in the Final Act bears reproduction:

> In view of the paramount importance of ensuring broad participation in the work of the Conference, which was of a fundamentally humanitarian nature, and because the progressive development and codification of international humanitarian law applicable in armed conflicts is a universal task in which the national liberation movements can contribute positively, the Conference . . . decided to invite also the national liberation movements recognized by the regional intergovernmental organizations concerned to participate fully in the deliberations of the Conference and its Main Committees, it being understood that only delegations representing States were entitled to vote

but their status was further enhanced by their being allowed to sign the Final Act of the conference. In addition to the organizations already mentioned, invitations were extended to the Mozambique Liberation Front (FRELIMO) and both the Angola National Liberation Front (FNLA) and the People's Movement for the Liberation of Angola (MPLA), although in view of the securing of independence by Mozambique and Angola, these organizations only attended the first and second sessions.

In accordance with the view already expressed by the General Assembly that struggles for national liberation amount to international conflicts, the conference agreed in Article 1 of Protocol I[46] that this concept includes "armed conflicts in which peoples are fighting against colonial domination and alien occupation and against racist regimes in the exercise of their right of self-determination." It went on in

---

[46] 16 Int'l Legal Materials 1391.

Article 44 to redefine the nature of combatants and prisoners of war. Having said

> all combatants are obliged to comply with the rules of international law applicable in armed conflict, [it states] violations of these rules shall not deprive a combatant of his right to be a combatant or, if he falls into the hands of an adverse party, of his right to be a prisoner of war.

It requires combatants "to distinguish themselves from the civilian population while they are engaged in an attack or in a military operation preparatory to attack." To this, there can of course be no objection. But,

> recognizing, however that there are situations in armed conflicts where, owing to the nature of the hostilities, an armed combatant cannot so distinguish himself, he shall retain his status as a combatant, provided that, in such situations, he carries his arms openly: (a) during each engagement, and (b) during such time as he is visible to the adversary while he is engaged in a military deployment preceding the launching of an attack in which he is to participate.

There is no guide as to the meaning of this latter provision. Moreover,

> any combatant who falls into the power of an adverse party while not engaged in an attack or in a military operation preparatory to an attack shall not forfeit his rights to be a combatant and a prisoner of war by virtue of his prior activities.

This means that any person in civilian clothing captured and charged with responsibility for terrorist activities will be able to plead that he is a member of a national liberation movement engaged in a struggle for self-determination and that acts with which he is charged were actually committed during a military engagement when he was in fact carrying his arms openly. As such, he will be able to maintain that he was not a terrorist subject to criminal law, but a legitimate combatant entitled to be treated as a prisoner of war. Once again, we have the situation where international law has granted legal status to terrorists and legalized their terrorist activities.

The implications of this provision have already

become apparent in Europe. During the Folkerts case[47] before the District Court of Utrecht in 1977, the accused, whose extradition was sought by the Federal German Republic as a member of the Baader-Meinhof group, officially known as the Rote Armee Fraktion (RAF), contested the jurisdiction of the court on the ground that the RAF was engaged in a class war not only with the Federal Republic but with every state in the world where such a class war exists. On this basis, he contended that the RAF was engaged in an international armed conflict and protected by the Geneva Conventions and Protocol I. The court rejected this, first, on the ground that the protocol has not yet come into force, but, more importantly, because the RAF is not a movement which, in the exercise of its right to self-determination, is fighting against colonial domination, alien occupation, or racist regimes, nor had Folkerts been able to prove that at the time of his arrest he was engaged in such a conflict. It is perhaps only a matter of time before a court in a country sympathetic to some terrorist organization decides to the contrary. It would only need a situation in which the accused happened to be a member of what that particular country regarded as a national liberation movement.

It is not the only nonaligned majority in the United Nations, the Organization of African Unity, and the League of Arab States that is prepared to legalize acts of terrorism. In 1977, the Council of Europe adopted the European Convention on the Suppression of Terrorism,[48] according to Article 1 of which a number of acts generally recognized as being terrorist in character are condemned and rendered extraditable without any possibility of the claim being frustrated by the political offense plea. These offenses are listed as being within the scope of the Hague and Montreal antihijacking conventions: those involving attacks against the life, physical integrity, or liberty of internationally protected persons, including diplomatic agents; those involving kidnapping, the taking of hostages, or serious unlawful detention; and those involving the use of bombs, grenades, rockets, automatic firearms, or letter or parcel bombs if their use

endangered persons. This treaty was signed by all the members of the Council of Europe except Ireland and Malta. Insofar as the former is concerned, it has made it clear to the United Kingdom that it is not prepared to regard acts that are committed by members of the Irish Republican Army and that fall within the treaty definition of terrorism or the British Terrorists Order[49] respecting Northern Ireland as other than political offenses. Yet again, political and ideological sympathy is considered more important than the suppression and punishment of terrorism, although in this case it might be argued that the acts have not been made lawful, but merely excepted from extradition.

There seems little chance of terrorism being controlled on anything like a universal basis so long as international organizations or individual states are prepared to apply a double standard whereby they confer legality and respectability upon acts of violence that are committed by those with whom they sympathize, especially when they can be presented in the language of the new international order that places self-determination and independence above any other principle or obligation. Nor can one expect the public to condemn such acts, when the media describe them as heroic activities full of glamour, rendered yet more respectable by abandoning the term "murder" in favor of the legal term "execution." One is tempted to remind such partisans of the comments of Milton and of Lord Acton:

> Licence they mean when they cry Liberty.

> There is no error so monstrous that it fails to find defenders among the ablest men. Murder may be done by legal means, by plausible and profitable war, by calumny, as well as by dose or dagger.

QUESTIONS FOR DISCUSSION

1 Do all states wish to control terrorism? What types of states do (or do not) wish such control?
2 What role does international law play in the control of international terrorism?
3 Is new international legislation needed to control terrorism? If so, what kind? If not, why not?

---

[47] 20 Dec. 1977, Rolno. 3853/77. I am grateful to Mr. Sam Bloembergen, legal adviser, Netherlands Ministry of Foreign Affairs, for providing me with the test and a summarized translation of this judgment.
[48] European Treaty Series, No. 90.

[49] See Ireland v. United Kingdom (1978, European Court of Human Rights, official text).

4 Is terrorism ever moral?
5 How can international terrorism be ended?

SUGGESTED READINGS

Alexander, Yonah, and Marjorie Brown (eds.). *Control of Terrorism: International Documents*. New York: Crane, Russak, 1979.

Alexander, Yonah, and Seymour Maxwell Finger (eds.). *Terrorism: Interdisciplinary Perspectives*. New York: John Jay Press, 1977.

Delaney, Robert F. "World Terrorism Today." *California Western International Law Journal* 9 (Summer 1979): 450–460.

Friedlander, Robert A. (ed.). *Terrorism: Documents of International and Local Control*. Dobbs Ferry, N.Y.: Oceana Publications, 1979.

Livingston, Marius H., with Lee Bruce Kress and Marie G. Wanek (eds.). *International Terrorism in the Contemporary World*. Westport, Conn.: Greenwood Press, 1978.

Lowe, E. Nobles, and Harry D. Shargel, cochairmen. *Legal and Other Aspects of Terrorism*. New York: Practicing Law Institute, 1979.

Murphy, John F. *Legal Aspects of International Terrorism: Summary Report of an International Conference*. St. Paul, Minn.: West, 1980.

Sterling, Claire. *The Terror Network: The Secret War of International Terrorism*. New York: Reader's Digest Press, Holt, Rinehart and Winston, 1981.

U.S. Congress. Senate. *International Terrorism*. Hearing before the Committee on Foreign Relations, 97th Cong., 1st Sess., 1981.

Wilkinson, Paul. *Political Terrorism*. New York: Wiley, 1974.

Chapter Six

Modes of Interaction

In world politics, states rely on different modes of interaction. Which methods a state uses depend in part on the strategy it adopts. Strategy may be defined as the political, economic, military, and psychological means used to achieve foreign-policy goals. In the nineteenth century, Britain's strategy in preserving its security was to rely on a balance of power in Europe and on a navy strong enough to support a nation or group of nations threatened by a dominating and aggressive state.

In the post-World War II period, states have devised different strategies to meet diverse goals—whether these goals be security, world domination, or economic development. Often, the stated goals of a country and its real intentions differ, or are perceived to differ. Soviet leaders view American foreign-policy actions as imperialistic rather than security-oriented, and American leaders evaluate Soviet foreign policy as expansionist rather than defensive.

This chapter deals with some of the strategic issues that states have considered since 1945. These issues involve détente, the "China card," and nuclear proliferation.

DÉTENTE

As mentioned in Chapter 3, United States policy, as devised by President Nixon and his national security advisor Henry Kissinger, was based on the premise that arms control and improved trade relations would contribute to changes in Soviet foreign policy that would temper Soviet adventurism. During the Nixon administration, the term "détente" was used to describe improved relationships between the superpowers.

As the Nixon administration gave way to the Ford administration, détente lost popularity in the United States. When the Yom Kippur war occurred, the Soviet Union called on the Arab oil states to embargo oil for the West. The Soviet Union continued to increase its military arsenal and sought to strengthen communism throughout the world. The Soviet invasion of Afghanistan in December 1979 seemed to galvanize public opinion in the United States into a more anti-Soviet position. That invasion undermined the prospects for the United States to ratify the SALT II Treaty that had been submitted by President Carter to the Senate earlier in 1979.

In spite of setbacks in achieving improved relations, détente continues to be an issue in deliberations about superpower strategy. Does détente have a future? Attorney Samuel Pisar thinks that it does. He argues that the United States is overestimating Soviet power. The Soviet Union has an incredibly strong military machine, but it cannot feed its own people or create an efficient agricultural and industrial sector. The Soviets, moreover, cannot count on the loyalty of their Warsaw Pact allies. The United States, Pisar says, should draw the poison from U.S.-Soviet relations by promoting trade, encouraging the forces of moderation in Soviet society, and strengthening arms control.

Defense analyst Charles M. Kupperman argues that the Soviet Union has not changed its views of the world in the postwar period. The Soviet Union seeks to be the dominant global power, a goal it can achieve by eliminating the United States as its major competitor. The Soviet Union does not believe in mutual security interests of the United States and the Soviet Union. Soviet global domination is the goal.

According to Kupperman, the Soviet Union perceives détente to be a policy forced on the United States because of increasing Soviet power and declining American power. The Soviets seek nuclear superiority. Their doctrine emphasizes that this superiority will be used in warfare.

In evaluating the future of détente, a number of questions should be considered. What actions can the Soviet Union realistically be expected to take that would allow critics of détente to be convinced that the Soviet Union is genuinely committed to peace? Is the détente relationship all one-sided against the West, or is the Soviet communist system threatened in any way by the policy? What is the relationship between détente and increased military expenditures, and between détente and foreign interventionism? What are the alternatives to détente?

THE CHINA CARD

The United States was allied with China during World War II. It sought to strengthen the Nationalist government of Chiang Kai-shek after the war. Communist insurgency grew, however, and in 1949, the communists seized control of the government, and the remnants of Chiang's forces fled to Taiwan.

In 1950, China and the Soviet Union signed a treaty of friendship. An appearance of unity was shown by Soviet leader Joseph Stalin and Chinese leader Mao Zedong, but there had been long-standing differences between the two men.

American foreign policy was generally not geared to deal with the diversities of communism, at least in the early postwar years. The wooing of Yugoslavia in the late 1940s served as an exception to what was a hard-line American foreign policy.

The rhetoric of American foreign policy was resistance to communism everywhere as asserted in the Truman Doctrine. The strategic doctrine was containment—a policy of opposing communist challenges everywhere. When the Korean war broke out in June 1950, the United States rushed to support the besieged South Korean army. After establishing a beachhead at Pusan, American forces, under UN auspices, launched a counterattack and drove the North Korean army out of South Korea. United States forces crossed into North Korea and moved toward the Yalu River, which separated North Korea from China. Chinese troops entered the fray, forcing the Americans to retreat southward.

By 1953, a stalemate had been achieved, and a truce was arranged. Bitter relations between China and the United States continued, although informal negotiations between the two governments were conducted in Warsaw. The United States refused to recognize the communist regime in China, and it opposed its representation in the UN. The Chinese support of North Vietnam in the 1960s contributed to bad relations between the two countries.

The Chinese, however, directed increasing criticism at the Soviet Union. Mao Zedong attacked the Soviet policy of peaceful coexistence, favoring a more bellicose policy of world revolution. Border disputes and some fighting along the border between the Soviet Union and China flared. There was even some talk about a Soviet nuclear strike against China after China detonated its first nuclear bomb in 1964, but no action was taken.

In 1971, Henry Kissinger made a secret trip to China and set the stage for a meeting between Nixon and Mao Zedong. It was from this period that the era of détente began between the two countries. Nixon, who had risen to national prominence as a staunch anti-communist, was able to achieve what was generally regarded as a great diplomatic triumph.

The relationship between the United States and Communist China has improved steadily ever since that meeting. A major issue separating the two countries involved the future of Taiwan. The United States had been a supporter of the Nationalist government. The Communist government, however, wanted the United States to withdraw its support of Taiwan—a step the United States has avoided. The United States extended full diplomatic recognition to Communist China during the Carter administration and has encouraged trade, cultural exchanges, and technical assistance for the purpose of helping China to modernize.

As the country with the largest population in the world and as a country that borders on the Soviet Union, China is an important component of Soviet and American strategy. Because of Sino-Soviet tension, an estimated 600,000 Soviet troops are tied down along the Sino-Soviet border. If the Soviet Union and China were to restore amicable ties, then those forces could be diverted elsewhere, such as to east Europe where they would face NATO forces.

What role China should play in American strategy is a fiercely debated question. Should the United States play the China card; that is, arm the Chinese militarily as well as help them economically so that they threaten the Soviet Union? Elias M. Schwarzbart, an expert in far eastern affairs, argues that the United States should play the China card because to do so would promote a balance-of-power system in the world. Because the Soviet Union is the strongest threat to world peace, he says, the United States should tilt toward China to preserve the peace. Schwarzbart makes the following points: (1) Russia and China have historic and geographic conflicts over vast borderlands. (2) China has emphasized modernization rather than expansionism in foreign policy; the Soviet Union has sought global hegemony. (3) United States support of China would encompass an integrated balance-of-power doctrine for the entire Eurasian land mass. (4) China and the United States have mutual interests in countering Russian expansionism in Asia and all other continents. (5) China's economic interests require a policy of peace and long-term collaboration with the United States and its Western allies.

Political scientist Allen S. Whiting argues against playing the China card. China is a poor country, and its military modernization would be a massive undertaking. Strengthening China militarily may arouse the opposition of some of China's neighbors against whom China has made territorial claims. These countries are the Soviet Union, India, Vietnam, Malaysia, the Philippines, and Japan. China has a dispute with Japan and South Korea about the continental shelf, and it has reserved the right to use force against Taiwan.

Whiting argues that the Soviets can counter an increasingly stronger Chinese military establishment. China's hostility toward the Soviet Union did not deter the Soviets from invading Afghanistan. The enlargement of Soviet military strength in eastern Europe, moreover, has not been slowed by the Soviet buildup against China. If the United States plays the China card, the Soviets are likely to strengthen their armed forces, accelerate the arms race, and increase tension between the superpowers.

China will have to improve its economy before it can develop a modern military establishment. The current leadership of the People's Republic is aging, and it is not possible to predict what the views of the new leadership will be in the decade ahead. By helping China to modernize economically, we can hope that China could be integrated into interdependent relationships with the world, rather than pursue a nationalistic and isolationist foreign policy, according to Whiting.

An evaluation of whether the United States should play the China card should consider matters involving international politics generally and specific aspects of the Soviet Union-China-United States relationship. What does history show about the predictability of long-term relationships in maintaining alliances? Can the United States be certain that a militarily strong China would act as the United States wishes? Would the United States have more or less leverage over China if it played the China card? Which country, the Soviet Union or China, has the most adventurous ambitions in foreign policy over the long run? Those who support the China card may consider the kinds of military support that the United States should give to China and what the consequences of that support would be to global and regional stability. Those who oppose playing the China card may evaluate the prospects of Sino-Soviet rapprochement and the consequences of a militarily weak China on global and regional stability.

NUCLEAR PROLIFERATION

Almost as soon as the nuclear-weapons age was born in 1945, it was recognized that the American nuclear monopoly would not last forever. Attempts to establish an international organization with full control of nuclear weapons failed because of the insecurity of nations. One country after another acquired nuclear weapons.

The proliferation of nuclear weapons resulted from a variety of factors. Security, bureaucratic pressures, and economic interests were the most prominent.

Some governments felt that in the final analysis, they could rely only on their own military forces to protect vital interests. Particularly as intercontinental delivery systems became available in abundance to the superpowers, the leaders of many countries believed that security guarantees by the superpowers had lost their credibility.

Bureaucratic pressures encouraged states to become nuclear-weapons powers. Once a governmental organization was formed that was concerned with nuclear energy, it seemed natural for it to expand its interests to include a nuclear-weapons field.

Economic forces played a role, too. As mentioned earlier, economic interests benefit from weapons development and production. Economic forces played a role in another way. Nuclear energy is not only important for weapons, it is also a vital source of energy for many energy-hungry countries in the world. The same technology that is designed to produce enriched uranium and plutonium necessary to build nuclear weapons also serves the peaceful nuclear energy needs of nations. As the price of oil soared after 1973, countries relied more and more on nuclear energy as a way to become less dependent on OPEC.

Even before 1973, however, countries had sought nuclear reactors for their energy programs. Although many of these reactors were supposed to be under international inspection so that no enriched uranium or plutonium could be diverted for military purposes, there was much doubt about the effectiveness of inspection measures to prevent such diversion. Business organizations in the United States, West Germany, and France sought contracts in other countries to build nuclear reprocessing plants in nonnuclear weapons states, such as Brazil and South Korea. Although ostensibly for nonmilitary purposes, the plants could produce weapons-grade material.

Both superpowers helped nonnuclear weapons states to become nuclear-weapons states. The United States shared information with Great Britain. The "special relationship" between Great Britain and the United States served to irritate leaders of other countries allied to the United States—most notably France. For a short time, moreover, the Soviet Union aided Communist China in its efforts to become a nuclear power.

The superpowers, however, generally favored a policy of nonproliferation. Whatever other differences existed between them, they shared the conviction that nuclear proliferation was dangerous. Many nonnuclear-weapons states recognized that if they built nuclear-weapons arsenals, so, too, would their adversaries. An arms race, consequently, would result, and security would be diminished for all parties engaged in such a race.

In 1968, the Nonproliferation Treaty was signed. As mentioned in Chapter 5, its main provisions governed nuclear-weapons states and nonnuclear-weapons states. The nuclear-weapons states committed themselves to reduce the level of armaments. The nonnuclear-weapons states agreed, for their part, not to build nuclear weapons.

The treaty had many loopholes. Not all states signed or ratified the treaty—most notably India, Pakistan, Israel, Egypt, South Africa, Spain, Argentina, and Brazil. The treaty did not cover peaceful nuclear explosions. Also, one could comply with the provisions of the treaty and build everything necessary for a nuclear weapon except the last pin. States, moreover, could withdraw from the treaty with 3 months notice if they found that extraordinary events jeopardized their supreme interests.

It is possible that between 50 and 100 states can develop and produce nuclear weapons by the year 2000. Is this a terrifying prospect? Daniel Yergin argues that nuclear proliferation is a danger to peace and stability by (1) undermining the balance of terror between the United States and the Soviet Union; (2) producing a "chain reaction" with each state ready to go nuclear to meet its neighboring nuclear enemy; (3) easing the taboo against the use of nuclear weapons; and (4) inducing microproliferation—the use of such weapons by terrorists and other groups.

Donald L. Clark argues that nuclear proliferation provides some benefits to states and to world peace. First, nuclear-weapons states are more secure than nonnuclear-weapons states. No nuclear-weapons state has ever had its border seriously attacked by another state. Second, although wars have occurred since World War II, no nuclear nation has used nuclear weapons in these wars.

Clark suggests the hypothesis: "If no nuclear possessor need fear attack, then the only place there can be wars is where nuclear weapons are not possessed, and if such places are diminished through nuclear proliferation, then war potential is also diminished." Nuclear proliferation, he argues, may be more likely to eliminate war than nonproliferation. The danger of use of these weapons by "wild-eyed fanatics" is exaggerated. Mad leaders, such as Stalin and Mao, possessed these weapons and did not use them. Clark supports a policy of controlled proliferation in which the United States would grant limited nuclear weaponry to some states.

In considering the merits of nuclear proliferation, attention may be given to the factors that contribute to a state becoming a nuclear-weapons power, the impact of security guarantees by nuclear-weapons states on nonproliferation, and the stability of a world of many nuclear-weapons states.

19   Does Détente Have a Future?

YES

Samuel Pisar

Drawing the Poison from U.S.-Soviet Relations

NO

Charles M. Kupperman

The Soviet World View

Drawing the Poison from U.S.-Soviet Relations
Samuel Pisar

Russia's intervention in Afghanistan, nervousness over the upheavals in Poland, and the American presidential election are provoking a sharp re-evaluation of the U.S. stance toward the Soviet Union. Unhappily, this is not taking the shape of a debate.

The message perceived by our political leaders is clear: The public has had its fill of weaknesses, or in the idiom of another generation, appeasement. The Carter administration has all but abandoned trade and SALT; the Reagan Convention has dismissed, almost with contempt, the Republican Party's only proven star, Henry Kissinger, in the mistaken notion that he is the symbol, if not the architect, of detente.

The reasoning behind these policy shifts is also clear: Military superiority over the Soviets thwarts their aggressive instincts, thereby promoting stability; arms control and detente encourage their mad ambition to dominate the world, inviting instability.

This view—now automatically endorsed by both political parties—is a dangerous oversimplification of contemporary international life. Both the Soviet Union and the U.S. already have incredibly powerful military establishments; but neither enjoys stability or internal strength. Neither has gained clearcut superiority; nor is a renewed arms race likely to add to either's security. We have not achieved a balance of power either; we have settled for an extremely precarious balance of weakness, while the rest of the world sinks deeper into poverty and the turbulence it spawns.

Weakness as a description of either the Soviet Union or the U.S. is less of a paradox than it may seem. The USSR may be able to destroy the world with its missiles, or in minor league efforts subdue the Afghan rebels or even the Polish strikers with its armor, but it cannot feed its own people. Its industry is not much more advanced than its agriculture. The Soviets may have many more tanks than NATO, but it takes Soviet workers at least twice as long to build each one; and 65 years of revolution have produced an industrial society that must ask an Italian car manufacturer to erect an automobile plant.

Part of Soviet armed might rests with the Warsaw Pact, but how reliable would its allies actually be at the crunch? As a boy in Soviet-occupied eastern Poland I watched Red Army soldiers don German uniforms and traitorously turn their guns eastward. And the loyal majority showed little inclination to fight—in fact the vaunted Red Army crumbled—until the savagery of Hitler's legions, deep inside the motherland, became evident.

As a survivor of the death camps of World War II I could never endorse unilateral disarmament. I once saw my home town occupied by Soviet troops; and then the destruction of my people and my family by the Nazis. My experience confirms that unpreparedness can indeed tempt aggressors.

Yet, having said that, we must ask where our renewed quest for military superiority may lead. The Russians, if they feel threatened, will build arms to the last crumb of bread, the last drop of blood. I know their regime and their paranoia about security. They have been invaded over and over from the East and West and their present leaders, old men who have been through a holocaust, will not ignore the lessons of history.

But the younger men and women, who stand on the threshold of power, do not have personally imprinted upon their psyches the scars of two World Wars. I have met and dealt with some of them. Understandably, they are less concerned with their parents' shibboleths than with their own desires for fulfillment: a start in the direction of economic well-being, political freedom, civil rights. In the long run, these preoccupations will become more important than ideological ambitions.

Think about these people for a moment. Think about the Germans and Japanese of the 1940s and 1980s. People we crushed, fire-bombed and atom-bombed 35 years ago are now our allies. I'm not a seer. I cannot say that Russians, threatened by a populous China in the East and an effervescent Islam in the South, could one day be our friends again.

But is their hostility now genetic or is it conceivable that a young Russian engineer, technician or manager today, cynical about the moribund bureaucracy that

From Samuel Pisar, "Drawing the Poison from U.S.-Soviet Relations," *Wall Street Journal*, Aug. 26, 1980, p. 32.

surrounds him, bored with ideological rhetoric, aware of the discontent of his country's consumers, intellectuals and ethnic groups, but intensely interested in accomplishing something constructive, just might be willing to look beyond the ideological divisions of the present day? At the very least, we should take care not to feed a paranoia that might be dying out.

The crucial question of our times is what we can do, while maintaining our strength, to turn the minds and energies of both societies in more productive directions.

To isolate the Soviet Union from world trade, even in the unlikely event that our allies could be held to such a policy, would be a serious error. Only the growth of living commercial and human tissue can draw the poison from Soviet-American relations and strengthen those in the USSR who are for pragmatism, moderation and liberalization. These are the people who are likely to inherit power in Moscow.

The CIA reports that, at present production rates, by the mid-1980s the USSR must import oil. At that point, its concern with the Middle East will shift from mere opportunism to critical strategic needs. Given the likelihood of increased pressure on supplies, prices and the political soft-spots of the Persian Gulf, are we really enhancing the security of America, Europe and Japan by denying Russia the technology which would enable it to get oil from its own plentiful Siberian reserves?

I know that my views go against the new wisdom—we have tried detente, coexistence and commerce and got nothing in return. The Russians probably feel the same way—SALT, trade, scientific and technical cooperation, the so-called "web of mutual interests," were never given a chance. Both sides have kept one foot on the accelerator and the other foot on the brake.

We must draw the line against Soviet expansion, to be sure, in order to protect ourselves, our interests and our friends. But at the same time we must also use our constructive intelligence to find another way. Break off the dialogue on trade and arms control and you insure that Russia's borders are sealed to Jewish emigration, that the dissidents are finally crushed, that a new iron curtain descends upon Eastern Europe, while we, with whatever allies stand by us, isolate ourselves behind an invincible screen of missiles.

Even if this course were not too risky, it is too costly. It will not only squander resources that are urgently needed elsewhere, it will profoundly alter our industry, our institutions, our government, our people. We, and the world, will have lost what we have struggled for over 200 years to preserve.

The Soviet World View
Charles M. Kupperman

The Soviet concept of what is "strategic" is much broader and more dynamic than the U.S. concept of "strategic." While the U.S. tends to compartmentalize the world, the Soviet Union views the world as a single strategic theater for the historic clash between capitalism and socialism. The basic strategic objective of the Soviet Union is to position itself as the dominant global power. This means possessing the capability to control global economic, political, and strategic affairs directly from Moscow. This can be accomplished only by eliminating the U.S. as its major competitor, by undermining U.S. power at minimal costs and risks to the Soviet Union.[1] This strategic objective becomes quite evident if one examines the strong synergism between Soviet political policies, strategies and tactics, and their enormous military programs.

The Soviet effort to achieve its basic strategic objective has been massive in scope and tempo and

[1] "Highlights of Selected Factors and Issues Bearing Upon Soviet Perceptions and Assessments Relative to the 'Correlation of World Forces,'" A Paper Prepared by the Center for Advanced International Studies, University of Miami, June 1975, p. 7.

From Charles M. Kupperman, "The Soviet World View," *Policy Review* No. **7** (Winter 1979): 45–67.

consistent over time.[2] The Soviet Union also utilizes increasingly sophisticated strategies to achieve this objective.[3] In pursuit of this objective, the Soviet Union requires less political and strategic "modeling" predictability than the U.S. and, therefore, approaches its strategic objective with the open-ended and firm conviction that strength and superiority over the U.S., wherever attainable, is highly desirable and definitely usable. It is a matter of Soviet policy to seek such strength.

In the Soviet world view, conflict and competition with the U.S. are normal states of affairs; these types of relationships must be anticipated and preparations must be made that will produce Soviet victories. And "since the Soviet leadership has gone to great lengths to spell out what it means by 'peaceful coexistence,' the limits of that concept, as well as its implications for Soviet foreign policies, there is no reason, as Soviet spokesmen themselves point out, why the West should harbor any 'illusions' about it or persist in basing its expectations on different assumptions concerning Moscow's policies and actions."[4] Indeed, "the main problem is not that the Soviets do not tell us what they are doing, but that we are reluctant to believe they mean what they say."[5] The result is a highly aggressive Soviet drive for global dominance and continued U.S. strategic lethargy.

The basic outcome of the U.S.-Soviet conflict is, for the Soviet Union, non-negotiable. There can be no common set of security interests between the two nations defined by the U.S. "Equal" security for the Soviet Union translates into absolute insecurity for all other Western nations. From the Soviet perspective,

all that is negotiable for the long-term is the method the West prefers that will ensure its collapse.[6] Thus far, the Soviet Union has structured the spectrum of choice from appeasement to preemptive concession to "conceptual breakthroughs" to surrender to strategic superiority. Basic Soviet policy will continue to pursue the spectrum.

The Soviet Union views the ultimate long-term clash as a "zero-sum" game in which a U.S. loss is counted as a Soviet gain and a Soviet gain is counted as a U.S. loss.[7] There is no Soviet sense of "fair play" or "spirit" about splitting the political, economic, social, or strategic differences that would transform the epic confrontation into a "non-zero-sum" game.

During the conduct of these "games," the Soviet Union will exploit all opportunities and internal divisions within the Western bloc by maintaining a flexible negotiating strategy and military capability that support their requirements for waging political warfare. The Soviet approach deplores rigidity and doctrinairism and emphasizes adaptability. It also demonstrates no hesitation to use illogical argumentation or inconsistency as long as they serve their strategic objective. For the Soviet Union, consistency is not a virtue in its own right.

GLOBAL COMPETITION—A 'REALISTIC VIEW'

The central concept in the Soviet world view is the "correlation of world forces," which the Soviet Union defines as a dynamic mixture of political, economic, social, and military factors. The "correlation" is fundamental to any Soviet assessment of its relation with the U.S. Of equal importance to this unifying concept is the Soviet perception of the movements or trends in the "correlation of world forces." The Soviets do not view the "correlation of world forces" as an abstract concept but, rather, as an "objective" assessment reflecting the "realities" of the world. In the Soviet world view, the major shift in the "correlation of world forces" has been in favor of the Soviet Union and at the core of this belief is the perception that the changed balance of U.S.-Soviet military

[2] Harold Brown, *Department of Defense Annual Report Fiscal Year 1979* (Washington, D.C.: Government Printing Office, 1978).

[3] Foy D. Kohler and Mose L. Harvey (eds.), *The Soviet Union: Yesterday, Today, Tomorrow: A Colloquy of American Long Timers in Moscow,* Monographs in International Affairs (University of Miami: Center for Advanced International Studies, 1975) p. 4.

[4] Leon Goure, Foy D. Kohler, and Mose L. Harvey, *The Role of Nuclear Forces in Current Soviet Strategy,* Monographs in International Affairs (University of Miami: Center for Advanced International Studies, 1974) p. xxi.

[5] Foy D. Kohler, Mose L. Harvey, Leon Goure, and Richard Soll, *Soviet Strategy for the Seventies: From Cold War to Peaceful Coexistence*, Monographs in International Affairs (University of Miami: Center for Advanced International Studies, 1973) p. 6.

[6] Colin S. Gray, "War and Peace—The Soviet View," *Air Force Magazine*, October 1976, p. 30.

[7] "Highlights of Selected Factors and Issues Bearing Upon Soviet Perceptions and Assessments Relative to the 'Correlation of World Forces,' " p. 6.

power has been the key to Soviet ascendancy. The SALT I Agreements of 1972[8] and the Final Act of the C.S.C.E. signed at Helsinki in 1975[9] are frequently cited as *hard* evidence of these new "objective realities" which influence U.S.-Soviet relations and which have actually "forced" the U.S. to adapt itself to Soviet initiatives.[10]

The cutting edge of the "correlation of world forces" is Soviet military power, and ". . . the Soviet authorities leave no doubt that they consider as basic to all else that has happened, or may happen in the way of a shift in the balance of world forces, the growth of Soviet military power, and more particularly, Soviet nuclear power."[11] "Soviet strategic nuclear power has been the elevator of Soviet status in international politics."[12] The state of the military balance and perceptions of this balance are critical factors in determining the character of U.S.-Soviet global competition. These assessments have important ideological as well as strategic implications and the Soviets pride themselves on their ability to make accurate and timely evaluations of the "correlation of world forces" and, more precisely, the military balance.

Briefly then, in the Soviet world view, "detente" was forced upon the U.S. due to the enormous across-the-board increase in Soviet military power, accompanied and reinforced by a precipitous decline in U.S. political will. Despite the enormous increase in Soviet power, the Soviets believe that "deterrence" is fragile and could fail—the result of U.S. resistance to Soviet initiatives. Therefore, Soviet leaders take the possibility of war at *all* levels far more seriously than their Western counterparts, whose guiding premise is to avoid war and particularly "nuclear"

war at all political and strategic costs. In order to strengthen "deterrence" and assure the survival of the Soviet Union should "deterrence" fail, the Soviets emphasize the need for expanding and enhancing their military power, the combat readiness of their forces, the morale and vigilance of the Soviet citizenry, and the vigilance of their "allied forces of Socialism."[13]

With this perspective, there is no inconsistency for the Soviets to follow on the one hand, the policy of "détente" while, on the other hand, engaging in the most massive strategic nuclear buildup in history.[14] Such a policy is in strict accord with common and monotonously repeated principles of Marxist-Leninist "dialectics." For the Soviet Union, military "sufficiency" is only a relative state, not an absolute benchmark of security. The Soviet world view does not regard strategic nuclear weapons as negative instruments having limited applicability to international politics. They are perceived to be important diplomatic instruments that can be utilized to further foreign policy goals and restrict U.S. international political and military activity. Above all else, the Soviet world view incorporates the desire to survive any potential political crisis or war with the U.S. and the Soviet approach is now being evaluated by more strategists on its own terms. A fundamental question remains—why the long delay?

ERRONEOUS PERCEPTIONS OF SOVIET STRATEGIC DOCTRINE

During the 1960s and even at SALT I, the U.S. exhibited a tendency to project Soviet force planning and strategy primarily on the basis of preferred U.S. concepts and assumptions. These "mirror-image" assumptions included such levels of ethnocentrism that U.S. strategic planning was actually an exercise in planning for both sides—hardly a competitive view of strategy—but entirely consistent with the American "hostility to hostility."

Another fundamental assumption of the "mirror-image" concerned the so-called U.S.-Soviet arms

---

[8] William R. Van Cleave, "Political and Negotiating Asymmetries: Insult in SALT I," A Paper Prepared for the Sixth International Arms Control Symposium, Philadelphia, November 2, 1973; and Donald G. Brennan, *Arms Treaties with Moscow: Unequal Terms Unevenly Applied?* (New York: National Strategy Information Center, 1975).

[9] George W. Ball, "Capitulation at Helsinki," *Atlantic Community Quarterly*, Fall 1975, pp. 286–288.

[10] G. Arbatov, "The Strength of A Policy of Realism," *Izvestia*, June 22, 1972, and *The Current Digest of the Soviet Press*, July 17, 1972, p. 4.

[11] Leon Goure, *et al.*, *The Role of Nuclear Forces in Current Soviet Strategy*, p. 2.

[12] Colin S. Gray, "War and Peace—the Soviet View," p. 28.

[13] *Communist of the Armed Forces*, November 1975, in Paul H. Nitze, "Deterring our Deterrent," *Foreign Policy*, Winter 1976–1977, p. 197.

[14] Leon Goure, *et al.*, *The Role of Nuclear Forces in Current Soviet Strategy*, p. 23.

race.[15] The basic premise in this chain of logic was that the U.S. was the initiator of arms "race" activity, while the Soviet Union was the reacting party. In order to break the mechanistic operation of the "arms spiral," unilateral U.S. self-restraint would (naturally) induce Soviet restraint. Such restraint would subsequently produce a strategic nuclear relationship in which each side would possess a highly survivable "assured destruction" capability that must not be threatened by the other side's strategic forces. There would be no need to procure strategic forces beyond those required for the statistical assured destruction mission. Because of the American belief that strategic forces had no extracurricular political utility, additional strategic forces were considered irrelevant.

Even when "unique" Soviet strategic programs began to appear in the mid-1960s, they were not evaluated on their own characteristics or strategic implications, but were forced to fit the conceptual model of the assured destruction mirror-image. Despite the obvious differences in throw-weight, warhead yield, and strategic doctrine, the Soviet Union was still stereotyped as an assured destroyer. In order to accommodate this strategic and intellectual confusion, new rationalizations had to be developed. Although the Soviets *might* be different strategic adversaries, nuclear technology was assumed to be immune to ideology, and it was, therefore, perceived to be the common denominator in the action-reaction model, which would soon produce a "plateau of stable deterrence."

This plateau, however, would be accompanied by the loss of American strategic superiority. For, by the late 1960s, U.S. officials saw "rough strategic parity" as the condition that would stabilize the then doubled Soviet threat and concluded that their Soviet counterparts would reciprocate the "mirror image" phenomenon. American analyses of Soviet strategic doctrine during this period were not derived from either a critical or comparative analysis of Soviet views. Soviet

strategic thought was perceived to be backward, quite unsophisticated, and in dire need of an American strategic education. Little consideration was given to the basic propositions that the Soviet Union might have its own set of strategic approaches and strategic objectives and that these might not conform to American expectations or preferences.

In order to rescue the mirror-image model, the discrepancies among Soviet literature, official Soviet pronouncements and strategic programs and U.S. concepts were rationalized away by the arguments of the "strategic educators."[16] These analysts argued that the Soviets would eventually change their views once they appreciated the foundation and merit of the U.S. assured destruction model and that it was only a matter of time, monotonous repetition, patience, and *more* strategic self-restraint for "strategic convergence" to occur.

Soviet convergence, however, did not occur, as explicit Soviet strategic doctrine demonstrated no equivalent concepts of mutual assured destruction (MAD), any sensitivity to the varieties of stability—strategic, arms competition, crisis, or substrategic (all of which are considered "reactionary" contradictions of "correct" Marxist-Leninist ideology), "deterrence," or "parity." Furthermore, the Soviet Union did not endorse the false distinction between deterrence and defense, but continued to develop and deploy strategic nuclear forces of a "war-fighting" nature.

Despite the fact that American strategic superiority had been the predominate condition of international politics for the previous fifteen years and had brought stability to international politics, America's faith in the non-utility of strategic nuclear superiority could not be shaken and the Soviet strategic buildup was seen as an opportunity to institutionalize a "new structure of peace." If one, however, had argued that "the Soviet Union has no inherent right to strategic parity or to a place in the sun co-equal to that occupied by the U.S.,"[17] one would have been for-

---

[15] The classic "mirror-image" texts are: Robert S. McNamara, *The Essence of Security* (New York: Harper and Row, 1968); and Alain C. Enthoven and K. Wayne Smith, *How Much Is Enough? Shaping the Defense Program, 1961–1969* (New York: Harper and Row, 1971). For refutations of these action-reaction arms race models, see Albert Wohlstetter, "Is There a Strategic Arms Race?", *Foreign Policy*, Spring and Fall 1974; and Colin S. Gray, *The Soviet-American Arms Race* (Lexington, Mass.: D.C. Heath & Co., 1976).

[16] Jeremy J. Stone, *Strategic Persuasion: Arms Limitation Through Dialogue* (New York: Columbia University Press, 1976); Roman Kolkowicz, *The Soviet Union and Arms Control: A Superpower Dilemma* (Baltimore: The Johns Hopkins University Press, 1970); and John Newhouse, *Cold Dawn: The Story of SALT* (New York: Holt, Rinehart and Winston, 1973).

[17] Colin S. Gray, *The Soviet-American Arms Race*.

warding a minority opinion, one which was outside the predominate view which defined strategic nuclear weapons as *sui generis* instruments of policy.[18]

Some "strategic convergence" has indeed occurred, but it has occurred in the opposite and unexpected direction of U.S. strategic thought converging with Soviet concepts. The present period of official strategic debate and academic ferment indicates the rapidity of the adverse shift in the central strategic balance. This state of affairs has forced the U.S. to rethink, re-evaluate, and reformulate its basic concepts of nuclear strategy and its requirements for "high quality deterrence" in light of a severe Soviet threat.

The shift in the U.S. approach toward Soviet strategic doctrine represents the reaction to "discovering" an enormous gap between U.S. expectations of Soviet behavior and actual Soviet strategic programs. It has been the Soviet Union which has increased the American learning curve and forced a new appreciation for Soviet strategic objectives and preferences. Unfortunately for the U.S., this education could be costly because, if not promptly offset, the dynamism of Soviet strategic programs indicates the emergence of a period of unprecedented strategic insecurity for the West—1980–1982—when the Soviets' new generation of large throw-weight fixed land-based MIRVed ICBMs are fully deployed and operational.

EXAMINING AND EVALUATING SOVIET STRATEGIC DOCTRINE

It is possible to analyze Soviet military thought and strategic doctrine as they are revealed in their military literature, military exercises, and strategic force deployments. Despite certain gaps in our knowledge, it is possible to reach reasonable conclusions about Soviet strategic doctrine—and it is indeed necessary —for to wait for the threat to appear is to court disaster and forefeit by default any compensatory countermeasures which could reduce or rechannel the threat. Furthermore, it is impossible to indoctrinate, train and equip the Soviet military establishment without utilizing specific doctrinal literature and this requires Western analysts to be discriminating when examining Soviet military literature and also to evaluate the content based on its intended audience.[19]

A complementary method of analysis is to examine the strategic capabilities the Soviet Union has procured and continues to develop. With this type of analysis, it is also possible to make reasonable inferences about Soviet strategic doctrine and, if there is congruence between Soviet military literature and strategic force deployments, it would seem to be entirely logical to postulate conclusions about Soviet strategic doctrine.[20] This method of analysis is further strengthened if there has been continuity and consistency in both the literary areas and actual force deployments.

It is crucial not to confuse the terms Soviet "doctrine," "military strategy," "military science," and "military art."[21] At the supreme level of this verbal hierarchy is Soviet "doctrine." Soviet strategic doctrine is "a single system of national directions free from individual views." Soviet strategic doctrine is the product of a command political system and is formulated at the highest political level in the Soviet Union. Soviet strategic doctrine has the official approval, the political imprimatur, of the ruling elite of the CPSU— the Politburo. Soviet strategic doctrine is fairly immutable, not subject to ex post facto debate,[22] nor is it a negotiable item with the U.S. Contrary to the role of the U.S. military, the Soviet military enjoys a significant political decision-making role in the formulation of strategic doctrine.

Despite the vertical chain of command, Soviet doctrine does not deprive the Soviet Union of enormous flexibility in shifting tactics in order to take advantage of real and perceived changes in the "cor-

---

[18] For a list of the Western analysts who acknowledge the political utility and military relevance of strategic nuclear forces, see Colin S. Gray, "The 'Second Wave': New Directions in Strategic Studies," *RUSI Journal*, December 1972.

[19] William F. Scott, *Soviet Sources of Military Doctrine and Strategy* (New York: Crane, Russak & Company, Inc., 1975); and Joseph D. Douglass, Jr., "Soviet Military Thought," *Air Force Magazine*, March 1976.

[20] William R. Van Cleave, "Soviet Doctrine and Strategy: A Developing American View," in Lawrence L. Whetten, ed., *The Future of Soviet Military Power* (New York: Crane, Russak & Company, Inc., 1976) p. 43.

[21] V. D. Sokolovskiy, *Soviet Military Strategy*, edited, with an analysis and commentary by Harriet Fast Scott (New York: Crane, Russak & Company, Inc., 3rd Edition, 1975).

[22] William F. Scott, "Soviet Military Doctrine and Strategy: Realities and Misunderstandings," *Strategic Review*, Summer 1975.

relation of world forces." Soviet doctrine, therefore, incorporates an extremely sensitive appreciation of the relative trends in military capabilities.

Soviet military strategy, military science, and military art are all subordinate to political considerations. At these levels of thought, differences of opinion are possible and even encouraged in order to insure the proper synthesis of military thought. These three categories of military thought represent "the fundamentals of preparing for and waging war as a whole and its campaigns."[23]

On the U.S. side of the doctrinal ledger, few believe that any Soviet-American armed conflict is at all likely. In the U.S., there has been made a sharp separation between the concepts of "deterrence" and "defense." The U.S. has emphasized prewar deterrence while neglecting the basic preparations and planning necessary to assure national survival and recovery from a strategic nuclear war with the Soviet Union. The basic belief has been that "deterrence won't ever fail" and that strategic nuclear war is, therefore, "unthinkable." Furthermore, strategic nuclear war *must be avoided at all costs* and this objective has become an end in itself. Until very recently, planning to prosecute different types of strategic nuclear war was secondary. The dominance of a simple single-exchange assured destruction nuclear war model, a basic revulsion against actually thinking through various hypothetical breakdowns in deterrence, and a substantially reduced Soviet threat all contributed to this American strategic doctrinal malaise.

The U.S. approach to arms control was also insensitive to either the stakes involved or the benefits of a coherent negotiating strategy. Rather, it was based on the erroneous perception of mutual U.S.-Soviet interests in solving each other's strategic problems, which were always assumed to be identical anyway. For the U.S., arms control was an end in itself, divorced from the political realities of U.S.-Soviet enmity and somehow placed within the preferred U.S. framework of the "harmony of interests." Arms control developed into a substitute for prudential U.S. national security policy and planning.

Soviet strategic doctrine, to the contrary, stresses the advantages and desirability of real and perceived strategic nuclear superiority. In the Soviet view, "to

press hard in strategic weaponry pays dividends,"[24] and the acquisition of strategic nuclear superiority over the U.S. can serve three interrelated objectives.[25]

First, strategic nuclear superiority confers on the Soviet Union the ability to prevail in strategic nuclear war with the U.S. at a tolerable cost to the Soviet regime. Second, the acquisition of strategic nuclear capabilities unmatched by the U.S. should yield significant military and political advantages that will either deter crisis situations or win them short of strategic nuclear war. Finally, the acquisition of a strategic force posture that looks more substantial and capable than the U.S. force confers additional usable political status on the Soviet Union.

The most important asymmetry between Soviet and American strategic doctrine is the Soviet Union's policy to design their strategic forces to fight and "win" a general nuclear war.[26] The Soviet war-fighting capability and doctrine are designed to achieve the most favorable post-exchange(s) balance and leave the Soviet Union as the dominant global power. When evaluating its strategic capabilities, the Soviet Union assesses the cumulative capabilities of its strategic forces and related programs. Unlike the U.S., the Soviet Union does not over-isolate its strategic weapons systems but emphasizes the synergistic qualities of its strategic forces, programs, and doctrine.

SOVIET STRATEGIC PROGRAMS

Soviet strategic forces are designed to maximize qualitative improvements and flexible war-fighting operations. Soviet strategic doctrine has an unmistakable counterforce emphasis and a premium is placed on surprise and preemption—from the highest political level to the lowest operational level. The Soviet Union is dedicated to the strategy of firing the first salvo, thereby linking counterforce and damage limitation.

[23] V.D. Sokolovskiy, *Soviet Military Strategy*, p. xvii.

[24] Colin S. Gray, *The Soviet-American Arms Race*, p. 64.
[25] Colin S. Gray, "Soviet-American Strategic Competition: Instruments, Doctrines, and Purposes," A Paper Prepared for the National Security Affairs Conference, "Long-Range U.S.-USSR Competition: National Security Implications" (Washington, D.C.: National Defense University, July 12–14, 1976) p. 38.
[26] Richard Pipes, "Why the Soviet Union Thinks It Could Fight and Win a Nuclear War," *Commentary*, July 1977.

Soviet targeting priorities cover the spectrum of counterforce targets: U.S. strategic nuclear missile forces; SAC bomber bases; SSBN bases; nuclear weapon facilities; general purpose forces, bases, and overseas deployments; military command, control, and communication centers; political leadership; and defense industry (particularly war-supporting industry).[27] Soviet coverage of U.S. military targets will grow categorically and geographically as Soviet targeting capabilities continue to expand.

The Soviet Union has invested heavily in its land-based ICBM force and this program has three major objectives: "expanded target coverage (particularly countermilitary) with MIRVs, improved pre-launch survivability with the new hard silo designs, and the attainment of a significant hard-target kill capability.[28] The fourth generation of Soviet land-based ICBMs—the SS-16, SS-17, SS-18, and SS-19—are MIRVed or MIRVable, have substantially greater throw-weights than the third generation of missiles, and incorporate all the advanced technologies necessary for high accuracy.[29] All are designed for a first-strike, hard-target, counterforce mission and the Soviet Union is deploying these systems at a rate of 100-150 a year.[30]

The Soviet Union "has made more rapid strides in accuracy than is generally appreciated and has shown an intense interest in various applications of terminal guidance."[31] New reentry vehicles with much higher betas are being developed by the Soviet Union. These RVs are designed for improved accuracy and will increase Soviet hard target, counterforce capabilities. According to Secretary of Defense Harold Brown,

the current deployment program of fourth generation ICBMs will give the Soviet Union the potential to attain "high single-shot kill probabilities against U.S. silos."[32] . . .

SOVIET DEFENSE CAPABILITIES

Soviet programs for strategic defense are no less impressive than the strategic nuclear offensive forces. These programs—ABM, air defense, civil defense, and related war-survival measures—are integral components of Soviet war-fighting, damage-limiting, and war-winning doctrine, and could have significant political and strategic impact. Soviet active and passive defenses are designed to defend against a residual U.S. second strike and to exploit the synergism of the various defenses. . . .

Soviet passive defenses, in conjunction with active defenses, are designed to reduce Soviet vulnerability to U.S. second-strike forces. An extensive network of blast shelters and evacuation procedures exist to protect the Soviet leadership and civilian population from nuclear weapon effects.[33] The Soviets estimate that population losses in a major nuclear war with the U.S. could be held to 3-4 percent of the urban population and 6-8 percent of the total population.[34] While any quantification of the effectiveness of Soviet

[27] William R. Van Cleave, "Soviet Doctrine and Strategy: A Developing American View," p. 51; and Colin S. Gray, "Soviet Strategic Rocket Forces: Military Capability, Political Utility," *Air Force Magazine*, March 1978.

[28] James R. Schlesinger, *Annual Defense Department Report FY 1976 and FY 1977* (Washington, D.C.: Government Printing Office, 1975) p. II-14.

[29] James R. Schlesinger, *Annual Defense Department Report FY 1976 and FY 1977,* p. II-6. This includes on-board software for guidance, a new inertial guidance system, and a new bus system.

[30] Harold Brown, *Department of Defense Annual Report Fiscal Year 1979* (Washington D.C.: Government Printing Office, 1978) p. 49. According to this report, "there now are over 100 SS-18 launchers converted from SS-9 launchers, along with more than 60 SS-17 and over 200 SS-19 launchers converted from SS-11 launchers."

[31] James R. Schlesinger, *Annual Defense Department Report FY 1976 and FY 1977*, p. II-8.

[32] Harold Brown, *Department of Defense Annual Report Fiscal Year 1979*, p. 63; and "SS-17, SS-18, and SS-19, All Potential Single Shot Silo Killers," *Defense Space Business Daily*, March 8, 1978, p. 43.

[33] "The Soviets probably have sufficient blast-shelter space in hardened command posts for virtually all the leadership elements at all levels (about 110,000 people). . . . Shelters at key economic installations could accommodate about 12 to 24 percent of the total work force . . . and a minimum of 10 to 20 percent of the total population in urban areas (including essential workers) could be accommodated at present in blast-resistant shelters." This figure could increase to 15 to 30 percent by 1985. See Director of Intelligence, *Soviet Civil Defense* (Washington, D.C.: July 1978); and Leon Goure, *Shelters in Soviet War Survival Strategy*, Monographs in International Affairs (University of Miami: Advanced International Studies Institute, 1978).

[34] P. T. Egorov, I. A. Shlyakov, and N. I. Alabin, *Civil Defense* (Moscow: Publishing House for Higher Education, 2nd Edition, 1970), translated and prepared by Oak Ridge National Laboratory, October 1972; U.S. Congress, House, Hearings by the Civil Defense Panel of the Subcommittee on Investigations of the Committee on Armed Services, "Civil Defense Review," 94th Congress, 2nd Session (Washington, D.C.: Government Printing Office, 1976) pp. 268–290.

civil defense is sensitive to basic assumptions about the scale and nature of the attack, the perception of having this damage-limiting capability (buttressed by strategic nuclear superiority) could have significant political and strategic impact.

The Soviets continue to stockpile, harden, and disperse their industrial and economic assets. Further, the Soviet Union has "established a goal to store reserves of grain adequate to feed the entire population for one year by the end of 1981.[35] These programs not only undercut the military effectiveness of the U.S. deterrent, but also undermine U.S. political will.[36]

There is no indication that the Soviets are reducing their defense research and development or industrial capacity in order to divert it to other areas.[37] The achievement of superiority in deployed military technology by the early 1980s remains a basic Soviet objective.[38] In terms of defense spending, in 1975, the CIA revised its estimate of Soviet defense spending—from 5-7 percent of their GNP to 11-13 percent of their GNP—and this revision contained the major caveat that "the new estimates should be viewed as interim and subject to change as work progresses."[39] Soviet defense expenditures now exceed those of the United States by a margin of between 20 and 40 percent and by 60 percent for strategic nuclear offensive forces.

The Soviet Union also has utilized another strategy in its drive for global dominance—"detente"—and like U.S.-Soviet strategic doctrines, there are striking asymmetries between the two nations' definitions, approaches, and expectations for "detente."

'DETENTE': THE U.S. VIEW

In the official Kissingerian view announced 19 September 1974,[40] "detente" was described as a continuing process, not a final condition. America's basic purpose in pursuing "detente" was to "encourage an improvement in which competitors can regulate and restrain their differences and ultimately move from competition to cooperation."[41] In seeking this "atmosphere," the U.S. would provide as many incentives as possible in return for Soviet actions most conducive to peace and individual well-being.

Progress created in one area, it was argued, would lead to momentum in other areas: "by acquiring a stake in this network of relationships with the West, the Soviet Union may become more conscious of what it would lose by a return to confrontation." Inherent in the original U.S. notion of "detente" was that it was "indivisible." Kissinger's earlier assessment that, "a tactical change sufficiently prolonged becomes a lasting transformation,"[42] sought to *adapt* the Soviet Union to preferred U.S. norms of peaceful international behavior.

Another of Kissinger's basic assumptions about "detente" was that "unfortunately the temptation to combine detente with increasing pressure on the Soviet Union will grow. Such an attitude will be disastrous. We will not accept it from Moscow; Moscow will not accept it from us."[43] The original primary criterion of the success or failure of "detente" was U.S. insistence on responsible international behavior by the Soviet Union:

> Let there be no question, however, that Soviet actions could destroy detente as well. If the Soviet Union uses detente to strengthen its military capacity in all fields; if in crises it acts to sharpen tension; if it does not contribute to progress towards stability; if it seeks to undermine our alliances; if it is deaf to the urgent needs of the least developed and the

[35] Statement of Lt. General Samuel V. Wilson, Director, Defense Intelligence Agency, in U.S. Congress, Senate, Hearings Before the Subcommittee on Priorities and Economy in Government of the Joint Economic Committee, "Allocation of Resources in the Soviet Union and China—1977," 95th Congress, 1st Session (Washington D.C.: Government Printing Office, 1977) p. 83.

[36] *Ibid*. According to Lt. General Wilson, ". . . Soviet civil defense, in conjunction with various offensive and defensive measures, has the potential to alter the strategic military relationship, possibly by the mid-1980s."

[37] Statement by Sayre Stevens, CIA Deputy Director for Intelligence, in U.S. Congress, Senate, Hearing Before the Joint Economic Committee, "Allocation of Resources in the Soviet Union and China—1977," p. 19.

[38] Clarence A. Robinson, Jr., "Soviet Press Technology Gains," *Aviation Week & Space Technology*, February 9, 1976, pp. 12–15.

[39] Central Intelligence Agency, *Estimated Soviet Defense Spending in Rubles, 1970–1975* (Washington, D.C., May 1975) p. 1.

[40] Statement by Dr. Henry A. Kissinger, "Detente: The American View," *Survival*, January–February 1975, pp. 35–42.

[41] *Ibid*., p. 35.

[42] *Ibid*., p. 40.

[43] *Ibid*., p. 41.

emerging issues of interdependence, then it in turn tempts a return to the tensions and conflicts we have made such efforts to overcome.[44]

The Soviet Union, contrary to original expectations, has refused to comply with the U.S. definition of detente. Kissinger's definition posed a false alternative between "detente" and "cold war," a dichotomy which also remains the perception of the present Administration. President Carter has stated that detente must be "broadly defined and truly reciprocal" and that "neither of us should entertain the notion that military supremacy can be attained or that transient military advantage can be politically exploited"[45] This political rhetoric is devoid of operational meaning and is categorically rejected by the Soviet Union.

Despite nearly a decade of "detente," the U.S. formulation of that concept continues to obscure the reality of Soviet imperialism and its threat to the West. The fundamental weakness of the U.S. approach to "detente" is that appeasement was and remains an integral part of it.[46] However, such a policy will not appease the Soviet Union.

'DETENTE IN SOVIET STRATEGY'

For the Soviet Union, detente is an offensive strategy designed to expand Soviet power while continuing to exploit the West.[47] The Soviets use the term "detente" almost exclusively in commentaries directed at Western audiences; the word rarely infiltrates Soviet literature. Although the latest Soviet policy of "detente" received its political imprimatur at the 24th Party Congress in 1971, "detente" is not a new element in Soviet strategy.[48]

What is unique about the present Soviet strategy of

detente is that the Soviet Union can bring unprecedented power against a U.S. that lacks the political will necessary to contain Soviet imperialism. For the Soviets, the key is to exploit these opportunities without "overplaying" the assault. The Soviets do not want to provoke a strong U.S. counterresponse that could delay or deny the Soviet drive for global dominance.[49]

In the Soviet view, detente is not a relaxation in the struggle or a reduction of tension with the U.S.; it is merely one form of the struggle—a dialectic complete with Soviet rules, perceptions, and tactics. Detente is, in fact, an *intensification* of the struggle between the two antagonists. The Soviet interpretation and policy of detente requires that the U.S. accept certain "objective" conditions. The first condition is that the U.S. must continue to recognize the state of U.S.-Soviet military parity while the Soviet Union continues to seek strategic superiority. The second Soviet condition for detente is U.S. recognition of the Soviet political sphere of influence—a sphere which now includes the preservation of the territorial integrity of nations well beyond the contiguous borders of Warsaw Pact nations.[50] Such a recognition reduces "detente" to the avoidance of a direct military collision between the U.S. and U.S.S.R., but leaves everything else wide open. The U.S. is expected to cease and desist in "exporting counterrevolution" into third world areas while permitting the Soviet Union and its proxies to support "wars of national liberation," free from the threat of U.S. opposition including the use of military power. Finally, Soviet detente is designed to slacken and choke off Western military programs and reduce Western defense expenditures. The Soviets clearly seek to continue their military buildup and, thus far, "detente" has proven to be *another* useful strategy for achieving the Soviet strategic objective.

The Soviet strategy of detente also includes several interrelated objectives that can assist in the drive for global dominance. The first and foremost objective is to foster the continued recession of U.S. power in

[44] *Ibid.*, p. 42.

[45] U.S. Department of Defense, "Selected Statements" (Washington D.C., July 1, 1978) p. 12.

[46] Theodore Draper, "Appeasement and Detente," *Commentary*, February 1976.

[47] Norman Podhoretz, "Making the World Safe for Communism," *Commentary*, April 1976; Mose L. Harvey and Mark Miller, "Detente Without Mutual Restraint: Fateful Choices for the United States?" Research Notes on U.S.-Soviet Affairs, No. 1 (University of Miami: Advanced International Studies Institute, July 1978).

[48] Department of Defense, Defense Intelligence Agency, *Detente in Soviet Strategy* (Washington, D.C., September 1975) p. 4.

[49] Leon Goure, "An Overview of Soviet Perceptions on the U.S.S.R.'s Position and Prospects in the Current International Situation," A Discussion Paper Prepared for the CAIS-ARPA Workshop on Soviet Perceptions," University of Miami, January 26, 1966, p. 4.

[50] "A Brezhnev Doctrine for the World," *Foreign Report*, May 26, 1976, p. 1; and Avigdor Haselkorn, *The Evolution of Soviet Security Strategy 1965–1975* (New York: Crane, Russak & Company, Inc., 1978).

Europe and replace it with Soviet power. To produce the power vacuum, the Soviet Union seeks the disintegration of the Western Alliance structure. Examples of Soviet activities designed to undermine and outflank NATO include its role in the 1973 Mid-East War, including the oil embargo; continued support for "Euro-communism"; the MBFR negotiations; Soviet-Turkish negotiation of a "non-aggression" treaty; Soviet-Cuban conquest in Africa; and coups in South Yemen and Afghanistan.

The attainment of qualitative nuclear superiority, as well as the maintainance of quantitative superiority, is necessary to meet theater objectives. The growth in Soviet military power allowed the Soviet Union to issue its first explicit nuclear threat to the U.S. during the 1973 Mid-East War (which, itself, became a road test for Soviet policy in Angola in 1976). The Soviet Union has manipulated "detente" to mask the enormous expansion of its military power and has aided the modernization of its strategic and conventional forces.

Securing access to Western (including Japanese) credits, capital goods, and technology to alleviate chronic Soviet economic problems is another important Soviet objective. This type of assistance also aids and abets the Soviet military buildup by subsidizing inefficient Soviet managerial sectors. Overall, this assistance helps the Soviet government to sustain high levels of military spending without forcing *more* difficult resource allocation decisions. Western technology transfers solve short-term Soviet problems, reduce research and development time, costs, and effort—and produce significant military benefits for the Soviet Union.

The fourth and last major objective of the Soviet strategy of detente is the isolation of China. China is perceived by the Soviet Union to be a long-term security problem, but basic remedial steps taken now could reduce some of the pressures of a classic "two-front problem" and insure future Soviet dividends. For the present period, China remains primarily an ideological rival to be isolated, and this can be accomplished by reducing the appeal of "Chinese Communism" while making the world more amenable to the Soviet brand.

CONCLUSION

Thus far, "detente" is clearly working to the advantage of the Soviet Union. The Soviet Union has made few (if any) concessions and has secured the West's

acceptance and endorsement of the Soviet right to control and expand its sphere of influence with means that would have been totally unacceptable in the days of "cold war" or "confrontation."[51] The Soviets have demonstrated their willingness to exploit crises to their advantage and, according to one strategist, "if this is detente, it would be interesting to see the kind of military program Soviet leaders would endorse for a renewal of the cold war."[52] As long as "positive" benefits, as defined by Moscow, continue to accrue from "detente," it will continue to be endorsed by the Politburo as one strategy designed to produce global dominance.

Unless the Carter Administration takes immediate steps to reverse the adverse trends in the military balance, views the world as a single strategic theater, and *leads* the West, international stability could be the result of a *Pax Sovietica*.

The proper intellectual epitaph for present U.S. policy can be found in the wise counsel of Mr. Walter Lippmann who wrote these lines over thirty years ago:

> I do not find much ground for reasonable confidence in a policy which can be successful only if the most optimistic prediction should prove to be true. Surely a sound policy must be addressed to the worst and hardest that may be judged to be probable, and not to the best and easiest that may be possible.[53]

QUESTIONS FOR DISCUSSION

1 What are the differences between Soviet and American concepts of détente?
2 Charles M. Kupperman contends that the Soviets perceive American interests in the third world as "exporting counterrevolution" and Soviet intervention in the third world as supporting "wars of national liberation." Are there differences between "exporting counterrevolution" and "wars of national liberation?"

[51] "The Kissinger Memorandum" *Foreign Report*; April 7, 1976. This report presents the "Sonnenfeldt Doctrine" and its bureaucratic evolution under the direction of Kissinger.
[52] Colin S. Gray, *The Soviet-American Arms Race*, p. 73.
[53] Walter Lippman, *The Cold War: A Study in U.S. Foreign Policy* (New York: Harper and Brothers, 1947) pp. 11–12.

3 Have the Soviet Union and the United States made genuine accommodations to each other's security interests?

4 What foreign policy should the United States pursue toward the Soviet Union?

5 Does détente favor the Soviet Union?

SUGGESTED READINGS

Arbatov, Georgi. "A Soviet View of U.S. Policy." *Wall Street Journal*, Apr. 29, 1980, p. 22.

Barghoorn, Frederick C. *Detente and the Democratic Movement in the USSR*. New York: Free Press, 1976.

Bell, Coral. *The Diplomacy of Detente: The Kissinger Era*. New York: St. Martin's Press, 1977.

Pipes, Richard. *U.S.-Soviet Relations in the Era of Detente*. Boulder, Colo.: Westview Press, 1981.

Podhoretz, Norman. "The Present Danger." *Commentary* (March 1980): 27–40.

Sheldon, Della W. (ed.). *Dimensions of Detente*. New York: Praeger, 1978.

Solzhenitsyn, Aleksandr Isaevich. *Detente: Prospects for Democracy and Dictatorship*. New Brunswick, N.J.: Transaction Books, 1976.

Steibel, Gerald L. *Detente: Promises and Pitfalls*. Foreword by Irving Kristol. New York: Crane, Russak, 1975.

Timberlake, Charles E. (ed.). *Detente: A Documentary Record*. New York: Praeger, 1978.

Urban, G. R. (ed.). *Detente*. London: Temple Smith, 1976.

20 Should the United States Play the China Card?

YES

Elias M. Schwarzbart

The China Card? Play It!

NO

Allen S. Whiting

Sino-American Military Relations

The China Card? Play It!
Elias M. Schwarzbart

Over six years elapsed between the reversal of American policy towards the People's Republic of China (PRC) begun by President Nixon's historic visit to Peking and the formal renewal of diplomatic ties. During the intervening years, the early promise of that initiative was aborted. These were the years during which Nixon, the true architect of the shift toward China ("playing the China card"), was rendered *hors de combat* by the long agony of Watergate. Henry Kissinger then took full charge of foreign policy, and, convinced that the Soviet Union alone could and would guarantee Hanoi's compliance with a peace settlement, decided instead to play the Russian card, with all the disastrous consequences of the destruction of South Vietnam's independence, the humiliating American withdrawal, and the decline of American power. Such was the terrible price paid for our first failure to play the China card to the end.

The Carter administration's recognition of China gave a renewed impetus to Chinese-American relations, but no sooner was this accomplished, than the administration, as if frightened by its unaccustomed boldness, shifted to the Russian side of the triangle with an attempted revival of the discredited policy of "detente." The bilateral SALT II negotiations were actively pursued, and Carter adopted a policy of passive "neutrality" on the China-Vietnam conflict where we should have made clear (without endorsing the Chinese punitive expedition) our agreement with China that it was Hanoi's expansionism, abetted by Russia, that was at the heart of the crisis and that a stable peace in Southeast Asia could not be achieved unless Hanoi abandoned her hegemonistic goals. Are we on the verge of repeating the same fatal mistake? This, then, is a good time to set down the underlying rationale for a policy of playing the China card and for urging its consistent application as a long-term strategy.

IMPORTANCE OF HISTORY

When dealing with contemporary events, a knowledge of a country's history and culture can give a deeper perspective. This is particularly true of China. Unfortunately, most observers' knowledge of China's history begins with 1949, Year One of the "new" China. Others, like the writer, see instead the Middle Kingdom, Chung Kuo, one of the world's oldest great civilizations with a continuous history beginning in the second millennium B.C.E. and the classical country of oriental despotism. We also see almost three centuries of Chinese-Russian hostility marked, under both czar and commissar, by an unceasing tearing away at and absorption of large chunks of the declining Chinese empire. This long-enduring antagonistic relationship was suspended during the honeymoon period following the Communist victory in China, only to be renewed with increased fervor once history and national interest reasserted their primacy over a supposedly common ideology.

In discussing the triangular relationship between the United States, Russia, and China which gives rise to the playing of the China card, I shall try to follow the excellent example of Raymond Aron, who in a recent article challenging George Kennan's neo-isolationism and appeasement of Russia, stated that "strategic speculation is not beyond the understanding of simple mortals"; that is, strategy is not the monopoly of the "experts."

We start with an assumption that has strong support in history: that a crucial role in maintaining the peace is played throughout history by the balance of power. When a rough balance prevails, peace reigns; when the power equilibrium becomes significantly unbalanced, war is the almost certain outcome. The classic *positive* example in modern history is the general European peace that prevailed in the one hundred years between the ending of the Napoleonic Wars in 1815 and the outbreak of World War I, owing to the arrangements made under the Treaty of Vienna and England's balancing role. The classic *negative* example is the appeasement policy toward Hitler, which gave Germany decisive strategic superiority and led inevitably to World War II. The balance of power as the lever of peace may not be the ideal solution but, as long as we have the system of

From Elias M. Schwarzbart, "The China Card? Play It!" *New America* (July/August 1979): 6–7.

nation-states, there is no workable alternative. To paraphrase Winston Churchill, the balance of power may be the worst method—excepting only all the others.

PEACE POLICY

It should also be borne in mind that the balance of power is a peace policy. Those nations which want or need peace, for whatever reason, will support a policy of balance of power. On the other hand, those nations which pursue a policy of expansionism and imperialism (even when in a revolutionary guise) will disturb and upset this balance, which sooner or later leads to war.

When we speak, then, of playing the China card, we mean applying balance-of-power principles to our present predicament. Most opponents of the China card see the problem of maintaining peace in terms of a two-handed game of table-stakes poker between the two superpowers, Russia and America. This becomes the theoretical justification for the Russian-American detente. However, we really are involved in a much more complicated global contest more closely resembling three-handed pinochle, where the third hand is held by China. As any denizen of Seventh Avenue can tell you, pinochle is a game of two against one. It is my thesis, in brief, that since Russia is today's and tomorrow's global threat, while China is likely to be quiescent until at least the end of the century, wisdom dictates that we tilt towards China in this three-handed game to help restore and maintain the balance of power and thus preserve peace for this generation.

That the global balance has already shifted in favor of Russia is conceded even by opponents of the China card. Indeed, Edward Luttwak, one of our most brilliant strategic thinkers, who wrote an article opposing the China card in the October 1978 *Commentary*, has paradoxically stated the premises of the argument in favor of playing the China card most cogently:

> The military balance in Europe, such as it is, already depends on the hostility between the Soviet Union and China which offsets in great part the uneven competition between NATO and the Warsaw Pact . . . it would be altogether overthrown if the Soviet Union were to diminish its forces on the Chinese border . . . the effort expended by the Soviet Union on the Chinese border has increased very greatly. . . . Accordingly, the Soviet military resources absorbed by the confrontation with China must be reckoned as withdrawn from the competition with the West. . . . As things now stand, a diplomatic adjustment between Moscow and Peking could quite suddenly undermine the balance in Europe and beyond. . . .
>
> *The premises of the argument* [for playing the China card] *are incontestable*; the hopes of the Kissingerian detente have now been exposed as vain; the Soviet Union, obdurately bent on achieving a broad military superiority, is steadily advancing over the West in one category of forces after another, and is already acting in a seriously disruptive fashion abroad while being more than usually nasty at home. As for the strategic arms limitation negotiations, they have already failed in substance, whatever the final outcome, since even the most ardent advocates of a new SALT treaty *now concede that it will not preserve strategic stability*. . . . Having tried our best to reach a stable accord with the Soviet Union, *we must now face the brutal fact that we have failed*—perhaps because our well-meaning intent has been mistaken for weakness, or perhaps because our weakness is all too real. [my emphases]

The question arises: if these premises are incontestible, why doesn't the conclusion follow? Instead of responding directly, Luttwak furnishes a catalogue of objections, the most serious of which relates to the risks involved, particularly the possibility of triggering a dangerous Soviet reaction, not excluding the use of nuclear force against China, However, in evaluating any policy, one must assume its ideal execution, reducing the risks to the greatest degree possible; otherwise no policy would meet the test, including any alternative to the China card. There are, of course, no riskless policies. But given the dangerous imbalance in favor of the Soviet Union, are not the risks of *not* playing the China card greater and more immediate? Indeed, does not the historic evidence point to the fact that the disastrous failures of America's post-war Far Eastern policy are in a great part attributable to our earlier failure to do so? And is it not more likely that playing the China card will persuade Russia to moderate her policies and seek better relations with the United States and the West?

Aren't we, in fact, beginning to see the first tokens of moderation? But given an unavoidable level of risk, what is most surprising in Luttwak's critique, as in the case of most critics of the China card, is the absence of an alternative policy.

WHY PLAY THE CARD?

Here, I should like to outline briefly the affirmative arguments for playing the China card as a particular application of the basic balance-of-power principles discussed earlier.

1 The Eurasian continent, a geopolitical unity, is the critical mass in the world balance of power upon which world peace depends. Nevertheless, from 1949 until the Nixon-Kissinger visit to China, we attempted to create separate balancing structures for Europe and Asia while, paradoxically, harboring the disastrous misconception of the Soviet Union and Communist China as a monolithic force bound by a common ideology. As events have amply demonstrated, behind the facade of ideological unity, Russia and China are locked by history and geography in an ineluctable struggle over the vast borderlands imperial Russia wrested from a weakened China. Our setbacks in East Asia—from Korea to Vietnam—can be attributed in large part to our failure to take these antagonisms into account.

2 Since 1965, when Mao Zedong returned to power under the banner of the Cultural Revolution, China has turned inward to cope with its vast internal problems, and following the liquidation of the Cultural Revolution, China under the tutelage of Zhou Enlai and his annointed successor Deng Xiaoping, have set the nation to the task of creating a modern industrial state which will diminish its challenge until the end of the century.

During the same period Russia's policy of military build-up and expansionism have grown apace and its behavior has become more intransigent, in Africa, the Middle East, and most recently, in Southeast Asia. The grand strategy of the Russian empire seeks nothing less than global hegemony through the containment of China in the East and the conquest or subjugation of Europe in the West. Let Europe fall and the rest will follow. Should Russia succeed, the world balance will have shifted decisively in its favor, with war or submission as the only alternative.

3 It follows that a sound American strategy should encompass an integrated balance-of-power doctrine for the entire Eurasian land mass whereby the outer ring of U.S. alliances—NATO in the West, Japan and South Korea in the East, supported by America's global power—responds to the contradictions between Russia and China, who occupy the inner heartlands, in order to maintain the balance under all changing conditions. Since expansionist Russia is today's and tomorrow's threat to peace and American security, while the potential Chinese threat lies beyond this century, this is the time to tilt toward China, leaving to the next generation the task of maintaining the balance in the unforseeable circumstances of the more distant future.

4 The PRC and the U.S. have long-term parallel interests in countering Russian expansionism in Asia and all other continents. In a letter I wrote to *The New York Times* in March of 1972, I argued for a shift of American policy towards China as the best means of achieving a satisfactory ending of the Vietnam conflict, stating that "the road to peace passes through Peking before it reaches Moscow." I urged that China and the U.S. have parallel interests in Indochina. I pointed out that since 1966 Russia, not China, had become the main support of North Vietnam as part of Russia's long-term plan to encircle China and reduce American power; that it was in China's interest, as well as ours, to have small independent states, not excluding an independent South Vietnam, as her southern neighbors, rather than a unified Vietnam whose true objective was hegemony over all of Indochina with Russia's full support. We have since seen North Vietnam's hegemonistic policy unfold in South Vietnam, Laos, and now Cambodia. The PRC, for its part, has recognized these parallel interests and has openly signalled its support for a strengthened NATO, urging the U.S. to maintain a strong presence in East Asia and the Pacific region.

5 I have left for last the economic dimension, which may ultimately prove the most promising and most stabilizing factor.

The extent and rapidity of the startling changes in economic policy already introduced under the redoubtable Deng Xiaoping should astound even the most seasoned China-watcher. China, under its present leadership is apparently determined to do all that is necessary to achieve rapid modernization and become a developed industrial state by the end of the century in fulfillment of Zhou Enlai's testament; this goal requires peace and long-term collaboration with the U.S. and its Western allies, including Japan.

ECONOMIC CHANGES

The figures are staggering; but even more than the figures are the fantastic changes foreshadowed in economic and social policy best summarized in Fox Butterfield's dispatches to *The New York Times* from Hong Kong: the new leaders are introducing a limited market economy; turning to foreign capitalist governments and multinational corporations for vast investments and internal development projects; transforming agricultural communes into efficient producing units for both agricultural and small industry; restoring factory discipline, differential wages based on productivity (although more recently there are reports that the Yugoslav system of factory autonomy and profit-sharing may be substituted); introducing the high interest rates for state loans; reviving profit incentives and *mirabile dictu*, urging that "the proletariat can and must learn from the bourgeoisie." Since then, more modest and realistic objectives have been set, without affecting the awesome dimensions.

Clearly these developments have the potential of altering the course of history. Think of this: "Communist" China is creating a new contemporary model for rapid modernization of a backward country premised on collaboration with the "capitalist" West, both in the economic and security spheres. This model is precisely the polar opposite of the prevailing Soviet model of unswerving hostility to the West and unceasing international class war, which has influenced many Third and Fourth World countries. If the Chinese model should prove successful, with a resulting discrediting of the Soviet model, it is possible that we might see the Third and Fourth World countries reversing gears and emulating the Chinese example, thus fulfilling the vision of those who grasped the symbiotic relationship—the relationship of mutual interdependence—between the advanced Western industrial countries and the developing nations.

In this sense, then, the addition of the crucial economic dimension makes playing the China card take on an even deeper significance in opening the realistic prospect of advancing world prosperity and leaving a peaceful world to the next generation. If this

should work out, it could be a whole new global ball game.

Some may ask: Have we not seen this before? Is this really different from the New Economic Policy (NEP) of 1921 in Soviet Russia? It is different because the whole historic context is different. In NEP, Lenin also sought Western aid to revive a ruined economy, but the policy was purely tactical, short-term, and confined to the realm of economics. In terms of strategy and foreign policy, the Soviet Union continued to proclaim its revolutionary aims of overthrowing world capitalism and actively supporting revolution and revolutionary parties throughout the world. By contrast, China is seeking the aid of the West within the context, not of sworn hostility to, but of long-term active collaboration with, the West also in political and strategic spheres against Soviet expansionism. (We have the spectacle of American Maoists bombing the PRC mission building in Washington on the eve of Deng's visit and condemning China's collaboration with "imperialism.") Although we should not drop our guard against unexpected developments, this difference nevertheless provides a sound underpinning for the China card.

Perhaps the biggest and most troublesome unanswered question is: "Can a Hundred Flowers Bloom in the Chinese Totalitarian Garden?" Once before, in 1957, Mao launched his Rectification Program to win over the intelligentsia under the slogan, "Let one hundred schools of thought contend and let one hundred flowers bloom." However, when the populace sought to take advantage of the new freedom to demand democracy and multiple parties and to utter dangerous thoughts, Mao mercilessly crushed the blossoming movement and launched the ill-fated Great Leap Forward. The recent suppression of wall-posters and demonstrations calling for democracy, the rule of law, and a better life for the people, as well as the revelations of the existence of a Chinese Gulag, have justifiably given rise to fears that the government's tolerance of dissent would prove all too limited.

China's leaders are confronted by a cruel dilemma: they must choose between the primacy of the party and of the nation, that is, between absolute monopolistic power and rapid modernization which can be achieved only with the long-term assistance of the West and the simultaneous unleashing of the creative powers of the people. In a crunch, which path will the leaders choose? To pose this question is to reckon with the fact that the stability of Chinese-American relations is more likely to depend on internal developments and that Chinese international policy will to a large extent be a reflection of internal tensions. Yet, there is reason to hope that as long as the present disciples of Zhou Enlai remain in power, they will faithfully execute his legacy and the instructions of the Tenth and Eleventh Party Congresses to give priority to the task of carrying China into the twenty-first century.

In China's classical age, under the middle and late Chou dynasties (774–256 *B.C.E.*), overlapping Greece's great classical age, learning, arts and crafts, philosophy, and remarkable technical progress flourished for several centuries. China moved from the bronze age to the iron age and the rise of cities. It was the time of Lao Tze, Confucious, and Mencius; of Yang and Yin and the I Ching. And what was the name given to this era? "The Era of the Hundred Schools!" (Again, the echoes in Chinese history.) However, with the further development of irrigation systems under the control of the emperor came the age of oriental despotism which has haunted Chinese history to this day (see Wittfogel, *Oriental Despotism*). Is it possible that China's new course may finally mark the beginning of the end of two millennia of oriental despotism and its more virulent modern variant, Communist totalitarianism? The answer lies in the unknown future, but on that answer may ultimately depend the success of the entire modernization program, the future direction of American-Chinese relations, and the hopes for a peaceful world.

A related question is whether we can trust the new Chinese leaders. The first answer is no, no more than the old leaders and no more than the Russian Communists. But the second answer is that the strategy of the balance of power does not depend on trust: it depends on self-interest. Indeed, if there were trust among nations to begin with, there would be no need for the balance of power. Just as we play the China card in our interest, the Chinese are playing the American card in theirs. The give and take must, therefore, be mutual and roughly balanced. It must not be all give by America and all take by China. A one-sided China detente would be no improvement over a one-sided Russian detente. We must hold Chinese credits, technical assistance, and trade on a tight leash, within limits of ability to pay and, at all times, in coordination with the pursuit of common political and strategic objectives.

This caution underlines the amateurish stupidity (not to mention the moral cowardice) of the Carter administration's handling of the Taiwan issue. At the least, we should have insisted on firm assurances, backed up by our military umbrella, against the use of force by the PRC to achieve reunification. The irony of the situation is that Deng had openly put Taiwan on the back burner in his anxiety to win the West and would have agreed to the American conditions if only they had been firmly insisted upon. Fortunately, the effects of the Carter blunder have been mitigated by the security provision adopted by Congress, and the internal situation in Taiwan has restabilized.

This brings us to the next question: Does playing the China card mean that the U.S. must have an anti-Russian policy? Here again, the answer is yes and no because the answer does not depend on us as much as it does on the Russians. If they come seeking conquest, we shall show them the sword; if they come seeking peace, we shall extend the hand of friendship. As I pointed out at the outset, the balance-of-power policy is an instrument for preserving the peace and not for making war. Our goal must be to persuade *both* Russia and China that it is in their best interests to join the world community as peaceful members and play according to civilized rules in the conduct of their internal and international affairs. But the question left unanswered by those who oppose playing the China card is: How do you persuade an expansionist Russia hell-bent on conquest other than on the one hand, by confronting her with sufficient strength to deter her from her present aggressive course and, on the other, by making a show of good-will if she takes the path of peace? At this historic moment, the truly remarkable opportunity of Chinese collaboration is a crucial element in the power balance and, therefore, a force for peace.

In my view, the next five years will be the most dangerous for the world. If Russia is to make her move for world hegemony, she must strike within that time; beyond that, the tide of history will begin to turn against her. We have waited much too long to strengthen our defense posture and play the China card, but now that we have begun to do so, we have improved the odds that the Russian leaders may decide that the fruits of peace will be' richer than the fruits of war. Whether they choose war or peace, we shall be better prepared to meet the test.

Sino-American Military Relations
Allen S. Whiting

INTRODUCTION

U.S.-China policy has accomplished many of its objectives since the historic visit of President Nixon to Beijing and the Shanghai Communique of February 1972. Full diplomatic relations between these two major Pacific powers have opened the door to an ever expanding range of trade, travel, scientific and cultural exchange. The United States is beginning to play a major role in China's economic modernization. A *modus vivendi* on Taiwan has obviated the need for an American defense commitment and ended our intervention in the Chinese civil war.

China's support for the U.S.-Japan security treaty strengthens the prospects for peace and stability in northeast Asia.[1] China's close cooperation with the Association of Southeast Asian Nations (ASEAN) in condemning the Vietnamese invasion of Cambodia is an important counter to expanded Soviet influence in the area. Sino-Pakistani consultations have reinforced South Asian resistance to the threat of Soviet expansionism, manifest in the invasion of Afghanistan.

The progress to date has been so swift and successful as to exceed the most optimistic expectations of those who labored over the past ten years to bring about a new relationship between China and the United States. Tactical bargaining and technical problems continue to impede solution of such matters as textile quotas, civil airline arrangements, and the final disposition of frozen assets and confiscated property claims. But the positive far outweighs the negative, to the credit of high officials in Beijing and Washington who committed their political prestige to a Sino-American detente.

However, the next stage in Sino-American relations raises new questions and problems. Having resolved most of the immediate issues between our two countries, the possibility arises of entering into a strategic partnership. This prospect was raised by Vice-President Walter Mondale, speaking on Chinese media at Beijing University in August 1979. In his words, "The fundamental challenges we face are to build concrete political ties in the context of mutual security."[2] Mutual security implies an alliance relationship. More recently, Assistant Secretary of State for East Asian Affairs Richard Holbrooke declared, "A China confident in its ability to defend its borders against foreign aggression enhances stability in the Pacific and on the Eurasian landmass, and therefore contributes to our own security and that of our allies."[3]

In pursuit of this goal, Mr. Holbrooke declared, "We can and we will assist China's drive to improve its security by permitting appropriate technology transfer, including the sale of carefully selected items of dual use technology and defensive military support equipment." While repeating previous administration policy against the sale of arms to China, he implied that this was subject to change by noting that "the *current* international situation does not justify our doing so." (Italics added)

The Mondale and Holbrooke speeches signal an impending Sino-American military entente directed against the Soviet Union, at least as seen from the vantage point of Moscow. While Holbrooke asserted that "relations with China are not a simple function of our relations with the Soviet Union," he warned that "the pace of their advance has been and will continue to be influenced by changes in the international environment," a clear hint of the triangular fix on policy which he elsewhere tried to deny.

These propositions deserve careful scrutiny. China's military modernization is a massive undertaking. It will require the total re-equipping of the air force

---

[1] Premier Hua Guofeng noted at his recent Tokyo press conference, "We appreciate Japan's efforts to strengthen its alliance with the United States." *Beijing Review*, No. 23, June 9, 1980, p. 12.

[2] *The New York Times*, August 28, 1980.

[3] Assistant Secretary Richard Holbrooke in address to the National Council for U.S.-China Trade, Washington, D.C., June 4, 1980, Department of State text.

From prepared statement of Allen S. Whiting in U.S. Congress, House of Representatives, *The United States and the People's Republic of China: Issues for the 1980's,* Hearings before the Subcommittee on Asian and Pacific Affairs of the Committee on Foreign Affairs, 96th Cong., 2d Sess., 1980, pp. 44–58.

which is wholly obsolete and the complete overhaul of the ground forces, where capabilities are sadly deficient compared with those of the Soviet Union. It will also require the retraining and upgrading of human skills involved in the management and maintenance of the vast People's Liberation Army. Only through this gargantuan effort can China feel truly confident "in its ability to defend its borders against foreign aggression."

But more than feasibility forces us to ask hard questions concerning our military relations with the People's Republic. The political consequences must also be weighed. The borders that China seeks to defend are disputed by its two largest neighbors, the Soviet Union and India. Incidents along the Sino-Vietnamese border contributed to China's invasion of Vietnam in 1979. China's territorial claims at sea conflict with those of Vietnam, Malaysia, the Philippines, and Japan. China's continental shelf position challenges that of Japan and the Republic of Korea. Last but not least, Beijing reserves the right to use force against Taiwan. These potential flash-points of controversy compel us to examine the assumptions and implications which underlie present and prospective policy.

In addition, of course, there is the larger question of the triangular relationship. How do we envisage our long run policy toward Moscow? Is it one of maximizing the force available to deter Soviet aggression and should deterrence fail, to win World War III? Or is it a mixed strategy of selective confrontation and cooperation in hope of stabilizing the relationship and reducing the risk of war? Should we strengthen one side militarily in the Sino-Soviet dispute, or should we limit our help to non-military activity?

Finally, what is our confidence in predicting future Chinese foreign policy? What are the prospects in the 1990s, when Beijing's modernization programs should begin to bear fruit? Does the past provide any precedent for prediction or is this a watershed period for the People's Republic and its interaction with the world?

These are only the most salient questions. They cannot be adequately addressed, much less answered, in the compass of a brief paper. Moreover, they should be considered in consultation with our allies and friends in Asia, especially Japan, whose interests in and knowledge of the area supercede our own. However, in the following pages, we can at least examine some of the implications of assisting China's military modernization as a guide to the extensive discussion and debate which will follow this committee's deliberations.

CHINA'S UNSETTLED TERRITORIAL CLAIMS

So long as China entertains a claim to territory disputed by a neighbor, any strengthening of Beijing's military capability to assert that claim logically should be of concern to that neighbor. Fighting between the PLA and another country triggered wholly or in part by such disputes has occurred with India (1962), the Soviet Union (1969), South Vietnam (1974), and North Vietnam (1980). In addition, a demonstration of armed force by Chinese fishing boats occurred near the Senkaku Islands administered by Japan (1978).

These territorial claims vary widely in their military, political, and economic importance as well as in their susceptibility to armed confrontation. The status quo between India and China has not been challenged by either side since 1962. The PLA victory at that time confirmed Beijing's ability to control a large disputed sector in the Ladakh area through which an important military road linked the potentially rebellious frontier areas of Xinjiang and Tibet.[4] While the PLA offensive simultaneously overran the entire Northeast Frontier Agency (NEFA), also in dispute, a unilateral withdrawal returned NEFA to New Delhi's control as a tacit *quid pro quo* for the Ladakh area. This followed a compromise formula proposed by Premier Zhou Enlai in 1960.

Until this border is formally agreed upon and demarcated as well as delimited, the potential for further fighting remains. This could arise through dissident activity in Tibet with guerrilla support from neighboring territories provoking Chinese patrols to pursue actual or suspected opposition through passes in the high Himalayas held by Indian outposts. Alternatively, clashes could occur in the context of renewed Pak-Indian hostilities, wherein China's tacit alliance with Pakistan prompts Beijing to show support for Islamabad. Both situations have arisen in the past. Their future possibility helps to explain India's recent agreement to accept $1.6 billion in military aid from the Soviet Union over the next five years.[5]

---

[4] Allen S. Whiting, *The Chinese Calculus of Deterrence: India and Indochina* (Ann Arbor: University of Michigan Press, 1975).

[5] *The New York Times*, May 30, 1980.

The Sino-Soviet border dispute involves considerably less territory, most of which has little or no strategic significance, but it continues to have a far higher potential for conflict. Two areas held by Moscow and claimed by Beijing are of military importance: the island at the juncture of the Amur and Ussuri Rivers overlooking Khabarovsk and the so-called "Pamir knot" adjoining the U.S.S.R., China, and Afghanistan.[6] The remainder involves islands in the Ussuri River and frontier land in Central Asia.

The potential volatility of this territorial dispute stems from the larger context of Sino-Soviet relations, manifest in the deployment of more than a million troops in confrontation along the 4,100-mile border. The lack of Soviet apprehension over an imminent conflict is reflected in the fact that of its forty-odd divisions arraigned against China, nearly half remain at one-third strength or less.[7] For its part, Beijing has muted the war alarm of its public media of a few years past. The size and composition of the Soviet forces justify this relatively relaxed posture, although the recent addition of Backfire bombers and SS-20 missiles has increased Moscow's ability to strike hard and deep at Chinese population and industrial centers. Thus, neither side seems concerned about war in the near future either as a defensive or offensive contingency. However, Soviet professed apprehension over the prospects of Chinese military modernization with foreign assistance appears genuine. In view of the vulnerability of the Trans-Siberian Railroad which supplies the key Far East base of Vladivostok, this apprehension has some basis in objective reality, however much it is exaggerated in manipulative posture or subjective paranoia.[8]

The border dispute with Vietnam is the least sizeable and the most recent of the three controversies over China's landed frontier, but it also has occasioned the most serious fighting. While few details are available in open sources, it appears that no area of strategic or economic importance is involved. As with the Sino-Soviet dispute, the boundary problem is more a function of the larger relationship than significant in itself. Yet the fact remains that China justified its invasion of Vietnam in part on allegations of border violation.[9]

It might be argued that because the U.S.S.R. and Vietnam are basically in an adversary relationship with the United States and its ASEAN friends, it is in the American interest to support China in its border disputes with both countries. The argument is open to challenge. In the short run, Vietnam's increased dependency on the Soviet Union as a consequence of Chinese economic and military pressure enhances the Soviet position in Indochina. The appearance of Moscow's military ships and planes in Cam Ranh Bay and Danang as a result of the Chinese invasion demonstrated this triangular interaction. In the long run, Vietnam's desire for full independence and its need for economic assistance from countries outside the Soviet bloc may provide an opportunity to reduce Soviet influence, provided that Sino-Vietnamese relations improve rather than deteriorate. This would be to the interest of ASEAN as well as of the United States.

China's offshore claims cover the entire South China Sea, extend to the island archipelago between Japan and Taiwan, and reach across the continental shelf to the waters between Japan and Korea. In January 1974 Beijing exercised its claim to the Paracel Islands by defeating South Vietnamese forces there in a brief encounter. Other islands in the South China Sea held by Vietnam, Malaysia, the Philippines, and Taiwan are contested by Beijing. Chinese maps ring the Sea with territorial boundary markers.[10] At a minimum, China's extension of the twelve-mile limit from its claimed islands, reefs, and shoals could obstruct passage through this main route between Japan and the Middle East. At a maximum, recourse to the 200-mile economic zone could provide Beijing with control over the use of the area for fishing and

[6] *International Boundary Study: China-USSR*, No. 64 (revised) (Washington: Bureau of Intelligence and Research, Department of State, February 13, 1978).

[7] *The Military Balance, 1979–1980* (London: International Institute for Strategic Studies, 1979), p. 10. Also John M. Collins, *Imbalance of Power* (San Rafael: Presidio Press, 1978), p. 130 notes, "About half of all Soviet divisions on the Chinese border are Category III. The Kremlin apparently anticipates no early aggression by either side in that area."

[8] The Trans-Siberian Railroad runs within ten miles of the Chinese border for a distance of 175 miles between Khabarovsk and Vladivostok, at one point being only 1.5 miles away. Data from U.S. Army Map Service. 1:250,000. (L–542, Sheet NL. 53–7, *Hu-lin, China*) (Washington, D.C.: Defense Mapping Agency, 1955).

[9] Harlan W. Jencks, "China's 'Punitive' War on Vietnam: A Military Assessment," *Asian Survey*, August 1979, Vol. 19, No. 8, p. 802.

[10] *Zhongguo Dituce* (Atlas of China) (Shanghai: 1974), p. 16.

offshore oil exploration, vital concerns for contiguous countries.

Beijing has confined its official protests over Japanese administration of the Senkaku (Diaoyutai) Islands to statements. However, a fleet of more than one hundred armed fishing boats sailed in the vicinity for a week in April 1978 with signs declaring the islands to be Chinese.[11] Although miniscule and uninhabited, they may provide access to offshore oil. Joint offshore oil exploration between Seoul and Tokyo has been protested by Beijing for many years as a violation of China's ownership of the continental shelf.[12] So long as Japan continues to play a major role in China's economic modernization, there is little danger that either issue will be pressed to the point of confrontation. However, China's relations with South Korea and Japan contain the seeds of serious controversy, depending upon how the three countries manage their pursuit of offshore oil.

Land-based controversies can be affected by changes in ground and air force capabilities; those at sea are susceptible to changes in naval and air power. All three services are potentially relevant for the future disposition of Taiwan, although an air-sea blockade is more likely than an all-out invasion across the 100 miles of strait separating the Nationalist island from the Communist mainland. In sum, the agenda of unsettled territorial issues confronting future Chinese regimes in Beijing makes it virtually impossible to strengthen the PLA without increasing the potential threat to countries whose interests are important to U.S. policy.

THE SOVIET FACTOR

Assistant Secretary Holbrooke's allusion to "stability on the Eurasian landmass" being enhanced by "a China confident in its ability to defend its borders against aggression" raises the relevance of other areas beyond the periphery of China. More specifically, it is sometimes argued that China provides a deterrent against Soviet aggression on the NATO front through the prospect of a two-front war, and China diverts Soviet forces that might be deployed elsewhere to facilitate Moscow's expansionist goals.[13]

In quantitative terms, this argument has some merit, although less than its advocates profess. The Sino-Soviet border has never been a demilitarized frontier like that between Canada and the United States. Even during the heyday of alleged "monolithic unity" between Moscow and Beijing, twelve to fifteen divisions were positioned in the Soviet republics adjacent to China. This increased to thirty-five divisions by 1969, the year of maximum fighting on the border and of implied Soviet threats to attack China's nuclear facilities.[14] Ten years later, an estimated 600,000 Soviet troops were arraigned in an arc extending from Central Asia through Mongolia to the Soviet Far East.[15]

None of this occurred as a result of an improvement in Chinese military capabilities. Conceivably such an improvement might prompt Moscow to deploy additional units which otherwise might confront NATO or move to trouble-spots in the Middle East and Africa. But this is not certain. Moreover, China's hostility did not deter the Soviet invasion of Afghanistan. As for NATO, the American troop presence and treaty commitment is almost certainly the operative deterrent, while the buildup of Soviet conventional and nuclear strength in East Europe has apparently not been significantly slowed by the buildup against China.[16] In sum, the advantages in global terms of strengthening China's military forces are highly conjectural and marginal at best.

While the disadvantages in terms of U.S.-Soviet relations are also conjectural, they further weaken the argument of those who cite alleged benefits. We know virtually nothing about Soviet decision-making at the highest levels. We can only speculate on the relative

[11] Chae-jin Lee, "The Making of the Sino-Japanese Peace and Friendship Treaty," *Pacific Affairs*, Fall 1979, Vol. 52, No. 3, pp. 430–31.

[12] See Chinese Government Statement, May 7, 1980, *Beijing Review*, No. 20, May 19, 1980, pp. 6–7.

[13] Ronald Reagan offered this analysis to support President Nixon's trip to Beijing in 1972. See Helen von Damm, *Sincerely Yours, Ronald Reagan* (Ottawa, Ill: Green Hill Press, 1976) pp. 74–75, letter to M. Stanton Evans, head of American Conservative Union.

[14] Information available to the author at the time.

[15] *Allocation of Resources in the Soviet Union and China—1978*; Hearings before the Subcommittee on Priorities and Economy in Government of the Joint Economic Committee, Congress of the United States, 95th Congress, 2nd session (Washington: 1978), Part 4: Soviet Union, p. 88.

[16] The Central Intelligence Agency estimated in 1978 that between 12 and 15 percent of the Soviet military expenditure was for forces arraigned against China; *ibid.*

weight of respective factions and in particular of civilian versus military interests.[17] However, both logic and analogy with other modern bureaucratic systems suggest that the stronger and more visible the Western role in China's military modernization, the more likely is the Kremlin to strengthen its armed forces, and the more hostile will it perceive Western policy to be. This in turn will maintain, if not accelerate, the arms race and the level of tension in Soviet-American relations.

The opposite possibility of arms control and detente does not necessarily follow from a refusal to arm China. Indeed, the dynamics of Soviet decision-making may drive Moscow's military expansionism further, necessitating additional countermeasures and perhaps an ultimate confrontation. But until we are confident that Soviet policy is inexorably set on a course of conquest, it is imperative that we advance the prospects for a debate in the Kremlin which will respond to our professed desire for a cooperative, not conflictual, co-existence.

It is difficult to determine the political volatility of the China factor in Soviet calculations. Objectively, Moscow's overwhelming preponderance of military power, at all levels and in all categories of weaponry, should provide ample reassurance that no serious threat from China need be contemplated for at least a decade and more likely until the end of the century. Subjectively, however, twenty years of bitter relations combine with a gross population disparity to produce an acute sensitivity to indicators of an anti-Soviet coalition which might include China. In part, this stems from the historic Russian recall of Moscovy and Kiev being overrun by the Mongol invasion. In part, it comes from the extreme xenophobia, directed especially against the Soviet Union, manifested in Red Guard rampages during the Cultural Revolution of 1966–68.

These fears are not all determining. They did not preclude Stalin providing Mao with an entire jet air force in 1951–53 or Khrushchev's delivery of important assistance in the manufacture of atomic weapons in 1958–60. They do not rule out a future Sino-Soviet detente, should both sides agree to a *modus vivendi*. But neither can they be dismissed out of hand as

irrelevant to Sino-American relations. At the very least, we are in no position to underwrite China's border claims against the Soviet Union or appear to strengthen Beijing's hand in its negotiations with Moscow over this issue. Least of all should we risk raising this perception in the Kremlin when Soviet-American communication is at a low ebb and a change in Soviet leadership appears imminent.

CHINA'S FUTURE AND U.S. POLICY

Given the obsolete state of the PLA, its size, and the human component of modernization, it is not likely that any major changes will occur in China's military capability before the middle of this decade, except perhaps in strategic nuclear weapons. The missile program may soon benefit from the translation of research and development into regular production. Otherwise, however, the cumulative efforts of improved ground, air, and naval weapons changes will only become operationally important in the late 1980s at the earliest.

So far as predicting Chinese policy at that time is concerned, particularly with respect to the foregoing agenda of issues, formidable obstacles exist. The present leadership is predominantly in its upper sixties and seventies. We do not know what mix of individuals and interests will dominate decision-making in a decade hence. There is good reason to hope that the integration of China into interdependent relationships will temper its recurring tendency toward xenophobic isolation and induce compromise in such matters as the management of ocean resources. However, factional political struggle may combine with frustrated economic development to produce an angry reaction against interdependency and compromise on nationalistic issues.

This possibility provides a powerful rationale for assisting China's economic modernization through loans, technology transfer, and training abroad. This supports goals articulated by the present leadership in Beijing, which are presumably shared by those being prepared for succession. These goals place military modernization last in sequence to be accomplished as the result of developing the civilian economy rather than through the "quick fix" acquisition of foreign weapons. If this order of priority continues to be observed, the spillover effects of advanced technology will eventually strengthen China's military capability.

[17] Arthur J. Alexander, *Decision-Making in Soviet Weapons Procurement*, Adelphi Paper No. 147/8, Winter 1978/79 (London: International Institute of Strategic Studies).

This should not exclude the sale of technology and equipment which may be used for military purposes as well as serve non-military needs. In fact, the Soviet Union sells long-range jet transport aircraft and "civilian" helicopters to China. However, the alleged line of distinction between so-called "defensive" and "offensive" weapons is generally too indistinct to permit clear and consistent policy application. Moreover, the incremental transition from one category to the other can be anticipated, contrary to fact, by friend or foe with disturbing consequences in either case. In short, the absolute prohibition against weapons sales to China should remain in force for U.S. policy.

Dual purpose technology raises complications which cannot be addressed here. In general, however, the potential use of such technology in a highly advanced economy such as the United States, or by a military superpower such as the Soviet Union, is not possible for China at its present stage of development. This argues against applying the same embargo list for both sides of the Sino-Soviet dispute. Furthermore, technology is more easily copied or acquired through a competitive world market than are advanced weapons. U.S. allies, particularly Japan, are less likely to agree to constraints in this area than they are to arms sales to China.

As a final note, we must be sensitive to the role of symbols as well as of substance. Perceptions and expectations are shaped by speeches, visits, and media messages triggered by calculated briefings and backgrounders. Short-run tactical maneuvers can cause long-run strategic problems if they are not carefully designed as part of an overall policy calculation of potential gains and risks. Sino-American relations, whether addressed unilaterally or through interaction between Beijing and Washington, must not be construed by either side or by third parties as based on any such concept as "mutual security." Many points of divergence exist between China's definition of its security and that held by the United States, its allies, and its friends in Asia. The more common terms, "parallel strategic interests," reminds us that parallel lines may be proximately or widely separated but they never meet. This overstates the divergence between China and the United States on such questions as the U.S.-Japan security treaty and the Soviet presence in Southeast Asia.

Given these complications, it would be better to abandon the effort for catch words and phrases that become cliches at best and policy traps at worst, the most notorious example being the so-called "China card." Rhetoric can not only obscure reality; it can create a reality of its own. The Sino-American relationship is now entering a stage where hard facts and plain speaking should determine the image as well as the content of U.S. policy, especially where military aspects are concerned.

QUESTIONS FOR DISCUSSION

1 Is it reasonable to suppose that the United States could successfully play the China card?
2 What are the potential advantages and disadvantages to the United States of attempting this?
3 What long-term relationships are probable between the Soviet Union and China?
4 Over the long term, what types of Sino-Soviet relationships are most likely to serve United States interests?
5 How are United States relationships with China or the Soviet Union likely to be affected by their degree of conflict or accommodation?

SUGGESTED READINGS

Boyd, Gavin. "Issues in China's Global Policy," in Gavin Boyd and Charles E. Pentland (eds.). *Issues in Global Politics*. New York: Free Press, 1981, pp. 156–99.

Hinton, Harold C. "The United States and Extended Security Commitments: East Asia." *The Annals of the American Academy of Political and Social Science* 457 (September 1981): 88–108.

Johnson, Chalmers. "The New Thrust in China's Foreign Policy." *Foreign Affairs* 57 (Fall 1978): 125–137.

Low, Alfred D. *The Sino-Soviet Dispute*. Madison, N.J.: Farleigh Dickinson University Press, 1978.

Segal, Gerald. *The Great Power Triangle*. London: Macmillan, 1981.

———. 'China's Nuclear Posture for the 1980's." *Survival* (January/February 1981): 11–18.

Shanor, Donald R. *The Soviet Triangle: Russia's Relations with China and the West in the 1980s*. New York: St. Martin's Press, 1980.

Simes, Dimitri K. "Washington's China Card." *New Leader*, Jan. 28, 1980, pp. 14–16.

U.S. Congress. House of Representatives. *Playing the China Card: Implications for United States-Soviet-Chinese Relations*. Report prepared for the Subcommittee on Asian and Pacific Affairs by the Foreign Affairs and National Defense Division, Congressional Research Service, Library of Congress. 96th Cong., 1st Sess., October 1979.

U.S. Congress. House of Representatives. *The United States and the People's Republic of China: Issues for the 1980s*. Hearings before the Subcommittee on Asian and Pacific Affairs, 96th Cong., 2d Sess., 1980.

21 Is Nuclear Proliferation a Danger to International Peace and Security?

YES

Daniel Yergin

The Terrifying Prospect: Atomic Bombs Everywhere

NO

Donald L. Clark

Could We Be Wrong?

The Terrifying Prospect: Atomic Bombs Everywhere
Daniel Yergin

In an automobile accident there is the long moment before impact, when you see the other vehicle coming toward you, and you realize that a collision is imminent, and yet you cannot believe that it is going to happen. At last, you hear the sound of colliding metal, and you know that it is too late.

The people of the world are at such a moment, on course for a nuclear collision. The question is whether it is already too late to change direction. Nuclear warfare has been a possibility for more than three decades. But suddenly the threat has intensified—not because of political instability, but simply because of the prospect of widespread proliferation of nuclear armaments. It is not too much to say that we are entering the Second Nuclear Age—the age of proliferation.

While many countries use nuclear energy as a source of power, there are only six "nuclear weapon states" today—the United States, the Soviet Union, Britain, China, France, and India. But recent technical, economic, and political changes have brought nuclear weapons within easy reach of many others. Israel seems very close to a nuclear weapons capability though it feels safer being secretive on the subject. A host of other countries could soon qualify for admission to what newspapers call "the nuclear club" —countries such as South Korea, Iran, Pakistan, South Africa, Brazil, Argentina, Taiwan, and Spain. Turkey's defense minister has publicly discussed his country's developing nuclear weapons and the Yugoslav Communist party newspaper not long ago suggested that some atomic bombs would contribute to that nation's security. A number of Arab countries are exploring ways to obtain nuclear weapons. Libya's president has said that in the future "atomic weapons will be like traditional ones, possessed by every state according to its potential. We will have our share of this new weapon." So eager is Libya that a few years ago it actually went shopping for a bomb. Both France and China are reported to have refused to sell.

In the First Nuclear Age, a country that wanted a bomb had to mount an expensive, complex program. In the Second Nuclear Age, a country acquires the capability to produce a nuclear weapon with relative ease—as a by-product of developing nuclear power. According to present plans, some forty countries will have nuclear energy programs by 1985. Each program would produce enough nuclear material for three or more bombs. Most of them would have enough material for thirty or more bombs.

Looking to 1990, projections indicate that reactors in the Third World alone could be producing enough nuclear material for 3000 Hiroshima-sized bombs a year. In such circumstances, so-called "subnational" groups—terrorists—could take as hostages not planes but a reactor, or even an atomic bomb, or nuclear waste products, and then their terror would reach to an entire city or even a nation. The problem gets worse year by year. In 1995, up to a hundred nations could have the knowledge, facilities, and raw materials that, with a little extra effort, would enable them to manufacture a bomb.

David Lilienthal is now seventy-seven years old. His experience with nuclear energy goes back almost to its beginnings. In 1946, he helped to draft America's first plan to control nuclear weapons and became the first chairman of the Atomic Energy Commission. He once shared the dream that the atom could bring good as well as bad into the world. But he now looks with something akin to horror at what is happening. He recently described the proliferated world as "the terrifying prospect for the young men and women who are looking forward to a future."

"I am glad," he added, "I am not a young man, and I am sorry for my children."

HOW WE GOT TO WHERE WE ARE

There were just three nuclear devices in the summer of 1945. The first, called "Trinity," was detonated in the New Mexico desert in July, proving that an atomic bomb would work. It was quickly followed by "Little Boy" over Hiroshima and "Fat Man" over Nagasaki. The American atomic arsenal was depleted, but it did not matter, for it had brought an end to the war with Japan. The First Nuclear Age had begun.

In 1945 there was still only one nuclear weapon state, the United States, which went on producing

From Daniel Yergin, "The Terrifying Prospect: Atomic Bombs Everywhere," *Atlantic* (April 1977): 46–49, 53–54, and 56–65. Reprinted with permission of The Helen Brann Agency.

bombs. Right from the beginning, two questions dominated all considerations. Who else would develop a bomb? And when? American leaders tried to find a way to keep the fearful new invention under surveillance. By the end of 1946, it was clear that the United States and the Soviet Union would not be able to agree on an international control system.

President Truman confidently pronounced the American monopoly a "sacred trust." Most U.S. leaders assumed that it would take the Russians many years to achieve their own capability. (A number of scientists did not agree.) The illusion was shattered in early September 1949, when it was learned that the Russians had successfully detonated an atomic device in Siberia in late August. So then there were two nuclear powers, and a process of mutual deterrence was begun.

The British felt they had been deprived of the payoff for their wartime collaboration on atomic developments with the United States. They could hardly be a Great Power without nuclear weapons. (The British chiefs of staffs had privately warned: "To have no share in what is recognized as the main deterrent in the Cold War and the only Allied offensive in a world war would seriously weaken British influence.") So on October 3, 1952, they tested a bomb on the Monte Bello islands off Australia. Now there were three atomic weapon states.

The French, especially under De Gaulle, also wanted to maintain the Great Power status, and they were not going to depend on the "Anglo-Saxons." They exploded their bomb in the Sahara on February 13, 1960. "Hurrah for France!" De Gaulle telegraphed the French minister in charge. Now there were four nuclear weapon states.

Between 1955 and 1959, the Soviets provided their Chinese comrades with nuclear know-how. In 1959, as the Sino-Soviet rift developed, the Russians withdrew their assistance, but it was too late. "Whether or not nuclear weapons help peace depends on who possesses them," the Chinese announced in 1963. And on October 16, 1964, the Chinese exploded their first nuclear weapon in the Takla Makan desert in the province of Sinkiang.

There were now five nuclear weapon states. They continued to test atomic and hydrogen bombs, to perfect them, and to increase their number. They developed stockpiles, as well as the planes and missiles required to deliver the bombs from the country of manufacture to their targets. But no new players joined the game. In the possession of nuclear weapons by these five, there seemed a kind of stability, a mutual deterrence. There was even something symmetrical and fitting about it, for the five were the Great Powers. Attention shifted to such issues as limited war, guerrillas, regional conflicts, nationalism, while proliferation and nuclear dangers receded as subjects of concern. That situation lasted for almost a decade after China's first explosion, that is, until May 18, 1974.

THE SECOND NUCLEAR AGE

On that day, shortly after nine in the morning, the Indian foreign minister received a phone message: "The Buddha is smiling." An hour or so earlier, in an underground site in the Rajasthan desert, a hundred miles from the Pakistan border, the Indian Atomic Energy Commission had set off a nuclear device. It was officially announced to the world as a "peaceful nuclear explosive experiment." But there is no discernible difference between a "peaceful nuclear explosion" and the detonation of a prototype for an atomic bomb. Indeed, no satisfactory peaceful use has yet been found for nuclear explosions. India had become, in the words of an official in the U.S. Arms Control and Disarmament Agency, "a fourth-rate nuclear power." The Indian device was similar in design and power to the Nagasaki bomb, and, while lacking a large arsenal or sophisticated delivery systems, India is certainly more advanced than the United States was after Hiroshima and Nagasaki.

Mrs. Gandhi congratulated her scientists: "They worked hard and have done a good, clean job." The Indian newspapers headlined, "Nation is Thrilled" and "Indian Genius Triumphs." Canada, which had shared its technology with India, expressed shock that a country with so many economic problems, and in the face of assurances it had given Canada, would divert precious resources in order to develop nuclear weapons. The Indians said they had not violated any assurances because they had used uranium mined in India to make the explosive. Canada suspended and then canceled its $100 million a year assistance program with India.

The Indian test in the Rajasthan desert ushered in the Second Nuclear Age. It dramatized the fact that we could soon be living in the midst of what has been called "a nuclear weapons crowd." As the director of the Indian Institute for Defense Studies reminded the rest of the world, "The nuclear powers thought they could simply lock up technology. It was absurd."

Powerful forces have promoted the spread of nuclear technology. To make sense of them, we need first to back up several months from the Indian explosion to the "October Revolution" effected by the OPEC oil cartel in the autumn of 1973. The October Revolution revealed several dangers to most industrial and developing countries. These countries were highly vulnerable for they were dependent primarily on a small number of Middle Eastern producers for their supplies. The price hikes delivered a stunning blow to their economies, and many people became convinced that the world will run out of oil within a few decades.

Fortunately, or so it seemed at the time, a "deus ex technologica" was standing in the wings to rescue the world from dependence on OPEC oil—nuclear power. "With the increase in the world of both population and industrialization, we will have no choice for the years after 2000 but to accept nuclear energy," observed a senior official concerned with energy for the European Community in the autumn of 1975. "Everybody is convinced that after 1980 nuclear energy will develop very quickly."

But as the renewed drive for nuclear power took shape, relatively few people were willing to face up to a most alarming fact—that when a country develops a nuclear capability, it is much of the way toward developing a nuclear device. "A great many countries," the strategist Albert Wohlstetter of the University of Chicago has pointed out, "as a result of their civilian nuclear energy programs and the policies of nuclear exporters, can come within days or hours of assembling nuclear explosives without plainly breaking any of their promises to abstain from making or receiving them."

"There are not two atoms, one peaceful and one military," he said. "They are the same atom."

THE PLUTONIUM ECONOMY

The central problem is the "nuclear fuel cycle." This term suggests something pleasing, fulfilling, natural. It is not natural, for it involves tampering with natural uranium to create a new form of uranium as well as a number of elements that do not exist in nature and are very dangerous.

The cycle has, depending on how detailed one gets, between seven and eleven steps. The first several involve the mining of uranium and its preparation for the reactor. Then comes its actual use as fuel. The last steps involve the storage and disposition of the nuclear waste—that is, the leftovers after the uranium has done its job.

Two points in this fuel cycle intersect with the manufacture of an atomic bomb. Both stages produce what is variously known as fissionable or "fissile" material, which could be used as an explosive rather than a source of nuclear power.

As it is mined, uranium is not quite suited for nuclear reactors. It consists mostly of the stable U-238, with typically a .7 percent concentration of the isotope U-235. It needs to be "enriched" to about 3 percent U-235 in order to sustain a controlled chain reaction in the type of reactor developed in the United States. A nation that has enrichment facilities can go ahead and enrich the uranium to a concentration of U-235 much higher than 3 percent. Then it is in a state suitable for use as the explosive core of an atomic bomb. Highly enriched uranium was the material used in the Hiroshima bomb.

Further along in the fuel cycle, at what is called the "back end," after the enriched uranium has been consumed, there is the nuclear waste or ash, containing many different radioactive and toxic materials. Some of these wastes can be "chemically separated" and used again as fuel in the reactor. The two principal materials so recoverable are uranium and plutonium, a man-made element. Plutonium was the substance of the Trinity and Nagasaki bombs.

The most intense concern today focuses on the plutonium at the back end. Uranium enrichment is a costly, complex process. While it is not easy to extract the plutonium from the other wastes, it can be done through what is now the rather standard and less costly process of chemical separation. So even nations dependent on outside sources of enriched uranium can use it to produce their own plutonium.

Plutonium is the nub of the proliferation problem today. It has two uses. It can be separated for use as a fuel in a reactor, and there are those who think such plutonium will become a major nuclear fuel in the future. (Currently, reprocessing for this purpose is being carried out only on a small-scale developmental basis in Europe and the United States. No one has yet found this procedure economical.) But plutonium can also be used as one of the two basic materials for an atomic bomb.

The important point is that no country need decide

that it specifically *wants* to accumulate stocks of plutonium. In buying a reactor from country Y, country X does not have to make a conscious decision to acquire nuclear weapons. The thought can be a mere haze, neither analyzed by planners in the foreign ministry nor costed by the economists in the budget office. The opportunity is simply handed over with the keys to the reactor. All that needs to be done is to start up the reactor, and plutonium becomes one of the country's resources. The plutonium used in the core of the Indian bomb was chemically separated from the radioactive exhaust materials produced in reactors outside Bombay.

A good-sized but still standard reactor could produce 200 kilograms of plutonium a year, while a crude implosion bomb requires a mere ten kilograms of plutonium. It is the contrast between these two numbers that causes so much alarm. For they indicate that a satisfactorily operating atomic reactor would produce enough material for the explosive core of a bomb every two or three weeks. And in *The Last Chance*, his new book on proliferation, William Epstein suggests that a plant for separating plutonium for the purpose of making a bomb could be constructed for as little as $3 million. If current plans and developments for nuclear power go ahead, there will be such a plutonium glut—as a source of fuel, in international trade, and in waste products—that people have begun to speak of the dangers of a widespread "plutonium economy." Plutonium will become extravagantly widespread if the breeder reactor comes into use.

"The real problem of proliferation today is not that there are numerous countries 'chomping at the bit' to get nuclear weapons," Albert Wohlstetter noted. "But rather that all the non-nuclear nations, without making any conscious decision to build nuclear weapons, are drifting upward to higher categories of competence."

Of course, a nation that has neither enrichment nor reprocessing facilities would find it very difficult to do anything with its fissile material except use it as a source of power. Therefore, much of the thinking about proliferation focuses on ways to "safeguard" enrichment and reprocessing.

INCENTIVES

The October Revolution gave another kind of boost to atomic energy. The East-West split has been the historic impetus for the nuclear arms race of the last three decades. The United States, Britain, and France on one side, and the Soviet Union and China on the other, built up their stockpiles primarily to deter the other side. (Although, in the last several years, China and Russia of course have also been deterring each other.) But the October Revolution dramatized a different division—between North and South—pitting the industrial world in the Northern Hemisphere against the Third World "developing nations" in the Southern Hemisphere. In the United Nations and many other councils, the Third World countries have been asserting their independence, declaiming on the subject of their equality, and, in general blaming the First World for all their problems. Some of them believe that the acquisition of nuclear weapons is one of the most visible ways to assert their power and influence. It does no good for Westerners to express worry about the dangers for everybody in the spread of nuclear weapons, for the Third World snaps back (in the words of a leading Indian spokesman) that such concerns are merely "modern versions of the doctrine of white man's burden." Nuclear weapons are taken as a sign of prestige and influence. After all, it was not Mrs. Gandhi but Charles de Gaulle who announced, on the day of its first nuclear explosion, that France was "stronger and prouder since this morning." But it is not only countries such as India that want to augment their prestige and influence with nuclear weapons. Now, as a result of the drastic increase in oil prices, a country such as Libya has not only the desire and egoism but also the wherewithal in cash to buy nuclear technology. It is unsettling, to say the least, to think of nuclear weapons in the hands of Libya's leader, Qaddafi, who even in the Arab world is thought of as erratic ("a mental case," Anwar Sadat has called him). "It is well known that Qaddafi would like to have an atomic weapon," said a CIA analyst. "Some people think he is too irrational and unstable but he has shown himself rational enough in managing Libya." Having failed to buy a bomb, Qaddafi is now reported to be trying to assemble Arab nuclear scientists to develop his own nuclear weapons capability.

There are more specific incentives at work as well. Such countries as India, Brazil, and Iran are striving for what is now known as "regional hegemony." Nuclear weapons are one way to assert their seigneurial rights. But such steps of course only encourage further proliferation. Just as China's nuclear test in

1964 helped induce India's effort to make the bomb, so India's test a decade later had much the same effect on Pakistan, whose prime minister warned that if India took any more steps in the direction of building an atomic arsenal, "We will eat leaves and grass, even go hungry, but we will have to get one of our own." Pakistan is now strenuously seeking to assure itself that it too has the weapons option. Iran has indicated that if other countries in the region come into possession of nuclear weapons, Iran will also develop them. The shah has said, "If every upstart in the region acquires atomic bombs, then Iran must have them as well."

For some there is the most basic incentive to go nuclear—to buttress national survival. Three million Israelis face a mostly hostile Arab world of over 100 million people. The nuclear weapon is the deterrent of last resort, and Israel may now be only "a screwdriver's turn away" from having a nuclear capability. But the Israelis have never said they have any bombs, for that would only increase the Arab urgency to obtain their own. The Israelis have concluded that, for the time being, their best deterrent is one clothed in calculated ambiguity.

There is a final incentive. For decades a number of nations have lived and prospered under America's "nuclear umbrella." It has been understood, or implicitly guaranteed by treaty, that if their security is at stake, the U.S. nuclear arsenal stands behind them. But the umbrella has lost some of its covering in recent years. South Korea is not sure that it is protected anymore. Taiwan worries that it will soon be excluded. Therefore, as nations fear that they will be standing in an exposed place, they are sorely tempted to raise their own umbrellas, to develop an independent deterrent.

LIVING IN A NUCLEAR CROWD: BAD DREAMS

Even if we cannot predict how a conflict might occur, we can develop the likely possibilities.

1 *Undermining the balance of terror.* So long as there was a sharp distinction between the nuclear weapon states and all the rest, a kind of stability— absurd but real—prevailed. The superpowers have, at least to date, been in agreement on an implicit rule to contain crises. The closest they ever came to breaking that rule was over Cuba in 1962. But as more and more states acquire nuclear capability, more and

more nations (including our own) will feel a heightened sense of insecurity. Nuclear proliferation raises havoc with all the calculations about the nuclear relationship between the United States and the Soviet Union. Current defense thinking is based on the notion that in order to have nuclear stability, there must be parity and balance between the two superpowers, so that no intelligent person will make a mistake.

"There cannot be a balance where there are many different parties with many different objectives, and with entirely different levels of technology," says scientist Herbert York, who has been involved in the American atomic weapons program since World War II. "So if there is—and there does seem to have been—a stability in the nuclear relationship between the United States and the Soviet Union, the stability will be wiped out by proliferation. Even its theoretical underpinnings will be wiped out."

On a visit to China before he became secretary of state, Cyrus Vance pointed to one form of the danger when, in a discussion with Teng Hsiao-p'ing, he said, "The hazards of accidental launch are real and could have devastating effects if one didn't know where the weapon was launched from. Accidental launching will become more likely with the indiscriminate spread of nuclear weapons."

2 *The chain reaction.* One can easily imagine Israel being pushed to the wall. Arab forces are advancing on Tel Aviv. The Israelis begin assembling nuclear weapons. The Russians learn of this and dispatch warheads to Egypt. The United States in turn detects the Soviet warheads in transit. And the world is on the edge of destruction. But the chain can start with any client states. Both Iran and Iraq could become nuclear weapon states. A border clash between them could escalate into a nuclear exchange between the two countries, one of them a key American ally, the other tied by treaty to the Soviet Union. How long could the superpowers stay out? Where would it all end?

3 *The easing of the taboo.* The world slowly becomes accustomed to the idea that nuclear weapons are not merely for deterrence, but actually of considerable value in a war. Perhaps India and Pakistan go to war, or Brazil and Argentina. Each side uses nuclear weapons, millions are killed, but one side emerges a decisive winner. While the superpowers are not drawn in, this spectacle reduces the taboo and makes it easier for other ambitious leaders to contemplate the use of nuclear weapons. There is also the Crazy State model. A Libya or a Uganda, almost like a terrorist, could in the future use its nuclear bombs as a bargaining chip to achieve some bizarre and self-aggrandizing aim.

4 *Microproliferation*. A terrorist group or even the Mafia attempts to steal plutonium—despite the toxic risks—from either a power station or a reprocessing plant, or while it is in transit. This they use to blackmail one or more governments, either for money or for some political aim. Physical security is never perfect. Not long ago, a lunatic walked unnoticed into the control room of a French nuclear plant and randomly threw several switches before being detected. Such a danger is so real that in the United States guards now have shoot-to-kill orders at fourteen federal nuclear installations. As the number of power stations increases, as the trade in nuclear materials and the plutonium economy expand, and as a covert, semilegal "gray market" in sensitive items grows, the threats become so serious that they result in security measures that have a corrosive effect on democratic institutions, for people come to fear that the dangers could not be met without a more authoritarian political system.

The microproliferation threats, however, are more likely to occur in the unstable political systems of the Third World. Thomas Schelling of Harvard University engaged in some chilling speculations in a recent issue of the journal *International Security*. How different might the course of events have been in Lebanon in late 1975 and early 1976, he asked, had that country had even a small pilot plant for extracting plutonium from spent fuel? "Who would have guarded the facilities? Who would have destroyed them, from nearby or from afar, at the risk of spreading deadly plutonium locally to keep bomb material from falling into mischievous hands? What outside country might have invaded if the spoils of war would have included a nuclear-weapon capability, even only to deny that capability to some other greedy neighbor?

"One thing is certain: in years to come there will be military violence in countries that have sizable nuclear power industries."

Perhaps such possibilities will encourage some caution. Would the president of Egypt or the shah of Iran really want to live with the risk that a terrorist group, or some ambitious colonels, might seize control of the country's atomic bombs in the course of attempting a coup? Argentina has already had a foretaste of what

microproliferation can mean. Not long ago a group of terrorists temporarily seized a nuclear power station (still under construction) some sixty miles north of Buenos Aires.

5 *New patterns*. We still tend to think that all major nuclear developments will involve advanced industrial states. But one can see the outline of new "atomic alliances" crisscrossing the world. Already, it is reported, Argentinian scientists are at work in Iran's nuclear program, and Egyptian scientists are being trained at the nuclear facility that gave India its device. (India has also noted that after its test, it received discreet inquiries from several countries interested in buying a bomb. The Indians say they refused to sell.)

AMERICA'S TWO ATOMS POLICY

From 1949, when the Americans realized that the Russians had the bomb, until 1974, when the Indians exploded their device and the Buddha smiled, proliferation was not of much concern in Washington. This omission seems very odd from the perspective of 1977. After all, one would think that the United States, as progenitor of nuclear weapons and nuclear power, would have had some proprietary interest in the subsequent spawning and that special attention would be given to the relationship between atomic power and the atomic bomb. Such was indeed the case in the years immediately after World War II. In 1946, Robert Oppenheimer pointed out that the "heart of the problem" of international control was "the close technical parallelism and interrelation of the peaceful and the military applications of atomic energy."

But this connection was quickly forgotten. After Hiroshima and Nagasaki, there was a powerful emotional drive to find peaceful uses, something good to do with the atom, in order, somehow, to compensate for its horrors. Furthermore, once the Russians had the bomb, the worst seemed to have happened, and fears about the spread were forgotten. There were also strong economic incentives. And so, in 1953, President Eisenhower proposed Project Plowshare and Atoms-for-Peace. The next year, the United States approved the export of nuclear power technology to other countries.

Thereafter, American interests in this realm were defined by a nuclear energy Establishment: government agencies such as the Atomic Energy Commission and the Defense Department; the congressional Joint Atomic Energy Committee; and such powerful industrial allies as Westinghouse and General Electric. Both the AEC and the Joint Committee were committed to the "maximum" utilization of atomic energy. The Joint Committee may well have been the most powerful congressional committee in history. It certainly did a masterful job of pushing a disproportionate share of government research funds into nuclear energy, to the detriment (as we know today) of other forms of energy research. Since the Establishment wanted to promote nuclear power on a worldwide basis, little thought was given to proliferation or to nuclear waste disposal. It has only recently been discovered that the Atomic Energy Commission lost track of sizable quantities of weapons-grade material leased to a score of foreign countries in the 1950s and 1960s. "For twenty years," said Victor Gilinsky, a member of the Nuclear Regulatory Commission, "[the nuclear export bureaucracy] had been freewheeling through the domains of diplomacy and international commerce—out of public view, and under the protection of a myopic Atomic Energy Commission and its own congressional committee."

When an organization or a group of organizations wants to "sell" something badly enough, whether it be nuclear power or a new drug, eyes tend to be shut to possible side effects, especially if they seem far off. Such is what happened with the Atoms-for-Peace program. "Many mistakes were made in the way we executed the idea," observed Fred Ikle, former director of the Arms Control and Disarmament Agency. "We now can see many forks in the road, many turning points where we could have taken a different technological direction. We could have chosen a course that might have greatly reduced the risks of nuclear proliferation without any loss in terms of economical operation of power reactors."

But we did not. The conventional American reactor, the so-called light-water reactor, is, after all, a spin-off from the World War II atom project, for which plutonium was a highly desired end product, and, more directly, from the subsequent development of the Navy's nuclear-powered submarines. Habit was strong, and little thought was given to designing reactors that would not involve the dangerous steps in the fuel cycle.

"What is used for reactor design in the United States today is not the same design as for making plutonium for military purposes," said George Kistiakowsky, one of the most prominent scientists in the Manhattan Project, subsequently science adviser to President Eisenhower, and currently professor emeritus of chemistry at Harvard. "But our commercial light-water reactors are derivative copies of the submarine reactor. This is the result of the AEC's having been staffed with people who had worked on Admiral Rickover's nuclear submarine program. There could have been other pathways. The Canadian design is in some ways less risky, because its spent fuel is not very desirable for plutonium extraction. The British design is different again. But there was a determined drive by the AEC to adopt the light-water reactor because people in the AEC were to a large degree Rickover's people." In addition, General Electric and Westinghouse were eager to capitalize commercially on their experience in the Navy's reactor program.

Those in the nuclear Establishment held to an underlying faith that the appropriate technological "fixes" would be found for all problems—at the appropriate time. Furthermore, proliferation dangers seemed pretty far away. By the 1960s, the United States was not much worried that its allies in the First World, beyond the French and the British, would seek their own nuclear arsenals. Certainly there was no need to worry that the Russians would be so reckless as to trust *their* potentially unreliable allies in Eastern Europe with nuclear weapons. And it was difficult to imagine in the 1950s and the 1960s that Third World nations would organize themselves sufficiently and acquire the wherewithal and skills to move on to a nuclear weapons capability. That was a severe miscalculation.

After the first Chinese test in 1964, President Johnson, at the instigation of Defense Secretary Robert McNamara, appointed a high-level committee under Roswell Gilpatric to assess the dangers of proliferation and recommend whether or not nonproliferation should be made a top priority of U.S. foreign policy. The preliminary international negotiations for a nuclear non-proliferation treaty (the NPT) had already begun. Johnson was also looking for gestures before the November presidential election that would show that he was "doing good."

One participant recalled what happened: "The committee worked through the fall of 1964 and the beginning of the winter. We had come up with what looked like a unanimous agreement that proliferation was very dangerous and should be made a very high priority concern. Shortly after Johnson's inauguration in 1965, we had a meeting with Johnson, McNamara, Rusk, and the chairman of the joint chiefs, where we presented our views. Then something very unpleasant happened. One of the most distinguished members of our committee announced that he would not read his part of the briefing papers, but instead would speak ad lib. Instead of speaking for the non-proliferation treaty, he argued that we should arm our NATO allies with nuclear weapons as part of the so-called multilateral force, that this was far more important than the NPT. This weakened the impact of all the other presentations. The impact was then destroyed totally by Dean Rusk, who violently attacked the whole idea of the NPT. He said our conclusions were very dangerous to the security of the United States, and that we should not prepare a written report because it would be leaked. Johnson himself was not very attentive. There was this business where he had a telephone under his desk. He dialed continuously and kept whispering into it. He did this dozens of times while we were talking. Rusk said that our report was unrealistic and unimportant. McNamara tried to defend it, but rather feebly. Johnson then curtly thanked us and ordered us not to write anything and not to discuss it. That was the end of that. Of course, two or three years later he changed his mind." A few crucial years had been lost.

HOW SAFE ARE SAFEGUARDS OR WHY THE NPT IS ONLY A MEDIUM YIELD DEVICE

Finally, in 1968, the United States did reach agreement with the Soviet Union and other states on a non-proliferation treaty. It went into force in 1970. The International Atomic Energy Agency became the "executive" for the NPT. Headquartered in Vienna, the IAEA was founded in 1957 as a result of the drive to find a peaceful atom that would do good around the world. The agency was supposed to promote peaceful uses of atomic energy, but at the same time to apply "safeguards" to prevent the diversion of peaceful developments to military purposes.

Today the IAEA is a relatively small, efficient body affiliated with, but not subject to, the United Nations. It is one of the last international organizations to have escaped the Third World agitation and politicking that has so disrupted the work of most other international organizations, including the UN General Assembly.

The IAEA's safeguard functions expanded with the non-proliferation treaty, and the IAEA is now the cornerstone of what might be called the NPT system.

Lately, there has been some tendency to judge too harshly the NPT system. Hedley Bull, a prominent arms control expert, has pointed out some of its accomplishments: "The NPT has made an important contribution to the control of proliferation by advertising the fact that the spread of nuclear weapons is not inevitable, and so strengthening the hand of anti-nuclear weapons forces in many countries; by enabling countries which wish to remain without nuclear weapons to reassure each other by an exchange of pledges; by contributing to the emergence of détente, especially in Europe; and by the encouragement it has given to the development of International Atomic Energy Agency safeguards. The treaty is not simply the instrument of the nuclear states that are parties to it, but also reflects the desire of many non-nuclear weapons parties to impose limitations on each other."

And an official of the United States Arms Control and Disarmament Agency added: "It's indispensable. We couldn't be where we are without it."

All that is true, but it is also now clear that all that is not enough. Since the technological and economic barriers to proliferation are coming down, the effective potential barriers are political, and the most important is certainly the non-proliferation treaty. Unhappily, it is a product of the First Nuclear Age, and is not very effective in the Second.

The NPT system has a number of notable problems. While the IAEA has been getting stronger all the time, it is still not up to the new pressures thrust upon it. It was fine in a world of relatively few nuclear states, but it will need many more trained people to carry out safeguards in a world with hundreds of reactors, and it is not at all obvious where such people will come from.

One can also read too much into safeguards. The IAEA can evaluate plans for atomic facilities, review records of the movement and use of nuclear materials, and carry out inspection and surveillance of plants—where and when allowed by the host country. It is an accounting system. What this comes down to is a threat, "the deterrence of nuclear materials diversion by detection." But detection can be evaded, and agreements canceled. What would happen if cheating were discovered? IAEA officials have no definite channels for making their findings public. To whom would the information be conveyed? Who would be the policeman? That mysterious and often sluggish creature "world public opinion"? What would be the punishment? Even if the United States and the USSR got together to apply heavy pressure on the violator, would not many nations see this as rather hypocritical —as two nations with tens of thousands of nuclear weapons getting mad at some developing country that only wants two or three little ones?

There is another problem with safeguards: reprocessing large quantities of plutonium for commercial use in a reactor is still a relatively complicated and demanding undertaking. But to reprocess for just a few bombs is a much easier task. The quantities needed are so much smaller. The requisite facility might require only a dozen people to operate it.

The rationale of safeguards—and here is the critical point—is that the diversion from peaceful use will be discovered well before the violator reaches a nuclear weapons capability, thus exposing him to the risks of international reaction. And yet when a nation has not only reactors and low-enriched uranium but also a stockpile of separated plutonium or facilities for separation, then the value of the safeguards—accounting and inspection procedures—is greatly diminished. Even though safeguarded and stockpiled for peaceful future uses, this plutonium is only a short step away from use as an explosive.

"Should the owner decide, for whatever reason, on a sudden move to appropriate the material for illicit purposes," Victor Gilinsky has said, "the time between diversion of plutonium and complete weapons can be sharply reduced to what might be a matter of weeks, or conceivably days. Under these circumstances, even if it were assumed that IAEA inspection and monitoring systems were improved, it is hard to imagine that an international reaction could be mustered before the assembly of nuclear weapons was completed."

The second problem with the NPT is that although over a hundred countries have ratified the treaty, China, France, India, Argentina, Brazil, Pakistan, Saudi Arabia, Israel, and Spain have given no indication of signing.

The third problem is the NPT's two-tier structure. Under its definition, there are two kinds of states, nuclear weapon states and non-nuclear weapon states. A country that carried out an explosion before 1967 is officially a nuclear weapon state. This distinction rather freezes the relationships, and has caused

non-weapon states to charge "discrimination." The weapon states do have special rights and privileges and can go on building up their nuclear arsenals. Thus discontent and permanent instability are built into the NPT system.

The fourth problem goes back to the essential issue. The NPT and the IAEA are caught in a contradiction. On the one hand, they aim to prevent the proliferation of nuclear weapons. On the other hand, they are charged with encouraging peaceful nuclear uses. But to repeat, there is only one atom. So the NPT system encourages the diffusion of the *capability* to become a nuclear weapon state swiftly, even while trying to prevent it. Also, a nation can opt out after having benefited from sharing the technology of other members. "I don't think withdrawal would be lightly treated," said one U.S. official much involved with the NPT. But after all, a country need give only ninety days' notice, and then it can legally quit the NPT.

THAT GERMAN-BRAZILIAN DEAL

In current nuclear lore the German-Brazilian deal ranks in importance with India's explosion. And this particular bargain shows how complex the whole problem of proliferation has become, how many different interests are involved.

On June 27, 1975, it was formally agreed that Brazil would purchase from West Germany an entire nuclear industry, that is, the technology required for the whole fuel cycle. Not only will this be the largest industrial nuclear deal ever, but it is also a huge deal in any terms—worth something over $8 billion to the Germans. In addition to reactors, Brazil will buy those gateways to becoming a nuclear weapon state: facilities for uranium enrichment and for chemical separation of plutonium. This means that Brazil will have two nuclear weapons options—to enrich uranium to bomb-level concentration, and to separate plutonium from the other wastes.

Rather late in the day, the United States realized what was happening: Germany was selling Brazil the wherewithal to manufacture atomic bombs. At one point, the American firm Bechtel had sought to team up with Westinghouse to offer a similar package, but the U.S. government had forbidden it, for techniques of uranium enrichment and chemical separation are considered too dangerous to export. To make matters worse, Brazil has refused to sign the NPT, and has signaled its interest at different times in acquiring atomic bombs.

Brazil had its own compelling motives for going ahead. The OPEC price hike had hit it very hard, and the Brazilians feared that their growing economy might soon be starved of adequate energy. In addition, there are enough uncertainties about U.S. policy on exporting enriched uranium that the Brazilians wanted to have their own source.

The Germans also had their good reasons to go ahead. They are worried about future sources of raw uranium. In this deal, they will share in putative Brazilian uranium strikes. They also regard American complaints as sour grapes—because an American company did not get the reactor business. The fierce, often mercantilist, economic rivalry to sell nuclear technology can be too easily overlooked. Where profits are the criteria, foreign policy considerations can be shoved to the background. The competition can get very rough. To get the business, the Brazilians made clear, the Germans had to sweeten the deal and do better than Westinghouse—and that meant adding the enrichment and reprocessing facilities that the U.S. government had stricken from the American offer.

The deal is of course of vast economic importance to the Germans, not only in terms of employment, but in providing orders for the troubled German reactor industry. "Wherever we look—in Italy, Spain, Sweden, Thailand, South Korea—the Americans have already been there." So rationalized an executive of the German reactor manufacturer. "The Third World is the only open market left. To fully exploit our nuclear power plant capacity, we have to land at least three contracts a year for delivery abroad. The market here is about saturated and the United States has cornered most of the rest of Europe, so we have to concentrate on the Third World."

The deal may still go ahead in its current form, though a number of major technical problems remain. As one joke has it, "The Germans have sold an enrichment process that does not work, to enrich Brazilian uranium that does not exist." The financial stability of the main German supplier is also questioned in some quarters. The Carter Administration is putting pressure on the West German government, as is a new anti-nuclear lobby within Germany. But at this stage, the deal is still on. Such things as this make large-scale proliferation seem inevitable, hardly to be stayed or deterred by reasonable fears.

AMERICA'S TWO ATOMS POLICY GOES UP IN SMOKE

The German-Brazilian deal caught the U.S. government mostly unawares. But the Indian explosion a year earlier had already severely shaken American complacency.

Initially several congressmen became alarmed at what was happening abroad—and what was not happening in Washington. "It became very apparent that no one was paying any attention," said Senator Abraham Ribicoff. "Here was an issue on which the United States and the Soviet Union saw eye to eye, but no one was trying to get them together. Meanwhile, France and West Germany were moving into the nuclear export business in a big way. No one cared very much about the issue in the U.S. government. It was out of sight of the State Department. The Atomic Energy Commission was not paying much attention to this stuff, nor was the Joint Atomic Energy Committee. I have no proof that the nuclear bureaucracy had a vested interest in keeping it quiet, but we certainly weren't doing anything."

The State Department and the Arms Control and Disarmament Agency joined the congressmen in taking up the issue.

The most important initiative was Henry Kissinger's convening of a "Suppliers Club" in London after the Indian test. It was composed of seven possible exporting nations—the United States, Russia, Britain, France, West Germany, Canada, and Japan. The Americans and the Russians were not far apart on the problem. As a Soviet arms controller said recently, "Our interests on proliferation are almost identical with you Americans." Indeed, a CIA analyst observed, "There is no more sincere antiproliferator than the USSR. One reason is that a number of the countries that might soon become nuclear weapon states are highly antagonistic to the Soviet Union and not too far away from it."

It was much more difficult for the Americans to work out a common position with the French and Germans, who suspected a plot by U.S. commercial interests to recapture the whole business. "The American case would be better if you still had your virginity," is the way a German diplomat put it recently. "You've had a good time for some years and now you want to be pure." After all, he might have added, it was the United States that had trained 1100 Indian nuclear scientists and engineers prior to 1974.

Nevertheless, a year ago, the seven supplier nations were able to arrive at a "code of conduct," an agreement of modest but significant impact. It provides for improved safeguards and agreement not to assist any nuclear explosions, even "peaceful" ones, and for more attention to physical security. "Frankly," said one ACDA official, "much more has been accomplished than could have been reasonably expected. It is a very useful process."

Last autumn the French indicated that their stance on proliferation was "parallel" to that of the United States and that they would cooperate with the other members of the Suppliers Club. "It has required more courage than you can imagine to change our policies," said an official in the French Foreign Ministry. "We have no domestic political pressure against proliferation, and very strong vested bureaucratic and commercial pressures for exports." The French have, though, refused to budge on the sale of a plutonium reprocessing plant to Pakistan, despite U.S. pressure. "And Pakistan was a matter of principle. We can go ahead with you in the future. But we can't go back on deals we've already made. Pakistan is the main one. In any event, it is a very small reprocessing plant. Much more important is the German-Brazilian deal."

The original seven members in the Suppliers Club have now been joined by eight others—Belgium, the Netherlands, Sweden, Italy, East Germany, Czechoslovakia, Poland, and Switzerland—and their secret deliberations continue in London.

U.S. policy, however, has remained schizophrenic. Nuclear power has strong advocates. The core of the now-defunct Atomic Energy Commission resides in the Energy Research and Development Administration and, as one official put it, "There's a lot of inertia in ERDA." It took two years before the Ford Administration would admit that U.S. nuclear materials were used for the Indian explosion. Official policy projected 200 new power plants in the United States by 1985—twenty a year—and encouraged exports. President Ford also wanted to invite private industry into the nuclear enrichment business (now a government monopoly), which would only have enlarged the constituency in favor of rapid expansion of the nuclear business.

The 1976 presidental election changed things. During the campaign, Jimmy Carter seemed to be personally involved with the proliferation issue. After all, he had once received a dangerous dose of radiation while helping to deactivate a damaged reactor in Canada. He spoke strongly about the dangers of proliferation, strongly enough to worry Ford. As a secret memorandum warned Ford in September, there was now "considerable sentiment for a forceful nonproliferation initiative domestically." On October 28, Ford announced a major shift in U.S. policy. He downgraded the emphasis on plutonium reprocessing. He said that future exports would go only to countries that have either signed the NPT or put their entire nuclear energy programs under international safeguards. He also promised that such nations would be guaranteed enriched uranium from the United States. While politics instigated the change, it was really the outcome of a rough struggle between two competing views. The first, representing the attitudes of the old nuclear bureaucracy, wanted to continue to push nuclear power development, especially the breeder reactor, which actually produces more plutonium than it consumes. On the other side was the new concern over proliferation, articulated by the Arms Control and Disarmament Agency. The vicissitudes of presidential politics helped to give ACDA a moderate victory.

The October 28 statement represented a substantial turn in U.S. policy, though hardly one of 180 degrees.

WHAT IS TO BE DONE?

"As forces for proliferation are rising, our historical leverage to impose restraints is eroding." warned the secret memorandum that was the basis for the turn-around by the Ford Administration last autumn. Such sentiments point to the crucial question facing the Carter Administration: How much power over proliferation does the United States have in the Second Nuclear Age?

Many argue that it is already too late. "The technology is not all that magical, and we're not a monopoly," William Anders, former chairman of the Nuclear Regulatory Commission, said last year. "The only way to have our way is to be involved, to not opt out, to set the pace, to set the moral tone, if you will." Those who stand to make money from nuclear technology—industry—agree, and are even more outspoken. They argue that the best way we can continue to influence events is by competing aggressively in the marketplace.

This is a distortion. The United States continues to hold dominant power. "We are still *numero uno*," said NRC Commissioner Gilinsky. The United States holds about 70 percent of the nuclear business worldwide. The reactor industries of the other major exporters—France, West Germany, Canada—are all deeply involved with the U.S. industry and technology, and of course these nations are our partners in the Western security system. A United States that put "antiproliferationism" at the top of its agenda would have a profound effect. It is likely that many in the Carter Administration will try to do so.

There is no single solution, of course, but a great number of initiatives can be taken, in addition to those of the last two years, to induce dramatic change and help reduce dangers. (Deftness is also required, especially as the United States does not come to the subject with an unblemished record. "We have to work out a political approach that doesn't set us up as morally superior," says a State Department official. "The sledgehammer approach is not the best way of getting others to see the problem the way we do. In fact, it will have exactly the opposite effect of what we want.")

U.S. policy might work toward the following goals:

1 Improve the nuclear non-proliferation treaty system and strengthen the International Atomic Energy Agency. Today, the safeguards mainly cover reactors; they should be expanded to the entire fuel cycle, the life of facilities, and research institutes, and they should be aimed not merely at "timely detection" but also at prevention of illicit activities.

2 Provide incentives for nations to eschew a nuclear weapons capability. For instance, other countries must be confident that they can rely *completely* on the United States to deliver a steady supply of slightly enriched uranium—so long as they observe safeguards. It was lack of such confidence, in part, that drove the Brazilians into German arms. The United States should copy the Soviet Union and only "lease" the enriched uranium so that it can control the waste products.

3 Keep uranium enrichment out of the hands of private enterprise—and thus avoid further economic

incentive to export the makings of proliferation. Instead, cooperative international ventures could enrich uranium and handle the waste. This would make national nuclear programs much more visible. People would know what is happening.

4 Discourage the belief that plutonium should be used in reactors. Evidence increasingly indicates that plutonium recycling may be uneconomic and impractical, and we should not let people think otherwise. Plutonium separation for power purposes in this country should not go forward. The federal government should, in particular, avoid any commitment to the breeder reactor.

5 Prevent situations that allow a country to play suppliers off against each other to get the enrichment and reprocessing facilities that are required to make a bomb. One helpful device is the London Suppliers Club, which might give rise to a market-sharing arrangment—as proposed by Senator Ribicoff—that would reduce dangerous competition. Such an arrangement might also help to limit a "gray market," where suppliers with too much capacity or too much enriched uranium sell secretly at higher prices to countries that want a weapons capability.

6 Tighten American export rules so that, in effect, the United States *discriminates against* countries that do not cooperate with the NPT system. Up to now, the United States has often seemed to discriminate *in favor* of the recalcitrants. We should no longer make available cheap credits to help spread nuclear power.

There are also a number of other political options.

1 *The demonstration effect.* By one estimate, the United States has some 30,000 nuclear weapons. In current lingo, the accumulation of nuclear weapons is known as "vertical proliferation." Some of those most worried about "horizontal proliferation" scoff at the notion that vertical proliferation has any relevance to the problem. But, in the minds of Third World citizens, the connection is real. Why should they be denied nuclear weapons, Third World leaders ask themselves, when the superpowers cheerily go along building up their arsenals? Under the NPT, the superpowers are obligated to reduce their own nuclear arsenals, but this obligation has not exactly been observed. When James Schlesinger was secretary of defense, he talked about creating a "credible response"—that is, suggesting that nuclear weapons are not merely weapons of last resort but also have a rather precise role to play in limited battlefield conditions. This sounded as if the United States was saying that nuclear weapons are after all quite useful tools. If that is true for the United States, the Third World countries say, it is also true for them. A serious effort to control the nuclear arms race between the superpowers would have major meaning for the proliferation problem. As Michael Nacht of Harvard's Program in Science and International Affairs has said, "Progress in SALT will positively affect the perception of some 'have-nots' toward the 'haves' and should influence the domestic debate in threshold countries in favor of restraint."

2 *The prohibition effect.* Prohibit all nuclear explosions, even the "peaceful" underground variety. The United States and the Soviet Union signed a treaty banning tests above a threshold of 150 kilotons in 1974. But this "threshold" is more than *ten times higher* than the strength of the Hiroshima bomb. Unfortunately, the Russians continue to hold to the mistaken belief that "peaceful nuclear explosions" can work wonders, like changing the direction of Siberian rivers, although, increasingly, it seems that such explosions are uneconomic, unbelievably crude for the task at hand, and dangerous. If the United States and the USSR agreed to do away with all peaceful nuclear explosions, it would help to remove the cloak behind which India can disguise its weapons tests.

3 *The reliability quotient.* Strengthen American security guarantees to our allies. This can greatly inhibit our allies' desire for nuclear weapons, even if it poses unattractive choices for us. For instance, if American troops are withdrawn from South Korea, South Korea is likely to grope for some different kind of security, perhaps a nuclear capability of its own. Then Japan would feel impelled to follow suit; then other nations in Asia.

4 *The "nuclear free zone" approach.* It is feasible—difficult, but feasible—to contemplate treaty arrangements under which in certain regions nuclear weapons are forbidden.

5 *The instability factor.* The case can be made that the acquisition of nuclear weapons by countries not now possessing them may invoke dangers that far outweigh any sense of security such weapons may imply. Many West Germans, for example, now realize that an independent German capability would make

central Europe more unstable, not less. The same can certainly be said for a number of other countries.

THE DECISIVE STEP?

Yet all these proposals could well prove inadequate. Even if they are all acted upon, we might nevertheless in the 1980s be living in a world glutted with plutonium. "At last we've reached the point where the people making decisions recognize the problem," observed Professor Irwin Bupp of the Harvard Business School's Energy Research Project, a leading analyst of the nuclear industry. "But they are putting more faith in institutional solutions than is justified. It's unlikely that you're going to be able to prevent further proliferation through international organizations and controls. The inevitable result of spreading nuclear power is a world of abundant plutonium, and that means a very high risk of malevolent use."

There is a final, bold step the United States could take—a retreat from nuclear power itself. A number of responsible observers have already called for such action. "We must hold back on a great expansion of nuclear power until the world gets better," said George Kistiakowsky. "It's just too damn risky right now."

When one looks at the decline in orders for new reactors in the United States in 1975 and 1976, one could conclude that such a retreat is already on. But the United States could go further and announce a moratorium on the new development of conventional fission nuclear power. (This would not preclude the continuing of research.) When all the doubts—about economics, safety, nuclear waste disposal, and proliferation—are added up, it becomes reasonable to ask whether fission power, at a billion dollars or so per reactor, is the wisest way to allocate resources for future needs.

An American moratorium could have a powerful demonstration effect, significantly slowing the spread of nuclear energy and thus the spread of nuclear weapons competence. A moratorium would announce that the world's technological leader, the progenitor of atomic power, had examined it and found it wanting. Then many other countries would surely recalculate their own programs and look in other directions. It is already clear that nuclear energy makes little sense for the Third World. (Several studies now suggest that it is nothing short of ludicrous for a developing country to make the huge capital investment required for nuclear power.) In Western Europe and Japan, as in the United States, nuclear development lags far behind the expectations of only three or four years ago. As in the United States, the delays result from concern about cost, safety, and proliferation.

It is a commonplace that nuclear warfare could extinguish civilized life. Yet that fact today is imbued with new urgency. While there is no one way to stop proliferation, there are many things to be done that could help to manage the Second Nuclear Age. Even in sum, they may not be enough. Yet there is no choice but to try, and swiftly, when the alternative is the terrifying prospect of atomic bombs almost everywhere.

Could We Be Wrong?

Donald L. Clark

The spread of nuclear capability threatens U.S. security and increases the chance of nuclear holocaust. The NPT and the IAEA are the major international instruments for controlling the spread of nuclear weapons.

U.S. Department of State,
Bureau of Public Affairs, August 1977

From the moment the atomic bomb was dropped on Hiroshima, the main question before the world has been whether the human race is intelligent enough to survive. . . . At least seven nations are manufacturing nuclear bombs and a dozen more know how to make them.

"Arms and Madness," [Norman Cousins]
Saturday Review, July 26, 1975

Although I don't exactly love the H-bomb, it comes close to my idea of what a bomb should be. . . . In the more than 25 years since it became popular, it has never been used against anybody. A person could get fond of a bomb like that.

Russell Baker, *New York Times Magazine*,
July 31, 1977

Many now argue that the most dangerous issue facing the world is that of nuclear proliferation, and that contention is widely reflected in the great amount of recent press and international discussion.[1] President Carter apparently shares this belief and is even willing to sacrifice more potential efficiency in the battle for energy in an effort to stop, dampen, or slow proliferation.[2] Additionally, this is the one subject on which both U.S. political parties, the most renowned scien-

---

[1] In recent months *The Atlantic, Atlas, Saturday Review, Washington Post, Foreign Affairs, Foreign Policy*, and *The Illustrated London News*, to mention a few, have featured articles on the question of nuclear proliferation. Additionally, the U.S. State Department and U.S. officials have spoken out publicly and in print citing the need for nonproliferation and the connection between proliferation of nuclear weapons and nuclear energy development.

[2] President Carter has delayed development of the fast breeder reactor in the U.S. and tried to persuade the United Kingdom, the Federal Republic of Germany, and Canada to stop nuclear energy agreements with other nations for fear they encourage the possibility of proliferation. Mike McCormack, "How Not to End Nuclear Proliferation," *Washington Post*, April 24, 1977, p. 5.

From Donald L. Clark, "Could We Be Wrong?" *Air University Review* **29** (September-October 1978): 28–37.

tists, the military, the public, our allies, and enemies all seem to agree. Though the means to ensure nonproliferation may not be agreed on, nearly unanimously, the leaders proclaim proliferation to be bad, and nonproliferation, indeed an extension of the Nuclear Non-Proliferation Treaty (NPT), to be good.

However, a growing number of reasonable and responsible people are questioning that near unanimous opinion.[3] The purpose of this article is not to advocate proliferation but to expose the reader to the logic and thought on that other side of the question. Nonproliferation seems so logical on the face of it, so moral and proper, that perhaps most of us have tended to approve of it with little or only cursory consideration. Reading this article may make the decision tougher—indeed, it might even raise the issue to the level of some other international dilemmas where the right or best answer is not quite so clear. Above all, it is designed to force the reader to go beyond gut reaction and think the issue through. Readers may—I am tempted to say probably will—continue to support NPT initiatives, but I suspect they will do so with slightly less assurance, while feeling more confident that they have considered the issue in depth. They may also conclude that nonproliferation could be counterproductive to the very conditions it seeks to promote.

THE QUESTION

The Nuclear Non-Proliferation Treaty was signed in 1968 amid great fanfare proclaiming that the world now had a means to avoid nuclear holocaust. It has since been signed or ratified by more than one hundred nations. These ratifications seem to be a giant step forward, yet nuclear weapons have proliferated in both total numbers and number of possessors and may be on the verge of even more rapid growth and expansion. In fact, the NPT, to date, simply has not achieved its avowed goal. Tonga, Zambia, and similar third world nations have rushed to the signing table, but most of the nations that have the technology or technological potential and the financial ability to produce nuclear weapons have not been so eager to sign; and two possessors, France and the People's Republic of China, have not signed. The list of nonsigners is impressive. The Federal Republic of Germany and Japan are the only nonpossessor nations with true nuclear potential that have signed and ratified, and they ratified only some six years later after pressures were applied by the U.S. and the U.S.S.R.[4] Significant nonsigners or ratifiers include Brazil, Israel,[5] South Africa,[6] India, Pakistan, Bangladesh, and Egypt among the nonpossessors;[7] France, the People's Republic of China (PRC), and India are among nuclear weapon possessors. The question we have to ask is Why? *If nonproliferation is so clearly in the best interests of the world, why are such key countries not responding to this call for what we see as sanity?*

THE ANSWER

Nuclear weapon possession is, after all, most valuable. Why else would the U.S. and the U.S.S.R. possess thousands of warheads when the weapon has only been used twice more than thirty years ago? Why else would the United Kingdom, France, the People's Republic of China, and India, at increasing degrees of sacrifice, devote the enormous amounts of investment (manpower, money, and resources) necessary to enter the nuclear club, even while the latter three were being pressured, sniped at, and criticized by the superpowers for so doing? Could it be just for the right of membership in the exclusive nuclear club? Could it be just for a seat of power on the Security Council of the United Nations? No. (Note that the People's Republic of China was denied her seat until

---

[3] R. Robert Sandoval in "Consider the Porcupine: Another View of Nuclear Proliferation." *Bulletin of the Atomic Scientists,* May 1976, p. 17, suggests nuclear weapon proliferation might have some advantages. Another article raising the question is: "Undue Alarm over Nuclear Spread?" *Wall Street Journal,* October 15, 1976 by Ernest W. Lefever, p. 12.

[4] The West Germans were very slow to ratify the NPT and finally did so by a slim margin only when the U.S. and Russia insisted that German ratification was needed before the Berlin agreement would be signed. Japan was equally slow, only ratifying in 1976. The issue is frequently debated in Japan with an increasing number of supporters opposing Japan's allegiance to the NPT.

[5] Some now are convinced that Israel has added nuclear weapons to her war stocks.

[6] The U.S. and U.S.S.R. recently joined forces in an attempt to pressure South Africa to turn away from nuclear development. The verdict is not yet in.

[7] For a more thorough study of the possibilities and needs of nuclear power development potentials, see Major Wayne Morawitz, "Nuclear Proliferation and U.S. Security," *Air University Review,* January-February 1977, pp. 19–28.

she acquired nuclear weapons.) As important as it may be to join the nuclear club and enter the ever less effective and weakened Security Council, those reasons alone would not appear to justify the expenditure of the six "haves." Nuclear weapon possession must be perceived to offer something more. I suggest that that something more is quite evident and that it becomes more evident as proliferation increases. It is, in a word, "security." There is one self-evident and undisputed fact associated with nuclear power possession: *no nation that possesses nuclear weapons has ever had its borders seriously attacked by another nation.* True, nuclear possession may not be the sole reason for this, but, if we consider the evidence of history, it appears to be significant.

In the early days of the nuclear era, soon after World War II, many proffered the conclusion that atomic weapons made war unthinkable. That early premise failed to come true. Since 1945, wars have occurred around the world—in the Middle East, Korea, Southeast Asia, Latin America, and elsewhere. These wars have involved possessors of nuclear power, either directly, by proxy, or in the weapon supplier role, but they have *never* involved the sovereign territory of a nuclear nation.[8] Thus, although *all* wars have not been prevented, one could posit that nuclear war has been *prevented* and, further, that superpower or nuclear possessor wars have been prevented. This leads to the consideration that nuclear weapons may provide what nations have long sought: *perfect territorial security.* If even the possibility of that utopia comes from nuclear possession, it could readily explain why nations want them, in spite of the expense and why nations decline to sign a solemn treaty of self-denial. Surely, a nation that is able to attain a weapon system which has even some possibility of guaranteeing security should not forego that option, for is that not the first and primary goal of every government? Would the U.S. sign the Nuclear Non-Proliferation Treaty if we were a nonpossessor?

Considering the history of the nuclear era, I would additionally suggest another possible conclusion: that the *proliferation* of nuclear weapons has actually made them a more effective deterrent while simultaneously diminishing the likelihood of their use, a most incongruous and unique occurrence. Remember that when only *one* nation had nuclear weapons, it used

them in spite of what, at least in retrospect, seems to have been questionable cause.[9] But since that near-single use and the acquisition of similar weapons by other states, all have foregone their use in spite of provocation and opportunity. Thus, it can be argued that weapon possession by a single state is most unstabilizing, at least for all the others, but as more acquire the weapon the less likely it will be used, except in the theoretical last ditch effort to ensure survival.

DISCUSSION

If this is true, nuclear weapon holders, in the current state of weapon technology, have both the ultimate defense and, at the same time because of nuclear proliferation, an almost useless offensive weapon.[10] On the surface, this combination could tend to achieve what the early prophets of nuclear weapons foretold, a nuclear guarantee against war. Further, if the foregoing is true, it follows that the proliferation of nuclear weapons, instead of threatening war, actually increases the probability of preventing war. This conclusion suggests the following hypothesis: If no nuclear possessor need fear attack, then the only place there can be wars is where nuclear weapons are not possessed, and if such places are diminished through nuclear proliferation, then war potential is also diminished. Thus, nonproliferation, our sacred cow, may be counterproductive to the very purpose for which we have established it, or, in other words, proliferation may be more likely to eliminate war than nonproliferation. A key point is that "proliferation" has changed this powerful offensive weapon into one that can be used only in a last-ditch defensive role.

Let us turn for a moment from the realm of pure speculation to the facts of recent history. The U.S. and U.S.S.R., in spite of numerous crises, have avoided war with one another, and at least one significant reason for that could be because they both recognize the exponentially increased risks to them as a result of nuclear weapons. In fact, a study of their

---

[8] There have, of course, been the Sino-Soviet clashes over disputed territories on their 5000 mile border.

[9] In retrospect, we have learned that the Japanese would probably have surrendered without invasion or the use of atomic weapons.

[10] Drew Middleton in "Thinking about the Unthinkable, Politics and the Arms Race," *The Atlantic,* August 1976, pp. 54–57, is only one of many international observers who argues that nuclear parity rules out the use of nuclear weapons except in extreme emergencies.

relations can detect that as their nuclear arsenals have become more equal, they have become more and more prudent and cautious in their relations with one another; while when one side had a clear advantage, they were even more at odds.

But specific wars have occurred, even involving the superpowers—the U.S. in Korea and Vietnam and the U.S.S.R. in its invasions of Hungary and Czechoslovakia. Additionally, the U.S. and the U.S.S.R., by proxy and supply line, have been involved in three Middle Eastern wars and other even smaller ones in Angola, Yemen, Dominican Republic, Ethiopia, Zaire, etc. In fact, it is the contention of many concerned voices in the world that these indirect superpower confrontations in nonsuperpower wars present the greatest danger of leading to superpower nuclear war as the result of escalation, miscalculations, etc. On the evidence available, one has to conclude, then, that nuclear weapons, if they are preventing wars between the possessors, clearly are not also preventing wars among nonpossessors and further conclude that this is dangerous. However, we seldom ask, could those small wars also have been prevented had the lesser powers possessed nuclear weapons?

The 1968 Soviet invasion of Czechoslovakia presents an interesting example. The Soviets are noted for a strong conservative bent in international affairs, especially as to involving Soviet forces outside the U.S.S.R.[11] In 1968, Soviet generals were able to assure the party leadership that (1) organized Czech military resistance was unlikely and, (2) even if it occurred, it would be squashed reasonably rapidly and with, say, at worst 10,000 to 40,000 Soviet military casualties, a relatively undramatic loss possibility of professional soldiers in a country with millions. But what if those Soviet generals faced a proliferated world and knew that Czechoslovakia possessed, say, just 10 to 20 Minuteman missiles or their like? Now, their worst-case analysis would have to indicate that an invasion of Czechoslovakia could mean the loss of several million at-home Russian civilians in an overnight holocaust. The "pucker"

factor goes way up, and the conservative decision-maker is forced to re-evaluate the gains versus losses of his decision to strike or not.

The same applies to the Israel/Egypt/Syria triangle and similar African, Latin American, and other rivalries. Thus, is it not reasonable to ask if proliferation might not mean less chance of war—rather than an increased likelihood?

THE FANATICS

By now you are surely saying, but what about all those wild-eyed fanatics around the world? Surely nonproliferation is valid if it means preventing Idi Amins, Black Septembers, el-Qaddafis, and the like from acquiring nuclear weapons. This is a strong argument and on the surface makes sense to most of us (if we are not Ugandans, Palestinians, and Libyans). But, like so many of the apparent truisms of nonproliferation, examination of the issue reduces the definiteness of the initial conclusion. Wild-eyed fanatics have, in fact, had nuclear weapons and for some reason (possibly the fact of proliferation) chosen not to use them. The world may be shocked by the actions of Amin and el-Qaddafi, and even of the Black Septembers and other Palestinian terrorists, *but* their actions pale when compared with the murders, death camps, and unbelievable horrors of Joseph Stalin. Still, even Stalin resisted the temptation to use nuclear weapons once acquired. Mao Tse-tung's record cannot match Stalin's—at least is less well documented—but many have thought him mad, unrestrained, and callous toward life; yet he, too, proved quite modest in the nuclear arena. Both these men saw the value of nuclear weapons, killed or caused the death of innumerable lives just by diverting resources to acquire the weapons,[12] yet both showed restraint after nuclear weapon acquisition.

The point is that no matter how badly a nation might want to use its nuclear weapons for evil gains, since proliferation all they can realistically do with them is point to them with pride and say, "don't tread on me." They cannot (at least have not) use them

---

[11] Note that even now, when some experts claim the Soviets have acquired nuclear and overall superiority, the Soviets choose to use "proxies" (the Cubans) for their African adventures. In a 1970 article in the *Air University Review* (January-February), I predicted direct Soviet intervention in Africa by the mid-70s.

[12] The best chroniclers of Stalin's madness and his obsession with acquiring nukes are Aleksander I. Solzhenitsyn in several of his books, including *The First Circle* and *The Gulag Archipelago, 1918-1956: An Experiment in Literary Investigation* Parts I and II; and Robert Conquest in *The Great Terror: Stalin's Purge of the Thirties*.

because once a nation acquires such weapons no other nation can afford to push so drastically that he might have to use his nukes. But, simultaneously, without being attacked and in ultimate danger of survival, the nation is inhibited in the use of its weapons against even a nonpossessor because it fears retaliation from some other of the ever growing number of possessors. Idi Amin and such types may appear mad, but it is a controlled madness. These powerful men are willing to murder, harass, and torture those *under their control* and too weak to defend. They are even ready to tweak the nose of superior powers up to the point that it is not really serious enough to invite a strong response. However, they do not foolishly attack or push too far those capable of squashing them. Few, if any, who have risen to such absolute power have ever attacked a foe when it was clear that the foe or his allies would easily be able to annihilate them. An Amin with ten nuclear missiles under his control would not be a very attractive alternative to the world, but realistically, neither does he add much to the threat of nuclear war. The world feels helpless now to stop his internal machinations (partly due to nuclear proliferation), and if he had nuclear weapons, the rest would be even more deterred from interference. But, conversely, Amin might then perceive himself as less threatened and, therefore, determine it unnecessary to strike out against his "imagined" threateners. My point is that, bad as it might be even if an Amin were a nuclear possessor, the only likely change is that there would then be less chance that any other nation would decide to remove Amin— "nukes" *protect* the good and the bad equally, but due to proliferation they offer only an unusable offensive threat. Amin types are disgusting aberrations, but no more so than the world has faced before; and the previous aberrations, once they acquired nuclear weapons and faced the fact of proliferation, actually demonstrated restraint about their use and protection. It is a hard fact to accept, but to much of the world it was the U.S. *alone* that used such weapons, and U.S. irrationality alone, as recently demonstrated by "Nixsonianlike" paranoia over national security, they most fear. The wild-eyed, fanatic fear may be exaggerated—I hope.

INEVITABILITY

I say "I hope" because there is another argument against support of the NPT concept. Many of the world's most renowned experts in weapons, international affairs, politics, and nuclear science are now concluding that the battle is lost; proliferation is inevitable if only because science cannot be withheld, and the science of nuclear weaponry is available.[13] I might add that it is inevitable also because many see these weapons as useful. But the point they make is, why fight the inevitable? It is worth fighting even for a lost cause if the cause is noble and correct, but it is not worth the candle if the cause is not clearly in the best interests of mankind; and the points related thus far at least raise the question that proliferation *might* well be better for mankind than nonproliferation so the candle's value is questionable. However, unmanaged proliferation is more dangerous than other alternatives—one of which I will describe later.

U.S. IMAGE

Another concept of the nonproliferation policy that may in fact not be what we think it is, is the image its support by the U.S. creates. In the U.S., we instinctively consider nonproliferation to be good and support of the NPT to be respected and proper. The failure of the NPT should have warned us that they may not be universally true, *but it did not*. The truth may be, however, that other nations, especially those verging on nuclear capability and properly desirous of its advantages, consider the U.S. NPT policy to be hypocritical and arrogant. They may well interpret our platitudes about the evils of nuclear weapons as merely propagandistic cover for our participation and perpetuation in superpower world domination rather than a sincere desire to avoid a nuclear Armageddon.

Think of it for a moment from their viewpoint. What the U.S. may be perceived as saying, in concert with the U.S.S.R. and the world's former preeminent colonialist, the United Kingdom, is: *We and our powerful friends have accumulated these super destructive weapons in numbers that can threaten the world. We need them, but of course you do not. In fact, in your hands they could be most dangerous. For us*

---

[13] *Nuclear Energy*, Report of the Fiftieth American Assembly, April 22–25, 1976, Arden House. This distinguished group joined many others that believe, try as the world might, nuclear weapons will proliferate, and that the knowledge to build is common knowledge and the cost ever decreasing.

they guarantee freedom from attack by any and all and near ultimate security, but for you such a guarantee is not necessary. Sign the NPT and if anything goes wrong, we might decide to protect or punish you, depending on how we interpret the circumstances. You should forswear such weapons and even some of the energy related benefits some aspects of nuclear production capability might afford you, since they can lead to weaponry. We, on the other hand, will keep ours, even constantly increasing the numbers and/or the capability of them to destroy efficiently. Now if that is the way many of the nuclear have-nots judge our nuclear stance (this ignores the specialized economic gripes the Germans, Japanese, and Brazilians have made in recent months),[14] it is rather easy to see why they not only do not sign on but, in fact, might harbor rather strong resentment over the policy.

I would posit that our NPT policy—plus SALT, détente, and related activities that have brought the U.S. and U.S.S.R. into close and frequent contact— could cloud the view of much of the world concerning the basic differences between the U.S. and U.S.S.R. Partly because of this NPT attitude, they might judge us as two superpowers striving to achieve even greater power and wealth while telling others that it is bad for them to follow our path.

However, I do not mean even remotely to suggest that détente is the wrong approach, for I feel quite strongly the other way. Yet as other nations observe summit meetings with our President and the Soviet General Secretary arm-in-arm, toasting in champagne and concurring in joint policies like the NPT, it could cause the third world and even some of our developed allies to wonder if the superpowers are not becoming more and more alike and conspiring to hold onto special wealth, might, and status at everyone else's expense.

I suggest that instead the U.S. should highlight the differences between our system and the Soviet's whenever possible. Agreements to reduce or limit nuclear weapons and to exchange cultural programs, etc., can easily be judged by the world as progressive steps for all if they diminish ever so slightly the superpower threat of war, and they should continue. But the NPT policy may be viewed through others' eyes as discriminating—an act of inequality and even

immorality favoring the greats while depriving the weak. This image is not consistent with the founding of the U.S.; our founders called for no entangling alliances, all people and all nations equal, and no plan for the U.S. to try to dominate others. Thus, in spite of our belief in its goodness, the NPT policy might in the eyes of many be viewed as a new kind of imperialism, one sponsored by Communist and democrat alike. Is there then an alternative, a middle ground that turns us away from the lost cause while simultaneously taking advantage of some of the pros for proliferation? I suggest there may be. It is an approach I call "controlled proliferation," which is designed to lessen the risks of war, reduce the costs of acquiring nuclear weapons and nuclear energy, improve the U.S. image as a *leader* and seeker of an equitable as well as peaceful world, while simultaneously avoiding for as long as possible—perhaps indefinitely—proliferation to those most unstable, undesirable states.

CONTROLLED PROLIFERATION

Under controlled proliferation (CP), the U.S. would publicly withdraw from the NPT for reasons of its failure, the clear inevitability of proliferation, and the possibility that proliferation may better achieve the goal of lessening the danger of war. We would then make it clear to the world that, *under certain circumstances*, we would be willing either to assist or even grant nuclear weapon acquisition or energy capability to certain have-nots. The circumstances are, of course, the key, and they would have to be carefully determined,[15] but as a starting basis I suggest the U.S. might grant limited nuclear weaponry:

• Where a government has a long history of stability and friendly relations with the U.S. (Canada, Switzerland, The Netherlands, as examples).
• Where possession of nuclear weapons or energy by the state in question would make the region more

[14] Daniel Yergin, "The Terrifying Prospect: Atomic Bombs Everywhere," *The Atlantic*, April 1977, p. 60.

[15] Daniel Yergin in his excellent article, "The Terrifying Prospect: Atomic Bombs Everywhere," *The Atlantic*, April 1977, suggests policies whereby the U.S. would use incentives to accomplish nonproliferation. The similarity between other goals (nonnuclear) we list is interesting. The Committee for Economic Development in an 88-page report issued in 1976 also urged a close connection between other U.S. foreign policy goals and nuclear nonproliferation.

stable by lessening the likelihood of war (Taiwan, Israel, Egypt, Greece, Turkey).

• Where human rights are at an acceptable level or have drastically improved and are still improving (Canada, Switzerland, Norway, Sweden).

• Where the recipient will sign a treaty not to use such weapons except in defense of his sovereign national territory that has been invaded or attacked.

• Where the recipient will agree not to add to the number of weapons supplied by the U.S. or to transfer them.

In essence, the U.S. would consider supplying a small number—10 to 50 nuclear weapons—to those nations in which we determine it to be in our interest and the world's to do so, *yet* limit the number given or developed and their range so the recipients and the world can recognize that they basically have only a defensive force; a force that would make an attack against them too great a risk to consider, yet a force too small to enable them to initiate an attack capable of totally destroying another. (Expert opinion considers 200 to 300 warheads sufficient to destroy any modern state.)[16]

Think how this might be used to assist U.S. foreign policy. What influence might we gain over an Israel or Egypt to settle their problems if, instead of promissory guarantees over which they have no control, we could trade 10 Minuteman missiles for a reasonable compromise allowing a Palestinian state on the West Bank. Israel and Egypt would remain independent and now have control themselves over assuring the settlement. Yet, the agreement would likely stand because the risk factor potential would then exceed the desire for change. We could also make a U.S. force withdrawal from South Korea result in increased South Korean security rather than lessened.

What would the reaction to controlled proliferation be? Obviously, the U.S.S.R. would protest. Not because the U.S. policy would be wrong but because without U.S. participation in the NPT their chance to dominate the world is lessened. Unfortunately for the U.S.S.R., they trust no one not under their control sufficiently to give them nuclear weapons, and their natural fear and insecurity plus their imposed alliances are too fragile for them to follow our lead within their bloc. Proliferation in Soviet eyes is a far greater threat than it is to the U.S.

Those who sought such weapons but could not or would not meet the U.S. standards might also be unhappy. But, so what? They are not very likely to be cooperative with us now, and they just might decide that meeting U.S. standards of human rights and foreign affairs conduct would be worth the effort if it gained them genuine security—something the offer of our friendship or money alone does not assure thus provides little leverage to the U.S.

However, two serious concerns remain. One, I have not refuted the idea that proliferation, via the numbers game alone, increases the chance of nuclear weapons use. I accept that possibility, but with this qualification—How much danger is added? There are already at least six nuclear nations and 40,000-plus warheads in the world. Would 10 or 20 nations and another small fractional increase in the total number of weapons change that likelihood significantly (say, at the peak, another 2000 weapons)? There is a risk, but it might not outweigh the gain.

The second concern is related to the first. It deals with guarantees and their flimsiness. How can the U.S. be sure a nation that passes some carefully developed criteria of friendship, stability, etc., will remain that way? The answer is simple: We cannot, but, frankly, that is also true today. We have no such guarantees that the current possessors, the U.S.S.R., the People's Republic of China, India, or France, will not decide to attack tomorrow. They are all more atomically powerful and in some cases more likely opponents than any logical recipients of CP would be—and perhaps in the case of France, the U.S.S.R., and the People's Republic of China, they are even less stable—e.g., How many governments in France since World War II? What succession lines exist in the U.S.S.R. and the People's Republic of China? In other words, in the danger area, nothing new is added, but in the stability area, perhaps there could be an improvement. Under CP the U.S. would probably not give missiles to a Uganda under an Amin or a Libya under el-Qaddafi, but we might to Belgium and The Netherlands; Egypt and Israel; Hungary, Czechoslovakia, and even Romania; Canada and Iceland. Would the world be more explosive or less so? I contend there is a legitimate possibility it might prove

---

[16] In a study, *1970 without Arms Control*, the National Planning Association indicated no more than 200 warheads are needed to destroy a large nation/state.

more stable, and in such a proliferated world the U.S. would have to lead by example rather than power alone—a worthy challenge in a more equal world. It would be a dangerous gamble, but one that could enhance peace and nudge the United States back into the more traditional leadership role of its past—leading by leadership rather than power quotient.

Have we been wrong? Has nuclear weapons' greatest use to the world been frittered away by a short-sighted policy decision designed not to save the world but to ensure a dominant position in it for the current possessors for as long as possible—an inequitable policy hidden, as so often in the past, by the cover of security? If so, it will fail, and unfortunately the evidence shows it to be failing. Proliferation is occurring. The controlled proliferation alternative proffers a chance to achieve the long sought grail—a world of peace. Should we not consider it on its merits without blind allegiance to non-proliferation on instincts alone?

QUESTIONS FOR DISCUSSION

1 Is nuclear weapon proliferation dangerous?
2 What significance has the possession of nuclear weapons had on the actual use of force in world politics since the end of World War II?
3 What would be the Soviet response to an American policy of controlled proliferation?
4 Can proliferation be stopped? How?
5 How are Soviet and/or American interests served by nonproliferation? How are their interests harmed?

SUGGESTED READINGS

Greenwood, Ted, George W. Rathjens, and Jack Ruina. *Nuclear Power and Weapons Proliferation.* London: International Institute for Strategic Studies, 1976.

Harkavy, Robert E. *Spectre of a Middle Eastern Holocaust: The Strategic and Diplomatic Implications of the Israeli Nuclear Weapons Program.* Denver, Colo.: University of Denver Graduate School of International Studies, 1977.

Jones, Rodney W. *Nuclear Proliferation: Islam, the Bomb, and South Asia.* Foreward by Amos A. Jordan. Beverly Hills, Calif.: Sage Publications, 1981.

Lovins, Amory B., L. Hunter Lovins, and Leonard Ross. "Nuclear Power and Nuclear Bombs." *Foreign Affairs* **58** (Summer 1980): 1137–1177.

Marks, Anne W., (ed.). *NPT: Paradoxes and Problems.* Washington, D.C.: Arms Control Association, 1975.

Quester, George H. *The Politics of Nuclear Proliferation.* Baltimore: Johns Hopkins University Press, 1973.

Stockholm International Peace Research Institute. *Internationalization to Prevent the Spread of Nuclear Weapons.* London: Taylor & Francis, 1980.

Weltman, John J. "Nuclear Devolution and World Order." *World Politics* **32** (January 1980): 169–193.

Wohlstetter, Albert. "Spreading the Bomb Without Quite Breaking the Rules." *Foreign Policy* No. **25** (Winter 1976–77): 88–96 and 145–180.

Yoder, Amos. *Chinese Policies Toward Limiting Nuclear Weapons.* Muscatine, Iowa: Stanley Foundation, 1980.

Chapter Seven

The Future World Order

The world has experienced the cataclysmic events of war and depressions in the twentieth century. It has also known peace and prosperity. What will the future world order be? Political leaders, scholars, and writers disagree about the future. Some are optimistic and others pessimistic.

Some of the more optimistic visions of the future are described in this book. The view that states will decline in importance as greater interdependence among nations requires cooperation rather than conflict is generally an optimistic vision of a peaceful future.

There are other optimistic views. Some observers foresee rising standards of living as the benefits of science and technology become available to all the peoples of the world. This is in keeping with liberal and Marxist thought of the nineteenth century that industrial society will usher in an age of unprecedented abundance of goods so that real improvement in the quality of life will be experienced everywhere.

Pessimistic visions of the future are more common today. Essential themes of this pessimistic outlook are also described in this book: the danger of nuclear war, the prevalence of widespread poverty among the masses of people in the third and fourth world, the persistence of nationalism and subnationalism, and the continuing activities of terrorists engaged in substate violence.

This chapter deals with one issue of the future: the character of the future economic and ecological system. Is the world heading toward economic and environmental disaster? Predictions of economic decline go back at least to Thomas Malthus, an eighteenth-century economist, who believed that population was increasing more rapidly than food supplies. Wars, plagues, earthquakes, floods, and other disasters were essential to allow some people to cope with their environment.

Neo-Malthusians of the twentieth century use computers and mathematical models to come to similar conclusions. In 1972, the Club of Rome sponsored a study, *The Limits of Growth*, that predicted a global disaster if economic growth and population growth were not sharply reduced. Some pessimists of the twentieth century have also pointed to ecological disasters ahead.

In 1977, President Carter asked the United States Department of State and the Council on Environmental Quality to produce a report dealing with economic and environmental trends as the world heads toward the year 2000. The major conclusion of the report, issued in 1980, is that, if present trends continue, "the world in 2000 will be more crowded, more polluted, less stable ecologically, and more vulnerable to disruption than the world we live in now." People will be poorer in 2000 than they are today. According to the report, the future need not be bleak if there are changes in public policies, institutions, and rates of technological advance.

The major conclusions of this study are printed below. They are challenged by Hudson Institute analysts Herman Kahn and Ernest Schneider who describe *The Global 2000 Report* as "globaloney" because they regard the report as wrong. They estimate that world population growth will decline, poverty will be reduced, energy resources will be sufficient for people's needs, and food production will increase. The dangers of the future are not those depicted in the report, the authors say, but are, rather, nuclear proliferation and runaway inflation.

An evaluation of the economic future must consider which facts are relevant to predict the future. Why do the same "facts" lead to different conclusions? What assumptions about economic development do the optimists and the pessimists make in their predictions? Which economic future is likely to lead to global political instability and war?

The evidence for the future allows for differing interpretations about its character. Economic and environmental trends are difficult to predict. Political developments, such as war and revolution, will play a role in determining the course of economic development and environmental protection. Only the future itself will reveal whether the optimists or the pessimists were correct.

22 Is the World Heading toward Economic and Environmental Disaster?

YES

Council on Environmental Quality and Department of State

The Global 2000 Report to the President

NO

Herman Kahn and Ernest Schneider

Globaloney 2000

The Global 2000 Report to the President

Council on Environmental Quality
Department of State

MAJOR FINDINGS AND CONCLUSIONS

If present trends continue, the world in 2000 will be more crowded, more polluted, less stable ecologically, and more vulnerable to disruption than the world we live in now. Serious stresses involving population, resources, and environment are clearly visible ahead. Despite greater material output, the world's people will be poorer in many ways than they are today.

For hundreds of millions of the desperately poor, the outlook for food and other necessities of life will be no better. For many it will be worse. Barring revolutionary advances in technology, life for most people on earth will be more precarious in 2000 than it is now—unless the nations of the world act decisively to alter current trends.

This, in essence, is the picture emerging from the U.S. Government's projections of probable changes in world population, resources, and environment by the end of the century, as presented in the Global 2000 Study. They do not predict what will occur. Rather, they depict conditions that are likely to develop if there are no changes in public policies, institutions, or rates of technological advance, and if there are no wars or other major disruptions. A keener awareness of the nature of the current trends, however, may induce changes that will alter these trends and the projected outcome.

Principal Findings

Rapid growth in world population will hardly have altered by 2000. The world's population will grow from 4 billion in 1975 to 6.35 billion in 2000, an increase of more than 50 percent. The rate of growth will slow only marginally, from 1.8 percent a year to 1.7 percent. In terms of sheer numbers, population will be growing faster in 2000 than it is today, with 100 million people added each year compared with 75 million in 1975. Ninety percent of this growth will occur in the poorest countries.

While the economies of the less developed countries (LDCs) are expected to grow at faster rates than those of the industrialized nations, the gross national product per capita in most LDCs remains low. The average gross national product per capita is projected to rise substantially in some LDCs (especially in Latin America), but in the great populous nations of South Asia it remains below $200 a year (in 1975 dollars). The large existing gap between the rich and poor nations widens.

World food production is projected to increase 90 percent over the 30 years from 1970 to 2000. This translates into a global per capita increase of less than 15 percent over the same period. The bulk of that increase goes to countries that already have relatively high per capita food consumption. Meanwhile per capita consumption in South Asia, the Middle East, and the LDCs of Africa will scarcely improve or will actually decline below present inadequate levels. At the same time, real prices for food are expected to double.

Arable land will increase only 4 percent by 2000, so that most of the increased output of food will have to come from higher yields. Most of the elements that now contribute to higher yields—fertilizer, pesticides, power for irrigation, and fuel for machinery—depend heavily on oil and gas.

During the 1990s world oil production will approach geological estimates of maximum production capacity, even with rapidly increasing petroleum prices. The Study projects that the richer industrialized nations will be able to command enough oil and other commercial energy supplies to meet rising demands through 1990. With the expected price increases, many less developed countries will have increasing difficulties meeting energy needs. For the one-quarter of humankind that depends primarily on wood for fuel, the outlook is bleak. Needs for fuelwood will exceed available supplies by about 25 percent before the turn of the century.

While the world's finite fuel resources—coal, oil, gas, oil shale, tar sands, and uranium—are theoretically sufficient for centuries, they are not evenly distributed; they pose difficult economic and environmental problems; and they vary greatly in their amenability to exploitation and use.

From Council on Environmental Quality and Department of State, *The Global 2000 Report to the President*. Washington, D.C.: Government Printing Office, 1980, vol. 1, pp. 1–5.

Nonfuel mineral resources generally appear sufficient to meet projected demands through 2000, but further discoveries and investments will be needed to maintain reserves. In addition, production costs will increase with energy prices and may make some nonfuel mineral resources uneconomic. The quarter of the world's population that inhabits industrial countries will continue to absorb three-fourths of the world's mineral production.

Regional water shortages will become more severe. In the 1970-2000 period population growth alone will cause requirements for water to double in nearly half the world. Still greater increases would be needed to improve standards of living. In many LDCs, water supplies will become increasingly erratic by 2000 as a result of extensive deforestation. Development of new water supplies will become more costly virtually everywhere.

Significant losses of world forests will continue over the next 20 years as demand for forest products and fuelwood increases. Growing stocks of commercial-size timber are projected to decline 50 percent per capita. The world's forests are now disappearing at the rate of 18-20 million hectares a year (an area half the size of California), with most of the loss occurring in the humid tropical forests of Africa, Asia, and South America. The projections indicate that by 2000 some 40 percent of the remaining forest cover in LDCs will be gone.

Serious deterioration of agricultural soils will occur worldwide, due to erosion, loss of organic matter, desertification, salinization, alkalinization, and water-logging. Already, an area of cropland and grassland approximately the size of Maine is becoming barren wasteland each year, and the spread of desert-like conditions is likely to accelerate.

Atmospheric concentrations of carbon dioxide and ozone-depleting chemicals are expected to increase at rates that could alter the world's climate and upper atmosphere significantly by 2050. Acid rain from increased combustion of fossil fuels (especially coal) threatens damage to lakes, soils, and crops. Radioactive and other hazardous materials present health and safety problems in increasing numbers of countries.

Extinctions of plant and animal species will increase dramatically. Hundreds of thousands of species —perhaps as many as 20 percent of all species on earth—will be irretrievably lost as their habitats vanish, especially in tropical forests.

The future depicted by the U.S. Government projections, briefly outlined above, may actually understate the impending problems. The methods available for carrying out the Study led to certain gaps and inconsistencies that tend to impart an optimistic bias. For example, most of the individual projections for the various sectors studied—food, minerals, energy, and so on—assume that sufficient capital, energy, water, and land will be available in each of these sectors to meet their needs, regardless of the competing needs of the other sectors. More consistent, better-integrated projections would produce a still more emphatic picture of intensifying stresses, as the world enters the twenty-first century.

Conclusions

At present and projected growth rates, the world's population would reach 10 billion by 2030 and would approach 30 billion by the end of the twenty-first century. These levels correspond closely to estimates by the U.S. National Academy of Sciences of the maximum carrying capacity of the entire earth. Already the populations in sub-Saharan Africa and in the Himalayan hills of Asia have exceeded the carrying capacity of the immediate area, triggering an erosion of the land's capacity to support life. The resulting poverty and ill health have further complicated efforts to reduce fertility. Unless this circle of interlinked problems is broken soon, population growth in such areas will unfortunately be slowed for reasons other than declining birth rates. Hunger and disease will claim more babies and young children, and more of those surviving will be mentally and physically handicapped by childhood malnutrition.

Indeed, the problems of preserving the carrying capacity of the earth and sustaining the possibility of a decent life for the human beings that inhabit it are enormous and close upon us. Yet there is reason for hope. It must be emphasized that the Global 2000 Study's projections are based on the assumption that national policies regarding population stabilization, resource conservation, and environmental protection will remain essentially unchanged through the end of the century. But in fact, policies are beginning to change. In some areas, forests are being replanted after cutting. Some nations are taking steps to reduce soil losses and desertification. Interest in energy conservation is growing, and large sums are being invested in exploring alternatives to petroleum dependence. The need for family planning is slowly becoming better understood. Water supplies are being improved and waste treatment systems built. High-yield seeds are widely available and seed banks are being expanded. Some wildlands with their genetic resources are being protected. Natural predators and selective pesticides are being substituted for persistent and destructive pesticides.

Encouraging as these developments are, they are far from adequate to meet the global challenges projected in this Study. Vigorous, determined new initiatives are needed if worsening poverty and human suffering, environmental degradation, and international tension and conflict are to be prevented. There are no quick fixes. The only solutions to the problems of population, resources, and environment are complex and long-term. These problems are inextricably linked to some of the most perplexing and persistent problems in the world—poverty, injustice, and social conflict. New and imaginative ideas—and a willingness to act on them—are essential.

The needed changes go far beyond the capability and responsibility of this or any other single nation. An era of unprecedented cooperation and commitment is essential. Yet there are opportunities—and a strong rationale—for the United States to provide leadership among nations. A high priority for this Nation must be a thorough assessment of its foreign and domestic policies relating to population, resources, and environment. The United States, possessing the world's largest economy, can expect its policies to have a significant influence on global trends. An equally important priority for the United States is to cooperate generously and justly with other nations—particularly in the areas of trade, investment, and assistance—in seeking solutions to the many problems that extend beyond our national boundaries. There are many unfulfilled opportunities to cooperate with other nations in efforts to relieve poverty and hunger, stabilize population, and enhance economic and environmental productivity. Further cooperation among nations is also needed to strengthen international mechanisms for protecting and utilizing the "global commons"—the oceans and atmosphere.

To meet the challenges described in this Study, the United States must improve its ability to identify emerging problems and assess alternative responses. In using and evaluating the Government's present capability for long-term global analysis, the Study found serious inconsistencies in the methods and assumptions employed by the various agencies in making their projections. The Study itself made a start toward resolving these inadequacies. It represents the Government's first attempt to produce an interrelated set of population, resource, and environmental projections, and it has brought forth the most consistent set of global projections yet achieved by U.S. agencies. Nevertheless, the projections still contain serious gaps and contradictions that must be corrected if the Government's analytic capability is to be improved. It must be acknowledged that at present the Federal agencies are not always capable of providing projections of the quality needed for long-term policy decisions.

While limited resources may be a contributing factor in some instances, the primary problem is lack of coordination. The U.S. Government needs a mechanism for continuous review of the assumptions and methods the Federal agencies use in their projection models and for assurance that the agencies' models are sound, consistent, and well documented. The improved analyses that could result would provide not only a clearer sense of emerging problems and opportunities, but also a better means for evaluating alternative responses, and a better basis for decisions of worldwide significance that the President, the Congress, and the Federal Government as a whole must make.

With its limitations and rough approximations, the Global 2000 Study may be seen as no more than a reconnaissance of the future; nonetheless its conclusions are reinforced by similar findings of other recent global studies that were examined in the course of the Global 2000 Study. . . . All these studies are in general agreement on the nature of the problems and on the threats they pose to the future welfare of humankind. The available evidence leaves no doubt that the world—including this Nation—faces enormous, urgent, and complex problems in the decades immediately ahead. Prompt and vigorous changes in public policy around the world are needed to avoid or minimize these problems before they become unmanageable. Long lead times are required for effective action. If decisions are delayed until the problems become worse, options for effective action will be severely reduced.

Globaloney 2000

Herman Kahn
Ernest Schneider

In July 1980, the White House issued *The Global 2000 Report to the President*. Its basic conclusions could hardly be more stark:

> If present trends continue, the world in 2000 will be more crowded, more polluted, less stable ecologically, and more vulnerable to disruption than the world we live in now. Serious stresses involving population, resources, and environment are clearly visible ahead . . . Barring revolutionary advances in technology, life for most people on earth will be more precarious in 2000 than it is now . . . unless the nations of the world act decisively to alter currect trends.

In short, unless we change our wicked ways, disaster lies ahead. This clarion call is not new. A decade ago, the same alarm was sounded even more shrilly, dogmatically, and dramatically by the Club of Rome, a group of distinguished industrialists and scientists who sponsored one of the most influential books of our time, *The Limits to Growth*.[1] Their message was simple: if economic growth and population growth are not drastically curbed, the world will collapse within the next century. This time the message was very similar, but its purveyor was President Carter, backed by the authority of the United States government.

Global 2000 was prepared by the State Department and the Council on Environmental Quality in response to a request made by the President in 1977; Council Chairman Gus Speth and Assistant Secretary of State Thomas Pickering put the study together. Their two agencies were aided by the Departments of Agriculture, Energy, and Interior, the Agency for International Development, the CIA, the EPA, the Federal Emergency Management Agency, NASA, the National Science Foundation, the National Oceanic and Atmospheric Administration, and the Office of Science and Technology Policy. Who could doubt that these sober and responsible outfits know what they are doing?

Indeed, compared to the Club of Rome report, Global 2000 seems rather moderate; it is certainly more carefully worded. Although, in our view, both studies are simply disgraceful, Global 2000 is far more reprehensible. Its authors seem oblivious to the intensive criticism to which *The Limits to Growth* has been subjected during the past eight years. Many of its more alarming arguments had already been largely discredited among most people who deal professionally with these rather abstruse matters, and other arguments need caveats or elaboration. More importantly, the U.S. government has a fiduciary role which cannot be attributed to the Club of Rome. As the designated servant of the American people, the executive branch has a serious obligation to do accurate work, and a clear responsibility for the policy implications of its research. By contrast, the Club of Rome is a purely private venture; while the Club should not behave irresponsibly, it certainly enjoys more freedom than the Washington establishment which produced Global 2000.

Before Global 2000 was even completed, President Carter had discussed its conclusions with other world leaders at an economic summit held in Italy. Immediately upon receiving the report, he established a Task Force to ensure that priority attention would be devoted to the problems signalled by the report. The Task Force was led by Mr. Speth; it included the Secretary of State, the OMB Director, the President's Assistant for Domestic Affairs, and the Director of the Office of Science and Technology Policy. The group's report was submitted to President Carter a few days before Ronald Reagan was inaugurated. In addition, the outgoing President told the State Department to arrange an international meeting of environmental and economic experts in Washington in 1981 to discuss the interrelated questions of population, natural resources, environment, and economic development, which are the focal point of the report.

[1] Meadows, Meadows, Randers and Behrens, (New York: Universe Books, 1972).

From Herman Kahn and Ernest Schneider, "Globaloney 2000," *Policy Review* No. **16** (Spring 1981): 129–147.

Meanwhile, Secretary of State Edmund Muskie used Global 2000 as the centerpiece for an address to the UN General Assembly, and the Joint Economic Committee of Congress launched a series of hearings on the report; by October a subunit of the Committee had issued a report on Global 2000 titled *Averting Catastrophe;* a UNESCO General Conference held in Belgrade last October also discussed related issues. Finally, in his farewell address to the nation, President Carter singled out the kind of concerns which Global 2000 addresses as one of the three most important problems facing the American people (the other two being arms control and human rights):

> The shadows that fall across the future are cast not only by the kinds of weapons we've built but by the kind of world we will either nourish or neglect. There are real and growing dangers to our simple and our most precious possessions: the air we breathe, the water we drink, and the land which sustains us. The rapid depletion of irreplaceable minerals, the erosion of topsoil, the destruction of beauty, the blight of pollution, the demands of increasing billions of people all combine to create problems which are easy to observe and predict, but difficult to resolve, If we do not act, the world of the year 2000 will be much less able to sustain life than it is now.[2]

The U.S. government has been actively promoting the report at home and abroad. Seventeen thousand copies had been distributed by early September, more were being printed, and summaries were being prepared in French and Spanish. An advertisement for a German version of Global 2000 which appeared in West Germany's most popular news magazine proclaimed:

> The new official environmental study: the oceans polluted, acid rain, drinking water running out, air becoming scarce.[3]

The response to Global 2000 by the media has been almost uniformly favorable; hardly a note of caution was heard, even from such presumably responsible sources as the World Future Society and the Ameri-

can Association for the Advancement of Science.[4] *Time* and *Newsweek* both gave prominent attention to the report, and *Time* commented that, compared to *Limits to Growth*, Global 2000 is "certainly restrained," even muted. *The Washington Post* observed that "the report's projections clearly err on the side of optimism."

Thus, as far as published comment is concerned, Global 2000 has been almost universally accepted at face value, and accorded great respect. Mr. Speth correctly described response to the report as "overwhelmingly positive," and added that those few who were concerned that the report would be counterproductive have been "proven wrong."

These rave reviews have their own consequences: the prevailing pessimism of our society has been powerfully reinforced. To quote Representative Henry Reuss of Wisconsin, co-chairman of a Joint Economic Committee subcommittee, the report

> documents a world a bare 20 years from now that is desolate and dying, the result of the past, present, and prospective follies of its people.

As it happens, we recently participated in a series of briefings for freshman congressmen. We learned that, with some exceptions, congressmen had not been particularly affected by Global 2000; many were not even aware of its existence. However, many members of their staffs knew a great deal about it. And the real importance of this document lies in its impact upon people who are professionally concerned with environmental issues. In addition to government officials, this includes many college professors and public school teachers who are eager to exploit any respectable material which tends to support their pessimistic attitudes toward the U.S. economic and political system. Global 2000 is tailor-made for this kind of exploitation.

President Carter's Task Force asked some 600 experts, constituency group leaders, and business leaders how the government can enhance its capability to work with the private sector to address these problems more effectively. At hearings on Global 2000, Representative Reuss asked rhetorically wheth-

---

[2] *The New York Times,* January 15, 1981.
[3] There is no indication that the ad was officially sponsored.

[4] The only exception known to us is Julian Simon, "Global Confusion 1980: A Hard Look at the Global 2000 Report," *The Public Interest* (Winter 1981). His article appeared just as this article was being completed.

er the world could not do a better job of averting "Apocalypse 2000" if the "insane arms race" were stopped. He added, "We've got a great thing here; let's not louse it up." In response to urging from Senator Russell Long of Louisiana, Assistant Secretary of State Pickering observed that a consortium of foundations and other private bodies might deal with the issues raised by Global 2000.

NOVUS ORDO SECLORUM

The Carter administration would obviously have liked to see Global 2000 become the centerpiece of a vast effort to save mankind. Of course, President Carter's mandate for such an effort has run out.

And why should the Global 2000 report not enjoy this status? Because it is biased, misleading, and sometimes plain wrong.

The bias of Global 2000 is toward pessimism on practically every issue; a pervasive tendency always to see every glass as half empty rather than half full, and to consider some which are two-thirds full to be two-thirds empty.

At the outset, Global 2000 asserts that "Despite great material output, the world's people will be poorer *in many ways* than they are today." (Emphasis ours) The reader is expected to understand that, although almost every country will technically have a higher real GNP per capita, something else, presumably quality, will suffer as time goes by—and that this is more important than mere quantity. We agree that quality is always important; indeed, a sufficient decline in quality can negate any increase in quantity. But many complaints about the quality of life today turn out to have more to do with the perceptions and misperceptions of the middle class in Western culture than with the welfare of most people in these societies. Thus as mass consumption societies develop and expand, the way of life of the upper middle class often declines in certain respects (for example, the disappearance of servants, crowded resorts, and less easy access to prestigious universities). Global 2000 seems to be projecting this problem on other countries as well as on other classes within this country.

Although the study projects a 90 percent increase in world food production from 1970 to 2000, and a per capita increase of "less than 15 percent," it adds that per capita consumption in South Asia, the Middle East, and the less developed countries (LDCs) of Africa "will scarcely improve or will actually decline

below present inadequate levels." In our view, about 300 million people now live in countries which are desperately poor and unlikely to improve much in the next decade or two. Examples are Bangladesh, the Sahel of Africa, Haiti, and Bolivia. About 700 million additional people live in what we call "coping" poor countries: such nations are not doing badly as a whole, but many of their citizens are very poor; India, northeastern Brazil, and the peasantry of Mexico are examples. As the world's population grows from the current 4.3 billion and levels out around 10 billion in the middle of the twenty-first century, about a billion people will almost surely still be very badly off. These problems are both very important and very difficult to deal with. But they will have little relevance for the great majority of the world's population.

Nowhere is Global 2000's pessimistic bias more blatant than in its preoccupation with the so-called gap between the rich and poor people of the world—although this is a conventional sin. The concept is painfully simple. Since some people are richer than other people, a gap divides them. If both groups are becoming richer, the best way to distract attention from this agreeable prospect is to focus on something else, especially if it stimulates guilt feelings in the likely consumer of the information. Following this formula, Global 2000 tells us:

> The present income disparities between the wealthiest and poorest nations are projected to widen. Assuming that present trends continue . . . industrial countries will have a per capita GNP of nearly $8,500 (in 1975 dollars) in 2000 . . . By contrast, per capita GNP in the LDCs will average less than $600. . . .

Only by consulting a statistical table in Global 2000 can the reader learn that GNP per capita is projected to rise from $382 for the LDCs in 1975 to $587 in 2000, an increase of over 50 percent in two decades.

After these and other doses of pessimism, the report disarmingly admits that it may not be objective; we are told that the methods available for carrying out the study "tend to impart an optimistic bias." At least we have been warned.

THE AUTHORS AND THEIR BIASES

Dr. Gerald O. Barney, the director of the study, states in Global 2000 that two groups of expert advisors actively participated in preparing the report. Listed among an inner circle of seven such experts are Mihaljo Mesarovic, Anne Ehrlich, and Kenneth E. F. Watt.[5] All three are closely identified with opposition to growth. Mrs. Ehrlich and her husband Paul (who wrote *The Population Bomb*) are leaders of the Zero Population Growth movement in this country; in 1974 they published a book called *The End of Affluence*; Mr. Mesarovic was co-author of the Club of Rome's second study of "the human predicament"; Mr. Watt added another volume to the literature of doom by publishing a book in 1974 on the "titanic effect"; his definition of this concept epitomizes the strategy of wolf-crying:

the magnitude of disasters decreases to the extent that people believe that they are possible and plan to prevent their effect.

The second advisory group consisted of some 134 individuals. Among them are Dennis and Donella Meadows, two of the authors of *The Limits to Growth,* and their acknowledged mentor, Professor Jay Forrester of MIT. The organizations identified with many of these individuals read like an honor role of certified opponents of the kind of economic growth that most Americans support; among them are: the Natural Resources Defense Council, the Population Reference Bureau, the Rachel Carson Trust, the Friends of the Earth, World Watch Institute, the Canadian Association for the Club of Rome, the World Population Society, Environmental Action, the Environmental Fund, the Population Crisis Committee, the National Wildlife Federation, the American Conservation Association, the U.S. Association for the Club of Rome, the World Wildlife Foundation, Zero Population Growth, the Massachusetts

Audubon Society, Nature Conservancy, the National Parks and Conservation Association, and the Population Council.[6] While such groups should be consulted in preparing a study of this kind, who can doubt that they are strongly inclined to put their concept of adequate environmental protection ahead of almost all other goals?

Global 2000 asserts that its conclusions were reinforced by those of similar studies which it examined; it claims that

all these studies are in general agreement on the nature of the problems and on the threats they pose to the future welfare of mankind. The available evidence leaves no doubt that the world— including this Nation(sic)—faces enormous, urgent, and complex problems in the decades immediately ahead.

No one argues that the world does not face "enormous, urgent, and complex problems," but do all the studies really agree on the nature of these problems?

Global 2000 compared the government's several models to five other global studies:

1 "Worlds 2 and 3," both commissioned by the Club of Rome; the latter model was the basis for *The Limits to Growth.*

2 The Mesarovic-Pestel World Model, also commissioned by the Club of Rome; both authors are Club of Rome members.

3 MOIRA [Model of International Relations in Agriculture] also commissioned by the Club of Rome; according to Global 2000, "the modelers were motivated by the sentiment that human suffering is morally wrong and by a desire to minimize world hunger." While few could dissent, we would argue that objectivity and realism are far better motivations for policy researchers.

4 The Latin American World Model; although this study was also inspired by the Club of Rome, it was, according to Global 2000 designed to address the question "How can the resources of the world be used

---

[5] The other four are Anne Carter of Brandeis University, Nicholas Carter of the World Bank, Peter Henriot of the Center of Concern, and Douglas N. Ross of the Joint Economic Committee of the U.S. Congress. While their attitudes toward growth are not known to us, the two Carters are professional and respected economists who specialize in the kind of complex and detailed quantitative models which we find most misleading. According to the *Encyclopedia of Associations*, the Center of Concern is devoted to human rights and, *inter alia*, "calls for a more equitable sharing of material resources." This is doubtless a worthy aim, but it suggests that its members would approach any study like Global 2000 with preconceived goals.

[6] The list is not totally one-sided. It includes individuals affiliated with such institutions as A.T.&T., First National City Bank, and the American Petroleum Institute. However, organizations of this kind are outnumbered by at least 5 to 1; furthermore, this minority apparently wielded little influence.

most effectively to improve the lots of all people?"; thus "it is almost the antithesis of what the Global 2000 study is seeking. Rather than dealing with the problems of resources and environment, the modelers began with an assumption of no problems—particularly no serious resource problems. Their analysis much resembles that presented by Herman Kahn in *The Next 200 Years*."[7] The Latin American study concluded that "the fate of man does not depend, in the last instance, on insurmountable physical barriers, but on social and political factors that man must modify."

5 The UN World Model; this study, led by the Nobel Laureate Wassily Leontieff, was published in 1977. Among its conclusions:

Known world resources of metallic minerals and fossil fuels are generally sufficient to supply world requirements through the remaining decades of this century . . . mineral resource endowment is generally adequate to support world economic development at relatively high rates, but . . . these resources will most probably become more expensive to extract as the century moves toward its conclusion.[8]

Thus, it turns out that, rather than uniformly agreeing with Global 2000, three of these models share its ideological bias, and two seem to dissent from its conclusions.

[7] This book (H. Kahn, W. Brown, L. Martel; New York: Morrow, 1976) did not assume that the world faces no environmental or resource problems. On the contrary, it explicitly argued that mankind faces two kinds of "issues," of which eight are basically "solvable," and eight are basically "uncertain"; among the latter are "possible damage to earth because of complicated, complex, and subtle ecological and environmental effects." The authors attempted to match resources against probable needs, and found few serious problems—if proper investments are carried out. In general, many problems which now preoccupy elites in affluent societies can be solved by relying on business-as-usual methods—many serious problems are likely to arise in the future, but those signalled by Global 2000 are not likely to be very prominent among them. The authors of Global 2000 are not Cassandras. It was Cassandra's fate to warn of real problems and not be believed. The fate of Global 2000 is to warn of mostly unreal problems and to be mostly believed. One reason for Cassandras is that the public is confused by false signals and incorrect analyses.

[8] *The Future of the World Economy* (New York: Oxford University Press, 1977), p. 6.

MANIPULATING THE EVIDENCE: POPULATION

As for being misleading or wrong, let's look first at population, perhaps the single most important topic for studies of this kind. The report first asserts that rapid world population growth will "hardly have altered" by 2000, adding that the world's population will reach 6.35 billion by 2000, a 50 percent increase over 1975; the growth rate is projected to drop from 1.8 percent per year in 1975 to 1.7 in 2000.[9] The report adds that "if the fertility and mortality rates projected for 2000 were to continue unchanged into the twenty-first century, the world's population would reach 10 billion by 2030 and nearly 30 billion before the end of the twenty-first century."

While this latter assertion could be interpreted as arising out of the available data, it clearly misrepresents conventional demographic wisdom; this includes the estimates of the Census Bureau. The best current data indicate that, after reaching a peak rate of about 2.1 percent in the mid-sixties, the world population growth rate declined sharply to 1.6 to 1.7 percent; this represents a 20 percent drop. These estimates are, by definition, uncertain; however, they are accepted by most of the world's demographers.[10] The overall world rate will almost surely continue to decline, certainly in the time period to which Global 2000 addresses itself. By assuming the opposite, Global 2000 seems to be engaging in deliberate scare tactics.

[9] Donald Bogue and Amy Tsui argue in "Zero World Population Growth?" (*The Public Interest*, Spring 1979) that "population in the year 2000 will be as much as 250 million less than the lowest of the current predictions, and 700 million less than anticipated by the U.S. Census Bureau and the United Nations." They project a world total between 5.7 and 5.9 billion people in 2000, and conclude that by then "the world will have largely brought the problem of high population growth under control."

[10] The most recent annual report of the UN Fund for Population Activities found, according to *The New York Times* of June 15, 1980, that "By the end of the century, the pace of (world) population growth is expected to fall by 20 percent." The World Fertility Survey, covering 400,000 women in 61 countries, has concluded that birth rates in Third World countries and developed nations diminished significantly during the 1970s (*The New York Times,* July 15, 1980, C1). Bogue and Tsui (*see* footnote 9) report that 81 percent of the earth's inhabitants live in nations which experienced population decline between 1968 and 1975; furthermore, they found that the nations with higher birth rates in 1968 tended to experience the largest fertility reductions.

The recent sharp decline seems likely to continue, reaching about 1.4 percent by the end of the century. Thus, the most important characteristic about the rate of population increase is its rapid rise and even more rapid decline; this should not be thought of as a long, drawn out process.

The misleading nature of excessive preoccupation with recent high rates of world population growth is dramatized by the three graphs shown below.

These three graphs put the whole question of population growth into a meaningful historical perspective. The first focuses on a 60-year period; it indicates that these rates have been rather stable during the past several decades, but are now declining rather rapidly. The second covers a much longer period: 400 years. It illustrates the nature of the current demographic transition. This transition initially resulted from a sharp decline in death rates, followed by a similarly sharp drop in birth rates; this continued until a rough balance was achieved. The third graph, which covers 16,000 years, is of course the most dramatic. It shows that population growth was very slow before the demographic transition, perhaps 0.1 percent; at this rate, total population goes up by a factor of 3 in 1,000 years. The peak is incredibly sharp, only 100 years wide at the one-percent point. In this perspective the current era can be characterized as a "Great Transition" from a world where:

> 200 years ago almost everywhere human beings were comparatively few, poor and at the mercy of the forces of nature to one 200 years ahead where, barring bad luck and/or bad management, almost everywhere they will be numerous, rich, and in control of the forces of nature.[11]

If such a transition really occurs, it will certainly cause all sorts of problems and other growing pains; in many ways, it might even be disaster prone. But Global 2000 contains hardly a hint that an exciting and basically constructive process of this kind may lie ahead.

Since the decline in world population growth rates reflects the changes which occur in values and ways of

[11] See Kahn, Brown, Martel, *op. cit.,* p. 1; this definition is paraphrased here.

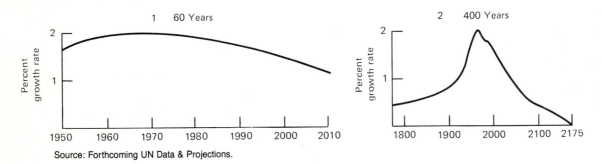

Source: Forthcoming UN Data & Projections.

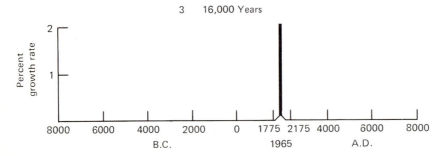

Source: Adapted from *Scientific American,* September 1974, pp. 36–37.

Three time-perspectives on world population growth.

life as most of the world's people gradually become more affluent, this trend is unlikely to change rapidly, if at all, within a decade or two. This basic pattern is unmistakably clear. Poor people tend to have large families, and affluent people small families.

As such diverse countries as the United States, Japan, the U.S.S.R., Brazil, and Mexico have become better off, their fertility rates have all declined. Spectacular decreases in fertility have taken place in China, Sri Lanka, Indonesia, and the Indian states of Kerala and Karnataka in recent years. In 1980, India's population growth rate dropped to 1.9 percent; since India represents one-sixth of the world's population, this is especially encouraging. And, according to Global 2000 itself, China, the world's most populous nation, will grow at an average annual rate of only 1.4 percent during the 1975-2000 period. This estimate was made before the new Chinese program which attempts to restrict Chinese families to one child.

WORLD NEEDS IN TRANSITION

Global 2000 puts much stress on its projection that 79 percent of the world's population in 2000 will be living in less developed countries. Whether this grim sounding prospect has much to do with reality depends, of course, upon how LDC is defined. By any traditional standard—say less than $500 annual per capita GNP in constant dollars—China, Thailand, Egypt, Nigeria, and the Philippines will probably no longer belong in this category by the year 2000. If Global 2000 had adopted the simple device of splitting the developing world into two groups—LDCs and those in transition to affluence—the LDC population in 2000 would be under 40 percent. On the whole, middle income and poor countries tend to attain faster economic growth than affluent countries; on a per capita basis, the results are about the same for both groups.

In dealing with energy, Global 2000 repeats the familiar litany which is almost certainly misleading:

During the 1990s, world oil production will approach geological estimates of maximum production capacity, even with rapidly increasing petroleum prices . . . richer industrial nations will be able to command enough oil and other commercial energy supplies to meet their rising demands through 1990, [but] many less developed countries will have increasing difficulties meeting energy needs. For the one-quarter of humankind that depends primarily on wood for fuel, the outlook is bleak . . . While the world's finite fuel resources— coal, oil, oil shale, tar sands, and uranium—are theoretically sufficient for centuries, they are not evenly distributed; they pose difficult economic and environmental problems; and they vary greatly in their amenability to exploitation and use.

The Global 2000 view that no early relief from the world's energy problems is in sight rests largely upon the notion that petroleum production capacity will not increase as rapidly as demand. This outlook is not unusual; it is based upon projections made by the Department of Energy in 1977. But agreement is growing that current high oil prices are rapidly bringing about the needed adjustments. Thus, projections for increased world demand for energy have been scaled down from about 3.5 percent per annum. For example, the U.S. Energy Department recently reduced its estimate of growth in U.S. energy demand to 1 percent annually, the latest in a series of reductions from a forecast of 2.5 percent in 1979.[12]

The important transition now being experienced reflects the world's ability to restructure its economics to produce desirable fuels at tolerable prices, and to adjust demand for those fuels accordingly. No doubt such adjustments will often be more painful to poor people in poor countries than to others, but this is a virtually inevitable result of poverty. By definition, a rich person can command more of the world's goods and services than a poor person; this is why most people prefer more money to less money. The solution, of course, is to eradicate poverty. This is happening; slowly and unevenly, but still happening.

In sum, on energy issues, Global 2000 is badly outdated; even when this is not the case, it tends to overstate demand and understate supply, while often ignoring the role of economic forces. In any case, there is little reason to place much credence in official forecasts of this kind; a cursory look at the record shows that they have consistently turned out to be wrong, almost always erring toward pessimism.[13]

[12] *The New York Times*, January 4, 1981, p. 1.
[13] An interesting list contrasting oil prophecies and realities since 1866 appears in *Presidential Energy Program*, Hearings Before the Subcommittee on Energy and Power of the Committee on Interstate and Foreign Commerce, February 17–21, 1975, Serial No. 94–20 (Washington, D.C.: USGPO, 1975), p. 643.

FEEDING THE WORLD

What about food? Global 2000 forecasts that world food production will grow by 2.5 percent per annum during the 1970-2000 period, but projects a 95 percent increase in the real price of food during those years. Food output in LDCs is expected to "barely keep ahead of population growth," and the outlook for improved diets for the poorest people in the poorest LDCs is described as "sobering."

Does this make much sense?

As for the real food prices, the world price for wheat and corn in constant dollars was roughly the same in 1977-1979 as it was in 1967-1969, despite sharp increases in 1973-1975. Such fluctuations can recur, and are indeed likely for 1980-1981, due mainly to the U.S. drought and the poor harvest in the Soviet Union. But an inexorable continuing rise in real terms has not occurred, nor is it particularly likely. While food prices in real terms are likely to go up in the immediate future, there is little reason to expect a long-term rise. The application of capital and technology should be able to overcome any tendency toward diminishing marginal returns.

In terms of numbers of people alone, China, India, Pakistan, Bangladesh, and Indonesia lie near the heart of any potential global food problem. These five nations account for 2 billion people today, and will number close to 2.75 billion by 2000. How are they doing?

China's agricultural situation today is not unsatisfactory in the sense that most of China's one billion people seem to be adequately fed. When shortages arise, the government has sufficient foreign exchange to import food from abroad. As for China's prospects, Global 2000 itself projects a 69 percent increase in food production during the 1970-2000 period, and a mere 42 percent increase in population between 1975-2000.

Under Indira Gandhi, India has increased food output by giving greater priority to agricultural development, improving incentives to farmers, and relaxing barriers to interstate grain trade. As a result:

1 India exported 700,000 tons of grain in 1980 (in 1975 she imported 7.5 million tons). India normally produces over 95 percent of her own grain requirements.

2 Substantial grain reserves have been accumulated.

3 7 million additional acres were irrigated in 1978.

In the longer run, India should be well off agriculturally. With twice the arable land per capita of China, India's intensity of fertilizer use is less than half that of China. India has extensive fertile river basins where water management is starting to take hold. And India's earlier emphasis upon industrialization has provided some of the infrastructure which is needed for rapid agricultural development.

Both Pakistan and Bangladesh dramatically improved their grain output in 1980—because of good weather and expanded fertilizer use. Indonesia has experienced two successive record rice harvests—by using more high yielding varieties, by higher fertilizer use, and by suffering less damage from floods and pests. Furthermore, multiple cropping and year-round irrigation are spreading fast in both countries.

In contrast to the hopeful outlook in Asia, the developing countries of the Sahel and Central Africa will probably need food aid on a continuing basis for at least a decade. Fortunately, the populations concerned are relatively small—about 40 million. If the Sudan, Ethiopia, and Somalia are included, the number rises to 120 million—still small compared to India's 670 million and China's one billion. And some faint signs are visible that the same awakening to agricultural technology that has taken place in South Asia is starting to happen in black Africa.[14]

This is not to argue that many millions in poor countries do not suffer from malnutrition. Fortunately, however, various technologies could solve or alleviate most of the world's nutritional problems in a few years. Their adoption has often depended upon effec-

[14] Richard Critchfield, a journalist specializing in peasant societies, has observed: "Is there something in the American psyche that feels more comfortable with a (fake) picture of Asian village misery and desperation? Do we really, deep down, *want* to hear bad news? This gap between reality in village Java and its perception in Washington . . . will not matter in the long run. Realities assert themselves in time." ("Javanese Village: The View from Below," *Society*, September-October 1980, p. 43.) The idea that the world is more or less permanently short of food has been propagated by prestigious organizations anxious to dramatize the plight of the few by making it appear to be the curse of many. The Food and Agricultural Organization (FAO) is the prime example of this tendency. Its director, Lord Boyd-Orr, claimed in 1950 that two-thirds of the world's people went to bed hungry. It was later shown that Lord Boyd-Orr's successors knew this statement was untrue; it had been based on a simple confusion compounded by inaccurate FAO statistics, but the FAO was loath to soften the impact of this assertion. See Colin Clark, *Starvation or Plenty?* (New York: Taplinger Publishing Company, 1970).

tive demand, i.e., demand with money behind it. If there is any single cause of world hunger, it is poverty, not a lack of food. Thus, the problem is financial rather than simple production.

The insistence of Global 2000 that the world is headed straight for disaster is intrinsically implausible. Gross World Product and Gross World Product per capita have been growing inexorably almost every year for at least a century. Life expectancy, the best single available indicator of human health and welfare, continues to lengthen almost everywhere, year after year. Pollution levels in the developed world are being reduced;[15] as the rest of the world becomes more affluent, this pattern will probably be repeated. Even more basic, of course, is the peaking of world population growth which occurred in the 1960s. Given these facts, it seems passing strange that the doomsdayism of Global 2000 is playing to rave reviews.

Of course things can go wrong. They often do, and this will surely happen again. But to argue that the whole world is heading straight for disaster within two decades borders on the foolish.

THE LURE OF DOOM

If Global 2000 is so biased toward doom, why did President Carter, a reasonably cheerful and responsible man, embrace its conclusions so eagerly, and why is the world press little more than a claque for its gloomy message?

One motivation behind these apparently mysterious phenomena seems to us more emotional than rational, and rather admirable at that. Who cannot sympathize with the pious wish of the rich and comfortable to help the poor and deprived? For this is what Global 2000 seems to be about: to the extent that this claim has some validity, it is an uncomfortable task to find fault with studies of this kind. But where compassion blooms with such entrepreneurial vigor, can guilt be entirely absent? This perhaps explains the preoccupation of Global 2000 and similar

studies[16] with the gap between rich and poor—which has little resonance among the poor. We feel sure that, in reality, the peasants of Bangladesh and the African Sahel are much more interested in self-improvement than they are in the difference between their lives and those of the affluent elites of New York, Dusseldorf, and Tokyo.

Why does Global 2000 proclaim, with such dismay, that the one-quarter of the world's population that inhabits industrial countries is projected to continue absorbing more than three-fourths of the world's nonfuel mineral production?

It would be odd if this were not the case; the problem of course is to create conditions under which the non-industrialized majority of the world's people can duplicate the high consumption of the industrialized world. But this is hardly the reason why Global 2000 revives this old chestnut. Guilt leads to compassion, and compassion may lead to action, to doing good deeds. Thus the insistent theme in Global 2000 that all is not (yet) lost:

> Prompt and vigorous changes in public policy around the world are needed to avoid or minimize these problems before they become unmanageable.

Crying wolf, then, is the strategy of the do-good establishment which specializes in proclaiming that disaster will strike—unless we follow their advice in a big way right away. Aurelio Peccei, the founder of the Club of Rome, conceded that this was the case when he commented that "the limits to growth report had served its purpose of 'getting the world's attention' focused on the ecological dangers of unplanned and uncontrolled population and industrial expansion."[17] He made this statement in the context of abandoning the Club's formerly negative attitude toward the desirability of further economic growth. By contrast, Global 2000 avoids taking a position for or against as such; its policy prescriptions are implied rather than stated. In his testimony before the Joint Economic Committee, Mr. Speth asserted that "the conflict between development and environmental protection is largely a myth"; adding that "we don't think that this report holds out a specter of limited or no

---

[15] For official data on improved U.S. air pollution levels, see Paul Portney, ed., *Current Issues in U.S. Environmental Policy,* published for Resources for the Future (Baltimore: Johns Hopkins University Press, 1978), p. 27, and Walter Rosenbaum, *The Politics of Environmental Concern,* (New York: Praeger, 1977), p. 152. The annual report for 1980 of the Council of Environmental Quality reported that the air in most American cities is becoming cleaner, including those with the dirtiest air (*The New York Times,* January 18, 1981).

[16] Notably the so-called Brandt report; for critical assessments of that study, *see Encounter,* December 1980, and Peter Day "Beneath Charity: The Brandt Report," *Policy Review,* Summer 1980.

[17] *The New York Times*, April 13, 1976.

growth." In this way, those responsible for Global 2000 seemingly want to avoid the onus of advocating limits to economic growth or resource use.

If, indeed, Global 2000 were the basis for U.S. policy over the next decade, what would happen? Solutions to the problems posed by Global 2000 are explored in the report delivered to President Carter by Mr. Speth and Secretary of State Edmund Muskie on the eve of Ronald Reagan's assumption of power. The report's tone is embodied in its title: *Global Future: Time to Act.* Among its recommendations are:

1 An expansion of U.S. foreign aid by 40 percent over the next five years.
2 A doubling of U.S. support for family planning.

In addition, the report makes dozens of suggestions for specific actions, many of them calling for the creation of new institutes, centers, task forces, and committees—as well as the expenditure of U.S. funds for such diverse purposes as aid to agriculture in poor countries, a conference on a conservation and management strategy for U.S. fisheries, and expanding efforts to train farmers in water management.[18] In general, *Global Future* is more restrained and reasonable than Global 2000, perhaps because it appears to reflect the thinking of bureaucrats more than the predispositions of professional environmentalists. As for the merits of its proposals, more U.S. foreign aid might be a good idea, but only if it is targeted on countries which need it most, and administered in ways which in fact encourage development rather than stifle it. On the record, this has often not been true. In any case, the affluent nations of the world clearly have a moral obligation to help the poor to improve their lot. To expand support for family planning is very probably desirable, given the strong likelihood that more and more people in developing countries will, for social and economic reasons, wish to limit their progeny, and need access to this information. Except for programs which penalize families for having excess children (for example, Singapore and China), such efforts are usually ineffective as propaganda, but can be very effective in providing information for people who want fewer children.

[18] According to *The Washington Post* of January 15, 1981, Gus Speth estimated that it would cost $1 billion to $1.5 billion annually to implement the recommendations of *Global Future.*

Some further policy clues are provided by Representative Reuss's report on *Averting Catastrophe.* While most of its recommendations are not policy specific, the report suggests focus on:

1 The relationship between economic development and the globe's resource base.
2 Dismantling barriers to the flow of capital and goods internationally.
3 The links between the arms race and other global problems.

While these goals are, to some extent, unexceptionable, their implications are not entirely harmless. The first certainly suggests that development may deplete scarce resources. Preoccupation with resource shortages may promote conservation, and more conservation is certainly an important aspect of a rational energy policy. But conservation, at least as a rhetorical goal, has hardly been neglected by the Nixon, Ford, and Carter administrations. The trouble is that, unless the price rises enough, rhetorical exhortation and conservation are remarkably ineffective. By now, however, the price has reached levels which really promote both conservation and production.

There is no rational basis for singling out military spending as a possible source of funds to save the world. While arms are certainly non-productive in the economic sense, this is no news. Indeed, it is arguable that no economic growth whatever could occur without the security shield provided by military strength.

But the real point lies elsewhere. Our society pays a heavy cost in terms of low morale when its establishment endorses the notion that our socio-economic system is, in effect, corrupt and evil. If the idea that more economic growth will pollute the environment and rob the world's poor further infiltrates our school system, we should not be surprised that young people prefer the Sierra Club and Nader's Raiders to Exxon and General Motors. The upper middle class youngsters who graduate from our most prestigious colleges generally lack the kind of direct experience with work and hardships of any kind which breeds realism. They tend to be sheltered and idealistic—easy prey to those who deplore industrialism and economic growth as vulgar and materialistic. It is precisely the prejudices, guilt feelings, and class interests (conscious and unconscious) of the affluent, the elite, and the privileged which inspire studies like Global 2000.

Since the advent of Global 2000 coincides with the demise of the Carter administration, the new team taking over in Washington should use Mr. Carter's Global 2000 swan song as an opportunity to show the differences between their respective world views in terms of sobriety, realism, and policy orientation. More importantly, a new study could identify problems more serious and pressing than those addressed by Global 2000: perhaps, for example, nuclear proliferation and runaway inflation. After all, Global 2000 arose from a worthy impulse to assess long range problems, and do something about them. If President Reagan decides to give us a more accurate and productive view of the future, he might help to inspire all of us to make a better world.

QUESTIONS FOR DISCUSSION

1 Is overpopulation a danger to the world?
2 Is the world running out of renewable resources?
3 Are supplies of nonrenewable necessities likely to be adequate over the long term?
4 Is the world facing a long-term trend toward environmental disaster?
5 What government policies, if any, are likely to help deal with the long-term problems we are likely to face?

SUGGESTED READINGS

Bruce-Briggs, B. "Against the Neo-Malthusians." *Commentary* (July 1974): 25–29.

Eberstadt, Nick. "Hunger and Ideology." *Commentary* (July 1981): 40–49.

Ehrlich, Paul R., Anne R. Ehrlich, and John P. Holdren. *Ecoscience*. San Francisco: Freeman, 1977.

Falk, Richard A. *A Study of Future Worlds*. New York: Free Press, 1975.

Kahn, Herman. *The Next 200 Years*. New York: Morrow, 1976.

Leontieff, Wassily, et al. *The Future of the World Economy*. New York: Oxford University Press, 1977.

Meadows, Donella H., Dennis L. Meadows, Jorgen Randers, and William W. Behrens. *The Limits to Growth*. New York: New American Library, 1974.

Pirages, Dennis. *Global Ecopolitics*. North Scituate, Mass.: Duxbury Press, 1978.

Pirages, Dennis, and Paul Ehrlich. *Ark II*. San Francisco: Freeman, 1974.

Toffler, Alvin. *The Third Wave*. New York: Morrow, 1980.